North American

Mission

Handbook

*US and Canadian Protestant
Ministries Overseas 2017–2019*

22nd Edition

Peggy E. Newell

EDITOR

WILLIAM CAREY
LIBRARY

North American Mission Handbook: US and Canadian Protestant Ministries Overseas 2017–2019, 22nd Edition

Executive editor, Marvin J Newell
Managing editor, Peggy E Newell
Associate editor, Michael VanHuis
Editorial assistant, Philip Newell
Database manager, Bill Morrison
Compilation assistant, Inge Donaldson
Compilation assistant, Joel Wright
Compilation assistant, Paul Erickson
Copyeditor, Melissa Hicks
Cover design, Kurtis Amundsen

For information about Missio Nexus
Website: www.MissioNexus.org
Email: Info@MissioNexus.org
Phone: 770.457.6677
Update your information at: www.missionexus.org/missionhandbook

Published by William Carey Library
1605 E. Elizabeth St.
Pasadena, CA 91104

ISBN: 978-0-87808-632-0

Printed in the United States of America
21 20 19 18 17   5 4 3 2 1 BP1500

Facts are our friends, and a fact-based missions resource is essential to help us understand the state of the mission force as we engage the mission field. The *Mission Handbook* is an exceedingly valuable resource, helping us to lead better because we know better.

ED STETZER, Billy Graham Distinguished Chair, Wheaton College

As a North American mission leader I am required to think regionally. However, to fully participate in God's mission I must also think globally. How does Wycliffe Bible Translators contribute globally to what God is doing to fulfill Matthew 28:18–20? How do we effectively partner with the Church in the US and with others regionally and globally? I am very excited that Missio Nexus has reinvigorated this handbook. May the information in this new volume better enable us to work more effectively together for the sake of the gospel.

BOB CRESON, President/CEO, Wycliffe Bible Translators USA

Every church missions leader needs the *Mission Handbook* on their bookshelf. You will reach for this resource to quickly discover the evangelical agencies working in any country around the world or to help a prospective worker identify organizations engaged in a particular type of ministry. When someone expresses interest in a mission agency you are unfamiliar with, this directory will provide information not readily available online. The survey data is an added bonus!

ELLEN LIVINGOOD, Catalyst Services

This informative handbook is a healthy reminder to busy churches and agencies that we are not alone in our efforts—many others are also striving to serve faithfully, often in similar ways and similar places! May this new version enable increased collaboration through dialogue, generosity, and a shared vision to reach the lost with the Good News.

ROB "MAGS" MAGWOOD, Host of the *Global Missions Podcast;* Executive Director of SEND Canada

Mission Handbook has established itself as the most reliable go-to guide for data on the state of North American mission activity. Readers will find not only useful statistics, but also insightful analysis essential to understanding current trends and developments. I look forward to using this updated edition for my own research and teaching.

CRAIG OTT, Professor of Mission and Intercultural Studies,
Trinity Evangelical Divinity School

To have such a rich diversity of information about missions, the global church, and the current needs in mission in one place is a great gift for the church. I pray that schools preparing missionaries, missions executives, and church leaders will read and study these pages together. Then the value of this gift will be realized.

SCOTT W. SUNQUIST, Dean, School of Intercultural Studies,
Professor of World Christianity, Fuller Theological Seminary

The *Mission Handbook* 2017 edition provides a wealth of information about the Protestant mission agencies and their missional context with profound insights into the growing role of the Global South and consequential call to the formation of new partnerships in mission. Missio Nexus expresses a new paradigm of collaboration toward the fulfillment of the Great Commission. The stage is set. Now is the time. Now is the opportunity.

LUIS BUSH, International Facilitator, Transform World Connections

For decades, the premier "go to" resource for mission agencies in North America has been the *Mission Handbook*. I've had the most recent copy on my ready reference bookshelf for over twenty-five years—and made many trips to the library before that. I've used it to guide students and colleagues, to research agencies, to explore trends, and to understand the world of mission agencies based in North America but mobilized globally.

SCOTT MOREAU, Associate Dean, Wheaton College Graduate School,
Professor of Intercultural Studies

I am pleased to endorse the newly published 22nd edition of the *Mission Handbook*. The handbook has a long tradition of serving Protestant North American overseas ministries. This newly researched data will prove to be a valuable tool for tracking efforts to complete the Great Commission and is a welcome addition to my library.

GREG MUNDIS, Executive Director,
Assemblies of God World Missions

I'm so grateful to Missio Nexus for taking on the monumental task of producing this latest edition of the *Mission Handbook*. This is a valuable tool that I keep close at hand and reach for often as I prepare for class lectures in which I want to include reliable statistics or highlight current missiological trends. I also find it incredibly useful as I am talking to students, who are preparing for missionary service, about possible mission agencies that work in specific countries or engage in certain types of ministry. While this kind of information may possibly be found scattered across the Internet, I find having it in one volume from a trustworthy source to be indispensable.

TIMOTHY R. SISK, Professor, Intercultural Studies,
Moody Bible Institute

With a legacy since 1953 and competency in data gathering, readers of *Mission Handbook: U.S. and Canadian Protestant Ministries Overseas* will find this resource valuable and helpful in many ways: **informative** (listings of global associations and networks with in-depth analysis), **inspiring** (for strategy formulation), and **innovative** (new surveys of Mission CEOs and Church Mission Leaders).

ENOCH WAN, past president of Evangelical Missiological Society,
Director, Doctor of Intercultural Studies program, Western Seminary

CONTENTS

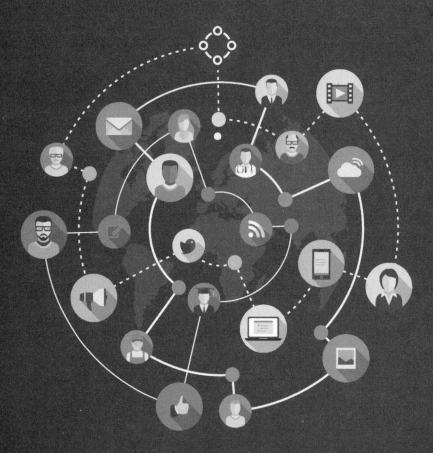

FOREWORD

Dear Friend,

The year 2017 is the 100th year anniversary of Missio Nexus, formed through the merge of CrossGlobal Link (founded in 1917) and The Mission Exchange (founded in 1945). Stop and think about all the changes that have happened in missions over this 100-year period. In all areas of life there have been massive changes. Evangelical mission has not been an exception. Over the past years as we have gone from boats to airplanes and from hard copy to digital, the means of doing mission has changed. At the same time, the foundational truths of the gospel remain the same.

The growth of the church worldwide over the past century has been breathtaking (see chapter 1, "Our Global Families" article). While we in the West fight against secularism, a different story is unfolding around the globe. His eternal purposes are evident on every continent. North Americans have played a significant role in this ever-expanding mission movement. With what I read in the book you hold in your hands, by God's grace we will continue to play that role.

When I talk with mission leaders I often hear an uncertainty about the status of the North American mission movement. Some feel that we continue to live in Bosch's state of uncertainty, which he outlined in his seminal book, *Transforming Mission*. Others think that missions from (and to) North America have been on the decline and that our future is unsure.

However, the data contained here should give one pause before writing an obituary on the North American mission movement. There is a growing vibrancy in missionary organizations, churches, and educational institutions as they grapple with the challenges of our day, as they strive to partner well, as they attempt to understand the task and stay focused.

I am beginning to conclude that the paradigm has begun to settle once again. There continues to be a role and place for North Americans in global missions! That role may be different, but in many ways, it is healthier as we now work together with our global brothers and sisters in Christ in ways our forbearers could only dream about.

A special thanks goes to Dr. Marv Newell who has overseen this project. Peggy Newell as managing editor and Michael VanHuis as research analyst also contributed substantially to the completion of this book. The whole Missio Nexus team hopes that this update on the status of the North American mission movement will not only be a blessing but also a helpful resource to the broader Great Commission community.

Ted Esler, PhD
President, Missio Nexus

Turn your insights into impact.

William Carey publishes books that shape and advance the missiological conversations in the world.

Our ambition is to overcome obstacles and pursue solutions, so that the last remaining, unreached people groups may also taste and see the goodness of Jesus.

FRONTIER VENTURES
SOME BARRIERS WERE MEANT TO BE BROKEN

Find out more at
www.frontierventures.org

INTRODUCTION

Missio Nexus is pleased to present the 22nd edition of the *Mission Handbook*. The purpose of this resource is to provide ready and easy access to vital and current information about US and Canada-based Protestant mission agencies[1] that are engaged in overseas ministries. It is the most comprehensive source of mission-related information available in a single location.

The *Mission Handbook* has incredible value for those going into missions and those who are part of the mission endeavor. It is a guide to help new inquirers discover what agency fits their passions, interests, and gifting. It is one of the best places to look when someone is considering joining an agency. The book's newly researched information and data guides the inquisitive person to a country of interest or specific ministry calling. Professors and researchers use the data to better understand the state of North American missions and to view trends in financial giving, resources, and personnel serving in short-term, mid-term, and long-term missions. **Mission leaders, both in North America and around the world, use this resource to discover peers and potential mission partners in various ministries and/or countries. It is a valuable resource in strategizing what areas of the world are without adequate witness.**

History of the Mission Handbook

The *Mission Handbook* first appeared in 1953 under the title *Foreign Missionary Agencies in the United States: A Check List*. It was compiled by the Missionary Research Library (MRL) in New York. In 1968 the publication

---

1. The term "agency" is used in the broad sense referring to all denominational and non-denominational boards and societies, including other specialized organizations involved in overseas missions.

became a cooperative effort of MRL and the Missions Advanced Research and Communication Center (MARC), a division of World Vision International. The title was changed to *North American Protestant Ministries Overseas Directory* to include ministries based in Canada. In 1973, the title included "Mission Handbook" because the publication began to incorporate related articles and expanded analyses of the surveyed data.

In 2000, the Evangelism and Missions Information Service (EMIS) of the Billy Graham Center at Wheaton College became the publisher. EMIS published through the 21st edition, which was released in 2010. The Billy Graham Center subsequently handed off the *Mission Handbook* rights to Missio Nexus in 2014. Missio Nexus adjusted the title to: *North American Mission Handbook: U.S. and Canadian Protestant Ministries Overseas 2017-2019*. Data collection was completed in 2016, resulting in a seven-year lapse between the previous and present edition.

History of Missio Nexus

Missio Nexus is the largest and most inclusive expression of Great Commission oriented evangelicals in North America (US and Canada) that fosters shared learning, provides opportunities for collaborative action, and produces increased effectiveness through its many mission-oriented products, programs, and services. The network is the result of the January 2012 merge of two long-standing mission associations: CrossGlobal Link (formerly Interdenominational Foreign Mission Association) and The Mission Exchange (formerly Evangelical Fellowship of Mission Agencies).

The Interdenominational Foreign Mission Association (IFMA) was founded in 1917 with the mission of strengthening Christian mission agencies by upholding standards of operation, assuring integrity, and cooperative resourcing to spread the gospel.

At its founding meeting on September 29, 1917 at the First Presbyterian Church of Princeton, NJ, fourteen mission leaders—ten men and four women—were present, representing seven founding missions. From that small cluster of mission leaders, over the next ninety-five years the IFMA expanded into a vast North American-wide mission association exclusively made up of "faith" or non-denominational mission agencies.

Over time they jointly fielded over 15,500 missionaries annually around the globe. At one time, it had over 100 mission agencies in membership.

The Evangelical Fellowship of Mission Agencies (EFMA) was the outgrowth of the National Association of Evangelicals (NAE), and primarily denominationally orientated. A group of mission executives met during the 1945 NAE convention and a committee was appointed to draw up bylaws and a constitution for a new mission association. On September 19, 1945 the constitution was approved and the incorporation was completed by December. The first EFMA convention was held in Minneapolis, MN in April 1946. Eleven mission agencies were received as charter members. Over time the EFMA comprised over 100 mission agencies that together annually fielded close to 20,000 missionaries globally.

In 2007 both associations updated their names. The EFMA changed its name to The Mission Exchange, while the IFMA changed theirs to CrossGlobal Link.

In the fall of 2010, the boards of the two associations met to discuss the possibility of merging with talks continuing into 2011. In September the triannual joint Annual Conference of the two was held in Phoenix, AZ. At their separate membership meetings on the morning of October 1, the membership of both associations voted overwhelmingly to merge. An interim board was established to carry forward the details of the merger. At its December meeting, the interim board agreed on adopting the new name of "Missio Nexus." Legally and practically the merger went into affect on January 1, 2012, but its name remained unannounced to await its official and public unveiling.

Subsequently, on February 6, 2012 at Tabernacle Church in Salem, Massachusetts, during the Bicentennial Celebration commemorating the commissioning of the first US missionaries sent out by a mission society, Missio Nexus was unveiled as the new name for the merged entity.

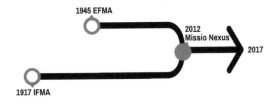

Using the Handbook

This edition of the *Mission Handbook* is designed to be a helpful resource in several ways. The opening articles relay information on the larger world of missions. A general overview by Todd M. Johnson and Cindy M. Wu provides insights into the global mission and church scene. That is followed by two helpful survey reports on overseas ministries seen from the vantage point of both North American mission CEOs and mission pastors. Next, an in-depth analysis, drawn from the book's primary survey, gives insights into current numbers and trends in North American missions. Chapter 5 is the Mission Directory, which is a ready guide to prominent mission agencies in North America. The following chapter is an index of Countries of Activities providing an easy guide for discovering which agencies are working in what countries and regions of the world. Finally, the chapter on Agencies by Ministry Activity enumerates the variety of ministries performed by the missions listed in the directory.

It is our hope that the data and statistics found in this volume will be a help to understanding the current state of the vast mission movement from North America to the rest of the world. Having said that, we are quite aware that there is a vibrant non-North American mission movement that parallels and even exceeds the number of missionaries, resources, and dollars that come from North America. We rejoice in this increasingly significant movement outside our continent and look with anticipation to even more effective collaborating and partnering with these like-minded Great Commission laborers in Kingdom ministries.

Marvin J. Newell, DMiss
Executive Editor

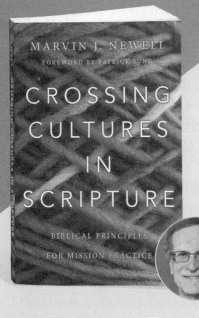
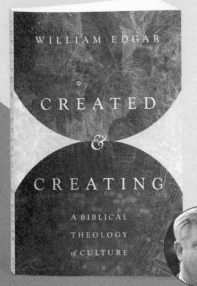

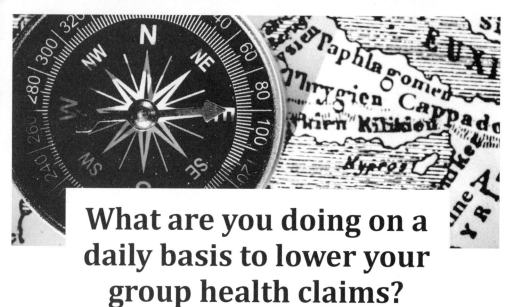

CHAPTER 1
OUR GLOBAL FAMILIES
Todd M. Johnson and Cindy M. Wu

We (the authors) were born into the human race—one of our global families.[1] As only two of more than 7 billion individuals, we are increasingly aware of both the joys and the challenges of getting along with this unfathomable mosaic of peoples, languages, ethnicities, religions, and cultures. For over 100 years the human family has come together every four years (only recently alternating in summer and winter) for a family reunion of sorts around our most accomplished athletes. These Olympic Games are generally a time of global solidarity and celebration. But other "get-togethers" are not so pleasant. In recent global meetings world leaders have had grave disagreements on trade, global warming, nuclear weapons, and a host of other issues. Consequently, while the global human family seems to have the know-how and resources to live well on our planet, we flounder when trying to work together to "save" it. Nonetheless, the human family overflows with creativity, producing technological marvels, impressive structures, dazzling works of art, poignant films, beautiful music, and stunning works of literature. It's a resourceful, chaotic family to belong to, and we are glad to be a part of it.

Our Global Christian Family

We are also part of the global Christian family. What does the global Christian family look like? How many Christians are there and where do they live? What languages do they speak, and what denominations or networks do they belong to? In the Western world we typically think

---

1. This article is excerpted and adapted from Chapter 1 and 2 from *Our Global Families: Christians Embracing Common Identity in a Changing World* by Todd M. Johnson and Cindy M. Wu (Grand Rapids: Baker Academic, 2015).

of a family as a nuclear family—mother, father, and a couple of children—while the Christian family is more of an extended family—a vast assemblage of aunts, uncles, cousins, and other relatives. Ever since the first century the Christian family has reflected a broad and far-reaching collection of people related by faith. Christians have never spoken just one language, represented just one ethnicity, or lived in just one country.[2]

In the many ways the story is framed, our global Christian family has a long and illustrious lineage. From the shores of Galilee in the first century to the remotest villages in the Himalayas today, followers of Jesus Christ have gradually spread to virtually everywhere in the world. David Barrett and I (Todd) estimated that there have been approximately 8 billion Christians since the time of Christ (out of 38 billion human beings).[3] Today the world's 2.4 billion Christians constitute 32.9 percent of the global population.

WHO IS A "CHRISTIAN"?

As we begin this journey into better understanding our global Christian family, invariably a question arises: "Are we talking about the 'true' invisible Church or everyone who considers themselves Christians?" Since the authors are both Evangelicals, you might expect us to say that our global Christian family is made up only of Evangelicals. However, for the purposes of this article, we are adopting the broader United Nations definition of a Christian as one who self-identifies as such.[4] Under this rubric, our global Christian family is made up of all who consider themselves

---

2. For a detailed enumeration of Christians past, present, and future see David B. Barrett, George T. Kurian, and Todd M. Johnson, *World Christian Encyclopedia: A Comparative Survey of Churches and Religions in the Modern World, 2nd edition* (New York: Oxford University Press, 2001), 2 vols.

3. David B. Barrett and Todd M. Johnson, *World Christian Trends* (Pasadena: William Carey Library, 2001), 97.

4. The starting point in any analysis of religious adherence is the United Nations' 1948 *Universal Declaration of Human Rights,* Article 18: "Everyone has the right to freedom of thought, conscience and religion; this right includes freedom to change his religion or belief, and freedom, either alone or in community with others and in public or private, to manifest his religion or belief in teaching, practice, worship and observance." The full text of the UN resolution can be found in Paul M. Taylor,

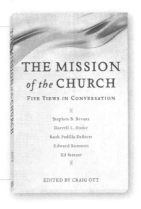
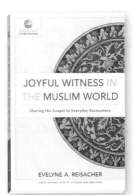

Christians, whether they fit into our ideals of what it means to be a Christian or not. This view doesn't make us any less committed to our tradition but it does mean that we are looking beyond our own network and expressing concern for all who call themselves Christians. This is how we use the term "Christian" throughout this article.

THE LONG VIEW: 2000 YEARS

When we take a long view of Christian history, stepping back and considering 2,000 years of Christian growth and decline, the demographics (or numbers) of Christians in this story are striking. Utilizing clues from historical records, we can track the numbers of Christians in every continent of the world across the entire history of Christianity.[5] The global percentage of Christians has gone up and down over time. Some high and low points are 700 CE (20%), 1000 (17%), 1300 (23%), 1600 (18%), and 1900 (24%). Asia had the most Christians for at least the first 700 years. Then by 1000 CE, Europe had that distinction and has held it to the present. Today, in 2017, three continents (Europe, Africa, and Latin America) all have approximately the same number of Christians. In a few short years, Africa will have, by far, the most Christians. In addition, Asia and Latin America will both have more Christians than Europe!

We can also group totals of Christians by Global North and Global South for the entire history of Christianity. By Global North, we are referring to Europe and Northern America; by Global South, we are referring to Africa, Asia, Latin America, and Oceania. For at least the first 900 years (until about 920 CE), Christians in the Global South outnumbered those in the Global North. Christians were all Southerners[6] at the time of Christ, gradually becoming more Northern until 1500 when fully 92 percent of all Christians were Northerners (Europeans). This percentage began to decline gradually until 1900, when it was 82 percent. After 1900 the percentage declined precipitously (or, from the Southern point of view,

---

Freedom of Religion: UN and European Human Rights Law and Practice (Cambridge: Cambridge University Press, 2005), 368–72.

5. A detailed analysis can be found in *Atlas of Global Christianity*, 212–13.

6. Ancient Palestine is located in the present-day UN region of Western Asia, defined above as part of the South.

rose meteorically). If these trends continue, by 2100 over three fourths of all Christians will be living in the South.[7] This not only represents a return to the demographic makeup of Christianity at the time of Christ (predominantly Southern) but also a vast extension of Christianity into all countries as well as thousands of peoples, languages, and cultures. The percentages are shown in Graph 1.1, "Christians by percentage in the North or South, 33–2100 CE."

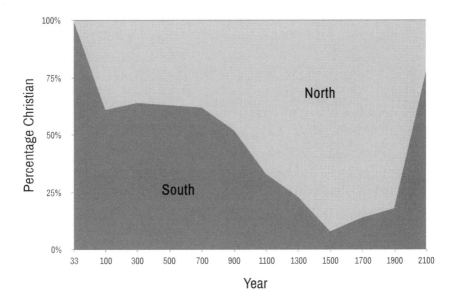

Source: Todd M. Johnson and Gina A. Zurlo, *World Christian Database*, (Leiden/ Boston: Brill) August 2016.

GRAPH 1.1 Christians by percentage in North or South, 33–2100 CE

THE SHORT VIEW: 115 YEARS

After 1900 something profound happened to the European dominance of global Christianity. Churches outside Europe and the Americas that had taken root in the nineteenth century grew rapidly in the twentieth

---

7.   Note as well that many of those Christians living in the North will be Southern Christians who have emigrated there!

century.[8] Africa, in particular, led this transformation, starting with only 10 million Christians in 1900, rising to 380 million by 2000, and to over 574 million by 2015. Table 1.1 below shows the changing status of Christianity by continent over the past 115 years.[9]

TABLE 1.1 Christians (C) by United Nations continent and Global North/South, 1900–2015

Region	Population 1900	C 1900	% 1990	Population 2015	C 2015	% 2015	C 1900–2015	Pop 1900–2015
GLOBAL SOUTH	1,135,392,000	98,674,000	8.7%	6,220,532,000	1,559,890,000	25.1%	2.43%	1.49%
Africa	107,808,000	9,918,000	9.2%	1,166,239,000	569,861,000	48.9%	3.59%	2.09%
Asia	956,196,000	21,914,000	2.3%	4,384,844,000	379,511,000	8.7%	2.51%	1.33%
Latin America	65,142,000	62,003,000	95.2%	630,089,000	581,730,000	82.3%	1.97%	1.99%
Oceania	6,246,000	4,839,000	77.5%	39,359,000	28,787,000	73.1%	1.56%	1.61%
GLOBAL NORTH	484,233,000	459,457,000	94.9%	1,104,251,000	860,433,000	77.9%	0.55%	0.72%
Europe	402,607,000	380,645,000	94.5%	743,123,000	579,789,000	78%	0.37%	0.53%
North America	81,626,000	78,812,000	96.6%	361,128,000	280,644,000	77.7%	1.11%	1.3%
GLOBE	1,619,625,000	558,131,000	34.5%	7,324,782,000	2,420,323,000	33%	1.28%	1.32%

Source: Todd M. Johnson and Gina A. Zurlo, *World Christian Database*, (Leiden/ Boston: Brill) August 2016.

This table illustrates several important trends. First, over the past 115 years Christianity changed very little as a proportion of the world's population. In 1900 it was 34.5 percent of the global population and today (2015) it is 32.9 percent. Second, one can see that Christianity has been growing more rapidly than the population in the Global South. Third, it has been growing more slowly than the population in the Global North. These dynamics together help to explain the rapid demographic shift of global Christianity to the South. While 82 percent of all Christians lived in the Global North in 1900, today nearly two-thirds of all Christians live in the Global South.

CHRISTIAN TRADITIONS AND MOVEMENTS

Table 1.2 below illustrates additional changes over the 115-year period from 1900–2015. Of the major traditions in Christianity, Roman Catholicism

---

8. Latin America was already 95 percent Christian (Roman Catholic) in 1900. The changes in Latin America since then refer to the growth of Protestantism and Pentecostalism.

9. The methodology and sources behind these estimates are explained in detail in Todd M. Johnson and Brian J. Grim, *The World's Religions in Figures: An Introduction to International Religious Demography* (Oxford: Wiley-Blackwell, 2013).

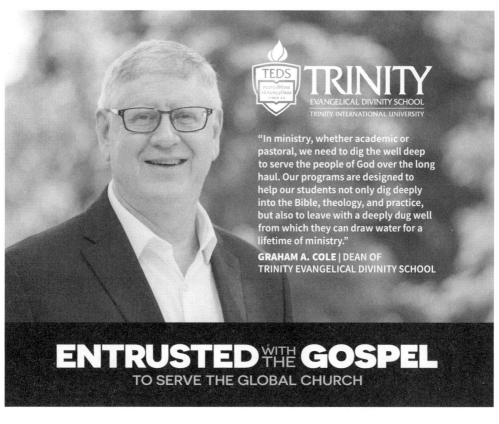

represents just over half of all Christians. Catholics' percentage of the global population stayed the same. This, however, masks a steep decline in adherents in Europe accompanied by a simultaneous rise in Africa, Asia, and Latin America. Since 1900, Orthodox declined as percentages of the population, both within Christianity and globally. Orthodoxy, decimated by the rise of communism in Europe, dropped from over 7 percent of the global population in 1900 to less than 4 percent today. At the same time, the Orthodox fell from 21 percent to less than 12 percent of all Christians. Protestant Christians have fallen slightly as a percentage of all Christians. Their share of the global population also decreased from 8.2 percent to 7.4 percent in the same period. Independents, on the other hand, increased their shares of the total Christian community and of the global population. Independent Christians, especially in Africa and Asia, represented only 1.6 percent of Christians in 1900 but rose meteorically to over 17 percent by 2015. Their share of the global population also increased, from 0.5 percent to 5.7 percent.

Movements within Christianity and across the traditions likewise experienced changes in size and percentage over the 115-year period (see Table 1.2 below). In 1900, Evangelicals, mainly Protestants in the Global North, represented 14.5 percent of all Christians and 5 percent of the global population. By 2015, these had dropped to 13.6 percent and 4.5 percent, respectively. Renewalists (Pentecostals and Charismatics), on the other hand, grew rapidly, from just 0.1 percent of the global population and 0.2 percent of all Christians in 1900 to 8.8 percent and 26.6 percent, respectively, by 2015.

TABLE 1.2 Christian (C) traditions and movements, 1900 and 2015

	Name	Adherents 1900	% world 1900	% all Cs 1900	Adherents 2015	% world 2015	% all Cs 2015
Traditions	Anglicans	30,578,000	1.9%	5.5%	94,226,000	1.3%	3.9%
	Independents	8,859,000	0.5%	1.6%	418,168,000	5.7%	17.3%
	Orthodox	115,855,000	7.2%	20.8%	282,967,000	3.9%	11.7%
	Protestants	103,028,000	6.4%	18.5%	449,418,000	6.1%	18.6%
	Catholics	266,566,000	16.5%	47.8%	1,239,808	16.9%	51.2%
Movements	Evangelicals	80,912,000	5.0%	14.5%	328,582,000	4.5%	13.6%
	Renewalists	981,000	0.1%	0.2%	643,661,000	8.8%	26.6%

Source: Todd M. Johnson and Gina A. Zurlo, *World Christian Database*, (Leiden/Boston: Brill) August 2016.
Note: Percentages do not add up to 100% because of double-counting between traditions.

ANTICIPATING THE CHRISTIAN FUTURE

What does it mean for the future of Christianity that the proportion of Christians in the Global South continues to increase? Until now, Western scholars have written the dominant theologies of Christianity, but the massive movements of Southern Christianity, whether they be Catholic, Orthodox, Protestant, Anglican, or Independent, will likely chart the future of Christian theology. Theologians such as the Ghanaian Kwame Bediako have begun to outline the enormous challenges this project holds for African Christians.[10] Malaysian Methodist Bishop Hwa Yung poses that as the Asian church grows rapidly, it needs to "self-theologize, developing a theology for itself that is rooted in one's culture, history and context."[11] The Northern church would do well to take on the posture of learning as British missiologist David Smith advises,

> We are witnesses to the emergence of new centres of spiritual and theological vitality as Christians from the southern continents add their insights to the church's total knowledge of the incomparable Christ. In the present transitional stage we are moving *from* a Christendom shaped by the culture of the Western world, *to* a world Christianity which will develop new spiritual and theological insights as the biblical revelation is allowed to interact with the many cultures in which Christ is now confessed as Lord.[12]

"THEY SPEAK IN MANY TONGUES"

The rapid growth of Christianity in non-Western, non-English-speaking countries also implies that the language of Christians is changing. Already

10. Kwame Bediako, *Christianity in Africa: The Renewal of a Non-Western Religion* (Maryknoll: Orbis, 1995).

11. Hwa Yung, "Theological Issues Facing the Asian Church," 2. Paper presented at ALCOE V, August 2002, Seoul. See also his more detailed proposal in *Mangoes or Bananas? The Quest for an Authentic Asian Christian Theology* (Oxford: Regnum Books International, 1997).

12. David Smith, *Mission After Christendom* (London: Darton, Longman and Todd Ltd, 2003), 61.

by 1980, Spanish was the leading language of church membership in the world (because of Latin America, not Spain).[13] European languages dominate the top ten, including English (2), Russian (4), German (6), French (7), Polish (8), and Ukrainian (9). But languages of the Global South are moving up the list: Portuguese (3, due primarily to Brazil), Chinese (5), and Tagalog (the Philippines) (10), with Amharic (Ethiopia), Korean, Yoruba (Nigeria), Igbo (Nigeria), and Cebuano (the Philippines) not far behind. Of course, Christians in Africa, Asia, Latin America, and Oceania worship in numerous other languages besides Spanish, Portuguese, Chinese, and Yoruba. Thus, the translation of the gospel into indigenous languages and cultures has become increasingly important.

Apart from the shift away from Northern languages as the dominant languages of Christianity, there is also a need for a change in the perception of missions as a Northern phenomenon. For the past several hundred years, Christians in Europe and the United States have been "the Church" and the rest of the world has been "the mission field." The shift of Christianity from Europe to the Southern hemisphere means that Africa, Asia, and Latin America can no longer be seen as the periphery. Instead, Christian mission to the whole world will require participation from all Christians—North and South—to be successful.

PERSECUTION

For some time now, most Christians in the North have experienced religious freedom and comfort.[14] The spread of Christianity to the South, where it often clashes with other religions, brings with it the reality of persecution and martyrdom experienced by the Church in the past. In places like the Middle East, Nigeria, Sudan/South Sudan, India, and China, many Christians live with the risk of losing their lives. The Pew

---

13. See Global Table 7 "Affiliated Christians (Church Members) Ranked by 96 Languages each with over a Million Native Speakers, AD 1980" in David B. Barrett, *World Christian Encyclopedia* (New York: Oxford University Press, 1982), 10. An updated table appears in the *Atlas of Global Christianity*, 213.

14. One exception among many is the Russian and Eastern European churches that suffered greatly under Communist rule. For a recent update on persecution see Paul Marshall, Lela Gilbert, and Nina Shea, *Persecuted: The Global Assault on Christians* (Nashville: Thomas Nelson, 2013).

Research Center reported in 2012 that Christians are the most widely-persecuted religious group (139 countries).[15] Christian discipleship, often defined in the New Testament by suffering and persecution, is taking on greater significance for the global Church. As increasing numbers of Christians suffer and die, the global Christian family suffers and takes on responsibility for mutual comfort, support, and advocacy.

All of these factors point toward a future for the global Christian family that represents both opportunity and peril. What is certain is that in either case Christianity will not be drawing on a dominant Northern or Southern cultural, linguistic, or political framework for the answers. Global Christianity is a phenomenon, not of uniformity, but of ever-increasing diversity. The unanswered question for Christians from both the North and the South is how well we will work, minister, and grow together as a family in the context of this astonishing diversity. Today, the global composition of our Christian family provides clues about where one might look to find both the answers and the leadership for that quest.

Our Global Human Family

We also belong to a larger diverse human family. Counting everyone who has ever lived, our human family is more than 80 billion people![16] Today some 7.3 billion people live on our planet. This embraces tropical peoples and mountain dwellers, high-rise executives and fishermen, and thousands of other locations and vocations. Diverse in language and customs, the world's peoples also practice a multitude of religions and philosophies.

Underlying the reality of a changing global religious landscape is increasing religious diversity. Religious diversity is present at two levels: intrareligious and interreligious diversity. Intrareligious diversity encompasses the diversity found within a given world religion (for example, traditions such as Roman Catholicism, Orthodoxy, and Protestantism within Christianity), whereas interreligious diversity describes the degree

---

15. Pew Research Center, "Rising Tide of Restrictions on Religion," September 23, 2012, http://www.pewforum.org/files/2012/09/RisingTideofRestrictions-fullreport.pdf.

16. See Steve Olson, *Mapping Human History: Genes, Race, and Our Common Origins* (Boston: Houghton Mifflin, 2002), 101.

of overall diversity of world religions (Christianity, Islam, Hinduism, Judaism, and so on) in a given population or geographic area.[17] It is important to note that, within a particular country, interreligious diversity can vary greatly from one locale to another because religious adherents often cluster in local communities. Such is often the case for countries receiving significant numbers of immigrants or refugees, many of whom settle in major metropolitan areas.

DIVERSITY VS. PLURALISM

In popular use, *diversity* and *pluralism* are sometimes considered interchangeable. We treat diversity as a descriptive, demographic characteristic that is distinct from pluralism, which scholars often treat as a relational characteristic.[18] So, for instance, a religiously *diverse* town in the United States might have a Christian church; a Native American spiritual center; a humanist society; a Jewish synagogue; a Muslim mosque; and Buddhist, Hindu, and Sikh temples. But the town would be considered to have religious *pluralism* only if these diverse groups contribute to a common civil society, accept one another, and approach differences respectfully.

RELIGIONS IN THE WORLD TODAY

Table 1.3 is a quick-reference for comparing the global strength of each of 18 religions as a percentage of the world's population in 1900 and 2015, as well as a way to compare a religion's growth rate with those of other religions and of the world's population as a whole (expressed as an average annual growth rate[19]). In addition, one can compare growth rates over the century (1900–2015) with those over the past 15 years (2000–2015).

---

17. For a complete survey of the intra-religious diversity of Christianity, see Johnson and Ross, *Atlas of Global Christianity*, parts II and III.

18. See Mark Silk, "Defining Religious Pluralism in America: A Regional Analysis," *The ANNALS of the American Academy of Political and Social Science*, July 2007, 62–81.

19. Calculated with the formula $[(\text{Adherents } 2015/\text{Adherents } 1900)1/115 - 1] \times 100$.

TABLE 1.3 World religions by adherents, 1900–2015

Religion	Adherents 1900	% 1900	Adherents 2015	% 2015	1900–2015 % p.a.	2000–2015 % p.a.
Agnostics	3,029,000	0.2%	698,258,000	9.5%	4.84%	0.37%
Atheists	226,000	0%	136,465,000	1.9%	5.73%	-0.02%
Baha'is	205,000	0%	7,904,000	0.1%	3.23%	1.69%
Buddhists	126,956,000	7.8%	521,232,000	7.1%	1.24%	0.95%
Chinese folk-religionists	379,974,000	23.5%	453,458,000	6.2%	0.15%	0.34%
Christians	558,131,000	34.5%	2,420,323,000	33%	1.28%	1.32%
Confucianists	840,000	0.1%	8,312,000	0.1%	2.01%	0.36%
Ethnoreligionists	117,437,000	7.3%	254,193,000	3.5%	0.67%	1.03%
Hindus	202,973,000	12.5%	983,750,000	13.4%	1.38%	1.26%
Jains	1,324,000	0.1%	5,755,000	0.1%	1.29%	1.55%
Jews	12,292,000	0.8%	13,863,000	0.2%	0.1%	0.3%
Muslims	199,818,000	12.3%	1,705,392,000	23.3%	1.88%	1.88%
New Religionists	5,986,000	0.4%	64,000,000	0.9%	2.08%	0.28%
Shintoists	6,720,000	0.4%	2,774,000	0%	-0.77%	0.09%
Sikhs	2,962,000	0.2%	25,870,000	0.4%	1.9%	1.59%
Spiritists	269,000	0%	14,271,000	0.2%	3.52%	0.89%
Daoists	375,000	0%	8,768,000	0.1%	2.78%	1.38%
Zoroastrians	109,000	0%	195,000	0%	0.51%	0.45%
TOTAL POPULATION	1,619,625,000	100%	7,324,782,000	100%	1.32%	1.2%

Source: Todd M. Johnson and Brian J. Grim, eds., *World Religion Database* (Leiden/ Boston: Brill) August 2016.

Four trends for the 115-year period are immediately apparent: (1) Christians' percentage of the world's population declined slightly; (2) Muslims have experienced the most significant change in proportion for any of the large religions; (3) Buddhists' and Chinese folk-religionists' combined share of the global population shrank by over half in that period; (4) agnostics and atheists experienced the largest percentage growth, from less than 1 percent of the world's population to well over 11 percent.

Two other profound changes are noteworthy when comparing the strengths of religions globally in 1900 with those of 2015. First, sub-Saharan Africa was predominantly tribal religionist in 1900; by 2015 tribal religionists had been displaced as a majority bloc, with either Christianity introduced from the south or Islam from the north now forming the majority in almost all provinces. Second, Eastern Asia has gone from a majority of Chinese folk-religionists to a plurality of agnostics and atheists. Table 1.3 shows the growth of agnostics and atheists globally.

Another important trend to note is that Christians and Muslims together are claiming an increasing percentage of the world's population.

If we were to go back to 1800, these two together would represent only about 33 percent of the world's population. Projections for 2100 show this increasing to 66 percent. So, in 1800, Christians and Muslims were one-third of the world's population—by 2100 they are expected to count for two-thirds. Surely the relationship between these two religions is a significant one.

RELIGIOUSLY AFFILIATED VS. UNAFFILIATED

Despite attempts to depict the twentieth century as a "secular" century, most of the people who lived during that period were, in fact, affiliated with a religion. In 1900, well over 99 percent of the world's population was religiously affiliated. By 2015 the figure had fallen below 89 percent, but this 115-year trend hides the fact that the high point for the nonreligious was around 1970, when almost 20 percent of the world's population was either agnostic or atheist (see Graph 1.2 below). The collapse of Soviet Communism in the late twentieth century was accompanied by a resurgence of religion, making the world more religiously affiliated in 2015 than in 1970. This resurgence of religious affiliation continues in the present (even though the number of atheists and agnostics continues to rise in the Western world), and the current growth of religions of all kinds in China (where the vast majority of the nonreligious live today) indicates that the future of the world is likely to be a religious one.

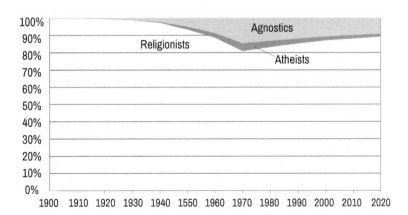

Source: Todd M. Johnson and Brian J. Grim, eds., *World Religion Database* (Leiden/Boston: Brill) August 2016.

GRAPH 1.2 Percentage of the world's population belonging to no religion or religion, 1900-2015

CLASH OR COOPERATION?

The shift of Christianity's demographic center to the South brings to the forefront the potential for conflict between Christians and non-Christians. How will Muslim-Christian tensions in countries like Nigeria, Sudan/South Sudan, Egypt, Indonesia, and the Philippines be resolved? What is the future of the Christian church in Hindu India? How will Buddhists and Christians coexist in Southeast Asia? Furthermore, although these religions are found primarily in Asia, increasing numbers of Muslims, Hindus, and Buddhists are living in North America and Europe. Christians around the globe have an opportunity to show hospitality to non-Christian neighbors and to take a genuine interest in their religions and cultures.

Looking Ahead

What difference does embracing our identity as members of both the global Christian family and the global human family make? Will we really be able to both witness to our faith and help to change the world? We have pointed out that considerable strife is present in both of our families. While they are both beautifully diverse, they are also tragically fragmented and disjointed.

We embrace a vision of our global Christian family getting along and of a world transformed by obedience to the gospel. We also embrace a vision of our global Christian family finding solidarity with our global human family to work together for the common good. We think these visions can change the world.

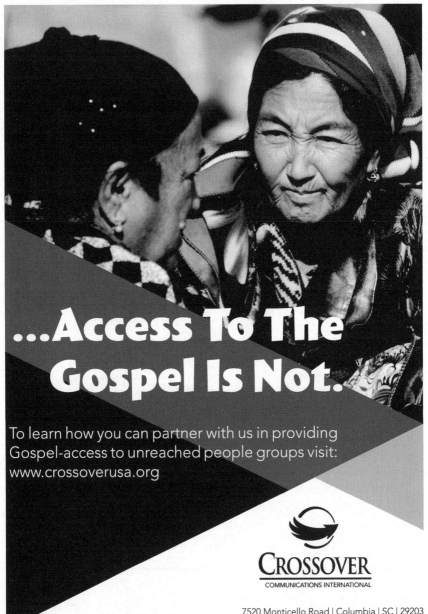

CHAPTER 2
MISSION CEO SURVEY SUMMARY

In 2016, Missio Nexus commissioned a second survey of mission agency CEOs. The goal was to provide peer information and perspective to enable leaders to more knowledgeably and carefully fulfill our charge of helping churches, organizations, and workers be fruitful in Great Commission ministry. The inaugural survey was fielded in early 2013 among chief executives from more than 150 mission organizations; in comparison, the 2016 survey represents 161 chief executives and mission leaders.

Mission CEO Priorities: Personal

CEOs were asked to identify their *Top Picked Personal Priorities*. The largest percentage emphasized a need for continued attention given to *Spiritual Discipline* as a guide for their leadership responsibilities. This is followed by an ability to provide *Servant Leadership* to their organizations. *Servant Leadership* and *Spiritual Discipline* lead the top priorities as they did in the

CHART **2.1** 2016 Top CEO Organizational Priorities

2013 study. These are followed by the ongoing need for continued *Leadership Training* and time given to *Fundraising*.

Mission CEO Priorities: Staff

The 2016 study identified that *Organizational Agility* and *Adaptability* was a high-level priority for staff effectiveness. With many millennials now working in mission offices, an increased desire for flexible hours, workspace, location, and less hierarchical processes has brought an increased need for adaptability from more traditional office structures to allow for more flexible working conditions.

An additional high level priority in 2016 was *Values—Driven Culture*. It is extremely important for staff of a mission organization to understand the underlying values of why they do what they do, and why leadership may need to make certain decisions that will not always win the popular vote. Reinforcing values among the staff on a regular basis creates and manages expectations more effectively.

Mission CEO Priorities: Organizational

In reviewing the last three to five years, CEOs identified both *Developing New Revenue* and *Fundraising* in their top five organizational priorities. *Attracting Qualified Staff* remained high over the past three years, and *Measuring Field Impact* moved into the top five priorities in ensuring effectiveness in the years to come.

Whether we examined priorities that are *Personal, Staff* or *Organizational* in focus, the consistent element was leadership, development, and the spiritual nurturing of our staff. As leaders, we must proactively seek to have the fitting heart and skills to lead our teams with passion and purpose.

2016 vs. 2013— How Far Have We Traveled?

CEOs ranked fifteen different categories in a question that asked them to compare how their organization looks today compared to 2013. CEOs reported in this section that in comparison to three years ago there were some very positive trends among North American mission organizations.

Sixty-one percent of CEOs reported that *Organizational Revenue* compared to three years ago had increased, twenty-three percent reported that it had stayed at the same level and fourteen percent expressed a decrease in revenue. Overall this is very encouraging news regarding the increase in revenue coming in to North American mission organizations over the last three years. Similarly, positive news was recorded for the *Number of Field Personnel* actively serving. Fifty-seven percent of CEOs reported that there was an increase in field personnel over the last three years. Twenty-six percent showed the number remaining the same and sixteen percent reported a decline in field personnel.

CHART **2.2** 2016 vs. 2013
Organization Revenue

CHART **2.3** 2016 vs. 2013
Number of Field Personnel

Although many who reported that field levels had increased, thirty-eight percent indicated that the number of people retiring from their mission was also increasing over the past three years. Fifty-two percent showed a stable number of retirees, and only 8.9% reported a decline in retirements.

One additional and significant area to highlight in this section is the reported changes in the *Percentage of Women in Leadership* roles within mission organizations. Over the last three years, a noted forty-five percent

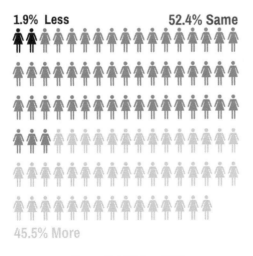

CHART **2.4** 2016 vs. 2013
Percentage of Women in Leadership

increase has been reported by participating organizations, while fifty-three percent have not changed. This continues to be an area of growth and discovery for many organizations. As we celebrate our sisters who are called to serve within our organizations, we still find many differing viewpoints about how and where they should serve. There is great diversity in the Great Commission community on this issue—driven by theological views, culture, upbringing, modern societal pressure, and the list could go on. There is clearly a need to engage in conversation with each other, within our churches and organizations and across the association on these issues. We need to be prepared to clearly articulate our beliefs about gender roles within mission and not just rest on our laurels and hope it takes care of itself.

How Well Have We Traveled?

CEOs were asked to reflect on how well they carry out specific activities as mission organizations. The first area to examine is *Enabling Global Teams to Work Effectively*. It was the only activity that registered a forty-nine percent for the category *Very Well*. There is evidence that intentionality is taking place within mission organizations to ensure that their teams are working as effectively as possible. Increases in leadership training and on-field member care are two areas which have been given increased attention and have facilitated healthier and more effective teams.

Another activity was *Intentionally Promote Mission, Vision, and Passion*. Forty-four percent of CEOs felt that their organization was doing a *Very Good* job of communicating who they are and what they are uniquely called to do. This is always an area of great focus for organizations as they try to communicate a message that is relevant across generations and culture yet remains in sync with ideology and mission.

Lastly, two areas registered *Slightly Well* to a greater degree than the others: *Spread Innovation Through Organizations Effectively* and *Monitoring the Spiritual Condition of Field Workers*. These are two very different activities, but both require intentionality on the part of the leader to be effective activities. Most organizations do not have a chief innovator who can work with both home office and field staff to analyze practices, ideas, and strategies and then utilize their platform to communicate them across the organization. Often organizations find it difficult to "enforce" innovation in practice across their organizations. Similarly, individual *Spiritual Condition of Workers* may be monitored at a field or regional level, but often it is difficult to gauge this over the breadth of the organizations. Intentionality in both areas would bring stronger, more effective and enduring ministry and workers

Metrics: Assessing Our Progress

Spiritual maturity of workers – 81%

Field ministry activities – 74%

Degree of partnership – 74%

Field ministry impact – 66%

Field worker retention – 52%

Percentage of work
among least reached – 47%

Number of field personnel – 46%

Revenue growth – 42%

Numbers of multiplying CPM/DMM's – 41%

Numbers of active ministry fields – 39%

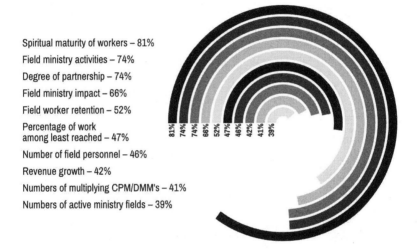

CHART 2.5 Effective Markers of Organizational Progress

Eighty-one percent of CEOs felt that understanding how their workers are doing spiritually is one of the most important markers for progress. When asked in a separate question how the spiritual condition and maturity of field workers compared to three years ago, forty-seven percent thought it was about the same, and fifty-two percent felt it was much better.

CEOs were asked what they measured and if they acted upon that data. *Revenue Growth* far exceeds other areas which are measured and acted upon. At the end of the day, the finances of an organization deeply matter to CEOs as they face the realities of running offices and ministries. The measurement of revenue is an easy metric to evaluate against ministry expenses. It is also an "easier" issue to give attention to and track results of development initiatives.

Field Ministry Impact, Worker Retention, and *Active Ministry Fields* are key indicators of effectiveness connected to the mission of organization. Field metric gathering can often be difficult but is extremely valuable. Organizations need to determine a strong rubric for field reporting. Clear terminology, process, and time lines with some form of accountability for field staff is ideal for gathering consistent and relevant information. This type of tracking will not only be valuable to field leaders but will also help with recruitment and fundraising efforts.

Looking Over the Horizon: External Forces Affecting Our Journey

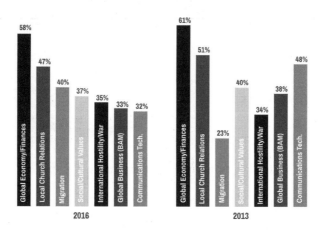

CHART 2.6 External Forces Affecting Change 2016 vs. 2013

Global Economy/Finances and *Local Church Relations* remain as the top two external forces CEOs believe will have an impact on the sustainability of their missions. Both external forces directly impact revenue and mobilization efforts of organizations.

Migration recorded the largest upward change, most likely in light of the crisis imposed by ISIS and the vast movement of people from the Middle East to Europe and North America over the last three years. This

NEW FROM FULLER SEMINARY:

A 100% ONLINE PROGRAM FOR MISSIONARIES

Fuller's Certificate of Christian Studies now equips missionaries for more effective work in an online format that allows them to learn in the field. New courses developed specifically for missionaries— Leadership for Transformation, Self-Care for Cross-Cultural Workers, and other topics requested by missionaries—are taught by Fuller's seasoned missiologists, at a substantial tuition discount available through partner mission agencies.

Fuller.edu/Missionaries

will continue to create opportunity for new ministry and a need to change mission methodologies to be able to engage with the growing migration. The global influences affecting this migration of people are also creating increased risk for workers around the world. The slight uptick in those listing *International Hostility/War* in their top five demonstrates that this is something that is on the minds of CEOs and no doubt on the minds of their boards. Proactive training, planning, and preparation for workers and leadership teams is invaluable as we continue to place people in locations that place them at physical risk.

Looking Over the Horizon: Internal Forces Affecting Our Journey

Personnel Recruitment continued to top the list of Internal Forces that will affect organizational change. In fact, fifty-two percent of non-denominational leaders chose this as the area of greatest impact compared to twenty-one percent of denominational leaders and sixty percent of mission support organizations. The most significant change was demonstrated in the area of *Business/Financial Model* category, moving up to thirty-three percent from twenty-six percent in 2013. Increased costs and the difficulty of home-based staff to raise support have led many organizations to start seeking new models for carrying on the business of missions. Some organizations are experimenting with shared office staff while others are utilizing outsourced companies to manage everything from finances to communications.

Governance and *Leadership* demonstrated the highest rate of CEOs that felt they were *Fully* prepared for change. The only times that CEOs listed that they were *Not Prepared* (albeit a small percentage) were in the areas of *Business Model* and *Crisis Prevention/Management*. These categories also had the highest ranking of *Minimally Prepared* out of all areas surveyed. Although CEOs felt they were *Minimally Prepared*, they did not rank either item high in the previous lists of internal or external forces facing their organizations. Organizations should be aware that the lack of priority or felt pressure in these areas could lead to a lack of preparation for change. Many would argue that both areas are key areas of importance for the future of mission organizations. Traditional business models are difficult to maintain and fund. Creative and innovative structures are needed for the future of mission organizations. Likewise, in the face of global and domestic terror threats mission organizations would be wise to proactively increase their level of knowledge and preparation for crisis at their home office and in relation to their global workers.

Evaluating Our Future: Innovation in Missions

CEOs were asked to reflect on areas of potential innovation in missions over the next three to five years. *Leadership Development* remained a top choice for CEOs as it was in the 2013 survey. *Financial Models, Mobilization,* and *Mission Structures* filled out the top six picks for 2016. A world of rapid change requires the ability of organizations to think innovatively when it comes to operations that have existed in a similar fashion for many decades. Time and resources spent on innovation, research, and testing ideas is rarely a wasted endeavor.

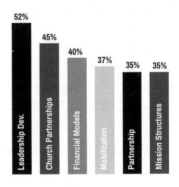

CHART 2.7 Innovation in Mission - All CEO's

Working with the Majority World Missions Movement

Many organizations are still seeking to adjust and blend strategies, resources, and leadership constructs in light of a growing non-western church missions movement. Among our group of respondents, forty-eight percent reported a growth of workers in their organizations originating from the majority world. Yet, there remains only a thirty-nine percent growth in North Americans reporting to those from the majority world. There is no doubt that change takes time, yet change is taking place.

Finances remains the biggest challenge when engaging with the majority world missions movement. As long as great extremes exist in global economies, finances will remain a source of potential tension. Clear communication, expectations, and engagement within organizations is essential in handling this issue. Sustainable and reproducible models of mission are essential to build, especially in light of radically changing global dynamics.

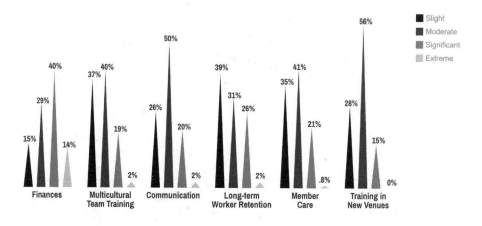

CHART 2.8 Challenges when engaging with the Majority World Missions Movement

Mission Organizations and the Local Church

The mission organization and local church relationship is strategic but not always easy to define or to carry out. Each mission organization and church has a unique perspective on their role in global missions and expectations about partnership.

CEOs were asked about their relationship with local churches. As was previously reported, they felt the local church played a key role in the internal and external forces facing their organizations in the next three to five years. *Church Partnerships* was fourth on the list of the top five internal forces creating impact and second on the list of external impactors. We also asked CEOs about challenges they face when working with the local church. Forty-nine percent of CEOs reported that *Increasing Local Church Relationships* was a *Significant* challenge, while an additional fourteen percent found it to be an *Extreme* challenge.

The majority of CEOs found that *Determining Partnership Models* was a challenge as they work with churches. Forums for ongoing interaction and discussion between both agencies and churches can be good starting points for open conversation on these challenges. Some mission organizations have made it a priority to host church partner forums to begin building relationships with the sending churches of their missionaries. This will go a long way in assisting with other noted challenges, such as missionary care and finances.

Summary—CEO Survey

Surveys and assessments increase in value if they bring about change. As leaders, we must prioritize internal investigation and assessment to determine the adjustments that need to be made to maximize our ministry efforts in order to accomplish the mission for which we have been called. Additional information, charts, and resources for further study can be found in the full 2016 Mission CEO and Church Mission Leader Survey at www.missionexus.org.

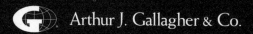

CHAPTER 3
MISSION PASTOR SURVEY SUMMARY

Missio Nexus conducted a survey among church mission leaders with a goal to gather and analyze data on the unique factors facing churches across North America who are engaged in global missions. Subsequently the information was analyzed in comparison to the data collected through the 2016 CEO survey, both studies will be conducted on a triennial basis.

Two hundred twelve church mission leaders participated in the inaugural survey, nearly split evenly between denominational and nondenominational churches. Forty-eight percent of the survey participants indicated that they were Full-time staff solely focused on their church's missions efforts. Eleven percent were staff with Split Roles who only give part of their time to missions, and eight percent were missions leaders serving in Part-time positions. Thirty-one percent of those leading their church's missions efforts indicated that they lead from a Volunteer position.

Eighty-nine of the participating churches had over a thousand in regular attendance, while one hundred twenty-eight had fewer than a thousand. Those over two thousand consisted of twenty denominational and thirty-one non-denominational churches.

Sixty percent of denominational churches and sixty-four percent of non-denominational listed the average age of attendees in their 40s. Only one percent had an average age in their 20s. Most churches represented late baby boomers, Gen X, and early millennials.

In summary, the largest percentage of churches had over a thousand in attendance, with an average age of attendees in their 40s. They were for the most part single-campus entities that have been in existence for at least a decade or, in most cases, longer. Sixty-seven percent had a staff member designated to lead their missions effort, and there was an even representation of denominational and non-denominational churches.

Church Missions Program Focus

In the last decade, there has been a substantial focus on Social Justice related issues in churches' global engagement. In light of this, our findings were quite interesting as we asked these churches to indicate their level of involvement in areas of Evangelism and Church Planting, Unreached People, Community Development, Humanitarian Aid and Social Justice.

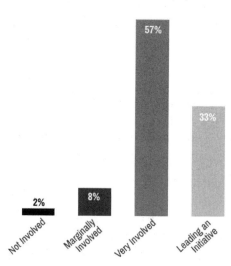

CHART 3.1 Focus of Church Missions Program *Evangelism and Church Planting*

Evangelism and Church Planting and Unreached People-focused ministry were by far the most engaged programs out of the five options. Fifty-seven percent of churches were Very Involved with Evangelism and Church Planting, and an encouraging thirty-three percent indicated that they were Actively Leading an Initiative.

Likewise, when asked about Unreached People, fifty percent were Very Involved in ministry and twenty-four percent were Leading an Initiative. In both of these areas, only two to three percent identified being Not Involved. In light of the call upon the church to be engaged with the proclamation of the gospel to the nations, the churches participating seemed to be taking this call and putting it into action through active work around the globe.

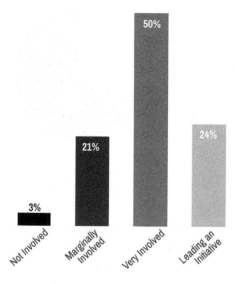

CHART 3.2 Focus of Church Missions Program *Unreached People*

Churches were less involved with Social Justice and Humanitarian Aid than we would have predicted. Although they are involved in some degree it was more marginal and a very small group were Actively Leading an Initiative in these areas. Forty-one percent indicated that they were Very Involved with Community Development, while only thirty percent were Very Involved with Humanitarian Aid and twenty percent in Social Justice ministry.

Long-Term Missionary Sending

The ongoing dialogue in the missions world would lead one to believe that churches are sending missionaries directly at a record level and the need of missionary sending agencies is decreasing.

For the churches taking part in this survey, they seemed to be using mission agencies more substantially than sending workers directly to the field without the aid of an agency. In fact, sixty-two percent reported using a mission agency as the primary means for sending workers. Wherever one may land on the sodality-modality framework for mission sending, it is apparent that partnership between the local church and mission organizations is essential, necessary, and not a thing of the past.

Fifty-nine percent of churches ranked themselves as Good to Very Good in regard to Internal Promotion of Missions within their church context. Interestingly, forty percent of churches with twenty to one hundred and two hundred fifty to five hundred in attendance ranked themselves as Very Good—a larger percentage than any other sized churches.

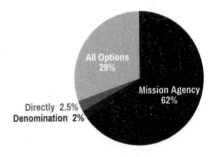

CHART 3.3 Platform for Sending Long-Term Workers

Although churches felt they were doing a good job of promoting missions, they did not feel that they were as well-equipped in the Identification of Potential Missionaries. Sixty-nine percent ranked themselves as Moderate to Poor in this area. Only six percent felt they were Very Good at identification.

The majority of churches not only expressed a weakness in the Identification of Potential Missionary Candidates but also in relation to the Training of Potential Missionaries. Both areas present opportunities for deeper agency and church partnerships. Agencies who specialize in mobilization and training could walk alongside churches to help them develop plans, training methods, and opportunities to educate and mobilize congregants toward global missions service.

Sixty-five percent of churches felt that they were engaging well with their missionaries while they are on the field. Care, connection, and interaction from a local church is an essential element for long-term workers to gain encouragement and resilience to stay actively engaged in their field work. For churches who send missionaries directly to the field, forty-three percent listed Field Supervision as their greatest weakness.

Scouting the Landscape: Short-Term Missions Trips

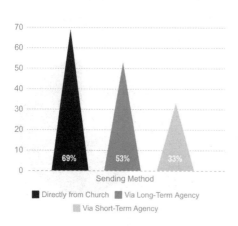

CHART 3.4 How Short-Term Teams are Sent

Short-term missions trips have been a substantial means of engaging North American young people and church attendees in missions projects around the globe. Hundreds of thousands of people each year pack up and head out "on mission" to visit new places, new people, and new cultures.

The data showed that sixty-nine percent of churches sent teams Directly from their Churches without using an agency to facilitate the trips. When they did use an agency, fifty-three percent used a Long-Term focused agency while thirty-three percent used a Short-Term Agency. Fifty-seven percent sent to Missionary Partners which could be executed directly or in connection with the missionary's

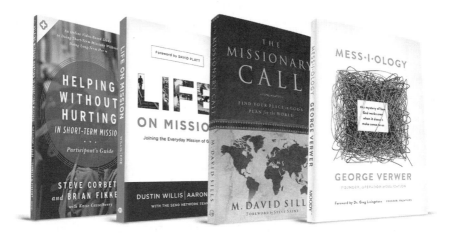

long-term agency. Seventeen percent sent to National Partners which would also account most likely for sending directly. This was followed by fifteen percent that sent to an agency location that was not directly tied to a ministry or relationship of the church.

Local Churches Engaged with the Nations Locally

The nations now live in our neighborhoods. The world is in a constant state of motion. What used to be ministry that only took place around the globe is now fast become essential in our hamlets, small towns, and large cities in North America.

Seventy-four percent of the churches taking part in this survey reported active engagement in some way with the internationals living in their local community. Over seventy-eight different people groups from sixty countries were being directly ministered to by our local church community.

Only ten percent of the churches felt like they were doing a Very Good job of Engaging with Internationals Locally. Forty-two percent expressed inadequacy in their ability to minister effectively. Significant opportunities exist for partnership in this area between local churches and mission agencies who have substantial experience ministering in these cultures.

Financing Mission

Eighty percent of churches participating in the survey gave a Percentage of Overall Budget toward global missions. For some that also included the salaries of their global ministries team. Thirty percent only utilized funds received from Individual Donations, and twenty-five percent only used Faith Promise Campaigns. As can be expected, the larger the church the more they were able to contribute toward the cause of global missions. Annual mission budgets in our survey ranged from twelve hundred to two and a half million annually.

We also asked church mission leaders about the challenges they faced in financing global missions. There was virtually no difference between denominational and non-denominational leaders. Thirty-two percent stated that the Lack of Missions Education was the main reason there is a challenge in raising the needed financial resources. There are many competing interests in our churches and world today for philanthropic giving, so it is essential that the plight of global missions is given voice and attention amidst other louder and more proclaimed needs.

80% 30% 25% 2.8%

A Percentage of the Overall Church Budget
From Individual Donations to Projects
Faith Promise Giving
Denominational Cooperative Funds

Chart 3.5 Funding of Church Missions Programs

The Trail Ahead: Churches and Mission Organizations

Partnership is essential. If we seek to traverse the trails ahead, we must face our task with a diversified team that takes each member's strength and maximizes it for the sake of the cause—a significant element of partnership. We must also seek to understand what we each value, identify our strengths and weaknesses, and discover how we can complement each other as we work together.

As we look at the Top Six Organizational Priorities of both groups over the next three to five years there are immediate observable areas of overlap and partnership. Both groups listed Developing Partnerships, Ministry Metrics, and New Ministry Structures in their top six. Churches also highlighted areas in which they need to do better: Assess Ministry Opportunities, Innovation in New Ministry Methods, and Communication to their Congregations. All three areas present opportunities in which many organizations would be able to walk alongside church leaders and provide very practical tools for helping them address these priorities and see notable change.

Many mission organizations could assist a church in developing diagnostics to assess missionary candidates or global partner opportunities, allowing them to evaluate each in more effective ways. In addition, many mission organizations have excellent communications teams with materials already produced that would be extremely beneficial for church

YOU'RE CHANGING THE WORLD

BUT YOU FACE MANY CHALLENGES

Your ministry reaches across the globe, taking the Gospel to those who haven't heard the good news. You are responsible for stewarding support to help get the message proclaimed. You need software that is efficient and effective, so you can focus on your mission. See why other ministries like yours have partnered with DonorDirect for their donor and missionary management needs.

YOUR MISSION IS WHAT'S IMPORTANT
OUR JOB IS GETTING YOU THERE

leaders looking for innovative ways to educate and communicate about missions to their congregations. Likewise, for mission organizations looking to Attract Qualified Staff, Increase Fundraising, and develop New Revenue Sources, they could seek to deepen their relationships with churches who are and could increase resourcing of workers and finances. By working together, we can actively raise up a new generation of mission workers who are encouraged, supported, commissioned, and sent out to our partner mission organizations.

CHART 3.6 Top 6 Organizational Priorities in the next 3-5 Years

The migration of people around the globe is no longer an issue that is just theorized or left to the periphery of ministry. Global migration is at the epicenter of issues facing our world today. Significant opportunities to engage with the nations as they are on the move are presented to our churches and organizations on a daily basis. There are great opportunities for mission organizations to adapt training for global workers and gear it toward local churches who are seeking to minister among the nations in their own neighborhoods. There are ways to improvise and innovate in cross-cultural training, education, and ministry within our communities that used to be only after a long boat or plane trip.

Global Economy/Finance and Business as Mission (BAM) are also issues both groups are needing to address. There are significant opportunities for the use and development of business that can fund and create platforms for global missions. In addition, rising global economies present significant opportunities for fundraising in locations outside of North America.

As organizations continue the pursuit of internationalization, there are new opportunities to create regional hubs not only for ministry leadership but also for tasks that may have only been done at a North American "home office."

Lastly, Social Cultural Values is another External Force that creates unavoidable issues for our ministries. Views on the definition of marriage, sexual orientation, and theology that may have been on the periphery in the past are now at the forefront of discussion. How will these issues affect our churches and non-profit organizations? We simply do not know. Unity as a community could never be more paramount. This is the time for unity among the body of Christ to bring together churches, mission organizations, non-profits, businesses, and individuals to stand firm, resolved, and in love—holding to the truth of the grace, mercy, and love afforded by the gospel we have been granted and seek to proclaim.

Summary

The local church is essential to the mission of global evangelism to the unengaged, unreached peoples of the world. The local church is the incubator to grow strong, gospel-centric believers who have a passion for the lost whether in their neighborhood, at their place of work, or in a distant and potentially forgotten corner of the world.

In a world that is consumed with itself, we are in desperate need of local church leaders who will be willing to point to a cause—a hope that is greater than their kingdom—and in so doing seek to build a Kingdom that is eternal and glorious. A church united in purpose, a church united in passion, a church united in Christ will transform the very landscape of our world.

In partnership together, individuals, churches, and mission organizations can take the command of gospel proclamation and see it become the very essence and reason for our unity. The vision is God glorified and His name heralded among the nations—nations in our neighborhood and around the globe. Together we are better, together we are stronger, together we are united.

Additional information, charts, and resources for further study can be found in the full 2016 Mission CEO and Church Mission Leader Survey at www.missionexus.org.

A NEW STEP FORWARD IN PUBLISHING FOR THE KINGDOM

WILLIAM CAREY
LIBRARY

WILLIAM CAREY
PRESS

WCL is the same traditional publishing house that you know and trust. We publish books that will shape and advance the missiological conversations in the world.

"The Press" is our new paid-publishing service for mission agencies. It is designed to answer all your publishing needs so you can focus on the work of spreading the Good News and we can help you do it by sharing our expertise in publishing.

THE WILLIAM CAREY STAFF is dedicated to helping mission agencies advance the Kingdom through our publishing expertise and doing so at the the lowest possible cost to agencies.

CONTACT US
For submitting your book to **William Carey Library** read our guidelines at missionbooks.org and send your inquiry to submissions@wclbooks.com.

For inquiries about publishing with the **William Carey Press** send an email with details to publishing@wclbooks.com.

We look forward to helping you publish for the Kingdom.

IMAGINE IF YOU NEEDED . . .

¤ A devotional created for donors

¤ A training manual printed for disciple-makers in Africa, Asia, etc.

¤ A reprint of a book you've published but at better rates than you can get as an individual print buyer

¤ A coffee table book to celebrate an organizational anniversary

¤ Curriculum published in multiple languages

¤ A history of your agency or the memoir of your president/founder

¤ Stories from your field workers

¤ Or any other publishing need you can imagine, *The Press is the answer!*

William Carey Publishing, which includes both William Carey Library and William Carey Press, collectively are ministries of Frontier Ventures.

faith in the process.

Tenfold BPO provides Christian organizations with affordable, high-quality accounting services so they can focus on their missions.

↓

Learn more at **tenfoldbpo.org**

Business Process Outsourcing

CHAPTER 4

MISSION HANDBOOK SURVEY
Perspective and Dynamics

J. Ted Esler, Marvin J. Newell, and Michael VanHuis

Section 1: Introduction

Seven years have passed since the last edition of the *Mission Handbook* was released. Much has changed in the North American and global landscape. Global leaders have changed; significant opportunities have been created through a mass refugee crisis; organizations have merged, closed, and changed names. This handbook is now being stewarded by Missio Nexus as we seek to carry on the long-held legacy of providing the North American community with a comprehensive resource for understanding and gauging the status of Protestant missions. Our goal and hope is that the updates will come more regularly, and that we will be able to identify trends and provide relevant analysis to serve the missions community. We believe that this information is essential to strategic Kingdom engagement and impact. However, we do not want to overinflate the value of data. It has a place, and it is a tool. But we all must seek the movement of the Holy Spirit as we gauge who and how we send workers to the field, seek partnerships around the world, and lead a missions movement that is sustainable and reproducible—whether it is in our home offices or among the most unreached peoples across the globe. Data is a great tool if we use it to monitor whether we are staying on course and allow it to draw us to our knees to call on the Almighty to send even more workers to the harvest fields.

CHART 4.1 Organizations by Country
Reflects combined 2008 and 2016 US & Canada Data

Data from 922 organizations is represented in this handbook, 778 from the United States of America and 144 from Canada. Our team worked diligently to interact with these organizations and acquire new data points from the last edition of the handbook. Out of the 922 organizations, we were able to acquire new data from 594. In order to give a more complete perspective on the status of North American missions, it was decided that for the 328 organizations from whom we were not able to acquire new data, we would use their 2008 information in this handbook. We know that many who read this text will be looking for trends and projection, so we have sought to be as clear as possible in our charts, tables, and text. We have made notations such as, "*Reflects combined 2008 and 2016 US & Canada Data." There are no duplicates; all are unique organizations from whom we have data, whether 2008 or 2016. You will also see notated, "*Reflects only 2016 Data." There were a few questions in the current survey that were not in the 2008 survey. In some instances, we used only the 2016 data because we had a large enough data group. Lastly, we sought to notate whether you are looking at US data, Canadian data or both. On issues like field staffing and finances we have provided a comparison between 2008 and 2016 for organizations from whom we had data in both periods.

In this type of analysis, it is always necessary to provide a disclaimer. A. Scott Moreau, who compiled the data for the 21st edition of this handbook wrote:

> "we [ask] our readers to keep in mind that the tables and graphs throughout are only as valid as the numbers reported by the organizations themselves. Several factors contribute softness to these numbers. First, the numbers themselves fluctuate during the year (e.g., people leave their field of service unexpectedly, budgets change, administrative staff come and go, field assignments are changed and so on). Second, the agencies we survey use different methods for counting their own personnel. While some carefully tabulate and report painstakingly exact numbers for the month the survey is completed, others provide either highs or averages for the year. Still others provide estimates based on their best guesses,

especially for categories such as short-term workers. Third, and finally, agencies do not always interpret the survey questions consistently with other agencies or even with their own answers in previous surveys."[1]

The data has been broken down into different categories throughout this chapter in an effort to make it as practical and relatable as possible. As stated previously, data is based on location and time—US and Canada, 2008 versus 2016—but it is also based on affiliation, which can be seen in Chart 2 and Table 1.

TABLE 4.1 Categories of Affiliation

Nondenominational	Denominational
Nondenominational / Denominational heritage	Denominational / Independent Sending Agency of Baptist Tradition
Nondenominational / Interdenominational	Denominational heritage
Nondenominational / Interdenominational / Denominational heritage	Denominational, African Methodist Episcopal Church
Nondenominational, affiliated with Grace Gospel Fellowship	Anabaptist
Fellowship	Independent Full Gospel
Interdenominational	**Other**
Transdenominational	Prefer that denominational orientation not be used
Ecumenical	Secular
	Service Agency
	Association

We have taken all the different types of affiliations and narrowed them down to four main categories:

Nondenominational
Interdenominational
Denominational
Other

---

1. Linda J. Webber, *Mission Handbook, U.S. and Canadian Protestant Ministries Overseas 21st Edition* (Wheaton: EMIS, 2010), 34.

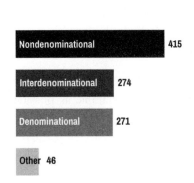

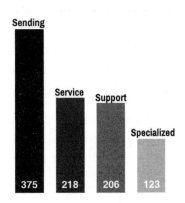

CHART 4.2 Organizations by Affiliation
*Reflects combined 2008 and 2016
US & Canada Data*

CHART 4.3 Organizations by
Agency Type
*Reflects combined 2008 and 2016
US & Canada Data*

When organizations identified multiple affiliations, we used the first one listed to categorize.

Lastly, we have broken the data down by agency type. There were four main agency types that were listed by organizations: sending, service, support, and specialized. Throughout the chapter, we show data for each of these and use these types for comparison purposes.

The chapter starts with a broad perspective and becomes more specific as you progress. We seek to show data related to personnel, primary activities of organizations, regional placement of field workers, and when organizations were founded. This is followed by analysis of organization type from multiple perspectives and then analysis on organizational finances.

Section 2: Personnel Overview

The question that most people will immediately ask upon picking up this text is whether the North American missions movement is growing or shrinking. The data collected in the process of creating this *Mission Handbook* was not designed for this question specifically, but does give us a clear answer. The North American mission movement is neither growing nor shrinking, but is maintaining its size and scope with relatively little overall change.

The data collected here has limitations that must be understood before accepting this conclusion. First, and most important, is that there exists no complete data set of all North American mission personnel. The number of organizations responding to this survey does not, of course, contain all potential agencies. Those that are newer or less well known may not have been contacted. Further, many responding agencies did not provide full data in both 2008 and 2016. Another limitation is the way that agencies count their staff; there is a great deal of inconsistency, and some agencies simply cannot provide the numbers because they do not have a categorization process in place.

For example, the survey asked for the number of single men, single women, and married couples that an organization employed. This number should correlate to the total of all employees noted in the section that asked for their regional placement. In few cases did these numbers match. Certainly, security concerns are one reason for this. Yet there is no other survey on mission agencies as complete as this one. We should be able to draw some conclusions from the data.

To understand if missionary agencies grew or shrank over the 8-year time span between *Mission Handbook* projects, we created a representative sampling of agencies. We diversified this list by size and agency type. Organizations that did not provide data in both collections processes were removed from the list, and outliers (those agencies with wide variances that could not be explained) were also removed from the sample set. We created a Canadian data set distinct from the US data.

The resulting analysis provides a strong indication that there were "winners" and "losers" in employee staff size. However, when taken in aggregate, the picture of a stable missionary force emerges. Perhaps the figures that give the most confidence are in the employee data set. A sampling of thirty sending agencies produced a variance of 1 percent growth in full-time staff over the 8-year period. There was growth in part-time staff of 16 percent. The sample data suggested that there was a downturn in the number of people serving 4 or more years. About the only numbers that had significant increase were the number of non-citizen employees and non-resident missionaries. In 2016, the number of non-citizens employed by the sample sending agencies was three times larger than 2008. Non-resident missionaries were reported to have grown by 65 percent.

And how will we know who has not yet heard?

Learn about more than 6,000 unreached people groups at

JoshuaProject.net

The number of "two week or less" missionaries also exploded in size among sending agencies. We do not feel confident that a percentage tells this story and so will not provide one. Five of nineteen agencies reported much higher numbers in 2016 than in 2008. However, almost all agencies increased the number of short-term missionaries in the 8-year period. It is accurate to say that the data indicates significant growth in this category. A separate study of short-term missionary efforts would be helpful.

The Canadian sending agency sample data set revealed similar changes, mostly mirroring the narrative of stability. The one area where there is variance to the US data is in the category "more than 4 years." Canadian sending agencies reported an increase of 38 percent in this category.

Based on the data available, we conclude that the missionary force from North America has remained stable in the 8 years between Mission Handbook projects.

PERSONNEL: LONG-TERM FIELD STAFF

Compared to data from the previous *Handbook* edition, the number of long-term field staff (those serving four years or more) from North America (US and Canada) has decreased by 7.5 percent. In real terms, the difference is 2,746 field missionaries. However, half of that decrease can be accounted for by the unusual step the largest reporting agency, the IMB of the Southern Baptist Convention, took just prior to this survey to intentionally decrease their members. Between September 2015 and February 2016 that mission saw a loss of 1,132 members through an

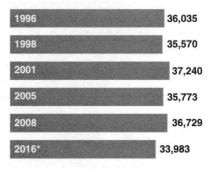

CHART 4.4 Long-Term Field Staff (4+ Years)
Reflects combined 2008 and 2016 US & Canada Data

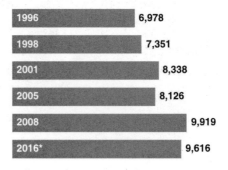

CHART 4.5 Mid-Term Field Staff (1-4 Years)
Reflects combined 2008 and 2016 US & Canada Data

early retirement option that was extended to both field and home staff. It cannot be determined how many of those members transferred to other mission organizations and thus stayed within the count of North American missions. Regardless, the decrease in numbers from that one agency did have an overall impact on the totals reported in our current survey.

PERSONNEL: MID-TERM FIELD STAFF

An increasingly important segment of field workers over the past two decades are those who opt to minister overseas 1–4 years. Those within this category slightly decreased from the previous data collection year. The difference is 3 percent, or a decrease of 303 workers. This is a combined count from our current survey (5035) plus 4581 from the 2008 survey.

PERSONNEL: TENTMAKER

Although some delineate between Business as Mission (BAM) and "tentmakers," we have combined the two into one category. Over the past 8 years the number of workers engaged in Business as Mission has experienced a healthy increase. The percentage of increase is 18 percent, which translates into 632 in real numbers.

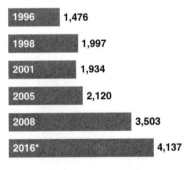

1996	1,476
1998	1,997
2001	1,934
2005	2,120
2008	3,503
2016*	4,137

CHART 4.6 Tentmakers
Reflects only 2016 US & Canada Data

PERSONNEL: MARRIED AND SINGLE WORKERS

The number of married individuals serving overseas continues to be substantially greater than singles. There are four times as many married individuals as singles. When it comes to single workers, women make up 72.26 percent of the group, whereas men are at 27.74 percent.

PERSONNEL: SHORT-TERM (LESS THAN 2 WEEKS)

As mentioned in the overview, the data shows significant growth in this category, an astonishing 80 percent. It must be remembered that the figure of 80,813 for 2016 represents short-term missionaries sent by agencies only. If short-termers sent directly from North American churches were factored in, the number would be exponentially higher.

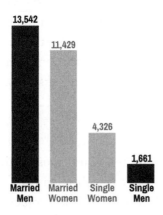

CHART 4.7 Married and Single)
*Reflects only 2016 Reported
US & Canada Data*

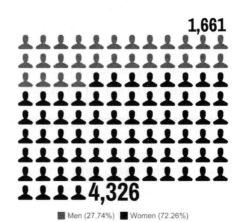

CHART 4.8 Single Men vs. Single Women
*Reflects only 2016
US & Canada Data*

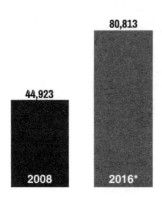

CHART 4.9 Short-Term
(Less than 2 Weeks)
*Reflects only 2016
US & Canada Data*

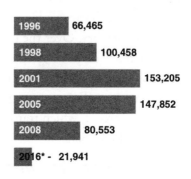

CHART 4.10 Short-Term (More than
2 Weeks, Less than 1 Year)
*Reflects only 2016
US & Canada Data*

PERSONNEL: SHORT-TERM
(MORE THAN 2 WEEKS, LESS THAN 1 YEAR)

Conversely, the category of short-term workers serving more than two weeks but less than one year, as sent by agencies, shows a significant decrease. The decrease is not just relative to 2008, but is significantly lower than the numbers recorded twenty years ago in 1996. Since its peak in 2001, this category has been in steady decline.

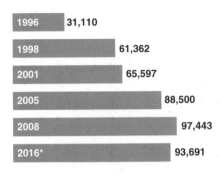

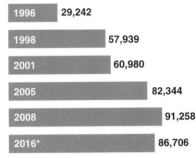

CHART 4.11 Non-US/CA Personnel
*Reflects combined 2008 and 2016
US & Canada Data*

CHART 4.12 Non-US/CA Personnel
Serving in Home Country
*Reflects combined 2008 and 2016
US & Canada Data*

PERSONNEL: NON-NORTH AMERICANS

US and Canadian agencies continue to substantially utilize non-US and Canadian citizens to engage in their work. There is no question of the effectiveness of these workers and there are definite financial efficiencies gained by utilizing them rather than North Americans. Compared to 2008, there is a small shift down in the numbers reported. However, the total number remains very high, at nearly 94,000. We believe that the 3.8 percent decrease is a result in variants of reporting compared to the 2008 survey.

PERSONNEL: NON-NORTH AMERICANS SERVING IN HOME COUNTRY

By far the number of non-North Americans serving with North American agencies work within their own countries. The extent to which these workers are actually serving as cross-cultural workers, rather than same-cultural workers, is unknown. Some undoubtedly work among their own people group. However, with the fluidity of people on the move, even within one country, this delineation is hard to make. Our data shows a worker decrease of 4.9 percent in this category.

PERSONNEL: NON-NORTH AMERICANS SERVING OUTSIDE OF HOME COUNTRY

Generally, it can be assumed that workers in this category are serving cross-culturally. However, in our globalized world it would also be easy to imagine an Indonesian working among same-culture Indonesians in Holland, or a Kenyan doing the same in England. Although there are numerous scenarios, it is encouraging to see an increase in this category. Compared to 2008, there has been a 13 percent increase.

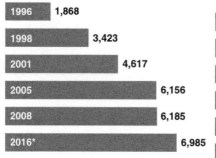

CHART 4.13 Non-US/CA Personnel Serving
Outside of Home Country
*Reflects combined 2008 and 2016
US & Canada Data

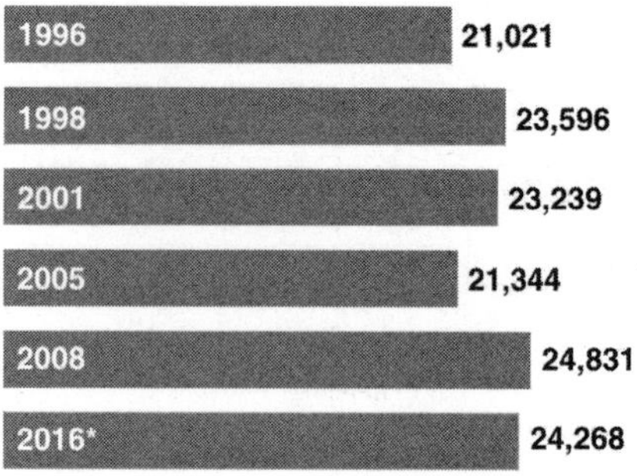

CHART 4.14 Full-Time Paid Office Staff
*Reflects combined 2008 and 2016
US & Canada Data

PERSONNEL: FULL-TIME PAID OFFICE STAFF

The value of supporting staff for the effectiveness of field workers is incalculable. Before sailing to India, William Carey said to the small band of brothers around him, "Well, I will go down into the mine, if you will hold the rope." This office staff category includes mobilizers, trainers, coaches, administrators, finance people, and a host of others that make the ministry of field workers possible. However, some agencies also include redeployments back to North America who work cross-culturally among diaspora peoples and within ethnic pockets located here. The change in number of full-time office staff reported between 2008 and 2016 is a negative 2.2 percent.

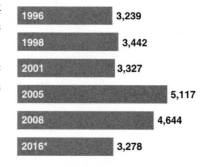

PERSONNEL: PART-TIME PAID OFFICE STAFF

Augmenting full-time office staff are those who are employed part-time by agency offices. Most of these do not go

CHART 4.15 Part-Time
Paid Office Staff
*Reflects combined 2008 and 2016
US & Canada Data

through the intense screening process of becoming a "member," but are hired as supplemental employees. Agencies appear to be finding ways to replace part-time paid staff. The number of staff in this category decreased 30 percent when compared to the 2008 survey.

PERSONNEL: DATA SUMMARY

TABLE 4.2 Full-Time Personnel Serving Overseas

	2001	2005	2008	2016	Notes
Full-Time Personnel Serving Overseas					
Long-Term (4+years)					
US	34,747	33,714	34,480		*2016 represents combined 2008 and 2016 data
CA	2,493	2,059	2,249		
Combined	**37,240**	**35,773**	**36,729**	**33,983**	
Mid-Term (1-4 years)					
US	8,001	7,615	9,427		*2016 represents combined 2008 and 2016 data
CA	337	511	492		
Combined	**8,338**	**8,126**	**9,919**	**9,616**	
Tentmakers					
US	1,780	1,934	3,354		*2016 represents only new 2016 data
CA	154	186	149		
Combined	**1,934**	**2,120**	**3,503**	**4,137**	
TOTAL	**47,512**	**46,019**	**50,151**	**47,736**	

TABLE 4.3 Other Personnel Serving Overseas

	2001	2005	2008	2016	Notes
Other Personnel Serving Overseas					
Short-Term (<2weeks)					
US			41,378		*2016 represents only new 2016 data
CA			3,545		
Combined			**44,923**	**80,813**	
Short-Term (>2weeks)					
US	149,810	144,318	77,281		*2016 represents only new 2016 data
CA	3,395	3,534	3,272		
Combined	**153,205**	**147,852**	**80,553**	**21,941**	
SUBTOTAL	**153,205**	**147,852**	**125,476**	**102,754**	
Non-Residential Full Support					
US	1610	3055	4166		*2016 represents only new 2016 data
CA	385	156	407		
Combined	**1995**	**3211**	**4573**	**8,361**	

	2001	2005	2008	2016	Notes
Other Personnel Serving Overseas					
Non-Residential Partial Support					
US	501	697	1489		* Full and Partial was not delineated in the 2016 survey
CA	27	38	50		
Combined	528	735	1539		
SUBTOTAL	2,523	3,946	6,112	8,361	
TOTAL	155,728	151,798	131,588	111,115	

TABLE 4.4 Non-US/CA Personnel Directly Supported

	2001	2005	2008	2016	Notes
Non-US/CA Personnel Directly Supported					
In Home Country					
US	59,852	80,834	86,471		*2016 represents combined 2008 and 2016 data
CA	1,128	1,510	4,787		
Combined	60,980	82,344	91,258	86,706	
Outside Home Country					
US	3,744	5,428	5,537		*2016 represents combined 2008 and 2016 data
CA	873	728	648		
Combined	4,617	6,156	6,185	6,985	
TOTAL	65,597	88,500	97,443	93,691	

TABLE 4.5 US/CA Ministry and Home Office Staff

	2001	2005	2008	2016	Notes
US/CA Ministry and Home Office Staff					
Full-Time Paid Staff					
US	20,724	19,199	22,296	22,423	*2016 represents combined 2008 and 2016 data
CA	2,515	2,145	2,535	1,845	
Combined	23,239	21,344	24,831	24,268	
Part-Time Staff/Associates					
US	2,896	4,547	3,852	2,805	*2016 represents combined 2008 and 2016 data
CA	431	570	792	473	
Combined	3,327	5,117	4,644	3,278	
SUBTOTAL	26,566	26,461	29,475	27,546	
Short-Term Support Staff					
US	1,866	2,882	2,616		*Question was not asked on the 2016 survey
CA	320	169	346		
Combined	2,186	3,051	2,962		
TOTAL	28,752	29,512	32,437	27,546	

TABLE **4.6** Total People Mobilized by North American Agencies

	2001	2005	2008	2016	Notes
Total People Mobilized by North American Agencies					
Full-Time On Location (Long-Term/Mid-Term/ Tentmakers)					
US	44,528	43,263	47,261		
CA	2,984	2,756	2,890		
Combined	**47,512**	**46,019**	**50,151**	**47,736**	
All Full-Time On Location (All US/CA & Non US/CA)					
US	108,124	129,525	139,269		
CA	4,985	4,994	8,325		
Combined	**113,109**	**134,519**	**147,594**	**141,427**	
All Overseas Any Duration (Everyone Except Home Office Staff)					
US	260,045	277,595	263,583		
CA	8,792	8,722	15,599		
Combined	**268,837**	**286,317**	**279,182**	**252,542**	
All Home Office Staff					
US	25,486	26,628	28,764	25,228	
CA	3,266	2,884	3,673	2,318	
Combined	**28,752**	**29,512**	**32,437**	**27,546**	
GRAND TOTAL	**297,589**	**315,829**	**311,619**	**280,088**	

Section 3: Primary Activities

PRIMARY ACTIVITIES: OVERVIEW

In our 2016 survey we asked agencies to identify up to six of their primary activities. We provided a list of eighty options from which to choose, including an "other" option that allowed them to identify additional activities not on the list. We also asked them to specify the one ministry activity that is most central to, or most characteristic of, their organization.

As was done in past *Handbook* editions, for the following analysis we assume that the self-identified primary activity receives a larger share of an agency's resources and attention than any other activity. For instance, if an agency selects "discipleship" as their primary activity, we assume that this receives more personnel and financial resources than any of the five other categories they selected.

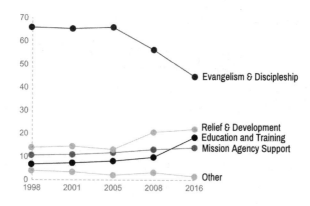

CHART 4.16 1998-2016 Activity Changes
US & Canada Data

Furthermore, as in past *Handbook* editions, we categorize each of the eighty activities into five mega-groupings: Evangelism and Discipleship, Education and Training, Relief and Development, Mission Support, and Other.

Chart 17 identifies the percentage of agencies engaged in those overarching categories.

PRIMARY ACTIVITIES: CHANGES

Since 1998, the *Handbook* has tracked the ebb and flow of agencies reporting a primary activity within each major category. From 1998 to 2016 the percentage of all agencies indicating a primary activity in the Evangelism and Discipleship category has dropped significantly. It has declined by almost nineteen points, from 62.8 percent to the current 44 percent. On the other hand, the percent of agencies indicating a primary activity in the Relief and Development category has doubled, from 11 percent to 23 percent. The other strong uptick in activity was in the Education and Training category, which jumped from 8.1 percent to 18 percent.

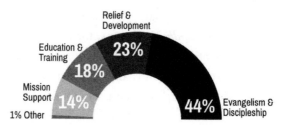

CHART 4.17 2016 Identified Primary Activities
US & Canada Data

PRIMARY ACTIVITIES: TOP 20

The top twenty primary activities are listed in chart 18. Notice that these are actual activities, rather than the categories noted earlier. The activity with which the most agencies identify or engage is Church Planting (Establishing). This activity has more than twice the agencies identified than the second, which is Evangelism.

Although all mission activities have their value, it is encouraging to see the ministry emphasis of the top twenty activities that are being performed by North American agencies.

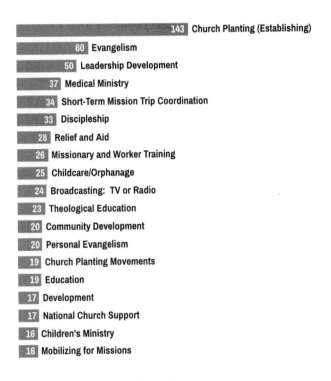

143 Church Planting (Establishing)
60 Evangelism
50 Leadership Development
37 Medical Ministry
34 Short-Term Mission Trip Coordination
33 Discipleship
28 Relief and Aid
26 Missionary and Worker Training
25 Childcare/Orphanage
24 Broadcasting: TV or Radio
23 Theological Education
20 Community Development
20 Personal Evangelism
19 Church Planting Movements
19 Education
17 Development
17 National Church Support
16 Children's Ministry
16 Mobilizing for Missions

CHART **4.18** Top 20 Primary Activities
By Number of Organizations

Section 4: Year Founded

It is interesting to note when most North American agencies were founded. Chart 19 indicates the number of agencies founded by century, over the past five centuries. Congruent with the development of both the US and Canada, agency founding's began slowly, gained momentum in the 1800s, and then shot up as North America emerged as a world influencer.

Probably of more interest to most readers is the founding of agencies from decade to decade over the past century. There was a significant increase of agency founding in the post-World War II years, as servicemen who had seen the world were burdened to take the gospel back to places where they had served. It is felt that the downward trend starting in the late 1990s is not an accurate portrayal of the past years, but rather is the result of incomplete data and the limitations of our current survey. Although there is a decline in the founding of "traditional mission agencies," there are a vast number of innovative missional NGOs that have been established that are not included in the current survey.

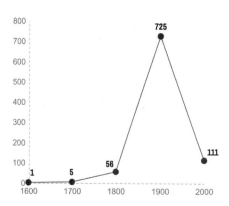

CHART 4.19 Founding of Mission Agencies
US & Canada Data

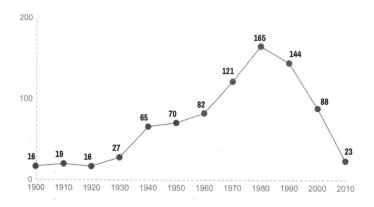

CHART 4.20 Founding of Mission Agenices by Decade (1900-2000)
US & Canada Data

Section 5: Regional Data

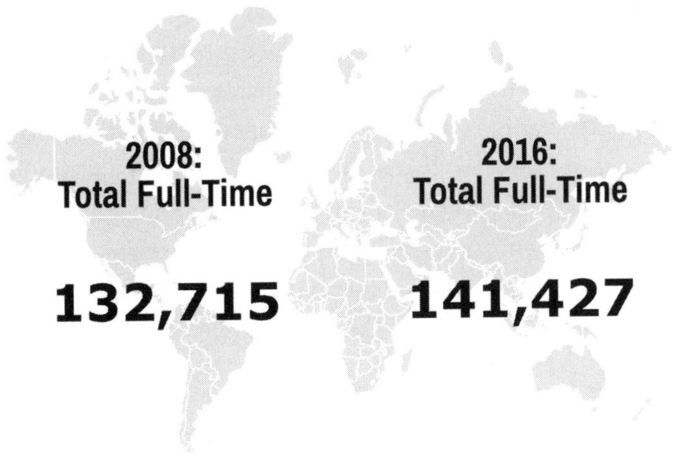

2008:
Total Full-Time

2016:
Total Full-Time

132,715   141,427

CHART **4.21** Field Deployment 2008 vs. 2016
Represents US/CA Full-Time and Non-US/CA Full-Time

The distribution of workers from North America is truly global. Our survey shows that North American mission agencies field workers in 228 countries. When compared with 2008, there is an increase of 8,712 workers worldwide. This number reflects the combined 2008 and 2016 data in the 2016 tally (without duplication). Also, the "head count" represents US and Canadian full-time workers along with their non-US and Canadian full-time associates. These figures do include tentmakers, but in order not to skew the totals, do not include non-resident personnel.

REGIONAL DATA: DEPLOYMENT

In our survey, we asked agencies to indicate where they have workers, either by country, by region, or by "global." The global category is new with this edition, as an increasing number of agencies find it unadvisable, mainly for security reasons, to indicate where their workers are located. Because an increasing number of agencies now have workers deployed in the US and Canada, reflecting the trend of international migration of peoples, we also added a "North America" region. This category reflects workers who are ministering cross-culturally within the US and Canada, but excludes any who are categorized as home office staff.

Chart 22 and Table 7 indicate that, with many agencies opting to list their workers in the "global" category, there is an artificial downturn in the totals for Asia and the Middle East. That outcome was expected given the new option for reporting. Although South America also experienced a decline in numbers, this is not thought to be a result of the "global" option of reporting. We believe there is a discernable downward trend in North American missionaries serving in South America, as indicated by both the 2008 and current surveys. This is due to the expansion and strength of the church in that region over the past decades, and also because the continent has become a strong mission sending center in its own right. On another note, surprisingly, there has been more than a doubling of workers sent to Oceania since the past survey. Africa and Europe/CIS remain relatively unchanged.

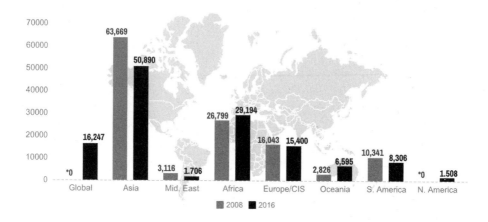

CHART 4.22 Regional Deployment 2008 vs. 2016
Represents US/CA Full-Time and Non-US/CA Full-Time

TABLE 4.7 Regional Field Comparison 2008 vs. 2016
*2016 data represents 2008 and 2016 US & Canada Data

2008 COMBINED US & CA	US & CA FULL-TIME	Change 2005 to 2008		Non-US & CA FULL-TIME	Change 2005 to 2008		All US & CA FULL-TIME	Change 2005 to 2008	
Africa	7,141	469	7.0%	19,658	7,807	66%	26,799	8,276	45%
Asia	9,362	300	3.3%	54,307	-4,385	-7%	63,669	-4,085	-6%
Central America/ Caribbean	4,007	397	11.0%	5,914	1,135	24%	9,921	1,532	18%
Europe/CIS	8,279	501	6.4%	7,764	1,835	31%	16,043	2,336	17%
Middle East	1,369	154	12.7%	1,747	548	46%	3,116	702	29%
Oceania	1,881	120	6.8%	945	246	35%	2,826	366	15%
South America	4,795	-538	-10.1%	5,546	2,291	70.0%	10,341	1,753	20.0%
TOTAL	36,834	1,403	4.0%	95,881	9,477	11%	132,715	10,880	9%

2016 COMBINED US & CA	US & CA FULL-TIME	Change 2008 to 2016		Non-US & CA FULL-TIME	Change 2008 to 2016		All US & CA FULL-TIME	Change 2008 to 2016	
Africa	7,368	227	3%	21,826	2,168	11%	29,194	2,395	9%
Asia	9,362	0	0%	41,528	-12,779	-24%	50,890	-12,779	-20.0%
Central America/ Caribbean	4,629	622	16%	6,952	1,038	18%	11,581	1,660	17%
Europe/CIS	8,183	-96	-1%	7,217	-547	-7%	15,400	-643	-4%
Middle East	942	-427	-31%	764	-983	-56%	1,706	-1,410	-45%
Oceania	2,868	987	52%	3,727	2,782	294%	6,595	3,769	133%
South America	3,731	-1,064	-22%	4,575	-971	-18%	8,306	-2,035	-20.0%
North America	470	470	100%	1,038	1,038	100%	1,508	1,508	100%
Global Ministry Non-Specified	10,183	10,183	100%	6,064	6,064	100%	16,247	16,247	100%
TOTAL	47,736	10,902	30.0%	93,691	-2,190	-2%	141,427	8,712	6%

REGIONAL DATA: TOP 50 COUNTRIES WITH ACTIVE WORK

TABLE **4.8** Top 50 Countries with Active Work
US & Canada Data

Country of Service	# of Orgs. with Active Work	Country of Service	# of Orgs. with Active Work
India	201	Paraguay	56
Mexico	195	Bangladesh	52
Kenya	175	Mozambique	52
Philippines	156	Cuba	50
Brazil	142	Hong Kong	50
Thailand	131	Papua New Guinea	50
Haiti	123	Zimbabwe	50
Ukraine	123	Czech Republic	49
Uganda	118	Ireland	49
South Africa	117	Jamaica	49
Peru	113	Korea, South	49
Japan	111	Austria	48
Guatemala	109	Poland	48
Spain	106	Singapore	48
Ecuador	105	Turkey	48
Honduras	105	Rwanda	47
United Kingdom	105	Venezuela	47
Russia	103	Vietnam	47
Bolivia	101	Bulgaria	46
Germany	99	Cameroon	46
Indonesia	96	Panama	45
Cambodia	94	Burkina Faso	44
France	92	Israel	44
Ghana	92	Netherlands	44
China	90	Albania	42

As stated previously, North American agencies' field workers in 228 countries of the world. That leaves about 10 countries that either do not have workers, or, as we suspect, workers there were reported in the "global" category for security concerns.

Table 8 shows the top 50 countries with active work according to the number of mission agencies that are present. Most probably it also indicates the countries with the highest number of workers connected to a North American agency. When the list is examined, there is no discernable pattern as to regional/continental preference for location of service.

Section 6: Organization Detail by Agency Type

AGENCY TYPE: INTRODUCTION

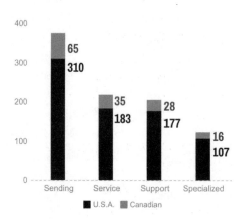

CHART 4.23 Country and Agency Type

A total of 778 US and 144 Canadian agencies answered the survey. There is no easy way to determine what percentage of all mission organizations this represents in the US and Canada. According to the National Center for Charitable Statistics, there were 50,456 registered religious charities in the US in 2013 (NCCS, 2017). Out of this number, 778 most likely represents a fraction of those that focus on global mission, yet it certainly represents the largest data set of which we are aware.

Each agency listed in the *Handbook* is identified as primarily functioning as one of four types:

- Sending: an agency whose primary function is to send North American workers overseas.
- Service: an agency whose primary function is to provide a service to overseas churches or other agencies.
- Support: an agency whose primary function is to supply financial support or other material help to national workers or churches overseas.
- Specialized: an agency whose primary function is to provide a specialty to the mission community or global church community.

In most cases, agencies placed themselves within one of these four categories. For those that did not, the editors identified in which category they belonged based on familiarity with those agencies.

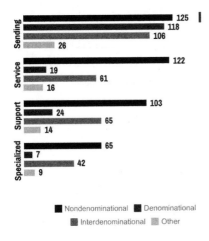

Nondenominational Denominational
Interdenominational Other

CHART 4.24 Affiliation and Agency Type
US & Canada Data

Chart 24 combines affiliation and agency type, revealing that non-denominational agencies make up the biggest sector of the data set. Interdenominational agencies (those agencies that purposefully work across or through multiple denominations or that have an ecumenical orientation) are somewhat of an outlier in their emphasis on being service agencies.

AGENCY TYPE: PRIMARY ACTIVITIES

The following four tables (9–12) list the primary activities indicated by agencies. Bolded text indicates those activities that are found on all four charts, indicating that the activity is pursued regardless of the agency type. For overall data without the type breakdown, refer to Chart 18. Church Planting (Establishing) is the most commonly cited primary activity for two of the agency types (support and sending). This number is even larger if one includes the category of Church Planting Movements.

TABLE 4.9 Sending Agency

Church Planting (Establishing)	115	Church Development	3
Evangelism	33	Church, School or General Christian Education	3
Discipleship	24	**Partnership Development**	3
Leadership Development	21	**Student Evangelism**	3
Church Planting Movements (CPM)	14	Bible Teaching	2
Missionary and Worker Training	12	Disciple-Making Movements (DMMs)	2
Personal or Small Group Evangelism	11	Fund Raising or Transmission	2
Childcare or Orphanage	10	Literacy	2
Mass Evangelism	10	**Member Care**	2
National Church Support	10	Mobilizing for Mission	2
Short-Term Mission Trip Coordination	10	Support of national workers	2
Recruiting or Mobilizing for Mission	8	Training, other	2
Theological Education	8	Agricultural Assistance	1
Education	7	Apologetics	1
Medical Ministry	6	**Aviation**	1
Relief and Aid	6	Camping Programs	1
Bible Translation	5	Children at Risk	1
Children's Ministry	5	Counseling	1

Development, community and/or other	5	Literature Production	1
Business as Mission	4	Networking, Partnership, or Coordination	1
Community Development	4	Orality or Storying	1
Youth Ministry	4	Orphan Care	1
Broadcasting: Radio or TV	3	Pastoral Training	1
		Video, Film Production or Distribution	1

TABLE 4.10 Service Agency

Leadership Development	15	Economic Development	2
Medical Ministry	12	Mass Evangelism	2
Broadcasting: Radio or TV	11	Personal or Small Group Evangelism	2
Short-Term Mission Trip Coordination	10	Prayer-Intercession	2
Missionary and Worker Training	9	Services for other agencies	2
Relief and Aid	9	Technical Assistance	2
Development, community and/or other	8	Translation	2
Evangelism	8	Advocacy	1
Community Development	7	Agricultural Assistance	1
Education	7	Aviation	1
Mobilizing for Mission	6	Business as Mission	1
Services for Mission Organizations	6	Business Solutions to Poverty	1
Theological Education	6	Children at Risk	1
Bible Distribution	5	Children's Education	1
Childcare or Orphanage	5	Children's Ministry	1
Discipleship	5	Church, School or General Christian Education	1
Member Care	5	Correspondence courses	1
Partnership Development	5	Disciple-Making Movements (DMMs)	1
Church Planting (Establishing)	4	Fund Raising or Transmission	1
Literature Production	4	Grants for Christian Healthcare Professionals	1
Recruiting or Mobilizing for Mission	4	Health & Technology Education	1
Bible Translation	3	Housing for Missionaries	1
Childcare	3	Music Ministry Evangelism	1
Church Planting Movements (CPM)	3	Orphan Care	1
Human Trafficking	3	Pastoral Training	1
Justice and Related Issues	3	Purchasing or Supply Services	1
Networking, Partnership, or Coordination	3	Research	1
Apologetics	2	Spiritual Renewal	1
Church Construction	2	Student Evangelism	1
Church Development	2	Support of national workers	1
Crisis Management and Security	2	Technical Training	1
Disabled Ministry	2	Video, Film Production or Distribution	1

Table 4.11 Support Agency

Church Planting (Establishing)	18	Aviation	2
Evangelism	17	Children at Risk	2
Leadership Development	10	Fund Raising or Transmission	2
National Church Support	10	Mass Evangelism	2
Relief and Aid	9	Member Care	2
Theological Education	9	Networking, Partnership, or Coordination	2
Childcare or Orphanage	8	Services for Mission Organizations	2
Bible Distribution	7	Video, Film Production or Distribution	2
Children's Ministry	7	Agricultural Assistance	1
Community Development	6	Audio Recording or Distribution	1
Medical Ministry	6	Bible Teaching	1
Personal or Small Group Evangelism	6	Business as Mission	1
Education	5	Camping Programs	1
Short-Term Mission Trip Coordination	5	Children's Education	1
Support of national workers	5	Church Planting Movements (CPM)	1
Training, other	5	Correspondence courses	1
Literature Distribution	4	Development, community and/or other	1
Orphan Care	4	Housing for Missionaries	1
Broadcasting: Radio or TV	3	Human Trafficking	1
Childcare	3	International Student Ministry	1
Church, School or General Christian Education	3	Missionary and Worker Training	1
Disabled Ministry	3	Orality or Storying	1
Discipleship	3	Partnership Development	1
Justice and Related Issues	3	Pastoral Training	1
Recruiting or Mobilizing for Mission	3	Support of Organizations	1
Student Evangelism	3	Technical Assistance	1
Youth Ministry	3	Tentmaking & related	1
		TESOL or TEFL	1

Table 4.12 Specialized Agency

Medical Ministry	12	Bible Teaching	1
Short-Term Mission Trip Coordination	9	Bible Translation	1
Broadcasting: Radio or TV	7	Church Planting Movements (CPM)	1
Church Planting (Establishing)	6	Counseling	1
Partnership Development	5	Disciple-Making Movements (DMMs)	1
Audio Recording or Distribution	4	Discipleship	1
Leadership Development	4	Environmental Missions	1
Missionary and Worker Training	4	Fund Raising or Transmission	1
Relief and Aid	4	Hearing Aids	1
Aviation	3	Information or Journalism	1
Bible Distribution	3	Internet Discipleship or Training	1
Children's Ministry	3	Internet Evangelism	1
Community Development	3	Literacy	1
Development, community and/or other	3	Mass Evangelism	1
Literature Distribution	3	Member Care	1
Business as Mission	2	National Church Support	1
Childcare	2	National Worker Support	1
Childcare or Orphanage	2	Networking, Partnership, or Coordination	1

Evangelism	2	Orality or Storying	1
Literature Production	2	**Personal or Small Group Evangelism**	**1**
Mobilizing for Mission	2	Publisher and Writer Training	1
Persecuted Church	2	**Recruiting or Mobilizing for Mission**	**1**
Services for Mission Organizations	2	Refugee Ministry	1
Sports Ministry	2	Services for other agencies	1
Technical Assistance	2	**Student Evangelism**	**1**
Video, Film Production or Distribution	**2**	TESOL or TEFL	1
Apologetics	1	Youth Ministry	1

AGENCY TYPE: SHORT-TERM MISSION SENDING

The short-term statistics presented here are from the 2016 data set only. One hundred nine sending agencies provided data on the extent of their short-term mission programs that lasted two weeks or less. The total number of short-term workers was 66,072. The other agency types send far fewer people on short-term trips of two weeks or less. The sum of the other three agency types is 14,741, just 22 percent of the sending agencies.

For short-term trips lasting longer than two weeks but less than one year, thirty-six sending agencies provided data and they sent 17,534 people in this capacity. Some have suggested that millennials prefer this shorter time-frame and some may find it surprising that there aren't more trips of this length. The other three agency types had a total of 4,407 assignments under one year but longer than two weeks.

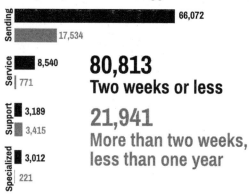

CHART 4.25 Short-Term Mission Sending
by Agency Type
US & Canada Data

Tables 13–16 show the organizations with the largest number of short-term missionaries. It is worth pointing out that among "sending" agencies, the largest two organizations account for more than half of all workers. The IMB of the Southern Baptist Convention and the Assemblies of God World Mission accounted for 30,489 of the 56,211 total for two week or less trips. The IMB of the Southern Baptist Convention and Adventures in Mission accounted for 13,500 of the 15,330 serving more than two weeks. A similar pattern can be seen in other tables as well.

TABLE 4.13 Sending Agency

TWO WEEKS OR LESS		MORE THAN TWO WEEKS LESS THAN ONE YEAR	
IMB of the Southern Baptist Convention	20,000	IMB of the Southern Baptist Convention	10,000
Assemblies of God World Missions	10,489	Adventures in Missions	3,500
Church of the Nazarene, Inc.	8,484	Assemblies of God World Missions	350
SCORE International	6,500	InterVarsity Christian Fellowship/USA	307
Foursquare Missions International	4,000	Church of the Nazarene, Inc.	302
Josiah Venture	1,725	The Navigators	280
The Christian and Missionary Alliance	1,615	Foursquare Missions International	200
American Baptist International Ministries	1,300	Operation Mobilization	148
Global Health Outreach	1,098	Christian Ministries International (CMI)	127
Kids Alive International	1,000	Pioneers USA	116

TABLE 4.14 Service Agency

TWO WEEKS OR LESS		MORE THAN TWO WEEKS LESS THAN ONE YEAR	
Azusa Pacific University - Mexico Outreach	3,000	Mission Nannys	350
Lifeline Christian Mission	886	Reach Beyond (HCJB Global)	80
Buckner International	550	Cup of Cold Water Ministries	45
DELTA Ministries International	541	Global Frontier Missions	40
Northwest Haiti Christian Mission	500	Buckner International	30
Global Frontier Missions	500	DELTA Ministries International	30
CSI Ministries, Inc.	414	Lifeline Christian Mission	23
NEXT Worldwide	405	Emmaus Road International	20
Real Impact Missions	308	Empowering Lives International	13
Bright Hope	200	Frontier Ventures (formerly USCWM)	13

TABLE 4.15 Support Agency

TWO WEEKS OR LESS		MORE THAN TWO WEEKS LESS THAN ONE YEAR	
Lifesong for Orphans	750	e3 Partners Ministry	3,000
AMG International	434	Heart To Heart International Ministries	230
TCM International Institute	200	Correll Missionary Ministries	23
Mission Possible USA	200	Village Schools International	18
Haitian Christian Outreach	150	TCM International Institute	14
Correll Missionary Ministries	150	Colorado Haiti Project Inc.	12
Heart for Lebanon Foundation	150	Lifesong for Orphans	10
Global Hope India	129	Mission Possible USA	10
India Gospel League	124	Global Hope India	10
Gospelink, Inc.	100	Working for Orphans and Widows	9

TABLE **4.16** Specialized Agency

TWO WEEKS OR LESS		MORE THAN TWO WEEKS LESS THAN ONE YEAR	
World Servants, Inc.	915	Christian Veterinary Mission	77
Christian Veterinary Mission	473	Indopartners Agency	32
Children's Lifeline	386	ERRC	26
Christ In Youth	264	World Servants, Inc.	15
Mission On The Move	200	Global Recordings Network	15
Missionary Athletes International	153	Trans World Radio	11
Caring Partners International	120	Blessing the Children International	10
FAME	96	Children's Lifeline	8
With Open Eyes	60	SAT-7 North America	7
Health Teams International	50	Mission On The Move	6

AGENCY TYPE: HOME OFFICE STAFF

Using combined data from the current and past survey, the number of home office staff is shown in Chart 26. The totals for full-time staff were derived from 280 sending agencies, 148 service agencies, 151 support agencies and 85 specialized agencies. For part time staff the totals were provided by 223 sending agencies, 98 service agencies, 102 support agencies and 54 specialized agencies.

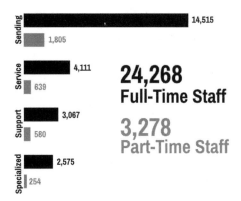

CHART **4.26** Home Office Staff by Agency Type
US & Canada Data

Tables 17–20 show the agencies with the largest home office staff by type. These tables combine the 2008 and 2016 data by using 2008 data when a count was not provided in 2016.

TABLE **4.17** Sending Agency

FULL-TIME STAFF		PART-TIME STAFF	
Campus Crusade for Christ (Cru)	6401	JAARS	324
Christian Broadcasting Network	1288	Wycliffe Bible Translators USA	160
World Relief	400	World Relief	75
Wycliffe Bible Translators USA	374	Pioneers USA	62
IMB of the Southern Baptist Convention	300	Chosen People Ministries, Inc.	50
Youth with a Mission Canada	275	Mennonite Mission Network	41
Ethnos360 (Fomerly New Tribes Mission)	264	Operation Mobilization	31
SIM USA	234	OneHope	31
Adventures in Missions	200	Youth with a Mission Canada, Inc.	30
Operation Mobilization	195	Frontiers	27

TABLE **4.18** Service Agency

FULL-TIME STAFF		PART-TIME STAFF	
World Vision, Inc.	1150	World Vision Canada	87
World Vision Canada	465	Rio Grande Bible Institute, Inc.	85
Our Daily Bread (formerly RBC Ministries)	300	Wycliffe Associates	70
Wycliffe Associates	180	Crossroads Christian Communications Inc. (ERDF)	67
ACSI (Association of Christian Schools International)	158	Holt International Children's Services, Inc.	49
Gideons International, The	106	Mercy Ships	20
Joni and Friends	99	ACSI (Association of Christian Schools International)	17
International Justice Mission	94	World Missionary Press, Inc.	12
Crossroads Christian Communications Inc. (ERDF)	88	Azusa Pacific University - Mexico Outreach	9
Holt International Children's Services, Inc.	86	International Justice Mission	8

TABLE **4.19** Support Agency

FULL-TIME STAFF		PART-TIME STAFF	
Compassion International, Inc.	762	Lutheran Hour Ministries	31
e3 Partners Ministry	400	Medical Teams International	21
Heifer Project International	259	Mission Aviation Fellowship	20
Inter-Varsity Christian Fellowship of Canada	108	Link Care Foundation	18
HOPE International	90	Global Recordings Network	11
Christ for the Nations, Inc.	80	Habitat for Humanity International	10
Gospel for Asia, Inc.	80	Awana Clubs International	8
Bread for the World	79	World Servants, Inc.	8
Operation Blessing International Relief and Development Corporation	78	International Aid	7
International Students, Inc (ISI)	72	Ravi Zacharias International Ministries, Inc.	7

TABLE 4.20 Specialized Agency

FULL-TIME STAFF		PART-TIME STAFF	
Samaritan's Purse	623	Christian Veterinary Mission	77
Habitat for Humanity International	558	Indopartners Agency	32
TWR (Trans World Radio)	246	ERRC	26
Mission Aviation Fellowship	150	World Servants, Inc.	15
Lutheran Hour Ministries	111	Global Recordings Network	15
Christian Medical & Dental Associations	76	Trans World Radio	11
International Aid	59	Blessing the Children International	10
Medical Teams International	56	Children's Lifeline	8
MAP International	55	SAT-7 North America	7
Women to the World, Inc.	45	Mission On The Move	6

AGENCY TYPE: NORTH AMERICAN DIASPORA FOCUS

The phenomenon of the acceleration of international migration is bringing an increasing number of "diaspora" peoples to North America. These new arrivals come as migrant workers, immigrants (legal and illegal), international students, and refugees. North American mission agencies are increasingly intentional about reaching out to this segment of society. In 2008, 266 agencies reported a total of 7,973 workers among diaspora peoples in North America. The 2016 survey added 142 organizations reporting 2,660 workers. The combined data shows 11,633 agency workers with this focus here in North America.

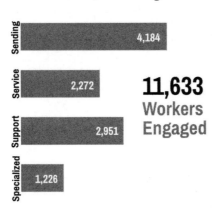

CHART 4.27 North American Diaspora
Engagement by Agency Type
US & Canada Data

Table 21 indicates that World Vision Canada is by far the largest agency providing immigration-oriented ministry. This is not surprising given the immigrant nature of the Canadian population.

TABLE **4.21** North American Diaspora Engagement by Agency Type
Combined 2008 and 2016 Data

SENDING AGENCY DIASPORA FOCUSED STAFF		SUPPORT AGENCY DIASPORA FOCUSED STAFF	
World Relief	475	Compassion International, Inc.	762
Youth with a Mission Canada, Inc.	305	Sidney and Helen Correll Ministries (dba Correll Missionary Ministries)	512
Power to Change Ministries	150	Heifer Project International	267
OneHope	127	International Students, Inc (ISI)	216
The Navigators	115	Inter-Varsity Christian Fellowship of Canada	178
Baptist Mid-Missions	110	Christ for the Nations, Inc.	110
Precept Ministries International	109	Bread for the World	90
Josiah Venture	105	Operation Blessing International Relief and Development Corporation	85
Biblical Ministries Worldwide	101	Gospel for Asia, Inc.	80
ABWE International	100	World Help	69
SERVICE AGENCY DIASPORA FOCUSED STAFF		**SPECIALIZED AGENCY DIASPORA FOCUSED STAFF**	
World Vision Canada	1150	Habitat for Humanity International	568
ACSI (Association of Christian Schools International)	552	Lutheran Hour Ministries	142
Crossroads Christian Communications Inc. (ERDF)	175	Medical Teams International	77
Holt International Children's Services, Inc.	155	International Aid	66
Rio Grande Bible Institute, Inc.	135	MAP International	58
Gideons International, The	118	Ravi Zacharias International Ministries, Inc.	41
International Justice Mission	107	Blessing the Children International	35
Samaritan's Purse - Canada	102	Christian Blind Mission International - Canada	31
Wycliffe Associates	73	Habitat for Humanity Canada	30
Opportunity International	70	Missionary Expediters, Inc.	21

Section 7: Finances

FINANCES: OVERVIEW

Because some organizations in the database did not provide financial numbers in 2016, data from 2008 was used. Charts are separated in some cases so that the reader can get a better understanding of this summarization.

Are agencies growing financially? Like the earlier section regarding staffing levels, the data is not conclusive. Some agencies gave data, some did not, while others gave it in ways that didn't match the given categories. Despite this, some trending could be identified.

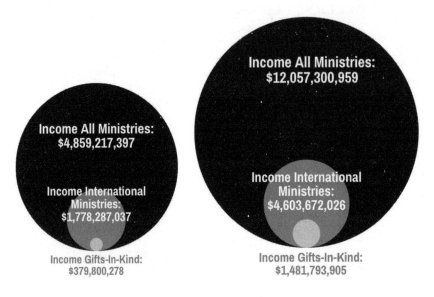

CHART 4.29 US & Canada Agency
2016 Only Income

CHART 4.28 US & Canada Agency Income
Reflects combined 2008 and 2016 data

Rather than relying on aggregate numbers, a sample data set of 29 organizations that provided financial information for international ministries in both 2016 and 2008 was selected. This group included agencies of different sizes and types to create a representative sample.

The result shows a net loss of 11 percent in revenues among the sample data set. However, one large organization reclassified income over this time between organizational entities. If this agency is removed, then overall revenue increased by 15 percent. It appears the aggregate numbers for 2016 lean toward a slight but insignificant growth over the eight-year period. The absolute numbers have most likely grown some, but when inflation is considered (11.5 percent over this timeframe) there is a small decrease.

This coincides with data collected by the Evangelical Council for Financial Accountability (ECFA) from its member agencies. It indicates that revenues have grown over the past few years but only by a very small amount. A similar Canadian sample data set produced almost identical results, with a few variations.

Taken together with the analysis of staffing the data suggests that missionary agencies in North America are stable, showing neither a growth or reduction pattern.

FINANCES: US AND CANADA AGENCY INCOME

Total income for US and Canadian agencies that reported data is just over 12 billion dollars. Chart 28 includes data from the 2008 research project for organizations that did not provide current financial information. This total number should be regarded as an estimate because the 2008 agencies may have grown or shrunk. The data set includes 276 organizations from 2008 and 438 organizations from 2016.

Chart 29 shows only the 2016 data. Note that the distribution of income types ("gifts in kind," "international ministries," and "all ministries") is roughly the same between the two charts. "Gifts in kind" refers to non-cash gifts (stock, machinery and other fixed assets, for example). "International ministries" and "all ministries" take into account fundraising done for global ministry as well as domestic, home office, and other types of funds raised.

FINANCES: INCOME BY AFFILIATION

Agencies were classified as to their larger affiliation. Those agencies that work across multiple denominations or that have an ecumenical orientation are classified as interdenominational. Non-denominational agencies are simply not affiliated with denominations in a purposeful way. Denominational agencies, of course, represent their respective denomination. The final category, "other," consists of specialized agencies, loose associations, or agencies that said "none" for affiliation. See Chart 30 for more information.

Interdenominational agencies have the largest income, followed by non-denominational agencies, denominational agencies, and other.

CHART **4.30** Income by Agency Affiliation

Interdenominational Agency

Income All Ministries:
$4.9 Billion

Income International
Ministries:
$1.7 Billion

Income Gifts-In-Kind:
$454K

Nondenominational Agency

Income All Ministries:
$3.6 Billion

Income International
Ministries:
$1.4 Billion

Income Gifts-In-Kind:
$838K

Denominational Agency

Income All Ministries:
$2.6 Billion

Income International
Ministries:
$912 Million

Income Gifts-In-Kind:
$15K

Other Agencies

Income All Ministries: $804K

Income International
Ministries: $532K

Income Gifts-In-Kind:
$173K

Reflects combined 2008 and 2016 data

FINANCES: INCOME BY AGENCY TYPE

Sending agencies make up the biggest portion of survey respondents and they also make up the largest portion of income. The second largest group is specialized agencies, which is no surprise considering the large agencies that are on the list, including Habitat for Humanity and Samaritan's Purse.

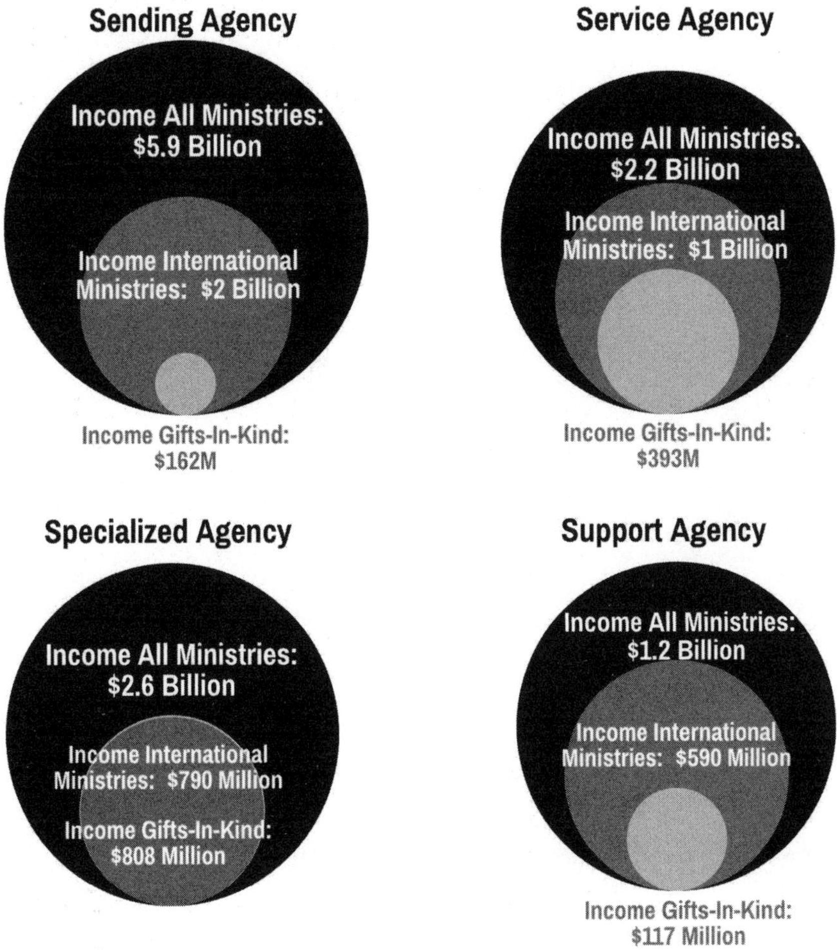

Sending Agency

Income All Ministries:
$5.9 Billion

Income International
Ministries: $2 Billion

Income Gifts-In-Kind:
$162M

Service Agency

Income All Ministries:
$2.2 Billion

Income International
Ministries: $1 Billion

Income Gifts-In-Kind:
$393M

Specialized Agency

Income All Ministries:
$2.6 Billion

Income International
Ministries: $790 Million

Income Gifts-In-Kind:
$808 Million

Support Agency

Income All Ministries:
$1.2 Billion

Income International
Ministries: $590 Million

Income Gifts-In-Kind:
$117 Million

CHART 4.31 Income by Agency Type
Reflects combined 2008 and 2016 data

TABLE 4.22 Sending Agency

Income All Ministries		Income International Ministries	
Seventh-day Adventists, General Conference—Global Mission	$864,314,130.00	IMB of the Southern Baptist Convention	$265,000,000.00
Campus Crusade for Christ (Cru in the US)	$682,870,000.00	Campus Crusade for Christ (Cru in the US)	$139,918,000.00
Christian Churches / Churches of Christ	$650,000,000.00	Christian Broadcasting Network Inc., The	$128,854,919.00
Christian Broadcasting Network Inc., The	$420,420,304.00	Food for the Hungry, Inc.	$82,768,788.00
IMB of the Southern Baptist Convention	$265,000,000.00	Seventh-day Adventists, General Conference–Global Mission	$53,959,359.00
Salvation Army—Canada and Bermuda Territory	$227,000,000.00	Christian Churches / Churches of Christ	$52,000,000.00
Evangelical Lutheran Church in America, Div. for Global Mission	$174,035,570.00	World Concern	$48,818,000.00
Wycliffe Bible Translators USA	$159,210,181.74	Pioneers USA	$46,840,000.00
Presbyterian Church (USA), Worldwide Ministries	$115,000,000.00	Presbyterian Church (USA), Worldwide Ministries	$40,000,000.00
InterVarsity Christian Fellowship/USA	$102,073,000.00	The Salvation Army USA National Headquarters	$38,700,651.00

TABLE 4.23 Service Agency

Income All Ministries		Income International Ministries	
World Vision, Inc.	$743,000,000.00	World Vision Canada	$306,600,000.00
World Vision Canada	$381,800,000.00	Christian Aid Ministries (CAM)	$183,415,214.00
Christian Aid Ministries (CAM)	$186,806,073.00	Opportunity International	$112,064,000.00
Gideons International, The	$115,000,000.00	Gideons International, The	$95,600,000.00
Opportunity International	$112,064,000.00	Network of International Christian Schools	$52,000,000.00
Church World Service	$70,967,349.00	Wycliffe Associates	$41,075,924.00
Network of International Christian Schools	$62,000,000.00	FH Canada	$40,874,000.00
Samaritan's Purse—Canada	$44,271,091.00	Every Home for Christ	$40,234,030.00
FH Canada	$41,977,000.00	Samaritan's Purse - Canada	$39,457,964.00
Wycliffe Associates	$41,075,924.00	Mercy Ships	$31,260,623.00

TABLE 4.24 Support Agency

Income All Ministries		Income International Ministries	
Compassion International, Inc.	$298,441,664.00	Compassion International, Inc.	$217,278,070.00
Operation Blessing International Relief and Development Corporation	$243,447,426.00	Heifer Project International	$81,973,237.00
Heifer Project International	$132,318,844.00	Gospel for Asia, Inc.	$47,842,080.00
IMA World Health	$96,166,173.00	IMA World Health	$20,511,465.00
Gospel for Asia, Inc.	$58,404,573.00	World Help	$18,872,269.00
World Help	$22,611,097.00	HOPE International	$17,400,000.00
e3 Partners Ministry	$18,000,000.00	One Child Matters (formerly Mission of Mercy)	$14,962,511.00
COMHINA	$17,959,465.00	Advancing Native Missions	$11,536,689.00
HOPE International	$17,400,000.00	World-Wide Missions	$11,396,421.00
Lifesong for Orphans	$16,609,034.00	Christian Aid Mission	$9,399,714.00

TABLE **4.25** Specialized Agency

Income All Ministries		Income International Ministries	
Habitat for Humanity International	$1,038,065,042.00	MAP International	$319,511,995.00
Samaritan's Purse	$599,821,688.00	Medical Teams International	$136,847,845.00
MAP International	$349,491,227.00	Habitat for Humanity International	$95,475,655.00
Medical Teams International	$138,921,034.00	International Aid	$36,611,986.00
The Voice of the Martyrs	$54,867,000.00	TWR (Trans World Radio)	$36,585,956.00
Mission Aviation Fellowship	$48,482,586.00	The Voice of the Martyrs	$35,631,000.00
International Aid	$42,906,011.00	Health Partners International of Canada	$28,521,262.00
Awana Clubs International	$37,271,269.00	Baptist Medical & Dental Mission International, Inc. (BMDMI)	$17,500,000.00
TWR (Trans World Radio)	$36,739,489.00	SAT-7 North America	$17,080,555.00
Caring Partners International	$29,986,423.00	American Leprosy Missions	$11,640,620.00

FINANCES: 2008 VS. 2016 COMPARISONS

FINANCES: US ALL INCOME 2008 VS. 2016

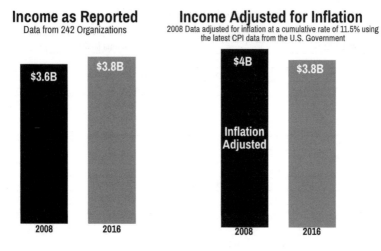

CHART **4.32** US All Income 2008 vs. 2016

This chart highlights the differences the 2008 and 2016 survey in reported income. This chart consists of only the 242 agencies that provided income amounts in both surveys. The numbers indicate that giving has increased until we take inflation into account. The $3.6 billion dollars reported by the 242 agencies in 2008 would have been worth $4 billion in today's currency.

Tables 26–29 show the twenty largest agencies in terms of income, sorted by largest to smallest using 2016 data. In almost every category we see significant growth or loss at particular agencies. While the overall missions community seems to have enjoyed a period of relative stability, there are certainly agencies that have weathered big changes.

TABLE 4.26 Sending Agency

SENDING AGENCY	Income All Ministries 2008	Income All Ministries 2016	Change	Change after 2008 oUHVUKTU at 11.5%
Campus Crusade for Christ (Cru in the US)	$514,449,000.00	$682,870,000.00	$168,421,000.00	$109,259,365.00
Wycliffe Bible Translators USA	$153,150,000.00	$159,210,181.74	$6,060,181.74	$(11,552,068.26)
Church of the Nazarene, Inc.	$92,952,943.00	$72,494,431.00	$(20,458,512.00)	$(31,148,100.45)
Word of Life Fellowship Inc	$26,168,293.00	$69,951,994.00	$43,783,701.00	$40,774,347.31
Ethnos360 (formerly New Tribes Mission)	$63,500,000.00	$61,271,541.00	$(2,228,459.00)	$(9,530,959.00)
Pioneers USA	$30,011,744.00	$55,337,000.00	$25,325,256.00	$21,873,905.44
SIM USA	$43,921,405.00	$50,724,661.00	$6,803,256.00	$1,752,294.42
Baptist International Missions, Inc.	$36,302,856.00	$36,587,420.00	$284,564.00	$(3,890,264.44)
Frontiers	$22,000,000.00	$32,000,000.00	$10,000,000.00	$7,470,000.00
Operation Mobilization	$23,751,000.00	$29,833,602.00	$6,082,602.00	$3,351,237.00
TEAM (The Evangelical Alliance Mission)	$26,635,000.00	$29,514,000.00	$2,879,000.00	$(184,025.00)
ReachGlobal	$29,090,078.00	$28,000,000.00	$(1,090,078.00)	$(4,435,436.97)
Jews for Jesus	$19,643,103.00	$25,800,000.00	$6,156,897.00	$3,897,940.16
Free Methodist World Missions	$24,997,668.00	$20,296,764.00	$(4,700,904.00)	$(7,575,635.82)
SEND International, Inc.	$19,400,000.00	$18,237,088.00	$(1,162,912.00)	$(3,393,912.00)
World Gospel Mission	$21,162,592.00	$18,170,403.00	$(2,992,189.00)	$(5,425,887.08)
CMF International	$10,000,000.00	$17,561,774.00	$7,561,774.00	$6,411,774.00
OMF International	$14,941,991.00	$17,020,874.00	$2,078,883.00	$360,554.04
East-West Ministries International	$12,240,000.00	$16,948,751.00	$4,708,751.00	$3,301,151.00
Crossworld	$16,706,200.00	$16,524,990.00	$(181,210.00)	$(2,102,423.00)

TABLE 4.27 Service Agency

SERVICE AGENCY	Income All Ministries 2008	Income All Ministries 2016	Change	Change after oUHVU KTUH 11.5%
World Vision, Inc.	$1,220,000,000.00	$743,000,000.00	$(477,000,000.00)	$(617,300,000.00)
Network of International Christian Schools	$3,895,814.00	$62,000,000.00	$58,104,186.00	$57,656,167.39
Wycliffe Associates	$17,785,492.00	$41,075,924.00	$23,290,432.00	$21,245,100.42
Reliant Mission, Inc. (formerly Great Commission Ministries, Inc.)	$13,966,351.00	$20,586,159.00	$6,619,808.00	$5,013,677.64

SERVICE AGENCY	Income All Ministries 2008	Income All Ministries 2016	Change	Change after oUHVU KTUH 11.5%
Christian Missions In Many Lands, Inc.	$12,700,000.00	$13,591,000.00	$891,000.00	$(569,500.00)
Bright Hope	$4,648,574.00	$11,196,889.00	$6,548,315.00	$6,013,728.99
Mission Eurasia (formerly Peter Deyneka Russian Ministries)	$4,552,857.00	$8,629,120.00	$4,076,263.00	$3,552,684.45
Our Daily Bread (formerly RBC Ministries)	$49,600,000.00	$8,600,000.00	$(41,000,000.00)	$(46,704,000.00)
Luis Palau Evangelistic Association	$22,000,677.00	$8,590,083.00	$(13,410,594.00)	$(15,940,671.86)
Joni and Friends	$23,304,649.00	$6,218,959.00	$(17,085,690.00)	$(19,765,724.64)
Back to the Bible	$12,798,352.00	$5,547,486.00	$(7,250,866.00)	$(8,722,676.48)
Association of Free Lutheran Congregations	$981,691.00	$3,200,000.00	$2,218,309.00	$2,105,414.54
Bibles For The World, Inc.	$3,712,988.00	$2,800,000.00	$(912,988.00)	$(1,339,981.62)
Medical Ambassadors International (Lifewind International)	$3,589,884.00	$2,301,502.00	$(1,288,382.00)	$(1,701,218.66)
Equip Inc & Equip International	$1,981,682.00	$1,792,578.00	$(189,104.00)	$(416,997.43)
visionSynergy	$500,000.00	$1,593,480.00	$1,093,480.00	$1,035,980.00
Servants in Faith & Technology (SIFAT)	$1,700,000.00	$1,500,000.00	$(200,000.00)	$(395,500.00)
Empowering Lives International	$1,121,300.00	$1,483,175.00	$361,875.00	$232,925.50
Celebrant Singers	$2,000,000.00	$1,200,000.00	$(800,000.00)	$(1,030,000.00)
Forward Edge International	$1,800,000.00	$1,200,000.00	$(600,000.00)	$(807,000.00)

TABLE 4.28 Support Agency

SUPPORT AGENCY	Income All Ministries 2008	Income All Ministries 2016	Change	Change after 2008 oUHVUKTU at 11.5%
HOPE International	$5,409,838.00	$17,400,000.00	$11,990,162.00	$11,368,030.63
Mission India	$10,452,433.00	$15,000,000.00	$4,547,567.00	$3,345,537.21
Christian Aid Mission	$10,566,602.00	$12,556,070.00	$1,989,468.00	$774,308.77
Advancing Native Missions	$6,692,053.00	$12,496,514.00	$5,804,461.00	$5,034,874.91
Evangelism Explosion III International, Inc.	$5,440,318.00	$6,108,000.00	$667,682.00	$42,045.43
AMG International	$6,246,530.00	$6,024,000.00	$(222,530.00)	$(940,880.95)
Blessings International	$23,847,067.00	$4,739,509.00	$(19,107,558.00)	$(21,849,970.71)
Development Associates Intl. (DAI)	$4,374,764.00	$4,222,319.00	$(152,445.00)	$(655,542.86)
TCM International Institute	$2,398,502.00	$3,056,404.00	$657,902.00	$382,074.27
Ambassadors for Christ International	$2,000,000.00	$3,000,000.00	$1,000,000.00	$770,000.00
Barnabas International	$1,483,224.00	$2,850,241.00	$1,367,017.00	$1,196,446.24
Good News for India	$1,100,000.00	$2,830,812.00	$1,730,812.00	$1,604,312.00
India Gospel League	$2,266,001.00	$2,720,730.00	$454,729.00	$194,138.88
Steer, Inc.	$1,477,024.00	$2,312,905.00	$835,881.00	$666,023.24
Help for Haiti Inc.	$27,000.00	$1,993,996.00	$1,966,996.00	$1,963,891.00
Final Frontiers Foundation	$916,932.00	$1,945,209.00	$1,028,277.00	$922,829.82

SUPPORT AGENCY	Income All Ministries 2008	Income All Ministries 2016	Change	Change after 2008 oUHVUKTU at 11.5%
Kinship United (formerly Warm Blankets Orphan Care Intl.)	$2,447,045.00	$1,895,751.00	$(551,294.00)	$(832,704.17)
Beyond Borders	$970,000.00	$1,600,000.00	$630,000.00	$518,450.00
Every Child Ministries, Inc.	$870,784.00	$1,257,406.00	$386,622.00	$286,481.84
Mission Possible USA	$792,232.00	$1,223,627.00	$431,395.00	$340,288.32

TABLE 4.29 Specialized Agency

SPECIALIZED AGENCY	Income All Ministries 2008	Income All Ministries 2016	Change	Change after 2008 oUHVUKTU at 11.5%
Samaritan's Purse	$313,256,181.00	$599,821,688.00	$286,565,507.00	$250,541,046.19
Mission Aviation Fellowship	$24,000,000.00	$48,482,586.00	$24,482,586.00	$21,722,586.00
Awana Clubs International	$34,599,942.00	$37,271,269.00	$2,671,327.00	$(1,307,666.33)
TWR (Trans World Radio)	$27,560,000.00	$36,739,489.00	$9,179,489.00	$6,010,089.00
Caring Partners International	$740,197.00	$29,986,423.00	$29,246,226.00	$29,161,103.35
SAT-7 North America	$5,500,000.00	$17,080,555.00	$11,580,555.00	$10,948,055.00
American Leprosy Missions	$7,960,969.00	$13,278,117.00	$5,317,148.00	$4,401,636.57
CLC Ministries International	$5,000,000.00	$4,086,642.00	$(913,358.00)	$(1,488,358.00)
Global Recordings Network	$2,189,352.00	$3,100,000.00	$910,648.00	$658,872.52
Christian Medical & Dental Associations	$16,103,647.00	$2,571,838.00	$(13,531,809.00)	$(15,383,728.41)
Good News Productions, International	$1,400,000.00	$2,407,734.00	$1,007,734.00	$846,734.00
Shelter for Life Intl. Inc.	$2,126,530.00	$2,110,000.00	$(16,530.00)	$(261,080.95)
World Compassion Terry Law Ministries	$3,227,256.00	$1,935,150.00	$(1,292,106.00)	$(1,663,240.44)
FAME	$12,080,322.00	$1,672,957.00	$(10,407,365.00)	$(11,796,602.03)
World Servants, Inc.	$1,575,102.00	$1,283,221.00	$(291,881.00)	$(473,017.73)
Media Associates International	$319,342.00	$797,246.00	$477,904.00	$441,179.67
Chosen Mission Project	$1,157,364.00	$787,622.00	$(369,742.00)	$(502,838.86)
Women to the World, Inc.	$255,183.00	$655,000.00	$399,817.00	$370,470.96
Alongside Ministries International	$613,831.00	$533,000.00	$(80,831.00)	$(151,421.57)
ERRC (Educational Resources & Referrals—China)	$367,828.00	$503,358.00	$135,530.00	$93,229.78

FINANCES: US INTERNATIONAL INCOME 2008 VS. 2016

Only 167 US agencies provided data in both 2008 and 2016 on the portion of their budget that went to International Ministries. Since the data set is smaller, the value of this chart is more in the comparison than the totals given. Even after adjusting for inflation, the amount spent on International Ministries has grown in the eight years between the two surveys.

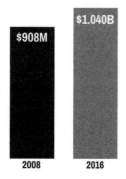

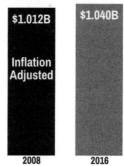

CHART 4.33 US International Ministries Income 2008 vs. 2016

Tables 30–33 show the ten largest agencies, sorted by largest to smallest using 2016 data, pertaining to income for International Ministries.

TABLE 4.30 Sending Agency

SENDING AGENCY	International Ministries 2008	International Ministries 2016	Change	Change after 2008 oUHVUKTU at 11.5%
Campus Crusade for Christ (Cru in the US)	$137,739,000.00	$139,918,000.00	$2,179,000.00	$(13,660,985.00)
Pioneers USA	$26,905,000.00	$46,840,000.00	$19,935,000.00	$16,840,925.00
TEAM (The Evangelical Alliance Mission)	$23,393,560.00	$27,409,000.00	$4,015,440.00	$1,325,180.60
Operation Mobilization	$17,227,000.00	$21,329,054.00	$4,102,054.00	$2,120,949.00
Wycliffe Bible Translators USA	$131,161,000.00	$19,018,113.45	$(112,142,886.55)	$(127,226,401.55)
CMF International	$10,000,000.00	$17,561,774.00	$7,561,774.00	$6,411,774.00
World Gospel Mission	$12,498,657.00	$16,744,455.00	$4,245,798.00	$2,808,452.45
East-West Ministries International	$12,240,000.00	$16,722,051.00	$4,482,051.00	$3,074,451.00
American Baptist Churches of the USA, International Ministries	$11,975,544.00	$16,159,360.00	$4,183,816.00	$2,806,628.44
United World Mission, Inc.	$7,260,015.00	$15,510,000.00	$8,249,985.00	$7,415,083.28

TABLE 4.31 Service Agency

SERVICE AGENCY	International Ministries 2008	International Ministries 2016	Change	Change after 2008 oUHVUKTU at 11.5%
Network of International Christian Schools	$2,659,301.00	$52,000,000.00	$49,340,699.00	$49,034,879.39
Wycliffe Associates	$11,992,503.00	$41,075,924.00	$29,083,421.00	$27,704,283.16
Every Home for Christ	$13,648,253.00	$40,234,030.00	$26,585,777.00	$25,016,227.91
Bright Hope	$4,648,574.00	$10,177,689.00	$5,529,115.00	$4,994,528.99
Mission Eurasia (formerly Peter Deyneka Russian Ministries)	$4,267,083.00	$8,629,120.00	$4,362,037.00	$3,871,322.46
Joni and Friends	$6,218,959.00	$4,796,959.00	$(1,422,000.00)	$(2,137,180.29)
Reliant Mission, Inc. (formerly Great Commission Ministries, Inc.)	$2,339,874.00	$3,276,380.00	$936,506.00	$667,420.49
visionSynergy	$325,000.00	$1,593,480.00	$1,268,480.00	$1,231,105.00
Association of Free Lutheran Congregations	$981,691.00	$1,400,000.00	$418,309.00	$305,414.54
Empowering Lives International	$600,464.00	$1,260,183.00	$659,719.00	$590,665.64

TABLE 4.32 Support Agency

SUPPORT AGENCY	International Ministries 2008	International Ministries 2016	Change	Change after 2008 oUHVUKTU at 11.5%
HOPE International	$5,409,838.00	$17,400,000.00	$11,990,162.00	$11,368,030.63
One Child Matters (formerly Mission of Mercy)	$13,736,718.00	$14,962,511.00	$1,225,793.00	$(353,929.57)
Advancing Native Missions	$4,509,182.00	$11,536,689.00	$7,027,507.00	$6,508,951.07
Christian Aid Mission	$10,566,602.00	$9,399,714.00	$(1,166,888.00)	$(2,382,047.23)
AMG International	$6,096,530.00	$6,000,000.00	$(96,530.00)	$(797,630.95)
Blessings International	$23,148,347.00	$4,739,509.00	$(18,408,838.00)	$(21,070,897.91)
TCM International Institute	$2,274,432.00	$3,056,404.00	$781,972.00	$520,412.32
Ambassadors for Christ International	$100,000.00	$3,000,000.00	$2,900,000.00	$2,888,500.00
India Gospel League	$3,370,519.00	$2,312,621.00	$(1,057,898.00)	$(1,445,507.69)
Evangelism Explosion III International, Inc.	$2,289,356.00	$2,290,000.00	$644.00	$(262,631.94)

TABLE **4.33** Specialized Agency

SPECIALIZED AGENCY	International Ministries 2008	International Ministries 2016	Change	Change after 2008 oUHVUKTU at 11.5%
TWR (Trans World Radio)	$20,560,000.00	$36,585,956.00	$16,025,956.00	$13,661,556.00
SAT-7 North America	$3,500,000.00	$17,080,555.00	$13,580,555.00	$13,178,055.00
American Leprosy Missions	$5,038,555.00	$11,640,620.00	$6,602,065.00	$6,022,631.18
Awana Clubs International	$5,005,665.00	$3,770,462.00	$(1,235,203.00)	$(1,810,854.48)
Global Recordings Network	$672,719.00	$2,480,000.00	$1,807,281.00	$1,729,918.32
Caring Partners International	$563,798.00	$2,140,783.00	$1,576,985.00	$1,512,148.23
World Compassion Terry Law Ministries	$1,810,982.00	$1,810,982.00	$-	$(208,262.93)
FAME	$11,464,097.00	$1,668,706.00	$(9,795,391.00)	$(11,113,762.16)
ERRC (Educational Resources & Referrals—China)	$252,188.00	$503,358.00	$251,170.00	$222,168.38
World Servants, Inc.	$450,070.00	$425,687.00	$(24,383.00)	$(76,141.05)

FINANCES: CANADIAN ALL INCOME 2008 VS. 2016

Thirty-four agencies provided data in both 2008 and 2016. As has been noted elsewhere in this report, there is not a significant amount of overall change. Both the US and Canadian data is in alignment, showing a relatively stable period over these eight years.

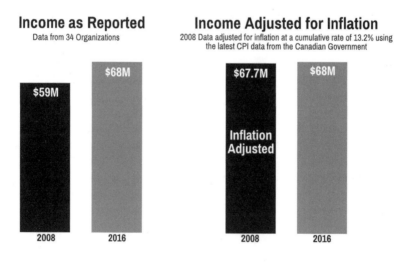

CHART **4.34** Canadian All Income 2008 vs. 2016

Table 34 shows all Canadian organizations that provided data regarding for the All Income category in both 2008 and 2016. It is sorted by largest to smallest using 2016 data.

TABLE **4.34** Canadian Agencies: Income All 2008 vs. 2016

SENDING AGENCY	Income All Ministries 2008	Income All Ministries 2016	Change	Change after oUHVU KTUH 13.2%
SIM Canada	$13,383,890.00	$9,267,067.00	$(4,116,823.00)	$(5,883,496.48)
Evangelical Free Church of Canada Mission	$3,700,000.00	$5,869,219.00	$2,169,219.00	$1,680,819.00
Pioneers Canada	$2,100,000.00	$5,812,000.00	$3,712,000.00	$3,434,800.00
OMF International—Canada	$3,584,764.00	$4,625,683.00	$1,040,919.00	$567,730.15
Africa Inland Mission Canada Intl.	$4,631,000.00	$3,637,968.00	$(993,032.00)	$(1,604,324.00)
SEND International of Canada	$3,262,402.00	$3,410,258.00	$147,856.00	$(282,781.06)
Avant Ministries Canada	$2,832,467.00	$2,999,845.00	$167,378.00	$(206,507.64)
WEC International Canada	$2,600,000.00	$2,555,000.00	$(45,000.00)	$(388,200.00)
Crossworld Canada	$1,298,799.00	$2,405,084.00	$1,106,285.00	$934,843.53
Baptist General Conference of Canada	$1,249,915.00	$1,940,804.00	$690,889.00	$525,900.22
Commission To Every Nation-Canada	$100,700.00	$1,801,537.00	$1,700,837.00	$1,687,544.60
Evangelical Mennonite Conference	$1,864,258.00	$1,755,500.00	$(108,758.00)	$(354,840.06)
Christar Canada	$740,000.00	$1,400,000.00	$660,000.00	$562,320.00
Chosen People Ministries (Canada)	$933,000.00	$1,223,363.00	$290,363.00	$167,207.00
Greater Europe Mission Canada	$1,425,675.00	$1,204,209.00	$(221,466.00)	$(409,655.10)
World Team Canada	$1,898,000.00	$1,160,000.00	$(738,000.00)	$(988,536.00)
Latin America Mission	$706,800.00	$1,125,580.00	$418,780.00	$325,482.40
Emmanuel Intl. Canada	$2,293,469.00	$850,353.00	$(1,443,116.00)	$(1,745,853.91)
Slavic Gospel Association—Canada	$1,132,178.00	$650,000.00	$(482,178.00)	$(631,625.50)
Liebenzell Mission of Canada	$329,136.00	$634,198.00	$305,062.00	$261,616.05
Into All The World	$625,000.00	$530,571.00	$(94,429.00)	$(176,929.00)
Camino Global Ministries Canada (formerly CAM International of Canada)	$277,511.00	$345,811.00	$68,300.00	$31,668.55
The Free Methodist Church in Canada	$1,700,000.00	$134,615.00	$(1,565,385.00)	$(1,789,785.00)
SERVICE AGENCY	Income All Ministries 2008	Income All Ministries 2016	Change	Change after oUHVU KTUH 13.2%
TWR Canada	$1,873,473.00	$4,828,000.00	$2,954,527.00	$2,707,228.56
Word & Deed Ministries Canada	$2,170,000.00	$3,873,970.00	$1,703,970.00	$1,417,530.00
Galcom International Canada	$745,000.00	$2,076,743.00	$1,331,743.00	$1,233,403.00
Evangelical Mennonite Mission Conference	$1,287,000.00	$1,100,000.00	$(187,000.00)	$(356,884.00)
Lutheran Bible Translators of Canada	$289,000.00	$370,000.00	$81,000.00	$42,852.00
Compassion	$50,000.00	$150,000.00	$100,000.00	$93,400.00

SPECIALIZED AGENCY	Income All Ministries 2008	Income All Ministries 2016	Change	Change after oUHVU KTUH 13.2%
Global Recordings Network Canada	$308,000.00	$245,765.00	$(62,235.00)	$(102,891.00)
SUPPORT AGENCY	Income All Ministries 2008	Income All Ministries 2016	Change	Change after oUHVU KTUH 13.2%
Mission Possible Canada	$189,000.00	$270,479.00	$81,479.00	$56,531.00
CSM Canada Intl. (Christian Salvage Mission)	$125,000.00	$60,000.00	$(65,000.00)	$(81,500.00)
Ukrainian Children's Christian Fund	$80,000.00	$10,000.00	$(70,000.00)	$(80,560.00)

FINANCES: CANADIAN INTERNATIONAL INCOME 2008 VS. 2016

Twenty-three organizations provided figures for International Ministries in both 2008 and 2016. The chart reveals a reduction in overall Canadian income for International Ministry. The $23.1 million given in 2008, when adjusted for inflation at a rate of 13.2%, is worth $26 million, surpassing the amount given in 2016.

Income as Reported
Data from 23 Organizations

$23.1M — 2008
$23.4M — 2016

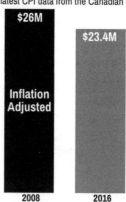

Income Adjusted for Inflation
2008 Data adjusted for inflation at a cumulative rate of 13.2% using the latest CPI data from the Canadian Government

$26M — Inflation Adjusted — 2008
$23.4M — 2016

CHART 4.35 Canadian International Ministries Income 2008 vs. 2016

TABLE 4.35 Canadian Agencies: International Ministries Income 2008 vs. 2016

SENDING AGENCY	International Ministries 2008	International Ministries 2016	Change	Change after 2008 oUHVUKTU at 13.2%
Evangelical Free Church of Canada Mission	$3,700,000.00	$4,922,402.00	$1,222,402.00	$734,002.00
SEND International of Canada	$2,319,719.00	$3,394,530.00	$1,074,811.00	$768,608.09
Africa Inland Mission Canada Intl.	$3,762,000.00	$2,500,000.00	$(1,262,000.00)	$(1,758,584.00)
Avant Ministries Canada	$2,026,282.00	$2,315,538.00	$289,256.00	$21,786.78
OMF International - Canada	$1,849,136.00	$2,167,847.00	$318,711.00	$74,625.05
WEC International Canada	$1,800,000.00	$1,890,000.00	$90,000.00	$(147,600.00)
Commission To Every Nation—Canada	$97,056.00	$1,801,537.00	$1,704,481.00	$1,691,669.61
Crossworld Canada	$1,008,726.00	$1,619,807.00	$611,081.00	$477,929.17
Greater Europe Mission Canada	$1,173,436.00	$1,170,547.00	$(2,889.00)	$(157,782.55)
Evangelical Mennonite Conference	$1,053,973.00	$1,136,000.00	$82,027.00	$(57,097.44)
Baptist General Conference of Canada	$553,515.00	$1,000,000.00	$446,485.00	$373,421.02
Latin America Mission	$611,828.00	$944,736.00	$332,908.00	$252,146.70
Christar Canada	$600,000.00	$750,000.00	$150,000.00	$70,800.00
Into All The World	$560,000.00	$508,694.00	$(51,306.00)	$(125,226.00)
The Free Methodist Church in Canada	$520,000.00	$322,557.00	$(197,443.00)	$(266,083.00)
Liebenzell Mission of Canada	$148,313.00	$214,581.00	$66,268.00	$46,690.68
Chosen People Ministries (Canada)	$32,400.00	$199,868.00	$167,468.00	$163,191.20
Camino Global Ministries Canada (formerly CAM International of Canada)	$262,000.00	$184,064.00	$(77,936.00)	$(112,520.00)
SERVICE AGENCY	**International Ministries 2008**	**International Ministries 2016**	**Change**	**Change after 2008 oUHVUKTU at 13.2%**
Evangelical Mennonite Mission Conference	$619,000.00	$632,000.00	$13,000.00	$(68,708.00)
Lutheran Bible Translators of Canada	$170,000.00	$300,000.00	$130,000.00	$107,560.00
Mennonite International Health Association	$53,942.00	$95,000.00	$41,058.00	$33,937.66
SPECIALIZED AGENCY	**International Ministries 2008**	**International Ministries 2016**	**Change**	**Change after 2008 oUHVUKTU at 13.2%**
Global Recordings Network Canada	$70,899.00	$120,165.00	$49,266.00	$39,907.33
SUPPORT AGENCY	**International Ministries 2008**	**International Ministries 2016**	**Change**	**Change after 2008 oUHVUKTU at 13.2%**
Mission Possible Canada	$156,000.00	$238,756.00	$82,756.00	$62,164.00

FINANCE: CONCLUSION

The overall picture is that the North American mission movement is neither growing nor shrinking financially. There has been a stable period over the past eight years. While within individual organizations there are some large financial shifts, aggregate revenues have remained largely unchanged.

Shifts in North American culture might cause one to conclude that North American mission agencies are in retreat, but financially they are holding their own. How long this will last, or if these agencies can grow in our current environment, remains to be seen.

Conclusion

We have sought to present the collected data in a manner that is clear and defined. In summary:

PERSONNEL:

- The missionary force from North America has not shrunk nor has it expanded since 2008.
- Short-term sending figures are substantially affected by just a few organizations.
- There was a much stronger reporting in the short-term category "2 weeks or less" (80 percent increase as compared to 2008).
- Over 24,000 people work in the home offices of agencies.
- Tentmaking and BAM continue to experience strong growth (18 percent increase).

ACTIVITIES:

- Evangelism and Discipleship continues to experience a notable decline as the primary activity of agencies.
- Discipleship and Training experienced the largest percentage of growth (125 percent) since the last survey.
- Although there is a decline in Evangelism and Discipleship as a category, the primary activity of Church Planting (Establishing) remains the top primary activity and something that is performed by all agency types.

REGIONAL FIELD WORK:

- Security concerns resulted in an increase in those designated as "Global."
- There is an increase in those designated as working in North America. This is most likely a response to an increased focus on diaspora ministry.

FOUNDING:

- The founding of new mission agencies seems to be tapering off.

FINANCES:

- Overall, the North American movement seems to be financially stable over the 2008 to 2016 period.
- While initial numbers indicate financial growth for agencies, when inflation-adjusted they are in slight decline.
- Surveyed agencies had over $12 billion in annual revenues in 2016.
- Agencies spent over $1 billion on international budgets in 2016.

In an effort to enable organizations to contribute more easily and regularly, our goal in upcoming years is to create new systems for data collection. By utilizing new technologies, we hope to provide the North American mission force with up-to-date analysis in new formats.

This data has been parsed in many different ways. It is not intended to create a perspective of competition between the US and Canada, or between denominational affiliations or agency types. We are clearly one body working together for the sake of the Great Commission. Hopefully, this chapter gave a clearer picture of where your organization stands and a better understanding of where we stand collectively from a North American perspective.

Let us not lose sight of the global church that is rising up in a new era of training and sending out of workers to the harvest. As North Americans, let us do all we can to stand alongside our sisters and brothers from around the globe, to learn together, to serve together, and—through our unity in Christ—see our mutual goal reached: the gospel taken to every tongue and tribe, until all have heard before Christ returns.

CHAPTER 5

DIRECTORY OF NORTH AMERICAN AGENCIES

This chapter contains the basic information for US and Canadian Protestant agencies engaged in Christian ministries outside of North America. It includes agencies that directly support the work of such ministries or the work of overseas national churches/workers. The agencies themselves supplied the data contained in these listings by way of a survey that is found at the end of this book. Where new data for individual agencies was not made available, data was used from the previous edition and is shown on the listing as follows:

(FPC-PE)	Field Personnel, Countries, or Regions of Service from previous edition
(DPE)	Data from previous edition
(DPE)(FPC16)	Data from previous edition but with updated Field Personnel and Countries or Regions of Service

In previous editions, this data was divided into two separate chapters: one for US agencies and another for Canada agencies. As a demonstration of solidarity of mission efforts, they are combined in this one chapter. For missions that are registered and active in both countries, if both submitted data, there are two listings.

Personnel are listed in two categories:

1. Fully supported personnel are serving cross-culturally more than 4 years, 1–4 years, or X-C in US or Canada, and non-residential are those living in the US or Canada but with ministry to other countries.
2. Other personnel include Short-Termers, Tentmakers or BAM, Non-North Americans serving in their own or another country, and home staff.

"Countries" are those where the agency sends North American personnel or regularly supports non-North American personnel. If a region or continent is indicated instead of a specific country it may be because of mission personnel whose ministry spans more than one country. Or, for security purposes, it was more prudent for the mission to report personnel in a general world region.

Refer to Chapter 6 for a list of what organizations work in each country, including details about number of personnel by length of service and non-North American personnel.

10/40 CONNECTIONS
PO Box 1141
Hixson, TN 37343 US
Phone: (423) 468-4871
Email: candles@1040connections.org
Website: 1040connections.org
Associations: Missio Nexus

An interdenominational service agency of Evangelical tradition engaged in apologetics, Bible teaching, CPM, addressing human trafficking, leadership development, and networking, partnership, or coordination.

Purpose: . . . to cast hope to unreached peoples so that they hear, experience and multiply the Good News of Jesus. We do so by connecting the Body of Christ, equipping believers, and engaging the unreached.

Year Founded in US: 2000
Countries/Regions: East Asia, Middle East, South Asia

20SCHEMES
PO Box 1491
Bardstown, KY 40004 US
Phone: (502) 601-0040
Email: info@20schemes.com
Website: 20schemes.com
Associations: Missio Nexus

A nondenominational sending agency of Baptist and Reformed tradition engaged in church planting (establishing), and training indigenous leaders.

Purpose: . . . to build healthy gospel centered churches for Scotland's poorest communities.

Year Founded in US: 2013

Other Personnel
  Home staff: 3

2ND MILE MINISTRIES
1650 Margaret St., Suite 302 #339
Jacksonville, FL 32204 US
Phone: (904) 372-3530
Email: jonathan@2ndmile-jax.com
Website: 2ndmile-jax.com

A denominational sending agency of Evangelical tradition engaged in children's ministry, justice or peace issues, missionary & worker training, and youth ministry.

Purpose: . . . to see the gospel renew lives and communities so they are transformed in every way.

Year Founded in US: 2003

A.C.T. INTERNATIONAL
Formerly: Artists in Christian Testimony
PO Box 1649
Brentwood, TN 37024-1649 US
Phone: (615) 376-7861
Email: info@actinternational.org
Website: actinternational.org
Associations: Missio Nexus

An interdenominational sending agency of Evangelical tradition engaged in arts ministry, missionary equipping and sending, church planting, discipleship, evangelism, funds transmission and mobilization for mission. (DPE)

Purpose: . . . to equip and mobilize artistic ministries, ministers and missionaries for Christ's Kingdom work worldwide.

Year Founded in US: 1973

Fully Supported US Personnel Working Cross-Culturally
  More than 4 years: 8
  Non-residential: 5
Other Personnel
  Short-Term less than 1 year: 5
  Tentmakers/BAM: 2
  Non-US in own/other country: 24
  Home staff: 4

Countries/Regions: Africa, Brazil, China (People's Republic of), France, Germany, Ghana, Hungary, Israel, Japan, Kenya, Lebanon, Russia, Tanzania, United Kingdom

ABWE CANADA (ACROSS BORDERS FOR WORLD EVANGELISM)
980 Adelaide St. S., Ste. #34
London, ON N6E 1R3 CA
Phone: (519) 690-1009
Email: office@abwecanada.org
Website: abwe.ca
A sending agency of Baptist and Evangelical tradition engaged in church planting, discipleship, theological education, evangelism, funds transmission and partnership development. (DPE)
Purpose: . . . to assist local churches to achieve their Canadian and international mission objectives.
Year Founded in CA: 2007
Income for International Min:
  $1,600,000
Fully Supported CA Personnel Working Cross-Culturally
  More than 4 years: 30
  1–4 years: 3
  Non-residential: 4
Other Personnel
  Short-Term less than 1 year: 68
  Home staff: 6
Countries/Regions: Africa, Asia, Brazil, Croatia, Europe, Liberia, Middle East, Portugal, Romania, Togo, Trinidad and Tobago, Ukraine, United Kingdom

ABWE INTERNATIONAL
PO Box 8585
Harrisburg, PA 17105-8585 US
Phone: (717) 774-7000
Email: abwe@abwe.org
Website: abwe.org
Associations: FOM, Missio Nexus

A denominational sending agency of Baptist tradition engaged in evangelism, camping programs, church planting, discipleship, theological education and medical work. (DPE)(FPC16)
Purpose: . . . to be a spiritually empowered family of servants committed to glorifying Him by following His command to preach the Gospel throughout the world.
Income for International Min:
  $36,000,000
Fully Supported US Personnel Working Cross-Culturally
  More than 4 years: 883
  1–4 years: 21
  X-C workers in US: 100
  Non-residential: 10
Other Personnel
  Short-Term less than 1 year: 275
  Home staff: 100
Countries/Regions: Argentina, Australia, Brazil, Bulgaria, Cambodia, Caribbean, Central America, Chile, Colombia, Costa Rica, Czech Republic, East Asia, Eastern Europe and Eurasia, Ecuador, France, Germany, Ghana, Greece, Haiti, Hungary, India, Ireland (Republic of), Italy, Jamaica, Japan, Mexico, Middle East, Nepal, Nicaragua, North Africa, Norway, Papua New Guinea, Paraguay, Peru, Philippines, Poland, Portugal, Romania, Saint Lucia, Slovakia, South America, South Asia, Spain, Taiwan (China), Thailand, Togo, Trinidad and Tobago, United Kingdom, Western Europe

ACCELERATING INTERNATIONAL MISSION STRATEGIES (AIMS)
PO Box 38301
Colorado Springs, CO 80937 US
Phone: (719) 266-3737
Email: aims@aims.org
Website: aims.org

An interdenominational service agency of Charismatic tradition engaged in CPM, missionary & worker training, networking, partnership, or coordination, and recruiting.

Purpose: . . . to mobilize, train, and network the global Church to work together to plant the Gospel in the world's least reached people groups, and to establish churches that reproduce themselves.

Fully Supported US Personnel Working Cross-Culturally
   More than 4 years: 12
   1–4 years: 10
Other Personnel
   Short-Term less than 1 year: 50
Countries/Regions: Central Asia, South Asia, Southeast Asia, Sub-Saharan Africa, Western Europe

ACCI (ADVENTIVE CROSS CULTURAL INITIATIVES)
89 Auriga Dr.
Nepean, ON K2E 7Z2 CA
Phone: (613) 298-1546
Email: lauren@adventive.ca
Website: adventive.ca
A nondenominational support agency of Evangelical tradition engaged in leadership development, Bible distribution, church planting, discipleship, support of national churches and partnership development. (DPE)

Purpose: . . . to attract, equip, send, and serve the vision of passionate, effective leaders and teams who are focused on cross-culturally advancing the Kingdom of Christ.
Year Founded in CA: 2002
Income for International Min:
   $189,000
Other Personnel
   Short-Term less than 1 year: 3

ACCI (ADVENTIVE CROSS CULTURAL INITIATIVES) – US
141 E. Main St.
Rock Hill, SC 29730 US
Phone: (704) 607-5029
Email: johnhaley@adventive.ca
Website: adventive.ca
A support agency of Evangelical tradition engaged in evangelism, support of national churches, mobilization for mission, relief and/or rehabilitation, short-term programs and missionary training. (DPE)

Purpose: . . . to bring the hope of Jesus to a lost and suffering world through the power of God and by the direction of His Holy Spirit.
Year Founded in US: 2004
Income for International Min:
   $109,193
Fully Supported US Personnel Working Cross-Culturally
   More than 4 years: 1
   1–4 years: 8
Other Personnel
   Short-Term less than 1 year: 3
   Non-US in own/other country: 8
Countries/Regions: Africa, Asia, Brazil, Ecuador, Guatemala, Italy, New Zealand, Sri Lanka, Zambia

ACM INTERNATIONAL
1270 Sandy Drive
Florissant, MO 63031 US
Phone: (314) 395-8823
Email: usoffice@acminternational.com
Website: acminternational.com
A nondenominational sending agency of Christian (Restoration Movement) tradition engaged in business as mission, community development, DMM, international student ministry, and youth ministry.

Purpose: . . . to see teams of Jesus disciples forming Kingdom churches and building global community, the Kingdom of God on earth.

Year Founded in US: 1947

Fully Supported US Personnel Working Cross-Culturally
　　More than 4 years: 11
　　X-C workers in US: 6
　　Non-residential: 2

Other Personnel
　　Short-Term less than 1 year: 1
　　Home staff: 5

Countries/Regions: Kenya, North Africa, Philippines, Tanzania

ACSI (ASSOCIATION OF CHRISTIAN SCHOOLS INTERNATIONAL)

PO Box 65130
Colorado Springs, CO 80962-5130 US
Phone: (719) 528-6906
Email: info@acsi.org
Website: acsi.org

A service agency of evangelical tradition engaged in Christian education K-12 and colleges, extension education, leadership development, management consulting/ training and short-term programs. (DPE)

Purpose: . . . to enable Christian educators and schools worldwide by offering effective Christian school education.

Income for International Min:
　$908,909

Fully Supported US Personnel Working Cross-Culturally
　　More than 4 years: 3
　　Non-residential: 3

Other Personnel
　　Short-Term less than 1 year: 1
　　Home staff: 175

Countries/Regions: Philippines, Ukraine

ACTION INTERNATIONAL MINISTRIES

PO Box 398
5502-232nd St. SW
Mountlake Terrace, WA 98043 US
Phone: (425) 775-4800
Email: pearl@actionusa.org
Website: actionintl.org
Associations: Missio Nexus

A nondenominational sending agency of Evangelical tradition engaged in business as mission, theological education, and medical ministry, including dental or public health.

Purpose: . . . to evangelize, disciple, equip and send multinational workers to the ends of the earth; especially among children in crisis, the poor, under-trained pastors and needy churches.

Year Founded in US: 1975

Income for International Min:
　$5,556,978

Fully Supported US Personnel Working Cross-Culturally
　　More than 4 years: 70
　　1–4 years: 3

Other Personnel
　　Short-Term less than 1 year: 18
　　Non-US in own/other country: 51

Countries/Regions: Austria, Brazil, Cambodia, Colombia, Ecuador, India, Malawi, Mexico, Philippines, Spain, Uganda, Zambia

ACTION INTERNATIONAL MINISTRIES – CANADA

3015 A 21st St. NE
Calgary, AB T2E 7T1 CA
Phone: (403) 204-1421
Email: info@actioncanada.net
Website: actioncanada.net

An interdenominational sending agency of Evangelical tradition engaged in training, camping programs, childcare/orphanage programs, discipleship, leadership development, literature distribution and urban ministry to the poor. (DPE)

Purpose: . . . network with local churches, national organizations and other mission agencies to reach people for Christ (evangelism), train them in Christian living (discipleship) and assist them in their physical and economic needs (development).

Year Founded in CA: 1985
Income for International Min:
$1,383,914

Fully Supported CA Personnel Working Cross-Culturally
More than 4 years: 17
1–4 years: 2
Non-residential: 1

Other Personnel
Short-Term less than 1 year: 36
Non-CA in own/other country: 11
Home staff: 2

Countries/Regions: Brazil, Colombia, Ecuador, Honduras, India, New Zealand, Philippines, Ukraine, Zambia

ACTS INTERNATIONAL MINISTRIES INC.

PO Box 64227
Colorado Springs, CO 80962 US
Phone: (888) 719-2287
Email: info@actsinternational.net
Website: actsinternational.net

A transdenominational support agency of Evangelical tradition engaged in church planting, theological education, leadership development, support of national churches, support of national workers and training. (DPE)

Purpose: . . . to equip indigenous missionaries for effective ministry and church planting among the unreached of Asia.

Other Personnel
Non-US in own/other country: 6
Home staff: 5

Countries/Regions: India, Myanmar (Burma), Nepal

ADRA (ADVENTIST DEVELOPMENT AND RELIEF AGENCY)

20 Robert St W
Newcastle, ON L1B 1C6 CA
Phone: (905) 446-2372
Email: info@adra.ca
Website: adra.ca

A service agency of Adventist tradition engaged in development, agricultural programs, medical work, relief and/or rehabilitation, children at risk and HIV/AIDS. (DPE)

Purpose: . . . to work with people in poverty and distress to create just and positive change through empowering partnerships and responsible action.

Income for International Min:
$3,899,496

Other Personnel
Home staff: 15

ADVANCING NATIVE MISSIONS

P. O. Box 5303, 10460 Critzers Shop Rd.
Charlottesville, VA 22905 US
Phone: (540) 456-7111
Email: davidt@advancingnativemissions.com
Website: advancingnativemissions.com

A nondenominational support agency of Evangelical tradition engaged in church planting (establishing), discipleship, medical supplies, and persecuted church. (FPC-PE)

Purpose: . . . to engage and support native missions groups working among the world's unreached peoples.

Year Founded in US: 1992
Income for International Min:
$11,536,689

Fully Supported US Personnel Working Cross-Culturally
    1–4 years: 1
Countries/Regions: Singapore

ADVENT CHRISTIAN WORLD OUTREACH

P O Box 690848
Charlotte, NC 28227 US
Phone: (704) 545-6161
Email: worldoutreach@acgc.us
Website: acgc.org
Associations: Missio Nexus

A denominational sending agency of Advent Christian tradition engaged in Bible teaching, church planting (establishing), discipleship, leadership development, and STM trip coordination.

Purpose: . . . to encourage, equip, and empower Advent Christian churches worldwide to be obedient to His great commandment and great commission.

Year Founded in US: 1865
Income for International Min:
    $790,204
Fully Supported US Personnel Working Cross-Culturally
    More than 4 years: 1
    1–4 years: 2
    X-C workers in US: 4
Other Personnel
    Short-Term less than 1 year: 22
    Non-US in own/other country: 33
    Home staff: 2
Countries/Regions: Australia, Burundi, Democratic Republic of Congo, Croatia, Ghana, Haiti, Honduras, India, Japan, Kenya, Liberia, Malawi, Malaysia, Mexico, Mozambique, Myanmar (Burma), New Zealand, Nigeria, Papua New Guinea, Philippines, South Africa, Tanzania, Thailand

ADVENTURES IN MISSIONS

6000 Wellspring Trail
Gainesville, GA 30506 US
Phone: (770) 983-1060
Email: neilbruinsma@adventures.org
Website: adventures.org

A nondenominational sending agency of Charismatic and Evangelical tradition engaged in discipleship, networking, partnership, or coordination, partnership development, recruiting or mobilizing for mission, and STM trip coordination. (FPC-PE)

Purpose: . . . to mobilize a generation of radical Christ followers, discipling and training them to establish the Kingdom of God.

Year Founded in US: 1989
Fully Supported US Personnel Working Cross-Culturally
    More than 4 years: 25
    1–4 years: 5
Other Personnel
    Short-Term less than 1 year: 3500
    Home staff: 200
Countries/Regions: Dominican Republic, Kenya, Mexico, New Zealand, Swaziland, United Kingdom

AEGA MINISTRIES INT'L INC. (ASSOCIATION OF EVANGELICAL GOSPEL ASSEMBLIES)

2149 Hwy 139
Monroe, LA 71203 US
Phone: (318) 345-1777
Email: pres@aega.org
Website: aega.org

A nondenominational support agency of Charismatic and Evangelical tradition engaged in church development, theological education, networking, partnership, or coordination, services for mission organizations, and youth ministry.

Purpose: . . . to send medicines around the world so souls are touched and brought into the Kingdom.
Year Founded in US: 1976
Income for International Min:
$1,000
Fully Supported US Personnel Working Cross-Culturally
More than 4 years: 10
Non-residential: 5
Other Personnel
Tentmakers/BAM: 10
Non-US in own/other country: 45
Countries/Regions: Global Ministry

AFRICA INLAND MISSION
PO Box 3611
Peachtree City, GA 30269 US
Phone: (800) 254-0010
Email: info.us@aimint.org
Website: AfricaInlandMission.org
Associations: Missio Nexus

A nondenominational sending agency of Evangelical tradition engaged in aviation, business as mission, discipleship, theological education, and personal or small group evangelism.
Purpose: . . . to establish Christ-centered churches among all African peoples.
Year Founded in US: 1895
Fully Supported US Personnel Working Cross-Culturally
More than 4 years: 488
X-C workers in US: 18
Non-residential: 382
Other Personnel
Non-US in own/other country: 197
Home staff: 31
Countries/Regions: Global Ministry, North Africa, Sub-Saharan Africa

AFRICA INLAND MISSION CANADA INTL.
1641 Victoria Park Ave
Scarborough, ON M1R 1P8 CA
Phone: (416) 751-6077
Email: general.ca@aimint.org
Website: ca.aimint.org
Associations: Missio Nexus

An interdenominational sending agency of Evangelical tradition engaged in Bible teaching, CPM, discipleship, theological education, missionary & worker training.
Purpose: . . . to see Christ-centered churches established and thriving among all African people.
Year Founded in CA: 1953
Income for International Min:
$2,500,000
Fully Supported CA Personnel Working Cross-Culturally
More than 4 years: 76
1–4 years: 10
X-C workers in CA: 5
Other Personnel
Short-Term less than 1 year: 15
Tentmakers/BAM: 3
Non-CA in own/other country: 84
Home staff: 14
Countries/Regions: Chad, Democratic Republic of Congo, Eastern Europe and Eurasia, Global Ministry, Kenya, Madagascar, North Africa, Oceania, South Sudan, Tanzania, Uganda, United States of America

AFRICAN CHILDREN'S MISSION
P.O Box 26470
Birmingham, AL 35260 US
Phone: (205) 620-4937
Email: acm-ea@att.net
Website: africanchildrensmission.org

An interdenominational support agency of Baptist and Fundamentalist tradition engaged in Bible teaching, children's ministry, discipleship, youth ministry, and sponsorship of children's education. (FPC-PE)

Purpose: . . . to reach out to children in destitute circumstances, physically, emotionally and with the Gospel of Jesus Christ.

Year Founded in US: 1996

Income for International Min:
  $225,000

Fully Supported US Personnel Working Cross-Culturally
  More than 4 years: 2
  X-C workers in US: 1

Other Personnel
  Short-Term less than 1 year: 26
  Home staff: 1

Countries/Regions: Kenya, Uganda

AFRICAN ENTERPRISE

PO Box 28190
Spokane, WA 99228 US
Phone: (509) 343-4011
Email: info@aeusa.org
Website: africanenterprise.org

A nondenominational support agency of Evangelical tradition engaged in counseling, discipleship, mass evangelism, leadership development, relief & aid, and spiritual renewal.

Purpose: . . . to evangelize the cities of Africa through word and deed in partnership with the church.

Year Founded in US: 1962

Other Personnel
  Non-US in own/other country: 279

Countries/Regions: Democratic Republic of Congo, Ethiopia, Ghana, Kenya, Malawi, Rwanda, South Africa, Tanzania, Uganda, Zimbabwe

AFRICAN ENTERPRISE CANADA

4509 11th Avenue West
Vancouver, BC V6R 2M5 CA
Phone: (604) 228 0930
Email: admin@africanenterprise.ca
Website: africanenterprise.ca

An interdenominational support agency of Evangelical tradition engaged in children's ministry, mass evangelism, student evangelism, leadership development, missionary & worker training, and partnership development. (FPC-PE)

Purpose: . . . to see the continent of Africa saved by the love of Jesus, and Africans discipled by the church and transformed for good works.

Year Founded in CA: 1965

Fully Supported CA Personnel Working Cross-Culturally
  More than 4 years: 3

Other Personnel
  Tentmakers/BAM: 2
  Non-CA in own/other country: 3

Countries/Regions: Africa

AFRICAN LEADERSHIP DEVELOPMENT

6159 Applewood Ridge Circle
Colorado Springs, CO 80918 US
Phone: (630) 280-9401
Email: bongani1@mac.com
Website: aldafrica.org

An interdenominational service agency of Evangelical tradition engaged in childcare or orphanage and leadership development.

Purpose: . . . to assist the church, by mentoring, empowering, and networking in Africa.

Year Founded in US: 2005

Fully Supported US Personnel Working Cross-Culturally
  Non-residential: 1

Other Personnel
  Short-Term less than 1 year: 15
  Non-US in own/other country: 5
  Home staff: 1

Countries/Regions: Sub-Saharan Africa

AGAPE GOSPEL MISSION
P.O. Box 1458
8811 Sudley Rd., Suite 225
Manassas, VA 20110 US
Phone: (703) 361-3331
Email: hholland@agapegospelmission.org
A nondenominational sending agency of
Charismatic tradition engaged in Bible
teaching, childcare or orphanage, church
planting (establishing), church, school or
general Christian education, personal or
small group evangelism, and leadership
development.
Purpose: . . . to reach the world with
God's love by evangelizing the lost,
empowering the Church, and embracing
the poor.
Year Founded in US: 1983
*Fully Supported US Personnel Working
Cross-Culturally*
    More than 4 years: 4
    1–4 years: 6
Other Personnel
    Short-Term less than 1 year: 45
    Home staff: 2
Countries/Regions: Ghana

AGAPE UNLIMITED
P.O. Box 50994
Midland, TX 79710 US
Phone: (877) 576-4504
Email: davidd@agapeunlimited.org
Website: agapeunlimited.org/
A nondenominational sending agency of
Evangelical tradition engaged in church
planting (establishing), personal or small
group evangelism, medical ministry,
including dental or public health, and STM
trip coordination.
Purpose: . . . to Go—where no one
wants to go, Help—those no one cares
about, Share—God's Love with everyone,
and Teach—others to do the same.
Year Founded in US: 1980

Income for International Min:
    $723,648
*Fully Supported US Personnel Working
Cross-Culturally*
    More than 4 years: 3
    Non-residential: 7
Other Personnel
    Short-Term less than 1 year: 35
    Non-US in own/other country: 18
    Home staff: 6
Countries/Regions: Eastern Europe and
Eurasia

AGATHOS INTERNATIONAL
18503 Teeside Lane
Arlington, WA 98223 US
Phone: (206) 353-2328
Email: agathosmarc@gmail.com
Website: agathosinternational.org/
A nondenominational sending agency
of Evangelical and Reformed tradition
engaged in childcare/orphanage programs,
agricultural programs, business as mission,
medical work, partnership development
and relief and/or rehabilitation. (DPE)
Purpose: . . . to provide a Christ centered
holistic approach to Sub-Saharan Africa's
orphan crisis. With orphans and widows
at our core, Agathos focuses programs
on pastoral training, church partnerships,
raising orphans, health care, and infra-
structure development.
Year Founded in US: 2002
Income for International Min:
    $11,500,000
*Fully Supported US Personnel Working
Cross-Culturally*
    More than 4 years: 1
    1–4 years: 5
Other Personnel
    Short-Term less than 1 year: 30
    Non-US in own/other country: 6
    Home staff: 3
Countries/Regions: Zambia

AIR MOBILE MINISTRIES
6250 N. Courtenay Parkway
Merritt Island, FL 32953 US
Phone: (321) 544-7757
Email: servingathirstyworld@gmail.com
Website: airmobile.org
A nondenominational support agency of
Evangelical tradition engaged in aviation,
Bible teaching, mass evangelism, personal
or small group evangelism, medical
supplies, and relief & aid.
Purpose: . . . to bring relief and Christ-
centered hope to those in need, wherever
they are.
Year Founded in US: 1978
Income for International Min:
  $163,700
*Fully Supported US Personnel Working
Cross-Culturally*
  X-C workers in US: 8
Other Personnel
  Short-Term less than 1 year: 22

ALBERTO MOTTESI EVANGELISTIC ASSOCIATION INC.
PO Box 6290
Santa Ana, CA 92706 US
Phone: (714) 265-0400
Email: info@albertomottesi.org
Website: albertomottesi.org
A nondenominational service agency
of Evangelical tradition engaged in
evangelism, audio recording/distribution,
broadcasting, TEE, literature distribution,
literature production and video/film
production/distribution. (DPE)
Purpose: . . . to equip Hispanic Christian
leaders and provide ministry resources for
worldwide Hispanic churches.
Year Founded in US: 1977
Income for International Min:
  $191,531

ALL ABOUT ORPHANS (DAVID LIVINGSTONE KURE FOUNDATION)
PO Box 716
Morgantown, WV 26507-0716 US
Phone: (304) 296-5873
Email: info@allaboutorphans.org
Website: allaboutorphans.org
A nondenominational service agency of
Independent tradition engaged in support
of national workers, childcare/orphanage
programs, Christian education and
development. (DPE)
Countries/Regions: India, Philippines,
Russia, Ukraine

ALL GOD'S CHILDREN INTERNATIONAL
1400 NE 136th Ave, Ste. 201
Vancouver, WA 98684 US
Phone: (503) 893-1350
Email: lmader@allgodschildren.org
Website: allgodschildren.org/
A nondenominational service agency of
Independent tradition engaged in adoption
and orphan care. (FPC-PE)
Purpose: . . . to answer God's call to
provide the love and care that every child
deserves.
*Fully Supported US Personnel Working
Cross-Culturally*
  1–4 years: 3
Other Personnel
  Non-US in own/other country: 181
Countries/Regions: China (People's
Republic of), Guatemala, Kazakhstan,
Nepal, Vietnam

ALLEGHENY WESLEYAN METHODIST CONNECTION
PO Box 357
2291 Depot Road
Salem, OH 44460-0357 US
Phone: (330) 337-9376
Email: awmc@juno.com

A denominational sending agency of Methodist and Wesleyan tradition engaged in children's ministry, church development, discipleship, church, school or general Christian education, mass evangelism, and international student ministry.

Purpose: . . . to promote and perform the Great Commission as it is recorded in the Holy Scriptures.

Income for International Min:
$279,143

Fully Supported US Personnel Working Cross-Culturally
More than 4 years: 10
X-C workers in US: 26

Other Personnel
Short-Term less than 1 year: 58
Tentmakers/BAM: 2
Non-US in own/other country: 2
Home staff: 6

Countries/Regions: Canada, Ghana, Global Ministry, Haiti, Peru

ALONGSIDE INC.
PO Box 587
Richland, MI 49083 US
Phone: (269) 447-2100
Email: info@alongsidecares.net
Website: alongsidecares.net
Associations: Missio Nexus

A nondenominational sending agency of Evangelical tradition engaged in counseling. (FPC-PE)

Purpose: . . . to encourage and empower Christian leaders and churches through an international network of prayer, partnership, and practical help.

Year Founded in US: 2000

ALONGSIDE MINISTRIES INTERNATIONAL
PO Box 610
Langley, WA 98260 US
Phone: (360) 331-7047
Email: office@alongside.org
Website: alongside.org

A nondenominational specialized agency of Evangelical and Presbyterian tradition engaged in camping programs, church planting (establishing), discipleship, evangelism, leadership development, partnership development, and youth ministry.

Purpose: . . . to help Christian pastors, missionaries, and their families grow in personal wholeness, healthy relationships, and ministry effectiveness.

Year Founded in US: 1983
Income for International Min:
$400,000

Fully Supported US Personnel Working Cross-Culturally
More than 4 years: 6
1–4 years: 7

Other Personnel
Non-US in own/other country: 5
Home staff: 4

Countries/Regions: Albania, Czech Republic, Estonia, France, Kosovo

AMAZON FOCUS INC.
P.O. Box 271109
Littleton, CO 80127 US
Phone: (720) 346-3000
Email: info@amazonfocus.com
Website: amazonfocus.com

A nondenominational support agency of Evangelical tradition engaged in discipleship, leadership development, networking, partnership, or coordination, and partnership development. (FPC-PE)

Purpose: . . . to facilitate the empowering and equipping of the indigenous tribes of the Amazon so that they can assume responsibility for their long-term spiritual, physical and survival needs.

Year Founded in US: 1995
Income for International Min:
$25,920

Fully Supported US Personnel Working Cross-Culturally
More than 4 years: 2

Other Personnel
Non-US in own/other country: 10
Home staff: 5
Countries/Regions: Peru

AMAZON OUTREACH
PO Box 794763
Dallas, TX 75379 US
Phone: (972) 931-5565
Email: jedt@amazonoutreach.org
Website: amazonoutreach.org
An interdenominational service agency
of Baptist tradition engaged in short-term
programs, evangelism, medical work,
support of national churches and water
well drilling. (DPE)
Purpose: . . . to support Brazilian
churches and other organized ministries
in spreading the Gospel message of Jesus
Christ throughout the Amazon Basin.
Income for International Min:
$1,667,671
Other Personnel
Short-Term less than 1 year: 300
Home staff: 4
Countries/Regions: Brazil

AMBASSADORS FOR CHRIST INC.
21 Ambassador Dr.
Paradise, PA 17562 US
Phone: (717) 687-8564
Email: afc@afcinc.org
Website: afcinc.org
A nondenominational support agency of
Evangelical tradition engaged in translation
and distribution of English language books
into Chinese, Bible distribution, literature
production and partnership development.
(DPE)
Purpose: . . . to evangelize and disciple
Chinese students and professionals in the
United States, and other parts of the world,
to motivate and equip them to impact the
culture for the Lord.
Year Founded in US: 1964

Income for International Min:
$135,000
Other Personnel
Short-Term less than 1 year: 2
Home staff: 13
Countries/Regions: China

AMBASSADORS FOR CHRIST INTERNATIONAL
PO Box 470
Tucker, GA 30085 US
Phone: (770) 921-4705
Email: info@afciworld.org
Website: afciworld.org
An interdenominational support agency
of Evangelical tradition engaged in
CPM, DMM, mass evangelism, personal
or small group evangelism, leadership
development, and persecuted church.
(FPC-PE)
Purpose: . . . to accelerate the spread
of the Gospel through local churches
worldwide.
Year Founded in US: 2001
Income for International Min:
$3,000,000
Other Personnel
Short-Term less than 1 year: 80
Home staff: 11

AMERICAN BAPTIST INTERNATIONAL MINISTRIES
P.O. Box 851
Valley Forge, PA 19482 US
Phone: (610) 768-2000
Email: BIMinfo@internationalministries.
org
Website: internationalministries.org
Associations: Missio Nexus
A denominational sending agency of
Baptist tradition engaged in discipleship,
theological education, addressing human
trafficking, justice or peace issues,
leadership development, and medical
ministry, including dental or public health.

Purpose: . . . to work cross-culturally to invite people to become disciples of Jesus Christ, and to proclaim—through both word and deed—God's reign of justice, peace, and abundant life for all creation.
Year Founded in US: 1814
Income for International Min:
   $16,159,360
Fully Supported US Personnel Working Cross-Culturally
   More than 4 years: 88
   Non-residential: 10
Other Personnel
   Short-Term less than 1 year: 1300
   Non-US in own/other country: 9
   Home staff: 44
Countries/Regions: Bolivia, Brazil, Bulgaria, Central America, Central Asia, Chile, Democratic Republic of Congo, Costa Rica, Dominican Republic, Ghana, Global Ministry, Haiti, Honduras, Hong Kong (China), Hungary, India, Japan, Lebanon, Mexico, Nepal, Nicaragua, Panama, Philippines, South Africa, Southeast Asia, Thailand, Turkey, United Kingdom, Western Europe

AMERICAN EVANGELICAL CHRISTIAN CHURCHES
PO Box 47312
Indianapolis, IN 46247-0312 US
Phone: (317) 788-9280
Email: aeccoffice@yahoo.com
Website: aeccministries.com
A nondenominational support agency of Evangelical tradition engaged in support of national churches, correspondence courses, extension education and evangelism. (DPE)
Purpose: . . . to provide credentials to workers, assisting with financial and prayer needs.
Year Founded in US: 1944

AMERICAN LEPROSY MISSIONS
1 Alm Way
Greenville, SC 29601 US
Phone: (800) 543-3135
Email: amlep@leprosy.org
Website: leprosy.org
Associations: Accord Network
A nondenominational specialized agency of Ecumenical tradition engaged in community development, disabled ministry, medical supplies, medical ministry, including dental or public health, and research.
Purpose: . . . to serve as a channel of Christ's love to persons affected by leprosy and related diseases, helping them to be healed in body and spirit and restored to lives of dignity and hope.
Year Founded in US: 1906
Income for International Min:
   $11,640,620
Fully Supported US Personnel Working Cross-Culturally
   More than 4 years: 2
   Non-residential: 3
Other Personnel
   Non-US in own/other country: 4
   Home staff: 15
Countries/Regions: Brazil, Ghana, Myanmar (Burma), Nepal, Norway, United Kingdom

AMG INTERNATIONAL
6815 Shallowford Rd.
Chattanooga, TN 37421 US
Phone: (423) 894-6060
Email: webcontactus@amginternational.org
Website: amginternational.org
A nondenominational support agency of Independent tradition engaged in children's ministry, church development, mass evangelism, medical ministry, including dental or public health, national worker support, and STM trip coordination. (FPC-PE)

Purpose: . . . to encourage, equip, and develop Christ-centered national leaders to become instruments of Gospel advancement and community transformation.

Income for International Min:
  $6,000,000

Fully Supported US Personnel Working Cross-Culturally
  More than 4 years: 14
  1–4 years: 7

Other Personnel
  Short-Term less than 1 year: 434
  Non-US in own/other country: 8315
  Home staff: 27

Countries/Regions: Argentina, Australia, Bangladesh, Brazil, Bulgaria, Cuba, Cyprus, Ghana, Greece, Guatemala, Haiti, India, Indonesia, Italy, Lebanon, Mexico, Mozambique, Myanmar (Burma), Peru, Philippines, Romania, Spain, Thailand, Turkey, Uganda

AMOR MINISTRIES
1664 Precision Park Ln.
San Diego, CA 92713 US
Phone: (619) 662-1200
Email: missionservices@amor.org
Website: amor.org

A nondenominational sending agency of Evangelical tradition engaged in development, support of national churches, partnership development, relief and/or rehabilitation and short-term programs. (DPE)

Year Founded in US: 1980
Income for International Min:
  $4,250,000

Fully Supported US Personnel Working Cross-Culturally
  1–4 years: 37

Other Personnel
  Non-US in own/other country: 10
  Home staff: 24

Countries/Regions: Mexico

ANGLICAN FRONTIER MISSIONS
PO Box 18038
Richmond, Va 23226 US
Phone: (804) 355-8468
Email: kristin@afm-us.org
Website: anglicanfrontiers.com
Associations: Missio Nexus

A denominational heritage sending agency of Anglican and Evangelical tradition engaged in business as mission, church planting (establishing), CPM, personal or small group evangelism, member care, and tentmaking & related.

Purpose: . . . to see biblically based, indigenous church planting movements multiplying in the largest, least evangelized people groups on earth.

Year Founded in US: 1993
Income for International Min:
  $600,000

Fully Supported US Personnel Working Cross-Culturally
  More than 4 years: 8
  1–4 years: 6
  X-C workers in US: 5
  Non-residential: 1

Other Personnel
  Short-Term less than 1 year: 15
  Non-US in own/other country: 6
  Home staff: 7

Countries/Regions: Central Asia, Global Ministry, Middle East, North Africa, Sub-Saharan Africa

APOSTOLIC CHRISTIAN CHURCH – MISSIONARY COMMITTEE
12666 Locust Rd.
Tremont, IL 61568 US
Phone: (309) 925-9040
Email: info@accm.org
Website: accm.org

A denominational sending agency of Anabaptist tradition engaged in funds transmission, church construction, relief aid, support of national workers and evangelism. (DPE)

Purpose: . . . exists to help fulfill Christ's Commission by sending out members of the AC Church who are called by God to become foreign missionaries.

Countries/Regions: Argentina, Australia, Brazil, Ghana, Japan, Mexico, Papua New Guinea, Paraguay

APOSTOLIC CHURCH IN CANADA, THE
220 Adelaide St. N.
London, ON N6B 3H4 CA
Phone: (519) 438-7036
Email: cheryl@apostolic.ca
Website: apostolic.ca

A denominational support agency of Charismatic and Apostolic tradition engaged in member care, discipleship and support of national churches. (DPE)

Purpose: . . . to establish a network of churches in apostolic relationship and reap a harvest through church planting.

Year Founded in CA: 1940

Other Personnel
  Home staff: 13
Countries/Regions: Brazil, India, Jamaica

APOSTOLIC CHURCH OF PENTECOST OF CANADA (GLOBAL HARVEST MISSIONS)
#119-2340 Pegasus Way NE
Calgary, AB T2E 8M5 CA
Phone: (403) 273-5777
Email: acop@acop.ca
Website: global-harvest.ca and acop.ca

A denominational sending agency of Pentecostal tradition engaged in business as mission, church planting (establishing), CPM, DMM, discipleship, and relief & aid.

Purpose: . . . to make disciples of all nations by proclaiming & demonstrating the good news of Jesus.

Year Founded in CA: 1921

Income for International Min:
  $1,700,000
Fully Supported CA Personnel Working Cross-Culturally
  More than 4 years: 15
  1–4 years: 6
  X-C workers in CA: 3
  Non-residential: 8
Other Personnel
  Short-Term less than 1 year: 1
  Non-CA in own/other country: 7
  Home staff: 7
Countries/Regions: Bolivia, Brazil, Cambodia, Central Asia, Costa Rica, Ecuador, El Salvador, Estonia, Global Ministry, Honduras, India, Malawi, Mali, Mexico, South Asia, Southeast Asia, Taiwan (China), Trinidad and Tobago, Zimbabwe

ARISE INTERNATIONAL MISSION
PO Box 1014
College Park, MD 20741 US
Phone: (301) 395-2385
Email: aim@arise-mission.org
Website: arise-mission.org

A support agency of Charismatic and Evangelical tradition engaged in leadership development, literature distribution, partnership development, mobilization for mission and technical assistance. (DPE)

Purpose: . . . to reach the least evangelized world through literature distribution and leadership development.

Other Personnel
  Short-Term less than 1 year: 5
  Non-US in own/other country: 9
  Home staff: 7
Countries/Regions: Africa, Asia

ASIAN ACCESS

PO Box 3307
Cerritos, CA 90703 US
Phone: (626) 914-8990
Email: info@asianaccess.org
Website: asianaccess.org
Associations: Missio Nexus

An interdenominational sending agency of Evangelical tradition engaged in CPM, DMM, leadership development, networking, partnership, or coordination, and persecuted church.

Purpose: . . . to identify, develop, and release emerging kingdom leaders to unite the church, multiply leaders and congregations, and extend the transforming power of the Gospel of Jesus Christ.

Year Founded in US: 1967
Income for International Min:
    $3,779,346
Fully Supported US Personnel Working Cross-Culturally
    More than 4 years: 23
    1–4 years: 4
    Non-residential: 7
Other Personnel
    Short-Term less than 1 year: 15
    Non-US in own/other country: 2
    Home staff: 7
Countries/Regions: Global Ministry, Japan

ASIAN OUTREACH INTERNATIONAL CANADA

2450 Milltower Court
Missisauga, ON L5N 5Z6 CA
Phone: (800) 779-262 x3067
Email: info@asianoutreach.ca
Website: asianoutreach.ca

A nondenominational support agency engaged in missions, Bible distribution, church planting, development, leadership development, literacy work and missionary training. (DPE)

Income for International Min:
    $356,478
Fully Supported CA Personnel Working Cross-Culturally
    More than 4 years: 1
Other Personnel
    Tentmakers/BAM: 1
    Non-CA in own/other country: 38
    Home staff: 2
Countries/Regions: Asia, Central Asia

ASSEMBLIES OF GOD WORLD MISSIONS

1445 N. Boonville Ave.
Springfield, MO 65802 US
Phone: (417) 862-2781
Email: acollins@ag.org
Website: AGWM.com
Associations: Missio Nexus

A denominational sending agency of Pentecostal tradition engaged in church planting (establishing), community development, discipleship, mass evangelism, leadership development, and recruiting or mobilizing for mission.

Purpose: . . . to engage in missionary endeavor pursuing the original and audacious commitment of our forefathers to unprecedented world evangelism, so all can hear.

Year Founded in US: 1914
Fully Supported US Personnel Working Cross-Culturally
    More than 4 years: 1920
    1–4 years: 858
    Non-residential: 274
Other Personnel
    Short-Term less than 1 year: 10839
    Home staff: 158
Countries/Regions: Albania, Angola, Antigua and Barbuda, Argentina, Armenia, Aruba, Austria, Belgium, Belize, Benin, Bolivia, Botswana, Brazil, Burkina Faso, Cambodia, Cameroon, Caribbean, Central America, Central Asia, Chad, Chile,

Colombia, Congo (Democratic Republic of), Congo (Republic of), Costa Rica, Côte d'Ivoire, Croatia, Czech Republic, Dominican Republic, East Asia, Eastern Europe and Eurasia, Ecuador, El Salvador, Estonia, Ethiopia, Fiji, France, Gabon, Georgia, Germany, Global Ministry, Greece, Guatemala, Haiti, Honduras, Hungary, Iceland, Indonesia, Ireland (Republic of), Republic of, Italy, Japan, Kenya, Latvia, Lesotho, Liberia, Lithuania, Macedonia, Madagascar, Malawi, Malaysia, Mali, Malta, Marshall Islands, Mexico, Micronesia, Federated States of, Middle East, Moldova, Mongolia, Mozambique, Namibia, Netherlands, Nicaragua, Niger, North Africa, Oceania, Palau, Panama, Papua New Guinea, Paraguay, Peru, Philippines, Poland, Portugal, Romania, Russia, Rwanda, Senegal, Serbia, Sierra Leone, Singapore, Slovakia, Slovenia, South Africa, South America, South Asia, South Korea, Southeast Asia, Spain, Sub-Saharan Africa, Swaziland, Sweden, Switzerland, Taiwan (China), Tanzania, Thailand, Togo, Tonga, Ukraine, United Kingdom, Uruguay, Vanuatu, Venezuela, Western Europe, Zambia, Zimbabwe

ASSIST (AID TO SPECIAL SAINTS IN STRATEGIC TIMES)

PO Box 609
Lake Forest, CA 92609 US
Phone: (949) 472-0974
Email: assistnews@aol.com
Website: assistnews.net

A nondenominational service agency of Evangelical tradition engaged in radio or TV broadcasting and news service. (FPC-PE)

Purpose: . . . to cover news from around the world from a Christian perspective, offering insight, commentary and relevant information on a host of contemporary and important issues affecting the world, Christians and the church.

Year Founded in US: 1989
Income for International Min:
$110,000
Other Personnel
Home staff: 1

ASSOCIATION OF FREE LUTHERAN CONGREGATIONS

3110 East Medicine Lake Blvd
Plymouth, MN 55441 US
Phone: (763) 545-5631
Email: president@aflc.org
Website: aflc.org

A fellowship service agency of Lutheran tradition engaged in Bible teaching, church development, church, school or general Christian education, personal or small group evangelism, STM trip coordination, and youth ministry.

Purpose: . . . to join together as free and living congregations for Christian fellowship, edification, and the salvation of souls.

Year Founded in US: 1962
Income for International Min:
$1,400,000
Fully Supported US Personnel Working Cross-Culturally
More than 4 years: 17
Non-residential: 1
Other Personnel
Tentmakers/BAM: 18
Non-US in own/other country: 5
Home staff: 5
Countries/Regions: Brazil, Czech Republic, Ecuador, Global Ministry, India, Mexico, Uganda

AUDIO SCRIPTURE MINISTRIES

760 Waverly Rd.
Holland, MI 49423 US
Phone: (616) 396-5291
Email: info@asmtoday.org
Website: asmtoday.org

A nondenominational specialized agency of Evangelical tradition engaged in audio recording/distribution, support of national workers, technical assistance and training. (DPE)

Purpose: . . . to facilitate the recording, duplication, and distribution of audio Scriptures primarily for non-readers around the world.

Year Founded in US: 1967
Income for International Min:
$490,052

Fully Supported US Personnel Working Cross-Culturally
   More than 4 years: 1
Other Personnel
   Short-Term less than 1 year: 3
   Non-US in own/other country: 1
   Home staff: 3
Countries/Regions: India

AURORA MISSION INC.

PO Box 1549
Bradenton, FL 34206 US
Phone: (941) 748-4100
Email: mission@auroramission.org
Website: auroramission.org

A nondenominational support agency of Baptist tradition engaged in theological education, church planting, leadership development, literature production and support of national churches. (DPE)

Purpose: . . . exists as an evangelical, conservative, nondenominational mission agency whose purpose is evangelism and discipleship with the goal of planting and strengthening churches and developing church leadership and church training centers.

Fully Supported US Personnel Working Cross-Culturally
   More than 4 years: 2
   1–4 years: 13
Other Personnel
   Short-Term less than 1 year: 1
   Home staff: 3
Countries/Regions: Italy

AVANT MINISTRIES

10000 N Oak Trafficway
Kansas City, MO 64155 US
Phone: (816) 734-8500
Email: donna.pace@avmi.org
Website: avantministries.org
Associations: Missio Nexus

An interdenominational sending agency of Baptist tradition engaged in business as mission, camping programs, church planting (establishing), church, school or general Christian education, member care, and video-film production or distribution.

Purpose: . . . to glorify God by helping others enjoy His presence through planting and developing new churches in the unreached areas of the world.

Year Founded in US: 1892
Income for International Min:
$8,683,509

Fully Supported US Personnel Working Cross-Culturally
   More than 4 years: 141
   X-C workers in US: 7
Other Personnel
   Short-Term less than 1 year: 39
   Non-US in own/other country: 8
   Home staff: 44
Countries/Regions: Argentina, Belgium, Belize, Bolivia, Brazil, Canada, Colombia, Czech Republic, Ecuador, France, Germany, Greece, India, Italy, Mali, Panama, Poland, Portugal, Russia, Senegal, Slovenia, Spain, Tajikistan, Tanzania, Thailand, Turkey, Ukraine, United Kingdom, Uruguay, Venezuela

AVANT MINISTRIES CANADA

2121 Henderson Hwy
Winnipeg, MB R2G 1P8 CA
Phone: (866) 812-8268
Email: mike.reimer@avmi.org
Website: avantministries.org
Associations: Missio Nexus

An interdenominational sending agency of Baptist and Evangelical tradition engaged in camping programs, church planting (establishing), counseling, discipleship, church, school or general Christian education, and member care.

Purpose: . . . to glorify God by helping others enjoy His presence through planting and developing new churches in the unreached areas of the world.

Year Founded in CA: 1949
Income for International Min:
  $2,315,538
Fully Supported CA Personnel Working Cross-Culturally
  More than 4 years: 37
  X-C workers in CA: 3
  Non-residential: 2
Other Personnel
  Short-Term less than 1 year: 16
  Non-CA in own/other country: 1
  Home staff: 6
Countries/Regions: Bolivia, Brazil, France, Kenya, Mali, Slovenia, South Sudan, Spain, Thailand, Uruguay

AWANA CLUBS INTERNATIONAL

1 E. Bode Road
Streamwood, Il 60103 US
Phone: (630) 213-2000
Email: customercare@awana.org
Website: awana.org/

A nondenominational with a denominational heritage specialized agency of Baptist and Evangelical tradition engaged in discipleship and youth ministry.

Purpose: . . . to reach the boys and girls of the world through Bible centered youth programs that bring all children and youth to a knowledge of, and relationship with, Jesus Christ as their personal Savior.

Year Founded in US: 1965
Income for International Min:
  $3,770,462
Fully Supported US Personnel Working Cross-Culturally
  More than 4 years: 5
  X-C workers in US: 2
Other Personnel
  Non-US in own/other country: 165
  Home staff: 27
Countries/Regions: Argentina, Australia, Bangladesh, Bolivia, Brazil, Burkina Faso, Burundi, Canada, Caribbean, Central America, Chile, Colombia, Costa Rica, Cuba, Czech Republic, Dominica, Dominican Republic, Ecuador, Egypt, Ethiopia, Fiji, Germany, Ghana, Guatemala, Haiti, Honduras, Hong Kong (China), India, Indonesia, Jamaica, Japan, Kazakhstan, Kenya, Latvia, Liberia, Malawi, Mexico, Moldova, Mozambique, Myanmar (Burma), Nepal, Nigeria, Pakistan, Panama, Papua New Guinea, Philippines, Portugal, Puerto Rico, Romania, Russia, Rwanda, Sierra Leone, Singapore, Slovakia, South Africa, South Asia, South Korea, Southeast Asia, Sri Lanka, Taiwan (China), Tanzania, Uganda, Ukraine, United Arab Emirates, Venezuela, Western Europe, Zambia, Zimbabwe

AZUSA PACIFIC UNIVERSITY – MEXICO OUTREACH

901 E. Alosta Ave.
Azusa, CA 91702 US
Phone: (626) 812-3027
Email: mo@apu.edu
Website: mexicooutreach.org

A nondenominational service agency of Evangelical and Wesleyan tradition engaged in children's ministry, personal or small group evangelism, medical ministry, including dental or public health, recruiting or mobilizing for mission, and STM trip coordination.

Purpose: . . . to provide educational assistance in Mexico.

Year Founded in US: 1899

Fully Supported US Personnel Working Cross-Culturally
    X-C workers in US: 4
Other Personnel
    Short-Term less than 1 year: 3000
    Home staff: 13

BACK TO THE BIBLE
6400 Cornhusker Highway
Lincoln, NE 68507 US
Phone: (402) 202-8405
Email: arniec@backtothebible.org
Website: backtothebible.org
Associations: Missio Nexus

A nondenominational service agency of Baptist and Evangelical tradition engaged in radio Bible teaching, radio or TV broadcasting, discipleship, and Bible engagement. (FPC-PE)

Purpose: . . . to connect with people and meet them where they are spiritually and help them grow into daily, biblically-engaged disciples of Jesus Christ.

Year Founded in US: 1939
Income for International Min:
    $312,368
Other Personnel
    Non-US in own/other country: 132
    Home staff: 21
Countries/Regions: Brazil, Ecuador, India, Indonesia, Jamaica, Japan, Nepal, Philippines, Sri Lanka, Trinidad and Tobago

BACK TO THE BIBLE CANADA
31087 Peardonville Road, Unit A
Abbotsford, BC V2T 6K4 CA
Phone: (800) 663-2425
Email: bttb@backtothebible.ca
Website: backtothebible.ca

An interdenominational service agency of Evangelical tradition engaged in broadcasting, audio recording/distribution and literacy work. (DPE)

Purpose: . . . to lead people into a dynamic relationship with God.

Year Founded in CA: 1964
Income for International Min:
    $233,543
Other Personnel
    Home staff: 7

BAPTIST BIBLE FELLOWSHIP INTERNATIONAL – WORLD MISSION SERVICE CENTER
PO Box 191
Springfield, MO 65801 US
Phone: (417) 862-5001
Email: info@bbfimissions.com
Website: bbfimissions.com

A denominational sending agency of Baptist tradition engaged in Bible teaching, business as mission, church planting (establishing), discipleship, mass evangelism, and missionary & worker training.

Purpose: . . . to serve churches and their missionaries as they endeavor to fulfill the Great Commission, as a bridge between those who give and those who go.

Year Founded in US: 1950
Income for International Min:
    $35,000,000
Fully Supported US Personnel Working Cross-Culturally
    More than 4 years: 674
    X-C workers in US: 26

Countries/Regions: Argentina, Australia, Bahamas, Belgium, Belize, Bolivia, Botswana, Brazil, Burkina Faso, Cambodia, Canada, Caribbean, Chile, Colombia, Republic of Congo , Costa Rica, Côte d'Ivoire, Croatia, Dominican Republic, Ecuador, Estonia, Ethiopia, France, Germany, Global Ministry, Greece, Guam, Guatemala, Haiti, Honduras, Hong Kong (China), Hungary, Indonesia, Ireland (Republic of), Israel, Italy, Jamaica, Japan, Kenya, South Korea, Lithuania, Madagascar, Mexico, New Zealand, Nicaragua, Panama, Papua New Guinea, Paraguay, Peru, Philippines, Portugal, Puerto Rico, Romania, Russia, Singapore, Slovakia, South Africa, South Asia, South Sudan, Spain, Sub-Saharan Africa, Taiwan (China), Tanzania, Thailand, Uganda, Ukraine, United Kingdom, Uruguay, Vanuatu, Zambia

BAPTIST BIBLE TRANSLATORS INSTITUTE

PO Box 1450
Bowie, TX 76230 US
Phone: (940) 872-5751
Email: info@baptisttranslators.com
Website: baptisttranslators.com
A denominational service agency of Baptist and Fundamental tradition engaged in missionary training, missionary education, linguistics and TESOL. (DPE)
Purpose: . . . missionaries training missionaries to plant New Testament Baptist churches in every Bible-less nation and translate the Scriptures into every Bible-less language.

BAPTIST GENERAL CONFERENCE OF CANADA

201, 8315 Davies Road NW
Edmonton, AB T6E 4N3 CA
Phone: (780) 438-9127
Email: diane@bgc.ca
Website: bgc.ca
Associations: CCRDA
A denominational sending agency of Baptist tradition engaged in church development, church planting (establishing), discipleship, personal or small group evangelism, networking, partnership, or coordination, and midwifery.
Purpose: . . . to build a network of churches that make disciples who live and spread the gospel of Jesus Christ in their communities, Canada and the Nations.
Year Founded in CA: 1982
Income for International Min:
   $1,000,000
Fully Supported CA Personnel Working Cross-Culturally
   More than 4 years: 14
   1–4 years: 1
   X-C workers in CA: 7
   Non-residential: 2
Other Personnel
   Home staff: 4
Countries/Regions: Argentina, China (People's Republic of), Global Ministry, Honduras, India, Philippines, Portugal, Rwanda

BAPTIST HAITI MISSION

13420 Eastpointe Centre Dr.
Louisville, KY 40223 US
Phone: (502) 491-0028
Email: bhmus@bhm.org
Website: bhm.org
A denominational heritage sending agency of Baptist tradition engaged in Bible teaching, church development, community development, church, school or general

Christian education, theological education, and medical ministry, including dental or public health.

Purpose: . . . to serve and strengthen the church of Haiti with the goal of seeing the people of Haiti transformed by the gospel of Jesus Christ for the glory of God.

Year Founded in US: 1963
Income for International Min:
  $1,924,072
Fully Supported US Personnel Working Cross-Culturally
  More than 4 years: 13
  Non-residential: 3
Other Personnel
  Short-Term less than 1 year: 163
  Non-US in own/other country: 1
  Home staff: 3
Countries/Regions: Haiti

BAPTIST INTERNATIONAL EVANGELISTIC MINISTRIES
121 Commerce Dr, Ste. 50
Danville, IN 46122 US
Phone: (317) 718-1633
Email: missions@baptistinternational.org
Website: baptistinternational.org
A denominational sending agency of Baptist tradition engaged in Bible distribution, children's ministry, church construction or financing, church planting (establishing), theological education, and personal or small group evangelism. (FPC-PE)

Purpose: . . . to help plant churches through partnership with nationals, serving the local church by helping fulfill the Great Commission.

Year Founded in US: 1981
Income for International Min:
  $1,200,000
Fully Supported US Personnel Working Cross-Culturally
  More than 4 years: 3

Other Personnel
  Short-Term less than 1 year: 10
  Non-US in own/other country: 93
  Home staff: 4
Countries/Regions: Asia, Belarus, Georgia, Kazakhstan, Kyrgyzstan, Moldova, Romania, Russia, Tajikistan, Turkmenistan, Ukraine, Uzbekistan

BAPTIST INTERNATIONAL MISSIONS INC.
PO Box 9
Harrison, TN 37341 US
Phone: (423) 344-5050
Email: directors@bimi.org
Website: bimi.org
A denominational sending agency of Baptist tradition engaged in Bible distribution, childcare or orphanage, church planting (establishing), and missionary & worker training.

Purpose: . . . to assist independent Baptist churches in the establishment of like churches around the world and to serve the local church as it sends missionaries into God's harvest field.

Year Founded in US: 1960
Fully Supported US Personnel Working Cross-Culturally
  More than 4 years: 683
  X-C workers in US: 25
  Non-residential: 35
Other Personnel
  Tentmakers/BAM: 2
  Home staff: 50
Countries/Regions: Anguilla, Antigua and Barbuda, Argentina, Australia, Austria, Bahamas, Barbados, Belize, Bolivia, Botswana, Brazil, Burkina Faso, Cambodia, Cameroon, Canada, Cape Verde Islands, Caribbean, Cayman Islands, Central America, Chile, Colombia, Costa Rica, Côte d'Ivoire, Dominican Republic, East Asia, Eastern Europe and Eurasia, Ecuador, El Salvador, Estonia, Fiji, France, Georgia,

Germany, Ghana, Global Ministry, Greece, Grenada, Guatemala, Guyana, Haiti, Honduras, Hong Kong (China), Indonesia, Ireland (Republic of), Italy, Jamaica, Japan, Kenya, Kiribati, South Korea, Madagascar, Mexico, Federated States of Micronesia, Moldova, Mongolia, Mozambique, Namibia, Nepal, New Zealand, Nicaragua, Niger, Nigeria, Palau, Panama, Papua New Guinea, Paraguay, Peru, Philippines, Puerto Rico, Romania, Russia, Rwanda, Saint Lucia, Samoa, São Tomé and Príncipe, Senegal, South Africa, South America, South Sudan, Southeast Asia, Spain, Sub-Saharan Africa, Taiwan (China), Tanzania, Thailand, Togo, Trinidad and Tobago, Turks and Caicos Islands, Uganda, United Kingdom, Uruguay, Venezuela, Virgin Islands of the USA, Western Europe, Zambia, Zimbabwe

BAPTIST INTERNATIONAL OUTREACH
PO Box 587, 1136 Romans Road
Jefferson City, TN 37760 US
Phone: (865) 262-0900
Email: yingling@biomissions.org
Website: biomissions.org
A denominational heritage sending agency of Baptist tradition engaged in Bible distribution, Bible teaching, church planting (establishing), CPM, personal or small group evangelism, and TESOL or TEFL.
Purpose: . . . to help missionaries enter limited access nations through symbiotic methods. We strive to accomplish this by seeking God, strengthening local churches, and by serving missionaries.
Year Founded in US: 1985
Income for International Min:
  $2,800,000

Fully Supported US Personnel Working Cross-Culturally
  More than 4 years: 89
  X-C workers in US: 7
  Non-residential: 28
Other Personnel
  Non-US in own/other country: 82
  Home staff: 11
Countries/Regions: American Samoa, Belarus, Bolivia, Botswana, Brazil, Burundi, Cambodia, Canada, Chile, China: (People's Republic of), Congo (Democratic Republic of), Congo (Republic of), Costa Rica, Cuba, Djibouti, Egypt, Eritrea, Ethiopia, Global Ministry, Hong Kong (China) Indonesia, Italy, Kazakhstan, Kenya, Kyrgyzstan, Mexico, Nicaragua, Nigeria, Panama, Peru, Philippines, Romania, Rwanda, Samoa, Somalia, South Africa, South Sudan, Tajikistan, Tanzania, Uganda, Uzbekistan, Venezuela, Vietnam, Zambia

BAPTIST MEDICAL & DENTAL MISSION INTERNATIONAL INC. (BMDMI)
11 Plaza Dr.
Hattiesburg, MS 39402 US
Phone: (601) 544-3586
Email: info@bmdmi.org
Website: bmdmi.org
A denominational specialized agency of Baptist tradition engaged in medical work, church planting, discipleship, evangelism and support of national churches. (DPE)
Purpose: . . . to evangelize the lost, disciple the saved, and minister to the needs of the poor.
Year Founded in US: 1974
Income for International Min:
  $17,500,000
Fully Supported US Personnel Working Cross-Culturally
  More than 4 years: 9
  1–4 years: 21

Other Personnel
Short-Term less than 1 year: 2158
Non-US in own/other country: 84
Home staff: 7
Countries/Regions: Honduras,
Nicaragua

BAPTIST MID-MISSIONS
PO Box 308011
Cleveland, OH 44130-8011 US
Phone: (440) 826-3930
Email: info@bmm.org
Website: bmm.org
Associations: FOM
A denominational sending agency of
Baptist tradition engaged in church
development, church planting
(establishing), discipleship, theological
education, personal or small group
evangelism, and Bible translation.
Purpose: . . . to strategically advance the
building of Christ's church, with His passion
and for His glory, in vital partnership with
Baptist churches worldwide.
Year Founded in US: 1920
*Fully Supported US Personnel Working
Cross-Culturally*
More than 4 years: 383
X-C workers in US: 110
Non-residential: 2
Other Personnel
Short-Term less than 1 year: 104
Tentmakers/BAM: 1
Non-US in own/other country: 60
Home staff: 45
Countries/Regions: Argentina,
Australia, Austria, Bangladesh, Brazil,
Cambodia, Cameroon, Canada, Central
African Republic, Chad, Chile, Côte
d'Ivoire, Dominican Republic, East
Asia, Ecuador, Ethiopia, Finland, France,
Germany, Ghana, Global Ministry,
Guam, Guyana, Haiti, Honduras, Hong
Kong (China), India, Indonesia, Ireland
(Republic of), Italy, Jamaica, Japan, Kenya,

Liberia, Malta, Mexico, Federated States
of Micronesia, Middle East, Mozambique,
Myanmar (Burma), Netherlands, New
Zealand, Papua New Guinea, Peru, Puerto
Rico, Romania, Russia, Saint Lucia, Saint
Vincent and the Grenadines, Slovakia,
South Africa, Spain, Taiwan (China),
Thailand, United Kingdom, Venezuela,
Zambia

BAPTIST MISSIONARY ASSOCIATION OF AMERICA (BMAA)
611 Locust Street
Conway, AR 72034 US
Phone: (501) 329-6891
Email: phil@bmaam.com
Website: bmamissions.org
A denominational sending agency of
Baptist tradition engaged in Bible teaching,
church planting (establishing), discipleship,
church, school or general Christian
education, theological education, and
medical ministry, including dental or
public health.
Purpose: . . . to focus on a discipleship-
based multiplication of new believers in
Jesus Christ, producing new leaders, and
planting new churches that are sustainable
and reproducible.
Year Founded in US: 1950
Income for International Min:
$8,000,000
*Fully Supported US Personnel Working
Cross-Culturally*
More than 4 years: 63
X-C workers in US: 5
Other Personnel
Short-Term less than 1 year: 160
Non-US in own/other country: 65
Home staff: 10
Countries/Regions: Argentina,
Armenia, Bolivia, Brazil, Cambodia,
Canada, China (People's Republic of),
Costa Rica, Cuba, Czech Republic,

Dominican Republic, Ecuador, Egypt, El
Salvador, Estonia, France, Ghana, Global
Ministry, Guatemala, Haiti, Honduras,
Hong Kong (China), India, Indonesia,
Japan, Jordan, Lebanon, Liberia, Mexico,
Myanmar (Burma), Nicaragua, Panama,
Papua New Guinea, Paraguay, Peru,
Philippines, Puerto Rico, Romania,
Thailand, Ukraine, Venezuela

BARNABAS AID

PO Box 6336, 6731 Curran Street
McLean, VA 22101 US
Phone: (703) 288-1681
Email: usa@barnabasaid.org

A nondenominational specialized agency
of Independent tradition engaged in
childcare or orphanage, church, school or
general Christian education, fund raising or
transmission, persecuted church, prayer-
intercession, and relief & aid.

Purpose: . . . to support Christians
where they are in a minority and
suffer discrimination, oppression, and
persecution as a consequence of their faith
and to strengthen Christian individuals,
churches, and their communities by
providing material and spiritual support
in response to needs identified by local
Christian leaders.

BARNABAS INTERNATIONAL

PO Box 11211, 431 S. Phelps Ave.,
Suite 608
Rockford, IL 61126 US
Phone: (815) 395-1335
Email: barnabas@barnabas.org
Website: barnabas.org
Associations: Missio Nexus

An interdenominational support agency of
Evangelical tradition engaged in counseling,
member care, and pastoral care.

Purpose: . . . to edify, encourage, enrich
and strengthen servants in ministry by
creatively seek ways through a variety of
ministry models.

Year Founded in US: 1986
Income for International Min:
  $2,201,621
*Fully Supported US Personnel Working
Cross-Culturally*
  More than 4 years: 4
  1–4 years: 4
  Non-residential: 153
Other Personnel
  Short-Term less than 1 year: 1
  Home staff: 3
Countries/Regions: Armenia, Australia,
Austria, Azerbaijan, Bermuda, Brazil,
Cambodia, China (People's Republic
of), Costa Rica, Croatia, Cuba, Ecuador,
Egypt, Estonia, Ethiopia, France, Germany,
Ghana, Hungary, India, Indonesia, Japan,
Kazakhstan, Kyrgyzstan, Lebanon, Mexico,
Nepal, Nigeria, Peru, Philippines, Poland,
Romania, Russia, Senegal, Singapore,
Slovakia, Slovenia, South Africa, Spain,
Swaziland, Switzerland, Tajikistan,
Thailand, Turkey, Uganda, Ukraine, United
Kingdom, Uzbekistan

BASIC MINISTRIES INC.

6406 Lakehurst Ave
Dallas, TX 75230 US
Phone: (214) 242-8951
Email: sudanproject@basicministries.info
Website: basicministries.info

A nondenominational support agency
of Evangelical and Presbyterian tradition
engaged in Bible distribution, childcare or
orphanage, church planting (establishing),
mass evangelism, and relief & aid.

Purpose: . . . to partner with our brothers
and sisters In Christ living in South Sudan,
NE DRC, and NW Uganda.
Year Founded in US: 1994
Income for International Min:
  $135,000
*Fully Supported US Personnel Working
Cross-Culturally*
  Non-residential: 1

Other Personnel
   Non-US in own/other country: 50
Countries/Regions: Sub-Saharan Africa

BCM INTERNATIONAL
201 Granite Run Dr, Ste. 260
Lancaster, PA 17601 US
Phone: (717) 560-9601
Email: info@bcmintl.org
Website: bcmintl,org
Associations: Missio Nexus

A nondenominational sending agency
of Evangelical tradition engaged in Bible
teaching, camping programs, children's
ministry, church development, church
planting (establishing), and leadership
development.

Purpose: . . . to make disciples of all age
groups for the Lord Jesus Christ through
evangelism, teaching and training so that
churches are established and The Church
strengthened.

Year Founded in US: 1936
Income for International Min:
   $1,209,053

*Fully Supported US Personnel Working
Cross-Culturally*
   More than 4 years: 11
   1–4 years: 12
   X-C workers in US: 19

Other Personnel
   Short-Term less than 1 year: 42
   Tentmakers/BAM: 7
   Non-US in own/other country: 697
   Home staff: 16

Countries/Regions: Antigua and
Barbuda, Belize, Bolivia, Brazil, Canada,
Democratic Republic of Congo, Cuba,
Dominican Republic, East Asia, France,
Germany, Guyana, Hungary, India,
Indonesia, Ireland (Republic of), Italy,
Jamaica, Mexico, Mozambique, Myanmar
(Burma), Nepal, Netherlands, Peru,
Philippines, Poland, Portugal, Romania,
Russia, Saint Vincent and the Grenadines,
South Africa, Spain, Sri Lanka, Suriname,
Swaziland, Ukraine, United Kingdom,
Zambia, Zimbabwe

BCM INTERNATIONAL
(CANADA) INC.
685 Main St. East
Hamilton, ON L8M 1K4 CA
Phone: (905) 548-9810
Email: director@bcmintl.ca
Website: bcmintl.ca

A nondenominational support agency
of Evangelical tradition engaged in
evangelism, camping programs, children's
programs, church planting, correspondence
courses and training. (DPE)

Purpose: . . . to make disciples of all age
groups for the Lord Jesus Christ through
evangelism, teaching, and training so that
churches are established and the Church
strengthened.

Year Founded in CA: 1977

Other Personnel
   Short-Term less than 1 year: 1
   Non-CA in own/other country: 4
   Home staff: 1
Countries/Regions: Italy, Netherlands,
Spain

BE ONE TOGETHER
PO Box 1001
Hiram, GA 30141 US
Phone: (770) 489-6834
Email: maryp@beonetogehter.com
Website: beonetogether.com
Associations: Missio Nexus

A nondenominational service agency of
Evangelical tradition engaged in Bible
teaching, children's ministry, church
planting (establishing), discipleship,
leadership development, and recruiting or
mobilizing for mission.

Purpose: . . . to engage all cultures by making God's Word real through collaboration in outreach, discipleship, and mobilization.

Year Founded in US: 2012
Income for International Min:
   $60,000
Fully Supported US Personnel Working Cross-Culturally
   X-C workers in US: 34
   Non-residential: 4
Other Personnel
   Short-Term less than 1 year: 1
   Tentmakers/BAM: 1
   Non-US in own/other country: 2017
Countries/Regions: Brazil, Germany, Portugal

BEAUTIFUL FEET

Formerly: Heart of God Ministries; Every Nation (merged in 2016)
3720 S. Hiwassee Rd.
Choctaw, OK 73020 US
Phone: (405) 737-9446
Email: info@beautifulfeet.us
Website: beautifulfeet.us

A nondenominational service agency of Evangelical tradition engaged in CPM, community development, and DMM.

Purpose: . . . to passionately and whole-heartedly pursue Jesus and His Kingdom through radical love for one another, and compassionate, holistic ministry that results in church planting movements.

Year Founded in US: 1997
Income for International Min:
   $1,000,405
Fully Supported US Personnel Working Cross-Culturally
   More than 4 years: 46
Other Personnel
   Non-US in own/other country: 5
   Home staff: 11

Countries/Regions: Bangladesh, Bulgaria, Cambodia, East Asia, Liberia, Middle East, Nigeria, South Asia, Southeast Asia, Sub-Saharan Africa, Suriname, Taiwan (China), Uganda, Ukraine

BEE WORLD (BIBLICAL EDUCATION BY EXTENSION)

990 Pinon Ranch View, Ste. 100
Colorado Springs, CO 80907 US
Phone: (719) 488-5837
Email: info@beeworld.org
Website: beeworld.org
Associations: Missio Nexus

A nondenominational sending agency of Evangelical tradition engaged in discipleship, TEE or other extension education, theological education, and leadership development. (FPC-PE)

Purpose: . . . to help the Church fulfill the Great Commission by providing Biblical training that results in the multiplication of servant leaders with priority given to countries with limited access to training.

Year Founded in US: 1994
Fully Supported US Personnel Working Cross-Culturally
   More than 4 years: 7
Other Personnel
   Non-US in own/other country: 2
Countries/Regions: Asia

BETHANY GATEWAYS

Formerly: Bethany International Ministries
6820 Auto Club Rd, Ste. D
Minneapolis, MN 55438 US
Phone: (952) 944-2121
Email: ministries@bethfel.org
Website: bethanyinternational.org
Associations: Missio Nexus

A nondenominational sending agency of Evangelical tradition engaged in church planting (establishing), literature production, missionary & worker training, networking, partnership, or coordination, and recruiting or mobilizing for mission.

Purpose: . . . to take the Church to where it is not by recruiting, equipping, and fielding followers of Jesus who are transformed by the cross, empowered by the Holy Spirit, and are effectively prepared with intercultural educational experience.

Year Founded in US: 1963
Income for International Min:
   $3,514,000
Fully Supported US Personnel Working Cross-Culturally
   More than 4 years: 42
   1–4 years: 45
   X-C workers in US: 1
   Non-residential: 2
Other Personnel
   Short-Term less than 1 year: 241
   Non-US in own/other country: 24
   Home staff: 14
Countries/Regions: Brazil, East Asia, Eastern Europe and Eurasia, France, Germany, Ghana, Global Ministry, Honduras, Japan, Kenya, Mexico, Netherlands, Panama, Philippines, Slovenia, Southeast Asia, Sri Lanka, Thailand, United Kingdom

BETHANYKIDS
PO Box 1297
Abingdon, VA 24212 US
Phone: (800) 469-1512
Email: tdavis@bethanykids.org
Website: bethanykids.org
A nondenominational support agency of Evangelical and Friends tradition engaged in children's ministry, disabled ministry, discipleship, medical ministry, including dental or public health, and surgical training program.

Purpose: . . . to transform the lives of African children with surgical conditions and disabilities through pediatric surgery, rehabilitation, public education, spiritual ministry, and training health professionals.

Year Founded in US: 2001
Income for International Min:
   $752,258
Fully Supported US Personnel Working Cross-Culturally
   Non-residential: 1
Other Personnel
   Short-Term less than 1 year: 10
   Non-US in own/other country: 38
   Home staff: 2
Countries/Regions: Canada, Ethiopia, Kenya, Madagascar, Sierra Leone, South Africa, Uganda

BETHANYKIDS CANADA
PO Box 1202
Kingston, ON K7L 4Y8 CA
Phone: (800) 469-1512
Email: mrobinson@bethanykids.org
Website: bethanykids.org
A nondenominational support agency of Evangelical and Friends tradition engaged in disabled ministry, church, school or general Christian education, medical ministry, including dental or public health, missionary & worker training, relief & aid, and surgical training program.

Purpose: . . . to transform the lives of African children with surgical conditions and disabilities through pediatric surgery, rehabilitation, public education, spiritual ministry, and training health professionals.

Year Founded in CA: 2001
Income for International Min:
   $752,258
Other Personnel
   Short-Term less than 1 year: 20
   Home staff: 1

BEYOND

Formerly: Mission to Unreached Peoples
P.O. Box 860548
Plano, TX 75086 US
Phone: (469) 814-8222
Email: info@beyond.org
Website: beyond.org
Associations: Missio Nexus

A nondenominational sending agency of
Evangelical tradition engaged in Church
Planting Movements.

Purpose: . . . to start church planting
movements to transform unreached
people groups—where obedient disciples
make obedient disciples and reproducing
churches make reproducing churches—
who make Jesus known by transforming
lives, relationships and communities.

BEYOND BORDERS

PO Box 2132
Norristown, PA 19404 US
Phone: (610) 277-5045
Email: mail@beyondborders.net
Website: beyondborders.net

An interdenominational support agency
of Ecumenical tradition engaged in
community development, addressing
human trafficking, justice or peace issues,
leadership development, literacy, and
networking, partnership, or coordination.

Purpose: . . . to support movements
in Haiti to end child slavery, guarantee
universal access to education, end
violence against women and girls, and
replace systems that oppress the poor with
systems that support dignified work and
sustainable livelihoods.

Year Founded in US: 1993
Income for International Min:
   $1,600,000
*Fully Supported US Personnel Working
Cross-Culturally*
   Non-residential: 6

Other Personnel
   Non-US in own/other country: 15
   Home staff: 6
Countries/Regions: Haiti

BIBLE LEAGUE CANADA

PO Box 5037
Burlington, ON L7R 3Y8 CA
Phone: (905) 00319-95
Email: ministry@bibleleague.ca
Website: bibleleague.ca

A specialized agency of Evangelical and
Reformed tradition engaged in Bible
distribution, children's programs, church
planting, discipleship, literacy work and
literature distribution. (DPE)

Purpose: . . . to provide Scriptures
and training worldwide, so that people
prepared by the Holy Spirit will be brought
into fellowship with Christ and His Church.

Year Founded in CA: 1971
Income for International Min:
   $4,368,550
*Fully Supported CA Personnel Working
Cross-Culturally*
   Non-residential: 2
Other Personnel
   Short-Term less than 1 year: 18
   Non-CA in own/other country: 5
   Home staff: 18
Countries/Regions: Africa, Asia,
Eastern Europe, Latin America

BIBLE LEAGUE INTERNATIONAL

3801 Eagle Nest Dr
Crete, IL 60417 US
Phone: (708) 367-8500
Email: info@bibleleague.org
Website: bibleleague.org

An interdenominational specialized agency
of Evangelical and Independent tradition
engaged in Bible distribution, church
planting (establishing), personal or small
group evangelism, and literacy. (FPC-PE)

Purpose: . . . to serve the under-resourced Church globally through the provision of Bibles, biblical resources, and training to transform lives worldwide through God's Word.
Year Founded in US: 1938

BIBLE TRAINING CENTRE FOR PASTORS
2030 Tucker Industrial Rd. #126
Tucker, GA 30084 US
Phone: (770) 938-6160
Email: info@btcp.com
Website: bibletraining.com
An interdenominational support agency of Evangelical tradition engaged in Bible teaching and training pastors & church leaders. (FPC-PE)
Purpose: . . . to extend non-formal theological training to the world's untrained pastors and church leaders.
Year Founded in US: 1990

BIBLES AND LITERATURE IN FRENCH
PO Box 629
Wheaton, IL 60187 US
Phone: (630) 221-1980
Email: info@blfusa.org
Website: blfusa.org
Associations: Missio Nexus
A nondenominational specialized agency of Evangelical tradition engaged in Bible distribution, literature distribution, and literature production.
Purpose: . . . to glorify God by facilitating the creation and distribution of Christian resources and materials for the evangelization and discipleship of the Francophone world.
Year Founded in US: 1958
Fully Supported US Personnel Working Cross-Culturally
    More than 4 years: 2

Other Personnel
    Short-Term less than 1 year: 11
    Home staff: 8
Countries/Regions: France

BIBLES FOR THE WORLD INC.
PO Box 49759
Colorado Springs, CO 80949 US
Phone: (888) 382-4253
Email: info@bftw.org
Website: biblesfortheworld.org
Associations: Missio Nexus
A nondenominational service agency of Evangelical tradition engaged in Bible distribution, church, school or general Christian education, TEE or other extension education, national worker support, and childcare sponsorship. (FPC-PE)
Purpose: . . . to be a catalyst for individual and cultural change through Christ and the power of His Word!
Year Founded in US: 1971
Other Personnel
    Non-US in own/other country: 400
Countries/Regions: India

BIBLICAL MINISTRIES WORLDWIDE
1595 Herrington Road
Lawrenceville, ga 30043 US
Phone: (770) 339-3500
Email: hqbmw@biblicalministries.org
Website: biblicalministries.org
Associations: FOM
A nondenominational sending agency of Independent tradition engaged in church planting (establishing), discipleship, theological education, personal or small group evangelism, leadership development, and deaf-blind ministries.
Purpose: . . . to serve the Lord and local churches by establishing reproducing churches through evangelism, discipleship, and leadership development.
Year Founded in US: 1989

Income for International Min:
$9,000,000
Fully Supported US Personnel Working Cross-Culturally
More than 4 years: 177
1–4 years: 25
X-C workers in US: 101
Non-residential: 4
Other Personnel
Tentmakers/BAM: 4
Non-US in own/other country: 202
Home staff: 9
Countries/Regions: Antigua and Barbuda, Argentina, Australia, Austria, Canada, Central Asia, Croatia, Denmark, Ecuador, Fiji, Finland, Germany, Guam, Honduras, Hong Kong (China), Indonesia, Italy, Japan, Kenya, Luxembourg, Mexico, Middle East, Netherlands, New Zealand, Palau, Philippines, Puerto Rico, Romania, Russia, Senegal, South Africa, Spain, Sweden, Tajikistan, United Kingdom, Vanuatu

BIC CANADA-GLOBAL
Formerly: Brethren in Christ World Missions – Canada
2700 Bristol Circle
Oakville, ON L6H 6E1 CA
Phone: (905) 339-2335
Email: bic.global@canadianbic.ca
Website: canadianbic.ca/global-ministry/
A denominational sending agency of Mennonite or Anabaptist and Brethren in Christ tradition engaged in childcare or orphanage, church planting (establishing), church, school or general Christian education, leadership development, national worker support, and relief and aid.
Purpose: . . . to follow Jesus, share his message, and extend his peace around the world.
Year Founded in CA: 2014
Income for International Min:
$335,187

Fully Supported CA Personnel Working Cross-Culturally
1–4 years: 5
Other Personnel
Short-Term less than 1 year: 42
Home staff: 4
Countries/Regions: Zambia

BILD INTERNATIONAL
2400 Oakwood Rd
Ames, IA 50014 US
Phone: (515) 292-7012
Email: info@bild.org
Website: bild.org
A denominational support agency of Evangelical tradition engaged in church development, church planting (establishing), CPM, theological education, leadership development, and translation.
Purpose: . . . to train networks of leaders—grassroots to national—in the way of Christ and His apostles, in partnership with church-planting movements in each of the nine major civilizations around the world.
Year Founded in US: 1974
Fully Supported US Personnel Working Cross-Culturally
More than 4 years: 17
X-C workers in US: 1
Other Personnel
Non-US in own/other country: 54
Home staff: 14
Countries/Regions: Albania, Australia, Bangladesh, Brazil, Cambodia, Chile, China (People's Republic of), Democratic Republic of Congo, Costa Rica, Cuba, Dominican Republic, Ecuador, Ethiopia, France, Guatemala, Hong Kong (China), India, Indonesia, Japan, Kosovo, Macedonia, Mongolia, Myanmar (Burma), Nepal, Nigeria, North Africa, Pakistan, Peru, Sri Lanka, Uganda, Vietnam

BLESSING THE CHILDREN INTERNATIONAL

2265 Fraser Road
Kawkawlin, MI 48631 US
Phone: (989) 667-8850
Email: Info@BlessingtheChildren.org
Website: blessingthechildren.org
An interdenominational specialized agency of Evangelical and Pentecostal tradition engaged in childcare or orphanage, children's ministry, community development, church, school or general Christian education, STM trip coordination, and work with widows.

Purpose: . . . to minister to the physical, mental, social, and spiritual needs of orphans and widows in Ethiopia.

Year Founded in US: 2001
Income for International Min:
$158,269
Fully Supported US Personnel Working Cross-Culturally
X-C workers in US: 35
Non-residential: 3
Other Personnel
Short-Term less than 1 year: 35
Non-US in own/other country: 56
Countries/Regions: Ethiopia

BLESSINGS INTERNATIONAL

1650 N. Indianwood Avenue
Broken Arrow, OK 74012 US
Phone: (818) 250-8101
Email: info@blessing.org
Website: blessing.org
Associations: Accord Network, CCRDA
An interdenominational support agency of Independent tradition engaged in medical supplies and medical ministry, including dental or public health. (FPC-PE)

Purpose: . . . to heal the hurting globally and locally by providing life-saving pharmaceuticals, vitamins, and medical supplies to medical mission teams, clinics and hospitals; to build healthy communities by treating the poor and victims of endemic medical problems and outbreak of disease.

Year Founded in US: 1981
Income for International Min:
$4,739,509
Other Personnel
Home staff: 22

BLF CANADA

256 Marc-Aurele-Fortin
Lachute, PQ J8H 3W7 CA
Phone: (450) 562-7859
Email: toeblake@sympatico.ca
Website: blfcanada.artisteer.net/
An interdenominational support agency of Evangelical tradition engaged in literature production, Bible distribution, discipleship, evangelism, literature distribution and short-term programs. (DPE)

Purpose: . . . to provide French literature to the French world at an affordable cost.

BOLD VENTURES

Formerly: Plead the Cause
365 NE Greenwood Ave #1
Bend, OR 97701 US
Phone: (541) 728-3340
Email: new@boldventures.global
Website: boldventures.global
A nondenominational sending agency of Charismatic and Independent tradition engaged in church planting (establishing), TEE or other extension education, personal or small group evangelism, missionary & worker training, networking, partnership, or coordination, and leadership development.

Purpose: . . . to mobilize missionaries for pioneer church planting.

Year Founded in US: 2016
Income for International Min:
$135,000
Fully Supported US Personnel Working Cross-Culturally
More than 4 years: 2
Other Personnel
Short-Term less than 1 year: 25
Tentmakers/BAM: 30
Non-US in own/other country: 23
Home staff: 1
Countries/Regions: Uganda

BOUNDLESS MINISTRIES INC.

Formerly: Great Commission Global
Ministries Inc. (GCGM)
6809 District Heights Parkway, Suite 100
District Heights, MD 20747 US
Phone: (301) 880-7056
Email: latkins@gcgm.org
Website: gcgm.org
Associations: Missio Nexus
A nondenominational sending agency of
Evangelical tradition engaged in church
planting (establishing), discipleship, mass
evangelism, leadership development,
partnership development, and recruiting or
mobilizing for mission.
Purpose: . . . to equip, network and
mobilized all people, but especially
African Americans for world missions.
Year Founded in US: 1998
Fully Supported US Personnel Working Cross-Culturally
X-C workers in US: 5
Other Personnel
Home staff: 13

BRAZIL GOSPEL FELLOWSHIP MISSION (BGFM)

125 W. Ash St.
Springfield, IL 62704 US
Phone: (217) 523-7176
Email: chrisbgfm@gmail.com
Website: bgfmission.com

A sending agency of Baptist and
Independent tradition engaged in church
planting, camping programs, Christian
education, TEE, evangelism and leadership
development. (DPE)
Purpose: . . . to aid the evangelization of
Brazil, South America.
Year Founded in US: 1955
Income for International Min:
$1,070,700
Fully Supported US Personnel Working Cross-Culturally
More than 4 years: 44
1–4 years: 1
Other Personnel
Short-Term less than 1 year: 6
Home staff: 4
Countries/Regions: Brazil

BREAD FOR THE WORLD

425 3rd Street SW, Suite 1200
Washington, DC 20024 US
Phone: (800) 822-7323
Email: bread@bread.org
Website: bread.org
A support agency of Ecumenical tradition
engaged in advocacy, poverty education
and justice. (DPE)
Purpose: . . . to urge our nation's
decision makers to end hunger at home
and abroad.
Other Personnel
Home staff: 90

BRETHREN IN CHRIST WORLD MISSIONS (BICWM)

PO Box 390
Grantham, PA 17027-0390 US
Phone: (717) 697-2634
Email: bicwm@bic-church.org
Website: bic-church.org/wm
Associations: Missio Nexus

A denominational sending agency of Brethren tradition engaged in church planting, apologetics, business as mission, discipleship, theological education and TEE. (DPE)

Purpose: A church for every people . . . the Gospel to every person . . . Jesus worshipped in the nations . . . a mission from every church . . . to extend the Kingdom of God by laboring cross-culturally with other believers.

Income for International Min: $1,325,192

Fully Supported US Personnel Working Cross-Culturally
More than 4 years: 35
Non-residential: 2

Other Personnel
Short-Term less than 1 year: 68
Tentmakers/BAM: 5
Non-US in own/other country: 3
Home staff: 12

Countries/Regions: Colombia, Honduras, Malawi, Mexico, Spain, Unspecified Country, Zambia, Zimbabwe

BRIDGE BUILDERS INTERNATIONAL

P.O. Box 4073
Salem, OR 97302 US
Phone: (541) 602-6968
Email: naomi@bridgebuildersint.com
Website: bridgebuildersint.com

A nondenominational support agency of Baptist tradition engaged in arts in mission, Bible teaching, childcare or orphanage, disabled ministry, networking, partnership, or coordination, and leadership development.

Purpose: . . . to see the nation of Latvia transformed by the love and power of Christ, and to help Latvians know and follow the Lord Jesus Christ with all their hearts.

Year Founded in US: 1994

Fully Supported US Personnel Working Cross-Culturally
More than 4 years: 5

Other Personnel
Short-Term less than 1 year: 15
Non-US in own/other country: 5
Home staff: 2

Countries/Regions: Latvia

BRIGHT HOPE

2060 Stonington Avenue
Hoffman Estates, IL 60169 US
Phone: (224) 520-6100
Email: Info@BrightHope.org
Website: BrightHope.org
Associations: Accord Network

A nondenominational service agency of Evangelical tradition engaged in agricultural assistance, church planting (establishing), community development, personal or small group evangelism, leadership development, and micro-finance.

Purpose: . . . to help those living on less than $1.00 a day.

Year Founded in US: 1968
Income for International Min: $10,177,689

Fully Supported US Personnel Working Cross-Culturally
More than 4 years: 2
1–4 years: 1

Other Personnel
Short-Term less than 1 year: 200
Non-US in own/other country: 5
Home staff: 10

Countries/Regions: Bolivia, Haiti, Kenya, Uganda, Zambia

BUCKNER INTERNATIONAL
5405 Shoe Dr
Mesquite, TX 75149 US
Phone: (214) 939-7194
Email: dhofmann@buckner.org
Website: buckner.org
Associations: Accord Network
A denominational service agency of Baptist tradition engaged in adoption, community development, medical ministry, including dental or public health, STM trip coordination, and spiritual renewal.
Purpose: . . . to transform the lives of vulnerable children, enrich the lives of senior adults, and build strong families through Christ-centered values.
Year Founded in US: 1879
Fully Supported US Personnel Working Cross-Culturally
  1–4 years: 1
Other Personnel
  Short-Term less than 1 year: 580
  Non-US in own/other country: 115
Countries/Regions: Dominican Republic, Guatemala, Honduras, Kenya, Mexico, Peru

CADENCE INTERNATIONAL
PO Box 1268
Englewood, CO 80150 US
Phone: (303) 762-1400
Email: info@cadence.org
Website: cadence.org
A nondenominational service agency of Evangelical tradition engaged in ministry to the military community, evangelism, children's programs, youth programs and discipleship. (DPE)
Purpose: . . . to exalt Christ in the nations through the lives of transformed military people.
Year Founded in US: 1954
Income for International Min:
  $3,683,602

Fully Supported US Personnel Working Cross-Culturally
  More than 4 years: 44
  1–4 years: 21
  Non-residential: 3
Other Personnel
  Short-Term less than 1 year: 16
  Home staff: 12
Countries/Regions: Germany, Italy, Japan, South Korea, Spain, Thailand, United Kingdom

CAFÉ 1040 INC.
PO Box 110
Alpharetta, GA 30009 US
Phone: (678) 938-5556
Email: information@cafe1040.com
Website: cafe1040.com
Associations: Missio Nexus
A sending agency of Evangelical tradition engaged in moblilization for missions, leadership development, missionary training, justice, discipleship and business as mission. (DPE)
Purpose: . . . to provide practical training inside the 10/40 Window, where students can learn daily lessons in language, culture, history, technology and relational evangelism, and apply those skills.
Income for International Min:
  $389,003
Fully Supported US Personnel Working Cross-Culturally
  1–4 years: 7
Other Personnel
  Home staff: 4
Countries/Regions: Asia, Middle East

CALVARY COMMISSION INC.
PO Box 100
Lindale, TX 75771 US
Phone: (903) 882-5501
Email: missions@calvarycommission.org
Website: calvarycommission.org

An interdenominational sending agency of Charismatic and Evangelical tradition engaged in childcare or orphanage, mass evangelism, national worker support, and STM trip coordination.

Purpose: . . . emphasize prison ministry, discipleship, ministry training, and missions work both foreign and domestic.

Year Founded in US: 1977

Fully Supported US Personnel Working Cross-Culturally
    More than 4 years: 19
Other Personnel
    Home staff: 45
Countries/Regions: Belize, Cuba, Mexico, Romania

CAMA SERVICES

Formerly: Compassion and Mercy Associates
8595 Explorer Dr
Colorado Springs, CO 80920 US
Phone: (719) 265-2039
Email: cama@camaservices.org
Website: camaservices.org
Associations: Accord Network

A denominational service agency of Evangelical tradition engaged in agricultural assistance, community development, HIV/AIDS ministry, relief & aid, sports ministry, and TESOL or TEFL.

Purpose: . . . to demonstrate Christ's compassion through immediate relief and long term development that transforms lives and restores communities.

Year Founded in US: 1972
Income for International Min:
    $2,760,000
Fully Supported US Personnel Working Cross-Culturally
    More than 4 years: 28
    1–4 years: 7

Other Personnel
    Short-Term less than 1 year: 20
    Tentmakers/BAM: 3
    Non-US in own/other country: 2
    Home staff: 6
Countries/Regions: Central Asia, China (People's Republic of), Guinea, Indonesia, Jordan, Kosovo, Mali, Mongolia, Myanmar (Burma), Niger, Senegal, Southeast Asia, Spain, Sub-Saharan Africa, Vietnam

CAMINO GLOBAL

Formerly: CAM International
8625 La Prada Drive
Dallas, TX 75228 US
Phone: (214) 327-8206
Email: info@caminoglobal.org
Website: caminoglobal.org
Associations: Missio Nexus

A nondenominational sending agency of Evangelical tradition engaged in business as mission, church development, community development, discipleship, theological education, and Internet discipleship or training.

Purpose: . . . to make disciples of Jesus Christ, serving among and with Spanish speakers globally.

Year Founded in US: 1890
Income for International Min:
    $6,037,397
Fully Supported US Personnel Working Cross-Culturally
    More than 4 years: 111
    1–4 years: 4
    X-C workers in US: 87
    Non-residential: 2
Other Personnel
    Short-Term less than 1 year: 243
    Non-US in own/other country: 19
    Home staff: 29
Countries/Regions: Albania, Colombia, Cuba, Guatemala, Honduras, Mexico, Nicaragua, Panama, Spain, Uruguay

CAMINO GLOBAL MINISTRIES CANADA

Formerly: CAM International of Canada
PO Box 37010 Stanley Park, 1005 Ottawa St. North
Kitchener, ON N2A 4A7 CA
Phone: (647) 977-3226
Email: kelliott@caminoglobal.com
Website: caminoglobal.org
Associations: Missio Nexus

An interdenominational sending agency of Baptist and Evangelical tradition engaged in Bible teaching, church planting (establishing), theological education, and STM trip coordination.

Purpose: . . . to journey with Spanish speakers everywhere to transform communities, equip believers, and reach the world.

Year Founded in CA: 1969
Income for International Min:
   $184,064
Fully Supported CA Personnel Working Cross-Culturally
   More than 4 years: 7
   1–4 years: 1901
   X-C workers in CA: 2
   Non-residential: 2
Other Personnel
   Short-Term less than 1 year: 6
   Home staff: 3
Countries/Regions: Cuba, Guatemala, Honduras, Mexico, United States of America

CAMPUS CRUSADE FOR CHRIST (CRU IN THE US)

100 Lake Hart Drive
Orlando, FL 32832 US
Phone: (888) 278-7233
Email: Thelly.Thomas@ccci.org
Website: cru.org
Associations: Missio Nexus

An interdenominational sending agency of Evangelical tradition engaged in CPM, discipleship, student evangelism, Internet evangelism, sports ministry, and video-film production or distribution.

Purpose: . . . to help fulfill the Great Commission by winning people to Christ, building them in their faith and sending them in the power of the Holy Spirit and helping the body of Christ do evangelism and discipleship.

Year Founded in US: 1951
Income for International Min:
   $139,918,000
Fully Supported US Personnel Working Cross-Culturally
   More than 4 years: 818
   1–4 years: 271
   Non-residential: 7
Countries/Regions: Albania, Australia, Belarus, Bosnia and Herzegovina, Botswana, Brazil, Chile, Costa Rica, Côte d'Ivoire, Croatia, Czech Republic, Dominican Republic, East Asia, Eastern Europe and Eurasia, Ecuador, Estonia, Ethiopia, France, Germany, Global Ministry, Greece, Hungary, Ireland (Republic of), Italy, Japan, Latvia, Lithuania, Macedonia, Mongolia, Montenegro, New Zealand, Niger, North Africa, Philippines, Poland, Portugal, Puerto Rico, Russia, Senegal, Singapore, Slovakia, Slovenia, South America, South Asia, South Sudan, Southeast Asia, Spain, Sub-Saharan Africa, Sweden, Tanzania, Thailand, Uganda, Ukraine, United Kingdom, Uruguay, Western Europe

CANADIAN ASSEMBLIES OF GOD – GENERAL CONFERENCE

5845 boul. Couture
St-Léonard, PQ H1P 1A8 CA
Phone: (514) 279-1100
Email: info@caogonline.org
Website: caogonline.org

A denominational support agency of Pentecostal tradition engaged in support of

national churches, association of missions, leadership development and youth programs. (DPE)

Year Founded in CA: 2005
Income for International Min:
  $85,867
Other Personnel
  Home staff: 1

CANADIAN BAPTIST MINISTRIES

7185 Millcreek Dr.
Missisauga, ON L5N 5R4 CA
Phone: (905) 821-3533
Email: administration@cbmin.org
Website: cbmin.org

A denominational sending agency of Baptist tradition engaged in leadership development, church planting, development and discipleship. (DPE)

Purpose: . . . to unite, encourage, and enable Canadian Baptist Churches in their national and international endeavors to fulfill the Great Commandment and the Great Commission of our Lord Jesus Christ, in the power of the Holy Spirit, proclaiming the Gospel and showing the love of God in word and deed.

Fully Supported CA Personnel Working Cross-Culturally
  More than 4 years: 22
Other Personnel
  Short-Term less than 1 year: 327
  Non-CA in own/other country: 10
  Home staff: 33
Countries/Regions: Angola, Argentina, Bolivia, Brazil, China (People's Republic of), El Salvador, Europe, India, Indonesia, Kenya, Lebanon, Middle East, Rwanda

CANADIAN BIBLE SOCIETY / LA SOCIETE BIBLIQUE CANADIENNE

10 Carnforth Rd.
Toronto, ON M4A 1S4 CA
Phone: (416) 757-4171
Email: info@biblesociety.ca
Website: biblesociety.ca

An interdenominational support agency of Ecumenical tradition engaged in Bible distribution, linguistics, literature distribution, literature production, and Bible translation. (FPC-PE)

Purpose: . . . to promote and encourage the translation, publication, distribution, and use of the Scriptures globally.

Year Founded in CA: 1904
Income for International Min:
  $2,694,000
Other Personnel
  Home staff: 40

CANADIAN CHURCHES FORUM FOR GLOBAL MINISTRIES

47 Queens Park Crescent East
Toronto, ON M1K 1T3 CA
Phone: (416) 924-9351
Email: director@ccforum.ca
Website: ccfroum.ca

An ecumenical service agency of Ecumenical tradition engaged in missionary and worker training. (FPC-PE)

Purpose: . . . to partner with others to foster intercultural leadership, learning, and ministry.

Year Founded in CA: 1921

CANADIAN NATIONAL BAPTIST CONVENTION (CNBC)

100 Convention Way
Cochrane, AB T4C 2G2 CA
Phone: (403) 932-5688
Email: office@cnbc.ca
Website: cnbc.ca

A denominational sending agency of Baptist tradition engaged in church planting, discipleship, evangelism, support of national churches, partnership development and mobilization for mission. (DPE)

Purpose: . . . churches in covenant giving ourselves away to advance the Kingdom of God.

Income for International Min: $362,462

Fully Supported CA Personnel Working Cross-Culturally
More than 4 years: 6
Non-residential: 26

Other Personnel
Non-CA in own/other country: 26
Home staff: 21

Countries/Regions: Africa, Asia, Botswana, Central Asia, Croatia, Europe, Germany, Mexico, Middle East, Niger

CANADIAN SOUTH AMERICA MISSION

1633 Dougall Ave
Windsor, ON N8X 1S4 CA
Phone: (866) 443-2250
Email: steve@southamericamission.ca
Website: southamericamission.org

A nondenominational sending agency of Evangelical tradition engaged in church leadership development, aviation services, church planting and development. (DPE)

Purpose: . . . building leaders to build churches.

Income for International Min: $158,590

Fully Supported CA Personnel Working Cross-Culturally
More than 4 years: 3
1–4 years: 2

Other Personnel
Non-CA in own/other country: 6
Home staff: 1

Countries/Regions: Bolivia, Brazil, Peru

CARE OF CREATION INC.

PO Box 44582
Madison, WI 53744 US
Phone: (608) 233-7048
Email: rness@careofcreation.org
Website: careofcreation.net

A nondenominational specialized agency of Evangelical tradition engaged in agricultural assistance, church, school or general Christian education, and environmental missions.

Purpose: . . . to pursue a God-centered response to environmental challenges that brings glory to the Creator, advances the cause of Christ, and leads to a transformation of the people and the land that sustains them.

Year Founded in US: 2005

Fully Supported US Personnel Working Cross-Culturally
More than 4 years: 2
Non-residential: 1

Other Personnel
Non-US in own/other country: 8
Home staff: 6

Countries/Regions: Global Ministry, Kenya, Tanzania

CARIBBEAN BAPTIST MISSION SOCIETY

PO Box 40247
Fort Worth, TX 76140-0247 US
Phone: (817) 447-3722
Email: michaelmanire@cbms.org
Website: cbms.org

A denominational sending agency of Baptist tradition engaged in business as mission, apologetics, church construction, church planting, evangelism and providing medical supplies. (DPE)

Purpose: . . . to collect and distribute support monies for national and international missionaries and mission organizations of like faith that practice and are actively proclaiming the Gospel.

Income for International Min:
$38,000
Fully Supported US Personnel Working
Cross-Culturally
1–4 years: 6
Countries/Regions: Haiti

CARIBBEAN LIFETIME MISSION
225 Main Street, #710
Dallas, GA 30157 US
Phone: (678) 574-3818
Email: info@clmissions.org
Website: lifetimemissions.org/
A nondenominational sending agency
of Evangelical and Pentecostal tradition
engaged in Bible teaching, childcare
or orphanage, children's ministry,
church development, church planting
(establishing), and CPM.
Purpose: . . . to REACH the Caribbean
with the message of the Gospel, TRAIN
(disciple) the (new) believers, and SEND
missionaries to the Caribbean and the rest
of the world.

CARING FOR OTHERS
3480 S. Highpointe Dr
New Berlin, WI 53151 US
Phone: (262) 641-9600
Email: john@caringforothers.org
Website: caringforothers.org
A nondenominational service agency
of Evangelical tradition engaged in
counseling, member care, and missionary
& worker training.
Purpose: . . . to increase the
effectiveness of missionaries and to reduce
their attrition rate by strengthening and
encouraging global Christian workers so
they can spread the Gospel of Jesus Christ
as effectively as possible, to as many as
possible, for as long as possible.
Year Founded in US: 2002

Fully Supported US Personnel Working
Cross-Culturally
More than 4 years: 2
Other Personnel
Home staff: 2
Countries/Regions: Global Ministry

CARING PARTNERS INTERNATIONAL
601 Shotwell Drive
Franklin, OH 45005 US
Phone: (937) 743-2744
Email: info@caringpartners.org
Website: caringpartners.org
An interdenominational specialized agency
of Evangelical tradition engaged in church
development, personal or small group
evangelism, medical supplies, medical
ministry, including dental or public health,
and STM trip coordination. (FPC-PE)
Purpose: . . . to equip churches to use
healthcare to share the Gospel of Jesus
Christ.
Year Founded in US: 1992
Income for International Min:
$2,140,783
Other Personnel
Short-Term less than 1 year: 120
Non-US in own/other country: 8
Home staff: 6
Countries/Regions: Cuba, Ecuador,
Guatemala

CASA VIVA
PO Box 120
Wheaton, IL 60187-0120 US
Phone: (630) 427-4040
Email: info@casaviva.org
Website: casaviva.org
A nondenominational support agency of
Evangelical tradition engaged in childcare
or orphanage and justice or peace issues.
Purpose: . . . to provide family-based
care for orphaned, abandoned, abused,
and neglected children worldwide.

Year Founded in US: 2008

Other Personnel
   Non-US in own/other country: 500
Countries/Regions: Costa Rica

CATALYST MISSIONS

7111 Grassland Cove
Arlington, TN 38002 US
Phone: (901) 378-5008
Email: doug@catalystmissions.org
Website: catalystmissions.org

A nondenominational service agency of
Baptist tradition engaged in Bible teaching,
church development, church planting
(establishing), discipleship, missionary &
worker training, and national worker support.

Purpose: . . . to train those who will train
others, believing that the biblical model of
discipleship in 2 Timothy 2:2 affords us no
other option.

Year Founded in US: 2007

*Fully Supported US Personnel Working
Cross-Culturally*
   1–4 years: 6
   X-C workers in US: 1
   Non-residential: 20
Other Personnel
   Short-Term less than 1 year: 15
   Tentmakers/BAM: 17
   Non-US in own/other country: 4
   Home staff: 3
Countries/Regions: Bolivia, Indonesia,
Sudan

CATALYST SERVICES

PO Box 152
Newtown, PA 18940 US
Phone: (215) 579-4346
Email: info@catalystservices.org
Website: CatalystServices.org
Associations: Missio Nexus

A nondenominational service agency
of Evangelical tradition engaged in
networking, partnership, or coordination,
partnership development, recruiting or
mobilizing for mission, and services for
mission organizations. (FPC-PE)

Purpose: . . . to assist mission
organizations, local churches, and
networks to expand their global impact by
engaging the untapped potential of local
congregations.

Year Founded in US: 2005

Other Personnel
   Home staff: 2

CAUSE CANADA

P.O Box 8100
Canmore, AB T1W 2T8 CA
Phone: (403) 678-3332
Email: info@cause.ca
Website: cause.ca

A nondenominational support agency
of Independent tradition engaged in
community development, disabled
ministry, literacy, medical ministry,
including dental or public health, and relief
& aid. (FPC-PE)

Purpose: . . . to be a catalyst for global
justice providing sustainable, integrated
community development in rural West
Africa and Central America through
authentic, collaborative long-term
relationships.

Income for International Min:
   $1,587,221
*Fully Supported CA Personnel Working
Cross-Culturally*
   1–4 years: 5
Other Personnel
   Non-CA in own/other country: 80
   Home staff: 8
Countries/Regions: Guatemala,
Honduras, Sierra Leone

CBMC INC.

Formerly: Connecting Businessmen to Christ, Inc.
PO Box 8009
Chattanooga, TN 37414 US
Phone: (423) 698-4444
Email: info@cbmc.com
Website: cbmc.com

A nondenominational specialized agency of Evangelical tradition engaged in discipleship, personal or small group evangelism, and leadership development. (FPC-PE)

Purpose: . . . to present Jesus Christ as Savior and Lord to business and professional men, and to develop Christian business and professional men to carry out the Great Commission.

Year Founded in US: 1930
Other Personnel
   Home staff: 20

CEDAR LANE MISSIONARY HOMES

103 Cedar Lane
Laurel Springs, NJ 08021 US
Phone: (856) 783-6525
Email: cedarlane@furloughhomes.org
Website: furloughhomes.org

A nondenominational service agency of Independent tradition engaged in housing for missionaries. (FPC-PE)

Purpose: . . . to provide comfortable housing and a safe environment for God's servants as they have need, either for home assignment or medical or transitional needs.

Year Founded in US: 1949

CEIFA INTERNATIONAL

PO Box 83
Bethalto, IL 62010 US
Phone: (618) 581-6134
Email: ceifaministryinternational@gmail.com
Website: goceifa.com

A transdenominational service agency of Evangelical tradition engaged in

TEE, Bible distribution, children at risk, children's programs, church planting, missionary education, evangelism, literature distribution, literature production, providing medical supplies, support of national workers, short-term programs, missionary training and youth programs. (DPE)

Purpose: . . . to proclaim and demonstrate in word and deed the Gospel of Jesus Christ in conjunction with the local church.

Income for International Min:
   $48,000
Fully Supported US Personnel Working Cross-Culturally
   More than 4 years: 18
   Non-residential: 4
Other Personnel
   Short-Term less than 1 year: 35
   Non-US in own/other country: 18
Countries/Regions: Albania, Asia, India, Nepal, Romania

CELEBRANT SINGERS

PO Box 1416
Visalia, CA 93291 US
Phone: (559) 740-4000
Email: celebrants@celebrants.org
Website: celebrants.org

An interdenominational service agency of Charismatic and Evangelical tradition engaged in audio recording or distribution, radio or TV broadcasting, ethno-musicology, and music ministry evangelism. (FPC-PE)

Purpose: . . . to teach young adults by proclaiming His greatness and sharing His love with a hurting world through music, testimony, the preaching of the Word, and our lives.

Year Founded in US: 1977
Other Personnel
   Home staff: 10

CENTER FOR MISSION MOBILIZATION

Formerly: Body Builders
PO Box 3556
Fayetteville, AR 72702 US
Phone: (479) 587-9598
Email: info@mobilization.org
Website: mobilization.org
Associations: Missio Nexus

A nondenominational sending agency of Evangelical tradition engaged in missionary & worker training, national worker support, networking, partnership, or coordination, partnership development, recruiting or mobilizing for mission, and services for mission organizations.

Purpose: . . . to engage, equip, and connect believers worldwide to their most strategic role in completing the Great Commission.

Year Founded in US: 2001
Income for International Min:
   $2,500,000
Fully Supported US Personnel Working Cross-Culturally
   More than 4 years: 20
   1–4 years: 10
   X-C workers in US: 20
Other Personnel
   Short-Term less than 1 year: 50
   Non-US in own/other country: 6
   Home staff: 86
Countries/Regions: East Asia, Ethiopia, Kenya, Malaysia, Peru, Russia

CENTRAL YEARLY MEETING OF FRIENDS MISSIONS

5601 E. Co. Rd. 650 S.
Muncie, IN 47302 US
Phone: (317) 896-5082
Email: cymsuper@gmail.com
Website: cymfriends.com/missions.html

A denominational sending agency of Friends tradition engaged in church planting, Bible distribution and evangelism. (DPE)

CHAPLAINCY ENDORSEMENT COMMISSION FOR THE CHRISTIAN CHURCH AND CHURCHES OF CHRIST

PO Box 861571
Vint Hill, VA 20187 US
Phone: (703) 965-1495
Email: chaplainec@gmail.com
Website: cec-chap.org

A nondenominational sending agency of Christian (Restoration Movement) tradition engaged in Bible teaching, counseling, discipleship, leadership development, recruiting or mobilizing for mission, and spiritual renewal.

Purpose: . . . to provide endorsement and pastoral care of chaplains and counselors in ministry who serve in a variety of agencies such as the military and hospitals.

Year Founded in US: 1969

CHILD EVANGELISM FELLOWSHIP INC.

PO Box 348
Warrenton, MO 63383 US
Phone: (636) 456-4321
Email: intlmin@cefonline.com
Website: cefonline.com

An interdenominational sending agency of Independent tradition engaged in children's ministry, mass evangelism, literature distribution, literature production, and partnership development.

Purpose: . . . to evangelize boys and girl, and establish them in the Word of God and the local church.

Year Founded in US: 1937
Fully Supported US Personnel Working Cross-Culturally
   More than 4 years: 109
Other Personnel
   Home staff: 132

Countries/Regions: Albania, Angola, Argentina, Armenia, Australia, Austria, Belgium, Belize, Benin, Bolivia, Botswana, Brazil, Burkina Faso, Burundi, Cameroon, Chad, Chile, Colombia, Democratic Republic of Congo, Côte d'Ivoire, Croatia, Cuba, Cyprus, Denmark, Ecuador, El Salvador, Estonia, Fiji, France, Gambia, Germany, Ghana, Greece, Guatemala, Guinea, Haiti, Hong Kong (China), Hungary, Israel, Japan, Jordan, Kenya, Liberia, Madagascar, Malawi, Mali, Mexico, Federated States of Micronesia, Moldova, Mozambique, Namibia, Nepal, Niger, Nigeria, Pakistan, Peru, Philippines, Poland, Russia, Serbia, Singapore, Slovakia, Slovenia, South Africa, Suriname, Switzerland, Ukraine, Zambia, Zimbabwe

CHILDCARE WORLDWIDE
1971 Midway Lane, Ste N
Bellingham, WA 98226 US
Phone: (360) 647-2283
Email: smiddleton@childcareworldwide.org
Website: childcareworldwide.org
A nondenominational service agency of Evangelical tradition engaged in child sponsorship, church/school/general Christian education, childcare/orphanage programs, children at risk, medical work and relief and/or rehabilitation. (DPE)
Purpose: . . . to build a bridge between concerned people in the West and children in the developing world . . . to help meet their spiritual and physical needs through a ministry that emphasizes education and is based on the Gospel of Jesus Christ.
Income for International Min:
$13,167,522
Other Personnel
Non-US in own/other country: 275
Home staff: 19

Countries/Regions: Haiti, India, Kenya, Liberia, Mexico, Peru, Philippines, Sri Lanka, Thailand, Uganda

CHILDREN OF PROMISE INTERNATIONAL
6844 Loop Rd.
Centerville, OH 45459-2159 US
Phone: (888) 667-7426
Email: info@promise.org
Website: promise.org
A sending agency of Evangelical tradition engaged in childcare/orphanage programs, evangelism, funds transmission and support of national workers. (DPE)
Purpose: . . . to care for orphans and love them into the Kingdom.
Income for International Min:
$994,559
Fully Supported US Personnel Working Cross-Culturally
More than 4 years: 16
1–4 years: 8
Non-residential: 7
Countries/Regions: Costa Rica, Guatemala, Haiti, Mexico, Venezuela

CHILDREN'S HAVEN INTL.
400 E. Minnesota
Pharr, TX 78577 US
Phone: (956) 787-7378
Email: chii@childrenshaven.org
Website: childrenshaven.org
A nondenominational service agency of Evangelical tradition engaged in childcare or orphanage and STM trip coordination.
Purpose: . . . to provide loving care to needy children.
Year Founded in US: 1972
Fully Supported US Personnel Working Cross-Culturally
More than 4 years: 22
Countries/Regions: Mexico

CHILDREN'S HOPECHEST
PO Box 1190
Palmer Lake, CO 80133 US
Phone: (719(487-7800
Email: rwright@hopechest.org
Website: hopechest.org

A nondenominational support agency of Evangelical tradition engaged in orphan sponsorship programs, childcare/orphanage programs, children at risk, discipleship, HIV/AIDS and mobilization for mission. (DPE)

Purpose: . . . to respond to God's desire to create a world where every orphan knows Him, experiences the blessing of family, and acquires the skills necessary for independent life.

Year Founded in US: 1998
Income for International Min: $3,398,782
Fully Supported US Personnel Working Cross-Culturally
   More than 4 years: 1
Other Personnel
   Short-Term less than 1 year: 480
   Non-US in own/other country: 162
   Home staff: 13
Countries/Regions: Ethiopia, Russia, Swaziland, Uganda

CHILDREN'S LIFELINE
P.O. Box 428
Hamilton, GA 31811 US
Phone: (606) 663-3459
Email: donna.webb@childrenslifeline.com
Website: childrenslifeline.com

An interdenominational specialized agency of Evangelical tradition engaged in Bible teaching, childcare or orphanage, church, school or general Christian education, medical ministry, including dental or public health, relief & aid, and STM trip coordination.

Purpose: . . . to disseminate the Word of God under Christian principles while providing food, clothing, medical supplies, facilities, and educational assistance for the underprivileged children and their families in undeveloped areas of Haiti.

Other Personnel
   Short-Term less than 1 year: 394
   Home staff: 2
Countries/Regions: Haiti

CHILDREN'S MINISTRY INTERNATIONAL INC. (CMI)
2331 Fourth Street, Suite 106
Tucker, GA 30084 US
Phone: (770) 493-8952
Email: childrensministry1@earthlink.net
Website: childministry.com

A specialized agency of Presbyterian and Reformed tradition engaged in children's programs, Christian education, evangelism, support of national churches, services for other agencies and short-term programs. (DPE)

Purpose: . . . to develop and distribute children's materials, translate materials with the help of missionaries and nationals, and teach missionary children at missionary regional conferences.

Year Founded in US: 1982
Income for International Min: $35,000
Other Personnel
   Short-Term less than 1 year: 20
   Home staff: 2

CHILDSPRING INTERNATIONAL
1328 Peachtree St. NE
Atlanta, GA 30309 US
Phone: (404) 228-7770
Email: alison@childspringintl.org
Website: childspringintl.org
Associations: Missio Nexus

A denominational support agency of Christian (Restoration Movement) tradition engaged in medical ministry, including dental or public health and partnership development. (FPC-PE)

Purpose: . . . to become internationally recognized as the leading facilitator of medical care for children in need, resulting in 5,000 transformed lives throughout the global community by 2020.

Year Founded in US: 2001

Other Personnel
  Home staff: 5

CHINA MINISTRIES INTERNATIONAL

1605 Elizabeth St.
Pasadena, CA 91104 US
Phone: (626) 398-2343
Email: samuelchao@msn.com
Website: cmius.org

A nondenominational support agency of Evangelical tradition engaged in Bible distribution, theological education, mass evangelism, missionary & worker training, and national worker support.

Purpose: . . . for the evangelization of China, the strengthening of the Chinese Church by engaging in ministries of research, training of workers, and sending them to the harvest field.

Year Founded in US: 1987

Fully Supported US Personnel Working Cross-Culturally
  More than 4 years: 12
  Non-residential: 2
Other Personnel
  Non-US in own/other country: 8
  Home staff: 6
Countries/Regions: Central Asia

CHINA OUTREACH MINISTRIES INC.

555 Gettysburg Pike, Ste. A200
Mechanicsburg, PA 17055 US
Phone: (717) 591-3500
Email: kimbaer@chinaoutreach.net
Website: chinaoutreach.net

An interdenominational support agency of Evangelical tradition engaged in evangelism. (DPE)

Purpose: . . . to focus on giving Christ to China's future leaders by showing them the love of Christ and by leading them to faith in Christ . . . to disciple, train, mentor, and equip them to minister creatively to other Chinese people.

Year Founded in US: 1959
Income for International Min: $105,639

Fully Supported US Personnel Working Cross-Culturally
  More than 4 years: 2
  Non-residential: 2
Other Personnel
  Short-Term less than 1 year: 8
  Tentmakers/BAM: 1
  Non-US in own/other country: 2
  Home staff: 10
Countries/Regions: Asia

CHINA PARTNERS

1205 Rio Grande Blvd
Denton, TX 76205 US
Phone: (214) 213-5459
Email: cpartneradmin@gmail.com
Website: china-partners.org

A nondenominational sending agency of Charismatic tradition engaged in discipleship, personal or small group evangelism, student evangelism, leadership development, partnership development, and TESOL or TEFL.

Purpose: . . . to serve the Chinese church by forming leaders through evangelism and discipleship.

Fully Supported US Personnel Working Cross-Culturally
  More than 4 years: 5
  1–4 years: 9
Other Personnel
  Non-US in own/other country: 1
Countries/Regions: China (People's Republic of)

CHINA SERVICE VENTURES

1407 Cleveland Ave. N.
St. Paul, MN 55108 US
Phone: (651) 659-1396
Email: revelness@aol.com
Website: chinaserviceventures.org

A denominational sending agency of Lutheran tradition engaged in children's education, children's programs, development, medical work and youth programs. (DPE)

Purpose: . . . to foster enriching relationships between Christian communities and individuals in North America with individuals and communities in China.

Income for International Min:
$380,000

Fully Supported US Personnel Working Cross-Culturally
More than 4 years: 3
1–4 years: 2
Non-residential: 2

Other Personnel
Short-Term less than 1 year: 30
Non-US in own/other country: 2
Home staff: 1

Countries/Regions: China

CHINASOURCE

PO Box 2160
Orange, CA 92859 US
Phone: (951) 968-0913
Email: info@chinasource.org
Website: chinasource.org
Associations: Missio Nexus

A nondenominational specialized agency of Evangelical and Independent tradition engaged in leadership development, missionary & worker training, partnership development, research, and services for mission organizations. (FPC-PE)

Purpose: . . . to engage the Christian community with the critical knowledge needed to collaborate with and serve the Chinese church and society.

Year Founded in US: 1995

Fully Supported US Personnel Working Cross-Culturally
More than 4 years: 1

Countries/Regions: China

CHINESE CHRISTIAN LIFE FELLOWSHIP INC.

670 Bonded Parkway
Streamwood, IL 60107 US
Phone: (630) 867-7551
Email: cclife@sbcglobal.net
Website: cclifefl.org

A nondenominational service agency of Evangelical tradition engaged in audio recording or distribution, Bible teaching, theological education, Internet evangelism, and evangelism publications.

Purpose: . . . to facilitate and mobilize the spiritual growth of PRC Christians and to raise up Christian leadership among Chinese intellectuals, through publications, overseas PRC ministry and China ministry.

Year Founded in US: 1996
Income for International Min:
$60,000

Fully Supported US Personnel Working Cross-Culturally
1–4 years: 2

Other Personnel
Short-Term less than 1 year: 2
Non-US in own/other country: 3
Home staff: 5

Countries/Regions: Canada, China (People's Republic of), Hong Kong (China)

CHOSEN MISSION PROJECT

3638 W. 26th St.
Erie, PA 16506 US
Phone: (814) 833-3023
Email: rick@chosenmissionproject.com
Website: chosenmissionproject.com

A nondenominational specialized agency of Evangelical tradition engaged in medical supplies and technical assistance. (FPC-PE)

Purpose: . . . to promote health care programs in conjunction with missionaries and national Christian health care workers in a tangible effort to bring the love of Christ to those least able to help themselves.

Year Founded in US: 1969

Other Personnel
   Home staff: 4

CHOSEN PEOPLE MINISTRIES (CANADA)

Dufferin-Lawrence, PO Box 58103
Toronto, ON M6A 3C8 CA
Phone: (416) 250-0177
Email: info@chosenpeople.ca
Website: chosenpeople.ca
Associations: Missio Nexus

An interdenominational sending agency of Evangelical tradition engaged in Bible teaching, church planting (establishing), discipleship, church, school or general Christian education, and personal or small group evangelism. (FPC-PE)

Purpose: . . . to pray for, evangelize, disciple, and serve Jewish people everywhere and to help fellow believers do the same.

Year Founded in CA: 1940
Income for International Min:
   $199,868

Fully Supported CA Personnel Working Cross-Culturally
   X-C workers in CA: 6
Other Personnel
   Short-Term less than 1 year: 2
   Home staff: 5

CHOSEN PEOPLE MINISTRIES INC.

241 E. 51st Street
New York, NY 01913 US
Phone: (212) 223-2252
Email: info@chosenpeople.com
Website: chosenpeople.com
Associations: Missio Nexus

A nondenominational sending agency of Evangelical tradition engaged in apologetics, church planting (establishing), theological education, mass evangelism, missionary & worker training, and STM trip coordination.

Purpose: . . . to pray for, evangelize, disciple, and serve Jewish people everywhere and to help fellow believers do the same.

Year Founded in US: 1894

Fully Supported US Personnel Working Cross-Culturally
   More than 4 years: 11
Other Personnel
   Short-Term less than 1 year: 100
   Non-US in own/other country: 95
   Home staff: 50
Countries/Regions: Argentina, Australia, Canada, Finland, France, Germany, Hong Kong (China), Israel, South Korea, Latvia, Netherlands, New Zealand, Russia, South Africa, Ukraine, United Kingdom

CHRIST FOR CHILDREN INTERNATIONAL

PO Box 260
Wheaton, IL 60187-0260 US
Phone: (205) 968-3004
Email: marydorset@aol.com
Website: christforchildren.com

An interdenominational sending agency of Anglican and Evangelical tradition engaged in Holistic care of impoverished families, children at risk, children's programs, discipleship and evangelism. (DPE)

Income for International Min:
$217,000
Fully Supported US Personnel Working Cross-Culturally
More than 4 years: 5
1–4 years: 2
Other Personnel
Non-US in own/other country: 3
Countries/Regions: Mexico, Angola, Brazil, Central African Republic, El Salvador, Ethiopia, Ghana, Guatemala, Haiti

CHRIST FOR INDIA INC.

PO Box 271086
Dallas, TX 75227 US
Phone: (972) 771-7221
Email: jtitus@christforindia.org
Website: christforindia.org
An interdenominational service agency of Charismatic and Pentecostal tradition engaged in theological education, childcare/orphanage programs, church construction, church planting, providing medical supplies and support of national workers. (DPE)
Purpose: . . . to fulfill Christ's Great Commission to India . . . to train nationals as pastors and evangelists . . . to establish native churches . . . to provide humanitarian aid . . . to educate India's future leaders.
Year Founded in US: 1981
Income for International Min:
$341,548
Fully Supported US Personnel Working Cross-Culturally
More than 4 years: 1
Non-residential: 1
Other Personnel
Short-Term less than 1 year: 4
Tentmakers/BAM: 1
Home staff: 2
Countries/Regions: India

CHRIST FOR THE CITY INTERNATIONAL

5332 S. 138th Street, Suite 200
Omaha, NE 68137 US
Phone: (402) 892-8332
Email: info@cfci.org
Website: cfci.org
An interdenominational sending agency of Evangelical tradition engaged in evangelism, childcare/orphanage programs, leadership development, children at risk, support of national churches and short-term programs. (DPE)
Purpose: . . . to help people transform cities by transforming lives.
Income for International Min:
$1,165,000
Fully Supported US Personnel Working Cross-Culturally
More than 4 years: 14
1–4 years: 10
Non-residential: 2
Other Personnel
Short-Term less than 1 year: 25
Tentmakers/BAM: 2
Non-US in own/other country: 63
Home staff: 1
Countries/Regions: Bolivia, Colombia, Costa Rica, Mali, Mexico, Nicaragua, Peru, Spain

CHRIST FOR THE NATIONS INC.

444 Fawn Ridge Drive
Dallas, TX 75224 US
Phone: (214) 376-1711
Email: info@cfni.org
Website: cfni.org
An interdenominational support agency of Pentecostal tradition engaged in missionary education, church construction, theological education, evangelism, literature distribution and literature production. (DPE)

Purpose: . . . to provide resources for the completion of church buildings, caring for orphans, supporting the nation of Israel, humanitarian relief efforts, establishing and strengthening international Bible schools and the distribution of Christian literature.

Income for International Min:
$1,500,000

Other Personnel
Short-Term less than 1 year: 400
Home staff: 110

CHRIST IN YOUTH
2201 N Main St
Joplin, MO 64801 US
Phone: (417) 781-2273
Email: rachel.grindle@ciy.com
Website: ciy.com/engage
A nondenominational specialized agency of Christian (Restoration Movement) and Evangelical tradition engaged in justice or peace issues, medical ministry, including dental or public health, missionary & worker training, recruiting or mobilizing for mission, and youth ministry.

Purpose: . . . to train students for a life of Kingdom work, amplifying the call on students' lives to become Kingdom workers through trips, events, and resources.

Other Personnel
Short-Term less than 1 year: 264
Home staff: 6

CHRIST TO THE NATIONS
PO Box 236713
Cocoa, FL 32923 US
Phone: (321) 504-0778
Email: harvesttoday@live.com
Website: cttn.org
An interdenominational sending agency of Baptist and Independent tradition engaged in childcare or orphanage, church planting (establishing), TEE or other extension

education, mass evangelism, missionary & worker training, and national worker support.

Purpose: . . . to help local churches and God's people reach the unreached millions with the Gospel of Jesus Christ and the Word of God.

Year Founded in US: 1991

Fully Supported US Personnel Working Cross-Culturally
More than 4 years: 12

Other Personnel
Home staff: 2

Countries/Regions: Bahamas, India, Kenya, Lithuania, Pakistan, Philippines, Romania, Sint Maarten

CHRISTAR
1500 International Parkway
Richardson, TX 75081 US
Phone: (800) 755-7955
Email: info@christar.org
Website: christar.org/
Associations: Missio Nexus
An interdenominational sending agency of Evangelical tradition engaged in business as mission, church planting (establishing), environmental missions, personal or small group evangelism, medical ministry, including dental or public health, and tentmaking & related.

Purpose: . . . to glorify God by establishing churches among least-reached Buddhists, Hindus, Muslims and other Asians worldwide.

Fully Supported US Personnel Working Cross-Culturally
More than 4 years: 157
1–4 years: 32
Non-residential: 22

Other Personnel
Tentmakers/BAM: 13
Non-US in own/other country: 1

Countries/Regions: Central Asia, East Asia, Eastern Europe and Eurasia, Global Ministry, Middle East, North Africa, South Asia, Southeast Asia, Western Europe

CHRISTAR CANADA
PO Box 20164
St. Catharines, ON L2M 7W7 CA
Phone: (905) 646-0228
Email: info@christar.ca
Website: Christar.ca
Associations: Missio Nexus
A nondenominational sending agency of Baptist and Evangelical tradition engaged in church planting (establishing), CPM, DMM, theological education, tentmaking & related, and TESOL or TEFL.
Purpose: . . . to glorify God by establishing churches among least-reached Buddhists, Hindus, Muslims, and other Asians worldwide.
Year Founded in CA: 1954
Income for International Min:
$750,000
Fully Supported CA Personnel Working Cross-Culturally
More than 4 years: 21
X-C workers in CA: 6
Other Personnel
Short-Term less than 1 year: 10
Home staff: 4
Countries/Regions: East Asia, Middle East, South Asia, Southeast Asia, Western Europe

CHRISTIAN AID MINISTRIES (CAM)
PO Box 360
Berlin, OH 44610 US
Phone: (330) 893-2428
Email: cam@camoh.org
Website: christianaidministries.org
A service agency of Mennonite tradition engaged in relief and/or rehabilitation, Bible distribution, childcare/orphanage programs, literature distribution and medical work. (DPE)

Purpose: . . . to help and encourage God's people . . . to help bring the Gospel to a lost and dying world.
Income for International Min:
$183,415,214
Fully Supported US Personnel Working Cross-Culturally
More than 4 years: 16
1–4 years: 47
Other Personnel
Short-Term less than 1 year: 15
Non-US in own/other country: 265
Home staff: 63
Countries/Regions: Haiti, Israel, Liberia, Moldova, Nicaragua, Romania, Ukraine

CHRISTIAN AID MISSION
1201 5th Street Extended
Charlottesville, VA 22906 US
Phone: (434) 977-5650
Email: info@christianaid.org
Website: christianaid.org
Associations: Missio Nexus
An interdenominational support agency of Evangelical tradition engaged in church planting (establishing), discipleship, mass evangelism, missionary & worker training, national worker support, and persecuted church. (FPC-PE)
Purpose: . . . to assist independent, indigenous missionary ministries reaching the unreached with the Gospel of Jesus Christ, especially in areas of poverty and persecution through prayer, advocacy and financial support.
Year Founded in US: 1953
Income for International Min:
$9,399,714
Other Personnel
Non-US in own/other country: 11036
Home staff: 54
Countries/Regions: Albania, Algeria, Argentina, Australia, Bangladesh, Belarus, Benin, Bhutan, Bolivia, Brazil, Bulgaria,

Burkina Faso, Burundi, Cambodia, Cameroon, Chad, Chile, China (People's Republic of), Colombia, Democratic Republic of Congo, Côte d'Ivoire, Cuba, Czech Republic, Ecuador, Egypt, Equatorial Guinea, Eritrea, Europe, Gabon, Gambia, Germany, Ghana, Guatemala, Guinea, Guinea-Bissau, Honduras, Hungary, India, Indonesia, Iraq, Jordan, Kazakhstan, Kenya, Kyrgyzstan, Laos, Lebanon, Liberia, Libya, Malawi, Mali, Mauritania, Mexico, Morocco, Mozambique, Myanmar (Burma), Nepal, Niger, Nigeria, Pakistan, Palestine, Papua New Guinea, Paraguay, Peru, Philippines, Poland, Russia, Senegal, Sierra Leone, South Africa, Sri Lanka, Sudan, Syria, Tanzania, Thailand, Togo, Uganda, Ukraine, Uruguay, Uzbekistan, Vietnam, Western Sahara, Zambia, Zimbabwe

CHRISTIAN AND MISSIONARY ALLIANCE IN CANADA, THE
30 Carrier Dr., Ste. 100
Toronto, ON M9W 5T7 CA
Phone: (416) 674-7878
Email: info@cmacan.org
Website: cmacan.org
Associations: Missio Nexus
A denominational sending agency of Evangelical tradition engaged in church planting, business as mission, theological education, evangelism, leadership development and tentmaking. (DPE)
Purpose: . . . a movement of churches transformed by Christ, transforming Canada and the world.
Income for International Min:
$9,200,000
Fully Supported CA Personnel Working Cross-Culturally
   More than 4 years: 175
   1–4 years: 9
   Non-residential: 199

Other Personnel
   Home staff: 28
Countries/Regions: Africa, Asia, Cambodia, Republic of Congo, Ecuador, France, Germany, Guatemala, Guinea, Hungary, Indonesia, Japan, Laos, Malaysia, Mexico, Middle East, Netherlands, Niger, Panama, Philippines, Poland, Russia, Senegal, Serbia, Spain, Taiwan (China), Thailand, Unspecified Country, Venezuela

CHRISTIAN AVIATION AND RADIO MISSION
PO Box 514
Ankeny, IA 50021 US
Phone: (515) 480-9099
Email: carmstan@aol.com
Website: carmus.org
A nondenominational specialized agency of Christian (Restoration Movement) tradition engaged in audio recording or distribution, aviation, radio or TV broadcasting, Internet discipleship or training, Internet evangelism, and video-film production or distribution.
Purpose: . . . to make available to ministers, evangelists and missionaries effective tools for carrying out the mission of the church to both members of Christ's body and to those previously unreached by the Gospel.
Year Founded in US: 1989
Income for International Min:
$19,689
Fully Supported US Personnel Working Cross-Culturally
   X-C workers in US: 1
   Non-residential: 1
Other Personnel
   Short-Term less than 1 year: 1
   Non-US in own/other country: 5
   Home staff: 3
Countries/Regions: Philippines

CHRISTIAN BLIND MISSION INTERNATIONAL – CANADA

3844 Stouffville Rd.
Stouffville, ON L4A 7Z9 CA
Phone: (9050 640-6464
Email: cbmi@cbmicanada.org
Website: cbmcanada.org

A nondenominational medical and rehabilitational agency engaged in the cure, prevention and care of disabling afflictions, including the training of nationals. (DPE)

Purpose: . . . to rescue and restore people trapped in poverty by disability.

Income for International Min:
$8,540,527

Other Personnel
Home staff: 31

CHRISTIAN BROADCASTING NETWORK INC., THE

977 Centerville Turnpike
Virginia Beach, VA 23463 US
Phone: (757) 226-7000
Email: cbnonline@cbn.com
Website: www1.cbn.com/home

An interdenominational sending agency of Evangelical tradition engaged in broadcasting, radio and/or TV and video/film production/distribution. (DPE)

Purpose: . . . to prepare the nations of the world for the coming of Jesus Christ and the establishment of His Kingdom on earth.

Income for International Min:
$128,854,919

Fully Supported US Personnel Working Cross-Culturally
More than 4 years: 6
1–4 years: 9
Non-residential: 7
Other Personnel
Non-US in own/other country: 853
Home staff: 1288

Countries/Regions: Brazil, Cambodia, China (People's Republic of), Costa Rica, Ghana, Hong Kong (China), India, Indonesia, Kazakhstan, Mexico, Nigeria, Philippines, Russia, Senegal, Singapore, South Africa, Thailand, Ukraine, United Kingdom

CHRISTIAN CHURCH (DISCIPLES OF CHRIST) – GLOBAL MINISTRIES

PO Box 1986
Indianapolis, IN 46206 US
Phone: (317) 709-8164
Email: dom@disciples.org
Website: globalministries.org

A denominational sending agency of Christian (Restoration Movement) and Congregational tradition engaged in support of national churches, development, Christian education, theological education, leadership development and partnership development. Working in partnership with United Church of Christ Global Ministries. Statistics include the United Church of Christ Global Ministries. (DPE)

Purpose: . . . committed to a ministry of critical presence where we meet God's people and creation at the point of deepest need: spiritually, physically, emotionally, and/or economically.

Income for International Min:
$3,760,519

Fully Supported US Personnel Working Cross-Culturally
1–4 years: 49
Other Personnel
Short-Term less than 1 year: 12
Home staff: 43

Countries/Regions: Angola, Botswana, Chile, China (People's Republic of), Colombia, East Timor, Egypt, Guadeloupe, Guatemala, Haiti, Hong Kong (China), Hungary, India, Indonesia, Japan, Kenya,

Laos, Lesotho, Mexico, Palestine, Poland, South Africa, Thailand, Turkey, Venezuela, Zimbabwe

CHRISTIAN CHURCHES / CHURCHES OF CHRIST

4001 Airport FWY, Ste. 550
Bedford, TX 76021 US

A body of autonomous congregations and agencies of Christian (Restoration Movement) tradition (using instrumental music in worship) which sends and supports missionaries directly from local congregations. Data provided by Missions Resource Network (all information based upon best estimates for an independent brotherhood of churches). No central office. (DPE)

Income for International Min:
$52,000,000

Fully Supported US Personnel Working Cross-Culturally
More than 4 years: 915
1–4 years: 100
Non-residential: 50

Other Personnel
Short-Term less than 1 year: 2000
Non-US in own/other country: 422

Countries/Regions: Africa, Argentina, Asia, Australia, Austria, Bahamas, Bangladesh, Barbados, Belgium, Bosnia and Herzegovina, Brazil, Cayman Islands, Chile, Côte d'Ivoire, Czech Republic, Dominica, Dominican Republic, Ecuador, Equatorial Guinea, Ethiopia, France, Germany, Ghana, Grenada, Guatemala, Guinea, Guyana, Haiti, Honduras, Hong Kong (China), India, Indonesia, Ireland (Republic of), Israel, Italy, Jamaica, Japan, Kenya, South Korea, Kosovo, Liberia, Mali, Mexico, Mozambique, Myanmar (Burma), New Zealand, Nigeria, Pakistan, Panama, Papua New Guinea, Philippines, Poland, Portugal, Puerto Rico, Russia, Singapore, South Africa, Spain, Taiwan (China),

Tanzania, Thailand, Ukraine, United Kingdom, Unspecified Country, Venezuela, Zimbabwe

CHRISTIAN CULTURAL DEVELOPMENT FOUNDATION

417 NE Third Ave
Fort Lauderdale, FL 33301 US
Phone: (954)828-1505
Email: robin@christiancultural.com
Website: christiancultural.com

An interdenominational service agency of Ecumenical and Evangelical tradition engaged in development, evangelism, prostitution ministry, justice, leadership development and support of national workers. (DPE)

Purpose: . . . to provide creative alternatives to prostitutes and street children in the Philippines who want to change their lifestyles and follow Jesus Christ.

Year Founded in US: 2002
Income for International Min:
$14,408

Fully Supported US Personnel Working Cross-Culturally
More than 4 years: 2
Non-residential: 1

Other Personnel
Tentmakers/BAM: 2
Non-US in own/other country: 6
Home staff: 1

Countries/Regions: Philippines

CHRISTIAN DENTAL SOCIETY

PO Box 296
Sumner, IA 50674 US
Phone: (563) 578-8887
Email: cdssent@netins.net
Website: christiandental.org

A nondenominational specialized agency of Christian tradition engaged in dental mission work. (FPC-PE)

Purpose: . . . to aspire to share the Good News of Jesus Christ, while encouraging and serving others at home and abroad.
Year Founded in US: 1965
Other Personnel
   Home staff: 1

CHRISTIAN DISCIPLESHIP INTERNATIONAL
Formerly: Rogma International, Inc.
PO Box 2008
Easley, SC 29641 US
Phone: (864) 855-2887
Email: jlittle@cdimin.org
Website: christiandiscipleshipintl.org
Associations: FOM

A nondenominational service agency of Baptist and Evangelical tradition engaged in Bible teaching, church planting (establishing), discipleship, and theological education.
Purpose: . . . to provide biblical resources to believers as they pursue the fulfillment of the Great Commission (Matt. 28:19-20).
Year Founded in US: 1985
Income for International Min: $24,000
Fully Supported US Personnel Working Cross-Culturally
   X-C workers in US: 5
Other Personnel
   Short-Term less than 1 year: 2
   Non-US in own/other country: 28
   Home staff: 2
Countries/Regions: Bolivia, Ghana, Haiti, India, Kenya, Liberia, Mexico, Middle East, Myanmar (Burma), Nepal, Philippines, Rwanda, Sierra Leone, Tanzania

CHRISTIAN EMERGENCY RELIEF TEAMS (CERT) INTERNATIONAL
Formerly: Children's Emergency Relief Teams International
PO Box 763
Crossville, TN 38557 US
Phone: (931) 707-9328
Email: michele@certinternational.org
Website: certinternational.org

A nondenominational service agency of Baptist tradition engaged in Bible distribution, personal or small group evangelism, medical ministry, including dental or public health, recruiting or mobilizing for mission, relief & aid, medical ministry, and STM.
Purpose: . . . to alleviate human suffering with medical/dental services in remote locations and provide relief in emergency or needy situations with the love of Christ.
Year Founded in US: 1974
Income for International Min: $25,562,400
Fully Supported US Personnel Working Cross-Culturally
   Non-residential: 93
Other Personnel
   Short-Term less than 1 year: 93
   Non-US in own/other country: 33
   Home staff: 5
Countries/Regions: Haiti, Jamaica, Mexico, Peru, Romania

CHRISTIAN FELLOWSHIP UNION INC.
PO Box 909
McAllen, TX 78505 US
Phone: (958) 686-5886
Email: cfunion@sbcglobal.net
Website: cfunion.org

An interdenominational support agency of Evangelical and Independent tradition engaged in leadership development, church planting, theological education, support of national churches, missionary training and discipleship. (DPE)

Purpose: . . . to proclaim Jesus Christ, make disciples, establish churches, and equip believers in Mexico and South Texas for worldwide ministry.

Income for International Min: $22,562

Fully Supported US Personnel Working Cross-Culturally
More than 4 years: 4
Non-residential: 2

Other Personnel
Tentmakers/BAM: 2
Home staff: 1

Countries/Regions: Mexico, Spain

CHRISTIAN FLIGHTS INTERNATIONAL

309 S Bragg St.
Perryville, KY 40468 US
Phone: (859) 262-9200
Email: scottmandl@aol.com
Website: christianflights.org/cgi/wp

A nondenominational sending agency of Ecumenical tradition engaged in Christian education, agricultural programs, development, medical work, short-term programs and supplying equipment. (DPE)

Purpose: . . . to further the Kingdom of God by providing resources and encouraging Haitians to facilitate wellness, community development, and excellence in education.

Year Founded in US: 1983
Income for International Min: $298,000

Fully Supported US Personnel Working Cross-Culturally
More than 4 years: 1
1–4 years: 1

Other Personnel
Short-Term less than 1 year: 70
Non-US in own/other country: 100
Home staff: 2

Countries/Regions: Haiti

CHRISTIAN LAYMEN'S MISSIONARY EVANGELISM ASSOCIATION

826 Ford St
Prosser, WA 99350 US
Phone: (509) 241-0530
Email: taylor.larry77@gmail.com
Website: clmea.com

An interdenominational support agency of Charismatic tradition engaged in radio or TV broadcasting, mass evangelism, and national worker support. (FPC-PE)

Purpose: . . . to raise up laymen for world evangelism, engaging in evangelism, broadcasting and support of national workers.

Year Founded in US: 1977

Other Personnel
Home staff: 1

CHRISTIAN LITERACY ASSOCIATES

541 Perry Highway
Pittsburgh, PA 15229 US
Phone: (412) 364-3777
Email: clapress@aol.com
Website: christianliteracy.org

An interdenominational specialized agency of Evangelical tradition engaged in children's ministry, personal or small group evangelism, literacy, services for mission organizations, and TESOL or TEFL. (FPC-PE)

Purpose: . . . to provide the key to eliminate illiteracy, build relationships, and share the Good News using The Christian Literacy Series.

Year Founded in US: 1975

Fully Supported US Personnel Working Cross-Culturally
X-C workers in US: 4

Other Personnel
Home staff: 4

CHRISTIAN MEDICAL & DENTAL ASSOCIATIONS

PO Box 7500
Bristol, TN 37621 US
Phone: (423) 844-1000
Email: main@cmda.org
Website: cmda.org

An interdenominational specialized agency of Evangelical tradition engaged in discipleship, church, school or general Christian education, mass evangelism, leadership development, medical ministry, including dental or public health, and member care.

Purpose: . . . to motivate, educate and equip Christian physicians, dentists and others serving through health care to glorify God by living out the character of Christ in their homes, practices, communities, and around the world.

Year Founded in US: 1931
Fully Supported US Personnel Working Cross-Culturally
   More than 4 years: 9
Other Personnel
   Home staff: 76
Countries/Regions: Central America, Central Asia, East Asia, Middle East, North Africa, South America, South Asia, Southeast Asia, Sub-Saharan Africa

CHRISTIAN MINISTRIES INTERNATIONAL (CMI)

2615 Serenity Circle N
Port St. Lucie, FL 34981 US
Phone: (772) 489-6721
Email: llhoodpsl@gmail.com
Website: cmimissions.com

An interdenominational sending agency of Charismatic tradition engaged in discipleship, leadership development, management consulting or training, and missionary & worker training.

Purpose: . . . to prepare national indigenous leaders of the local church to be empowered by New Testament principles of leadership to assist them in world evangelization and church planting in their generation.

Year Founded in US: 1985
Income for International Min:
   $250,000
Fully Supported US Personnel Working Cross-Culturally
   More than 4 years: 4
Other Personnel
   Short-Term less than 1 year: 127
   Non-US in own/other country: 28
   Home staff: 4
Countries/Regions: Brazil, Colombia, Global Ministry, Thailand

CHRISTIAN MISSION FOR THE DEAF

PO Box 1651
Aledo, TX 76008 US
Email: info@cmdeaf.org
Website: cmdeaf.org

A denominational support agency of Brethren tradition engaged in Christian education, camping programs and funds transmission. (DPE)

Purpose: . . . to organize, operate, maintain, promote and encourage Gospel and education work among the deaf of Africa.

Income for International Min:
   $114,047
Fully Supported US Personnel Working Cross-Culturally
   More than 4 years: 2
Other Personnel
   Short-Term less than 1 year: 1
   Home staff: 2
Countries/Regions: Democratic Republic of Congo

CHRISTIAN MISSIONS IN MANY LANDS INC.

PO Box 13
Spring Lake, NJ 07762 US
Phone: (732) 449-8880
Email: cmml@cmml.us
Website: cmml.us

A nondenominational service agency of Christian (Plymouth Brethren) tradition engaged in services for mission organizations. (FPC-PE)

Purpose: . . . to assist missionaries commended by (Plymouth Brethren) assemblies; to bridge the gap between the missionaries on the field and the assemblies at home, and provide necessary services.

Year Founded in US: 1921

Other Personnel
Home staff: 12

CHRISTIAN OUTREACH INTERNATIONAL

PO Box 2823
Vero Beach, FL 32966 US
Phone: (772) 778-0575
Email: groupscoi@coiusa.org
Website: coiusa.com

An interdenominational specialized agency of Evangelical tradition engaged in TEE or other extension education, mass evangelism, relief & aid, STM trip coordination, and sports ministry.

Purpose: . . . to specialize in short-term projects that empower believers to action, volunteerism, leadership, full-time service, and disciple making through local and international outreach.

Year Founded in US: 1984

Fully Supported US Personnel Working Cross-Culturally
More than 4 years: 5

Other Personnel
Home staff: 2

Countries/Regions: Belize, Dominican Republic, Haiti, Honduras, Ukraine

CHRISTIAN REFORMED WORLD MISSIONS

1700 28th Street SE
Grand Rapids, MI 49508 US
Phone: (616) 224-0700
Email: crwm@crcna.org
Website: crwm.org
Associations: Missio Nexus

A denominational sending agency of Reformed tradition engaged in church development, discipleship, church, school or general Christian education, personal or small group evangelism, and leadership development.

Purpose: . . . to glorify God by leading the CRC to respond obediently to our Lord's commission to witness to the good news of God's Kingdom and make disciples of all nations.

Year Founded in US: 1888
Income for International Min:
$12,000,000

Fully Supported US Personnel Working Cross-Culturally
More than 4 years: 71
1–4 years: 10

Other Personnel
Short-Term less than 1 year: 372
Tentmakers/BAM: 6
Home staff: 33

Countries/Regions: Bangladesh, Cambodia, Costa Rica, Dominican Republic, Eastern Europe and Eurasia, Egypt, Global Ministry, Guatemala, Guinea, Haiti, Honduras, Japan, Kenya, Lithuania, Mali, Mexico, Nepal, Nicaragua, Nigeria, Philippines, Romania, Russia, South Africa, Ukraine

CHRISTIAN RELIEF FUND, THE

P.O. Box 19670
Amarillo, TX 79114 US
Phone: (806) 352-5030
Email: crfinfo@christianrelieffund.org
Website: christianrelieffund.org
A sending agency of Christian (Restoration Movement) tradition engaged in childcare/orphanage programs, development, HIV/AIDS and relief and/or rehabilitation. (DPE)
Purpose: . . . to follow Christ's example by feeding the hungry, healing disease and heartbreak, fighting ignorance and poverty through education, and preaching the Gospel through word and deed.
Income for International Min:
$2,783,995
Other Personnel
Short-Term less than 1 year: 2
Tentmakers/BAM: 2
Non-US in own/other country: 42
Home staff: 10
Countries/Regions: Belarus, Dominican Republic, Ecuador, El Salvador, Ethiopia, Guatemala, Haiti, Honduras, India, Jamaica, Kenya, Liberia, Lithuania, Malawi, Mexico, Nicaragua, Niger, Nigeria, Romania, Uganda, Ukraine, Zambia, Zimbabwe

CHRISTIAN RESOURCES INTL.

PO Box 356
Fowlerville, MI 48836 US
Phone: (517) 223-3193
Email: admin@mycrimission.com
Website: mycrimission.com
A nondenominational specialized agency of Evangelical and Fundamentalist tradition engaged in Bible and literature distribution. (FPC-PE)
Purpose: . . . to evangelize the world by distributing free Christian literature to spiritually-needy people.

Year Founded in US: 1956
Other Personnel
Home staff: 5

CHRISTIAN VETERINARY MISSION

Formerly: CRISTA
19303 Fremont Ave N
Seattle, WA 98133 US
Phone: (206) 546-7311
Email: cvminfo@cvmusa.org
Website: cvmusa.org
Associations: Missio Nexus
An interdenominational specialized agency of Evangelical tradition engaged in agricultural assistance, church planting (establishing), community development, international student ministry, STM trip coordination, and veterinary.
Purpose: . . . to challenge, empower, and facilitate veterinary professionals to serve others by living out their Christian faith.
Year Founded in US: 1976
Income for International Min:
$352,000
Fully Supported US Personnel Working Cross-Culturally
More than 4 years: 22
1–4 years: 15
Other Personnel
Short-Term less than 1 year: 550
Tentmakers/BAM: 2
Non-US in own/other country: 2
Home staff: 8
Countries/Regions: Bolivia, Ethiopia, Ghana, Haiti, India, Italy, Kenya, Middle East, Mongolia, Nicaragua, South Africa, Southeast Asia, Tanzania, Thailand, Uganda, Zambia

CHRISTIANS IN ACTION MISSIONS INTERNATIONAL

1318 E Shaw Ave, Ste. 308
Fresno, CA 93710 US
Phone: (559) 370-4103
Email: stephanie@cinami.org
Website: cinami.org
Associations: Missio Nexus

An interdenominational sending agency of Evangelical tradition engaged in evangelism, church planting, support of national churches, mobilization for mission, short-term programs and missionary training. (DPE)

Purpose: . . . to proclaim Christ to the nations by preparing and sending missionaries, planting indigenous churches, empowering national leaders, and personal evangelism.

Year Founded in US: 1958
Income for International Min:
  $843,111
Fully Supported US Personnel Working Cross-Culturally
  More than 4 years: 13
Other Personnel
  Short-Term less than 1 year: 15
  Non-US in own/other country: 40
  Home staff: 5
Countries/Regions: Brazil, Colombia, Ecuador, Germany, Ghana, Guatemala, Guinea-Bissau, Honduras, India, Japan, South Korea, Macau (China), Mexico, Peru, Philippines, Sierra Leone, United Kingdom

CHURCH LEADERSHIP DEVELOPMENT INTERNATIONAL

8000 Research Forest Dr.
The Woodlands, TX 77382-1506 US
Phone: (281) 363-2534
Email: craig@cldi.org
Website: cldi.org

A nondenominational support agency of Evangelical tradition engaged in training pastors, church planting, leadership development and literature distribution. (DPE)

Purpose: . . . to equip pastors in Eurasia and India with training, encouragement and resources to strengthen and multiply their churches.

Other Personnel
  Non-US in own/other country: 7
  Home staff: 1
Countries/Regions: Central Asia, Georgia, India, Ukraine

CHURCH MINISTRIES INTL.

2001 W. Plano Pkwy, Ste. 3100
Plano, TX 75075-8632 US
Phone: (972) 941-4422
Email: cmioffice@churchministries.org

An interdenominational support agency of Evangelical tradition engaged in church construction or financing, church planting (establishing), partnership development, and services for mission organizations.

Purpose: . . . to reach nations for Christ by serving as a catalyst for urban churches toward strategic planning, partnerships, leadership training, and ministries that address the goal of evangelizing and discipling entire countries.

Year Founded in US: 1989
Fully Supported US Personnel Working Cross-Culturally
  More than 4 years: 1
Other Personnel
  Home staff: 4
Countries/Regions: Ecuador

CHURCH OF GOD (CLEVELAND TN) WORLD MISSIONS

PO Box 8016
Cleveland, TN 37320-8016 US
Phone: (423) 478-7190
Email: kcooper@cogwm.org
Website: cogwm.org

A denominational sending agency of Pentecostal tradition engaged in church planting, childcare/orphanage programs, church construction, TEE, theological education and evangelism. (DPE)

Purpose: . . . committed to obeying God by fulfilling Christ's Great Commission by proclaiming the Gospel through the power of the Holy Spirit to the unconverted everywhere and by discipling those Christ adds to His Kingdom.

Fully Supported US Personnel Working Cross-Culturally
　　More than 4 years: 159
　　1–4 years: 31
　　Non-residential: 55
Other Personnel
　　Short-Term less than 1 year: 98
　　Non-US in own/other country: 55
　　Home staff: 66
Countries/Regions: Albania, Aruba, Australia, Austria, Bahrain, Belgium, Brazil, Bulgaria, Caribbean, Chile, China (People's Republic of), Colombia, Croatia, Czech Republic, Ecuador, Europe, Fiji, France, Germany, Ghana, Greece, Guatemala, Haiti, Honduras, Indonesia, Ireland (Republic of), Italy, Kenya, Liberia, Malaysia, Mexico, Nicaragua, Nigeria, Pakistan, Panama, Paraguay, Peru, Philippines, Romania, Russia, Singapore, South Africa, South America, Spain, Ukraine, United Kingdom, Unspecified Country, Venezuela, Vietnam, Zambia

CHURCH OF GOD (HOLINESS) WORLD MISSION DEPT. INC.
PO Box 4711
Overland Park, KS 66204 US
Phone: (913) 432-0303
Email: worldmissions@cogh.net
Website: coghworldmissions.org

A denominational sending agency of Holiness and Wesleyan tradition engaged in church planting (establishing), church, school or general Christian education, personal or small group evangelism, medical ministry, including dental or public health, and Bible translation.

Purpose: . . . to promote God's kingdom through proclaiming the Gospel of Jesus Christ and providing opportunities to develop mission fields into self-propagating missionary forces.

Fully Supported US Personnel Working Cross-Culturally
　　1–4 years: 5
　　X-C workers in US: 2
Other Personnel
　　Short-Term less than 1 year: 7
　　Non-US in own/other country: 35
Countries/Regions: Cayman Islands, Ghana, Haiti, Papua New Guinea

CHURCH OF GOD MINISTRIES (ANDERSON) – GLOBAL STRATEGY
PO Box 2420
Anderson, IN 46018-2420 US
Phone: (765) 648-2140
Email: bedwards@chog.org
Website: chogglobal.org

A sending agency of Holiness and Wesleyan tradition engaged in leadership development, TEE, theological education, member care, support of national churches and missionary training. (DPE)(FPC16)

Purpose: . . . committed to world evangelism and discipleship, we will send missionaries, resource global ministry, and network through interdependent partnerships with the Church around the world.

Income for International Min:
　　$5,255,506

Fully Supported US Personnel Working Cross-Culturally
More than 4 years: 22
1–4 years: 20
X-C workers in US: 8
Non-residential: 11
Other Personnel
Short-Term less than 1 year: 1700
Tentmakers/BAM: 8
Non-US in own/other country: 5
Home staff: 8
Countries/Regions: Belize, Bolivia, Brazil, Costa Rica, Côte d'Ivoire, Eastern Europe and Eurasia, Ecuador, Germany, Haiti, Honduras, Japan, Kenya, Malawi, Middle East, Netherlands, New Zealand, Northern Mariana Islands, Paraguay, South America, Southeast Asia, Spain, Sri Lanka, Tanzania, Thailand, Uganda, United Kingdom, Vietnam, Western Europe

CHURCH OF GOD OF THE APOSTOLIC FAITH INC., THE
PO Box 244
Ramona, OK 74061 US
Phone: (918) 437-7652
Email: office@cogaf.org
Website: cogaf.org
A denominational sending agency of Pentecostal tradition engaged in Bible distribution, church construction or financing, church planting (establishing), theological education, mass evangelism, and literature distribution.
Purpose: . . . knowing Him . . . making Him known . . . that others may believe.
Year Founded in US: 1914
Fully Supported US Personnel Working Cross-Culturally
More than 4 years: 2
Other Personnel
Home staff: 2
Countries/Regions: Honduras, Mexico

CHURCH OF THE BRETHREN – GLOBAL MISSION PARTNERSHIPS
1451 Dundee Ave.
Elgin, IL 60120 US
Phone: (847) 742-5100
Email: mission@brethren.org
Website: brethren.org
A denominational sending agency of Brethren tradition engaged in peace and reconciliation, justice, support of national churches, Christian education, TEE and missionary training. (DPE)
Purpose: . . . to extend the church's witness around the world, leading out in God's mission, serving as a bridge between the local and the global, and creating opportunities for service and partnership.
Income for International Min:
$1,807,162
Fully Supported US Personnel Working Cross-Culturally
More than 4 years: 3
1–4 years: 36
Non-residential: 1
Other Personnel
Home staff: 7
Countries/Regions: Bosnia and Herzegovina, Brazil, Dominican Republic, El Salvador, France, Germany, Guatemala, Haiti, Honduras, Hungary, Ireland (Republic of), Japan, Mexico, Netherlands, Nicaragua, Nigeria, Serbia, Slovakia, Sudan, Switzerland, Vietnam

CHURCH OF THE NAZARENE INC.
Formerly: General Board Church of the Nazarene
17001 Prairie Star Pkwy
Lenexa, KS 66220 US
Phone: (913) 577-0500
Email: gm@nazarene.org
Website: nazarene.org
Associations: Accord Network, Missio Nexus

A denominational sending agency of Holiness and Wesleyan tradition engaged in church development, church planting (establishing), discipleship, theological education, mass evangelism, and leadership development.

Purpose: . . . to make Christlike disciples in the nations.

Year Founded in US: 1908

Fully Supported US Personnel Working Cross-Culturally
    More than 4 years: 215
    X-C workers in US: 24
    Non-residential: 599

Other Personnel
    Short-Term less than 1 year: 8786
    Tentmakers/BAM: 291
    Non-US in own/other country: 166
    Home staff: 196

Countries/Regions: Albania, Angola, Argentina, Armenia, Australia, Bangladesh, Barbados, Benin, Bolivia, Brazil, Bulgaria, Burkina Faso, Burundi, Cambodia, Cameroon, Canada, Cape Verde Islands, Central Asia, Chile, Colombia, Congo (Democratic Republic of), Costa Rica, Côte d'Ivoire, Croatia, Curaçao, Denmark, Dominica, Dominican Republic, East Asia, Ecuador, El Salvador, Ethiopia, France, Germany, Ghana, Guatemala, Guinea-Bissau, Guyana, Haiti, Honduras, Hungary, India, Indonesia, Ireland (Republic of), Israel, Italy, Japan, Jordan, Kenya, Kosovo, Lebanon, Madagascar, Malawi, Mali, Mexico, Mongolia, Morocco, Mozambique, Namibia, Netherlands, New Zealand, Panama, Papua New Guinea, Paraguay, Peru, Philippines, Poland, Portugal, Romania, Russia, Senegal, Singapore, South Africa, South Korea, Southeast Asia, Spain, Swaziland, Switzerland, Thailand, Togo, Tonga, Trinidad and Tobago, Uganda, Ukraine, United Kingdom, Vanuatu, Zambia

CHURCH PLANTING INTERNATIONAL

5186 Cressingham Drive
Fort Mill, SC 29707 US
Phone: (419) 353-7437
Email: info@churchplantinginternational. org
Website: churchplantinginternational.org

A nondenominational support agency of Evangelical and Reformed tradition engaged in Bible teaching, church planting (establishing), personal or small group evangelism, leadership development, relief & aid, and STM trip coordination. (FPC-PE)

Purpose: . . . to preach the Gospel, train leaders, and aid in the planting, strengthening, and multiplying of churches around the world.

Year Founded in US: 1986

Countries/Regions: Myanmar (Burma), Portugal, Uganda

CHURCH WORLD SERVICE

28606 Phillips St.
Elkhart, IN 46515 US
Phone: (800) 297-1516
Email: info@churchworldservice.org
Website: churchworldservice.org

A denominational service agency of Ecumenical tradition engaged in development, agricultural programs, HIV/AIDS, justice, literacy work and relief and/or rehabilitation. (DPE)

Purpose: . . . working with partners to build interfaith and intercultural coalitions to eradicate hunger and poverty and promote peace and justice around the world.

CHURCHES OF GOD – GENERAL CONFERENCE

700 E. Melrose Ave.
Findley, OH 45839 US
Phone: (419) 424-1961
Email: missions@cggc.org
Website: cggc.org
Associations: Missio Nexus

A denominational sending agency of Evangelical tradition engaged in support of national churches, church planting, Christian education, leadership development, medical work and support of national workers. (DPE)

Purpose: . . . to make Jesus Christ known to all people as Savior and Lord . . . to lead them into a personal relationship with God through Jesus Christ as Savior.

Year Founded in US: 1867
Income for International Min:
$980,394

Fully Supported US Personnel Working Cross-Culturally
More than 4 years: 8
Other Personnel
Short-Term less than 1 year: 5
Home staff: 6
Countries/Regions: Brazil, Haiti

CIS – CHRISTIAN INVOLVEMENT IN SERVICE

PO Box 768
St. Joseph, MI 49085 US
Phone: (269) 926-8819
Email: j_agens@yahoo.com

A nondenominational specialized agency of Baptist and Evangelical tradition engaged in Bible distribution, Bible teaching, church planting (establishing), leadership development, national worker support, and orphan ministry.

Purpose: . . . to stimulate in American churches an awareness of the necessity for prayer and financial support for the national missionaries who received theological education, know the language, culture and their people and are prepared to preach the gospel and establish new churches.

Year Founded in US: 2004
Income for International Min:
$56,500

Fully Supported US Personnel Working Cross-Culturally
Non-residential: 1
Other Personnel
Short-Term less than 1 year: 1
Non-US in own/other country: 21
Countries/Regions: Russia, Ukraine

CITYTEAM MINISTRIES – NEW GENERATIONS INTERNATIONAL

2304 Zanker Rd.
San Jose, CA 95131 US
Phone: (408) 232-5600
Email: mhunsicker@cityteam.org
Website: cityteam.org

A nondenominational support agency engaged in church planting, discipleship, partnership development, relief and/or rehabilitation and training. (DPE)

Purpose: . . . serving people in need, proclaiming the gospel, and establishing disciples among disadvantaged people of cities.

Fully Supported US Personnel Working Cross-Culturally
More than 4 years: 1
Non-residential: 3
Other Personnel
Non-US in own/other country: 11
Countries/Regions: Côte d'Ivoire, Ethiopia, Indonesia, Sierra Leone, South Africa

CLC MINISTRIES INTERNATIONAL

701 Pennsylvania Ave., PO Box 1449
Fort Washington, PA 19034 US
Phone: (215) 542-1242
Email: missions@clcusa.org
Website: clcusa.org
Associations: Missio Nexus

A nondenominational specialized agency of Evangelical tradition engaged in Bible distribution, business as mission, literacy, literature distribution, literature production, and purchasing or supply services.

Purpose: . . . to make Evangelical Christian literature available to all nations, so that people may come to faith and maturity in the Lord Jesus Christ.

Year Founded in US: 1947
Income for International Min:
 $169,335

Fully Supported US Personnel Working Cross-Culturally
 More than 4 years: 6

Other Personnel
 Short-Term less than 1 year: 2
 Home staff: 18

Countries/Regions: Central Asia, Thailand, Western Europe

CMF INTERNATIONAL

PO Box 501020, 5525 E 82nd St
Indianapolis, IN 46250 US
Phone: (317) 578-2700
Email: missions@cmfi.org
Website: cmfi.org
Associations: Missio Nexus

A nondenominational sending agency of Christian (Restoration Movement) tradition engaged in CPM, community development, DMM, international student ministry, leadership development, and urban poor.

Purpose: . . . to create dynamic Christ-centered communities that transform the world.

Year Founded in US: 1949

Income for International Min:
 $17,561,774

Fully Supported US Personnel Working Cross-Culturally
 More than 4 years: 101
 1–4 years: 121
 Non-residential: 3

Other Personnel
 Short-Term less than 1 year: 26
 Non-US in own/other country: 220
 Home staff: 36

Countries/Regions: Australia, Brazil, Burkina Faso, Chile, Côte d'Ivoire, East Asia, Ecuador, Ethiopia, Germany, Global Ministry, India, Indonesia, Kenya, Mexico, Peru, Southeast Asia, Spain, Sri Lanka, Tanzania, Thailand, Ukraine, United Kingdom, Uruguay

CMTS MINISTRIES

1119 N. Boundary Rd
Bernville, PA 19506 US
Phone: (610) 488-6975
Email: cmtsmin@aol.com
Website: cmtsministries.com

A nondenominational service agency of Evangelical tradition engaged in technical assistance, discipleship, furloughed missionary support, purchasing services, services for other agencies and supplying equipment. (DPE)

Purpose: . . . to provide technical assistance, materials, and equipment for use by Christian organizations and Bible-believing missionaries at home and abroad.

Year Founded in US: 1983
Income for International Min:
 $106,626

Fully Supported US Personnel Working Cross-Culturally
 Non-residential: 1

Other Personnel
   Short-Term less than 1 year: 65
   Non-US in own/other country: 2
Countries/Regions: Mexico

COLORADO HAITI PROJECT INC.
908 Main St, Ste. 245
Louisville, CO 80027 US
Phone: (303) 938-5021
Email: office@coloradohaitiproject.org
Website: coloradohaitiproject.org
A denominational heritage support
agency of Episcopal or Anglican
tradition engaged in church, school or
general Christian education, leadership
development, medical ministry, including
dental or public health, and partnership
development.
Purpose: . . . to share Christ's love
through partnership with our brothers
and sisters in Haiti to improve the human
condition.
Year Founded in US: 1989
Income for International Min:
   $472,000
Other Personnel
   Short-Term less than 1 year: 12
   Non-US in own/other country: 23
   Home staff: 3
Countries/Regions: Haiti, Argentina,
Bolivia, China (People's Republic of),
Honduras, Hungary, Japan, Kenya, Mexico,
Nigeria, Papua New Guinea, Paraguay,
Peru, South Sudan, Uganda, Ukraine

COMCARE INTERNATIONAL
3027 Split Rock Circle
Bulverde, TX 78163 US
Phone: (210) 317-9998
Email: cci@comcareinternational.org
Website: comcareinternational.org
An interdenominational specialized agency
of Evangelical tradition engaged in medical
supplies and production of hearing aids.
(FPC-PE)

Purpose: . . . to engage in producing and
distributing solar powered hearing aids for
unreached people.
Year Founded in US: 1989
Income for International Min:
   $24,000
*Fully Supported US Personnel Working
Cross-Culturally*
   More than 4 years: 2
Other Personnel
   Non-US in own/other country: 2
Countries/Regions: Mexico

COMHINA
P.O. Box 3342
Reston, VA 20195 US
Phone: (407) 992-7726
Email: comhinanacional@comhina.org
Website: comhina.org
An interdenominational support agency of
Christian (Restoration Movement) tradition
engaged in mobilization for mission,
children at risk, missionary education,
leadership development and partnership
development. (DPE)
Purpose: . . . to glorify God by fulfilling the
mandate that our Lord Jesus Christ gave us in
the Great Commission, collaborating with the
Hispanic local churches in the United States
and Canada in its missionary action.
Income for International Min:
   $1,672,125
*Fully Supported US Personnel Working
Cross-Culturally*
   Non-residential: 4
Other Personnel
   Short-Term less than 1 year: 2
   Home staff: 4

COMMA
400 S. Main Pl.
Carol Stream, IL 60188 US
Phone: (630) 306-7956
Email: roy.oksnevad@gmail.com
Website: commanetwork.com
A nondenominational network of
Evangelical tradition engaged in
association of missions, personal or small
group evangelism, missionary & worker
training, and networking, partnership, or
coordination.
Purpose: . . . to network believers
together to equip and teach so as to reach
and disciple Muslims in North America.
Year Founded in US: 1999

COMMISSION TO EVERY NATION
PO Box 291307
Kerrville, TX 78028 US
Phone: (830) 896-8326
Email: usa@cten.org
Website: cten.org
An interdenominational sending agency of
Evangelical tradition engaged in childcare
or orphanage, church development,
community development, discipleship,
church, school or general Christian
education, and personal or small group
evangelism.
Purpose: . . . to help ordinary people
partner with God to accomplish the
extraordinary.
Year Founded in US: 1994
*Fully Supported US Personnel Working
Cross-Culturally*
    More than 4 years: 173
    1–4 years: 65
Other Personnel
    Non-US in own/other country: 240
    Home staff: 27
Countries/Regions: Albania, Asia,
Belize, Bolivia, Brazil, Burkina Faso,
Cambodia, Cameroon, Chile, Costa
Rica, Cyprus, Ecuador, El Salvador,
Germany, Guatemala, Honduras, India,
Ireland (Republic of), Kenya, Liberia,
Mexico, Mozambique, Nicaragua, Peru,
Philippines, Poland, Romania, Rwanda,
South Africa, Spain, Suriname, Sweden,
Tanzania, Thailand, Trinidad and Tobago,
Uganda, Ukraine, Zambia

COMMISSION TO EVERY NATION-CANADA
PO Box 22017, 11500 Tecumseh Rd E
Windsor, ON N8N 5G6 CA
Phone: (888) 863-4810
Email: canada@cten.org
Website: cten.org
A nondenominational sending agency
of Evangelical and Independent tradition
engaged in childcare or orphanage,
church planting (establishing), community
development, church, school or general
Christian education, medical ministry,
evangelism, and youth ministry.
Purpose: . . . to help ordinary people
partner with God to achieve the
extraordinary.
Year Founded in CA: 2005
Income for International Min:
    $1,801,537
*Fully Supported CA Personnel Working
Cross-Culturally*
    More than 4 years: 35
    1–4 years: 7
Other Personnel
    Non-CA in own/other country: 5
    Home staff: 3
Countries/Regions: Bolivia, Burkina
Faso, Costa Rica, Ecuador, Global Ministry,
Guatemala, Honduras, Madagascar,
Mexico, Philippines, Rwanda, Tanzania,
United States of America

COMMUNITAS INTERNATIONAL

Formerly: Christian Associates International
2221 E. Arapahoe Rd, #3338
Denver, CO 80161 US
Phone: (888) 242-5930
Email: usoffice@christianassociates.org
Website: gocommunitas.org/
Associations: Missio Nexus

A nondenominational sending agency of Evangelical and Independent tradition engaged in church planting (establishing), CPM, and personal or small group evangelism.

Purpose: . . . to establish churches who follow Jesus in transforming their world.

Year Founded in US: 1968

Fully Supported US Personnel Working Cross-Culturally
    More than 4 years: 60
    1–4 years: 1
    Non-residential: 13
Other Personnel
    Short-Term less than 1 year: 1
    Tentmakers/BAM: 50
    Non-US in own/other country: 34
    Home staff: 13
Countries/Regions: Caribbean, Central America, Eastern Europe and Eurasia, Global Ministry, South America, United States of America, Western Europe

COMPASIO

PO Box 77015
Ottawa, ON K1S 5N2 CA
Phone: (613) 686-5535
Email: info@compasio.org
Website: compasio.org

A service agency of Evangelical tradition engaged in counseling, addressing human trafficking, justice or peace issues, and relief & aid.

Purpose: . . . to engage in trafficking/slavery issues, children at risk, development, justice, psychological counseling, and relief and/or rehabilitation.

Year Founded in CA: 2006

Other Personnel
    Non-CA in own/other country: 40
    Home staff: 3
Countries/Regions: Australia, New Zealand, Norway, Thailand, United Kingdom

COMPASSION CANADA

985 Adelaide St. S
London, ON N6E 4A3 CA
Phone: (519) 668-0224
Email: info@compassion.ca
Website: compassion.ca

A service agency of Evangelical tradition engaged in holistic child development, children at risk, discipleship, leadership development and partnership development. (DPE)

Purpose: . . . exists as an advocate for children to release them from their spiritual, economic, social and physical poverty and enable them to become fulfilled, Christian adults, in response to the Great Commission.

Other Personnel
    Home staff: 60

COMPASSION INTERNATIONAL INC.

12290 Voyager Pkwy.
Colorado Springs, CO 80921 US
Phone: (719) 487-7000
Email: ciinfo@us.ci.org
Website: compassion.com

A support agency engaged in children's programs, development, Christian education, evangelism, leadership development and medical work. (DPE)

Purpose: . . . an advocate for children, to release them from their spiritual, economic, social, and physical poverty and enable them to become responsible and fulfilled Christian adults.

Year Founded in US: 1956
Income for International Min:
$217,278,070
Fully Supported US Personnel Working Cross-Culturally
More than 4 years: 6
1–4 years: 5
Other Personnel
Non-US in own/other country: 1531
Home staff: 762
Countries/Regions: Asia, Bangladesh, Bolivia, Brazil, Burkina Faso, Colombia, Dominican Republic, Ecuador, El Salvador, Ethiopia, Ghana, Guatemala, Haiti, Honduras, India, Indonesia, Kenya, Mexico, Nicaragua, Peru, Philippines, Rwanda, Tanzania, Thailand, Togo, Uganda

CONGREGATIONAL METHODIST MISSIONS
PO Box 9
Florence, MS 39073 US
Phone: (601) 845-8787
Email: info@cmcmissions.com
Website: cmmission.com
A denominational sending agency of Methodist and Wesleyan tradition engaged in church planting (establishing), mass evangelism, leadership development, partnership development, and STM trip coordination.
Purpose: . . . to promote evangelism of non-Christians, equipping of believers, empowering of leaders, and the planting of churches both within the U.S. and abroad.
Year Founded in US: 1852
Fully Supported US Personnel Working Cross-Culturally
More than 4 years: 4

Other Personnel
Home staff: 25
Countries/Regions: Belize, Haiti, Mexico

CONSERVATIVE CONGREGATIONAL CHRISTIAN CONFERENCE-MISSIONS COMMITTEE
8941 33rd St. North
Lake Elmo, MN 55042 US
Phone: (651) 739-1474
Email: missions@cccusa.com
Website: cccusa.org
A denominational specialized agency of Congregational and Evangelical tradition engaged in national worker support and STM trip coordination.
Purpose: . . . to encourage and stimulate missionary interests in the local churches of the Conference.
Year Founded in US: 1948
Fully Supported US Personnel Working Cross-Culturally
More than 4 years: 4
Other Personnel
Home staff: 8
Countries/Regions: Federated States of Micronesia

CONVERGE
11002 Lake Hart Dr, Mail Code 200
Orlando, FL 32832 US
Phone: (800) 323-4215
Email: missions@converge.org
Website: converge.org
Associations: Missio Nexus
A denominational sending agency of Baptist tradition engaged in church development, church planting (establishing), discipleship, theological education, and medical ministry, including dental or public health.

Purpose: . . . to develop an expanding network of leaders and leadership teams serving together to mobilize and multiply vital, reproducing churches.

Year Founded in US: 1945

Fully Supported US Personnel Working Cross-Culturally
   More than 4 years: 101
Other Personnel
   Home staff: 7

COOPERATIVE BAPTIST FELLOWSHIP – GLOBAL MISSIONS

160 Clairemont Avenue, Suite 500
Decatur, GA 30030 US
Phone: (800) 352-8741
Email: rclark@cbf.net
Website: cbf.net/missions

A sending agency of Baptist tradition engaged in development, agricultural programs, justice, leadership development, support of national churches and tentmaking. (DPE)

Purpose: . . . to serve Christians and churches as they discover and fulfill their God-given mission.

Year Founded in US: 1991

Fully Supported US Personnel Working Cross-Culturally
   More than 4 years: 54
   1–4 years: 21
   Non-residential: 66
Other Personnel
   Short-Term less than 1 year: 275
   Tentmakers/BAM: 37
   Home staff: 63

Countries/Regions: Africa, Asia, Belgium, Belize, China (People's Republic of), Greece, Haiti, Hungary, India, Kenya, Macedonia, Mexico, Middle East, Netherlands, Peru, Slovakia, South Africa, Spain, Uganda, Ukraine

CRESCENT PROJECT

PO Box 50986
Indianapolis, IN 46250 US
Phone: (888) 446-5457
Email: info@crescentproject.org
Website: crescentproject.org

An interdenominational specialized agency of Evangelical tradition engaged in mass evangelism, literature distribution, literature production, and missionary & worker training. (FPC-PE)

Purpose: . . . to inspire, equip, and serve the Church to reach Muslims with the Gospel of Christ for the Glory of God.

Year Founded in US: 1994

Income for International Min:
   $200,000

CRISIS CONSULTING INTERNATIONAL

9452 Telephone Rd, #223
Ventura, CA 93004 US
Phone: (805) 642-2549
Email: info@cricon.org
Website: cricon.org
Associations: Missio Nexus

A nondenominational service agency of Independent tradition engaged in leadership development, management consulting or training, missionary & worker training, services for mission organizations, and crisis management & security. (FPC-PE)

Purpose: . . . to assist the global Christian community in fulfilling the Great Commission by providing security, training, and crisis management services.

Year Founded in US: 1986

Other Personnel
   Short-Term less than 1 year: 14
   Home staff: 2

CRM

1240 N. Lakeview, Ste. 120
Anaheim, CA 92807 US
Phone: (714) 779-0370
Email: kevin.brown@crmleaders.org
Website: crmleaders.org
Associations: Missio Nexus

A nondenominational sending agency of
Evangelical tradition engaged in business
as mission, church planting (establishing),
CPM, DMM, discipleship, and leadership
development.

Purpose: . . . to create movements of
committed followers of Jesus.

Income for International Min:
$8,685,000

*Fully Supported US Personnel Working
Cross-Culturally*
More than 4 years: 76
1–4 years: 9
X-C workers in US: 25
Non-residential: 4

Other Personnel
Short-Term less than 1 year: 4
Non-US in own/other country: 167
Home staff: 26

Countries/Regions: Australia, Burundi,
Cambodia, Canada, Central Asia,
Colombia, Croatia, East Asia, Eastern
Europe and Eurasia, Germany, Guatemala,
Honduras, Hungary, Italy, Japan, Kenya,
Middle East, Moldova, Nigeria, Poland,
Romania, Serbia, Singapore, South Africa,
South Asia, South Korea, Spain, United
Kingdom, Venezuela

CROSS-CULTURAL MINISTRIES – CHURCHES OF GOD GENERAL CONFERENCE

Formerly: Church of God in North
America
PO Box 926, 700 E Melrose Ave.
Findlay, OH 45849 US
Phone: (724) 419-1691
Email: ccm@cggc.org
Website: cggc.org
Associations: Missio Nexus

A denominational sending agency of
Wesleyan tradition engaged in Bible
teaching, church planting (establishing),
community development, church, school
or general Christian education, personal
or small group evangelism, and medical
ministry, including dental or public health.

Purpose: . . . to glorify God by
mobilizing churches to have a biblical
vision of reproducing Christ's followers in
other cultures.

Income for International Min:
$1,000,000

*Fully Supported US Personnel Working
Cross-Culturally*
More than 4 years: 3
X-C workers in US: 4

Other Personnel
Short-Term less than 1 year: 100
Tentmakers/BAM: 1
Non-US in own/other country: 7
Home staff: 4

CROSSOVER COMMUNICATIONS INTERNATIONAL

7520 Monticello Rd
Columbia, SC 29203 US
Phone: (803) 691-0688
Email: info@innovativeaccess.org
Website: crossoverusa.org
Associations: Missio Nexus

An interdenominational sending agency of Evangelical tradition engaged in church planting (establishing) and CPM.

Purpose: . . . to be a catalyst to plant multiplying churches among the unreached peoples of the world.

Year Founded in US: 1987
Income for International Min:
$1,700,000

Fully Supported US Personnel Working Cross-Culturally
More than 4 years: 6
1–4 years: 9

Other Personnel
Short-Term less than 1 year: 39
Non-US in own/other country: 21
Home staff: 14

Countries/Regions: Australia, China (People's Republic of), Cyprus, Germany, Indonesia, Iran, Jordan, Moldova, New Zealand, Spain, Turkey

CROSSROADS CHRISTIAN COMMUNICATIONS INC. (ERDF)

PO Box 5100
Burlington, ON L7R 4M2 CA
Phone: (905) 332-6400
Email: knuttall@crossroads.ca
Website: crossroads.ca

A nondenominational service agency of Evangelical and Pentecostal tradition engaged in broadcasting, agricultural programs, development, funds transmission, relief and/or rehabilitation and supplying equipment. (DPE)

Income for International Min:
$2,680,897

Other Personnel
Home staff: 155

Countries/Regions: Haiti, India, Kenya, Uganda, Ukraine, Zambia

CROSSWAY INTERNATIONAL

14 Fabra Oaks Road
Boerne, TX 78006-7901 US
Phone: (930) 249-2322
Email: dean@gocrossway.org
Website: gocrossway.org

An interdenominational sending agency of Evangelical tradition engaged in Bible teaching, TEE or other extension education, mass evangelism, personal or small group evangelism, national worker support, and relief & aid.

Purpose: . . . to present a clear presentation of the gospel of grace.

Year Founded in US: 1997

Fully Supported US Personnel Working Cross-Culturally
Non-residential: 13

Other Personnel
Non-US in own/other country: 27

Countries/Regions: Ethiopia, Kenya, Liberia, Nicaragua

CROSSWORLD

10,000 N. Oak Trafficway
Kansas City, MO 64155 US
Phone: (816) 479-7300
Email: info@crossworld.org
Website: crossworld.org
Associations: Missio Nexus

A nondenominational sending agency of Baptist and Independent tradition engaged in business as mission, children's ministry, church planting (establishing), discipleship, theological education, and leadership development.

Purpose: . . . to help disciple-makers from all professions bring God's love to life in the world's least-reached marketplaces.

Year Founded in US: 1941
Income for International Min:
$12,847,854

Fully Supported US Personnel Working Cross-Culturally
  More than 4 years: 210
  1–4 years: 8
  X-C workers in US: 26
  Non-residential: 2
Other Personnel
  Short-Term less than 1 year: 98
  Tentmakers/BAM: 3
  Non-US in own/other country: 8
  Home staff: 43
Countries/Regions: Brazil, Cambodia, Canada, Central Asia, Democratic Republic of Congo, Dominican Republic, East Asia, Eastern Europe and Eurasia, Ecuador, France, Germany, Global Ministry, Guyana, Haiti, Ireland (Republic of), Italy, Kenya, Mexico, Middle East, Oceania, Philippines, Romania, Senegal, Slovakia, South Africa, Southeast Asia, Spain, Sweden, Switzerland, Thailand, Ukraine, United Kingdom

CROSSWORLD CANADA
1020 Matheson Blvd E #11
Mississauga, ON L4W 4J9 CA
Phone: (905) 238-0904
Email: canada@crossworld.org
Website: crossworld.ca
Associations: Missio Nexus

A nondenominational sending agency of Baptist and Independent tradition engaged in business as mission, children's ministry, church planting (establishing), discipleship, theological education, and leadership development.

Purpose: . . . to help disciple-makers from all professions bring God's love to life in the world's least-reached marketplaces.

Year Founded in CA: 1931
Income for International Min:
  $1,619,807
Fully Supported CA Personnel Working Cross-Culturally
  More than 4 years: 21
  X-C workers in CA: 9

Other Personnel
  Short-Term less than 1 year: 7
  Non-CA in own/other country: 6
  Home staff: 6
Countries/Regions: Brazil, Cambodia, East Asia, Eastern Europe and Eurasia, Haiti, Ireland (Republic of), Italy, Middle East, Senegal, Togo, Ukraine

CSI MINISTRIES INC.
Formerly: Christian Service International
PO Box 841, 1714 W Royale Dr.
Muncie, IN 47308 US
Phone: (800) 286-5773
Email: hensley@csiministries.org
Website: csiministries.org

A nondenominational service agency of Evangelical tradition engaged in STM trip coordination.

Purpose: . . . to bring people closer to Christ through short-term missions.

Year Founded in US: 1967
Income for International Min:
  $645,000
Fully Supported US Personnel Working Cross-Culturally
  1–4 years: 1
Other Personnel
  Short-Term less than 1 year: 414
  Home staff: 5
Countries/Regions: Jamaica

CSM CANADA INTL. (CHRISTIAN SALVAGE MISSION)
120 Lansing Dr., Unit #3
Hamilton, ON L8W 3A1 CA
Phone: (905) 574-3334
Email: info@csmcanada.org

A nondenominational support agency of Evangelical and Fundamentalist tradition engaged in Bible distribution and services for mission organisations. (FPC-PE)

Purpose: . . . to supply Bibles and evangelical materials to Christian pastors and students around the world.

Year Founded in CA: 1994

Other Personnel
 Home staff: 1

CTI MUSIC MINISTRIES (CARPENTER'S TOOLS INTERNATIONAL)
PO Box 100
Willmar, MN 56201-0100 US
Phone: (329) 235-0155
Email: info@ctimusic.org
Website: ctimusic.org

An interdenominational support agency of Evangelical tradition engaged in evangelism, short-term programs, music performance and youth programs. An associate ministry of Youth for Christ International. (DPE)

Purpose: . . . to recruit, train and send music teams to work with established Christian ministries worldwide to reach young people with the Gospel.

Year Founded in US: 1989
Income for International Min:
 $230,000

Other Personnel
 Short-Term less than 1 year: 45
 Home staff: 7

CULTURELINK
PO Box 6623
Marietta, GA 30065 US
Phone: (404) 513-0668
Email: info@culturelinkinc.org
Website: culturelinkinc.org

A nondenominational service agency of Independent tradition engaged in discipleship, leadership development, management consulting or training, missionary & worker training, services for mission organizations, and STM trip coordination.

Purpose: . . . to make disciples of those who will make disciples of all nations.

Year Founded in US: 2010

Other Personnel
 Short-Term less than 1 year: 28
 Home staff: 3

CUMBERLAND PRESBYTERIAN CHURCH BOARD OF MISSIONS
8207 Traditional Place
Cordova, TN 38016 US
Phone: (901) 276-9988
Email: watkr@mac.com
Website: cpcmc.org/mmt/global

A denominational sending agency of Presbyterian tradition engaged in church planting, missions information service, leadership development, partnership development, relief and/or rehabilitation and short-term programs. (DPE)

Year Founded in US: 1964
Income for International Min:
 $437,720

Other Personnel
 Short-Term less than 1 year: 30
 Tentmakers/BAM: 4
 Home staff: 11

CUP OF COLD WATER MINISTRIES
PO Box 318
Newark, IL 60541 US
Phone: (815) 228-1442
Email: director@ccwm.org
Website: ccwm.org

A nondenominational service agency of Evangelical tradition engaged in childcare or orphanage, church planting (establishing), church, school or general Christian education, medical ministry, including dental or public health, relief & aid, and STM trip coordination.

Purpose: . . . to glorify our Lord Jesus Christ by faithful proclamation of His Word and by loving service to our fellow man, especially the poor and disadvantaged, both at home and abroad.

Year Founded in US: 1978

Income for International Min:
  $397,567
Fully Supported US Personnel Working Cross-Culturally
  More than 4 years: 17
  1–4 years: 5
  X-C workers in US: 1
  Non-residential: 2
Other Personnel
  Short-Term less than 1 year: 45
  Tentmakers/BAM: 3
  Non-US in own/other country: 22
  Home staff: 2
Countries/Regions: Bolivia, Canada, Guatemala, India, Mongolia

CWE MISSIONS
4301 West South Avenue
Tampa, FL 33614 US
Phone: (813) 877-8420
Email: office@cwe-missions.org
Website: cwe-missions.org
A nondenominational service agency of Evangelical tradition engaged in agricultural assistance, church construction or financing, medical ministry, including dental or public health, and STM trip coordination. (FPC-PE)

Purpose: . . . to assist the local church in fulfilling the Great Commission by providing and facilitating spiritually effective mission opportunities throughout the world.
Year Founded in US: 1991
Other Personnel
  Home staff: 4

CYBERMISSIONS
Formerly: Asian Internet Bible Institute – International
21615 Berendo Ave, Ste. 400
Torrance, CA 90502 US
Phone: (310) 748-9274
Email: johned@aibi.ph
Website: cybermissions.org

A nondenominational specialized agency of Charismatic and Pentecostal tradition engaged in Bible teaching, TEE or other extension education, Internet discipleship or training, Internet evangelism, missionary & worker training, and technical assistance.

Purpose: . . . to provide life-changing and strategic content, primarily as freely transmissible digital resources, for Christian workers and for the developing world.
Year Founded in US: 2004
Income for International Min:
  $165,800
Fully Supported US Personnel Working Cross-Culturally
  More than 4 years: 2
  X-C workers in US: 2
  Non-residential: 2
Other Personnel
  Short-Term less than 1 year: 1
  Tentmakers/BAM: 5
  Home staff: 2
Countries/Regions: Brazil, Philippines

D&D MISSIONARY HOMES INC.
13702 Green Isle Dr
Clermont, FL 34711 US
Phone: (727) 522-0522
Email: info@ddmissionry.com
Website: ddmissionary.com
A nondenominational service agency of Evangelical tradition engaged in services for mission organizations. (FPC-PE)

Purpose: . . . to provide temporary housing to Bible-believing missionaries doing deputation, on furlough, or during the first year of retirement.
Year Founded in US: 1949
Other Personnel
  Home staff: 13

DAVAR PARTNERS INTERNATIONAL
1015 Tyrone Rd, Ste. 420
Tyrone, GA 30290 US
Phone: (404) 902-6026
Email: info@davarpartners.com
Website: davarpartners.com
Associations: Missio Nexus

An interdenominational specialized agency of Evangelical tradition engaged in audio recording or distribution, Bible distribution, Bible teaching, discipleship, orality or storying, and partnership development.

Purpose: . . . to enable oral learners to have access to the spoken Word of God in their language by the year 2035.

Year Founded in US: 2009
Income for International Min:
$967,222

Fully Supported US Personnel Working Cross-Culturally
   More than 4 years: 1
Other Personnel
   Tentmakers/BAM: 1
   Non-US in own/other country: 22
   Home staff: 5
Countries/Regions: Israel, South Africa

DAYSTAR U.S.
8011 34th Ave S
Bloomington, MN 55425 US
Phone: (952) 928-2551
Email: info@daystarus.org
Website: daystarus.org

An interdenominational sending agency of Evangelical tradition engaged in church, school or general Christian education, TEE or other extension education, theological education, and leadership development. (FPC-PE)

Purpose: . . . to educate Christ-centered servant leaders to transform Africa.

Year Founded in US: 1982

Fully Supported US Personnel Working Cross-Culturally
   More than 4 years: 4
Other Personnel
   Home staff: 6
Countries/Regions: Kenya

DEAF MISSIONS INTERNATIONAL INC.
PO Box 8514
Clearwater, FL 33758 US
Phone: (727) 530-3020
Email: dmi@dminetwork.org
Website: dminetwork.org

A transdenominational specialized agency of Evangelical tradition engaged in radio or TV broadcasting, camping programs, disabled ministry, mass evangelism, Bible translation, and video-film production or distribution. (FPC-PE)

Purpose: . . . to provide deaf children and deaf adults access to health, education and understanding of moral values.

Year Founded in US: 1967

DENIKE MINISTRIES
PO Box 1231
McAlester, OK 74502 US
Phone: (918) 423-2431
Email: info@denikeministries.org
Website: denikeministries.org

A nondenominational support agency of Charismatic and Independent tradition engaged in short-term programs, training the nationals in Mexico and Kenya, church construction, church planting, theological education, partnership development and supplying equipment. (DPE)

Purpose: . . . to encourage others to come alongside of them to provide the necessary resources, both spiritual and physical, for the training and strengthening of God's people in Mexico, so they can more effectively fulfill their burden to reach the lost for Jesus as stated in Matt. 28:18–20.

*Fully Supported US Personnel Working
Cross-Culturally*
    More than 4 years: 1
Other Personnel
    Short-Term less than 1 year: 120
    Home staff: 1
Countries/Regions: Mexico

DEVELOPMENT ASSOCIATES INTL. (DAI)

13710 Struthers Rd, Ste. 120
Colorado Springs, CO 80921 US
Phone: (719) 598-7970
Email: info@daintl.org
Website: daintl.org
Associations: Missio Nexus

A nondenominational support agency
of Evangelical tradition engaged in
discipleship, theological education,
leadership development, and partnership
development.

Purpose: . . . to enhance the integrity
and effectiveness of Christian leaders
worldwide so that the Church can fulfill its
role in extending the Kingdom of God.

Year Founded in US: 1996
Other Personnel
    Non-US in own/other country: 14
    Home staff: 15
Countries/Regions: Australia, Belgium,
Côte d'Ivoire, Egypt, Ghana, India, Liberia,
Nepal, Nigeria, Russia, South Africa, Togo,
Uganda, United Kingdom

DISCIPLE MAKERS

4393 Boron Drive
Latonia, KY 41015 US
Phone: (859) 491-2620
Email: info@disciplemakers.org
Website: disciplemakers.org

A nondenominational service agency of
Christian (Restoration Movement) tradition
engaged in church planting (establishing),
CPM, DMM, discipleship, and leadership
development.

Purpose: . . . to establish indigenous and
reproducing churches among the unsaved,
unreached and unengaged peoples of the
world.

Year Founded in US: 1989
*Fully Supported US Personnel Working
Cross-Culturally*
    More than 4 years: 6
Other Personnel
    Tentmakers/BAM: 313
    Non-US in own/other country: 311
Countries/Regions: Central America,
Global Ministry, Southeast Asia

DISCIPLES INTERNATIONAL

PO Box 466
Wallingford, PA 19086 US
Phone: (610) 872-8742
Email: david.komarnicki@verizon.net
Website: disciplesinternational.org

A specialized agency of Evangelical
tradition engaged in leadership
development, Bible memorization,
correspondence courses, discipleship,
evangelism and literature distribution.
(DPE)

Purpose: . . . to obtain translations of and
distribute copies of the Apostles' Creed
and certain Bible verses into the 100 most
widely spoken languages.

Income for International Min:
    $2,000

DISCIPLESHIP INTERNATIONAL

Suite 400, 604 Columbia Street
New Westminster, BC V3M 1A5 CA
Phone: (604) 275-0850
Email: office@discipleshipint.org
Website: discipleshipint.org

A specialized agency of Evangelical
tradition engaged in Bible teaching,
discipleship, church, school or general
Christian education, and Internet
discipleship or training.

Purpose: . . . to walk alongside other disciples in order to encourage, equip and challenge one another in love to grow towards maturity in Christ.
Year Founded in CA: 1994
Income for International Min:
  $100,000
Other Personnel
  Short-Term less than 1 year: 22
  Home staff: 7

DOOR OF HOPE INTERNATIONAL
PO Box 303
Glendale, CA 91209 US
Phone: (877) 440-3644
Email: info@dohi.org
Website: dohi.org
An interdenominational support agency engaged in Bible distribution, childcare/orphanage programs, missions information service, relief and/or rehabilitation, Bible translation and youth programs. (DPE)
Purpose: . . . to provide help and bring spiritual, practical and humanitarian assistance to Eastern Europe through the development and support of leadership in the indigenous church and the education of believers in the West.
Income for International Min:
  $158,985
Other Personnel
  Home staff: 4

DUALREACH
PO Box 427
Dana Point, CA 92629 US
Phone: (949) 248-1236
Email: info@DualReach.org
Website: DualReach.org
A transdenominational service agency of Evangelical tradition engaged in mobilizing for mission and services for mission organizations.

Purpose: . . . to provide resources, training and consulting to churches and mission agencies to help them mobilize local congregations' potential to reach the world globally and locally.
Year Founded in US: 2001
Income for International Min:
  $25,000
Fully Supported US Personnel Working Cross-Culturally
  Non-residential: 1
Other Personnel
  Short-Term less than 1 year: 6
  Home staff: 1
Countries/Regions: Global Ministry

E3 PARTNERS MINISTRY
2001 W. Plano Pkwy, Ste. 3100
Plano, TX 75075 US
Phone: (214) 440-1101
Email: help@e3partners.org
Website: e3partners.org
An interdenominational support agency of Evangelical tradition engaged in church planting (establishing), mass evangelism, leadership development, and STM trip coordination. (FPC-PE)
Purpose: . . . to equip God's people to evangelize His world and establish His Church.
Year Founded in US: 1987
Other Personnel
  Short-Term less than 1 year: 3000
  Home staff: 400

EARTH MISSION INC.
PO Box 6411
Siloam Springs, AR 72761 US
Phone: (479) 524-0776
Email: earth@earth-mission.org
Website: earth-mission.org
A nondenominational service agency of Evangelical tradition engaged in community development, medical

ministry, including dental or public health, prayer-intercession, relief & aid, technical assistance, and health & technology education.

Purpose: . . . to demonstrate God's love by offering hope to those in need. We do this by providing practical, culturally sensitive, and sustainable solutions to problems that require technical or medical skills, and by mobilizing prayer, supporters and donors for this cause.

Year Founded in US: 1983

Fully Supported US Personnel Working Cross-Culturally
   More than 4 years: 2
Other Personnel
   Tentmakers/BAM: 2
   Home staff: 1
Countries/Regions: Southeast Asia

EAST AFRICAN MINISTRIES

Formerly: Radler Foundation
1320 S. University Dr, Ste. 500
Fort Worth, TX 76107 US
Phone: (817) 632-5200
Email: canderson@radlerfoundation.org
Website: eamafrica.org
Associations: Accord Network

A nondenominational specialized agency of Evangelical tradition engaged in Bible teaching, community development, mass evangelism, leadership development, relief & aid, and water wells.

Purpose: . . . to practically demonstrate the love of Jesus Christ and strengthen God's Kingdom by promoting sustainable solutions for clean water, health and leadership development to unreachable communities in East Africa.

Year Founded in US: 2009
Income for International Min:
   $1,308,000

Fully Supported US Personnel Working Cross-Culturally
   More than 4 years: 1
   Non-residential: 7
Other Personnel
   Short-Term less than 1 year: 5
   Non-US in own/other country: 83
   Home staff: 6
Countries/Regions: South Sudan

EAST EUROPEAN MISSIONS NETWORK

2111 Golf Course Rd. SE, Ste. C
Rio Rancho, NM 87124 US
Phone: (505) 994-3278
Email: PastorDavid@EEMN.org
Website: EEMN.org

A denominational heritage sending agency of Lutheran tradition engaged in discipleship, church, school or general Christian education, student evangelism, leadership development, networking, partnership, or coordination, and partnership development.

Purpose: . . . to partner in building and equipping the Body of Christ in Eastern Europe and the former Soviet Union.

Year Founded in US: 1992
Income for International Min:
   $455,000

Fully Supported US Personnel Working Cross-Culturally
   More than 4 years: 14
   1–4 years: 2
   Non-residential: 150
Other Personnel
   Short-Term less than 1 year: 75
   Tentmakers/BAM: 4
   Non-US in own/other country: 82
   Home staff: 5
Countries/Regions: Albania, Belarus, Bulgaria, Czech Republic, Eastern Europe and Eurasia, Estonia, Latvia, Poland, Russia, Slovakia, Turkey, Ukraine

EAST WEST INTERKNIT
PO Box 270333
St. Paul, MN 55127 US
Phone: (651) 765-2550
Email: info@ew-interknit.org
Website: ew-interknit.org
A nondenominational support agency
of Evangelical tradition engaged in
fund raising or transmission, literature
distribution, and national worker support.
(FPC-PE)
Purpose: . . . to provide training, tools
and resources that enhance the outreach
efforts of developing world Christians
serving to meet the spiritual and physical
needs of people in their sphere of
influence.
Year Founded in US: 1992
Other Personnel
  Home staff: 2

EAST-WEST MINISTRIES INTERNATIONAL
2001 W. Plano Parkway, Suite 3000
Plano, TX 75075 US
Phone: (972) 941-4500
Email: kshuler@eastwest.org
Website: eastwest.org
Associations: Missio Nexus
A nondenominational sending agency of
Evangelical tradition engaged in CPM,
DMM, mass evangelism, personal or small
group evangelism, recruiting or mobilizing
for mission, and STM trip coordination.
Purpose: . . . to mobilize the Body of
Christ to evangelize the lost and equip
local believers to multiply disciples of
healthy churches among unreached
peoples and/or restricted access
communities.
Year Founded in US: 1993
Income for International Min:
  $16,722,051

Fully Supported US Personnel Working Cross-Culturally
  More than 4 years: 24
  1–4 years: 70
  X-C workers in US: 2
  Non-residential: 99
Other Personnel
  Short-Term less than 1 year: 544
  Tentmakers/BAM: 7
  Non-US in own/other country: 9
  Home staff: 58
Countries/Regions: Caribbean, Central
Asia, East Asia, Eastern Europe and Eurasia,
Global Ministry, Middle East, South Asia,
Southeast Asia, Sub-Saharan Africa,
Western Europe

EASTERN MENNONITE MISSIONS
PO Box 458, 53 West Brandt Blvd
Salunga, PA 17538 US
Phone: (717) 898-2251
Email: info@emm.org
Website: emm.org
Associations: Missio Nexus
A denominational sending agency
of Mennonite or Anabaptist tradition
engaged in church development, church
planting (establishing), CPM, discipleship,
leadership development, and recruiting or
mobilizing for mission.
Purpose: . . . to serve and strengthen the
Church so that all peoples will encounter
Christ and become His disciples in
reproducing Kingdom communities.
Year Founded in US: 1914
Income for International Min:
  $4,101,976
Fully Supported US Personnel Working Cross-Culturally
  More than 4 years: 56
  1–4 years: 28
  X-C workers in US: 5
  Non-residential: 6

Other Personnel
Short-Term less than 1 year: 106
Tentmakers/BAM: 11
Non-US in own/other country: 4
Home staff: 42
Countries/Regions: Albania, Bahrain, Belize, Cambodia, Chile, China (People's Republic of), Czech Republic, Gambia, Germany, Guatemala, Guinea-Bissau, Honduras, Hong Kong (China), India, Indonesia, Kenya, Kyrgyzstan, Laos, Morocco, Netherlands, Peru, Saudi Arabia, Senegal, South Africa, Tajikistan, Tanzania, Thailand, Turkey, United Kingdom, Vietnam

EASY ENGLISH OUTREACH
Formerly: Teach My Children English, Inc
3560 W Dawson Rd
Sedalia, CO 80135 US
Phone: (303) 688-6626
Email: teacheasyenglish@gmail.con
Website: teacheasyenglish.org
A nondenominational support agency of Charismatic and Evangelical tradition engaged in addressing human trafficking, linguistics, literature production, STM trip coordination, TESOL or TEFL, and teaching English speaking skills to teachers-ministers of third world countries.

Purpose: . . . to empower ministry leaders and English teachers with easy-to-use materials which teach clear English pronunciation skills through advanced brain-training techniques and multi-media.
Income for International Min:
$10,000
Other Personnel
Short-Term less than 1 year: 4
Home staff: 2

ECHO
17391 Durrance Road
North Fort Myers, FL 33917 US
Phone: (239) 543-3246
Email: info@echonet.org
Website: echonet.org
A nondenominational support agency of Evangelical tradition engaged in agricultural training and assistance, community development, missionary & worker training, networking, partnership, or coordination, research, and technical assistance.

Purpose: . . . to follow Jesus by reducing hunger and improving lives worldwide through partnerships that equip people with agricultural resources and skills.
Year Founded in US: 1973
Income for International Min:
$3,081,066
Fully Supported US Personnel Working Cross-Culturally
More than 4 years: 10
1–4 years: 3
Other Personnel
Non-US in own/other country: 20
Home staff: 53
Countries/Regions: Burkina Faso, Caribbean, Central America, Global Ministry, Tanzania, Thailand

ECHOCUBA
PO Box 546135
Miami, FL 33154 US
Phone: (305) 884-0441
Email: raiza@echocuba.org
Website: echocuba.org
A nondenominational service agency of Evangelical tradition engaged in camping programs, children's ministry, church development, church, school or general Christian education, services for mission organizations, and STM trip coordination.

Purpose: . . . to collaborate with local leaders throughout Cuba and with others to bring hearts, minds, and resources together.

We believe in the equipping and strengthening of the independent evangelical institutions of Cuba.

Year Founded in US: 1994

Fully Supported US Personnel Working Cross-Culturally
   More than 4 years: 5
   Non-residential: 5

Other Personnel
   Non-US in own/other country: 5
   Home staff: 5

Countries/Regions: Cuba

EFFECT HOPE

Formerly: The Leprosy Mission Canada
200-90 Allstate Pkwy
Markham, ON L3R 6H3 CA
Phone: (805) 886-2885
Email: info@effecthope.org
Website: effecthope.org

An interdenominational service agency of Congregational and Evangelical tradition engaged in church, school or general Christian education, medical supplies, medical ministry, including dental or public health, and relief & aid.

Purpose: . . . to free people from neglected tropical diseases that isolate and impoverish.

Year Founded in CA: 1892
Income for International Min:
   $7,133,250

Other Personnel
   Home staff: 30

Countries/Regions: Bangladesh, Democratic Republic of Congo, Côte d'Ivoire, Ethiopia, Ghana, India, Indonesia, Kenya, Liberia, Myanmar (Burma), Nepal, Nigeria

ELIM FELLOWSHIP

1703 Dalton Road
Lima, NY 14485 US
Phone: (585) 582-2790
Email: tcase@elimfellowship.org
Website: elimfellowship.org/
Associations: Missio Nexus

A nondenominational sending agency of Evangelical and Pentecostal tradition engaged in Bible teaching, childcare or orphanage, church planting (establishing), personal or small group evangelism, student evangelism, and spiritual renewal.

Purpose: . . . to strengthen the leader, to equip the church, to reach the world.

Year Founded in US: 1933
Income for International Min:
   $2,948,840

Fully Supported US Personnel Working Cross-Culturally
   More than 4 years: 99
   1–4 years: 1
   X-C workers in US: 28
   Non-residential: 32

Other Personnel
   Home staff: 18

Countries/Regions: Andorra, Argentina, Australia, Bosnia and Herzegovina, Brazil, Democratic Republic of Congo, East Asia, Egypt, Germany, Guam, Haiti, India, Japan, Kazakhstan, Kenya, Malaysia, Mali, Mexico, Nepal, New Zealand, Niger, Nigeria, Paraguay, Peru, Philippines, Poland, Rwanda, Tanzania, Thailand, Vietnam, Western Europe

EMAS CANADA

1295 North Service Road
Burlington, ON L7R 4M2 CA
Phone: (905) 319-3415
Email: info@emascanada.rog
Website: emascanada.org

A transdenominational specialized agency of Evangelical tradition engaged in medical work, development, extension education and short-term programs. (DPE)

Purpose: . . . to reveal Christ's love by working with national groups and to provide assistance in healing and teaching.

Year Founded in CA: 1971
Income for International Min:
  $1,611,035
Other Personnel
  Short-Term less than 1 year: 341
  Home staff: 2
Countries/Regions: Angola, Cambodia, China (People's Republic of), Cuba, Ecuador, Haiti, Hong Kong (China), Malawi, Philippines, Romania, Russia, Vietnam

EMMANUEL INTL. CANADA
PO Box 1179
Stouffville, ON L4A 8B6 CA
Phone: (905) 640-2111
Email: info@eicanada.org
Website: eicanada.org
Associations: CCRDA

An interdenominational sending agency of Evangelical tradition engaged in discipleship, TEE or other extension education, leadership development, partnership development, and relief & aid.

Purpose: . . . to encourage, strengthen, and assist churches worldwide to meet the spiritual and physical needs of the poor in accordance with the holy Scriptures.

Year Founded in CA: 1975
Fully Supported CA Personnel Working Cross-Culturally
  More than 4 years: 10
Other Personnel
  Home staff: 8
Countries/Regions: Australia, Brazil, Haiti, Malawi, Philippines, Somalia, Tanzania, Uganda, United Kingdom, United States of America

EMMAUS ROAD INTERNATIONAL
7150 Tanner Court
San Diego, CA 92111 US
Phone: (858) 292-7020
Email: Neal_Pirolo@eri.org
Website: eri.org

An interdenominational service agency of Evangelical tradition engaged in leadership development, member care, missionary & worker training, partnership development, spiritual renewal, and resources for cross-cultural ministry. (FPC-PE)

Purpose: . . . to work with any church, agency, university that adheres to the all-inclusive Gospel message to mobilize, train, and network.

Year Founded in US: 1983
Income for International Min:
  $60,000
Other Personnel
  Short-Term less than 1 year: 20
  Home staff: 2

EMPOWERING LIVES INTERNATIONAL
PO Box 67
Upland, Ca 91786 US
Phone: (909) 931-1311
Email: info@empoweringlives.org
Website: empoweringlives.org

A denominational heritage service agency of Evangelical and Methodist tradition engaged in agricultural assistance, business as mission, childcare or orphanage, community development, and STM trip coordination.

Purpose: . . . to empower the poor with knowledge, confidence and measurable growth that impacts their spiritual and economic life so that they become an example that others will be drawn to imitate and surpass.

Year Founded in US: 1994
Income for International Min:
  $1,260,183

Fully Supported US Personnel Working Cross-Culturally
  More than 4 years: 2
  1–4 years: 1
  X-C workers in US: 2
Other Personnel
  Short-Term less than 1 year: 41
  Non-US in own/other country: 56
  Home staff: 6
Countries/Regions: Democratic Republic of Congo, Kenya, South Sudan, Tanzania

ENCOMPASS WORLD PARTNERS
Formerly: Grace Brethren International Missions
PO Box 620067
Atlanta, GA 30362 US
Phone: (574) 992-5313
Email: info@encompassworld.org
Website: encompassworldpartners.org/
Associations: Missio Nexus
A denominational sending agency of Brethren and Evangelical tradition engaged in business as mission, church development, church planting (establishing), discipleship, leadership development, and relief & aid.
Purpose: . . . to mobilize, equip, deploy and nurture multinational teams of disciple-makers who live and proclaim the good news of Jesus Christ through engaging in sacrificial service, intentional evangelism and whole-life discipleship, resulting in the creation of healthy spiritual communities (churches).
Year Founded in US: 1900
Income for International Min:
  $6,600,000
Fully Supported US Personnel Working Cross-Culturally
  More than 4 years: 76
  1–4 years: 5
  X-C workers in US: 8

Other Personnel
  Short-Term less than 1 year: 152
  Non-US in own/other country: 61
  Home staff: 21
Countries/Regions: Argentina, Bahamas, Brazil, Cambodia, Cameroon, Central African Republic, Chad, Chile, Democratic Republic of Congo, Republic of Congo , Czech Republic, France, Germany, Guatemala, Haiti, Ireland (Republic of), Japan, Kyrgyzstan, Mexico, Nigeria, Paraguay, Philippines, Poland, Portugal, Sudan, Thailand, Turkey, United Kingdom, Uruguay, Vietnam

ENDPOVERTY.ORG
PO Box 3380
Oakton, VA 22124 US
Phone: (240) 396-1146
Email: for-more-info@endpoverty.org
Website: endpoverty.org
A nondenominational service agency of Evangelical tradition engaged in microenterprise development, community development, HIV/AIDS, partnership development, technical assistance and training. (DPE)
Purpose: . . . to demonstrate God's love by enabling the poor to free themselves from poverty.
Income for International Min:
  $858,649
Other Personnel
  Short-Term less than 1 year: 10
  Non-US in own/other country: 1
  Home staff: 6
Countries/Regions: Africa

ENGINEERING MINISTRIES INTERNATIONAL (EMI)

130 E. Kiowa St, Ste. 200
Colorado Springs, CO 80903 US
Phone: (719) 633-2078
Email: info@emiworld.org
Website: emiworld.org
Associations: Accord Network

An interdenominational specialized agency of Ecumenical tradition engaged in camping programs, church, school or general Christian education, medical ministry, including dental or public health, relief & aid, and technical assistance.

Purpose: . . . to design a world of hope for the physically and spiritually poor.

Year Founded in US: 1982

Other Personnel
   Non-US in own/other country: 57
   Home staff: 6
Countries/Regions: Canada, India, Uganda, United Kingdom

ENRICH MISSIONS INC.

PO Box 02-5640
Miami, FL 33102-5640 US
Phone: (407) 777-3743
Email: office@enrichmissions.org
Website: enrichmissions.org

A nondenominational support agency of Evangelical tradition engaged in children's ministry, community development, church, school or general Christian education, student evangelism, literacy, and relief & aid.

Purpose: . . . to serve children in extreme poverty so they can fully engage in educational opportunities.

Year Founded in US: 2015
Income for International Min:
   $35,000
Other Personnel
   Short-Term less than 1 year: 21

ENTRUST

PO Box 25520
Colorado Springs, CO 80936 US
Phone: (719) 622-1980
Email: info@entrust4.org
Website: entrust4.org

An interdenominational sending agency of Evangelical tradition engaged in discipleship, TEE or other extension education, theological education, HIV/AIDS ministry, leadership development, and missionary & worker training.

Purpose: . . . to multiply church leaders through accessible, locally owned, reproducible training systems.

Year Founded in US: 1979
Income for International Min:
   $2,360,761
Fully Supported US Personnel Working Cross-Culturally
   More than 4 years: 66
   X-C workers in US: 18
   Non-residential: 1
Other Personnel
   Non-US in own/other country: 19
   Home staff: 8
Countries/Regions: Austria, Bulgaria, Czech Republic, Global Ministry, Hungary, Iraq, Kenya, Mozambique, Netherlands, Russia, Slovakia, South Africa, Spain, Thailand, Turkey

ENVOY INTERNATIONAL

2051 Warrington
Rochester Hills, MI 48307 US
Phone: (248) 650-8974
Email: dandersen@envoyseminars.org
Website: envoyseminars.org

A nondenominational service agency of Baptist and Evangelical tradition engaged in information or journalism, leadership development, partnership development, services for mission organizations, STM Trip coordination, and mobilizing for mission. (FPC-PE)

Purpose: . . . to help the local church develop and implement a personalized involvement in world evangelization and discipleship.
Year Founded in US: 1995

EPC WORLD OUTREACH
5850 T.G. Lee Blvd, Ste. 510
Orlando, FL 32822 US
Phone: (734) 838-6945
Email: Phil.linton@epc.org
Website: epcwo.org
Associations: Missio Nexus

A denominational sending agency of Evangelical and Presbyterian tradition engaged in business as mission, church planting (establishing), CPM, DMM, theological education, and medical ministry, including dental or public health.
Purpose: . . . to send Evangelical Presbyterians to start reproducing churches among people with least access to the gospel.
Year Founded in US: 1982
Income for International Min:
  $4,900,000
Fully Supported US Personnel Working Cross-Culturally
  More than 4 years: 47
  1–4 years: 1
  Non-residential: 1
Other Personnel
  Short-Term less than 1 year: 10
  Home staff: 30
Countries/Regions: Afghanistan, Belarus, Cambodia, China (People's Republic of), France, Germany, Guatemala, India, Indonesia, Ireland (Republic of), Jordan, Kyrgyzstan, Lebanon, Malaysia, Middle East, Pakistan, Romania, Russia, Singapore, Spain, Taiwan (China), Thailand, Uzbekistan

EPISCOPAL CHURCH USA – DOMESTIC & FOREIGN MISSIONARY SOCIETY
815 Second Ave.
New York, NY 10017 US
Phone: (212) 922-5461
Email: yfourcand@episcopalchurch.org
Website: episcopalchurch.org

A denominational sending agency of Anglican and Episcopal tradition engaged in support of national churches, Christian education, evangelism, furloughed missionary support, partnership development and youth programs. (DPE)
Purpose: . . . to ensure, in the most comprehensive and coordinated manner possible, the full participation of Episcopalians in the worldwide mission of the Church.
Income for International Min:
  $13,000,000
Fully Supported US Personnel Working Cross-Culturally
  More than 4 years: 42
  1–4 years: 26
  Non-residential: 68
Other Personnel
  Short-Term less than 1 year: 14
Countries/Regions: Belize, Colombia, Israel, Namibia, Sierra Leone, Spain, Taiwan (China)

EQUIP CANADA
PO Box 683
Duncan, BC V9L 3Y1 CA
Phone: (250) 743-7171
Website: equipinternational.com

An interdenominational sending agency of Evangelical tradition engaged in development, community and/or other, agricultural programs, childcare/orphanage programs, children at risk, justice and medical work. (DPE)

Purpose: . . . to prepare, send, and support evangelical missionaries to assist the Church around the world to be responsive to the poor, sensitive to the Holy Spirit, focused on personal evangelism, and practically engaged in strengthening the Body of Christ.

Income for International Min:
$155,313

Fully Supported CA Personnel Working Cross-Culturally
More than 4 years: 6
Non-residential: 6
Other Personnel
Home staff: 3

Countries/Regions: Liberia, Nigeria, Uganda

EQUIP INC & EQUIP INTERNATIONAL

126 Rockhouse Rd
Marion, NC 28752 US
Phone: (828) 738-3891
Email: business@equipinternational.org
Website: equipinternational.org
Associations: Missio Nexus

An interdenominational service agency of Evangelical tradition engaged in agricultural assistance, Bible distribution, community development, literature distribution, medical ministry, including dental or public health, and missionary & worker training.

Purpose: . . . to prepare, send, and support evangelical missionaries to assist the church around the world to be: responsive to the poor, sensitive to the Holy Spirit, focused on personal evangelism, and practically engaged in strengthening the Body of Christ.

Income for International Min:
$1,030,310

Fully Supported US Personnel Working Cross-Culturally
More than 4 years: 21
1–4 years: 2007
Other Personnel
Non-US in own/other country: 13
Home staff: 10

Countries/Regions: Belize, Brazil, Canada, Colombia, Ethiopia, Honduras, India, Japan, Kenya, Mexico, Myanmar (Burma), Nicaragua, Nigeria, Spain, Uganda

EQUIP INTERNATIONAL MINISTRIES

2050 Sugarloaf Circle
Duluth, GA 30097 US
Phone: (321) 752-0072
Email: webmaster@equipministries.org
Website: iequip.org

An interdenominational support agency engaged in leadership development and discipleship. (DPE)

Purpose: . . . to see effective Christian leaders fulfill the Great Commission in every nation.

EQUIPPING THE SAINTS

1254 Keezletown Road
Weyers Cave, VA 24486 US
Phone: (540) 234-6222
Email: ets.usa@hotmail.com
Website: etsusa.org

An interdenominational service agency of Evangelical tradition engaged in Bible distribution, literature distribution, medical supplies, networking, partnership, or coordination, purchasing or supply services, and services for mission organizations. (FPC-PE)

Purpose: . . . to serve evangelical Christian ministries worldwide by providing all types of information, materials and equipment so that the body of Christ may be built up.

Year Founded in US: 1991
Income for International Min:
$428,756
Other Personnel
Home staff: 2

ERDO – EMERGENCY RELIEF AND DEVELOPMENT

7575 Danbro Crescent
Missisauga, ON L7L 5X3 CA
Phone: (905) 542-7400
Email: info@erdo.ca
Website: erdo.ca

A denominational support agency of Pentecostal tradition engaged in relief and/ or rehabilitation, agricultural programs, childcare/orphanage programs, children at risk, development, HIV/AIDS, justice and food aid. (DPE)

Purpose: . . . to respond to human need where there is poverty, hunger, disaster and injustice, on behalf of the Pentecostal Assemblies of Canada.

Year Founded in CA: 2003
Income for International Min:
$4,810,000
Fully Supported CA Personnel Working Cross-Culturally
Non-residential: 1
Other Personnel
Short-Term less than 1 year: 1
Home staff: 6

ERRC (EDUCATIONAL RESOURCES & REFERRALS – CHINA) – US

3824 Buell St, Ste. B
Oakland, CA 94619 US
Phone: (510) 486-8170
Email: errc@errchina.com
Website: errchina.com/
Associations: Missio Nexus

An interdenominational specialized agency of Evangelical and Reformed tradition engaged in Bible teaching, theological education, student evangelism, STM trip

coordination, TESOL or TEFL, and youth ministry. (FPC-PE)

Purpose: . . . to touch the heart and soul of China by inspiring, educating, and equipping its future leaders by sending teachers and professors to high-ranking universities.

Year Founded in US: 1986
Income for International Min:
$503,358
Fully Supported US Personnel Working Cross-Culturally
1–4 years: 1
Other Personnel
Short-Term less than 1 year: 26
Tentmakers/BAM: 3
Non-US in own/other country: 46
Home staff: 12
Countries/Regions: China

ERRC EDUCATIONAL SOCIETY

4974 Kingsway Avenue, Box 592
Burnaby, BC V5H 4M9 CA
Email: errc_canada@hotmail.com
Website: errchina.com

A transdenominational specialized agency of Evangelical and Reformed tradition engaged in cross-cultural education, training/orientation, discipleship, theological education, evangelism, leadership development and short-term programs. (DPE)

Purpose: . . . to offer educational services and academic resources to China . . . to send teachers, professionals, and academics to serve in educational institutions . . . to conduct local and international culturally relevant long-term programs, short-term seminars, conferences, and events of an educational nature consistent with the key values endorsed by the board.

Income for International Min:
$252,188

Fully Supported CA Personnel Working Cross-Culturally
1–4 years: 1
Non-residential: 4
Other Personnel
Short-Term less than 1 year: 8
Tentmakers/BAM: 3
Non-CA in own/other country: 46
Home staff: 3
Countries/Regions: China

ETERNAL HOPE IN HAITI
PO Box 307
Hoschton, GA 30548 US
Phone: (706) 367-7304
Email: thaynes123@aol.com
Website: eternalhopeinhaiti.org
An interdenominational sending agency of Baptist and Evangelical tradition engaged in Bible distribution, childcare or orphanage, discipleship, TEE or other extension education, medical ministry, including dental or public health, and partnership development.

Purpose: . . . to provide healthcare to the most impoverished Haitians and to help each child at Hope Haven to grow up healthy and safe in an atmosphere guided by the love of Jesus Christ.

Year Founded in US: 1996
Fully Supported US Personnel Working Cross-Culturally
More than 4 years: 4
Countries/Regions: Haiti

ETHNOS360
Formerly: New Tribes Mission
1000 E 1st St
Sanford, FL 32771 US
Phone: (407) 323-3430
Email: ntm@ntm.org
Website: ethnos360.org
Associations: Missio Nexus
A nondenominational sending agency of Evangelical tradition engaged in aviation,

Bible teaching, church planting (establishing), discipleship, missionary & worker training, and Bible translation.

Purpose: . . . to assist the ministry of the local church through the mobilizing, equipping, and coordinating of believers to evangelize unreached people groups, translating the Scriptures, and seeing indigenous churches established that glorify God.

Year Founded in US: 1942
Income for International Min:
  $31,000,000
Fully Supported US Personnel Working Cross-Culturally
  More than 4 years: 720
  1–4 years: 154
  Non-residential: 7
Other Personnel
  Short-Term less than 1 year: 30
  Home staff: 282
Countries/Regions: Bolivia, Brazil, Cambodia, Canada, Colombia, Germany, Global Ministry, Mexico, Oceania, Papua New Guinea, Paraguay, Philippines, Singapore, Sub-Saharan Africa, Thailand, United Kingdom

EURASIAN BAPTIST MISSION
6847 N. 9th Ave, Ste. A#332
Pensacola, FL 32504 US
Phone: (850) 910-7122
Email: chapmaneric57@gmail.com
Website: eurasianbaptistmission.com
A denominational heritage support agency of Baptist tradition engaged in Bible teaching, church planting (establishing), discipleship, theological education, mass evangelism, and medical ministry, including dental or public health.

Purpose: . . . to assist the local church and individual missionaries in carrying out the Great Commission as an extension of the local church to assist them in this commission.

A THRIVING CHURCH FOR EVERY PEOPLE

Year Founded in US: 1996
Income for International Min:
  $210,000
*Fully Supported US Personnel Working
Cross-Culturally*
  More than 4 years: 4
Other Personnel
  Short-Term less than 1 year: 20
  Non-US in own/other country: 10
Countries/Regions: Malawi, Moldova

EUROPEAN CHRISTIAN
MISSION INTL. – USA

5550 Tech Center Dr, Ste. 307
Colorado Springs, CO 80919 US
Phone: (419) 924-2056
Email: ecmi.usa@ecmi.org
Website: ecmi-usa.org
Associations: Missio Nexus

An interdenominational sending agency
of Evangelical tradition engaged in church
planting (establishing), discipleship,
theological education, mass evangelism,
and national worker support.

Purpose: . . . to establish and develop
local reproducing churches that evangelize
and disciple the peoples of Europe.

Year Founded in US: 1923
*Fully Supported US Personnel Working
Cross-Culturally*
  More than 4 years: 238
Other Personnel
  Short-Term less than 1 year: 50
  Home staff: 2
Countries/Regions: Albania,
Austria, Belguim, Bulgaria, Bosnia and
Herzegovina, Croatia, France, Germany,
Hungary, Ireland (Republic of), Italy,
Netherlands, Poland, Protugal, Romania,
Serbia, Slovenia, Spain, Sweden, Ukraine

EVANGEL BIBLE TRANSLATORS

PO Box 669
Rockwall, TX 75087-0669 US
Phone: (469) 480-8519
Email: connect.ebt@gmail.com
Website: evangelbible.org

A nondenominational sending agency
of Pentecostal tradition engaged in Bible
distribution, church planting (establishing),
literacy, and Bible translation.

Purpose: . . . to bring the Word of God
to all people in their mother tongue and
equip people with skills to read and write
in their language.

Year Founded in US: 1976
Other Personnel
  Non-US in own/other country: 33
  Home staff: 2
Countries/Regions: Benin, Ghana,
Guatemala, India, Liberia, Myanmar
(Burma)

EVANGELICAL BIBLE MISSION
– EBM INTERNATIONAL

5200 SE 145th St
Summerfield, FL 34491 US
Phone: (352) 245-2560
Email: ebminternational@gmail.com
Website: ebminternational.com

An interdenominational support agency
of Evangelical and Wesleyan tradition
engaged in radio or TV broadcasting,
childcare or orphanage, church
development, church, school or general
Christian education, medical ministry,
including dental or public health.

Purpose: . . . to empower other countries
with the Gospel and assist them in
carrying on the work that we help them
start so they become self sufficient and
continue to share Jesus with their nation.

Year Founded in US: 1941

EVANGELICAL CHRISTIAN CHURCH IN CANADA, THE

410-125 Lincoln Rd.
Waterloo, ON N2J 2N9 CA
Phone: (519) 880-9110
Email: cecc@rogers.com
Website: cecconline.com

A denominational sending agency of Christian (Restoration Movement), Evangelical, and Holiness tradition engaged in training, church planting, correspondence courses, TEE and support of national workers. (DPE)

Fully Supported CA Personnel Working Cross-Culturally
  More than 4 years: 5
  Non-residential: 1
Other Personnel
  Short-Term less than 1 year: 1
  Tentmakers/BAM: 5
  Non-CA in own/other country: 5
  Home staff: 3
Countries/Regions: Africa, China (People's Republic of), India, Russia, South America

EVANGELICAL CONGREGATIONAL CHURCH – GLOBAL MINISTRIES COMMISSION

100 W. Park Ave.
Myerstown, PA 17067 US
Phone: (717) 866-7584
Email: ecglobal@eccenter.com
Website: eccenter.com/Our-Structure/
Commissions/Global-Ministries-
Commission.aspx

A service agency of Wesleyan tradition engaged in missionary kids' education, support of national churches, aviation services, church planting and Bible translation. Additional missionaries are sent under other mission agencies. (DPE)
Income for International Min:
  $760,000

Fully Supported US Personnel Working Cross-Culturally
  More than 4 years: 23
Other Personnel
  Home staff: 3
Countries/Regions: Belize, Brazil, Caribbean, Kenya, Papua New Guinea, Spain, Thailand, Ukraine

EVANGELICAL COVENANT CHURCH OF CANADA

PO Box 23117, RPO McGillvray
Winnipeg, MB R3T 5S3 CA
Phone: (204) 269-3437
Email: messengr@escape.ca
Website: covchurch.ca

A denominational conference of Covenantal and Evangelical tradition engaged in denominational funds transmission and mission mobilization for evangelism and church planting. (DPE)
Income for International Min:
  $52,280
Other Personnel
  Home staff: 3

EVANGELICAL FREE CHURCH OF CANADA MISSION

PO Box 850, Langley Stn. LCD 1
Langley, BC V3A 8S6 CA
Phone: (604) 513-2183
Email: info@efccm.ca
Website: efccm.ca
Associations: Missio Nexus

A denominational sending agency of Evangelical tradition engaged in business as mission, childcare or orphanage, church planting (establishing), community development, personal or small group evangelism, and medical ministry, including dental or public health.

Purpose: . . . to help lives be transformed by the power of the gospel.
Income for International Min:
  $4,922,402

Fully Supported CA Personnel Working Cross-Culturally
    More than 4 years: 51
    1–4 years: 3
    Non-residential: 60
Other Personnel
    Tentmakers/BAM: 21
    Non-CA in own/other country: 4
    Home staff: 13
Countries/Regions: Bolivia, Republic of Congo, Cuba, East Asia, Eastern Europe and Eurasia, El Salvador, Ethiopia, Germany, Guatemala, Honduras, Hungary, Japan, Kenya, Liberia, Mexico, Nicaragua, North Africa, Panama, Philippines, Rwanda, Thailand, Ukraine, Zimbabwe

EVANGELICAL FRIENDS CHURCH SOUTHWEST

18639 Yorba Linda Blvd.
Yorba Linda, CA 92886-1436 US
Phone: (888) 704-9393
Email: office@friendschurchsw.org
Website: friendschurchsw.org
A denominational sending agency of Friends tradition engaged in church planting, association of missions, TEE, leadership development and member care. (DPE)
Purpose: . . . to seek to live our lives as Jesus would live if He were in our shoes, and together fuel a worldwide church multiplication movement that our grandchildren's grandchildren will be compelled to expand.
Fully Supported US Personnel Working Cross-Culturally
    1–4 years: 2
    Non-residential: 12
Other Personnel
    Short-Term less than 1 year: 33
    Non-US in own/other country: 7
    Home staff: 4
Countries/Regions: Cambodia

EVANGELICAL FRIENDS MISSION

PO Box 525
Arvada, CO 80001 US
Phone: (303) 421-8100
Email: efm@friendsmission.com
Website: friendsmission.com
Associations: Missio Nexus
A denominational sending agency of Evangelical and Friends tradition engaged in church planting (establishing), discipleship, theological education, personal or small group evangelism, medical ministry, including dental or public health, and discipling for development.
Purpose: . . . to fuel a worldwide movement of people who seek first the kingdom of God; planting churches that live and die to carry out the Great Commission in the spirit of the Great Commandment.
Year Founded in US: 1976
Income for International Min: $1,970,275
Fully Supported US Personnel Working Cross-Culturally
    More than 4 years: 8
    1–4 years: 6
    X-C workers in US: 2
Other Personnel
    Short-Term less than 1 year: 2
    Non-US in own/other country: 11
    Home staff: 15
Countries/Regions: Bangladesh, Bhutan, Ecuador, India, Ireland (Republic of), Mexico, Middle East, Nepal, Philippines, Rwanda

EVANGELICAL LUTHERAN CHURCH IN AMERICA – DIV. FOR GLOBAL MISSION

8765 W. Higgins Rd.
Chicago, IL 60631 US
Phone: (773) 380-2656
Email: GMInfo@elca.org
Website: elca.org

A denominational sending agency of Lutheran tradition engaged in partnership development, development, evangelism, leadership development and relief and/or rehabilitation. (DPE)

Purpose: . . . Marked with the cross of Christ forever, we are claimed, gathered and sent for the sake of the world.

Income for International Min:
$34,434,240

Fully Supported US Personnel Working Cross-Culturally
More than 4 years: 101
1–4 years: 62

Other Personnel
Short-Term less than 1 year: 83
Non-US in own/other country: 15
Home staff: 44

Countries/Regions: Argentina, Brazil, Cameroon, Central African Republic, China (People's Republic of), Costa Rica, Denmark, Egypt, El Salvador, Ethiopia, Germany, Guam, Guyana, Honduras, Hong Kong (China), India, Indonesia, Jamaica, Japan, Kenya, South Korea, Lebanon, Liberia, Madagascar, Mexico, Namibia, Nigeria, Palestine, Papua New Guinea, Russia, Senegal, Singapore, Slovakia, South Africa, Tanzania, Thailand

EVANGELICAL MENNONITE CONFERENCE

440 Main Street
Steinbach, MB R5G 1Z5 CA
Phone: (204) 326-6401
Email: info@emconf.ca
Website: emconference.ca

A denominational sending agency of Evangelical and Mennonite tradition engaged in church planting (establishing), CPM, DMM, TEE or other extension education, personal or small group evangelism, and leadership development.

Purpose: . . . to glorify God by building His Kingdom by proclaiming the gospel, ministering to people, establishing churches, building community, coordinating resources, and connecting with the global church.

Year Founded in CA: 1959
Income for International Min:
$1,136,000

Fully Supported CA Personnel Working Cross-Culturally
More than 4 years: 19
1–4 years: 2
X-C workers in CA: 6

Other Personnel
Short-Term less than 1 year: 19
Home staff: 4

Countries/Regions: Bolivia, Burkina Faso, Mexico, Paraguay

EVANGELICAL MENNONITE MISSION CONFERENCE

757 St. Anne's Road
Winnipeg, MB R2N 4G6 CA
Phone: (204) 253-7929
Email: info@gomission.ca
Website: gomission.ca

A denominational service agency of Evangelical and Mennonite tradition engaged in church development, church planting (establishing), community development, discipleship, church, school or general Christian education, and recruiting or mobilizing for mission.

Purpose: . . . to equip and encourage our churches for effective ministry, empowering them to participate in God's work in the world.

Year Founded in CA: 1959

Income for International Min:
$632,000
Fully Supported CA Personnel Working Cross-Culturally
More than 4 years: 5
Other Personnel
Non-CA in own/other country: 1
Home staff: 6
Countries/Regions: Belize, Bolivia, Mexico

EVANGELICAL METHODIST CHURCH INC. – BOARD OF MISSIONS

6838 South Gray Road
Indianapolis, IN 46237 US
Phone: (317) 780-8017
Email: generalsuperintendent@emchurch.org
Website: emchurch.org
A denominational sending agency of Wesleyan tradition engaged in evangelism, children's programs, church planting, discipleship and theological education. (DPE)
Year Founded in US: 1960
Income for International Min:
$344,145
Fully Supported US Personnel Working Cross-Culturally
More than 4 years: 5
Non-residential: 1
Other Personnel
Non-US in own/other country: 1
Home staff: 3
Countries/Regions: Mexico, Spain

EVANGELICAL MISSION MINISTRIES

P.O. Box 636
Pharr, TX 78577 US
Phone: (956) 787-3543
Email: office@emm-mexico.net
Website: emm-mexico.net
Associations: ANAM

A nondenominational sending agency of Evangelical tradition engaged in children's ministry, church construction or financing, church planting (establishing), correspondence courses, church, school or general Christian education, and theological education.
Purpose: . . . to reach Spanish-speaking people throughout the world with the Good News of salvation through our Lord Jesus Christ and disciple them for Christian ministry.
Year Founded in US: 1954
Income for International Min:
$284,101
Fully Supported US Personnel Working Cross-Culturally
More than 4 years: 4
Other Personnel
Non-US in own/other country: 3
Home staff: 4
Countries/Regions: Mexico

EVANGELICAL MISSIONARY CHURCH OF CANADA

Formerly: Merged: Missionary Church of Canada and Evangelical Church of Canada
4031 Brentwood Road NW
Calgary, AB T2L 1L1 CA
Phone: (403) 250-2759
Email: wp@emcc.ca
Website: emcc.ca
A denominational sending agency of Evangelical tradition engaged in community development, DMM, discipleship, theological education, leadership development, and relief & aid.
Purpose: . . . to strategically recruit, deploy and sustain workers globally by engaging in relief & development, resources, networks, and empowering people to bring change to the suffering people of this world.
Year Founded in CA: 1993

Fully Supported CA Personnel Working Cross-Culturally
  More than 4 years: 68
  1–4 years: 2
  Non-residential: 6
Other Personnel
  Short-Term less than 1 year: 60
  Home staff: 3
Countries/Regions: Afghanistan, Angola, Brazil, Burkina Faso, Central Asia, China (People's Republic of), Ghana, Guatemala, Haiti, Hungary, Ireland (Republic of), Italy, Madagascar, Mexico, Mongolia, Nigeria, Papua New Guinea, Paraguay, Philippines, Romania, Singapore, South Africa, Spain, Sudan, Thailand, Ukraine, United States of America

EVANGELISM EXPLOSION III INTERNATIONAL INC.

PO Box 753
Arden, NC 28704 US
Phone: (954) 491-6100
Email: info@eeworks.org
Website: evangelismexplosion.org
A nondenominational support agency of Evangelical tradition engaged in discipleship, theological education, and personal or small group evangelism.
Purpose: . . . to glorify God by equipping believers in and through local churches to multiply through friendship, evangelism, discipleship, and healthy growth.
Year Founded in US: 1970
Income for International Min:
  $2,290,000
Fully Supported US Personnel Working Cross-Culturally
  More than 4 years: 3
  X-C workers in US: 4
  Non-residential: 1
Other Personnel
  Non-US in own/other country: 570
  Home staff: 22

Countries/Regions: Albania, Argentina, Armenia, Bangladesh, Benin, Bolivia, Botswana, Brazil, Bulgaria, Burkina Faso, Burundi, Cambodia, Cameroon, Chile, Colombia, Republic of Congo , Costa Rica, Côte d'Ivoire, Dominican Republic, East Asia, Eastern Europe and Eurasia, Ecuador, El Salvador, Fiji, Finland, Georgia, Ghana, Global Ministry, Guatemala, Honduras, Hungary, India, Indonesia, Jamaica, Jordan, Kazakhstan, Kenya, Lesotho, Liberia, Macedonia, Malawi, Malaysia, Mali, Mexico, Moldova, Mongolia, Mozambique, Namibia, Nepal, Nicaragua, Niger, Nigeria, Oceania, Pakistan, Papua New Guinea, Paraguay, Peru, Philippines, Puerto Rico, Romania, Russia, Rwanda, Sierra Leone, Solomon Islands, South Africa, South America, Southeast Asia, Spain, Sub-Saharan Africa, Suriname, Swaziland, Tajikistan, Tanzania, Thailand, Togo, Tonga, Uganda, United Kingdom, Uzbekistan, Vanuatu, Vietnam, Zambia, Zimbabwe

EVANGELISM RESOURCES INC.

425 Epworth Ave.
Wilmore, KY 40390 US
Phone: (859) 858-0777
Email: eroffice@qx.net
Website: erinfo.org
A sending agency of Evangelical tradition engaged in evangelism, church planting, Christian education, evangelism, leadership development and literature distribution. (DPE)
Purpose: . . . to deliver time-tested curriculum, blended with cutting-edge practices . . . to equip churches to make evangelism an everyday, every-member, every-activity way of life.
Income for International Min:
  $739,016

Fully Supported US Personnel Working Cross-Culturally
　1–4 years: 2
Other Personnel
　Short-Term less than 1 year: 7
　Non-US in own/other country: 2
　Home staff: 2
Countries/Regions: India, Nigeria

EVANGELISTIC FAITH MISSION INC.

PO Box 609, 168 Ikerd Lane
Bedford, IN 47421 US
Phone: (812) 275-7521
Email: efm.pres@gmail.com
Website: efm-missions.org
Associations: Missio Nexus
An interdenominational sending agency of Holiness and Wesleyan tradition engaged in church planting (establishing), TEE or other extension education, and medical ministry, including dental or public health.
Purpose: . . . to glorify God by planting the church where it does not yet exist and by partnering with national believers in training, facilitating, and motivating them to fulfill the Great Commission in their culture and beyond.
Year Founded in US: 1905
Income for International Min:
　$891,417
Fully Supported US Personnel Working Cross-Culturally
　1–4 years: 10
　Non-residential: 4
Other Personnel
　Short-Term less than 1 year: 6
　Non-US in own/other country: 3
　Home staff: 6
Countries/Regions: Bolivia, Costa Rica, Cuba, Dominican Republic, East Asia, Egypt, Eritrea, Ethiopia, Guatemala, Honduras, South Asia

EVANGELIZE CHINA FELLOWSHIP INC.

437 S. Garfield Ave.
Monterey Park, CA 91754 US
Phone: (626) 288-8828
Email: info@ecfusa.org
Website: ecfinternational.org
A support agency of Baptist tradition engaged in evangelism, broadcasting, childcare/orphanage programs, church construction, Christian education and relief and/or rehabilitation. (DPE)
Year Founded in US: 1956
Other Personnel
　Short-Term less than 1 year: 17
　Non-US in own/other country: 2
　Home staff: 10
Countries/Regions: Hong Kong (China), Philippines

EVERY CHILD MINISTRIES INC.

P O Box 810, 875 South State Road 2
Hebron, IN 46341 US
Phone: (219) 996-4201
Email: ecmafrica@ecmafrica.org
Website: ecmafrica.org
A nondenominational support agency of Evangelical tradition engaged in childcare or orphanage, children's ministry, community development, student evangelism, and addressing human trafficking.
Purpose: . . . to offer hope, practical help and dignity to African children and their families in the name of Jesus, with special emphasis on those who are broken or outcast for any reason—"the forgotten children of Africa."
Year Founded in US: 1985
Income for International Min:
　$1,257,406

Fully Supported US Personnel Working Cross-Culturally
    More than 4 years: 10
    1–4 years: 2
    Non-residential: 2
Other Personnel
    Short-Term less than 1 year: 10
    Non-US in own/other country: 94
    Home staff: 7
Countries/Regions: Democratic Republic of Congo, Ghana, Sub-Saharan Africa, Uganda

EVERY HOME FOR CHRIST

640 Chapel Hills Drive
Colorado Springs, CO 80920 US
Phone: (800) 423-5054
Email: info@ehc.org
Website: ehc.org
A service agency of Evangelical tradition engaged in Bible distribution, Bible teaching, church planting (establishing), correspondence courses, personal or small group evangelism, and literature distribution.
Purpose: . . . to serve, mobilize and train the Church to actively participate and pray for the systematic, personal presentation of a printed or repeatable message of the Gospel of Jesus Christ to every home in the whole world, adding new believers as functioning members of the body of Christ.
Year Founded in US: 1946
Income for International Min:
    $40,234,030
Other Personnel
    Non-US in own/other country: 1500
    Home staff: 58
Countries/Regions: Global Ministry

FAIR

Formerly: Fellowship Agency for International Relief
PO Box 457
Guelph, ON N1H 6K9 CA
Phone: (519) 821-4830
Email: international@fellowship.ca
Website: fellowship.ca/FAIR
A denominational support agency of Baptist tradition engaged in relief and/or rehabilitation. The relief arm of FEBInternational. (DPE)
Income for International Min:
    $180,741
Other Personnel
    Home staff: 1

FAITH BAPTIST MISSION

Formerly: Evangelical Baptist Mission
PO Box 866
Eagle Lake, FL 33893 US
Phone: (863) 293-0689
Email: pbrockfbm@gmail.com
Website: faithbaptistmission.org
A denominational sending agency of Baptist tradition engaged in radio or TV broadcasting, church planting (establishing), church, school or general Christian education, theological education, medical ministry, including dental or public health, and Bible translation.
Purpose: . . . to meet the biblical mandate of training, equipping, evaluating and supporting missionaries by assisting churches as an integrated auxiliary/mission society of Faith Baptist Church of Winter Haven, Inc.
Year Founded in US: 2010
Income for International Min:
    $1,100,000
Fully Supported US Personnel Working Cross-Culturally
    More than 4 years: 21
    X-C workers in US: 3

Other Personnel
Home staff: 2
Countries/Regions: Benin, Canada, Mali, Niger, Nigeria

FAITH CHRISTIAN FELLOWSHIP INTL.
PO Box 35443
Tulsa, OK 74153 US
Phone: (918) 492-5800
Email: info@fcf.org
Website: fcf.org
A nondenominational sending agency of Charismatic tradition engaged in church planting (establishing), discipleship, church, school or general Christian education, theological education, leadership development, and partnership development.
Purpose: . . . to reach the world for Christ . . . to demonstrate the power of the Holy Spirit . . . to build covenant relationships.
Year Founded in US: 1977
Other Personnel
Non-US in own/other country: 22
Countries/Regions: Belgium, Czech Republic, Germany, Guatemala, India, Ireland (Republic of), Jamaica, Kenya, South Korea, Malawi, Mexico, Russia, Singapore, South Africa, Sri Lanka, Turkey, Zimbabwe

FAITHLIFE MINISTRIES INC.
6170 Crescent Landing Dr.
Cumming, GA 30028 US
Phone: (770) 492-4903
Email: barry.voss@faithlifeministries.net
Website: faithlifeministries.net
A nondenominational service agency of Lutheran tradition engaged in discipleship, leadership development, and management consulting or training.

Purpose: . . . to train and equip church leaders with Biblical, practical and basic leadership and management tools and information.
Year Founded in US: 2001
Income for International Min: $90,000
Other Personnel
Short-Term less than 1 year: 5
Non-US in own/other country: 33
Home staff: 1
Countries/Regions: Bhutan, Brazil, Burkina Faso, Cameroon, Côte d'Ivoire, Cuba, Ghana, Guinea, India, Kenya, Liberia, Mali, Nepal, Niger, Nigeria, Pakistan, Panama, Philippines, Sierra Leone, Tanzania, Togo, Uganda

FAME
4545 Southeastern Ave.
Indianapolis, IN 46203 US
Phone: (317) 358-2480
Email: fame@fameworld.org
Website: FAME@Fameworld.org
A nondenominational specialized agency of Christian (Restoration Movement) tradition engaged in community development, medical supplies, medical ministry, including dental or public health, and STM trip coordination. (FPC-PE)
Purpose: . . . to send help and hope in the name of Christ to the world through medical evangelism.
Year Founded in US: 1970
Income for International Min: $1,668,706
Other Personnel
Short-Term less than 1 year: 96
Home staff: 7

FAR CORNERS MISSIONS
Formerly: World Missions Far Corners
8401 Jacksboro Hwy, Ste. 130
Lakeside, TX 76135 US
Phone: (817) 237-3000
Email: roni@fc-usa.org
Website: fc-usa.org
Associations: Missio Nexus

A nondenominational sending agency of Evangelical tradition engaged in Bible teaching, childcare or orphanage, church planting (establishing), mass evangelism, medical ministry, including dental or public health, and missionary & worker training.

Purpose: . . . to communicate and demonstrate the Gospel of Jesus Christ to hard-to-reach people groups. We seek to accomplish the mission of God in four ways: sending, proclaiming, educationg, and demonstrating.

Year Founded in US: 1958
Income for International Min:
    $713,517
Other Personnel
    Home staff: 5

FAR EAST BROADCASTING ASSOCIATES OF CANADA (FEB CANADA)
3200 - 8888 Odlin Crescent
Richmond, BC V6X 3Z8 CA
Phone: (604) 717-8369
Email: international@fellowship.ca
Website: febcanada.org

A denominational sending agency of Baptist and Evangelical tradition engaged in church planting, discipleship, evangelism, leadership development, medical work and relief and/or rehabilitation. (DPE)

Purpose: . . . to develop reproducing churches among strategic populations and to facilitate humanitarian development.

Income for International Min:
    $2,729,335
Fully Supported CA Personnel Working Cross-Culturally
    More than 4 years: 50
    1–4 years: 15
Other Personnel
    Short-Term less than 1 year: 6
    Non-CA in own/other country: 6
    Home staff: 7
Countries/Regions: Bulgaria, Cambodia, Chile, Colombia, France, Honduras, India, Indonesia, Italy, Japan, Kazakhstan, Kenya, Mexico, Middle East, Netherlands, Pakistan, Philippines, Poland, Spain, Venezuela

FAR EAST BROADCASTING COMPANY
PO Box 1
La Mirada, CA 90637 US
Phone: (562) 947-0391
Email: info@febc.org
Website: febc.org

A nondenominational sending agency of Evangelical tradition engaged in audio recording or distribution, radio or TV broadcasting, mass evangelism, and national worker support.

Purpose: . . . to develop radio programming and deliver it to listeners in Asia in such a way that they move toward Jesus Christ and into His Kingdom, that they know Him as Savior, Lord, and King, following His teaching, and live in obedience to Him..

Year Founded in US: 1945
Income for International Min:
    $12,000,000
Other Personnel
    Non-US in own/other country: 9
    Home staff: 47

Countries/Regions: Cambodia, Finland, Indonesia, Mongolia, Northern Mariana Islands, Philippines, Russia, South Korea, United Kingdom

FARMS INTERNATIONAL INC.
PO Box 270
Knife River, MN 55609 US
Phone: (218) 834-2676
Email: joe@farmsinternational.com
Website: farmsinternational.com
A nondenominational specialized agency of Evangelical tradition engaged in agricultural assistance, church development, CPM, community development, discipleship, and persecuted church.
Purpose: . . . to release Christians from poverty by combining sustainable revolving loans and the practice of biblical stewardship enabling evangelistic outreach.
Year Founded in US: 1961
Income for International Min:
   $122,000
Other Personnel
   Short-Term less than 1 year: 3

FELLOWSHIP INTERNATIONAL MISSION
555 South 24th Street
Allentown, PA 18104 US
Phone: (610) 435-9099
Email: reports@fim.org
Website: fim.org
Associations: Missio Nexus
An interdenominational sending agency of Baptist and Evangelical tradition engaged in church development, church planting (establishing), discipleship, personal or small group evangelism, and leadership development.
Purpose: . . . to provide flexibility in ministry with integrity and accountability.
Year Founded in US: 1950

Income for International Min:
   $2,370,048
Fully Supported US Personnel Working Cross-Culturally
   More than 4 years: 57
   1–4 years: 2
   X-C workers in US: 6
Other Personnel
   Short-Term less than 1 year: 2
   Non-US in own/other country: 30
   Home staff: 7
Countries/Regions: Argentina, Australia, Bolivia, Brazil, Canada, France, Germany, Ghana, Global Ministry, Greece, Ireland (Republic of), Japan, Mexico, New Zealand, Niger, Nigeria, Peru, Poland, Senegal, Sweden, Togo, Uganda, Venezuela

FELLOWSHIP OF COMPANIES FOR CHRIST INTERNATIONAL (FCCI)
11675 Great Oaks Way, Suite 150
Alpharetta, GA 30011 US
Phone: (705) 746-1521
Email: terence@fcci.org
Website: fcci.org
A specialized agency of Evangelical tradition engaged in business as mission, discipleship, evangelism, leadership development, management consulting/ training and training. (DPE)
Purpose: . . . to equip and encourage Christian business leaders to operate their businesses and conduct their personal lives in accordance with Biblical principles.
Income for International Min:
   $182,115
Other Personnel
   Non-US in own/other country: 4
   Home staff: 4
Countries/Regions: Africa, Asia, Europe, Latin America

FELLOWSHIP OF EVANGELICAL CHURCHES – INTERNATIONAL MINISTRIES

1420 Kerrway Ct.
Fort Wayne, IN 46805 US
Phone: (260) 423-3649
Email: fecministries@fecministries.org
Website: fecministries.org
Associations: Missio Nexus

A denominational sending agency of Evangelical and Anabaptist tradition engaged in leadership development, church planting, discipleship, extension education and evangelism. (DPE)

Purpose: . . . to facilitate local churches to spread the Gospel among unreached and unevangelized peoples with the goal of generating and reproducing a church planting movement.

Year Founded in US: 1946
Income for International Min:
  $947,780
Fully Supported US Personnel Working Cross-Culturally
  More than 4 years: 21
  Non-residential: 1
Other Personnel
  Short-Term less than 1 year: 57
  Tentmakers/BAM: 1
  Home staff: 3
Countries/Regions: Albania, Asia, Hungary, Middle East, Spain, United Kingdom, Venezuela, Zimbabwe

FH CANADA

1-31741 Peardonville Rd
Abbotsford, BC V2T 1L2 CA
Phone: (604) 853-4262
Email: info@fhcanada.org
Website: fhcanada.org

A nondenominational service agency engaged in development, Christian education, leadership development, providing medical supplies, partnership development and relief and/or rehabilitation. (DPE)

Purpose: . . . to serve a suffering world by sending appropriate people, ideas and resources to needy communities influencing society to become advocates for the poor and empowering the Christian community with a Biblical view of poverty, social action and injustice.

Income for International Min:
  $40,874,000
Fully Supported CA Personnel Working Cross-Culturally
  More than 4 years: 5
  1–4 years: 12
  Non-residential: 1
Other Personnel
  Short-Term less than 1 year: 24
  Tentmakers/BAM: 2
  Non-CA in own/other country: 1
  Home staff: 26
Countries/Regions: Bolivia, Brazil, Cambodia, Ethiopia, Indonesia, Peru, Romania, Thailand, Uganda

FINAL FRONTIERS FOUNDATION

1200 Peachtree Street
Louisville, GA 30434 US
Phone: (800) 522-4324
Email: postmaster@finalfrontiers.org
Website: finalfrontiers.org

A denominational support agency of Baptist tradition engaged in Bible distribution, childcare or orphanage, children's ministry, church planting (establishing), persecuted church, and STM trip coordination. (FPC-PE)

Purpose: . . . to fund national preachers, endeavoring to effectively advance the gospel where it has never been preached before.

Year Founded in US: 1986
Income for International Min:
  $1,772,765

Other Personnel
Short-Term less than 1 year: 60
Non-US in own/other country: 1010
Home staff: 8
Countries/Regions: Africa, Asia,
Caribbean, Central Asia, Eastern Europe,
Europe, Latin America, Middle East,
Oceania

FINISHING THE TASK
26895 Aliso Creek Rd., B-156
Aliso Viejo, CA 92656 US
Phone: (949) 600-7223
Email: cindy.deibert@ccci.org
Website: finishingthetask.com
A nondenominational network of
Evangelical tradition engaged in research.
Purpose: . . . to see every people group
in the world engaged with an indigenously
led church planting movement.
Year Founded in US: 2005

FIREFALL INTERNATIONAL INC.
133 Parkridge Street
Hot Springs, AR 71901 US
Phone: (501) 620-6026
Email: firefall777@gmail.com
Website: firefallinternational.org
An interdenominational support agency
of Charismatic and Evangelical tradition
engaged in Bible distribution, Bible
teaching, leadership development, national
worker support, persecuted church, and
sports ministry.
Purpose: . . . to transform nations
through compassionate partnerships.
Year Founded in US: 1994
*Fully Supported US Personnel Working
Cross-Culturally*
More than 4 years: 2
1–4 years: 5
Non-residential: 2
Other Personnel
Home staff: 2
Countries/Regions: Southeast Asia

FISHHOOK INTERNATIONAL
Formerly: The Ford Philpot Evangelistic
Association
PO Box 910691
Lexington, KY 40591 US
Phone: (859) 215-0178
Email: info@fishhook.org
Website: fishhook.org/
A nondenominational support agency of
Evangelical and Holiness tradition engaged
in business as mission, childcare or
orphanage, church planting (establishing),
personal or small group evangelism,
missionary & worker training, and prayer-
intercession.
Purpose: . . . to bring the transforming
power of the Gospel to India through
evangelism and discipleship, care for
destitute widows and orphans, and helping
the poor become self reliant
Year Founded in US: 1955
Income for International Min:
$577,516
Other Personnel
Short-Term less than 1 year: 23
Non-US in own/other country: 4
Home staff: 1
Countries/Regions: India

FLYING DOCTORS OF AMERICA
Formerly: Medical Mercy Missions Inc.
PO Box 923563
Norcross, GA 30010 US
Phone: (404) 273-8348
Email: missiontrip@aol.com
Website: fdoamerica.org
An interdenominational service agency of
Ecumenical tradition engaged in medical
supplies and medical ministry, including
dental or public health. (FPC-PE)
Purpose: . . . to help people help people
by creating a network of God's love that
reaches into the farthest corners of the
world and the human heart.
Year Founded in US: 1990

Income for International Min:
$200,000
Other Personnel
Short-Term less than 1 year: 100
Countries/Regions: Guatemala,
Honduras, Mexico, Peru

**FOCAS (FOUNDATION
OF COMPASSIONATE
AMERICAN SAMARITANS)**
PO Box 428760
Cincinnati, OH 45242 US
Phone: (513) 621-5300
Email: FOCAS@focas-us.org
Website: focas-us.org
An interdenominational service agency of
Charismatic tradition engaged in medical
work, children's programs, Christian
education, evangelism and short-term
programs. (DPE)
Purpose: . . . to seek the transformation
of lives by proclaiming the gospel of
Jesus Christ and, through discipleship and
practical expressions of God's love, to
open hearts to the work of the Holy Spirit.
Year Founded in US: 1986
Income for International Min:
$400,000
Other Personnel
Non-US in own/other country: 8
Home staff: 3
Countries/Regions: Haiti

FOOD FOR THE HUNGRY INC.
1224 E. Washington St.
Phoenix, AZ 85034 US
Phone: (480) 998-3100
Email: marc.kyle@fh.org
Website: fh.org
An interdenominational sending agency
of Evangelical tradition engaged in
development, agricultural programs,
children at risk, children's programs, HIV/
AIDS and justice. (DPE)

Purpose: . . . to walk with churches,
leaders, and families in overcoming all
forms of human pover.
Income for International Min:
$82,768,788
*Fully Supported US Personnel Working
Cross-Culturally*
More than 4 years: 19
1–4 years: 63
Non-residential: 2
Other Personnel
Non-US in own/other country: 6
Home staff: 4
Countries/Regions: Bangladesh,
Bolivia, Brazil, Cambodia, China (People's
Republic of), Democratic Republic of
Congo, Costa Rica, Dominican Republic,
Ethiopia, Guatemala, India, Kenya, Laos,
Malaysia, Mongolia, Mozambique,
Nicaragua, Nigeria, Peru, Philippines,
Romania, Rwanda, Tajikistan, Thailand,
Uzbekistan

FOR GOD'S CHILDREN INTL.
PO Box 434
Council Bluffs, IA 51502-0434 US
Phone: (712) 328-3776
Email: fgci@fgci.org
Website: fgci.org
A nondenominational specialized agency
of Christian (Restoration Movement)
tradition engaged in camping programs,
children's ministry, mass evangelism, relief
& aid, and youth ministry.
Purpose: . . . to provide hope, dignity
and love in Jesus' name for God's children.
Year Founded in US: 1995
*Fully Supported US Personnel Working
Cross-Culturally*
More than 4 years: 2
Other Personnel
Non-US in own/other country: 7
Home staff: 5
Countries/Regions: Moldova, Romania

FOR HAITI WITH LOVE INC.

P O Box 1017, 4767 Simcoe Street
Palm Harbor, FL 34683 US
Phone: (727) 938-3245
Email: ForHaiti@aol.com
Website: forhaitiwithlove.org

An interdenominational support agency of Evangelical tradition engaged in medical supplies, medical ministry, including dental or public health, and providing food, clothing, and housing. (FPC-PE)

Purpose: . . . to serve God through helping the poorest of the poor in Northern Haiti, making life better for them in Haiti and helping them maintain independence, and by increasing the awareness stateside of those needs.

Year Founded in US: 1982
Income for International Min:
  $470,940

Fully Supported US Personnel Working Cross-Culturally
  More than 4 years: 7
Other Personnel
  Tentmakers/BAM: 2
  Non-US in own/other country: 7
  Home staff: 2
Countries/Regions: Haiti

FOR HIS GLORY EVANGELISTIC MINISTRIES

P.O. Box 922
St. Charles, MO 63302 US
Phone: (630) 728-8012
Email: rob.welch@forhisglorymin.org
Website: forhisglorymin.org

An interdenominational specialized agency of Evangelical tradition engaged in evangelism and leadership development. (DPE)

Purpose: . . . to proclaim the Good News of Jesus Christ . . . to equip and mobilize His Church to reach those without Christ.

Income for International Min:
  $91,520
Other Personnel
  Short-Term less than 1 year: 17
  Home staff: 2

FOREFRONT EXPERIENCE

Formerly: The Global Forefront
9500 Feather Grass Lane, Suite 120-186
Fort Worth, TX 76177 US
Phone: (417) 342-1256
Email: kyle@forefrontexperience.com
Website: forefrontexperience.com
Associations: Missio Nexus

An interdenominational sending agency of Evangelical tradition engaged in business as mission, DMM, international student ministry, missionary & worker training, recruiting or mobilizing for mission, and services for mission organizations.

Purpose: . . . to reach the unreached by equipping and empowering young adults for a lifetime of effective ministry while pursuing disciple making movements among the lost.

Year Founded in US: 2014
Fully Supported US Personnel Working Cross-Culturally
  1–4 years: 2
  X-C workers in US: 5
Other Personnel
  Home staff: 1
Countries/Regions: Uganda

FORGOTTEN VOICES INTL.

1215 Gettysburg Pike
Dillsburg, PA 17019 US
Phone: (717) 506-3144
Email: info@forgottenvoices.org
Website: forgottenvoices.org

An interdenominational support agency of Brethren and Evangelical tradition engaged in childcare or orphanage, counseling, HIV/AIDS ministry, and leadership development.

Purpose: . . . to demonstrate the love of Jesus Christ by equipping local churches in southern Africa to met the physical and spiritual needs of children orphaned by AIDS in their communities.

Year Founded in US: 2005

Other Personnel
   Non-US in own/other country: 21
   Home staff: 6

Countries/Regions: Malawi, Zambia, Zimbabwe

FORWARD EDGE INTERNATIONAL
15121 - A NE 72nd Ave
Vancouver, WA 98686 US
Phone: (360) 574-3343
Email: fei@forwardedge.org
Website: forwardedge.com

A transdenominational service agency of Evangelical tradition engaged in children's ministry, relief & aid, and STM trip coordination.

Purpose: . . . to partner with God to transform the lives of vulnerable children, disaster victims, and those who go to serve them.

Year Founded in US: 1983

Fully Supported US Personnel Working Cross-Culturally
   More than 4 years: 6

Other Personnel
   Home staff: 13

Countries/Regions: Mexico, Nicaragua

FOUNDATION FOR HIS MINISTRY
PO Box 74000
San Clemente, CA 92673-0134 US
Phone: (949) 492-2200
Email: charla@ffhm.org
Website: ffhm.org

An interdenominational service agency of Charismatic and Evangelical tradition engaged in radio or TV broadcasting, childcare or orphanage, church planting (establishing), disabled ministry, discipleship, and mass evangelism.

Purpose: . . . to glorify God by making disciples of Jesus Christ by sharing and demonstrating God's love through the power of the Holy Spirit by meeting basic spiritual, emotional, physical and educational needs of those in Mexico and beyond.

Year Founded in US: 1967

Fully Supported US Personnel Working Cross-Culturally
   More than 4 years: 20

Other Personnel
   Home staff: 8

Countries/Regions: Mexico

FOUR CORNERS MINISTRIES
715 Avenue A, Ste. 206
Opelika, AL 36801 US
Phone: (334) 737-6338
Email: kris@fourcorners.org
Website: fourcorners.org

An interdenominational sending agency of Baptist and Reformed tradition engaged in church planting (establishing), community development, discipleship, church, school or general Christian education, personal or small group evangelism, and STM trip coordination.

Purpose: . . . to communicate and demonstrate the gospel to hard-to-reach people groups.

Year Founded in US: 2003

Income for International Min: $496,650

Fully Supported US Personnel Working Cross-Culturally
   More than 4 years: 4
   Non-residential: 2

Other Personnel
   Short-Term less than 1 year: 71
   Non-US in own/other country: 1
   Home staff: 5

Countries/Regions: South Sudan, Uganda

FOURSQUARE MISSIONS INTERNATIONAL

1910 W Sunset Blvd, Ste. 700
Los Angeles, CA 90026 US
Phone: (213) 989-4320
Email: fmi@foursquare.org
Website: foursquaremissions.org
Associations: Missio Nexus

A denominational sending agency of Charismatic and Pentecostal tradition engaged in CPM, discipleship, mass evangelism, member care, missionary & worker training, and STM trip coordination.

Purpose: . . . to partner with the Foursquare family to evangelize, disciple, plant churches, and multiply national Foursquare church planting movements around the world.

Year Founded in US: 1925
Income for International Min:
   $7,205,350

Fully Supported US Personnel Working Cross-Culturally
   More than 4 years: 146
   1–4 years: 2
   X-C workers in US: 4

Other Personnel
   Short-Term less than 1 year: 4200
   Tentmakers/BAM: 4
   Non-US in own/other country: 3
   Home staff: 24

Countries/Regions: Albania, Australia, Austria, British Virgin Islands, Bulgaria, Cambodia, Caribbean, Central Asia, Chile, Costa Rica, Czech Republic, Dominican Republic, Ecuador, El Salvador, Estonia, France, Germany, Global Ministry, Greece, Grenada, Guam, Guatemala, Hong Kong (China), Hungary, Ireland (Republic of), Jamaica, Japan, Kenya, Mexico, Middle East, Oceania, Papua New Guinea, Peru, Philippines, Russia, Senegal, South Africa, South America, South Asia, Southeast Asia, Spain, Sub-Saharan Africa, Taiwan (China), Thailand, United Kingdom, Venezuela, Western Europe

FREE METHODIST WORLD MISSIONS

770 N High School Rd
Indianapolis, IN 46214 US
Phone: (317) 244-3660
Email: jennifer.veldman@fmcusa.org
Website: fmcusa.org/fmmissions/
Associations: Missio Nexus

A denominational sending agency of Methodist and Wesleyan tradition engaged in church development, church planting (establishing), community development, leadership development, and STM trip coordination.

Purpose: . . . to love God, love people, and make disciples

Year Founded in US: 1881
Income for International Min:
   $14,856,026

Fully Supported US Personnel Working Cross-Culturally
   More than 4 years: 61
   1–4 years: 16
   X-C workers in US: 3
   Non-residential: 13

Other Personnel
   Short-Term less than 1 year: 693
   Tentmakers/BAM: 2
   Home staff: 9

Countries/Regions: Brazil, Bulgaria, Chile, Colombia, Costa Rica, East Asia, Ecuador, Global Ministry, Greece, Haiti, Hungary, Iraq, Japan, Kenya, Mexico, Middle East, Nigeria, Philippines, Rwanda, South America, South Asia, Southeast Asia, Spain, Sub-Saharan Africa, Taiwan (China), Thailand, Uruguay

FREE WILL BAPTIST INTERNATIONAL MISSIONS
PO Box 5002
Antioch, TN 37011 US
Phone: (615) 760-6120
Email: cyndi@fwbgo.com
Website: fwbgo.com
Associations: Missio Nexus

A denominational sending agency of Baptist and Aremenian tradition engaged in Bible teaching, church planting (establishing), theological education, member care, partnership development, and STM trip coordination.

Purpose: . . . to labor with the Body of Christ to fulfill the Great Commission.

Year Founded in US: 1935
Income for International Min:
 $5,000,000
Fully Supported US Personnel Working Cross-Culturally
 More than 4 years: 61
 X-C workers in US: 8
 Non-residential: 4
Other Personnel
 Short-Term less than 1 year: 177
 Non-US in own/other country: 4
 Home staff: 11
Countries/Regions: Brazil, Bulgaria, Central Asia, Côte d'Ivoire, Cuba, France, Global Ministry, India, Japan, Kenya, Panama, Russia, Spain, Uruguay

FREEDOM FIRM
PO Box 33056
Denver, CO 80233 US
Phone: (720) 423-1607
Email: contactffusa@freedomfirm.org
Website: freedom.firm.in

A service agency of Ecumenical tradition engaged in addressing human trafficking.

Purpose: . . . to eliminate child prostitution in India and enable them to engage in effective rehabilitation.

Year Founded in US: 2006
Fully Supported US Personnel Working Cross-Culturally
 More than 4 years: 2
Other Personnel
 Non-US in own/other country: 30
 Home staff: 3
Countries/Regions: India

FREEDOM IN CHRIST MINISTRIES - USA
9051 Executive Park Dr, Ste. 503
Knoxville, TN 37923 US
Phone: (865) 342-4000
Email: info@ficm.org
Website: ficm.org

A nondenominational service agency of Evangelical tradition engaged in Bible teaching, counseling, discipleship, Internet discipleship or training, leadership development, and youth ministry. (FPC-PE)

Purpose: . . . to help people realize their new identity and freedom in Christ.

Year Founded in US: 1989

FREEDOM TO LEAD INTERNATIONAL
PO Box 3
Cary, NC 27511 US
Phone: (919) 961-4560
Email: rick@freedomtolead.net
Website: freedomtolead.net

A nondenominational service agency of Evangelical tradition engaged in leadership development and orality or storying.

Purpose: . . . to cultivate Christ-centered leaders through story, symbol, and song to unleash the whole Gospel in local communities.

Year Founded in US: 2009
Income for International Min:
 $700,000

Fully Supported US Personnel Working Cross-Culturally
1–4 years: 10065
Non-residential: 18
Other Personnel
Short-Term less than 1 year: 2
Countries/Regions: Côte d'Ivoire, Ethiopia, Gambia, India, Kenya, Nepal, Senegal

FRIENDS IN ACTION INTERNATIONAL – CANADA
27 Long Stan
Stouffville, ON L4A 1P5 CA
Phone: (905) 642-9531
Email: FIA-CAN@fiaintl.org
Website: fiaintl.org
A support agency of Baptist tradition engaged in services for other agencies, agricultural programs, church planting, development and support of national workers. (DPE)

Purpose: . . . to assist missionary groups and individuals around the world with similar purposes in helping to lighten their loads in some way . . . to enable them to continue in their work of reaching the unreached.
Year Founded in CA: 2008
Income for International Min:
$478,138
Fully Supported CA Personnel Working Cross-Culturally
More than 4 years: 3
1–4 years: 1
Other Personnel
Short-Term less than 1 year: 24
Home staff: 1
Countries/Regions: Burkina Faso, Papua New Guinea

FRIENDS IN ACTION INTL.
PO Box 323
Elizabethtown, PA 17022-0323 US
Phone: (717) 546-0208
Email: FIA-usa@fiaintl.org
Website: fiaintl.org
A nondenominational service agency of Evangelical tradition engaged in national worker support, partnership development, and services for mission organizations.

Purpose: . . . to accelerate the work of proclaiming the Gospel to people groups around the world that have not had the opportunity to hear the Good News of Jesus Christ.

Year Founded in US: 1992
Fully Supported US Personnel Working Cross-Culturally
More than 4 years: 7
Other Personnel
Home staff: 5
Countries/Regions: Bolivia, Burkina Faso, India, Moldova, Nicaragua, Papua New Guinea, Vanuatu

FRIENDS OF ISRAEL GOSPEL MINISTRY INC.
PO Box 908
Bellmawr, NJ 08099 US
Phone: (800) 257-7843
Email: info@foi.org
Website: foi.org
A nondenominational support agency of Evangelical tradition engaged in audio recording or distribution, radio or TV broadcasting, personal or small group evangelism, literature distribution, and literature production.

Purpose: . . . to communicate Biblical truth about Israel and the Messiah, while fostering solidarity with the Jewish people.
Year Founded in US: 1938

Fully Supported US Personnel Working Cross-Culturally
Non-residential: 1
Other Personnel
Non-US in own/other country: 32
Home staff: 37
Countries/Regions: Global Ministry

FRIENDS UNITED MEETING
101 Quaker Hill Dr.
Richmond, IN 47374 US
Phone: (765) 962-7573
Email: info@fum.org
Website: fum.org
A denominational sending agency of Friends tradition engaged in foreign missions, support of national churches, childcare/orphanage programs, theological education, leadership development, literature production and medical work. (DPE)
Purpose: . . . to energize and equip Friends, through the power of the Holy Spirit, to gather people into fellowships where Jesus Christ is known, loved, and obeyed as teacher and Lord.
Year Founded in US: 1966
Income for International Min: $1,080,015
Fully Supported US Personnel Working Cross-Culturally
More than 4 years: 3
1–4 years: 3
Other Personnel
Short-Term less than 1 year: 23
Non-US in own/other country: 1
Home staff: 6
Countries/Regions: Belize, Cuba, Jamaica, Kenya, Palestine

FRIENDSHIP INTERNATIONAL MINISTRIES INC.
PO Box 50884
Colorado Springs, CO 80949-0884 US
Phone: (719) 386-8808
Email: FRINT@aol.com
Website: friendshipintl.org
An interdenominational specialized agency of Evangelical tradition engaged in camping programs, discipleship, mass evangelism, STM trip coordination, and youth ministry.
Purpose: . . . to assist people in meeting their intellectual, physical and spiritual needs. We are committed to building up the body of Christ by communicating the gospel and by equipping and training Christians in using music, evangelism, discipleship training, short-term programs and youth programs.
Year Founded in US: 1990
Fully Supported US Personnel Working Cross-Culturally
More than 4 years: 8
Other Personnel
Home staff: 4
Countries/Regions: Chile, Hungary, Romania, United Kingdom

FRONTIER VENTURES
Formerly: US Center for World Mission (USCWM)
1605 E Elizabeth St.
Pasadena, CA 91104 US
Phone: (626) 797-1111
Email: info@frontierventures.org
Website: FrontierVentures.org
Associations: Missio Nexus
An interdenominational service agency of Evangelical tradition engaged in information or journalism, literature production, networking, partnership, or coordination, recruiting or mobilizing for mission, research, and services for mission organizations.

Purpose: . . . to initiate and accelerate breakthrough of the gospel within every least reached people group by discerning and disseminating insights, mobilizing and equipping people, and launching innovations that overcome barriers to following Jesus.

Year Founded in US: 1976
Income for International Min:
  $528,400
Fully Supported US Personnel Working Cross-Culturally
  More than 4 years: 5
  1–4 years: 2
Other Personnel
  Short-Term less than 1 year: 40
  Home staff: 7
Countries/Regions: Brunei, Eastern Europe and Eurasia, Indonesia, Turkey

FRONTIERS
P.O. Box 60670
Phoenix, AZ 85082 US
Phone: (800) 462-8436
Email: info@frontiersusa.org
Website: frontiersusa.org
Associations: Missio Nexus

A nondenominational sending agency of Evangelical tradition engaged in business as mission, CPM, DMM, member care, missionary & worker training, and recruiting or mobilizing for mission.
Purpose: . . . to invite all Muslim Peoples to follow Jesus with love and respect.
Year Founded in US: 1982
Income for International Min:
  $32,000,000
Fully Supported US Personnel Working Cross-Culturally
  More than 4 years: 578
  X-C workers in US: 16
Other Personnel
  Short-Term less than 1 year: 50
  Home staff: 123
Countries/Regions: Global Ministry

FRONTIERS CANADA
Box 48004
Winnipeg, MB R2J 4A3 CA
Phone: (204) 962-7712
Email: info@frontiers.ca
Website: frontiers.ca
Associations: Missio Nexus

An interdenominational sending agency of Evangelical tradition engaged in church planting (establishing), CPM, DMM, and recruiting or mobilizing for mission. (FPC-PE)
Purpose: . . . to invite all Muslim Peoples to follow Jesus with love and respect.
Year Founded in CA: 2011
Fully Supported CA Personnel Working Cross-Culturally
  More than 4 years: 37
Other Personnel
  Non-CA in own/other country: 2
Countries/Regions: Africa, Asia, Central Asia, Europe, Middle East

FULL GOSPEL EVANGELISTIC ASSOCIATION
PO Box 702378
Tulsa, OK 74170-2378 US
Phone: (918) 749-3432
Email: admin@fgeaonline.org
Website: fgeaonline.org

An association of missions of Pentecostal and Full Gospel tradition helping to support full-time missionaries and national churches engaged in church construction, church planting, member care and services for other agencies. (DPE)
Year Founded in US: 1951
Fully Supported US Personnel Working Cross-Culturally
  More than 4 years: 12
  1–4 years: 6
  Non-residential: 1
Other Personnel
  Short-Term less than 1 year: 25
  Non-US in own/other country: 2
  Home staff: 2

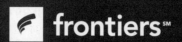

Countries/Regions: El Salvador, Honduras, Kenya, Mexico, Nicaragua, Pakistan, Russia

FUNDAMENTAL BAPTIST MISSION OF TRINIDAD & TOBAGO

P.O. Box 58201
Charleston, WV 25358 US
Phone: (304) 415-2566
Email: fbmtt@earthlink.net
Website: fbmtt.org
A sending agency of Baptist and Fundamental tradition engaged in church planting, evangelism and support of national workers. (DPE)
Countries/Regions: Trinidad and Tobago

FUNDAMENTAL BAPTIST MISSIONS INTERNATIONAL

507 State Street
Hammond, IN 46320 US
Phone: (219) 932-0711
Email: helpdesk@fbmi.org
Website: fbmi.org
An Independent sending agency of Baptist tradition engaged in church planting, Bible distribution, Christian education, evangelism, funds transmission and Bible translation. (DPE)
Income for International Min:
  $6,470,000
Other Personnel
  Home staff: 21

GAIN (GLOBAL AID NETWORK)

2001 West Plano Parkway, Suite 2200
Plano, TX 75075 US
Phone: (972) 234-0800
Email: info@gainusa.org
Website: gainusa.org
An interdenominational specialized agency of Evangelical tradition engaged in relief and/or rehabilitation, humanitarian aid, children at risk, evangelism, providing medical supplies and short-term programs,

with short-term mission trips to more than 10 countries. (DPE)
Purpose: . . . to demonstrate the love of God, in word and deed, to hurting and needy people around the world.
Income for International Min:
  $33,854,534
Fully Supported US Personnel Working Cross-Culturally
  Non-residential: 1
Other Personnel
  Short-Term less than 1 year: 235
  Non-US in own/other country: 6
  Home staff: 58
Countries/Regions: Eastern Europe, France

GALCOM INTERNATIONAL CANADA

115 Nebo Rd
Hamilton, ON L8W 2E1 CA
Phone: (905) 574-4626
Email: galcom@galcom.org
Website: galcom.org
A nondenominational service agency of Evangelical tradition engaged in audio recording or distribution and radio or TV broadcasting. (FPC-PE)
Purpose: . . . to multiply missionary impact through audio technology and by providing durable technical equipment for communicating the Gospel worldwide.
Year Founded in CA: 1989

GALCOM INTERNATIONAL USA INC.

PO Box 270956
Tampa, FL 33688 US
Phone: (813) 933-8111
Email: administration@galcomusa.com
Website: galcomusa.com
A nondenominational service agency of Evangelical tradition engaged in audio recording or distribution, radio broacasting, and technical assistance. (FPC-PE)

Purpose: . . . to provide durable technical equipment for communicating the Gospel worldwide.
Year Founded in US: 1989

GATE BREAKER MINISTRIES
824 E. Sicily Court
Meridian, ID 83642 US
Phone: (208) 290-4007
Email: sfleming@gatebreakers.com
Website: gatebreakers.com
A nondenominational sending agency of Charismatic and Pentecostal tradition engaged in apologetics, church, school or general Christian education, addressing human trafficking, leadership development, networking, partnership, or coordination, and STM trip coordination.
Purpose: . . . to equip the church to dispel darkness by promoting the truth.
Year Founded in US: 2007
Income for International Min:
   $95,165
Fully Supported US Personnel Working Cross-Culturally
   Non-residential: 2
Other Personnel
   Short-Term less than 1 year: 13
   Non-US in own/other country: 15
   Home staff: 1
Countries/Regions: Kenya, Pakistan

GATEWAY TRAINING FOR CROSS-CULTURAL SERVICE
21233 - 32nd Avenue
Langley, BC V2Z 2E7 CA
Phone: (604) 530-4283
Email: registrar@gatewaytraining.org
Website: gatewaytraining.org
An interdenominational specialized agency of Evangelical tradition engaged in missionary training and missionary education. A division of WEC International. (DPE)
Other Personnel
   Home staff: 9

GENERAL BAPTISTS INTERNATIONAL
100 Stinson Dr.
Poplar Bluff, MO 63901 US
Phone: (573) 785-7746
Email: mark.powell@generalbaptist.com
Website: generalbaptist.com
Associations: Missio Nexus
A denominational sending agency of Baptist tradition engaged in church planting, agricultural programs, childcare/orphanage programs, literacy work, short-term programs and training. (DPE)
Purpose: . . . to win and disciple people around the world.
Fully Supported US Personnel Working Cross-Culturally
   More than 4 years: 20
   1–4 years: 7
   Non-residential: 16
Other Personnel
   Short-Term less than 1 year: 500
   Non-US in own/other country: 1
   Home staff: 5
Countries/Regions: Honduras, India, Mexico, Northern Mariana Islands, Philippines, Unspecified Country

GIDEONS INTERNATIONAL, THE
PO Box 140800
Nashville, TN 37214-0800 US
Phone: (615) 564-5000
Email: jburden@gideons.org
Website: gideons.org
An interdenominational service agency of Evangelical and Fundamental tradition engaged in Bible distribution and evangelism. (DPE)
Purpose: . . . to win others to Christ through personal witnessing and scripture distribution.
Year Founded in US: 1910
Income for International Min:
   $95,600,000

Fully Supported US Personnel Working Cross-Culturally
Non-residential: 8
Other Personnel
Short-Term less than 1 year: 150
Non-US in own/other country: 58
Home staff: 107
Countries/Regions: Africa, Asia, Europe, Latin America

GLOBAL ACTION
PO Box 51063
Colorado Springs, CO 80949 US
Phone: (719) 528-8728
Email: globalaction@globalaction.com
Website: globalaction.com
A nondenominational sending agency of Evangelical tradition engaged in children's ministry, church planting (establishing), mass evangelism, STM trip coordination, and youth ministry.
Purpose: . . . to proclaim the Kingdom of God in word and deed around the world and to serve the Church by empowering, training, motivating, and mobilizing people to become fully devoted followers of Christ.
Year Founded in US: 1998
Income for International Min:
$966,077
Fully Supported US Personnel Working Cross-Culturally
More than 4 years: 9
Other Personnel
Home staff: 4
Countries/Regions: Guatemala, Honduras, India, Ukraine

GLOBAL ADOPT A PEOPLE CAMPAIGN
1443 E Washington Blvd
Pasadena, CA 91104 US
Phone: (818) 510-3272
Email: philbogosian@gaapc.org
Website: globaladoptapeoplecampaign.org

An interdenominational service agency of Evangelical tradition engaged in literature distribution, literature production, prayer-intercession, recruiting or mobilizing for mission, and services for mission organizations.
Purpose: . . . to reach all peoples with the gospel as soon as possible by equipping and educating local denominational church members, through seminars, videos, and publications, to pray regularly for their own denominational missionaries who are working to plant Christ's church among unreached peoples.
Year Founded in US: 1995
Income for International Min:
$230,000
Fully Supported US Personnel Working Cross-Culturally
More than 4 years: 6
Other Personnel
Home staff: 2
Countries/Regions: Philippines

GLOBAL AID NETWORK INC. – CANADA
20385 - 64 Ave.
Langley, BC V2Y 1N5 CA
Phone: (604) 514-2026
Email: info@globalaid.net
Website: globalaid.net
A sending agency of Evangelical tradition engaged in development, childcare/orphanage programs, church planting, psychological counseling and relief and/or rehabilitation. (DPE)
Purpose: . . . to demonstrate the love of God in word and deed to hurting and needy people around the world through relief and development projects.
Income for International Min:
$2,015,693

Fully Supported CA Personnel Working Cross-Culturally
More than 4 years: 25
1–4 years: 25
Other Personnel
Short-Term less than 1 year: 34
Home staff: 2
Countries/Regions: Africa

GLOBAL FELLOWSHIP INC.
PO Box 1
Meadow Vista, CA 95772 US
Phone: (530) 888-9208
Email: don@globalfellowship.org
Website: globalfellowship.org
An interdenominational sending agency of Evangelical tradition engaged in church planting (establishing), mass evangelism, missionary & worker training, and national worker support.
Purpose: . . . to serve indigenous ministries including financial assistance, technological assistance, prayer relief, and human resources as well as spiritual encouragement, exhortation and equipping.
Year Founded in US: 1989
Income for International Min:
$500,000
Fully Supported US Personnel Working Cross-Culturally
More than 4 years: 8
Other Personnel
Home staff: 4
Countries/Regions: Singapore, South Asia

GLOBAL FOCUS
PO Box 1058
Acworth, GA 30101 US
Phone: (770) 529-0861
Email: contact.info@globalfocus.info
Website: globalfocus.info
A nondenominational service agency of Baptist and Evangelical tradition engaged

in church mobilization, church mission development, missions information service and Acts 1:8 strategies. (DPE)
Purpose: . . . to glorify God by helping pastors or church leaders to be more effective in mobilizing the church to reach the world for Christ.
Year Founded in US: 1995
Other Personnel
Home staff: 8

GLOBAL FRONTIER MISSIONS
PO Box 327
Clarkston, GA 30021 US
Phone: (770) 676-2851
Email: gfmstaff@gmail.com
Website: globalfrontiermissions.org
Associations: Missio Nexus
A nondenominational service agency of Evangelical tradition engaged in church development, DMM, missionary & worker training, prayer-intercession, STM trip coordination, and TESOL or TEFL.
Purpose: . . . as a movement of Christ-centered communities dedicated to mobilizing, training, and multiplying disciples and churches to meet the physical and spiritual needs of the unreached people groups of the earth.
Year Founded in US: 2000
Income for International Min:
$50,000
Fully Supported US Personnel Working Cross-Culturally
1–4 years: 8
X-C workers in US: 44
Other Personnel
Short-Term less than 1 year: 540
Countries/Regions: Australia, India

GLOBAL GATES

236 W. 72nd Street
New York, NY 10023 US
Phone: (917) 243-4979
Email: info@globalgates.info
Website: GlobalGates.info
Associations: Missio Nexus

A nondenominational sending agency of Evangelical tradition engaged in Bible distribution, CPM, personal or small group evangelism, networking, partnership, or coordination, prayer-intercession, and recruiting or mobilizing for mission.

Purpose: . . . to reach the ends of the earth through global gateway cities.

Year Founded in US: 2012
Income for International Min:
  $1,980,000
Fully Supported US Personnel Working Cross-Culturally
  More than 4 years: 26
  1–4 years: 2012
  X-C workers in US: 27
Other Personnel
  Short-Term less than 1 year: 6
  Home staff: 3
Countries/Regions: Afghanistan, Bangladesh, Canada, India, Iran, Mali, Pakistan, Palestine, Saudi Arabia, Somalia, Thailand, Turkey, Yemen

GLOBAL HEALTH MINISTRIES

7831 Hickory St. NE
Minneapolis, MN 55432 US
Phone: (763) 586-9590
Email: ghmoffice@cs.com
Website: ghm.org

An interdenominational support agency of Lutheran tradition engaged in providing medical supplies, development, management consulting/training, medical work, partnership development and mobilization for mission. Ongoing programs in 21 countries. (DPE)

Purpose: . . . to enhance the health care programs of Lutheran churches in the developing world.

Income for International Min:
  $2,255,177
Other Personnel
  Short-Term less than 1 year: 6
  Non-US in own/other country: 2
  Home staff: 8
Countries/Regions: Central African Republic, Madagascar

GLOBAL HEALTH OUTREACH

P.O. Box 7500
Bristol, TN 37621 US
Phone: (423) 844-1000
Email: ghoapps@cmda.org
Website: ghotrips.org
Associations: Accord Network

A nondenominational sending agency of Evangelical tradition engaged in discipleship, addressing human trafficking, medical ministry, including dental or public health, and STM trip coordination.

Purpose: . . . to demonstrate the love and compassion of Jesus, offering hope to mind, body and spirit through medical and dental care and influence those around them to a right relationship with Jesus Christ.

Year Founded in US: 1931
Income for International Min:
  $6,600,892
Other Personnel
  Short-Term less than 1 year: 1098
  Non-US in own/other country: 2
  Home staff: 9
Countries/Regions: Afghanistan, Albania, Armenia, Cambodia, China (People's Republic of), Dominican Republic, Ecuador, Egypt, El Salvador, Ethiopia, Ghana, Guatemala, Haiti, Honduras, Indonesia, Jordan, Kenya,

Lebanon, Mexico, Moldova, Morocco, Myanmar (Burma), Nepal, Nicaragua, Nigeria, Ukraine, Vietnam

GLOBAL HOPE INDIA
Formerly: The Compassion Network
400 Fayetteville St, Ste. E
Raleigh, NC 27601 US
Phone: (919) 438-2444
Email: info@globalhopeindia.org
Website: globalhopeindia.org
A nondenominational support agency of Baptist tradition engaged in childcare or orphanage, church planting (establishing), leadership development, medical ministry, including dental or public health, networking, partnership, or coordination, and STM trip coordination.
Purpose: . . . to engage the Church globally to empower the local church in India.
Year Founded in US: 2003
Other Personnel
    Short-Term less than 1 year: 139
    Home staff: 6

GLOBAL IMPACT SERVICES
PO Box 336
Jenison, MI 49429 US
Phone: (616) 821-7117
Email: mark@globalimpactservices.org
Website: globalimpactservices.org
A nondenominational service agency of Evangelical tradition engaged in management consulting/training, missions information service and mission-related research. (DPE)
Purpose: . . . to maximize the resources and mobilize the people of the Church and her agencies for greater global impact.
Other Personnel
    Home staff: 1

GLOBAL MEDIA OUTREACH
7160 Dallas Parkway, Ste. 200
Plano, TX 75204 US
Phone: (972) 975-9444
Email: contact@gmomail.org
Website: globalmediaoutreach.com
A nondenominational specialized agency of Evangelical tradition engaged in Bible distribution, discipleship, mass evangelism, Internet discipleship or training, Internet evangelism, and prayer-intercession.
Purpose: . . . to give every man, woman, and child multiple opportunities to experience the gospel of Jesus Christ. Our goal is to stay on the cutting edge of emerging technologies and use these technologies to reach the world for Christ.
Year Founded in US: 2004
Fully Supported US Personnel Working Cross-Culturally
    X-C workers in US: 4000
Other Personnel
    Tentmakers/BAM: 1375
    Home staff: 43
Countries/Regions: Albania, Angola, Argentina, Australia, Austria, Bahrain, Bangladesh, Belarus, Belgium, Benin, Bolivia, Brazil, Burkina Faso, Burundi, Cameroon, Canada, Central African Republic, Chile, China (People's Republic of), Colombia, Costa Rica, Côte d'Ivoire, Democratic Republic of Congo, Ecuador, Egypt, El Salvador, Ethiopia, Federated States of Micronesia, Finland, France, Gambia, Germany, Ghana, Global Ministry, Greece, Guatemala, Guyana, Honduras, Hong Kong (China)Hungary, India, Indonesia, Ireland (Republic of), Republic of, Israel, Italy, Japan, Jordan, Kenya, Kuwait, Lebanon, Madagascar, Malawi, Malaysia, Mali, Mauritius, Mexico, Morocco, Namibia, Nepal, Netherlands, New Zealand, Nicaragua, Nigeria, Norway, Pakistan, Palestine, Panama, Paraguay, Peru, Philippines, Puerto Rico,

Republic of Congo, Romania, Russia,
Rwanda, Saint Lucia, Senegal, Seychelles,
Singapore, Slovenia, South Africa, South
Korea, South Sudan, Spain, Sri Lanka,
Sweden, Switzerland, Syria, Tanzania,
Thailand, Togo, Trinidad and Tobago,
Turkey, Uganda, Ukraine, United Arab
Emirates, United Kingdom, Uruguay,
Venezuela, Vietnam, Zambia, Zimbabwe

GLOBAL MISSIONS (UNITED PENTECOSTAL CHURCH INTL.)
8855 Dunn Rd.
Hazelwood, MO 63042 US
Phone: (314) 837-7300
Email: bhowell@upci.org
Website: globalmissions.com/
A denominational sending agency of
Pentecostal and Apostolic tradition
engaged in evangelism, church planting,
discipleship, theological education,
evangelism and leadership development.
(DPE)
Fully Supported US Personnel Working Cross-Culturally
  1–4 years: 340
  Non-residential: 551
Other Personnel
  Short-Term less than 1 year: 300
  Non-US in own/other country: 236
  Home staff: 35
Countries/Regions: Albania, American
Samoa, Argentina, Armenia, Aruba,
Australia, Austria, Azerbaijan, Bahamas,
Bangladesh, Belarus, Belgium, Belize,
Benin, Bhutan, Bolivia, Bosnia and
Herzegovina, Botswana, Brazil, Bulgaria,
Burkina Faso, Burundi, Cambodia,
Cameroon, Caribbean, Cayman Islands,
Central African Republic, Chile, China
(People's Republic of), Colombia,
Democratic Republic of Congo, Costa
Rica, Côte d'Ivoire, Croatia, Cuba,
Cyprus, Czech Republic, Dominican
Republic, Ecuador, Egypt, El Salvador,

Equatorial Guinea, Europe, Fiji, Finland,
France, French Guiana, Gabon, Gambia,
Georgia, Germany, Ghana, Greece,
Grenada, Guam, Guatemala, Guyana,
Haiti, Honduras, Hong Kong (China),
Hungary, India, Indonesia, Israel, Italy,
Jamaica, Japan, Jordan, Kazakhstan, Kenya,
South Korea, Laos, Latvia, Lebanon,
Lesotho, Liberia, Lithuania, Macedonia,
Madagascar, Malawi, Malaysia, Malta,
Mauritius, Mexico, Federated States
of Micronesia, Middle East, Morocco,
Mozambique, Myanmar (Burma), Namibia,
Nepal, Netherlands, New Caledonia,
New Zealand, Nicaragua, Niger, Nigeria,
Norway, Oceania, Pakistan, Palestine,
Panama, Papua New Guinea, Paraguay,
Peru, Philippines, Poland, Portugal,
Puerto Rico, Réunion, Romania, Russia,
Rwanda, Samoa, Serbia, Seychelles, Sierra
Leone, Singapore, Slovakia, Solomon
Islands, South Africa, Spain, Sri Lanka,
Sudan, Suriname, Swaziland, Sweden,
Switzerland, Taiwan (China), Tanzania,
Thailand, Togo, Tonga, Trinidad and
Tobago, Turkey, Uganda, Ukraine, United
Kingdom, Uruguay, Vanuatu, Venezuela,
Vietnam, Zambia, Zimbabwe

GLOBAL MISSIONS OF OPEN BIBLE CHURCHES
Formerly: International Ministries
2020 Bell Avenue
Des Moines, IA 50315 US
Phone: (515) 288-6761
Email: missions@openbible.org
Website: globalmissionsobc.org
Associations: Missio Nexus
A denominational sending agency of
Pentecostal tradition engaged in Bible
teaching, childcare or orphanage, church
construction or financing, church planting
(establishing), discipleship, and church,
school or general Christian education.

Purpose: . . . to globally make disciples, develop leaders and plant churches.

Fully Supported US Personnel Working Cross-Culturally
More than 4 years: 19
1–4 years: 6
Other Personnel
Non-US in own/other country: 44
Countries/Regions: Argentina, Bolivia, Brazil, Cambodia, Canada, Cayman Islands, Chile, Costa Rica, Cuba, Dominican Republic, El Salvador, Ghana, Grenada, Guatemala, Guinea, Guyana, Hungary, India, Jamaica, Japan, Kenya, South Korea, Liberia, Mexico, Nicaragua, Nigeria, North Africa, Papua New Guinea, Paraguay, Peru, Philippines, Puerto Rico, Romania, Saint Vincent and the Grenadines, Sierra Leone, South America, Spain, Suriname, Thailand, Trinidad and Tobago, Uganda, Ukraine, United Kingdom, Uruguay, Venezuela

GLOBAL OPPORTUNITIES – GLOBAL INTENT
6900 Daniels Parkway, Ste 29-309
Fort Myers, FL 33912 US
Phone: (239) 243-0881
Email: info@intent.org
Website: intent.org
An interdenominational specialized agency of Evangelical and Independent tradition engaged in business as mission, church planting (establishing), DMM, tentmaking & related. (FPC-PE)

Purpose: . . . to help the church to understand and engage the Biblical model of tent making by sending committed, everyday, workplace Christians as mission workers, and to mobilize and equip these Christians to serve abroad as effective tentmakers, primarily to least reached peoples.

Year Founded in US: 1984
Other Personnel
Home staff: 2

GLOBAL OUTREACH INTERNATIONAL
PO Box 1
Tupelo, MS 38802 US
Phone: (662) 842-4615
Email: go@globaloutreach.org
Website: globaloutreach.org
A nondenominational sending agency of Evangelical tradition engaged in missionary training, childcare/orphanage programs, church construction, evangelism, leadership development and medical work. (DPE)

Income for International Min:
$4,789,009
Fully Supported US Personnel Working Cross-Culturally
More than 4 years: 165
Other Personnel
Short-Term less than 1 year: 1007
Non-US in own/other country: 9
Home staff: 9
Countries/Regions: Argentina, Barbados, Belize, Brazil, Cambodia, Cameroon, Chile, China (People's Republic of), Costa Rica, Ecuador, Guatemala, Guyana, Haiti, Honduras, India, Kenya, Mexico, Moldova, Mozambique, Myanmar (Burma), Nicaragua, Peru, Philippines, Poland, Romania, Rwanda, Slovakia, Sudan, Uganda, Ukraine, United Kingdom, Vietnam

GLOBAL OUTREACH MISSION INC.
PO Box 2010
Buffalo, NY 14231-2010 US
Phone: (716) 688-5048
Email: gom@missiongo.org
Website: missiongo.org
A nondenominational sending agency of Evangelical and Independent tradition engaged in church planting, broadcasting,

evangelism, medical work, support of national workers, relief and/or rehabilitation and short-term programs. (DPE)

Purpose: . . . to share the Gospel of Jesus Christ around the world . . . to plant and encourage His church . . . to help the hurting physically and to serve in every area of Christian development.

Income for International Min:
 $3,421,928
Fully Supported US Personnel Working Cross-Culturally
 More than 4 years: 178
 1–4 years: 10
Other Personnel
 Short-Term less than 1 year: 95
 Home staff: 14
Countries/Regions: Antigua and Barbuda, Australia, Austria, Belgium, Belize, Bolivia, Brazil, Chile, Republic of Congo, Costa Rica, Dominican Republic, France, Gabon, Germany, Ghana, Guatemala, Haiti, Honduras, India, Ireland (Republic of), Jamaica, Jordan, Kosovo, Mexico, Myanmar (Burma), Netherlands, Paraguay, Peru, Romania, Russia, Sierra Leone, Sint Maarten, Spain, Switzerland, Thailand, Ukraine, United Kingdom

GLOBAL OUTREACH MISSION INC. CANADA
PO Box 1210
St. Catherines, ON L2R 7A7 CA
Phone: (905) 684-1402
Email: glmiss@on.aibn.com
Website: missiongo.org

A nondenominational sending agency of Evangelical and Independent tradition engaged in church planting, broadcasting, evangelism, medical work, support of national workers, mobilization for mission and short-term programs. (DPE)

Purpose: . . . to share the Gospel . . . to plant and encourage His church . . . to help those who are hurting physically and to serve in every area of Christian development.

Income for International Min:
 $1,176,212
Fully Supported CA Personnel Working Cross-Culturally
 More than 4 years: 40
 1–4 years: 1
Countries/Regions: Belgium, Brazil, Republic of Congo, France, Guatemala, Hong Kong (China), India, Ireland (Republic of), Kazakhstan, Romania, United Kingdom

GLOBAL PARTNERS (THE WESLEYAN CHURCH WORLD HEADQUARTERS)
PO Box 50434
Indianapolis, IN 46250 US
Phone: (317) 774-7950
Email: globalpartners@wesleyan.org
Website: globalpartnersonline.org/
Associations: Missio Nexus

A denominational sending agency of Wesleyan tradition engaged in Bible teaching, church planting (establishing), discipleship, personal or small group evangelism, leadership development, and medical ministry, including dental or public health.

Purpose: . . . to amplify local church mission for global transformation.

Income for International Min:
 $10,119,708
Fully Supported US Personnel Working Cross-Culturally
 More than 4 years: 151
 1–4 years: 6
 Non-residential: 23
Other Personnel
 Home staff: 18

Countries/Regions: Albania,
Australia, Austria, Bangladesh, Bosnia and
Herzegovina, Brazil, Cambodia, Caribbean,
Croatia, Czech Republic, East Asia, Ecuador,
El Salvador, Global Ministry, Guyana, Haiti,
India, Japan, Macedonia, Mexico, Middle
East, Mozambique, Nepal, Niger, Panama,
Philippines, Russia, Sierra Leone, Singapore,
South Africa, South America, Swaziland,
Thailand, Uganda, Zambia

GLOBAL RECORDINGS NETWORK
41823 Enterprise Circle N #200
Temecula, CA 92590 US
Phone: (951) 719-1650
Email: dalerickards@globalrecordings.net
Website: globalrecordings.net
Associations: Missio Nexus
A nondenominational specialized agency
of Evangelical tradition engaged in audio
recording or distribution, discipleship,
mass evangelism, personal or small group
evangelism, Internet evangelism, and
orality or storying. (FPC-PE)
Purpose: . . . to effectively communicate
the Good News of Jesus Christ by means
of culturally appropriate audio and audio-
visual materials in every language.
Year Founded in US: 1939
Income for International Min:
$2,480,000
*Fully Supported US Personnel Working
Cross-Culturally*
More than 4 years: 7
Non-residential: 3
Other Personnel
Short-Term less than 1 year: 30
Tentmakers/BAM: 10
Non-US in own/other country: 133
Home staff: 26
Countries/Regions: Australia, Austria,
Bangladesh, Belgium, Brazil, Burkina
Faso, Cameroon, Canada, Central African
Republic, Chad, Colombia, Democratic
Republic of Congo, Côte d'Ivoire, Ecuador,

France, Gambia, Germany, Ghana,
Guinea, India, Indonesia, Kenya, South
Korea, Liberia, Mauritania, Mexico,
Myanmar (Burma), Nepal, Netherlands,
Nigeria, Pakistan, Philippines, Sierra Leone,
South Africa, Spain, Switzerland, Tanzania,
Thailand, Togo, United Kingdom, Vanuatu

GLOBAL RECORDINGS
NETWORK CANADA
115 Nebo Road
Hamilton, ON L8W 2E1 CA
Phone: (905) 574-8220
Email: ca@globalrecordings.net
Website: globalrecordings.net/en/ca
A nondenominational specialized agency
of Baptist and Evangelical tradition
engaged in audio recording or distribution
and recording Bible stories in minority
languages.
Purpose: . . . to tell the story of Jesus in
all languages by preparing and distributing
equipment and recorded audio-visual
materials to communicate the Gospel of
Jesus Christ both at home and abroad.
Year Founded in CA: 1969
Income for International Min:
$120,165
Other Personnel
Non-CA in own/other country: 4
Home staff: 5
Countries/Regions: Kenya

GLOBAL SCHOLARS
International Institute for Christian Schools
PO Box 12147
Overland Park, KS 66282-2147 US
Phone: (913) 962-4422
Email: swallace@global-scholars.org
Website: global-scholars.org
Associations: Missio Nexus
An interdenominational sending agency of
Evangelical tradition engaged in extension
education, theological education,
evangelism, HIV/AIDS and TESOL. (DPE)

Purpose: . . . to bring glory to God and impact the world by developing godly leaders for every sector of society— government, business, home, church, the arts, law, the sciences, education - as we provide key universities and academic institutions outside North America with educational services and Christian faculty who teach and live in such a way as to draw others to faith and transformation in Christ.

Income for International Min:
$1,850,386

Fully Supported US Personnel Working Cross-Culturally
More than 4 years: 29
1–4 years: 9

Other Personnel
Short-Term less than 1 year: 10
Tentmakers/BAM: 25
Non-US in own/other country: 38
Home staff: 8

Countries/Regions: Brazil, Bulgaria, Czech Republic, Japan, Kazakhstan, Lithuania, Mexico, Nigeria, Romania, Uganda, Unspecified Country

GLOBAL SPHERES
Formerly: Global Harvest Ministries
P.O. Box 1601
Denton, TX 76202 US
Phone: (940) 382-7231
Email: info@globalharvest.org
Website: globalspheres.org

A transdenominational support agency of Evangelical and Charismatic tradition engaged in leadership development and training. (DPE)

Purpose: . . . to strengthen global forces for evangelism; engage in apostolic ministries to train, encourage, network, and resource leaders; mobilize prayer for world evangelization; train leaders in prayer, spiritual warfare, practical ministry and deliverance.

Other Personnel
Short-Term less than 1 year: 8
Home staff: 19

GLOBAL TEAMS INTERNATIONAL INC.
3821 Mount Vernon Ave.
Bakersfield, CA 93306 US
Phone: (661) 323-1214
Email: inquiries@global-teams.net
Website: global-teams.net
Associations: Missio Nexus

An interdenominational sending agency of Evangelical tradition engaged in church planting, business as mission, leadership development, member care, mobilization for mission and Bible translation. (DPE)

Purpose: . . . to equip and send teams of missionaries from many nations to multiply disciples of Jesus within cultures least familiar with the Gospel.

Income for International Min:
$1,128,000

Other Personnel
Short-Term less than 1 year: 9
Home staff: 5

GLOBAL TRAINING NETWORK
7558 W. Thunderbird Rd. Ste. 1, PMB 449
Peoria, AZ 85381 US
Phone: (623) 217-3867
Email: joshuakienzle@globaltrainingnetwork.org
Website: globaltrainingnetwork.org

A nondenominational support agency of Evangelical tradition engaged in church development, discipleship, leadership development, and pastoral training.

Purpose: . . . to train Majority World church planters, pastors, and Christian leaders so that they can more effectively equip their congregations to evangelize and disciple their communities for Christ.

Year Founded in US: 2004

Income for International Min:
$3,400,000
Fully Supported US Personnel Working Cross-Culturally
More than 4 years: 34
1–4 years: 53
Non-residential: 84
Other Personnel
Short-Term less than 1 year: 20
Non-US in own/other country: 3
Home staff: 4
Countries/Regions: Global Ministry, South America, South Asia, Sub-Saharan Africa

GLOBAL WITNESS AND MINISTRY-AME CHURCH
PO Box 30396,
1587 Savannah Highway, Ste. A
Charleston, SC 29417 US
Phone: (843) 852-2645
Email: gwmame@bellsouth.net
Website: amecglobalmissions.org
Associations: CCRDA

A denominational sending agency of Methodist tradition engaged in childcare or orphanage, church, school or general Christian education, HIV/AIDS ministry, partnership development, relief & aid, and STM trip coordination.

Purpose: . . . to pursue a Global Mission in ministry, witness and gospel proclamation so that the people of God may be liberated spiritually and materially and reconciled to each other through the Holy Spirit.
Year Founded in US: 1866

GLOBALLEAD
Formerly: Global Youth Ministry Network
91 Park Ave. W. Ste. G
Mansfield, OH 44902-1630 US
Phone: (419) 756-4433
Email: office@globallead.world
Website: globallead.world

A transdenominational specialized agency of Evangelical and Reformed tradition engaged in leadership development, evangelism, support of national workers, support of national churches, training and youth programs. (DPE)
Income for International Min:
$75,000
Fully Supported US Personnel Working Cross-Culturally
More than 4 years: 1
Other Personnel
Non-US in own/other country: 6
Home staff: 2
Countries/Regions: Africa, Asia, Latin America, Unspecified Country

GLOBE INTERNATIONAL
8590 Hwy 98 West
Pensacola, FL 32506 US
Phone: (850) 453-3453
Email: info@globeintl.org
Website: globeintl.org
Associations: Missio Nexus

An interdenominational sending agency of Charismatic and Evangelical tradition engaged in church planting, discipleship, evangelism, funds transmission, leadership development and missionary training. (DPE)

Purpose: . . . to carry the Gospel across cultural boundaries to unreached people, encouraging them to accept Christ as Lord and Savior . . . to draw disciples together into clusters of churches . . . to help the churches, under the Holy Spirit's leadership, to multiply, serve their communities and send out their own cross-cultural missionaries.
Year Founded in US: 1973
Income for International Min:
$3,000,000

Fully Supported US Personnel Working Cross-Culturally
    More than 4 years: 97
    1–4 years: 4
Countries/Regions: Africa, Albania, Argentina, China (People's Republic of), Costa Rica, Ecuador, Germany, Guatemala, Haiti, Honduras, India, Indonesia, Israel, Italy, Kenya, Laos, Malaysia, Mexico, Mozambique, Nepal, Nicaragua, Philippines, Russia, South Africa, Sri Lanka, Taiwan (China), Thailand, Ukraine, United Kingdom, Vietnam

GMI
Formerly: Global Mapping International
PO Box 63719
Colorado Springs, CO 80962 US
Phone: (719) 531-3599
Email: info@gmi.org
Website: gmi.org
Associations: Missio Nexus

A nondenominational service agency of Evangelical tradition engaged in information or journalism, leadership development, missionary & worker training, networking, partnership, or coordination, research, and technical assistance. (FPC-PE)

Purpose: . . . to leverage research and technology to create, cultivate, and communicate mission information leading to insight that inspires Kingdom service.

Fully Supported US Personnel Working Cross-Culturally
    X-C workers in US: 4
Other Personnel
    Home staff: 9

GO TO NATIONS
Formerly: Calvary International
3771 Spring Park Rd.
Jacksonville, FL 32207 US
Phone: (904) 398-6559
Email: mobassist@gotonations.org
Website: gotonations.com

An interdenominational sending agency of Charismatic and Evangelical tradition engaged in leadership development, children's programs, church planting, development, evangelism and missionary training. (DPE)

Purpose: . . . a servant ministry helping the body of Christ reap a global harvest.
Year Founded in US: 1981
Income for International Min:
    $3,506,976
Fully Supported US Personnel Working Cross-Culturally
    More than 4 years: 65
    1–4 years: 9
    Non-residential: 6
Other Personnel
    Short-Term less than 1 year: 110
    Non-US in own/other country: 62
    Home staff: 59
Countries/Regions: Asia, Australia, Burkina Faso, Cambodia, Colombia, Costa Rica, Cuba, Ecuador, Equatorial Guinea, Estonia, Ethiopia, Ghana, Guatemala, Honduras, India, Indonesia, Jamaica, Jordan, North Korea, Latvia, Malaysia, Mexico, Nepal, Netherlands, Niger, Nigeria, Peru, Philippines, Russia, Singapore, South Africa, Tanzania, Thailand, Turkey, Ukraine, United Kingdom, Venezuela

GO YE FELLOWSHIP

PO Box 539
Monrovia, CA 91017 US
Phone: (626) 386-5493
Email: info@goyefellowship.org
Website: goyefellowship.org
Associations: Missio Nexus

An interdenominational sending agency of Evangelical tradition engaged in church planting (establishing), disabled ministry, discipleship, personal or small group evangelism, addressing human trafficking, and international student ministry.

Purpose: . . . to enable cross-cultural workers to carry out their distinct God-given vision to make reproducing disciples of Jesus among all peoples.

Year Founded in US: 1932
Income for International Min:
$1,315,000
Fully Supported US Personnel Working Cross-Culturally
More than 4 years: 64
X-C workers in US: 6
Non-residential: 10
Other Personnel
Short-Term less than 1 year: 1
Tentmakers/BAM: 1
Non-US in own/other country: 57
Home staff: 6
Countries/Regions: Argentina, Austria, Brazil, Central Asia, East Asia, France, Germany, Global Ministry, Indonesia, Kenya, South Korea, Mexico, Middle East, Philippines, Slovakia, Tanzania, Thailand, United Kingdom

GOCORPS

6736 Regent Ave N
Brooklyn Center, MN 55429 US
Phone: (314) 643-8376
Email: info@gocorps.org
Website: gocorps.org
Associations: Missio Nexus

A nondenominational specialized agency of Evangelical tradition engaged in arts in mission, business as mission, community development, addressing human trafficking, medical ministry, mobilizing for mission, and youth ministry.

Purpose: . . . to cultivate a culture of mid-term missions in the American church and campus.

Year Founded in US: 2009
Other Personnel
Home staff: 12

GOD REPORTS

PO Box 7022
Capistrano Beach, CA 92624 US
Phone: (949) 230-2843
Email: mark@Godreports.com
Website: Godreports.com

A nondenominational specialized agency of Evangelical tradition engaged in information or journalism, Internet evangelism, networking, partnership, or coordination, persecuted church, and recruiting or mobilizing for mission. (FPC-PE)

Purpose: . . . to spread the Gospel of Jesus Christ and support and encourage Christian missions by sharing stories from missionaries and mission organizations.
Year Founded in US: 2007

GOGF MINISTRIES

158 E. Main St
Lansdale, PA 19446 US
Phone: (215) 361-8111
Email: admin@gogf.org
Website: gogf.org

A nondenominational specialized agency of Brethren and Christian (Plymouth Brethren) tradition engaged in radio or TV broadcasting, church planting (establishing), and national worker support.

Purpose: . . . to plant churches, to prepare leaders, and to proclaim the Gospel until the whole world hears.
Year Founded in US: 1961
Income for International Min:
$50,000
Other Personnel
Short-Term less than 1 year: 20
Non-US in own/other country: 2
Home staff: 2
Countries/Regions: Global Ministry

GOOD NEWS FOR INDIA
PO Box 7576
La Verne, CA 91750 US
Phone: (909) 376-9579
Email: gnficea@gmail.com
Website: goodnewsforindia.org
An interdenominational support agency of Charismatic and Pentecostal tradition engaged in church planting (establishing), community development, discipleship, church, school or general Christian education, theological education, and national worker support.
Purpose: . . . to train national Christian leaders to strengthen the Church in the Indian subcontinent; train nationals to preach the Gospel and start churches in unreached areas and among unreached people groups.
Year Founded in US: 1986
Income for International Min:
$2,198,637
Other Personnel
Short-Term less than 1 year: 37
Non-US in own/other country: 350
Home staff: 3
Countries/Regions: India

GOOD NEWS PRODUCTIONS INTERNATIONAL
2111 Main St
Joplin, MO 64801 US
Phone: (417) 782-0060
Email: gnpi@gnpi.org
Website: gnpi.org
A nondenominational specialized agency of Christian (Restoration Movement) tradition engaged in audio recording or distribution, radio or TV broadcasting, mass evangelism, Internet evangelism, translation, and video-film production or distribution. (FPC-PE)
Purpose: . . . to accelerate global evangelism through media and technology.
Year Founded in US: 1976
Other Personnel
Home staff: 20
Countries/Regions: Africa, India, Mexico, Myanmar (Burma), Philippines, Singapore, Thailand, Ukraine

GOOD SHEPHERD MINISTRIES INC.
PO BOX 2624
Clanton, AL 35046 US
Phone: (712) 324-9709
Email: lamar@gsmi-haiti.org
Website: gsmi-haiti.org
An interdenominational support agency of Baptist and Evangelical tradition engaged in theological education, extension education, evangelism, literature distribution, providing medical supplies, medical work and supplying equipment. (DPE)
Income for International Min:
$203,343
Fully Supported US Personnel Working Cross-Culturally
More than 4 years: 2
Non-residential: 1

Other Personnel
Short-Term less than 1 year: 6
Non-US in own/other country: 48
Home staff: 1
Countries/Regions: Haiti

GOOD SHEPHERD
MINISTRIES INTL.
PO Box 11909
San Bernardino, CA 92423 US
Phone: (909) 478-3330
Email: info@isom.org
Website: isom.org
A nondenominational sending agency
of Charismatic and Pentecostal tradition
engaged in correspondence courses,
discipleship, church, school or general
Christian education, video-film production
or distribution, and youth ministry.
Purpose: . . . to train laborers for the
end-time harvest with training schools in
146 nations and in over 75 languages.
Year Founded in US: 1991
Other Personnel
Home staff: 20

GOSENDME GLOBAL
PO Box 913106
Sherman, TX 75091 US
Phone: (214) 717-4562
Email: info@gosendme.us
Website: gosendmeglobal.org
A nondenominational sending agency
with a denominational heritage of Baptist
tradition engaged in church planting
(establishing), discipleship, missionary &
worker training, recruiting or mobilizing
for mission, relief & aid, and STM trip
coordination. (FPC-PE)
Purpose: . . . to engage, encourage and
equip those in physical, emotional, and
spiritual need worldwide.
Year Founded in US: 2016
Income for International Min:
$35,000

*Fully Supported US Personnel Working
Cross-Culturally*
X-C workers in US: 5
Other Personnel
Short-Term less than 1 year: 5
Tentmakers/BAM: 5
Home staff: 1
Countries/Regions: Greece, India,
Nicaragua, Peru, Sierra Leone

GOSPEL FELLOWSHIP
ASSOCIATION
1809 Wade Hampton Blvd., #110
Greenville, SC 29609 US
Phone: (864) 609-5500
Email: GFA@gfamissions.org
Website: gfamissions.org
A nondenominational sending agency
of Fundamental tradition engaged in
church planting, camping programs,
correspondence courses, theological
education, evangelism and medical work.
(DPE)
Purpose: . . . to get the Gospel to as
many people as possible in the shortest
time possible.
Year Founded in US: 1939
*Fully Supported US Personnel Working
Cross-Culturally*
More than 4 years: 163
1–4 years: 35
Non-residential: 3
Other Personnel
Home staff: 9
Countries/Regions: Albania, Argentina,
Australia, Austria, Brazil, Cambodia,
Cameroon, Costa Rica, Dominica,
Ecuador, Germany, Italy, Japan, South
Korea, Marshall Islands, Mexico,
Netherlands, New Zealand, Panama,
Papua New Guinea, Philippines, Puerto
Rico, South Africa, Spain, United Kingdom,
Unspecified Country, Zambia

GOSPEL FOR ASIA CANADA
245 King St. E.
Stony Creek, ON L8G 1L9 CA
Phone: (905) 662-2101
Email: infocanada@gfa.org
Website: gfa.ca
An interdenominational support agency of
Evangelical tradition engaged in support
of national workers totaling approximately
16,000 native missionaries, Bible
distribution, broadcasting, church planting,
evangelism and literature production. (DPE)
Other Personnel
   Home staff: 13
Countries/Regions: Bangladesh,
Bhutan, Cambodia, China (People's
Republic of), India, Laos, Myanmar
(Burma), Nepal, Sri Lanka, Thailand

GOSPEL FOR ASIA INC.
1116 St. Thomas Way
Wills Point, TX 75169 US
Phone: (800) 946-2742
Email: info@gfa.org
Website: gfa.org
An interdenominational service agency
of Evangelical tradition engaged in
church planting, broadcasting, children's
programs, leadership development,
support of national workers and missionary
training. (DPE)
Purpose: . . . to be devout followers of
Christ and fulfill the Great Commission
among the unreached in Asia through
training, sending, and assisting qualified
laborers who will win the lost and plant
local churches in partnership with the
Body of Christ.
Income for International Min:
   $47,842,080
Other Personnel
   Non-US in own/other country: 9523
   Home staff: 80
Countries/Regions: Asia

GOSPEL LITERATURE INTERNATIONAL (GLINT)
9650 Business Center Dr, Ste. 111
Rancho Cucamonga, CA 91730 US
Phone: (909) 481-5222
Email: glintint@aol.com
Website: glint.org
A nondenominational service agency of
Evangelical tradition engaged in Bible and
other translation. (FPC-PE)
Purpose: . . . to provide resources for
literature projects worldwide for effective
Bible teaching and learning materials
in national languages, with the goal
of making disciples, developing godly
Christian leaders, and building the Church.
Year Founded in US: 1961

GOSPEL MISSION OF SOUTH AMERICA INC.
1401 SW 21st Ave.
Fort Lauderdale, FL 33312 US
Phone: (954) 587-2975
Email: gmsausa@gmsa.org
Website: gmsa.org
Associations: FOM
A nondenominational sending agency of
Baptist and Fundamental tradition engaged
in church planting, theological education
and leadership development. (DPE)
Purpose: . . . to evangelize the people
of Latin America by means of itinerant
and localized work, with the object of
establishing and developing indigenous
churches.
Year Founded in US: 1944
Income for International Min:
   $930,930
*Fully Supported US Personnel Working
Cross-Culturally*
   More than 4 years: 24
Other Personnel
   Short-Term less than 1 year: 5
   Home staff: 4
Countries/Regions: Argentina, Chile,
Uruguay

GOSPEL MISSION OF SOUTH AMERICA OF CANADA
PO Box 150
St. Charles, ON P0M 2W0 CA
Phone: (705) 967-1262
Email: canada@gmsa.org
Website: gmsa.org
Associations: FOM

A sending agency of Baptist tradition engaged in church planting, discipleship, evangelism, furloughed missionary support and support of national churches. (DPE)

Purpose: . . . to glorify God by serving sending churches as we help their missionaries establish reproducing churches in Latin America through evangelism, discipleship, and leadership development.

Income for International Min:
$103,203
Fully Supported CA Personnel Working Cross-Culturally
More than 4 years: 3
Other Personnel
Short-Term less than 1 year: 2
Non-CA in own/other country: 5
Countries/Regions: Argentina, Chile

GOSPEL OUTBOUND
2738 E. Main St.
Millville, NJ 08332 US
Phone: (609) 602-1410
Email: info@gospeloutbound.org
Website: gospeloutbound.org

A nondenominational sending agency of Charismatic and Pentecostal tradition engaged in Bible teaching, radio or TV broadcasting, business as mission, missionary & worker training, and orphan education. (FPC-PE)

Purpose: . . . to provide various missions training in Uganda, and S. Sudan. From these raise up national missionaries, particularly to the unreached villages and peoples of those countries.

Year Founded in US: 1997
Income for International Min:
$69,828
Fully Supported US Personnel Working Cross-Culturally
More than 4 years: 1
Other Personnel
Home staff: 1
Countries/Regions: Guatemala, India, Myanmar (Burma), Uganda

GOSPEL OUTREACH MINISTRIES INTL.
PO Box 380
Hillsboro, MO 63050-0380 US
Phone: (636) 948-9836
Email: gomint@aol.com

A nondenominational support agency of Evangelical tradition engaged in evangelism, church planting, support of national workers, mission-related research, literacy work, development, childcare/orphanage programs, leadership development, short-term programs and relief and/or rehabilitation. Primary focus is the most unreached people groups in India. (DPE)

Purpose: . . . to fulfill the responsibility of the Great Commission to disciple the lost through a relationship with God and forming a community of local believers.

Income for International Min:
$144,000
Other Personnel
Short-Term less than 1 year: 7
Non-US in own/other country: 250
Home staff: 2
Countries/Regions: India

GOSPEL REVIVAL MINISTRIES
PO Box 705
Desoto, TX 75123-0705 US
Phone: (469) 245-8140
Email: president@gogoodnews.com
Website: gogoodnews.com

A nondenominational support agency of Independent tradition engaged in Bible distribution, church construction or financing, mass evangelism, national worker support, relief & aid, and unreached tribes.

Purpose: . . . to preach the Gospel of God's grace at home and abroad, to support by prayers and gifts, individuals, churches, and organizations which are true to the faith, in all parts of the world.

Year Founded in US: 1980
Income for International Min:
   $54,243
Other Personnel
   Non-US in own/other country: 1100
   Home staff: 4
Countries/Regions: Global Ministry

GOSPEL TIDE BROADCASTING ASSOCIATION

P. O. Box 399
Chambersburg, PA 17201 US
Phone: (717) 264-7288
Email: donshenk@thetide.org
Website: thetide.org

A nondenominational with a denominational heritage service agency of Evangelical tradition engaged in audio recording or distribution, Bible distribution, radio or TV broadcasting, church planting (establishing), correspondence courses, and discipleship.

Purpose: . . . to creatively share the good news of Jesus Christ worldwide through media and partnerships

Year Founded in US: 1946
Other Personnel
   Short-Term less than 1 year: 8
   Tentmakers/BAM: 10
   Non-US in own/other country: 16
   Home staff: 3
Countries/Regions: Albania, Bhutan, India, Kosovo, Nepal, Nigeria, Zimbabwe

GOSPELINK INC.

PO Box 4299
Lynchburg, VA 24502 US
Phone: (434) 485-7007
Email: info@gospelink.org
Website: gospelink.org

A nondenominational support agency of Evangelical tradition engaged in childcare or orphanage, church development, church planting (establishing), theological education, and personal or small group evangelism.

Purpose: . . . to advance the Gospel of Jesus Christ by assisting national preachers.

Year Founded in US: 1998
Income for International Min:
   $2,100,000
Other Personnel
   Short-Term less than 1 year: 100
   Non-US in own/other country: 1300
   Home staff: 18
Countries/Regions: Global Ministry

GRACE & TRUTH INC.

210 Chestnut St.
Danville, IL 61832 US
Phone: (217) 442-1120
Email: gtpress@gtpress.org
Website: gtpress.org

A nondenominational specialized agency of Brethren tradition engaged in literature distribution. (FPC-PE)

Purpose: . . . to publish and print Christian literature and send it to many countries for distribution.

Year Founded in US: 1931

GRACE MINISTRIES INTERNATIONAL

1011 Aldon St SW, PO Box 9405
Grand Rapids, MI 49509 US
Phone: (616) 241-5666
Email: mo@gracem.org
Website: gracem.org
Associations: Missio Nexus

A nondenominational sending agency of Evangelical tradition engaged in church planting (establishing), theological education, personal or small group evangelism, and leadership development.

Purpose: . . . to send missionaries into various countries of the world with the purpose of preaching the gospel of God's grace, establishing indigenous churches, training and equipping men and women to do the work of the ministry in the churches, and meeting the needs of people through medical, educational and community development ministries.

Year Founded in US: 1939
Income for International Min:
$1,880,611

Fully Supported US Personnel Working Cross-Culturally
More than 4 years: 30
1–4 years: 5993

Other Personnel
Short-Term less than 1 year: 28
Non-US in own/other country: 15
Home staff: 5

Countries/Regions: Bolivia, Caribbean, Costa Rica, Malawi, Mozambique, Nicaragua, Paraguay, Puerto Rico, Tanzania

GRACE MISSION INC.
PO Box 126
Henderson, NE 68371 US
Phone: (402) 723-4700
Email: gmiese@mainstaycomm.net
Website: gracemission.info

A nondenominational support agency of Evangelical tradition engaged in radio or TV broadcasting, childcare or orphanage, church planting (establishing), church, school or general Christian education, STM trip coordination, and seniors home.

Purpose: . . . to unleash the power of the gospel through national ministers in Haiti and Mexico.

Year Founded in US: 1981
Income for International Min:
$300,000

Fully Supported US Personnel Working Cross-Culturally
More than 4 years: 4

Other Personnel
Short-Term less than 1 year: 69
Non-US in own/other country: 101
Home staff: 2

Countries/Regions: Haiti, Mexico

GREAT CITIES MISSIONS
Formerly: Continent of Great Cities
3939 Belt Line Rd, Ste. 705
Addison, TX 75001 US
Phone: (214) 466-6200
Email: info@greatcities.org
Website: greatcities.org

A denominational sending agency of Christian (Restoration Movement) tradition engaged in church planting (establishing), member care, missionary & worker training, and national worker support.

Purpose: . . . to see a "main avenue" church planted in every major city of the Latin World.

Year Founded in US: 1976

Fully Supported US Personnel Working Cross-Culturally
More than 4 years: 2

Other Personnel
Home staff: 19

Countries/Regions: Central America, South America

GREAT COMMISSION CENTER INTERNATIONAL
848 Stewart Dr., Ste. 200
Sunnyvale, CA 94085 US
Phone: (408) 636-0030
Email: info@gcciusa.org
Website: gcciusa.org

An interdenominational support agency of Evangelical tradition engaged in mobilization for mission, missions information service, literature production, mission-related research and training. (DPE)

Purpose: . . . to serve alongside the evangelical churches and para-church groups for the progressive realization of the Great Commission.

Income for International Min: $178,217

Other Personnel
Home staff: 5

GREAT COMMISSION MEDIA MINISTRIES

Formerly: International Russian Radio/TV
3–1335 Trans Canada Way SE
Medicine Hat, AB T1B 1J1 CA
Phone: (877) 674-5630
Email: info_irrtv@irrtv.org
Website: gcmediaministries.org/

An interdenominational sending agency of Evangelical and Pentecostal tradition engaged in video/film production/distribution, association of missions, broadcasting, Christian education, evangelism and leadership development. (DPE)

Purpose: . . . to win, build, train and send.

Income for International Min: $501,764

Other Personnel
Non-CA in own/other country: 48
Countries/Regions: Israel, Russia, Ukraine

GREATER EUROPE MISSION

18950 Base Camp Road
Monument, CO 80132 US
Phone: (719) 488-8008
Email: info@gemission.com
Website: gemission.org
Associations: Missio Nexus

An interdenominational sending agency of Evangelical tradition engaged in arts in mission, Bible teaching, business as mission, CPM, discipleship, and personal or small group evangelism.

Purpose: . . . to reach Europe by multiplying disciples and growing Christ's Church.

Year Founded in US: 1944

Fully Supported US Personnel Working Cross-Culturally
More than 4 years: 132
1–4 years: 40

Other Personnel
Non-US in own/other country: 3
Countries/Regions: Austria, Belarus, Belgium, Bulgaria, Croatia, Czech Republic, Eastern Europe and Eurasia, Estonia, France, Georgia, Germany, Greece, Hungary, Iceland, Ireland (Republic of), Italy, Kosovo, Latvia, Luxembourg, Macedonia, Netherlands, Poland, Portugal, Romania, Spain, Sweden, Switzerland, United Kingdom, Western Europe

GREATER EUROPE MISSION CANADA

100 Ontario Street
Oshawa, ON L1G 4Z1 CA
Phone: (866) 241-3579
Email: GEMCanada@GEMission.com
Website: gemission.org
Associations: Missio Nexus

An interdenominational sending agency of Evangelical tradition engaged in Bible distribution, camping programs, CPM, discipleship, and STM trip coordination. (FPC-PE)

Purpose: . . . to reach Europe by multiplying disciples and growing Christ's Church.

Year Founded in CA: 1961
Income for International Min: $1,170,547

Fully Supported CA Personnel Working Cross-Culturally
  More than 4 years: 17
  1–4 years: 3
Other Personnel
  Short-Term less than 1 year: 73
  Home staff: 3
Countries/Regions: Croatia, Germany, Hungary, Ireland (Republic of), Latvia, Luxembourg, Portugal

GREATER GRACE WORLD OUTREACH
6025 Moravia Park Drive
Baltimore, MD 21206 US
Phone: (410) 483-3700
Email: missions@ggwo.org
Website: GreaterGraceMissions.org
A nondenominational sending agency of Evangelical tradition engaged in Bible teaching, radio or TV broadcasting, church planting (establishing), discipleship, church, school or general Christian education, and personal or small group evangelism.
Purpose: . . . to propagate the finished work Gospel of Jesus Christ locally, nationally, and internationally; to teach, in word and deed, those within our sphere of influence; and to practice and promote a Christian lifestyle.
Fully Supported US Personnel Working Cross-Culturally
  More than 4 years: 6
  1–4 years: 7
  Non-residential: 2
Other Personnel
  Tentmakers/BAM: 63
  Non-US in own/other country: 271
Countries/Regions: Albania, Argentina, Azerbaijan, Benin, Brazil, Burkina Faso, Cambodia, Canada, Chile, China (People's Republic of), Costa Rica, Côte d'Ivoire, Czech Republic, Democratic Republic of Congo, Dominican Republic, Ecuador, Finland, France, Gabon, Germany, Ghana,

Haiti, Hungary, India, Israel, Japan, Kazakhstan, Kenya, Kyrgyzstan, Liberia, Lithuania, Malawi, Mali, Mexico, Middle East, Mozambique, Nepal, Nicaragua, Niger, Pakistan, Peru, Philippines, Poland, Puerto Rico, Romania, Russia, Rwanda, Serbia, South Africa, South Korea, Tajikistan, Tanzania, Thailand, Togo, Turkey, Turkmenistan, Uganda, Ukraine, United Arab Emirates, United Kingdom, Uzbekistan, Zambia, Zimbabwe

HABITAT FOR HUMANITY CANADA
477 Mount Pleasant Road, Suite 403
Toronto, ON M4S 2L9 CA
Phone: (416) 644-0988
Email: habitat@habitat.ca
Website: habitat.ca
A nondenominational specialized agency of Ecumenical tradition engaged in affordable housing, development, relief and/or rehabilitation and short-term programs. (DPE)
Purpose: . . . to mobilize volunteers and community partners in building affordable housing and promoting homeownership as a means to breaking the cycle of poverty.
Income for International Min:
  $2,355,678
Other Personnel
  Short-Term less than 1 year: 1387
  Home staff: 30

HABITAT FOR HUMANITY INTERNATIONAL
121 Habitat St.
Americus, GA 31709 US
Phone: (229) 924-6935
Email: publicinfo@habitat.org
Website: habitat.org
An interdenominational specialized service agency of Ecumenical tradition engaged in building low-income housing in partnership with/for people in need. Since 1976, Habitat has built more than 200,000 houses in nearly 100 countries. (DPE)

Purpose: . . . works in partnership with God and people everywhere to develop communities with God's people in need by building and renovating houses . . . in which people can live and grow into all that God intended.

Income for International Min:
$95,475,655

Fully Supported US Personnel Working Cross-Culturally
More than 4 years: 22
1–4 years: 184
Non-residential: 50

Other Personnel
Short-Term less than 1 year: 4600
Non-US in own/other country: 206
Home staff: 568

Countries/Regions: Afghanistan, Australia, Bangladesh, Botswana, Brazil, China (People's Republic of), Democratic Republic of Congo, Costa Rica, Dominican Republic, Ecuador, Fiji, Ghana, Hong Kong (China), Hungary, India, Indonesia, Jordan, Kenya, Lesotho, Malawi, Mongolia, Mozambique, Nepal, Nicaragua, Philippines, Senegal, Singapore, South Africa, Sri Lanka, Tanzania, Thailand, Uganda, United Kingdom, Vietnam

HAITI ARISE – CANADA
PO Box 85267, Albert Park PO
Calgary, AB T2A 7R7 CA
Phone: (403) 272-6493
Email: info@haitiarise.org
Website: haitiarise.org

A nondenominational sending agency of Charismatic tradition engaged in technical/ trade college education, agricultural programs, church planting, theological education, providing medical clinics & supplies, and TESOL. (DPE)

Purpose: . . . to educate and relieve poverty in Haiti.

Income for International Min:
$211,000

Fully Supported CA Personnel Working Cross-Culturally
More than 4 years: 2

Other Personnel
Short-Term less than 1 year: 157

Countries/Regions: Haiti

HAITI LUTHERAN MISSION SOCIETY
PO Box 22544
Lincoln, NE 68542-2544 US
Phone: (402) 474-2063
Email: rnnbuethe@yahoo.com
Website: haitilutheran.org

A denominational support agency of Lutheran tradition engaged in church planting, Christian education, theological education, medical work and relief and/or rehabilitation. (DPE)

Purpose: . . . to minister to the spiritual and physical needs of the Haitian people so that they might be won by the Holy Spirit to be disciples of Jesus Christ.

Income for International Min:
$250,000

Other Personnel
Short-Term less than 1 year: 300
Non-US in own/other country: 75

Countries/Regions: Haiti

HAITIAN CHRISTIAN OUTREACH
P O Box 1052
Mahomet, IL 61853 US
Phone: (217) 778-6950
Email: hco@haitianchristian.org
Website: haitianchristian.org
Associations: Missio Nexus

A nondenominational support agency of Evangelical and Independent tradition engaged in Bible teaching, church development, church planting (establishing), community development, discipleship, church, and school or general Christian education.

Purpose: . . . to partner with Haitian Christians to transform a culture for Christ through church planting, education, community development, and health care ministries.

Year Founded in US: 1985
Income for International Min:
  $1,000,000

Other Personnel
  Short-Term less than 1 year: 154
  Non-US in own/other country: 1
  Home staff: 3
Countries/Regions: Haiti

HARVEST BRIDGE

Formerly: Evangelical Fellowship International
P.O Box 284
Grove City, PA 16127 US
Phone: (724) 506-8266
Email: info@harvestbridge.org
Website: harvestbridge.org
Associations: Missio Nexus

An interdenominational support agency of Evangelical tradition engaged in childcare or orphanage, church planting (establishing), church, school or general Christian education, missionary & worker training, persecuted church, and relief & aid.

Purpose: . . . to equip indigenous Christian ministries in South Asia to serve more effectively, so that Christ will be glorified and individuals in these countries will have greater physical, mental, emotional, and spiritual well-being.

Year Founded in US: 2009
Income for International Min:
  $332,167

Fully Supported US Personnel Working Cross-Culturally
  1–4 years: 2
  Non-residential: 2

Other Personnel
  Short-Term less than 1 year: 4
  Tentmakers/BAM: 268
  Home staff: 3
Countries/Regions: Bangladesh, Bhutan, China (People's Republic of), India, Myanmar (Burma), Nepal, Pakistan, South Asia, Sri Lanka

HARVEST FOUNDATION

P O BOX 2670
Phoenix, AZ 85002 US
Phone: (602) 258-1083
Email: usofficeteam@harvestfoundation. org
Website: harvestfoundation.org

An interdenominational service agency of Evangelical tradition engaged in church development, discipleship, church, school or general Christian education, leadership development, missionary & worker training, networking, and partnership, or coordination.

Purpose: . . . to envision and equip the church to reflect Jesus, the chief Servant.

Year Founded in US: 1978
Income for International Min:
  $775,077

Other Personnel
  Non-US in own/other country: 138
Countries/Regions: Armenia, Bolivia, Brazil, Burundi, Central America, Central Asia, Democratic Republic of Congo, Djibouti, Dominican Republic, Ethiopia, Ghana, Global Ministry, Guinea, Haiti, Honduras, India, Kenya, Mali, Myanmar (Burma), Nepal, Nigeria, Peru, Rwanda, South America, Southeast Asia, Sub-Saharan Africa, Togo, Venezuela

HARVEST INTERNATIONAL INC.
PO Box 6690
Ocala, FL 34478-6690 US
Phone: (352) 622-1818
Email: danny@harvestinternational.org
Website: harvestinternational.org
A sending agency of Evangelical tradition engaged in short-term programs, childcare/orphanage programs, church construction, evangelism, providing medical supplies and services for other agencies. (DPE)
Purpose: . . . to meet the physical needs of people in order to earn the right to minister to their spiritual needs.
Year Founded in US: 1987
Income for International Min:
   $1,366,382
Fully Supported US Personnel Working Cross-Culturally
   1–4 years: 11
   Non-residential: 2
Other Personnel
   Short-Term less than 1 year: 120
   Non-US in own/other country: 12
   Home staff: 5
Countries/Regions: Haiti, India, Kenya, Romania, Uganda, Ukraine, Zimbabwe

HARVEST MISSION TO THE UNREACHED
Post Box 16656
Sugar Land, TX 77496 US
Phone: (281) 499-7086
Email: harvestmission@gmail.com
Website: harvestmission.org
A nondenominational support agency of Independent tradition engaged in Bible teaching, children's ministry, church planting (establishing), missionary & worker training, national worker support, and relief & aid. (FPC-PE)
Purpose: . . . to reach the unreached through national pastors; win people for Christ, teach them Scripture, and send disciples to plant churches.

Year Founded in US: 1998
Income for International Min:
   $211,000
Other Personnel
   Short-Term less than 1 year: 5
   Non-US in own/other country: 120
   Home staff: 1
Countries/Regions: India

HARVESTING IN SPANISH (HIS)
VIP SAL 723
Miami, FL 33102-5364 US
Email: don.benner@harvesting.org
Website: harvesting.org
An interdenominational sending agency of Evangelical, Independent, and Pentecostal tradition engaged in childcare/orphanage programs, Bible distribution, Christian education, literature distribution, medical work and short-term programs. (DPE)
Purpose: . . . to prepare disadvantaged children to become ethical, productive Christian men and women through superior scholastic and spiritual education which promotes intellectual growth, social grace, an attitude of servanthood, and emotional stability.
Year Founded in US: 1980
Income for International Min:
   $624,550
Fully Supported US Personnel Working Cross-Culturally
   More than 4 years: 3
   Non-residential: 3
Other Personnel
   Short-Term less than 1 year: 125
   Non-US in own/other country: 3
   Home staff: 6
Countries/Regions: El Salvador

HBI GLOBAL PARTNERS
PO Box 584
Forest, VA 24551 US
Phone: (336) 595-3891
Email: info@globalpartners.org
Website: globalpartners.org
A sending agency of Baptist tradition engaged in leadership development, church planting, discipleship, support of national workers, relief and/or rehabilitation and short-term programs. (DPE)
Purpose: . . . enabling the North American Church to develop partnerships with national movements to reach the unreached in India and beyond.
Year Founded in US: 1950
Income for International Min:
  $1,069,020
Other Personnel
  Short-Term less than 1 year: 40
  Non-US in own/other country: 605
  Home staff: 2
Countries/Regions: India, Nepal

HEALTH PARTNERS INTERNATIONAL OF CANADA
3633 des Sources Boulevard, Suite 212
Dollard-des-Ormeaux, PQ H9B 2K4 CA
Phone: (514) 822-1112
Email: info@hpicanada.ca
Website: hpicanada.ca
Associations: CCRDA
A nondenominational specialized agency of Evangelical and Independent tradition engaged in management consulting or training, medical ministry, including dental or public health, and relief & aid. (FPC-PE)
Purpose: . . . to increase access to medicine in vulnerable communities by working with partner agencies to provide strategic, sustainable solutions that help communities transform themselves.
Year Founded in CA: 1987
Income for International Min:
  $28,521,262

HEALTH TEAMS INTERNATIONAL
10056 Applegate Ln.
Brighton, MI 48114 US
Phone: (810) 229-9346
Email: ddchar@earthlink.net
Website: healthteamsintl.org
An interdenominational specialized agency of Ecumenical tradition engaged in personal or small group evangelism, medical supplies, medical ministry, including dental or public health, and STM trip coordination. (FPC-PE)
Purpose: . . . to assist in the evangelization of the unreached through the ministration of short-term Christian health care teams.
Year Founded in US: 1986
Other Personnel
  Short-Term less than 1 year: 50
  Home staff: 1
Countries/Regions: Cameroon, China (People's Republic of), Global Ministry, India, Myanmar (Burma)

HEART FOR HONDURAS
22601 Lutheran Church Rd.
Tomball, TX 77377 US
Phone: (281) 290-1206
Email: kpieper@salem4u.com
Website: heartforhonduras.org
A denominational service agency of Lutheran tradition engaged in evangelism, medical work, partnership development and short-term programs. (DPE)
Purpose: . . . to obey Jesus Christ's great commandment.
Income for International Min:
  $180,526
Other Personnel
  Short-Term less than 1 year: 60
  Home staff: 3
Countries/Regions: Honduras

HEART FOR LEBANON FOUNDATION

PO Box 1294
Black Mountain, NC 28711 US
Phone: (828) 505-8432
Email: admin@heartforlebanon.org
Website: heartforlebanon.org
Associations: Missio Nexus

A nondenominational support agency of Evangelical tradition engaged in Bible teaching, children's ministry, community development, discipleship, church, school or general Christian education, and relief & aid.

Purpose: . . . as defined in the Bible to "go and make disciples" we work to see lives changed and communities transformed in the country of Lebanon.

Year Founded in US: 2007
Income for International Min:
$4,000,000

Other Personnel
Short-Term less than 1 year: 150
Non-US in own/other country: 54
Countries/Regions: Lebanon

HEART OF THE BRIDE MINISTRIES

PO Box 786
Niceville, FL 32588 US
Phone: (850) 678-9008
Email: info@heartofthebride.org
Website: heartofthebride.org

A nondenominational sending agency of Baptist tradition engaged in childcare/orphanage programs, children at risk, children's programs, discipleship, evangelism and HIV/AIDS. (DPE)

Purpose: . . . to send people and resources from places of abundance to places of need within the body of Christ . . . to care for and disciple orphans in developing countries through partnerships with indigenous believers.

Income for International Min:
$871,170

Fully Supported US Personnel Working Cross-Culturally
1–4 years: 7
Non-residential: 2
Other Personnel
Short-Term less than 1 year: 45
Tentmakers/BAM: 2
Home staff: 5
Countries/Regions: Kenya, Uganda, Zambia

HEART TO HEART INTERNATIONAL MINISTRIES

P.O. Box 1832
Ramona, CA 92065 US
Phone: (760) 789-8798
Email: jodi@h2hint.org
Website: h2hinternational.org

An interdenominational support agency of Evangelical tradition engaged in Bible teaching, camping programs, childcare or orphanage, discipleship, church, school or general Christian education, and orphan care.

Purpose: . . . to share God's love with the poor and orphans in Romania by proclaiming the Gospel message, offering physical help to those in need, and training people to become faithful followers of the Lord Jesus Christ.

Year Founded in US: 1993
Income for International Min:
$540,474

Fully Supported US Personnel Working Cross-Culturally
More than 4 years: 6
1–4 years: 1
Other Personnel
Short-Term less than 1 year: 230
Home staff: 3
Countries/Regions: Romania

HEART FOR LEBANON:
MOVING HURTING COMMUNITIES FROM DESPAIR TO HOPE,
ONE PERSON AT A TIME.

Relief and Community Care

Children at Risk Education

Bible Studies and Discipleship

Hope on Wheels Mobile Children's Ministry

Driven by the compassionate heart of Jesus Christ, Heart for Lebanon exists to see lives changed and communities transformed. In October of 2006 Heart for Lebanon was formed in response to the overwhelming needs created by the devastating war. Since then Lebanon has received over 1 million refugees within its borders. Heart for Lebanon continues to reach out to the lost and broken with the love of Jesus Christ.

BY JOINING HANDS WE CAN MAKE A DIFFERENCE IN LEBANON AND THE MIDDLE EAST
www.heartforlebanon.org

قلبنا مع لبنان

P.O. BOX 1294 • BLACK MOUNTAIN, NC 28711
WWW.HEARTFORLEBANON.ORG

HEIFER PROJECT INTERNATIONAL
1 World Ave.
Little Rock, AR 72202 US
Phone: (501) 907-2600
Email: info@heifer.org
Website: heifer.org

A transdenominational support agency of Independent tradition engaged in development, agricultural programs, justice and training. (DPE)

Purpose: . . . to work with communities to end hunger and poverty and to care for the earth.

Income for International Min:
$81,973,237

Other Personnel
Short-Term less than 1 year: 50
Home staff: 267
Countries/Regions: Asia, Europe, Latin America

HELIMISSION INC. – USA
7245 College St.
Lima, NY 14485 US
Phone: (585) 624-5509
Email: helimission-usa@rochester.rr.com
Website: helimission.org/en

A nondenominational service agency of Charismatic and Pentecostal tradition engaged in evangelism, aviation services, church planting, services for other agencies, Bible translation and natural disaster relief. (DPE)(FPC16)

Purpose: . . . to use helicopters to bring medical material and spiritual help to people in remote and inaccessible areas to assist in catastrophic emergencies in cooperation with international relief organizations.

Year Founded in US: 2007
Income for International Min:
$30,774

Fully Supported US Personnel Working Cross-Culturally
More than 4 years: 1
1–4 years: 4
Other Personnel
Short-Term less than 1 year: 1
Non-US in own/other country: 12
Home staff: 3
Countries/Regions: Ethiopia, Indonesia, Madagascar

HELLENIC MINISTRIES USA
25W560 Geneva Rd, Ste. 5
Carol Stream, IL 60188 US
Phone: (630) 520-0372
Email: info@hmnet.org
Website: hellenicministries.org

A denominational heritage sending agency of Evangelical tradition engaged in church planting (establishing), discipleship, personal or small group evangelism, and youth ministry.

Purpose: . . . to share Christ for Greece and the nations.

Year Founded in US: 1986
Income for International Min:
$986,659

Fully Supported US Personnel Working Cross-Culturally
More than 4 years: 15
Other Personnel
Short-Term less than 1 year: 6
Non-US in own/other country: 12
Home staff: 2
Countries/Regions: Global Ministry

HELP FOR HAITI INC.
1129 South B Street
Lake Worth, FL 33460 US
Phone: (561) 768-1518
Email: helpforhaiti.inc@gmail.com
Website: helpforhaitiinc.org

A nondenominational support agency of Evangelical tradition engaged in relief &

aid, services for mission organizations, and handicapped groups. (FPC-PE)

Purpose: . . . to serve the poorest of the poor of Haiti regardless of race, creed or religious affiliation or belief through spiritual and material immediate and long term relief.

Year Founded in US: 1995
Income for International Min:
$1,883,196

Fully Supported US Personnel Working Cross-Culturally
X-C workers in US: 2

Other Personnel
Short-Term less than 1 year: 10
Tentmakers/BAM: 1
Non-US in own/other country: 3
Home staff: 2
Countries/Regions: Haiti

HELPS MINISTRIES
1340 Patton Ave, Ste. J
Asheville, NC 28806 US
Phone: (828) 277-3812
Email: dprice@helpsmission.org
Website: helpsmission.org
A nondenominational specialized agency of Evangelical tradition engaged in agricultural assistance, children's ministry, community development, national worker support, partnership development, and and video-film production or distribution.

Purpose: . . . to provide professional services that strengthen Christian ministries and missionaries for God's kingdom purposes worldwide.

Year Founded in US: 1976
Income for International Min:
$1,800,000

Fully Supported US Personnel Working Cross-Culturally
More than 4 years: 29
X-C workers in US: 6
Non-residential: 1

Other Personnel
Non-US in own/other country: 18
Home staff: 10
Countries/Regions: Bahamas, Cambodia, Costa Rica, Estonia, Ethiopia, France, India, Israel, Japan, South Africa, Spain, Thailand, Uganda

HERMANO PABLO MINISTRIES
2080 Placentia Ave.
Costa Mesa, CA 92627 US
Phone: (949) 645-0676
Email: hpm@box100.org
Website: message2conscience.com
A nondenominational service agency of Evangelical tradition engaged in evangelistic broadcasting, audio recording/distribution, evangelism and video/film production/distribution, whose program "A Message to the Conscience" is broadcast 4,600 times each day in 32 countries throughout the Spanish-speaking world. (DPE)

Purpose: . . . to be God's voice to the conscience of every Hispanic in the world.
Year Founded in US: 1971
Income for International Min:
$320,260
Other Personnel
Home staff: 6

HIGH ADVENTURE MINISTRIES
PO Box 197569
Louisville, KY 40259 US
Phone: (502) 254-9960
Email: mail@highadventure.net
Website: highadventure.org
An interdenominational service agency of Evangelical tradition engaged in radio or TV broadcasting, personal or small group evangelism, and relief & aid.

Purpose: . . . to provide broadcasting, evangelism, and relief.
Year Founded in US: 1972

Other Personnel
Non-US in own/other country: 3
Home staff: 6
Countries/Regions: Israel

HISPORTIC CHRISTIAN MISSION
PO Box 2313
Elizabethton, TN 37644 US
Phone: (541) 324-9258
Email: cbookout@hcm.org
Website: hcm.org
A denominational support agency of
Christian (Restoration Movement) tradition
engaged in church planting. (DPE)
Purpose: . . . enables mission-minded
Christians to evangelize and plant churches
among Portuguese speaking people.
Income for International Min:
$1,200
Other Personnel
Tentmakers/BAM: 18
Non-US in own/other country: 1
Home staff: 5
Countries/Regions: Guinea-Bissau

HOLT INTERNATIONAL CHILDREN'S SERVICES INC.
250 Country Club Rd
Eugene, OR 97401 US
Phone: (888) 355-4658
Email: info@holtinternational.org
Website: holtinternational.org
A nondenominational service agency of
Evangelical tradition engaged in adoption,
childcare/orphanage programs, children
at risk, children's programs and disability
assistance programs. (DPE)
Purpose: . . . to carry out God's plan for
every child to have a permanent, loving
family.
Income for International Min:
$8,550,000
Fully Supported US Personnel Working Cross-Culturally
Non-residential: 2

Other Personnel
Non-US in own/other country: 102
Home staff: 135
Countries/Regions: Cambodia,
China (People's Republic of), Ethiopia,
Guatemala, Nepal, Ukraine, Vietnam

HOPE FOR THE HUNGRY
627 Hope for the Hungry Street
Belton, TX 76513 US
Phone: (254) 939-0124
Email: mlawson@hopeforthehungry.org
Website: hopeforthehungry.org
An interdenominational sending agency of
Evangelical tradition engaged in childcare
or orphanage, children's ministry, member
care, missionary & worker training,
services for mission organizations, and
STM trip coordination. (FPC-PE)
Purpose: . . . to share Jesus Christ with
those in the world who do not know Him
and will suffer eternal death without Him.
Year Founded in US: 1982
Income for International Min:
$478,285
Fully Supported US Personnel Working Cross-Culturally
More than 4 years: 16
1-4 years: 3
Other Personnel
Short-Term less than 1 year: 53
Non-US in own/other country: 24
Home staff: 8
Countries/Regions: Asia, Colombia,
Costa Rica, Ghana, Guatemala, Haiti,
India, Israel, Japan, Kenya, South Africa, Sri
Lanka, Taiwan (China), Uganda, Zimbabwe

HOPE HAVEN INTERNATIONAL MINISTRIES
1800 19th St.
Rock Valley, IA 51247 US
Phone: (712) 476-2737
Email: hopehavencanada@hotmail.com
Website: hopehaven.org

A denominational support agency of Reformed tradition engaged in disability assistance programs and camping programs. (DPE)

Purpose: . . . to assist persons with disabilities . . . to develop opportunities for improving the economic and social welfare and independence of people with disabilities within countries and cultures throughout the world.

Year Founded in US: 1964
Income for International Min:
   $2,084,582

Fully Supported US Personnel Working Cross-Culturally
   More than 4 years: 1
   Non-residential: 1

Other Personnel
   Short-Term less than 1 year: 50
   Non-US in own/other country: 16
   Home staff: 5

Countries/Regions: Guatemala, Romania, Vietnam

HOPE INTERNATIONAL

227 Granite Run Drive
Lancaster, PA 17601 US
Phone: (717) 464-3220
Email: sschultz@hopeinternational.org
Website: hopeinternational.org

A nondenominational support agency of Ecumenical tradition engaged in business as mission, church development, discipleship. (FPC-PE)

Purpose: . . . to invest in the dreams of families in the world's underserved communities as we proclaim and live the Gospel.

Year Founded in US: 1997
Income for International Min:
   $17,400,000

Fully Supported US Personnel Working Cross-Culturally
   More than 4 years: 4
   1–4 years: 7

Other Personnel
   Non-US in own/other country: 7
   Home staff: 101

Countries/Regions: Afghanistan, Burundi, China (People's Republic of), Democratic Republic of Congo, Republic of Congo, Haiti, India, Rwanda, Ukraine

HOPE INTERNATIONAL DEVELOPMENT AGENCY

214 Sixth Street
New Westminster, BC V3L 3A2 CA
Phone: (604) 525-5481
Email: hope@hope-international.com
Website: hope-international.com

A nondenominational service agency engaged in development, agricultural programs, leadership development, relief and/or rehabilitation and training. (DPE)

Purpose: . . . supports water resource development, agriculture, health care, education and micro-enterprise projects in Africa, South Asia, Southeast Asia, Central and Latin America. We provide volunteer opportunities for people with skills in the above areas. We also offer short-term serving and learning opportunities for students and young North Americans in various countries.

Income for International Min:
   $18,000,000

Fully Supported CA Personnel Working Cross-Culturally
   1–4 years: 1
   Non-residential: 1

Other Personnel
   Short-Term less than 1 year: 6
   Non-CA in own/other country: 23
   Home staff: 10

Countries/Regions: Afghanistan, Cambodia, Ethiopia, South Africa

IBMGLOBAL
P. O. Box 607
Nashua, NH 03061 US
Phone: (603) 821-5232
Email: deejoki1963@ibmglobal.org
Website: ibmglobal.org
Associations: FOM

A denominational and independent specialized agency of Baptist tradition engaged in business as mission, camping programs, childcare or orphanage, church construction or financing, church planting (establishing), and personal or small group evangelism.

Purpose: . . . to facilitate the American church in sending their missionaries around the world in fulfillment of the Great Commission.

Year Founded in US: 2011
Income for International Min:
 $2,700,000

Fully Supported US Personnel Working Cross-Culturally
 More than 4 years: 7
 1–4 years: 29
 X-C workers in US: 3
Other Personnel
 Non-US in own/other country: 4
 Home staff: 6
Countries/Regions: Chile, Ecuador, Italy, Japan, Panama, Paraguay, Peru, Russia, South Africa, South Sudan, Thailand, Turkey, Ukraine, Zambia

IDENTIFY
1950 Dartford Way
Hoschton, GA 30548 US
Phone: (404) 590-4908
Email: info@identifythemission.org
Website: identifythemission.org
Associations: Missio Nexus

A nondenominational service agency of Baptist and Christian (Restoration Movement) tradition engaged in children's ministry, church, school or general

Christian education, personal or small group evangelism, medical ministry, including dental or public health, STM coordination, and spiritual renewal.

Purpose: . . . to engage a spirit of global awareness and initiate life change through mission experiences and relationships in the name of Jesus Christ.

Year Founded in US: 2013
Income for International Min:
 $22,551

Fully Supported US Personnel Working Cross-Culturally
 Non-residential: 6
Other Personnel
 Short-Term less than 1 year: 58
 Non-US in own/other country: 1
 Home staff: 3
Countries/Regions: Ecuador, Guatemala, Venezuela

IFCA WORLD MISSIONS
1294 Rutledge Rd.
Transfer, PA 16154 US
Phone: (724) 962-3501
Email: ifcaworldimpact@verizon.net
Website: ifcaministry.org

A denominational support agency of Pentecostal tradition engaged in mobilization for mission, church planting, funds transmission, support of national churches, support of national workers and missionary training. (DPE)

Purpose: . . . to accelerate the Gospel to the unreached peoples of the world.

Year Founded in US: 1942
Income for International Min:
 $393,332

Fully Supported US Personnel Working Cross-Culturally
 More than 4 years: 8
Other Personnel
 Non-US in own/other country: 20
 Home staff: 2

Countries/Regions: Argentina,
Australia, Barbados, Bolivia, Botswana,
Brazil, Chile, Colombia, Ecuador,
Guyana, India, Italy, Madagascar, Malawi,
Philippines, South Africa, Ukraine,
Uruguay, Venezuela

IHOPE INTERNATIONAL
2754 Redbud Lane
Fort Mill, SC 29715 US
Phone: (803) 207-2670
Email: ihopeinternational@yahoo.com
Website: ihopeinternational.com
An interdenominational sending agency
of Evangelical and Independent tradition
engaged in apologetics, Bible teaching,
childcare or orphanage, discipleship,
theological education, and Internet
discipleship or training.
Purpose: . . . to equip Christians to
evangelize, minister to needs, disciple
believers, defend the historic Christian
faith, and fulfill the Great Commission.
Year Founded in US: 2010
*Fully Supported US Personnel Working
Cross-Culturally*
   More than 4 years: 6
Other Personnel
   Short-Term less than 1 year: 2
   Non-US in own/other country: 4
   Home staff: 5
Countries/Regions: East Asia, Global
Ministry, South Asia, Southeast Asia, Sub-
Saharan Africa

IMA WORLD HEALTH
1730 M Street, NW, Suite 1100
Washington, DC 20036 US
Phone: (202) 888-6200
Email: imainfo@worldhealth.org
Website: imaworldhealth.org
An interdenominational support agency of
Christian ("Restoration Movement") and
Ecumenical tradition distributing medical

supplies to healthcare facilities in more
than 50 countries affiliated with member
and associate organizations. (DPE)
Purpose: . . . to provide essential
products and services for emergency,
health and development programs of
interest to members, which serve people in
need with preference given to the poorest
of the poor.
Year Founded in US: 1960
Income for International Min:
   $20,511,465
Other Personnel
   Home staff: 23

IMB OF THE SOUTHERN BAPTIST CONVENTION
3806 Monument Ave.
Richmond, VA 23230 US
Phone: (804) 355-0151
Email: gric@imb.org
Website: imb.org
Associations: Missio Nexus
A denominational sending agency of
Baptist tradition engaged in church
planting (establishing), CPM, discipleship,
theological education, orality or storying,
and research.
Purpose: . . . to evangelize, disciple,
and plant reproducing churches among
all peoples in fulfillment of the Great
Commission.
Year Founded in US: 1845
Income for International Min:
   $265,000,000
*Fully Supported US Personnel Working
Cross-Culturally*
   More than 4 years: 2337
   1–4 years: 1335
Other Personnel
   Short-Term less than 1 year: 30000
   Home staff: 300
Countries/Regions: Global Ministry

Directory of North American Agencies   247

IMPACT CANADA MINISTRIES INC.
Formerly: Western Tract Mission, Inc.
2222 Avenue C North
Saskatoon, SK S7L 6C3 CA
Phone: (306) 244-0446
Email: impactcanadaforchrist@gmail.com
Website: westerntractmission.org
A nondenominational service agency
of Evangelical tradition engaged in
correspondence courses, evangelism and
literature distribution. (DPE)
Other Personnel
  Home staff: 6

IMPACT INTERNATIONAL INC.
PO Box 160
Boca Raton, FL 33429 US
Phone: (561) 338-7000
Email: bdm4@msn.com
A nondenominational sending agency
of Baptist tradition engaged in radio
or TV broadcasting, church planting
(establishing), personal or small group and
evangelism. (FPC-PE)
Purpose: . . . to evangelize the lost and
edify the Church in the Spanish-speaking
world.
Year Founded in US: 1959
Income for International Min:
  $500,000
*Fully Supported US Personnel Working
Cross-Culturally*
  More than 4 years: 4
Other Personnel
  Non-US in own/other country: 18
  Home staff: 4
Countries/Regions: Argentina, El
Salvador, Guatemala, Honduras, Mexico,
Federated States of Micronesia, Peru,
South America, Venezuela

IMPACT NATIONS INTERNATIONAL MINISTRIES
3620 Wyoming Blvd NE, Ste. 222
Albuquerque, NM 87111 US
Phone: (877) 736-0803
Email: info@impactnations.com
Website: impactnations.com/
A nondenominational support agency
of Charismatic tradition engaged in
childcare or orphanage, addressing human
trafficking, medical ministry, including
dental or public health, prayer-intercession,
relief & aid, and STM trip coordination.
Purpose: . . . to partner with leaders in
the developing world to rescue lives and
transform communities by engaging people
in practical and supernatural expressions
of the Kingdom of God.
Year Founded in US: 2014

IN MOTION MINISTRIES
P.O. Box 337507
Greeley, CO 80631 US
Phone: (970) 352-5640
Email: norma@inmotionministries.org
Website: inmotionministries.org
A nondenominational sending agency
of Independent tradition engaged in
discipleship, personal or small group
evangelism, leadership development,
missionary & worker training, services
for mission organizations, and STM trip
coordination. (FPC-PE)
Purpose: . . . to provide Christ-centered,
full-service short-term cross-cultural
ministry opportunities, which are high
quality and purpose driven with a lasting
impact.
Year Founded in US: 1986
Other Personnel
  Short-Term less than 1 year: 375
  Home staff: 7

IN NETWORK DBA
INTERNATIONAL NEEDS USA
5570 32nd Ave
Hudsonville, MI 49426 US
Phone: (616) 209-5420
Email: chris.vanreg@internationalneeds.us
Website: internationalneeds.us/
A nondenominational service agency of
Evangelical tradition engaged in children's
ministry, church planting (establishing),
community development, church, school
or general Christian education, and relief
& aid.
Purpose: . . . to fulfill the commission
of Jesus Christ, by supporting each other
to see transformed lives, families and
communities.
Year Founded in US: 1975
Income for International Min:
    $1,861,088
Other Personnel
    Short-Term less than 1 year: 37
    Non-US in own/other country: 115
    Home staff: 14
Countries/Regions: Bangladesh,
Colombia, Czech Republic, Egypt,
Ethiopia, Ghana, India, Kenya, Nepal,
Philippines, Romania, Slovakia, Turkey,
Uganda, Vietnam, Zambia

IN TOUCH MISSION
INTERNATIONAL
PO Box 7575
Tempe, AZ 85281 US
Phone: (480) 968-4100
Email: itmi@intouchmission.org
Website: intouchmission.org
A nondenominational sending agency of
Evangelical tradition engaged in support
of national workers, childcare/orphanage
programs, support of national churches,
partnership development, relief and/or
rehabilitation and Bible translation. (DPE)

Purpose: . . . to find and partner with
Christians who are already living and
doing ministry in their home country for
the purpose of connecting them with
resources that will empower them to fulfill
their calling by exposing their ministries to
others in the Body of Christ.
Income for International Min:
    $767,620
*Fully Supported US Personnel Working
Cross-Culturally*
    More than 4 years: 10
    1–4 years: 1
    Non-residential: 1
Other Personnel
    Short-Term less than 1 year: 2
    Non-US in own/other country: 30
    Home staff: 3
Countries/Regions: India, Poland,
Romania, South Africa

INDEPENDENT FAITH
MISSION INC.
PO Box 7791
Greensboro, NC 27417 US
Phone: (336) 292-1255
Email: kurtz.robert@ifmnews.com
Website: ifmnews.com
A denominational heritage sending agency
of Baptist tradition engaged in church
planting (establishing), personal or small
group evangelism, STM trip coordination,
and Bible translation.
Year Founded in US: 1950
Income for International Min:
    $2,650,000
*Fully Supported US Personnel Working
Cross-Culturally*
    More than 4 years: 94
Other Personnel
    Short-Term less than 1 year: 14
    Non-US in own/other country: 14
    Home staff: 7

Countries/Regions: Botswana, Global Ministry, Israel, Kenya, South Korea, Marshall Islands, Mexico, Philippines, South Africa, Suriname, Zambia, Zimbabwe

INDEPENDENT GOSPEL MISSIONS: A BAPTIST MISSION AGENCY
990 Calkins Rd
Rochester, NY 14623 US
Phone: (585) 334-9048
Email: igm@igmonline.or
Website: igmonline.org
A nondenominational sending agency of Baptist and Independent tradition engaged in childcare or orphanage, church planting (establishing), leadership development, national worker support, and STM trip coordination. (FPC-PE)
Purpose: . . . to serve the church, missionary, and national pastor to produce a concerted effort in the areas of accountability, responsibility, need, and the harvest of souls for the glory and kingdom of God.
Year Founded in US: 1968
Other Personnel
   Home staff: 1

INDIA EVANGELICAL MISSION INC.
PO Box 1633
Lakewood, CA 90716 US
Phone: (562) 484-0881
Email: iem@indiaevangelical.org
Website: indiaevangelical.org
A nondenominational support agency of Evangelical tradition engaged in childcare or orphanage, church planting (establishing), theological education, mass evangelism, leadership development, and national worker support.

Purpose: . . . to build and equip Indian nationals to fulfill the Great Commission of our Lord, seeking to provide for the physical, spiritual, and material needs of the people.
Year Founded in US: 1966
Income for International Min: $488,000
Fully Supported US Personnel Working Cross-Culturally
   More than 4 years: 2
   1–4 years: 1
   X-C workers in US: 2
   Non-residential: 3
Other Personnel
   Short-Term less than 1 year: 13
   Tentmakers/BAM: 2
   Non-US in own/other country: 64
   Home staff: 3
Countries/Regions: India

INDIA GOSPEL LEAGUE
1521 Georgetown Rd, Ste. 305
Hudson, OH 44236 US
Phone: (330) 650-5900
Email: ksmith@iglworld.org
Website: iglworld.org/
An interdenominational support agency of Evangelical tradition engaged in children's ministry, church planting (establishing), community development, discipleship, leadership development, and medical ministry, including dental or public health.
Purpose: . . . to promote and establish the kingdom of God through the ministry of India Gospel League, India, which exists to promote and establish the kingdom of God and reach the unreached in South Asia.
Year Founded in US: 1994
Income for International Min: $2,312,621

Other Personnel
  Short-Term less than 1 year: 124
  Tentmakers/BAM: 6653
  Non-US in own/other country: 347
  Home staff: 10
Countries/Regions: India

INDIA GOSPEL OUTREACH INC.
PO Box 550
Rancho Cucamonga, CA 91729-0550 US
Phone: (909) 948-2404
Email: igo@indiago.org
Website: indiago.org
A service agency of Charismatic and
Evangelical tradition engaged in church
planting, evangelism, leadership
development, support of national workers,
mobilization for mission and training
evangelists. (DPE)
Purpose: . . . dedicated to evangelizing
all 3,000 ethnic groups of India by planting
dynamic churches in all 27,000+ zip codes.
Income for International Min:
  $2,018,160
*Fully Supported US Personnel Working
Cross-Culturally*
  More than 4 years: 1
  Non-residential: 1
Other Personnel
  Short-Term less than 1 year: 26
  Non-US in own/other country: 2540
  Home staff: 7
Countries/Regions: Bhutan, India,
Nepal

INDIA PARTNERS
PO Box 5470
Eugene, OR 97405-0470 US
Phone: (541) 683-0696
Email: info@indiapartners.org
Website: indiapartners.org
A nondenominational service agency
engaged in childcare/orphanage programs,
Christian education, medical work,
partnership development, short-term
programs and trafficking/slavery issues. (DPE)

Purpose: . . . to partner with the
people of India in ministry by cultivating
relationships, sharing resources, and
encouraging self-sufficiency through the
compassion and wisdom of Jesus Christ.
Income for International Min:
  $254,676
Other Personnel
  Short-Term less than 1 year: 10
  Non-US in own/other country: 1
  Home staff: 5
Countries/Regions: India

INDOPARTNERS AGENCY
550 W. Baseline Road, Suite 102-509
Mesa, AZ 85210 US
Phone: (408) 676-7472
Email: indopartners@gmail.com
Website: indopartners.com
Associations: Missio Nexus
A nondenominational specialized agency
of Evangelical tradition engaged in CPM,
discipleship, church, school or general
Christian education, Internet discipleship
or training, Internet evangelism, and STM
trip coordination.

Purpose: . . . to be a channel in reaching
Indonesian Unreached People Groups for
Christ through: partnering with indigenous
Indonesian churches and missions,
serving as a catalyst to inspire innovative
ministries, and engaging in direct
evangelism.
Year Founded in US: 2003
Income for International Min:
  $400,000
*Fully Supported US Personnel Working
Cross-Culturally*
  More than 4 years: 5
  1–4 years: 3
  Non-residential: 4
Other Personnel
  Short-Term less than 1 year: 32
  Non-US in own/other country: 2
  Home staff: 7
Countries/Regions: Indonesia, Tanzania

INDOPARTNERS

IS FOCUSED ON

INDONESIA'S UNREACHED

Seeking to reach Indonesia's more than 120 unreached people groups

ROOTED IN INDONESIA
Launched by Indonesian-American businessmen with a heart to reach their country of origin with the gospel.

IN PARTNERSHIP WITH INDONESIANS
– Indopartners serves alongside like-minded Indonesian churches, agencies and schools.

WWW.INDOPARTNERS.COM/MAKE-AN-IMPACT

- **LEARN MORE** - How you can get involved and make a kingdom impact:
- **INVEST** in digital evangelism
- **JOIN** a short term team
- **PRAY** - Become part of a Prayer Movement
- **PARTNER** with Indonesian church planters
- **SCHOLARSHIP** - Equip local Indonesians to reach the unreached

INDOPARTNERS AGENCY, INC. | WWW.INDOPARTNERS.COM | INDOPARTNERS@GMAIL.COM
(408)676-7472 | 550 W. BASELINE ROAD, SUITE 102-509, MESA, AZ 85210

INTER-VARSITY CHRISTIAN FELLOWSHIP OF CANADA

1 International Boulevard
Toronto, ON M9W 6H3 CA
Phone: (416) 443-1170
Email: info@ivcf.ca
Website: ivcf.ca

A nondenominational support agency of Evangelical tradition engaged in campus ministry, camping programs, evangelism and youth programs. (DPE)

Purpose: . . . to be shaped by God's Word and led by the Holy Spirit, the purpose of Inter-Varsity Christian Fellowship of Canada is the transformation of youth, students, and graduates into fully committed followers of Jesus Christ.

Year Founded in CA: 1944
Income for International Min:
$1,361,000
Other Personnel
Home staff: 178
Countries/Regions: Azerbaijan, China (People's Republic of), France, Kazakhstan, Ukraine

INTERACT MINISTRIES

31000 SE Kelso Rd.
Boring, OR 97009 US
Phone: (503) 668-5571
Email: info@interactministries.org
Website: InterActMinistries.org
Associations: Missio Nexus

An interdenominational sending agency of Evangelical and Independent tradition engaged in church planting (establishing), discipleship, personal or small group evangelism, leadership development, TESOL or TEFL, and youth ministry.

Purpose: . . . to make disciples among least-reached peoples in cooperation with like-minded churches and organizations.

Year Founded in US: 1951

Fully Supported US Personnel Working Cross-Culturally
More than 4 years: 30
X-C workers in US: 21
Other Personnel
Short-Term less than 1 year: 5
Home staff: 7
Countries/Regions: Canada, Russia

INTERACT MINISTRIES OF CANADA

Box 559
Crossfield, AB T0M 0S0 CA
Phone: (403) 946-5567
Email: canada@interactministries.org
Website: InterActMinistries.ca
Associations: Missio Nexus

An interdenominational sending agency of Evangelical and Independent tradition engaged in camping programs, church planting (establishing), correspondence courses, discipleship, personal or small group evangelism, and youth ministry.

Purpose: . . . to make disciples among least-reached peoples in cooperation with like-minded churches and organizations, reproducing disciples across Russia, Alaska and western Canada, the North Pacific Crescent.

Year Founded in CA: 1967
Fully Supported CA Personnel Working Cross-Culturally
More than 4 years: 1
X-C workers in CA: 30
Countries/Regions: United States of America

INTERACTION INTERNATIONAL

PO Box 863
Wheaton, IL 60189 US
Phone: (630) 653-8780
Email: office@interactionintl.org
Website: interactionintl.org

An interdenominational service agency of Evangelical tradition engaged in training and orientation of missionaries/

third-culture kids, Christian education, furloughed missionary support, member care and services for other agencies. (DPE)

Purpose: . . . to be a catalyst and resource working cooperatively in the development of programs, services and publications to provide and contribute to a flow of care that meets the needs of third-culture kids (TCKS) and internationally mobile personnel.

Year Founded in US: 1977

Other Personnel
  Home staff: 7

INTERCEDE INTERNATIONAL
Formerly: Christian Aid Mission
201 Stanton St.
Fort Erie, ON L2A 3N8 CA
Phone: (905) 871-1773
Email: friends@IntercedeNow.ca
Website: IntercedeNow.ca

A nondenominational support agency of Evangelical tradition engaged in Bible distribution, childcare or orphanage, church planting (establishing), church, school or general Christian education, mass evangelism, and persecuted church. (FPC-PE)

Purpose: . . . to aid, encourage and strengthen indigenous New Testament Christianity, particularly where Christians are impoverished or persecuted; and to encourage Christian witness and ministry to the international community in North America.

Year Founded in CA: 1953

Fully Supported CA Personnel Working Cross-Culturally
  X-C workers in CA: 1

Other Personnel
  Short-Term less than 1 year: 4
  Non-CA in own/other country: 64
  Home staff: 7

Countries/Regions: China (People's Republic of), Haiti, India, Indonesia, Jordan, Kenya, Liberia, Myanmar (Burma), Nepal, Nigeria, Pakistan, Philippines, Senegal, Sudan, Thailand, Turkey, Ukraine, Vietnam

INTERCOMM INC.
PO Box 618
Winona Lake, IN 46590 US
Phone: (574) 267-5774
Email: lanejill@intercommedia.org
Website: intercommedia.org

A nondenominational support agency of Evangelical tradition engaged in mass and media evangelism. (FPC-PE)

Purpose: . . . to equip National Christian Leaders with appropriate media to assist their vision of sharing Christ in their country.

Income for International Min:
  $300,000

Other Personnel
  Home staff: 2

INTERNATIONAL AID
17011 W. Hickory St.
Spring Lake, MI 49456 US
Phone: (616) 846-7490
Email: ia@internationalaid.org
Website: internationalaid.org

A nondenominational specialized agency of Evangelical tradition engaged in services for other agencies, development, providing medical supplies, relief and/or rehabilitation, supplying equipment and training. (DPE)

Purpose: . . . responding to Biblical mandates by providing and supporting solutions in healthcare.

Income for International Min:
  $36,611,986

Other Personnel
  Home staff: 66

INTERNATIONAL ASSOCIATION FOR REFUGEES

1515 East 66th Street
Minneapolis, MN 55423 US
Phone: (612) 200-0321
Email: info@iafr.org
Website: iafr.org

A nondenominational specialized agency of Evangelical tradition engaged in leadership development, national worker support, research, and refugee ministry.

Purpose: . . . to seek the welfare of forcibly displaced people with the church.

Year Founded in US: 2009
Income for International Min: $284,689

Fully Supported US Personnel Working Cross-Culturally
  More than 4 years: 4
  1–4 years: 5
  X-C workers in US: 5
  Non-residential: 8

Other Personnel
  Short-Term less than 1 year: 15
  Non-US in own/other country: 2
  Home staff: 5

Countries/Regions: Austria, France, Italy, Kenya, Malawi, Malta, Turkey

INTERNATIONAL BOARD OF JEWISH MISSIONS INC.

5106 Genesis Ln
Hixson, TN 37343 US
Phone: (423) 876-8150
Email: amolam@ibjm.org
Website: ibjm.org

A denominational heritage sending agency of Baptist and Evangelical tradition engaged in radio or TV broadcasting, personal or small group evangelism, literature distribution, and missionary & worker training.

Purpose: . . . to engage in missionary training, broadcasting, evangelism, and literature distribution.

Year Founded in US: 1949

Fully Supported US Personnel Working Cross-Culturally
  More than 4 years: 8
  1–4 years: 9

Other Personnel
  Short-Term less than 1 year: 3
  Non-US in own/other country: 3
  Home staff: 19

Countries/Regions: Global Ministry

INTERNATIONAL CHILD CARE (CANADA) INC.

500 Alden Rd., Ste. 210
Markham, ON L3R 5H5 CA
Phone: (905) 752-0501
Email: canada@intlchildcare.org
Website: ca.internationalchildcare.org/

An interdenominational sending agency of Evangelical tradition engaged in childcare/orphanage programs, children's programs, development, disability assistance programs, medical work and short-term programs. (DPE)

Purpose: . . . to respond to Jesus Christ through caring service by sharing and promoting health and wholeness to those in need, especially children.

Fully Supported CA Personnel Working Cross-Culturally
  More than 4 years: 2
  1–4 years: 4

Countries/Regions: Dominican Republic, Haiti

INTERNATIONAL CHILD CARE USA

240 West Michigan
Kalamazoo, MI 49007 US
Phone: (800) 722-4453
Email: iccusa@intlchildcare.org
Website: internationalchildcare.org

An interdenominational service agency of Methodist tradition engaged in fundraising/funds transmission to national organizations, Christian education, HIV/AIDS, missions information service and support of national workers. (DPE)

Purpose: . . . to respond to a loving God by promoting health and well-being for the children and families of Haiti and the Dominican Republic through caring service and the education of others.

Income for International Min:
$551,994

Other Personnel
Home staff: 4

INTERNATIONAL CHRISTIAN MINISTRIES

4201 Ardmore Ave., Ste. 6
Bakersfield, CA 93309 US
Phone: (661) 832-9740
Email: info@icmusa.org
Website: icmusa.org

An interdenominational sending agency of Evangelical tradition engaged in theological education, TEE, leadership development and partnership development. (DPE)

Purpose: . . . to serve the Church by discipling and equipping its leaders.

Income for International Min:
$1,500,000

Fully Supported US Personnel Working Cross-Culturally
More than 4 years: 2
1–4 years: 2
Non-residential: 4

Other Personnel
Short-Term less than 1 year: 20
Non-US in own/other country: 33
Home staff: 5

Countries/Regions: Democratic Republic of Congo, Egypt, Ethiopia, Kenya, Nigeria, Sierra Leone, South Africa, Tanzania, Uganda

INTERNATIONAL CHRISTIAN MINISTRIES CANADA (ICM)

#304 19978 - 72 Ave.
Langley, BC V2Y 1R7 CA
Phone: (604) 575-8686
Email: icmcanada@cs.com
Website: icmcanada.org

An interdenominational sending agency of Evangelical tradition engaged in leadership development, extension education, theological education, literature production, support of national churches and mentoring/coaching. (DPE)

Purpose: . . . to serve the Church by discipling and equipping its leaders.

Fully Supported CA Personnel Working Cross-Culturally
More than 4 years: 14
1–4 years: 2
Non-residential: 4

Other Personnel
Non-CA in own/other country: 14
Home staff: 4

Countries/Regions: Africa, Eastern Europe, Latin America, Russia

INTERNATIONAL COOPERATING MINISTRIES (ICM)

1901 Armistead Ave.
Hampton, VA 23666 US
Phone: (757) 224-7102
Email: egoodwin@icm.org
Website: icm.org

A transdenominational support agency of Evangelical tradition engaged in national church nurture/support, broadcasting, church planting and sports program ministry. (DPE)

Purpose: . . . to nurture believers and assist Church growth worldwide.

Income for International Min:
$6,924,906

Other Personnel
Home staff: 25

Countries/Regions: Africa, Asia, Caribbean, Eastern Europe, Latin America, South America

INTERNATIONAL CRISIS AID
PO Box 510167
St. Louis, MO 63151 US
Phone: (888) 740-7779
Email: info@crisisaid.org
Website: crisisaid.org
A nondenominational service agency of Evangelical tradition engaged in relief and/or rehabilitation, childcare/orphanage programs, children's programs, development, medical work and trafficking/slavery issues. (DPE)
Year Founded in US: 2002
Income for International Min:
$1,117,855
Other Personnel
    Short-Term less than 1 year: 40
    Non-US in own/other country: 5
    Home staff: 1
Countries/Regions: Ethiopia

INTERNATIONAL FAITH MISSIONS
5553 CR 79A
St. Joe, IN 46785 US
Phone: (330) 439-6468
Email: ifm.hdr@gmail.com
Website: ifmhaiti.org
A denominational heritage sending agency of Evangelical and Anabaptist tradition engaged in Bible teaching, childcare or orphanage, church development, church, school or general Christian education, leadership development, and medical ministry, including dental or public health.
Purpose: . . . to present Christ by word and deed, bringing people to a saving knowledge of Christ.
Year Founded in US: 1984
Income for International Min:
$500,000

Fully Supported US Personnel Working Cross-Culturally
    1–4 years: 12
Other Personnel
    Short-Term less than 1 year: 28
    Non-US in own/other country: 1
    Home staff: 2
Countries/Regions: Haiti

INTERNATIONAL FOUNDATION FOR EWHA WOMAN'S UNIVERSITY
475 Riverside Dr. Rm. 1359
New York, NY 10115 US
Phone: (212) 864-5759
Email: ewhafdn@aol.com
Website: ewhafoundation.org
An interdenominational support agency of Ecumenical tradition providing financial and other support to EWHA University in South Korea. (DPE)

INTERNATIONAL FRIENDSHIPS INC.
2500 N. High Street
Columbus, OH 43202 US
Phone: (614) 294-2434
Email: info@ifiusa.org
Website: ifipartners.org, ifiusa.org
A nondenominational support agency of Evangelical tradition engaged in discipleship, student evangelism, international student ministry
Purpose: . . . to serve internationals and partner with them to make Christ known among the nations.
Year Founded in US: 1979
Income for International Min:
$50,000
Fully Supported US Personnel Working Cross-Culturally
    1–4 years: 4
    X-C workers in US: 66
    Non-residential: 5

Other Personnel
Tentmakers/BAM: 5
Non-US in own/other country: 8
Home staff: 2
Countries/Regions: China (People's Republic of), Italy, Japan, Middle East, North Africa

INTERNATIONAL GOSPEL OUTREACH

PO Box 1008
Semmes, AL 36575-1008 US
Phone: (251) 645-2117
Email: infor@igoministries.org
Website: igoministries.org

An interdenominational sending agency of Evangelical and Wesleyan tradition engaged in CPM, discipleship, theological education, international student ministry, missionary & worker training, and STM trip coordination.

Purpose: . . . to serve the body of Christ in missions by educating, equipping, and sending missionaries in partnership with their local church or group.

Year Founded in US: 1975

Fully Supported US Personnel Working Cross-Culturally
More than 4 years: 92
1–4 years: 7
X-C workers in US: 22
Non-residential: 48

Other Personnel
Short-Term less than 1 year: 115
Tentmakers/BAM: 50
Non-US in own/other country: 99
Home staff: 14

Countries/Regions: Argentina, Burkina Faso, Burundi, Cameroon, Chile, Côte d'Ivoire, Cuba, Ethiopia, Gambia, Georgia, Ghana, Guatemala, Guinea, Guinea-Bissau, Honduras, Hong Kong (China), India, Italy, Kenya, Liberia, Mexico, Mongolia, Myanmar (Burma), Nepal,

Nicaragua, Pakistan, Philippines, Russia, Rwanda, Saudi Arabia, Sierra Leone, South Sudan, Tanzania, Uganda, Vietnam

INTERNATIONAL JUSTICE MISSION

PO Box 58147
Washington, DC 20037-8147 US
Phone: (703) 465-5495
Email: contact@ijm.org
Website: ijm.org

A nondenominational service agency engaged in justice, Christian education, relief and/or rehabilitation and trafficking/slavery issues. (DPE)

Purpose: . . . to secure justice for victims of slavery, sexual exploitation, and other forms of violent oppression . . . to work with local governments to ensure victim rescue . . . to prosecute perpetrators . . . to strengthen the community and civic factors that promote functioning public justice systems.

Income for International Min:
$8,000,000

Fully Supported US Personnel Working Cross-Culturally
1–4 years: 15
Non-residential: 3

Other Personnel
Short-Term less than 1 year: 85
Non-US in own/other country: 234
Home staff: 102

Countries/Regions: Bolivia, Cambodia, Guatemala, India, Kenya, Philippines, Rwanda, Thailand, Uganda, Zambia

INTERNATIONAL MESSENGERS

PO Box 618, 110 Orchard Ct.
Clear Lake, IA 50428 US
Phone: (641) 357-6700
Email: office@im-usa.org
Website: internationalmessengers.org

A nondenominational sending agency of Evangelical tradition engaged in discipleship, personal or small group evangelism, missionary & worker training, recruiting or mobilizing for mission, STM trip coordination, and TESOL or TEFL.

Purpose: . . . to make disciples of all nations through partnering with local churches to renew, train and mobilize believers for active involvement in reaching the world for Christ.

Fully Supported US Personnel Working Cross-Culturally
    More than 4 years: 110
    1–4 years: 53
Other Personnel
    Non-US in own/other country: 163
Countries/Regions: Canada, Cyprus, Czech Republic, East Asia, Eastern Europe and Eurasia, Hungary, North Africa, Peru, Poland, Romania, Slovenia, South Africa, Uganda, Ukraine, United Kingdom

INTERNATIONAL PARTNERSHIP ASSOCIATES
PO Box 1331
Edmonds, WA 98020 US
Phone: (425) 775-3362
Email: tricia@interdev.org
Website: ipassociates.org
A nondenominational service agency of Evangelical tradition engaged in partnership development. (DPE)

Purpose: . . . to serve the Church in its mission to the least-reached peoples by equipping, encouraging, and catalyzing the partnering movement.

Income for International Min:
    $45,000
Fully Supported US Personnel Working Cross-Culturally
    Non-residential: 1
Other Personnel
    Home staff: 1

INTERNATIONAL PARTNERSHIP MINISTRIES INC.
100 Spring Ave.
Hanover, PA 17331 US
Phone: (717) 637-7388
Email: ipm@ipmworld.org
Website: ipmworld.org
A sending agency of Baptist and Independent tradition engaged in church planting, childcare/orphanage programs, theological education, evangelism and partnership development. (DPE)

Purpose: . . . to glorify God through the reaching of men and women with the Gospel, the training of Christian leaders, and the planting of fundamental churches through partnerships with national missionaries and indigenous national ministries.

Income for International Min:
    $1,511,447
Fully Supported US Personnel Working Cross-Culturally
    More than 4 years: 3
    Non-residential: 1
Other Personnel
    Tentmakers/BAM: 4
    Non-US in own/other country: 390
    Home staff: 19
Countries/Regions: Bangladesh, Bhutan, Bolivia, Chad, Chile, China (People's Republic of), Côte d'Ivoire, Cuba, Dominican Republic, Ghana, Guatemala, Haiti, India, Iraq, Lebanon, Liberia, Mexico, Myanmar (Burma), Nepal, Peru, Philippines, Puerto Rico, Spain, Taiwan (China), Togo, Uruguay, Zambia

INTERNATIONAL PENTECOSTAL HOLINESS CHURCH
P. O. Box 12609
Oklahoma City, OK 73157 US
Phone: (405) 792-7171
Email: wmminfo@iphc.org
Website: iphc.org

A denominational sending agency of Holiness and Pentecostal tradition engaged in childcare or orphanage, church planting (establishing), fund raising or transmission, leadership development, missionary & worker training, and STM trip coordination. (FPC-PE)

Purpose: . . . to fulfill the Great Commission of our Lord Jesus Christ.

Year Founded in US: 1911
Income for International Min:
  $7,508,227
Fully Supported US Personnel Working Cross-Culturally
  More than 4 years: 128
  1–4 years: 7
Other Personnel
  Tentmakers/BAM: 2
  Non-US in own/other country: 35
  Home staff: 15
Countries/Regions: Albania, Argentina, Australia, Azerbaijan, Barbados, Belgium, Belize, Benin, Bolivia, Botswana, Brazil, Burundi, Cameroon, Chile, Colombia, Democratic Republic of Congo, Costa Rica, Côte d'Ivoire, Croatia, Cuba, Dominican Republic, Ecuador, Egypt, Estonia, Ethiopia, France, Germany, Ghana, Guatemala, Guyana, Haiti, Honduras, Hong Kong (China), Hungary, India, Indonesia, Italy, Jamaica, Japan, Kenya, South Korea, Lesotho, Liberia, Malawi, Malaysia, Malta, Mauritius, Mexico, Moldova, Mozambique, Myanmar (Burma), Netherlands, Nicaragua, Nigeria, Norway, Panama, Paraguay, Peru, Philippines, Portugal, Romania, Rwanda, Seychelles, Sierra Leone, Singapore, South Africa, Spain, Sri Lanka, Sudan, Swaziland, Tanzania, Thailand, Togo, Trinidad and Tobago, Turkey, Uganda, Ukraine, United Kingdom, Unspecified Country, Uruguay, Venezuela, Vietnam, Zambia, Zimbabwe

INTERNATIONAL PROJECT
Formerly: NYCIP
PO Box 1646, Apt 1
New York, NY 10026 US
Phone: (509) 225-0018
Email: nycipasst@outlook.com
Website: internationalproject.org/
Associations: Missio Nexus

A nondenominational sending agency of Evangelical tradition engaged in Bible teaching, CPM, DMM, personal or small group evangelism, student evangelism, and missionary & worker training.

Purpose: . . . to partner with the local church to equip and send people into the world with the truth of Jesus Christ.

Year Founded in US: 1999
Fully Supported US Personnel Working Cross-Culturally
  More than 4 years: 9
  1–4 years: 22
Other Personnel
  Tentmakers/BAM: 8
Countries/Regions: Global Ministry

INTERNATIONAL STREET KIDS OUTREACH MINISTRIES (ISKOM)
PO Box 8551
Clearwater, FL 33758-8551 US
Phone: (800) 265-1970
Email: contactus@internationalstreetkids.com
Website: internationalstreetkids.com

A support agency of Evangelical tradition engaged in children at risk, discipleship, childcare/orphanage programs, justice and trafficking/slavery issues. (DPE)

Purpose: . . . to reach, rescue, and make disciples of orphaned & abandoned children where the gospel of Christ has little or no access.

Income for International Min:
  $337,531

Fully Supported US Personnel Working Cross-Culturally
More than 4 years: 2
1–4 years: 2
Non-residential: 4
Other Personnel
Non-US in own/other country: 232
Countries/Regions: Asia, Brazil, Eastern Europe

INTERNATIONAL STUDENTS INC (ISI)

PO Box C
Colorado Springs, CO 80901-2901 US
Phone: (719) 576-2700
Email: president@isiwebnet.net
Website: isionline.org

A transdenominational support agency of Ecumenical tradition engaged in evangelism, discipleship, mobilization for mission and training. (DPE)

Purpose: . . . exists to share Christ's love with international students and to equip them for effective service in cooperation with the local church and others.

Fully Supported US Personnel Working Cross-Culturally
1–4 years: 2
Other Personnel
Non-US in own/other country: 2
Home staff: 216
Countries/Regions: China (People's Republic of), Hong Kong (China)

INTERNATIONAL TEAMS CANADA (EVANGELICAL INTERNATIONAL CRUSADES CANADA INC.)

1 Union St.
Elmira, ON N3B 3J9 CA
Phone: (519) 669-8844
Email: canada@iteams.org
Website: iteams.ca

A sending agency of Brethren tradition engaged in compassionate evangelism,

children's programs, church planting and youth programs. (DPE)

Purpose: . . . engages in authentic partnerships with local churches and other missions to mobilize teams of people around the world to compassionate evangelism and training next generation leaders.

Year Founded in CA: 1959
Income for International Min:
$1,094,000

Fully Supported CA Personnel Working Cross-Culturally
More than 4 years: 10
1–4 years: 3
Non-residential: 3
Other Personnel
Short-Term less than 1 year: 98
Home staff: 16
Countries/Regions: Austria, Bolivia, Costa Rica, Ecuador, Greece, Rwanda, Unspecified Country

INTERNATIONAL TEAMS U.S.A.

411 W. River Rd.
Elgin, IL 60123-1570 US
Phone: (847) 429-0900
Email: info@iteams.org
Website: iteams.org
Associations: Missio Nexus

An interdenominational sending agency of Evangelical tradition engaged in discipleship, children at risk, development, support of national churches, relief and/or rehabilitation and trafficking/slavery issues. (DPE)

Purpose: . . . mobilizing international teams to build transforming communities.

Income for International Min:
$8,647,062

Fully Supported US Personnel Working Cross-Culturally
More than 4 years: 211
1–4 years: 38

Other Personnel
 Short-Term less than 1 year: 710
 Non-US in own/other country: 487
 Home staff: 34
Countries/Regions: Albania, Argentina,
Australia, Austria, Belarus, Belgium,
Bhutan, Bolivia, Bosnia and Herzegovina,
Brazil, Bulgaria, Cambodia, Colombia,
Costa Rica, Cuba, Czech Republic,
Ecuador, Fiji, France, Greece, Honduras,
Indonesia, Ireland (Republic of), Israel,
Italy, Japan, Kenya, Kosovo, Mexico,
Nepal, Netherlands, New Zealand,
Nicaragua, Norway, Philippines, Romania,
Russia, Rwanda, Spain, Taiwan (China),
Thailand, Turkey, Uganda, Ukraine, United
Kingdom, Unspecified Country, Zambia

INTERSERVE CANADA
Formerly: International Service
Fellowship
10 Huntingdale Blvd.
Toronto, ON M1W 2S5 CA
Phone: (416) 499-7511
Email: communications@
interservecanada.org
Website: interservecanada.org
A sending agency of Evangelical tradition
engaged in mobilization for mission,
business as mission, development, medical
work, services for other agencies and
tentmaking. (DPE)
Purpose: . . . to make Christ known
where He is least known among the
neediest peoples in Asia and the Arab
world.
Year Founded in CA: 1967
Income for International Min:
 $1,600,000
*Fully Supported CA Personnel Working
Cross-Culturally*
 More than 4 years: 36
 1–4 years: 21
 Non-residential: 8

Other Personnel
 Tentmakers/BAM: 7
 Home staff: 6
Countries/Regions: Africa, Asia,
Central Asia, Middle East, United Kingdom

INTERSERVE USA
P.O. Box 418
Upper Darby, PA 19082 US
Phone: (800) 809-4440
Email: info@interserveusa.org
Website: interserveusa.org
Associations: Missio Nexus
An interdenominational sending agency of
Evangelical tradition engaged in business
as mission, community development,
addressing human trafficking, medical
ministry, including dental or public health,
technical assistance, and TESOL or TEFL.
(FPC-PE)
Purpose: . . . to make Jesus Christ known
through holistic ministry, in partnership
with the global church, amongst the
neediest peoples of Asia and the Arab
World.
Year Founded in US: 1860
Income for International Min:
 $6,201,000
*Fully Supported US Personnel Working
Cross-Culturally*
 X-C workers in US: 7
Other Personnel
 Short-Term less than 1 year: 13
 Home staff: 14
Countries/Regions: Afghanistan,
Bahrain, Bangladesh, Cambodia, China
(People's Republic of), Cyprus, Egypt,
India, Indonesia, Jordan, Oman, Pakistan,
Tajikistan, Turkey, United Arab Emirates,
Uzbekistan, Yemen

INTERVARSITY CHRISTIAN FELLOWSHIP/USA

PO Box 7895
Madison, WI 53707 US
Phone: (608) 274-9001
Email: info@intervarsity.org
Website: intervarsity.org
Associations: Missio Nexus

An interdenominational sending agency of Evangelical tradition engaged in Bible teaching, student evangelism, international student ministry, missionary & worker training, prayer-intercession, and recruiting or mobilizing for mission.

Purpose: . . . to establish and advance witnessing communities of students and faculty who follow Jesus as Savior and Lord: growing in love for God, God's Word, God's people of every ethnicity and culture, and God's purposes in the world.

Fully Supported US Personnel Working Cross-Culturally
   1–4 years: 49
Other Personnel
   Short-Term less than 1 year: 405
Countries/Regions: Armenia, Australia, Belgium, Bulgaria, Cambodia, Cayman Islands, East Asia, Eastern Europe and Eurasia, Ecuador, France, Germany, Ghana, Global Ministry, Israel, Japan, Kenya, Mexico, Netherlands, Puerto Rico, Romania, Singapore, South Asia, Switzerland, Ukraine, United Kingdom, Western Europe

INTO ALL THE WORLD

5256 Victoria Ave.
Niagara Falls, ON L2E 4E7 CA
Phone: (226) 706-1701
Email: david@iatw.ca
Website: iatw.ca

An interdenominational sending agency of Evangelical and Pentecostal tradition engaged in church development, community development, discipleship,

member care, partnership development, and prayer-intercession. (FPC-PE)

Purpose: . . . to mobilize the church and equip individuals to fulfill the Great Commission.

Year Founded in CA: 1981
Income for International Min:
   $508,694

Fully Supported CA Personnel Working Cross-Culturally
   More than 4 years: 15
   1–4 years: 2
   X-C workers in CA: 17
Other Personnel
   Tentmakers/BAM: 1
   Home staff: 2
Countries/Regions: Belize, Bolivia, Dominican Republic, Ethiopia, Kenya, Papua New Guinea, Peru, South Africa, Tanzania, Uganda

IRANIAN CHRISTIANS INTERNATIONAL

PO Box 25607
Colorado Springs, CO 80936 US
Phone: (719) 596-0010
Email: ici@iranchristians.org
Website: iranchristians.org

A transdenominational support agency of Evangelical tradition engaged in helping persecuted Christians, refugees & immigration, evangelism, justice, leadership development, literature distribution and literature production. (DPE)

Year Founded in US: 1981
Income for International Min:
   $2,000
Other Personnel
   Home staff: 2

ISOH/IMPACT

25182 W. River Rd.
Perrysburg, OH 43551 US
Phone: (419) 878-8548
Email: ministries@impactwithhope.org
Website: isohimpact.org

A nondenominational service agency of Holiness tradition engaged in relief and/ or rehabilitation, children's programs, development, evangelism, providing medical supplies and partnership development. (DPE)

Purpose: . . . to reach out and serve others in the name of Christ through disaster relief and development projects at home, across the United States, and around the world.

Year Founded in US: 1982
Income for International Min:
   $6,000,372
Fully Supported US Personnel Working Cross-Culturally
   More than 4 years: 4
Other Personnel
   Short-Term less than 1 year: 16
   Home staff: 4
Countries/Regions: Bulgaria, Honduras, Tajikistan

ISSACHAR INITIATIVE

26895 Aliso Creek Rd., B-156
Aliso Viejo, CA 92656 US
Phone: (717) 269-2450
Email: davidp@issacharinitiative.org
Website: issacharinitiative.org

A nondenominational specialized agency of Evangelical tradition engaged in networking, partnership, or coordination, partnership development, research, and services for mission organizations.

Purpose: . . . to serve the body of Christ by bringing vision and focus so its resources are strategically directed towards the fulfillment of the Great Commission.

Year Founded in US: 2010

ITALY FOR CHRIST INC.

1301 Shiloh Rd NW, #1820
Kennesaw, GA 30144 US
Phone: (770) 274-2800
Email: info@italyforchrist.com
Website: italyforchrist.it

A nondenominational sending agency of Evangelical tradition engaged in Bible distribution, church planting (establishing), discipleship, mass evangelism, student evangelism, and leadership development.

Purpose: . . . to present the Gospel of Christ to every Italian in this generation, in cooperation with the local churches.

Year Founded in US: 1983
Income for International Min:
   $369,774
Fully Supported US Personnel Working Cross-Culturally
   More than 4 years: 2
   X-C workers in US: 2
Other Personnel
   Short-Term less than 1 year: 106
   Non-US in own/other country: 3
   Home staff: 1
Countries/Regions: Italy

JAARS INC.

PO Box 248, 7601 Radin Road
Waxhaw, NC 28173 US
Phone: (704) 843-6000
Email: info_jaars@jaars.org
Website: jaars.org
Associations: Missio Nexus

An interdenominational sending agency of Evangelical tradition engaged in aviation, missionary & worker training, recruiting or mobilizing for mission, services for mission organizations, and Bible translation.

Purpose: . . . to make Bible translation and language development possible, especially in the most remote and difficult places on earth. We do that by enabling locally-appropriate and sustainable solutions in transportation, technology, media, and training.

Year Founded in US: 1948
Income for International Min:
$941,330
*Fully Supported US Personnel Working
Cross-Culturally*
More than 4 years: 500
Other Personnel
Non-US in own/other country: 5
Home staff: 505
Countries/Regions: Global Ministry

JAPANESE EVANGELICAL MISSIONARY SOCIETY (JEMS)
948 E 2nd St
Los Angeles, CA 90012 US
Phone: (213) 613-0022
Email: info@jems.org
Website: jems.org
An interdenominational service agency
of Evangelical tradition engaged in
association of missions, camping programs,
personal or small group evangelism, and
STM trip coordination.
Purpose: . . . to enable Japanese and
those of asian descent to be authentic
disciples of Jesus Christ by creatively
developing and providing ministry
opportunities in partnership with churches.
Year Founded in US: 1950
Income for International Min:
$300,000
*Fully Supported US Personnel Working
Cross-Culturally*
More than 4 years: 15
1–4 years: 3
Other Personnel
Short-Term less than 1 year: 11
Home staff: 13
Countries/Regions: Japan

JARON MINISTRIES INTERNATIONAL
4710 N Maple Ave
Fresno, CA 93726 US
Phone: (559) 227-7997
Email: office@jaron.org
Website: jaron.org
An interdenominational support agency
of Baptist tradition engaged in theological
education, leadership development,
literature production, and STM trip
coordination. (FPC-PE)
Purpose: . . . to teach, disciple, counsel,
and encourage Christian leaders; to
produce and provide biblically sound
and currently relevant written, audio, and
video training materials.
Year Founded in US: 1992
Income for International Min:
$96,328
Other Personnel
Short-Term less than 1 year: 25
Home staff: 50
Countries/Regions: Global Ministry,
Kenya, Philippines, Romania

JEWISH AWARENESS MINISTRIES INC.
P.O. BOX 1808
Angier, NC 27501 US
Phone: (919) 275-4477
Email: office@jewishawareness.org
Website: jewishawareness.org
A nondenominational sending agency of
Baptist and Fundamental tradition engaged
in evangelism, broadcasting, discipleship,
literature distribution, literature production
and missionary training. (DPE)(FPC16)
Purpose: . . . to proclaim the Messiah,
preach the Word and pray for Israel.
Year Founded in US: 1946
Income for International Min:
$37,500

Fully Supported US Personnel Working Cross-Culturally
  More than 4 years: 6
Other Personnel
  Non-US in own/other country: 6
  Home staff: 12
Countries/Regions: Ecuador, Israel

JEWS FOR JESUS
60 Haight Street
San Francisco, CA 94102 US
Phone: (415) 864-2600
Email: JFJ@jewsforjesus.org
Website: jewsforjesus.org
Associations: Missio Nexus

A nondenominational sending agency of Evangelical tradition engaged in arts in mission, Bible teaching, camping programs, mass evangelism, Internet evangelism, and missionary & worker training.

Purpose: . . . to make the messiahship of Jesus an unavoidable issue to our Jewish people worldwide.

Year Founded in US: 1973
Income for International Min:
  $3,400,000
Fully Supported US Personnel Working Cross-Culturally
  More than 4 years: 6
  X-C workers in US: 1
Other Personnel
  Non-US in own/other country: 61
  Home staff: 93
Countries/Regions: Australia, Canada, France, Germany, Hungary, Israel, Russia, South Africa, Switzerland, Ukraine, United Kingdom

JEWS FOR JESUS CANADA
10 Huntingdale Blvd
Toronto, ON M1W 2S5 CA
Phone: (416) 444-7020
Email: toronto@jewsforjesus.ca
Website: jewsforjesus.ca
Associations: Missio Nexus

An interdenominational sending agency of Evangelical tradition engaged in discipleship, church, school or general Christian education, mass evangelism, personal or small group evangelism, Internet discipleship or training, and Internet evangelism. (FPC-PE

Purpose: . . . to make the Messiahship of Jesus an unavoidable issue to our Jewish people worldwide.

Year Founded in CA: 1981
Income for International Min:
  $75,000
Fully Supported CA Personnel Working Cross-Culturally
  X-C workers in CA: 2
Other Personnel
  Home staff: 4

JONI AND FRIENDS
PO Box 3333
Agoura Hills, CA 91376 US
Phone: (818) 707-5664
Email: shunt@joniandfriends.org
Website: joniandfriends.org
Associations: Missio Nexus

An interdenominational service agency of Evangelical tradition engaged in radio or TV broadcasting, disabled ministry, church, school or general Christian education, mass evangelism, missionary & worker training, and STM trip coordination. (FPC-PE)

Purpose: . . . to communicate the Gospel and equip Christ-honoring churches worldwide to evangelize and disciple people affected by disabilities.

Year Founded in US: 1979
Other Personnel
  Home staff: 99

JOSHUA EXPEDITIONS
6841 Virginia Pkwy
McKinney, TX 75071 US
Phone: (972) 542-3024
Email: contact@joshuaexpeditions.org
Website: joshuaexpeditions.org

A nondenominational service agency of Evangelical tradition engaged in STM trip coordination and Christian educational travel. (FPC-PE)

Purpose: . . . to assist Christian organizations to inspire purpose, develop leaders, and share Christ through travel.
Year Founded in US: 1987

JOSIAH VENTURE
209 E. Liberty Drive
Wheaton, IL 60187 US
Phone: (630) 221-9332
Email: tkerns@josiahventure.com
Website: josiahventure.com

A nondenominational sending agency of Evangelical and Independent tradition engaged in Bible teaching, church planting (establishing), DMM, mass evangelism, student evangelism, and youth ministry.

Purpose: . . . to equip young leaders to fill Christ's commission through the local church.

Year Founded in US: 2001
Income for International Min:
    $11,254,199
Fully Supported US Personnel Working Cross-Culturally
    More than 4 years: 78
    1–4 years: 12030
    X-C workers in US: 105
    Non-residential: 2
Other Personnel
    Short-Term less than 1 year: 1800
    Tentmakers/BAM: 14
    Non-US in own/other country: 175
    Home staff: 6

Countries/Regions: Bulgaria, Croatia, Czech Republic, Estonia, Germany, Hungary, Latvia, Poland, Romania, Serbia, Slovakia, Slovenia, Ukraine

JOSUE YRION WORLD EVANGELISM & MISSIONS INC.
P.O. Box 768
La Mirada, CA 90637 US
Phone: (562) 928-8892
Email: josueyrion@josueyrion.org
Website: josueyrion.org

An interdenominational sending agency of Evangelical and Pentecostal tradition engaged in Bible distribution, Bible teaching, theological education, mass evangelism, literature production, and video-film production or distribution.

Purpose: . . . to serve the body of Christ, to edify, teach, and prepare an effective evangelistic ministry that can change lives by the power of God's word.

Year Founded in US: 2003
Income for International Min:
    $140,000
Other Personnel
    Non-US in own/other country: 55
    Home staff: 3
Countries/Regions: Caribbean, Central America, East Asia, Eastern Europe and Eurasia, North Africa, Oceania, South America, South Asia, Southeast Asia, Sub-Saharan Africa, Western Europe

KERUS GLOBAL EDUCATION
245 Newman Ave., Ste. B
Harrisonburg, VA 22801 US
Phone: (540) 438-8782
Email: kerus@kerusglobal.org
Website: kerusglobal.org

A nondenominational support agency engaged in training, childcare/orphanage programs, children at risk, development, Christian education, HIV/AIDS, services for other agencies and youth programs. (DPE)

Fully Supported US Personnel Working Cross-Culturally
   Non-residential: 2
Other Personnel
   Short-Term less than 1 year: 15
   Home staff: 3

KEY COMMUNICATIONS
P.O. Box 13620
Portland, OR 97213 US
Phone: (503) 233-7680
Email: feedback@keycom.org
Website: keycom.org
A nondenominational specialized agency of Christian (Restoration Movement) tradition engaged in radio or TV broadcasting, church planting (establishing), Internet evangelism, and literature production. (FPC-PE)
Purpose: . . . to provide people, particularly from a Muslim background, with enough information to make an intelligent decision about accepting Christ, and help those who accept Christ form congregations.
Year Founded in US: 1976
Countries/Regions: Pakistan

KIDS ALIVE INTERNATIONAL
2507 Cumberland Drive
Valparaiso, IN 46383 US
Phone: (219) 464-9035
Email: kidsalive@kidsalive.org
Website: kidsalive.org
A nondenominational sending agency of Evangelical tradition engaged in childcare or orphanage, children's ministry, church, school or general Christian education, relief & aid, STM trip coordination, and youth ministry.

Purpose: . . . to reflect the love of Christ by rescuing suffering children in crisis, nurturing them with quality holistic care, and introducing them to the transforming power of Jesus Christ so they are enabled to instill hope in others.
Year Founded in US: 1916
Income for International Min:
   $9,775,000
Fully Supported US Personnel Working Cross-Culturally
   More than 4 years: 38
   1–4 years: 19
Other Personnel
   Short-Term less than 1 year: 1040
   Non-US in own/other country: 14
   Home staff: 32
Countries/Regions: Dominican Republic, East Asia, Guatemala, Haiti, Kenya, Lebanon, Papua New Guinea, Peru, Zambia

KIDS AROUND THE WORLD
4750 Hydraulic Rd.
Rockford, IL 61109 US
Phone: (815) 229-8731
Email: info@kidsaroundtheworld.com
Website: kidsaroundtheworld.com
Associations: Missio Nexus
A nondenominational sending agency of Evangelical tradition engaged in children's ministry, church, school or general Christian education, networking, partnership, or coordination, orality or storying, STM trip coordination, and playgrounds.
Purpose: . . . to impact the lives of kids globally with God's transforming hope.
Year Founded in US: 1994
Other Personnel
   Short-Term less than 1 year: 256
   Home staff: 24
Countries/Regions: Caribbean, Central America, Central Asia, East Asia, Eastern Europe and Eurasia, Middle East,

North Africa, South America, South Asia, Southeast Asia, Sub-Saharan Africa, Western Europe

KIDS FOR CHRIST INTERNATIONAL
1485 Saint Anthony Lane
Florissant, MO 63033 US
Phone: (314) 972-7880
Email: chuck@kidsforchristonline.com
Website: kidsforchristonline.com
A nondenominational support agency of Christian (Restoration Movement) and Independent tradition engaged in children's programs, Bible distribution, Bible memorization, children at risk, church planting, discipleship, Christian education, missionary education, evangelism, mobilization for mission, TESOL and missionary training. (DPE)
Purpose: . . . to bring hope to children in a hopeless world.
Year Founded in US: 1988
Fully Supported US Personnel Working Cross-Culturally
  Non-residential: 1
Other Personnel
  Short-Term less than 1 year: 1
  Non-US in own/other country: 5
  Home staff: 1
Countries/Regions: China (People's Republic of), Liberia, Myanmar (Burma), Philippines, Thailand

KIDZANA MINISTRIES
13230 12th Pl W
Everett, WA 98204 US
Phone: (425) 954-4006
Email: info@kidzana.org
Website: kidzana.org
A nondenominational support agency of Evangelical tradition engaged in children's ministry, discipleship, student evangelism, leadership development, literature production, and missionary & worker training.

Purpose: . . . to equip local people to reach and disciple local kids around the world for Christ.
Year Founded in US: 1998
Income for International Min:
  $131,003
Fully Supported US Personnel Working Cross-Culturally
  More than 4 years: 6
Other Personnel
  Short-Term less than 1 year: 2
  Home staff: 1
Countries/Regions: Canada, Global Ministry

KINSHIP UNITED
Formerly: Warm Blankets Orphan Care International
5105 Tollview Dr, Ste. 155
Rolling Meadows, IL 60008 US
Phone: (847) 577-1070
Email: info@kinshipunited.org
Website: kinshipunited.org
A nondenominational support agency of Evangelical tradition engaged in childcare or orphanage, children's ministry, community development, and relief & aid.
Purpose: . . . to unite people separated by war and tragedy, rebuild loving families for orphans and widows, and create networks of local churches and rescue centers.
Year Founded in US: 1999
Other Personnel
  Home staff: 14
Countries/Regions: Burkina Faso, Cambodia, Dominican Republic, Global Ministry, India, Indonesia, Kenya, Pakistan, Thailand, Uganda

KORE FOUNDATION
695 Nashville Pike #101
Gallatin, TN 37066 US
Phone: (904) 610-7898
Email: Jennifer@korefoundation.org
Website: korefoundation.org
A nondenominational service agency of
Christian (Restoration Movement) tradition
engaged in agricultural assistance, business
as mission, community development, mass
evangelism, partnership development, and
STM trip coordination.
Purpose: . . . to provide sustainable
solutions for extreme poverty for the
Christians in Haiti.
Year Founded in US: 2010
Income for International Min:
  $1,100,000
*Fully Supported US Personnel Working
Cross-Culturally*
  More than 4 years: 5
  X-C workers in US: 5
  Non-residential: 1
Other Personnel
  Short-Term less than 1 year: 100
  Tentmakers/BAM: 2
  Non-US in own/other country: 25
  Home staff: 5
Countries/Regions: Haiti

LATIN AMERICA MISSION
500 Coldstream Avenue
Toronto, ON M6B 2K6 CA
Phone: (905) 569-0001
Email: execdirector@lamcanada.ca
Website: lamcanada.ca
A nondenominational sending agency
of Evangelical and Presbyterian tradition
engaged in Bible teaching, business as
mission, church planting (establishing),
community development, Economic
development, leadership development,
and recruiting or mobilizing

Purpose: . . . to partner with Latin
and Canadian churches, organizations
and projects to strengthen the body of
Christ and advance His kingdom in Latin
America and beyond.
Income for International Min:
  $944,736
*Fully Supported CA Personnel Working
Cross-Culturally*
  More than 4 years: 11
  1–4 years: 2
  X-C workers in CA: 3
Other Personnel
  Short-Term less than 1 year: 5
  Non-CA in own/other country: 6
  Home staff: 4
Countries/Regions: Brazil, Colombia,
Costa Rica, Honduras, Mexico

LATIN AMERICAN LUTHERAN MISSION
3517 Salinas Ave.
Laredo, TX 78041 US
Phone: (956) 722-4047
Email: misionaguaviva@hotmail.com
Website: lutheranmission.wordpress.
com/
Associations: ALMA
A denominational support agency of
Lutheran tradition engaged in support of
national workers, leadership development,
support of national churches, short-term
programs and training. (DPE)
Purpose: . . . to develop the capacities of
the Lutheran churches in Mexico and stir
up vision for cross-cultural mission among
USA Lutherans.
Year Founded in US: 1941
Income for International Min:
  $130,000
*Fully Supported US Personnel Working
Cross-Culturally*
  More than 4 years: 3
  Non-residential: 3

Other Personnel
   Short-Term less than 1 year: 350
   Tentmakers/BAM: 1
   Non-US in own/other country: 1
   Home staff: 3
Countries/Regions: Mexico

LATIN AMERICAN MISSIONS ASSOCIATION
3952-D Clairemont Mesa Blvd #135
San Diego, CA 92117 US
Phone: (858) 270-2345
Email: info@LAMAministry.org
Website: LAMAministry.org
An interdenominational sending agency
of Evangelical and Pentecostal tradition
engaged in Bible teaching, business
as mission, community development,
personal or small group evangelism,
prayer-intercession, and youth ministry.
Purpose: . . . to bring hope, love &
support to Latin Americans; to educate,
teach, inform & equip economically &
spiritually poor.
Year Founded in US: 2009
Income for International Min:
   $30,000
*Fully Supported US Personnel Working
Cross-Culturally*
   Non-residential: 2
Other Personnel
   Short-Term less than 1 year: 12
   Non-US in own/other country: 4
Countries/Regions: Peru

LAUNCH OUT MINISTRIES INTERNATIONAL
PO Box 543102
Merritt Island, FL 32954 US
Phone: (321) 637-0722
Email: office@launchoutministries.com
Website: launchoutministries.com
A nondenominational sending agency
of Evangelical tradition engaged in
mobilization for mission, childcare/

orphanage programs, HIV/AIDS, relief and/
or rehabilitation, short-term programs and
trafficking/slavery issues. (DPE)
Purpose: . . . to take the Gospel to the
unreached . . . however . . . whenever . . .
wherever.
Year Founded in US: 2004
Income for International Min:
   $101,000
*Fully Supported US Personnel Working
Cross-Culturally*
   1–4 years: 2
Other Personnel
   Short-Term less than 1 year: 100
   Tentmakers/BAM: 1
   Non-US in own/other country: 20
   Home staff: 2
Countries/Regions: Botswana, Brazil,
Malawi, Mozambique, South Africa,
Swaziland, Tanzania, Thailand, Zambia

LEADACHILD
Formerly: Children's Christian Concern
Society
1000 SW 10th Ave.
Topeka, KS 66604 US
Phone: (785) 357-7688
Email: dsaving@leadachild.org
Website: leadachild.org
A denominational support agency of
Lutheran tradition engaged in children's
ministry, discipleship, church, school or
general Christian education, theological
education, networking, partnership, or
coordination, and partnership development.
Purpose: . . . to share the Love of Jesus
with children around the world through
Christian Education.
Year Founded in US: 1968
Income for International Min:
   $500,000
Other Personnel
   Short-Term less than 1 year: 35
   Home staff: 5

LEADERSHIP MINISTRIES WORLDWIDE

3755 Pilot Point
Chattanooga, TN 37416 US
Phone: (423) 855-2181
Email: info@outlinebible.org
Website: outlinebible.org/

A nondenominational service agency of Evangelical tradition engaged in leadership development, Bible distribution, Christian education, literature production, training and translation work. (DPE)

Purpose: . . . to equip ministers, teachers, and laymen in their understanding, preaching, and teaching of God's Word by publishing and distributing worldwide The Preacher's Outline & Sermon Bible and related Outline Bible Resources to reach and disciple men, women, boys, and girls for Jesus Christ.

Year Founded in US: 1992
Income for International Min:
$215,405
Other Personnel
Short-Term less than 1 year: 2
Home staff: 9

LEADERSHIP RESOURCES INTERNATIONAL

12575 S. Ridgeland Ave
Palos Heights, IL 60463 US
Phone: (708) 489-0022
Email: mlachcik@leadershipresources.org
Website: leadershipresources.org
Associations: Missio Nexus

A nondenominational service agency of Evangelical and Reformed tradition engaged in Bible teaching and leadership development.

Purpose: . . . to equip and encourage pastors around the world to teach God's word with God's heart.

Income for International Min:
$3,338,382

Fully Supported US Personnel Working Cross-Culturally
Non-residential: 33
Other Personnel
Home staff: 14
Countries/Regions: Central America, Central Asia, East Asia, Global Ministry, South America, Southeast Asia, Sub-Saharan Africa

LEADERSHIP TRAINING INTERNATIONAL

PO Box 9882
Chesapeake, VA 23321 US
Phone: (757) 673-6581
Email: ltiadmin@ltiworld.org
Website: ltiworld.com

An interdenominational service agency of Charismatic and Evangelical tradition engaged in leadership development. (DPE)

Purpose: . . . to provide training and resources to multiply ministry leaders to fulfill the Great Commission.

Income for International Min:
$23,000
Other Personnel
Home staff: 6

LEADERSHIP VISTAS INTERNATIONAL MINISTRIES

2001 W Plano Pkwy, Ste. 3436
Plano, TX 75075 US
Phone: (972) 941-4464
Email: Jerry@LeadershipVistas.org
Website: LeadershipVistas.org

A nondenominational service agency of Evangelical tradition engaged in Bible distribution, Bible teaching, theological education, and leadership development.

Purpose: . . . to equip African church leaders to fulfill their calling from God.

Year Founded in US: 2002
Income for International Min:
$190,575

Fully Supported US Personnel Working Cross-Culturally
  Non-residential: 30
Other Personnel
  Short-Term less than 1 year: 10
  Non-US in own/other country: 6
  Home staff: 1
Countries/Regions: Kenya, Rwanda, Uganda

LEADERTREKS
25W560 Geneva Rd., #30
Carol Stream, IL 60188 US
Phone: (630) 668-0936
Email: info@leadertreks.com
Website: leadertreks.com
An interdenominational service agency engaged in leadership development. (DPE)
Purpose: . . . developing leaders to fulfill the Great Commission.
Fully Supported US Personnel Working Cross-Culturally
  1–4 years: 18
Other Personnel
  Short-Term less than 1 year: 1100
  Home staff: 17
Countries/Regions: Bolivia, Costa Rica, South Africa

LIBERTY CORNER MISSION
PO Box 204
Liberty Corner, NJ 07938-0204 US
Phone: (908) 647-1777
Email: mariabaha@mac.com
Website: lcmissionusa.com/
An interdenominational sending agency of Evangelical tradition engaged in evangelism, church planting and discipleship. (DPE)
Year Founded in US: 1933
Income for International Min:
  $147,000

Fully Supported US Personnel Working Cross-Culturally
  More than 4 years: 3
  Non-residential: 9
Other Personnel
  Short-Term less than 1 year: 1
  Non-US in own/other country: 9
  Home staff: 3
Countries/Regions: Japan, Taiwan (China)

LIEBENZELL MISSION OF CANADA
12168 First Line, RR#1
Moffat, ON L0P 1J0 CA
Phone: (519) 822-9748
Email: mission@liebenzell.ca
Website: liebenzell.ca
Associations: Missio Nexus
A nondenominational sending agency of Evangelical tradition engaged in church planting (establishing), discipleship, theological education, personal or small group evangelism, missionary & worker training, and retreat ministries.
Purpose: . . . to obey the Great Commission of making disciples of the nations (Matthew 28:18–20) through the ministries of church planting, education, Bible translation, etc.
Year Founded in CA: 1966
Income for International Min:
  $214,581
Fully Supported CA Personnel Working Cross-Culturally
  1–4 years: 5
  X-C workers in CA: 2
Other Personnel
  Short-Term less than 1 year: 5
  Non-CA in own/other country: 3
  Home staff: 4
Countries/Regions: Bangladesh, Ecuador, Germany, Malawi

LIEBENZELL MISSION OF USA INC.

PO Box 66
Schooleys Mtn., NJ 07870 US
Phone: (908) 852-3044
Email: missions@liebenzellusa.org
Website: liebenzellmission.org/

An interdenominational sending agency of Evangelical tradition engaged in church planting, Christian education, extension education, theological education, leadership development, Bible translation and discipleship. (DPE)(FPC16)

Purpose: . . . to help fulfill the Great Commission of our Lord by sharing the Gospel of Jesus Christ and by instructing believers in obedience to the Word of God and to Scriptural maturity wherever God may lead around the world.

Income for International Min:
$997,424
Fully Supported US Personnel Working Cross-Culturally
More than 4 years: 7
1–4 years: 4
Countries/Regions: Ecuador, Guam, Middle East, Nigeria, Palau, Zambia

LIFE IMPACT INC.

P. O. Box 9753
Bend, OR 97702 US
Phone: (541) 593-7415
Email: info@lifeimpactministries.net
Website: lifeimpactoregon.org
Associations: Missio Nexus

A nondenominational service agency of Evangelical tradition engaged in counseling and member care.

Purpose: . . . to strengthen and increase effectiveness and sustainability in Christian workers globally by renewing their hearts, minds, and bodies through safe and caring hosted places of renewal.

Year Founded in US: 2003
Income for International Min:
$405,702

Fully Supported US Personnel Working Cross-Culturally
More than 4 years: 12
Other Personnel
Non-US in own/other country: 12
Home staff: 6
Countries/Regions: Brazil, Costa Rica, East Asia, Italy, Middle East, Slovakia, South Africa

LIFE IN MESSIAH INTERNATIONAL

PO Box 5470
Lansing, IL 60438 US
Phone: (708) 418-0020
Email: ltaber@lifeinmessiah.org
Website: lifeinmessiah.org
Associations: Missio Nexus

A nondenominational sending agency of Evangelical tradition engaged in Bible distribution, Bible teaching, discipleship, personal or small group evangelism, Internet evangelism, and literature distribution.

Purpose: . . . to share God's heart for the Jewish People.

Year Founded in US: 1887
Income for International Min:
$826,282
Fully Supported US Personnel Working Cross-Culturally
More than 4 years: 7
X-C workers in US: 25
Other Personnel
Short-Term less than 1 year: 19
Tentmakers/BAM: 2
Non-US in own/other country: 16
Home staff: 10
Countries/Regions: Argentina, Canada, France, Hong Kong (China), Israel, Mexico, Netherlands

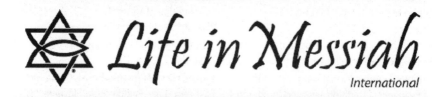

Life in Messiah
International

IN SEARCH OF
SHALOM
שלום

LIFE INTERNATIONAL

72 Ransom Ave NE
Grand Rapids, MI 49503 US
Phone: (616) 248-3300
Email: diane@lifeinternational.com
Website: lifeinternational.com
Associations: Missio Nexus

A nondenominational support agency of Evangelical tradition engaged in Bible teaching, Internet discipleship or training, leadership development, management consulting or training, partnership development, and prayer-intercession.

Purpose: . . . to partner with Gospel leaders to multiply life-giving ministry wherever abortion exists.

Year Founded in US: 2001

Other Personnel
  Home staff: 16

LIFELINE CHRISTIAN MISSION

921 Eastwind Dr, Ste. 104
Westerville, OH 43081 US
Phone: (614) 794-0108
Email: Connect@Lifeline.org
Website: Lifeline.org

A nondenominational service agency of Christian (Restoration Movement) tradition engaged in church planting (establishing), church, school or general Christian education, STM trip coordination, nutrition ministries, home building, and child sponsorship.

Purpose: . . . to restore hope by expressing love, growing followers, and making missionaries.

Year Founded in US: 1980
Income for International Min:
  $6,391,572

Other Personnel
  Short-Term less than 1 year: 909
  Home staff: 25

LIFELINE MALAWI

10556 Sumac Place
Surrey, BC V4N 1Y4 CA
Phone: (604) 498-3551
Email: info@lifelinemalawi.com
Website: lifelinemalawi.com

A nondenominational service agency of Evangelical tradition engaged in medical ministry, including dental or public health.

Purpose: . . . to provide community-based medical services and incorporate preventative initiatives that act to strengthen the health of local communities through compassion and loving service.

Year Founded in CA: 2003
Income for International Min:
  $339,931

Other Personnel
  Short-Term less than 1 year: 8

LIFESONG FOR ORPHANS

Formerly: Life International
202 N Ford Street
Gridley, IL 61744 US
Phone: (309) 747-4527
Email: kory@lifesongfororphans.org
Website: lifesongfororphans.org

A nondenominational support agency of Evangelical tradition engaged in adoption, business as mission, childcare or orphanage, discipleship, church, school or general Christian education, and missionary & worker training.

Purpose: . . . to bring joy and purpose to orphans.

Year Founded in US: 1994
Income for International Min:
  $6,541,138

Fully Supported US Personnel Working Cross-Culturally
  More than 4 years: 12
  1–4 years: 10
  Non-residential: 10

Other Personnel
Short-Term less than 1 year: 760
Tentmakers/BAM: 1
Non-US in own/other country: 593
Home staff: 24
Countries/Regions: Bolivia, Cambodia, Ethiopia, Guatemala, Haiti, India, Liberia, Mexico, Tanzania, Uganda, Ukraine, Zambia

LIFEWATER INTERNATIONAL INC.

PO Box 3131
San Luis Obispo, CA 93403-3131 US
Phone: (805) 541-6634
Email: info@lifewater.org
Website: lifewater.org
A nondenominational specialized agency of multi-denominational tradition engaged in development, extension education, medical work, partnership development, technical assistance and training. (DPE)
Purpose: . . . to equip partner organizations and work with them to empower communities in developing countries to gain safe water, adequate sanitation, effective hygiene, and the knowledge of Jesus' love.
Year Founded in US: 1984
Income for International Min:
$2,427,614
Fully Supported US Personnel Working Cross-Culturally
Non-residential: 4
Other Personnel
Short-Term less than 1 year: 8
Home staff: 17

LINK CARE FOUNDATION

1734 West Shaw Ave.
Fresno, CA 93711 US
Phone: (559) 439-5920
Email: philcollier@linkcare.org
Website: linkcare.org
Associations: Missio Nexus

A nondenominational specialized agency of Evangelical tradition engaged in radio or TV broadcasting, counseling, management consulting or training, member care, missionary & worker training, and networking, partnership, or coordination. (FPC-PE)
Purpose: . . . to serve God by helping people grow in emotional health, personal integrity, and spiritual wholeness.
Other Personnel
Home staff: 30

LINK INTERNATIONAL MINISTRIES

PO Box 23
New Westminster, BC V3L 4X9 CA
Phone: (604) 707-0222
Email: linkinternationalministries@hotmail.com
Website: linkinternational.org
An interdenominational support agency of Evangelical and Pentecostal tradition engaged in leadership development, childcare/orphanage programs, church planting, development, providing medical supplies and support of national workers. (DPE)
Purpose: . . . to make sure that all humanity, regardless of ethnicity or social status, are helped, empowered with the resources available to us, to become what they are created to be.
Year Founded in CA: 1989
Income for International Min:
$7,000
Fully Supported CA Personnel Working Cross-Culturally
Non-residential: 6
Other Personnel
Short-Term less than 1 year: 1
Non-CA in own/other country: 27
Countries/Regions: Belgium, Côte d'Ivoire, Kenya, Nigeria

THANK YOU
to the people+organizations whom we serve...

For *over 50 years*, *Link Care Center* has provided a safe haven for mission and ministry leaders and their families to receive care and counsel. *Over 75% of these servants have returned to service,* ready to continue on their various callings. We are honored and grateful to have played an important part in their healing and growth.

LINKCARE CENTER 50+
years of caring

Over 5,000 missionaries & families impacted!

If you or your people are interested in creating your own stories of healing with us, we'd love to hear from you.

Contact us for more information about our other programs:

> Member Care Training
> Member Care Organizational Audits
> Online Learning & Consulting
> On-Field Training

> Restoration & Personal Growth
> Pastoral Care
> Whole Family Involvement
> Psychotherapy

LINKCARE CENTER *restoring hearts • celebrating wholeness*
559.439.5920 // www.linkcare.org

LITERACY & EVANGELISM INTERNATIONAL
1800 S. Jackson Avenue
Tulsa, OK 74107 US
Phone: (918) 585-3826
Email: info@LiteracyInternational.net
Website: LiteracyEvangelism.org
An interdenominational sending agency of Evangelical and Presbyterian tradition engaged in personal or small group evangelism, literacy, missionary & worker training, services for mission organizations, and TESOL or TEFL.
Purpose: . . . to equip the Church to share the message of Jesus Christ through the gift of reading.
Year Founded in US: 1967
Income for International Min: $191,752
Fully Supported US Personnel Working Cross-Culturally
   More than 4 years: 5
   X-C workers in US: 13
   Non-residential: 6
Other Personnel
   Short-Term less than 1 year: 21
   Tentmakers/BAM: 2
   Non-US in own/other country: 31
   Home staff: 2
Countries/Regions: Benin, Brazil, Bulgaria, Burundi, Canada, Democratic Republic of Congo, Dominican Republic, Germany, Ghana, Guatemala, Haiti, India, Kenya, South Korea, Malawi, Mongolia, Nigeria, Peru, Sierra Leone

LIVING HOPE MINISTRIES INTERNATIONAL INC.
P.O. Box 1931
Jasper, GA 30143 US
Phone: (770) 917-1307
Email: info@lhmi.org
Website: lhmi.org
An interdenominational service agency of Baptist tradition engaged in childcare/orphanage programs, Bible distribution, children at risk, development and evangelism. (DPE)
Purpose: . . . to build Hope House Orphanages to care for the beautiful children of Kenya who have lost their parents to disease or the AIDS pandemic and who otherwise grow up with no hope for the future, physically or spiritually . . . to meet all their physical needs but most importantly, to teach them about our Lord and Savior Jesus Christ.
Other Personnel
   Short-Term less than 1 year: 7
Countries/Regions: Kenya

LIVING WATER INTERNATIONAL
4001 Greenbriar Dr.
Stafford, TX 77477 US
Phone: (281) 207-7800
Email: info@water.cc
Website: water.cc
An interdenominational service agency of Baptist and Evangelical tradition engaged in water project construction, partnership development, Bible distribution, evangelism, relief and/or rehabilitation, short-term programs and training. (DPE)
Purpose: . . . to demonstrate the love of God by helping communities acquire desperately needed clean water, and to experience "living water," the Gospel of Jesus Christ, which alone satisfies the deepest thirst.
Income for International Min: $10,588,000
Fully Supported US Personnel Working Cross-Culturally
   Non-residential: 4
Other Personnel
   Short-Term less than 1 year: 10
   Home staff: 39

Countries/Regions: Honduras, India, Kenya, Liberia, Malawi, Mexico, Namibia, Nicaragua, Nigeria, Peru, Romania, Rwanda, Sierra Leone, Sudan, Tanzania, Uganda, Zambia

LIVING WATER TEACHING
PO Box 1190
Caddo Mills, TX 75135 US
Phone: (903) 527-4160
Email: lwt@lwtusa.org
Website: livingwaterteaching.org
A nondenominational sending agency of Evangelical and Pentecostal tradition engaged in theological education, children's programs, evangelism, medical work, short-term programs, missionary training and youth programs. (DPE)
Purpose: . . . to make disciples through training and demonstration.
Year Founded in US: 1982
Fully Supported US Personnel Working Cross-Culturally
    More than 4 years: 15
    1–4 years: 2
Other Personnel
    Short-Term less than 1 year: 205
    Non-US in own/other country: 10
    Home staff: 7
Countries/Regions: Belize, Brazil, El Salvador, Guatemala, Honduras, Nicaragua, Panama, Paraguay

LIVING WORD MISSIONS
PO Box 687
Wilmington, MA 01887 US
Phone: (978) 258-3188
Email: admin@lwmcentral.com
Website: livingwordmissions.org
An interdenominational sending agency of Charismatic tradition engaged in Bible teaching, church planting (establishing), discipleship, literature distribution, literature production, and translation.

Purpose: . . . to provide support, training and resources for affiliated missionaries and majority world ministers with emphasis to unreached people groups in Muslim-dominated regions.
Year Founded in US: 1993
Income for International Min:
    $200,000
Fully Supported US Personnel Working Cross-Culturally
    More than 4 years: 25
    1–4 years: 1
Other Personnel
    Short-Term less than 1 year: 5
    Tentmakers/BAM: 1
    Non-US in own/other country: 27
    Home staff: 4
Countries/Regions: Burkina Faso, Central African Republic, Chad, Colombia, Côte d'Ivoire, Gambia, Guatemala, Indonesia, Liberia, Philippines, Sierra Leone, Switzerland, Thailand

LOGOI MINISTRIES
12900 SW 128 St, Suite 204
Miami, FL 33186 US
Phone: (305) 232-5880
Email: logoi@logoi.org
Website: logoi.org
A nondenominational service agency of Reformed tradition engaged in national Spanish pastoral training & resources, discipleship, theological education, leadership development and support of national churches. (DPE)
Purpose: . . . to prepare God's people for works of service, so that the body of Christ may be built up. Eph. 4:12–13
Fully Supported US Personnel Working Cross-Culturally
    Non-residential: 12

Other Personnel
Short-Term less than 1 year: 6
Tentmakers/BAM: 12
Non-US in own/other country: 19
Home staff: 9
Countries/Regions: Argentina, Bolivia, Chile, Colombia, Cuba, Ecuador, Mexico, Peru, Uruguay, Venezuela

LOTT CAREY BAPTIST FOREIGN MISSION CONVENTION
8201 Corporate Drive - Suite 1245
Landover, MD 20785 US
Phone: (301) 429-3300
Email: lottcarey@lottcarey.org
Website: lottcarey.org
A transdenominational sending agency of Baptist tradition engaged in support of national churches, theological education, HIV/AIDS, medical work, trafficking/slavery issues and youth programs. (DPE)
Purpose: . . . to help churches extend their Christian witness to the ends of the earth.
Income for International Min:
$2,250,000
Other Personnel
Short-Term less than 1 year: 125
Non-US in own/other country: 730
Home staff: 10
Countries/Regions: Guyana, India, Jamaica, Kenya, Liberia, Nigeria, South Africa, Zimbabwe

LUIS PALAU EVANGELISTIC ASSOCIATION
PO Box 50
Portland, OR 97207 US
Phone: (503) 614-1500
Email: info@palau.org
Website: palau.org
A nondenominational service agency of Evangelical tradition engaged in radio or TV broadcasting and mass evangelism.

Purpose: . . . to proclaim the Gospel, mobilize the Church, and equip the next generation.
Year Founded in US: 1978
Other Personnel
Non-US in own/other country: 18
Home staff: 50
Countries/Regions: Argentina, South America, United Kingdom

LUKE SOCIETY
3409 S. Gateway Blvd
Sioux Falls, SD 57106 US
Phone: (605) 373-9686
Email: office@lukesociety.org
Website: lukesociety.org
An interdenominational service agency of Reformed tradition engaged in Bible teaching, church planting (establishing), community development, church, school or general Christian education, medical ministry, including dental or public health, and partnership development.
Purpose: . . . to be a Christ-centered ministry of evangelism and discipleship, transforming communities by reconciling man to man and man to God through the truth of the Gospel.
Year Founded in US: 1964
Countries/Regions: Bolivia, Colombia, Ecuador, Guatemala, Honduras, Mexico, Nicaragua, Paraguay, Peru

LUTHERAN BIBLE TRANSLATORS INC.
PO Box 789
Concordia, MO 64020 US
Phone: (660) 225-0810
Email: info@lbt.org
Website: lbt.org
Associations: Missio Nexus
A denominational sending agency of Lutheran tradition engaged in Bible distribution, literacy, literature distribution, and Bible translation.

Purpose: . . . to help bring people to faith in Jesus Christ by making the Word of God available to those who do not yet have it in the language of their hearts.
Year Founded in US: 1964
Income for International Min:
$3,498,296
Other Personnel
Short-Term less than 1 year: 1
Non-US in own/other country: 94
Home staff: 16
Countries/Regions: Global Ministry

LUTHERAN BIBLE TRANSLATORS OF CANADA
137 Queen Street S
Kitchener, ON N2G 1W2 CA
Phone: (519) 742-3361
Email: jkeller@lbtc.ca
Website: lbtc.ca
A denominational service agency of Lutheran tradition engaged in audio recording or distribution, Bible distribution, Bible teaching, literacy, literature distribution, and Bible translation.
Purpose: . . . to help bring people to faith in Jesus Christ by making the Word of God available to those who do not yet have it in the language of their hearts.
Year Founded in CA: 1974
Income for International Min:
$300,000
Fully Supported CA Personnel Working Cross-Culturally
More than 4 years: 3
Other Personnel
Short-Term less than 1 year: 1
Non-CA in own/other country: 1
Home staff: 2
Countries/Regions: Cameroon

LUTHERAN BRETHREN INTERNATIONAL MISSION
PO Box 655
Fergus Falls, MN 56538 US
Phone: (218) 739-3336
Email: lbim@clba.org
Website: lbim.org
Associations: Missio Nexus
A denominational sending agency of Evangelical and Lutheran tradition engaged in church planting (establishing), community development, leadership development, literature production, partnership development, and Bible translation.
Purpose: . . . to glorify God by being a church that proclaims the gospel with an intensity and scope proportionate to our responsibility within the larger body of Christ, so that the Great Commission is fulfilled in and on behalf of our generation.
Year Founded in US: 1900
Income for International Min:
$1,000,000
Fully Supported US Personnel Working Cross-Culturally
More than 4 years: 18
Other Personnel
Short-Term less than 1 year: 7
Home staff: 5
Countries/Regions: Cameroon, Chad, China (People's Republic of), Japan, Taiwan (China)

LUTHERAN CHURCH MISSOURI SYNOD – WORLD MISSION
1333 S. Kirkwood Rd.
St. Louis, MO 63122-7295 US
Phone: (800) 433-3954
Email: roger.drinnon@lcms.org
Website: lcms.org/mission-and-outreach
A denominational sending agency of Lutheran tradition engaged in church planting, Christian education, theological education, TEE, leadership development and support of national churches. (DPE)

Purpose: . . . praying to the Lord of the harvest, LCMS World Mission, in collaboration with its North American and worldwide partners, will share the Good News of Jesus with 100 million unreached people or uncommitted people by the 500th anniversary of the Reformation in 2017.

Year Founded in US: 1847
Income for International Min:
$13,408,952

Fully Supported US Personnel Working Cross-Culturally
   More than 4 years: 59
   1–4 years: 9
Other Personnel
   Short-Term less than 1 year: 247
   Home staff: 71
Countries/Regions: Argentina, Asia, Central Asia, Guatemala, Jamaica, Japan, Kenya, Macau (China), Nigeria, Panama, Papua New Guinea, Poland, Puerto Rico, Russia, Taiwan (China), Togo, Venezuela

LUTHERAN HOUR MINISTRIES
660 Mason Ridge Center Dr.
St. Louis, MO 63141 US
Phone: (314) 317-4100
Email: lh_min@lhm.org.
Website: lhm.org
A denominational specialized agency of Lutheran tradition engaged in evangelism through broadcasting in 41 countries through 290 national staff. (DPE)

Purpose: . . . to bring Christ to the nations and the nations to the church through Christian radio and TV programming, the internet, print communications, dramas, music and congregational outreach training.
Income for International Min:
$650,000

Fully Supported US Personnel Working Cross-Culturally
   More than 4 years: 1
   Non-residential: 4
Other Personnel
   Short-Term less than 1 year: 72
   Non-US in own/other country: 290
   Home staff: 142

LUTHERAN WORLD RELIEF
700 Light St.
Baltimore, MD 21230 US
Phone: (410) 230-2800
Email: lwr@lwr.org
Website: lwr.org
A denominational service agency of Lutheran tradition engaged in agricultural assistance, leadership development, and relief or rehabilitation. (FPC-PE)

Purpose: . . . to alleviate suffering caused by natural disaster, conflict or poverty; through development efforts to enable marginalized people to realize more fully their God-given potential; and through education and advocacy efforts to promote a peaceful, just and sustainable global community.
Year Founded in US: 1945
Other Personnel
   Home staff: 80

MACEDONIA WORLD BAPTIST MISSION INTERNATIONAL
407 Rue St-Alexis
Trois-Rivieres, PQ G8W 2E2 CA
Phone: (819) 375-3655
Email: jasonhamby@mwbm.org
Website: mwbm.org
A denominational support agency of Baptist tradition engaged in Bible teaching, disabled ministry, church, school or general Christian education, and theological education.

Purpose: . . . to preach and advance the teachings of the Christian faith by undertaking missionary work.

Year Founded in CA: 2011

Fully Supported CA Personnel Working Cross-Culturally
  More than 4 years: 1
  X-C workers in CA: 1

Countries/Regions: Puerto Rico

MACEDONIA WORLD BAPTIST MISSIONS INC.

P.O. Box 519
Braselton, GA 30517 US
Phone: (706) 654-2818
Email: dhamby@mwbm.org
Website: mwbm.org

A denominational sending agency of Baptist tradition engaged in childcare or orphanage, children's ministry church planting (establishing), disabled ministry, church, school or general Christian education, and theological education.

Purpose: . . . to glorify God in the salvation of souls through the preaching of the Gospel of Jesus Christ, assisting local independent Baptist churches as they send their missionaries to both foreign fields of the world and to needy areas of the United States to propagate the Gospel of the Lord Jesus Christ and the establishing of New Testament, independent, Baptist churches.

Year Founded in US: 1967

Income for International Min:
  $550,000

Fully Supported US Personnel Working Cross-Culturally
  More than 4 years: 121
  1–4 years: 45995
  X-C workers in US: 8
  Non-residential: 2

Other Personnel
  Non-US in own/other country: 19
  Home staff: 8

Countries/Regions: Argentina, Bahamas, Belgium, Belize, Brazil, Burkina Faso, Canada, Chile, China (People's Republic of), Colombia, Cyprus, Egypt, Germany, Ghana, Guyana, Haiti, Honduras, India, Indonesia, Italy, Japan, Kenya, Kyrgyzstan, Mexico, Morocco, Nicaragua, Panama, Peru, Puerto Rico, Saint Kitts and Nevis, Saint Vincent and the Grenadines, Slovenia, South Africa, South Korea, Spain, Taiwan (China), Thailand, Tunisia, United Kingdom, Venezuela

MACEDONIAN MISSIONARY SERVICE

PO Box 68
Polk City, FL 33868-0068 US
Phone: (863) 984-4060
Email: leon@macedoniansms.org
Website: macedonianms.org

A denominational service agency of Baptist tradition engaged in Bible distribution, radio or TV broadcasting, church construction or financing, church planting (establishing), correspondence courses, and medical ministry, including dental or public health.

Purpose: . . . to serve missionaries with equipment and by encouragement.

Year Founded in US: 1973

Income for International Min:
  $25,000

Other Personnel
  Home staff: 5

MAILBOX CLUB INTERNATIONAL INC., THE

404 Eager Rd.
Valdosta, GA 31602 US
Phone: (229) 244-6812
Email: email@mailboxclub.org
Website: mailboxclub.org

A nondenominational support agency of Evangelical tradition engaged in correspondence courses, children's programs, discipleship, evangelism and literature distribution. (DPE)

Purpose: . . . to win the children and young people of the world to Christ, help nurture them into spiritual maturity through Bible correspondence courses and into local churches . . . accomplished through direct ministry and by multiplying our efforts through key partnerships and the body of Christ around the world.

Income for International Min:
$3,096,000

Fully Supported US Personnel Working Cross-Culturally
Non-residential: 4

Other Personnel
Non-US in own/other country: 14
Home staff: 11

Countries/Regions: Cameroon, India, Kenya, Nicaragua, Poland, Russia, South Africa, Uganda, Uruguay

MAKE WAY PARTNERS
PO Box 459
Chelsea, AL 35043 US
Phone: (205) 240-8597
Email: info@makewaypartners.org
Website: makewaypartners.org

An interdenominational service agency of Evangelical tradition engaged in childcare or orphanage, church, school or general Christian education, addressing human trafficking, persecuted church, relief & aid, and child sponsorship.

Purpose: . . . to prevent and combat human trafficking and all forms of modern-day oppression by educating and mobilizing the Body of Christ.

Year Founded in US: 2003
Income for International Min:
$2,678,759

Other Personnel
Short-Term less than 1 year: 12
Home staff: 8

MAP INTERNATIONAL
4700 Glynco Pkwy
Brunswick, GA 31525-6901 US
Phone: (912) 265-6010
Email: jelliott@map.org
Website: map.org

A nondenominational specialized agency engaged in providing medical supplies, children's programs, development, theological education, partnership development and relief and/or rehabilitation. (DPE)

Purpose: . . . to promote the total health of people living in the world's poorest communities by partnering in the provision of essential medicines, prevention and eradication of disease and the promotion of community health development.

Year Founded in US: 1954
Income for International Min:
$319,511,995

Other Personnel
Non-US in own/other country: 111
Home staff: 58

Countries/Regions: Bolivia, Côte d'Ivoire, Ecuador, Honduras, Indonesia, Kenya, Tanzania, Uganda

MASTER'S RESOURCING COMMISSION
Formerly: Missionary Revival Crusade
PO Box 4040
Seattle, WA 98194 US
Phone: (972) 283-8900
Email: finance@mrcpartners.org
Website: mrcpartners.com

A denominational specialized agency of Charismatic and Pentecostal tradition engaged in audio recording or distribution, radio or TV broadcasting, church planting (establishing), correspondence courses, discipleship, and leadership development.

Purpose: . . . to bring revival among God's people, to prepare workers for the harvest, and to reach the lost, at any cost, with the saving message of Jesus Christ.

Year Founded in US: 1955

Fully Supported US Personnel Working Cross-Culturally
    More than 4 years: 8
Other Personnel
    Home staff: 1

Countries/Regions: Argentina, Brazil, Colombia, France, Mexico, Nicaragua, Norway, Spain

MATS INTERNATIONAL
1400 E. Main St.
Richmond, IN 47374 US
Phone: (888) 776-7211
Email: mark@mats.org
Website: mats.org

A nondenominational service agency engaged in providing services for mission organizations. (FPC-PE)

Purpose: . . . to provide reliable and affordable transportation to ministries and their staff.

Year Founded in US: 1977

Other Personnel
    Home staff: 27

MB MISSION
Formerly: MBMS International
4867 Townsend Ave
Fresno, CA 93727 US
Phone: (559) 456-4600
Email: mbmission@mbmission.org
Website: mbmission.org
Associations: Missio Nexus

A denominational sending agency of Mennonite or Anabaptist tradition engaged in CPM, community development, discipleship, missionary & worker training, recruiting or mobilizing for mission, and STM trip coordination.

Purpose: . . . to multiply healthy disciples and missional leaders.

Year Founded in US: 1900

Countries/Regions: Austria, Burkina Faso, Burundi, Colombia, Democratic Republic of Congo, East Asia, Eastern Europe and Eurasia, France, Germany, India, Japan, Lithuania, Mexico, North Africa, Panama, Paraguay, Peru, Philippines, Portugal, South Africa, Southeast Asia, Sub-Saharan Africa, Thailand, Turkey, Ukraine, Western Europe

MB MISSION CANADA
Formerly: MBMS International
300-32040 Downes Rd
Abbotsford, BC V4X 1X5 CA
Phone: (604) 859-6267
Email: mbmission@mbmission.org
Website: mbmission.org
Associations: Missio Nexus

A denominational sending agency of Mennonite or Anabaptist tradition engaged in CPM, community development, discipleship, missionary & worker training, recruiting or mobilizing for mission, and STM trip coordination.

Purpose: . . . to multiply healthy disciples and missional leaders.

Year Founded in CA: 1900

Fully Supported CA Personnel Working Cross-Culturally
    More than 4 years: 54
    1–4 years: 2
Other Personnel
    Short-Term less than 1 year: 429
    Non-CA in own/other country: 210
    Home staff: 41

Countries/Regions: Austria, Burkina Faso, Burundi, Colombia, Democratic Republic of Congo, East Asia, Eastern Europe and Eurasia, France, Germany, India, Japan, Lithuania, Mexico, North Africa, Panama, Paraguay, Peru,

Philippines, Portugal, South Africa, Southeast Asia, Sub-Saharan Africa, Thailand, Turkey, Ukraine, Western Europe

MEDA – MENNONITE ECONOMIC DEVELOPMENT ASSOCIATES
155 Frobisher Drive, Suite I-106
Waterloo, ON N2V 2E1 CA
Phone: (519) 725-1633
Email: lwhitmore@meda.org
Website: meda.org
A denominational heritage service agency of Mennonite or Anabaptist tradition engaged in agricultural assistance, business as mission, community development, management consulting or training, technical assistance, and economic development. (FPC-PE)
Purpose: . . . to share abilities and resources by creating business solutions to alleviate poverty.
Income for International Min: $18,000,000
Other Personnel
 Non-CA in own/other country: 186
Countries/Regions: Afghanistan, Ethiopia, Nicaragua, Pakistan, Peru, Tajikistan, Tanzania, Zambia

MEDIA ASSOCIATES INTERNATIONAL
351 S. Main Place, Ste. 230
Carol Stream, IL 60188 US
Phone: (630) 260-9063
Email: mai@littworld.org
Website: littworld.org
An interdenominational specialized agency of Evangelical tradition engaged in information or journalism, leadership development, literature distribution, literature production, management consulting or training, and publisher & writer training. (FPC-PE)

Purpose: . . . to equip and encourage Christian publishers and writers in hard places of the world to create excellent content that enriches the church and influences society.
Year Founded in US: 1985
Other Personnel
 Short-Term less than 1 year: 30
 Home staff: 4

MEDICAL AMBASSADORS INTERNATIONAL (LIFEWIND INTERNATIONAL)
Formerly: Lifewind International
PO Box 1302, 5012 Salida Blvd
Salida, CA 95368 US
Phone: (888) 403-0600
Email: info@med-amb.org
Website: MedicalAmbassadors.org
Associations: Accord Network, CCRDA
A nondenominational service agency of Evangelical tradition engaged in children's ministry, church planting (establishing), community development, personal or small group evangelism, leadership development, and orality or storying.
Purpose: . . . to equip communities through Christ-centered health and development.
Year Founded in US: 1980
Other Personnel
 Home staff: 18

MEDICAL CENTERS OF WEST AFRICA (MCWA)
PO Box 66066
Baton Rouge, LA 70896 US
Phone: (225) 343-1814
Email: headquarters@mcwanet.org
Website: mcwestafrica.com
Associations: Missio Nexus
A nondenominational service agency of Evangelical tradition engaged in CPM, DMM, medical ministry, including dental or public health, and national worker support.

Purpose: . . . to plant churches among the Fulbe people and other unreached people groups. We believe God is glorified among the nations as we manifest the love of Christ by offering compassionate, competent medical care in Jesus' name.

Year Founded in US: 1989

Income for International Min:
$1,079,019

Fully Supported US Personnel Working Cross-Culturally
 More than 4 years: 2
 Non-residential: 3

Other Personnel
 Short-Term less than 1 year: 9
 Home staff: 4

Countries/Regions: Cameroon

MEDICAL MINISTRY INTERNATIONAL

PO Box 1339
Allen, TX 75013 US
Phone: (972) 727-5864
Email: mmitx@mmint.org
Website: mmint.org

An interdenominational support agency engaged in medical work. (DPE)

Year Founded in US: 1995

Income for International Min:
$3,700,426

Fully Supported US Personnel Working Cross-Culturally
 More than 4 years: 2
 1–4 years: 4

Other Personnel
 Non-US in own/other country: 35
 Home staff: 10

Countries/Regions: Armenia, Bolivia, Colombia, Dominican Republic, Ecuador, Ethiopia, Fiji, Ghana, Haiti, Honduras, Jamaica, Jordan, Mexico, Nicaragua, Peru, Philippines

MEDICAL MINISTRY INTERNATIONAL CANADA INC.

PO Box 56086
Stoney Creek, ON L8G 5C9 CA
Phone: (905) 524-3544
Email: mmican@mmicanada.ca
Website: mmint.org

An interdenominational service agency of Evangelical tradition engaged in discipleship, medical supplies, medical ministry, including dental or public health, and STM trip coordination. (FPC-PE)

Purpose: . . . to serve Jesus Christ by providing spiritual and physical health care in this world of need.

Year Founded in CA: 1968

Income for International Min:
$1,400,000

Other Personnel
 Short-Term less than 1 year: 3
 Tentmakers/BAM: 1
 Non-CA in own/other country: 14

Countries/Regions: Bolivia, Dominican Republic, Ecuador, Haiti, Jordan, Peru

MEDICAL TEAMS INTERNATIONAL

PO Box 10
Portland, OR 97207 US
Phone: (503) 624-1000
Email: info@medicalteams.org
Website: medicalteams.org

An interdenominational specialized agency of Ecumenical and Evangelical tradition engaged in short-term medical teams, development, HIV/AIDS, providing medical supplies, medical work and relief and/or rehabilitation. (DPE)

Purpose: . . . to demonstrate the love of Christ to those affected by disaster, conflict, and poverty around the world.

Year Founded in US: 1984

Income for International Min:
$136,847,845

Fully Supported US Personnel Working Cross-Culturally
  1–4 years: 6
Other Personnel
  Short-Term less than 1 year: 500
  Non-US in own/other country: 8
  Home staff: 77
Countries/Regions: Guatemala, Indonesia, Liberia, Mexico, Mozambique, Sri Lanka, Uganda

MEDSEND

Formerly: Project MedSend
999 Oronoque Lane
Stratford, CT 06614-1379 US
Phone: (203) 891-8223
Email: info@medsend.org
Website: medsend.org
Associations: Missio Nexus

A nondenominational service agency of Evangelical and Christian tradition engaged in fund raising or transmission, medical ministry, including dental or public health, missionary & worker training, services for mission organizations, and grants for Christian healthcare professionals.

Purpose: . . . to strategically fund highly qualified and committed healthcare professionals so that they can care for the physical and spiritual needs of people around the world who live with poverty and spiritual oppression.

Other Personnel
  Home staff: 8

MEN FOR MISSIONS INTERNATIONAL

PO Box A
Greenwood, IN 46142 US
Phone: (317) 881-6752
Email: whardig@omsinternational.org
Website: menformissions.org/

A nondenominational support agency of Wesleyan tradition engaged in short-term programs, action groups, church planting, and providing medical supplies. (DPE)

Purpose: . . . to do, go, and give of your God-given talents.

Other Personnel
  Short-Term less than 1 year: 473

MENNONITE ECONOMIC DEVELOPMENT ASSOCIATES (MEDA)

1891 Santa Barbara Dr, Ste. 201
Lancaster, PA 17601 US
Phone: (800) 665-7026
Email: meda@meda.org
Website: meda.org

A denominational heritage service agency of Mennonite or Anabaptist tradition engaged in agricultural assistance, business solutions to poverty, community development, management consulting or training, partnership development, and technical assistance.

Purpose: . . . so that all people may experience God's love and unleash their potential to earn a livelihood, provide for families and enrich their communities.

Year Founded in US: 1953

MENNONITE INTERNATIONAL HEALTH ASSOCIATION

15 Coleridge Park Dr
Winnipeg, MB R3K 0B2 CA
Phone: (204) 299-8651
Email: dad6@mymts.net
Website: mennonitemha.org

An interdenominational service agency of Mennonite or Anabaptist tradition engaged in medical supplies and medical ministry, including dental or public health. (FPC-PE)

Purpose: . . . to provide resources and services to Mennonite health care facilities in low resource countries.

Year Founded in CA: 2001
Income for International Min:
  $95,000
Other Personnel
  Home staff: 1

Countries/Regions: Democratic Republic of Congo, India, Paraguay, Zimbabwe

MENNONITE MISSION NETWORK
PO Box 370
Elkhart, IN 46515-0370 US
Phone: (574) 294-7523
Email: info@mennonitemission.net
Website: mennonitemission.net
A denominational sending agency of Mennonite tradition engaged in support of national churches, church planting, theological education, leadership development, partnership development and short-term programs. (DPE)

Purpose: . . . for every congregation and all parts of the Church to be fully engaged in God's mission, reaching from across the street, all through the market places to around the world.

Fully Supported US Personnel Working Cross-Culturally
    More than 4 years: 40
    1–4 years: 16
    Non-residential: 4
Other Personnel
    Short-Term less than 1 year: 78
    Tentmakers/BAM: 4
    Non-US in own/other country: 35
    Home staff: 95
Countries/Regions: Argentina, Australia, Benin, Bolivia, Botswana, Brazil, Burkina Faso, China (People's Republic of), Colombia, Democratic Republic of Congo, Ecuador, France, Germany, Ghana, India, Israel, Japan, South Korea, Lebanon, Lithuania, Macau (China), Middle East, Mongolia, Nepal, Nigeria, Senegal, South Africa, Spain, Sweden, Thailand, Ukraine, United Kingdom

MERCY PROJECTS
Formerly: Eastern European Outreach
PO Box 685
Murrieta, CA 92564 US
Phone: (951) 696-5244
Email: info@mercyprojects.org
Website: mercyprojects.org
A nondenominational support agency of Evangelical tradition engaged in camping programs, children's ministry, national worker support, STM trip coordination, youth ministry, and child sponsorship.

Purpose: . . . to strengthen the existing family of an at-risk child through sponsorship assistance, working to keep children in loving homes and out of orphanages and institutions.

Year Founded in US: 1980
Income for International Min:
    $795,000
Fully Supported US Personnel Working Cross-Culturally
    More than 4 years: 1
Other Personnel
    Short-Term less than 1 year: 20
    Non-US in own/other country: 35
    Home staff: 6
Countries/Regions: Kosovo, Russia, Ukraine

MERCY SHIPS
PO Box 2020
Lindale, TX 75771 US
Phone: (903) 939-7000
Email: arlene.harris@mercyships.org
Website: mercyships.org
An interdenominational service agency of Evangelical tradition engaged in medical work/surgical intervention, agricultural programs, development, leadership development, psychological counseling and training. (DPE)

Purpose: . . . Mercy Ships, a global charity, has operated a fleet of hospital ships in developing nations since 1978. Following the model of Jesus, Mercy Ships brings hope and healing to the poor, mobilizing people and resources worldwide.

Income for International Min:
  $31,260,623
Fully Supported US Personnel Working Cross-Culturally
  More than 4 years: 50
  1–4 years: 400
  Non-residential: 300
Other Personnel
  Short-Term less than 1 year: 1200
  Non-US in own/other country: 90
  Home staff: 40
Countries/Regions: Africa

MERCY SHIPS CANADA
5-3318 Oak St
Victoria, BC V8X 1R1 CA
Phone: (250) 381-2160
Email: msca@mercyships.ca
Website: mercyships.ca
A nondenominational service agency of Ecumenical tradition engaged in leadership development, medical supplies, and medical ministry, including dental or public health. (FPC-PE)
Purpose: . . . to follow the example of Jesus by bringing hope and healing to the world's forgotten poor.
Year Founded in CA: 1989
Income for International Min:
  $458,000
Other Personnel
  Home staff: 7

MESSIANIC JEWISH MOVEMENT INTERNATIONAL INC., THE (MJMI)
P.O. Box 41071
Phoenix, AZ 85080 US
Phone: (480) 786-6564
Email: office@mjmi.org
Website: mjmi.org
A Messianic Jewish support agency of Charismatic tradition engaged in evangelism, church planting, discipleship, leadership development and missionary training. (DPE)
Income for International Min:
  $120,000
Other Personnel
  Tentmakers/BAM: 1
  Non-US in own/other country: 7
  Home staff: 2
Countries/Regions: Israel

MEXICAN MEDICAL MINISTRIES
7850 Lester Ave
Lemon Grove, CA 91945 US
Phone: (619) 463-4777
Email: information@mexicanmedical.com
Website: mexicanmedical.com
A nondenominational service agency of Evangelical tradition engaged in medicine, incl. dental and public health, children's programs, evangelism, providing medical supplies, short-term programs and health education. (DPE)
Purpose: . . . to bring healing and hope to the people of Mexico . . . to bring God's healing touch to the total person. The redemptive work of God touches the physical, emotional, intellectual, and spiritual condition of humankind. In accomplishing this mission, Mexican Medical Ministries seeks to empower people to work together to accomplish the Great Commission.
Year Founded in US: 1965
Income for International Min:
  $1,615,000

Fully Supported US Personnel Working Cross-Culturally
    More than 4 years: 13
    Non-residential: 2
Other Personnel
    Short-Term less than 1 year: 2006
    Non-US in own/other country: 11
    Home staff: 7
Countries/Regions: Mexico

MEXICO MEDICAL MISSIONS

1302 Waugh Drive #685
Houston, TX 77019 US
Phone: (970) 315-0374
Email: vicky@mexicomedical.org
Website: mexicomedical.org
An interdenominational support agency of Evangelical tradition engaged in medical work, aviation services, development and support of national churches. (DPE)
Purpose: . . . to provide an excellent level of integrated health care to the indigenous people of the Sierra Madre of Mexico, thereby proclaiming the transforming love of Jesus Christ.
Year Founded in US: 1989
Income for International Min:
    $1,083,326
Other Personnel
    Short-Term less than 1 year: 45
    Non-US in own/other country: 45
    Home staff: 1
Countries/Regions: Mexico

MICAH CHALLENGE USA

1033 SW Yamhill St, Ste. 102
Portland, OR 97205 US
Phone: (888) 789-4660
Email: info@micahchallengeusa.org
Website: micahchallengeusa.org
Associations: Accord Network
An interdenominational service agency of Evangelical tradition engaged in advocacy.

Purpose: . . . to mobilize Christians to end extreme poverty through changing attitudes, behavior, and policies that perpetuate injustice and deny God's will for all creation to flourish.

MIDDLE EAST CHRISTIAN OUTREACH (MECO CANADA)

P.O. Box 610
Burlington, ON L7M 0Z1 CA
Phone: (905) 335-7329
Email: info@mecocanada.org
Website: mecocanada.org
An interdenominational service agency of Evangelical tradition engaged in association of missions, church, school or general Christian education, information or journalism, prayer-intercession, recruiting or mobilizing for mission, and relief & aid.
Purpose: . . . to partner in mission with Middle Eastern churches and Christians.
Year Founded in CA: 1978
Income for International Min:
    $48,797
Fully Supported CA Personnel Working Cross-Culturally
    More than 4 years: 4
    1–4 years: 2
    X-C workers in CA: 1
Other Personnel
    Short-Term less than 1 year: 2
    Home staff: 1
Countries/Regions: Egypt, Lebanon, Middle East

MIDDLE EAST MEDIA – USA

PO Box 4949
Wheaton, IL 60189-4949 US
Phone: (425) 488-9429
Email: director.usa@mem.org
Website: mem.org

A nondenominational support agency engaged in video/film production/ distribution, broadcasting, evangelism, support of national churches, missionary training, literature production and translation work. (DPE)

Income for International Min:
$286,870

Fully Supported US Personnel Working Cross-Culturally
More than 4 years: 2
Other Personnel
Non-US in own/other country: 89
Home staff: 4
Countries/Regions: Africa, Iran, Middle East, Turkey, Unspecified Country

MINISTRY TO EDUCATE AND EQUIP INTL. (MTEE)
PO Box 29792
Henrico, VA 23242 US
Phone: (804) 320-6456
Email: mtee@verizon.net
Website: mtee.org
Associations: Missio Nexus

A transdenominational sending agency of Pentecostal tradition engaged in church, school or general Christian education, TEE or other extension education, theological education, and leadership development.

Purpose: . . . to equip God's people for works of service so the body of Christ may be build up.

Year Founded in US: 1986
Fully Supported US Personnel Working Cross-Culturally
More than 4 years: 3
Other Personnel
Non-US in own/other country: 50
Home staff: 2
Countries/Regions: Bulgaria, Moldova, Ukraine

MISSION AVIATION FELLOWSHIP
P.O. Box 47
Nampa, ID 83687 US
Phone: (208) 498-0800
Email: MAF-us@maf.org
Website: maf.org
Associations: Accord Network, CCRA, Missio Nexus

A nondenominational specialized agency of Evangelical and Pentecostal tradition engaged in aviation, networking, partnership, or coordination, relief & aid, and technical assistance. (FPC-PE)

Purpose: . . . to share the love of Jesus Christ through aviation and technology, so that isolated people will be physically and spiritually transformed.

Year Founded in US: 1945
Fully Supported US Personnel Working Cross-Culturally
More than 4 years: 117
1–4 years: 44
Other Personnel
Non-US in own/other country: 28
Home staff: 170
Countries/Regions: Africa, Asia, Brazil, Democratic Republic of Congo, Costa Rica, Ecuador, Guatemala, Haiti, Indonesia, Lesotho, Mexico, Mozambique, Uganda

MISSION AVIATION FELLOWSHIP OF CANADA (MAFC)
264 Woodlawn Rd. W
Guelph, ON N1H 1B6 CA
Phone: (877) 351-9344
Email: info@mafc.org
Website: mafc.org
A nondenominational specialized agency of Evangelical tradition engaged in aviation services. (DPE)

Purpose: . . . to share God's love through aviation and technology.

Year Founded in CA: 1973

Income for International Min:
$3,732,455
Fully Supported CA Personnel Working Cross-Culturally
    More than 4 years: 32
    1–4 years: 9
    Non-residential: 44
Other Personnel
    Home staff: 20
Countries/Regions: Angola, Australia, Botswana, Central Asia, Chad, Haiti, Indonesia, Kenya, Laos, Lesotho, Madagascar, Mongolia, Papua New Guinea, Uganda, Zambia

MISSION CATALYST INTL. INC.
PO Box 73047
Houston, TX 77273-3047 US
Phone: (281) 507-8888
Email: jre@mci3.org
Website: mci3.org
Associations: Missio Nexus

An interdenominational support agency of Charismatic tradition engaged in church planting (establishing), discipleship, leadership development, missionary & worker training, national worker support, and research.

Purpose: . . . to help finish the Great Commission in this generation by training national workers in the 10/40 Window to plant effective, reproducing churches among the world's least-reached peoples.

Year Founded in US: 2002
Fully Supported US Personnel Working Cross-Culturally
    1–4 years: 6
Other Personnel
    Home staff: 4
Countries/Regions: Central Asia, East Asia, Middle East, North Africa, South Asia, Southeast Asia

MISSION DATA INTERNATIONAL
PO Box 16446
St Louis, MO 63125 US
Phone: (479) 530-5987
Email: davida@mdat.org
Website: mdat.org

An interdenominational specialized agency of Evangelical tradition engaged in networking, partnership, or coordination, services for mission organizations, and STM trip opportunities and coordination. (FPC-PE)

Purpose: . . . to bring people and missions together using internet technology.

Year Founded in US: 2000

MISSION EURASIA
Formerly: Peter Deyneka Russian Ministries
PO Box 496
Wheaton, IL 60187 US
Phone: (630) 462-1739
Email: info@missioneurasia.org
Website: missioneurasia.org
Associations: Missio Nexus

A nondenominational service agency of Evangelical tradition engaged in Bible distribution, children's ministry, church, school or general Christian education, mass evangelism, leadership development, and relief & aid.

Purpose: . . . to train, equip, and mobilize Christian leadership throughout Eurasia, who will engage in indigenous evangelism, church-planting, holistic ministries, and church growth by developing creative and strategic ministries and by facilitating partnerships between nationals and Western Christians.

Year Founded in US: 1991
Income for International Min:
$8,629,120

Fully Supported US Personnel Working Cross-Culturally
   More than 4 years: 2
Other Personnel
   Short-Term less than 1 year: 56
   Non-US in own/other country: 91
   Home staff: 10
Countries/Regions: Azerbaijan, Belarus, Georgia, Israel, Kazakhstan, Kyrgyzstan, Moldova, Mongolia, Russia, Tajikistan, Turkmenistan, Ukraine, Uzbekistan

MISSION GENERATION INC.
PO Box 720746
Norman, OK 73070 US
Phone: (405) 831-3299
Email: hmendoza@missiongeneration.org
Website: missiongeneration.org
A Christian development organization of Evangelical and Independent tradition engaged in children at risk, children's programs, evangelism and leadership development. (DPE)
Purpose: . . . to give children the tools they need to make quality life decisions.
Year Founded in US: 1999
Income for International Min:
   $39,029
Fully Supported US Personnel Working Cross-Culturally
   More than 4 years: 2
Other Personnel
   Short-Term less than 1 year: 4
   Non-US in own/other country: 60
Countries/Regions: Bolivia, Colombia, Costa Rica, Dominican Republic, Palestine, Paraguay, Peru

MISSION INDIA
PO Box 141312
Grand Rapids, MI 49514 US
Phone: (616) 453-8855
Email: info@missionindia.org
Website: missionindia@org

A nondenominational support agency of Evangelical tradition engaged in children's ministry, church planting (establishing), mass evangelism, literacy, and missionary & worker training. (FPC-PE)
Purpose: . . . to assist Indian churches and indigenous mission agencies in planting reproducing churches in a systematic, measureable way.
Year Founded in US: 1981
Other Personnel
   Non-US in own/other country: 2
   Home staff: 40
Countries/Regions: India

MISSION NANNYS
PO Box 61805
Santa Barbara, CA 93110 US
Phone: (805) 683-7476
Email: missionnannys@gmail.com
Website: missionnannys.org
Associations: Missio Nexus
A nondenominational service agency of Evangelical tradition engaged in childcare or orphanage, children's ministry, missionary & worker training, and domestic help & homeschooling for missionary families.
Purpose: . . . to seek to glorify God among missionary families through the domestic and teaching services of spiritually mature women who willingly volunteer to travel and meet particular needs.
Income for International Min:
   $30,000
Fully Supported US Personnel Working Cross-Culturally
   Non-residential: 84
Other Personnel
   Short-Term less than 1 year: 350
Countries/Regions: Albania, Belize, Bolivia, Brazil, Cameroon, Canada, Chad, China (People's Republic of), Costa Rica,

Croatia, Denmark, Fiji, French Guiana, Guatemala, India, Italy, Jordan, Kenya, Mexico, Romania, South Africa, Spain, Sweden, Taiwan (China), Uganda, Vanuatu

MISSION OF MERCY CANADA
4104-97 St.
Edmonton, AB T6E 5Y6 CA
Phone: (780) 485-9955
Email: info@missionofmercy.ca
Website: missionofmercy.ca
An interdenominational service agency of Pentecostal tradition engaged in constructing churches & children's homes, extension education, children's programs, partnership development and relief and/or rehabilitation. (DPE)
Purpose: . . . to help meet the physical and spiritual needs of the hurting children and adults of North and East India by feeding, housing, educating, and providing health and wellness care . . . to see the children of India who live in poverty, experience transformation and wholeness through God's love.
Year Founded in CA: 1978
Income for International Min:
   $2,134,000
Fully Supported CA Personnel Working Cross-Culturally
   1–4 years: 4
Other Personnel
   Home staff: 4
Countries/Regions: India

MISSION ON THE MOVE
P.O. Box 206
Springfield, GA 31329 US
Phone: (912) 754-3349
Email: ernie@missiononthemove.org
Website: missiononthemove.org
Associations: Missio Nexus
An interdenominational specialized agency of Evangelical tradition engaged in childcare or orphanage, children's ministry,

discipleship, church, school or general Christian education, personal or small group evangelism, and youth ministry.
Purpose: . . . to answer Christ's call to feed the hungry, welcome the stranger, visit the sick, clothe the naked & bring hope to a world in need.
Year Founded in US: 1986
Income for International Min:
   $260,000
Fully Supported US Personnel Working Cross-Culturally
   More than 4 years: 2
   1–4 years: 4
Other Personnel
   Short-Term less than 1 year: 206
   Non-US in own/other country: 17
   Home staff: 1
Countries/Regions: Honduras, Kenya, Mexico

MISSION ONE INC.
PO Box 5960
Scottsdale, AZ 85261 US
Phone: (480) 951-0900
Email: info@mission1.org
Website: mission1.org
Associations: Missio Nexus
A denominational heritage sending agency of Evangelical tradition engaged in business as mission, church planting (establishing), community development, and discipleship. (FPC-PE)
Purpose: . . . to train and mobilize the Church, focusing on cross-cultural partnerships to engage the unreached and serve the poor and oppressed.
Year Founded in US: 1991
Income for International Min:
   $386,882
Other Personnel
   Short-Term less than 1 year: 10
   Non-US in own/other country: 409
   Home staff: 5

Countries/Regions: Asia, Benin, Ethiopia, Ghana, India, Kenya, Middle East, Nepal, Nigeria, Pakistan, South Sudan, Sudan, Tanzania, Thailand, Togo, Uganda

MISSION POSSIBLE
PO Box 248
Mount Prospect, IL 60056 US
Phone: (800) 729-2425
Email: mpusa@mp.org
Website: mp.org

An interdenominational support agency of Evangelical tradition engaged in Bible teaching, childcare or orphanage, church, school or general Christian education, mass evangelism, leadership development, and relief & aid.

Purpose: . . . to equip the local Christians and churches in Eastern Europe for works of service in order for them to more effectively reach suffering and searching people. Bringing them the Gospel message, Biblical teaching and physical and social help.

Year Founded in US: 1974
Income for International Min:
  $850,000
Fully Supported US Personnel Working Cross-Culturally
  Non-residential: 5
Other Personnel
  Tentmakers/BAM: 95
  Home staff: 2
Countries/Regions: Eastern Europe and Eurasia

MISSION POSSIBLE CANADA
PO Box # 35034
London, ON N5W 5Z6 CA
Phone: (519) 285-2644
Email: missionpossible@odyssey.on.ca
Website: OurMissionIsPossible.org

A nondenominational support agency of Evangelical tradition engaged in

discipleship, church, school or general Christian education, leadership development, medical ministry, including dental or public health, STM trip coordination, and leadership development.

Purpose: . . . to equip the next generation of Christ-centred leaders.

Year Founded in CA: 1994
Income for International Min:
  $238,756

MISSION POSSIBLE USA
PO Box 1026, 306 W. Bigelow Ave.
Findlay, OH 45840 US
Phone: (419) 422-3364
Email: office@OurMissionIsPossible.org
Website: OurMissionIsPossible.org

A nondenominational support agency of Evangelical tradition engaged in church, school or general Christian education, theological education, student evangelism, leadership development, medical ministry, including dental or public health, and STM trip coordination.

Purpose: . . . to equip the next generation of Christ-centered leaders.

Year Founded in US: 1979
Income for International Min:
  $934,273
Other Personnel
  Short-Term less than 1 year: 210
  Non-US in own/other country: 248
  Home staff: 8
Countries/Regions: Dominican Republic, Haiti

MISSION SAFETY INTERNATIONAL
328 E. Elk Ave. #1
Elizabethton, TN 37643 US
Phone: (423) 542-8892
Email: info@msisafety.org
Website: msisafety.org

A nondenominational specialized agency of Evangelical tradition engaged in aviation and services for mission organizations. (FPC-PE)

Purpose: . . . to provide educational and consulting services to mission aviation training organizations and related agencies in the areas of operational safety and organizational security.
Year Founded in US: 1983
Income for International Min:
$100,000
Other Personnel
Home staff: 3

MISSION SERVICES ASSOCIATION INC.
2004 E. Magnolia Ave
Knoxville, TN 37917-8026 US
Phone: (865) 577-9740
Email: info@missionservices.org
Website: missionservices.org
A nondenominational support agency of Christian (Restoration Movement) tradition engaged in communication, print publishing, web development and missions information service. (DPE)
Income for International Min:
$400,000
Other Personnel
Home staff: 4
Countries/Regions: Global Ministry

MISSION TO CHILDREN
425 West Fifth Ave, Ste. 201
Escondido, CA 92025 US
Phone: (760) 839-1600
Email: skip@missiontochildren.org
Website: missiontochildren.org
A nondenominational specialized agency of Evangelical tradition engaged in association of missions, Bible teaching, childcare or orphanage, DMM, church, school or general Christian education.
Purpose: . . . to care for and cultivate Christ-like character in children—especially those at risk.
Year Founded in US: 1971

Income for International Min:
$293,507
Other Personnel
Short-Term less than 1 year: 1
Home staff: 7
Countries/Regions: Afghanistan, Bangladesh, Bolivia, Canada, Costa Rica, Egypt, El Salvador, Grenada, Guatemala, Guyana, India, Indonesia, Jordan, Kenya, Lebanon, Liberia, Lithuania, Nepal, Philippines, Romania, South Africa, South Sudan

MISSION TO THE WORLD (PCA) INC.
1600 N Brown Rd
Lawrenceville, GA 30043 US
Phone: (678) 823-0004
Email: info@mtw.org
Website: mtw.org
Associations: Missio Nexus
A denominational sending agency of Presbyterian tradition engaged in support of national churches, church planting, theological education, leadership development, medical work and youth programs. (DPE)
Purpose: . . . to fulfill the Great Commission by advancing Reformed and covenantal church-planting movements through word and deed in strategic areas worldwide.
Income for International Min:
$38,588,608
Fully Supported US Personnel Working Cross-Culturally
More than 4 years: 517
1–4 years: 145
Non-residential: 9
Other Personnel
Short-Term less than 1 year: 6520
Home staff: 99
Countries/Regions: Australia, Austria, Bangladesh, Belgium, Belize, Bolivia, Brazil, Bulgaria, Cambodia, Chile,

Colombia, Costa Rica, Czech Republic, Ecuador, Ethiopia, France, Germany, Guam, Haiti, Honduras, Hong Kong (China), India, Ireland (Republic of), Italy, Japan, Kenya, South Korea, Latvia, Mexico, Nicaragua, Panama, Papua New Guinea, Peru, Philippines, Portugal, Puerto Rico, Romania, Singapore, Slovakia, South Africa, Spain, Sweden, Taiwan (China), Thailand, Trinidad and Tobago, Uganda, Ukraine, United Kingdom, Unspecified Country, Zambia

MISSION TRAINING INTERNATIONAL
PO Box 1220
Palmer Lake, CO 80133 US
Phone: (719) 487-0111
Email: info@mti.org
Website: mti.org
Associations: Missio Nexus

An interdenominational service agency of Evangelical tradition engaged in linguistics, member care, missionary & worker training, and services for mission organizations. (FPC-PE)

Purpose: . . . to serve mission boards, churches and other sending organizations by developing and equipping their cross-cultural workers for the furtherance of Christ's Kingdom.

Year Founded in US: 1954

MISSION WITHOUT BORDERS CANADA
PO Box 2007
Abbotsford, BC V2T 3T8 CA
Phone: (604) 855-9126
Email: mwbcanada@mwbi.org
Website: mwbca.org

A nondenominational service agency of Evangelical tradition engaged in agricultural assistance, Bible teaching, camping programs, childcare or orphanage, correspondence courses, and relief & aid. (FPC-PE)

Purpose: . . . to serve children, families and elderly people suffering poverty and oppression, through practical and spiritual support, giving hope by meeting urgent needs and building self-sufficient communities.

MISSIONAIRE INTERNATIONAL
P.O. Box 446
Winchester, TN 37398 US
Phone: (931) 247-3660
Email: serve@missionaire.org
Website: missionaire.org

An interdenominational service agency of Evangelical tradition engaged in aviation services, missionary education, leadership development, services for other agencies, training and youth programs. (DPE)

Purpose: . . . to prepare people and aircraft for Christian mission service throughout the world.

Year Founded in US: 1988
Other Personnel
   Home staff: 11

MISSIONARY ATHLETES INTERNATIONAL
1020 Crews Rd N
Matthews, NC 28105 US
Phone: (704) 841-8644
Email: info@maisoccer.com
Website: maisoccer.com

A nondenominational specialized agency of Evangelical tradition engaged in discipleship, personal or small group evangelism, sports ministry, and youth ministry. (FPC-PE)

Purpose: . . . to communicate the message of Jesus Christ through the environment of soccer.

Year Founded in US: 1983
Income for International Min:
   $579,995

SENDING MESSENGERS TO ANOTHER CULTURE?

ARE THEY
READY?

for what makes or breaks
cross-cultural messengers
of the gospel

MISSION TRAINING
INTERNATIONAL

WE CAN HELP

develop and equip them for
effectiveness, endurance, and
personal vitality

TRUSTED TRAINING SINCE 1954

25,000 + Alumni from more than 350 evangelical sending agencies

Fully Supported US Personnel Working Cross-Culturally
   More than 4 years: 1
   1–4 years: 1
Other Personnel
   Short-Term less than 1 year: 153
   Home staff: 23
Countries/Regions: Asia, Global Ministry, Ukraine

MISSIONARY EXPEDITERS INC.
5620 Tchoupitoulas St.
New Orleans, LA 70115 US
Phone: (504) 891-6300
Email: matthewg@mxshipping.com
Website: missionaryexpediters.com
A specialized agency engaged in logistics and shipping GIK & personal effects. (DPE)
Other Personnel
   Home staff: 21

MISSIONARY FLIGHTS INTL.
3170 Airmans Dr.
Ft. Pierce, FL 34951 US
Phone: (772) 462-2395
Email: mfi@missionaryflights.org
A nondenominational support agency of Evangelical tradition engaged in aviation, Bible distribution, and relief & aid.
Purpose: . . . to spread the good news of Jesus Christ in partnership with Bible-centered missions by providing reliable transportation and logistical services.
Year Founded in US: 1964
Other Personnel
   Home staff: 22

MISSIONARY GOSPEL FELLOWSHIP
PO Box 1535
Turlock, CA 95380 US
Phone: (209) 634-8575
Email: bruce.leary@gmail.com
Website: mgfhq.org
A nondenominational sending agency of Evangelical tradition engaged in Bible

teaching, children's ministry, church development, personal or small group evangelism, international student ministry, and leadership development. (FPC-PE)
Purpose: . . . to evangelize and disciple according to the command of our Lord Jesus Christ, people groups in or near the USA who are unreached with the gospel.
Year Founded in US: 1941
Fully Supported US Personnel Working Cross-Culturally
   More than 4 years: 11
   1–4 years: 6
Other Personnel
   Non-US in own/other country: 17
Countries/Regions: Mexico

MISSIONARY RETREAT FELLOWSHIP
63 Missionary Retreat Rd
Jefferson Twp, PA 18436 US
Phone: (570) 689-2984
Email: mrf@missionaryretreat.org
Website: missionaryretreat.org
A nondenominational support agency of Evangelical tradition engaged in housing for missionaries.
Purpose: . . . by love serve one another. Gal. 5:13
Year Founded in US: 1965

MISSIONARY TECH TEAM
25 FRJ Drive
Longview, TX 75602 US
Phone: (903) 757-4530
Email: rharris@techteam.org
Website: techteam.org
Associations: ANAM
A nondenominational service agency of Fundamentalist tradition engaged in arts in mission, church construction or financing, community development, leadership development, services for mission organizations, and technical assistance. (FPC-PE)

Purpose: . . . to accelerate the vision of churches and missions worldwide through technical services.

Year Founded in US: 1968

Fully Supported US Personnel Working Cross-Culturally
    X-C workers in US: 4

Other Personnel
    Home staff: 16

MISSIONARY VENTURES CANADA

210B - 727 Woolwich St
Guelph, ON N1H 3Z2 CA
Phone: (519) 824-9380
Email: mvcanada@mvcanada.org
Website: missionaryventures.ca

An interdenominational service agency of Evangelical tradition engaged in recruiting or mobilizing for mission and STM trip coordination.

Purpose: . . . to identify, equip and empower indigenous Christian leadership to reach the world for Jesus Christ, fulfilling the call of the Great Commission and the Great Commandment.

Year Founded in CA: 1924

Fully Supported CA Personnel Working Cross-Culturally
    1–4 years: 2
    Non-residential: 1

Other Personnel
    Non-CA in own/other country: 24

Countries/Regions: Bolivia, Cuba, Global Ministry, Guatemala, Malawi, Mexico, Nicaragua, Peru, South Sudan, Swaziland, Ukraine, Zambia

MISSIONARY VENTURES INTL.

PO Box 593550
Orlando, FL 32859-3550 US
Phone: (407) 859-7934
Email: info@mvi.org

An interdenominational specialized agency of Evangelical tradition engaged

in children's ministry, national church support, and STM trip coordination.

Purpose: . . . to encourage and support indigenous missions through personal involvement, financial sponsorship and ministry development.

Year Founded in US: 1984

Fully Supported US Personnel Working Cross-Culturally
    More than 4 years: 68

Other Personnel
    Home staff: 14

Countries/Regions: Belize, Bolivia, Costa Rica, Dominican Republic, Ecuador, Gabon, Guatemala, Haiti, Honduras, Indonesia, Ireland (Republic of), Israel, Malaysia, Marshall Islands, Mexico, Nicaragua, Nigeria, Paraguay, Peru, Philippines, Russia, Singapore, South Africa, Thailand, Uganda, United Kingdom, Zambia

MISSIONNEXT

Formerly: Finishers Project
2518 Burnsed Blvd, PMB 327
The Villages, FL 32163 - 2704 US
Phone: (480) 584-5448
Email: floffice@missionnext.org
Website: missionnext.org
Associations: Missio Nexus

A nondenominational service agency of Evangelical tradition engaged in recruiting or mobilizing for mission.

Purpose: . . . to help Christian organizations connect with and mobilize qualified personnel.

Year Founded in US: 1998

MISSIONPREP INC.
Formerly: Missionary Internship Canada Inc.
PO Box 92204, 2900 Warden Ave
Toronto, ON M1W 3Y9 CA
Phone: (416) 840-5488
Email: admin@missionprep.ca
Website: missionprep.ca
Associations: Missio Nexus

An interdenominational specialized agency of Evangelical tradition engaged in missionary & worker training.

Purpose: . . . to facilitate high quality accessible training for effective cross-cultural ministry by pooling resources, providing courses, and fostering collaboration among agencies, churches and schools.

Year Founded in CA: 1984
Other Personnel
  Home staff: 4

MISSIONS DOOR
2530 Washington St.
Denver, CO 80205-3142 US
Phone: (303) 308-1818
Email: info@missionsdoor.org
Website: missionsdoor.org
Associations: Missio Nexus

An associational sending agency of Baptist and Evangelical tradition engaged in church planting, discipleship, TEE, leadership development and support of national churches. (DPE)(FPC16)

Purpose: . . . to assist local churches of like faith and practice in their efforts to evangelize, disciple and plant churches among the unreached, including economic development and humanitarian ministries, in obedience to the Gospel of Jesus Christ.

Year Founded in US: 1951
Income for International Min:
  $1,656,289

Fully Supported US Personnel Working Cross-Culturally
  X-C workers in US: 14
Other Personnel
  Short-Term less than 1 year: 150
  Non-US in own/other country: 22
  Home staff: 14
Countries/Regions: Bahamas, Belize, Bolivia, Brazil, Cambodia, Canada, Costa Rica, Dominican Republic, Ecuador, El Salvador, Ethiopia, Guatemala, Haiti, Honduras, Kenya, Liberia, Mexico, Nicaragua, Panama, Peru, Sierra Leone, Ukraine

MISSIONS RESOURCE NETWORK
1903 Central Dr, Ste. 410
Bedford, TX 76021 US
Phone: (817) 267-2727
Email: missions@MRNet.org
Website: MRNet.org
Associations: Missio Nexus

A nondenominational network of Christian (Restoration Movement) and Congregational tradition engaged in DMM, church, school or general Christian education, member care, missionary & worker training, networking, partnership, or coordination, and recruiting or mobilizing for mission.

Purpose: . . . to help disciples make disciples worldwide.

Year Founded in US: 1917
Fully Supported US Personnel Working Cross-Culturally
  More than 4 years: 39
Countries/Regions: Australia, Austria, Czech Republic, New Zealand, Rwanda, Ukraine

MISSIONS TO MILITARY INC.
2221 Centerville Turnpike
Virginia Beach, VA 23464 US
Phone: (757) 479-2288
Email: hqs@missionstomilitary.org
Associations: FOM
A nondenominational sending agency of
Baptist tradition engaged in discipleship,
mass evangelism, and literature
distribution.
Purpose: . . . to win and train the military
for Jesus Christ.
Year Founded in US: 1958
*Fully Supported US Personnel Working
Cross-Culturally*
    More than 4 years: 12
Other Personnel
    Home staff: 5
Countries/Regions: France, Ukraine

MMS AVIATION (MISSIONARY MAINTENANCE SERVICES)
PO Box 1118
Coshocton, OH 43812 US
Phone: (740) 622-6848
Email: admin@mmsaviation.org
Website: mmsaviation.org
A nondenominational support agency of
Evangelical tradition engaged in aviation
and missionary & worker training. (FPC-PE)
Purpose: . . . to prepare people and
planes for worldwide mission service.
Year Founded in US: 1975
Other Personnel
    Home staff: 23

MOBILE MEMBER CARE TEAM
4306 Heathbrook Ct.
Midlothian, VA 23112 US
Phone: (804) 748-8045
Email: mmct@mmct.org
Website: mmct.org
An interdenominational service agency
of Evangelical tradition engaged in

counseling, management consulting or
training, member care, missionary &
worker training, networking, partnership,
or coordination, and crisis response
training and care for missionaries.
Purpose: . . . to envision resilient
communities of cross cultural workers
caring for each other, equipped to thrive in
the midst of life's challenges and traumas.
Year Founded in US: 2000
Income for International Min:
    $201,837
*Fully Supported US Personnel Working
Cross-Culturally*
    More than 4 years: 3
    1–4 years: 5
Other Personnel
    Short-Term less than 1 year: 28
    Non-US in own/other country: 1
    Home staff: 3
Countries/Regions: Global Ministry,
Sub-Saharan Africa

MORAVIAN CHURCH IN NORTH AMERICA – BOARD OF WORLD MISSION
PO Box 1245
Bethlehem, PA 18016-1245 US
Phone: (610) 868-1732
Email: bwm@mcsp.org
Website: moravianmission.org
A denominational sending agency of
Ecumenical and Moravian tradition engaged
in short-term programs, Christian education,
leadership development, missionary training
and youth programs. (DPE)
Year Founded in US: 1949
Income for International Min:
    $1,200,000
*Fully Supported US Personnel Working
Cross-Culturally*
    Non-residential: 6

Other Personnel
Short-Term less than 1 year: 12
Non-US in own/other country: 4
Home staff: 5
Countries/Regions: Honduras, Kenya, Tanzania

MORELLI MINISTRIES INTL. INC.
PO Box 700026
Tulsa, OK 74170 US
Phone: (918) 645-4024
Email: michael@morelliministries.org
Website: morelliministries.org
A nondenominational support agency of Pentecostal tradition engaged in church planting (establishing), discipleship, mass evangelism, and national worker support.
Purpose: . . . to win millions to Christ one village at a time.
Year Founded in US: 1995
Fully Supported US Personnel Working Cross-Culturally
More than 4 years: 3
Other Personnel
Home staff: 1
Countries/Regions: Central America, East Asia, South America

MOST MINISTRIES
655 Phoenix Drive
Ann Arbor, MI 48108 US
Phone: (734) 994-7909
Email: dsuchyta@mostministries.org
Website: mostministries.org
Associations: ALMA
A denominational sending agency of Lutheran tradition engaged in STM trip coordination.
Purpose: . . . to impact the world for Jesus Christ through short-term mission by empowering the found in reaching the lost.
Year Founded in US: 1989

Fully Supported US Personnel Working Cross-Culturally
Non-residential: 5202
Other Personnel
Short-Term less than 1 year: 350
Home staff: 9
Countries/Regions: Argentina, Belize, Bolivia, Brazil, Cambodia, Chile, China (People's Republic of), Costa Rica, Côte d'Ivoire, Czech Republic, Dominican Republic, Ecuador, El Salvador, Ghana, Guatemala, Guinea, Haiti, Honduras, India, Indonesia, Jamaica, Kenya, Kyrgyzstan, Latvia, Liberia, Macau (China), Madagascar, Mexico, Mongolia, Nicaragua, Palestine, Panama, Paraguay, Peru, Philippines, Poland, Puerto Rico, Russia, Sierra Leone, Slovakia, South Africa, Sri Lanka, Tanzania, Uruguay, Venezuela

MPOWER APPROACH
106 North Watterson Trail
Louisville, KY 40243 US
Phone: (502) 544-9031
Email: lbordas@mpowerapproach.org
Website: mpowerapproach.org
A nondenominational service agency of Evangelical tradition engaged in community development, medical ministry, including dental or public health, and tentmaking & related. (FPC-PE)
Purpose: . . . to empower indigenous believers with the tools and training to take the Gospel to the ends of the Earth.
Fully Supported US Personnel Working Cross-Culturally
X-C workers in US: 37
Other Personnel
Short-Term less than 1 year: 37
Home staff: 3

MULTIPLICATION NETWORK MINISTRIES

22515 Torrence Ave
Sauk Village, IL 60411 US
Phone: (708) 414-1050
Email: multiplicationnetwork@gmail.com
Website: multiplicationnetwork.org
Associations: Missio Nexus

A nondenominational service agency of Evangelical tradition engaged in Bible distribution, children's ministry, church planting (establishing), CPM, leadership development, and translation.

Purpose: . . . to equip church leaders with the tools and resources to strengthen and multiply healthy churches.

Year Founded in US: 2007
Income for International Min:
$2,909,726
Other Personnel
Short-Term less than 1 year: 12
Home staff: 11

MUSLIM HOPE

PO Box 144441
Austin, TX 78714 US
Phone: (512) 218-8022
Email: webmaster@muslimhope.com
Website: muslimhope.com

An interdenominational specialized agency of Baptist tradition engaged in apologetics, theological education, evangelism, services for other agencies and missionary training. (DPE)

Other Personnel
Tentmakers/BAM: 1

MUSTARD SEED INTERNATIONAL

P.O. Box 91569
Austin, TX 78709 US
Phone: (843) 388-9314
Email: info@mustardseed.org
Website: mustardseed.org

An interdenominational sending agency of Evangelical tradition engaged in Christian education, agricultural programs, childcare/orphanage programs, church planting, TEE and medical work. (DPE)

Purpose: . . . to present Christ to all we meet, to heal disease and all manner of suffering and to love sincerely and deeply those people whose lives we are privileged to touch.

Year Founded in US: 1953
Income for International Min:
$837,916
Fully Supported US Personnel Working Cross-Culturally
More than 4 years: 7
Other Personnel
Short-Term less than 1 year: 100
Countries/Regions: India, Indonesia, Papua New Guinea, Sudan, Taiwan (China)

MUSTARD SEED MISSION CANADA INC.

#226 - 1885 Clements Rd.
Pickering, ON L1W 3V4 CA
Phone: (905) 427-5189
Email: mustardseed@canada.com
Website: mustardseedcanada.org

A nondenominational service agency engaged in Christian education, missionary education, evangelism, leadership development and support of national workers. (DPE)

Purpose: . . . to bear witness to the Lord Jesus Christ through education, skills training, medical assistance, basic improvement in living conditions, evangelistic outreach, and discipleship training among the indigenous people whom it serves.

Income for International Min:
$207,665

MUTUAL FAITH MINISTRIES INTL.

PO Box 951060
Mission Hills, CA 91395-1060 US
Phone: (818) 837-3400
Email: mail@mutualfaith.org
Website: mutualfaith.org

A nondenominational support agency of Independent tradition engaged in mass evangelism and STM trip coordination.

Purpose: . . . to help people join their faith to increase dynamic life-giving assistance in the nations of the world.

Year Founded in US: 1984

Fully Supported US Personnel Working Cross-Culturally
    1–4 years: 9
Other Personnel
    Home staff: 7
Countries/Regions: Costa Rica, Côte d'Ivoire, Ghana, Guatemala, Lebanon, Liberia, Nigeria, Philippines

NARRAMORE CHRISTIAN FOUNDATION

250 W. Colorado Blvd. Ste. 200
Arcadia, CA 91007 US
Phone: (626) 821-8400
Email: cscoon@ncfliving.org
Website: ncfliving.org

A nondenominational specialized agency of Evangelical tradition providing missionary kids reentry training and literature and also helps develop and support overseas missionary counseling and training programs. NCF's ministries include a Christian mental health website, literature on psychological problems and issues, reentry programs for missionary children and overseas seminars for missionaries. (DPE)

Purpose: . . . to serve individuals and families through biblically-based psychological counseling, consulting, publications, education, research and training . . . targeting toward missionaries and pastors and their families, laypersons and counseling/psychology students.

Income for International Min:
    $48,000
Other Personnel
    Home staff: 8

NATIONAL ASSOCIATION OF CONGREGATIONAL CHRISTIAN CHURCHES

PO Box 288, 8473 S. Howell Ave.
Oak Creek, WI 53154 US
Phone: (414) 856-1618
Email: lmiller@naccc.org
Website: naccc.org

A denominational sending agency of Congregational tradition engaged in Bible teaching, childcare or orphanage, church planting (establishing), discipleship, church, school or general Christian education, and medical ministry, including dental or public health.

Purpose: . . . to bring together Congregational Christian Churches for mutual care and outreach to our world in the name of Jesus Christ.

Year Founded in US: 1959
Income for International Min:
    $200,000
Fully Supported US Personnel Working Cross-Culturally
    More than 4 years: 1
    X-C workers in US: 10
Other Personnel
    Short-Term less than 1 year: 20
    Tentmakers/BAM: 37
    Non-US in own/other country: 197
    Home staff: 1

Countries/Regions: Argentina, Cameroon, Democratic Republic of Congo, Ghana, Haiti, Honduras, India, Kenya, Mexico, Myanmar (Burma), Nigeria, Philippines

NATIONAL BAPTIST CONVENTION OF AMERICA – FOREIGN MISSION BOARD

P. O. Box 4840
Dallas, TX 75208 US
Phone: (214) 942-3311
Email: info@nbcainc.com
Website: nbca-inc.com

A denominational support agency of Baptist tradition engaged in evangelism, Christian education, providing medical supplies and medical work. (DPE)

Purpose: . . . to operate as 'partner in ministry' with indigenous Christians and church bodies.

Income for International Min:
    $325,200
Other Personnel
    Non-US in own/other country: 118
    Home staff: 4
Countries/Regions: Ghana, Haiti, Jamaica, Panama, Virgin Islands of the USA

NATIONAL BAPTIST CONVENTION USA INC. – FOREIGN MISSION BOARD

701 South 19th St
Philadelphia, PA 19146 US
Phone: (215) 735-7868
Email: fmbnbc@comcast.net
Website: nationalbaptist.com

A denominational sending agency of Baptist tradition engaged in evangelism, children at risk, church planting, Christian education, furloughed missionary support and HIV/AIDS. (DPE)

Purpose: . . . to accomplish the Great Commission by training ministers and mission workers and providing health services and occupational training and services at each mission station with the goal of self-sufficiency.

Fully Supported US Personnel Working Cross-Culturally
    More than 4 years: 2
    1–4 years: 2
Other Personnel
    Non-US in own/other country: 130
    Home staff: 6
Countries/Regions: Barbados, Guinea, Lesotho, Malawi, Nicaragua, Sierra Leone, South Africa, Swaziland

NATIONAL RELIGIOUS BROADCASTERS

1 Massachusetts Avenue NW, Suite 333
Washington, DC 20001 US
Phone: (202) 543-0073
Email: JSmith@nrb.org
Website: nrb.org

A nondenominational service agency of Evangelical tradition engaged in radio or TV broadcasting, church, school or general Christian education, networking, partnership, or coordination, and services for mission organizations. (FPC-PE)

Purpose: . . . to advance biblical truth, promote media excellence, and defend free speech. In addition to promoting standards of excellence, integrity, and accountability, NRB provides networking, educational, ministry, and fellowship opportunities for its members.

Year Founded in US: 1944
Other Personnel
    Home staff: 23

NAVIGATORS OF CANADA, THE
PO Box 27070
London, ON N5X 3X5 CA
Phone: (519) 660-8300
Email: navscanada@navigators.ca
Website: navigators.ca

An interdenominational sending agency of Evangelical tradition engaged in discipleship, Bible memorization, evangelism and leadership development. (DPE)

Purpose: . . . to advance the Gospel of Jesus and His Kingdom into the nations through spiritual generations of labourers living and discipling among the lost.

Income for International Min:
$900,000

Fully Supported CA Personnel Working Cross-Culturally
More than 4 years: 17
1–4 years: 2
Other Personnel
Short-Term less than 1 year: 40
Tentmakers/BAM: 3
Home staff: 12
Countries/Regions: Africa, Asia, Chile, Hungary, Indonesia, Slovakia, Thailand, Turkey

NAZARENE COMPASSION MINISTRIES CANADA
20 Regan Rd., Unit 9
Brampton, ON N4L 1W5 CA
Phone: (888) 808-7490
Email: dmccrae@nazarene.ca
Website: ncmc.ca

A denominational support agency of Holiness tradition engaged in children at risk, HIV/AIDS, leadership development, providing medical supplies, medical work and relief and/or rehabilitation. (DPE)

Income for International Min:
$275,000

NEHEMIAH TEAMS INTERNATIONAL
PO Box 86
Buffalo Gap, SD 57722 US
Phone: (605) 833-2244
Email: chamberlandm@hotmail.com
Website: nehemiahteams.com/

A nondenominational specialized agency of Fundamental and Independent tradition engaged in short-term programs, church construction, discipleship, leadership development and services for other agencies. (DPE)

Purpose: . . . to assist in the construction of mission-related building projects.

Year Founded in US: 2006
Income for International Min:
$32,000

Other Personnel
Short-Term less than 1 year: 22

NETWORK OF INTERNATIONAL CHRISTIAN SCHOOLS
3790 Goodman Rd. E.
Southaven, MS 38672 US
Phone: (662) 892-4300
Email: joehale@nics.org
Website: nics.org

A nondenominational service agency of Evangelical and Fundamentalist tradition engaged in discipleship, church, school or general Christian education, student evangelism, international student ministry, and youth ministry.

Purpose: . . . to establish a worldwide network of international Christian schools staffed by qualified Christian educators, instilling in each student a Biblical worldview in an environment of academic excellence and respect for people of all cultures and religion

Year Founded in US: 1991
Income for International Min:
$52,000,000

Fully Supported US Personnel Working Cross-Culturally
More than 4 years: 182
1–4 years: 278
Other Personnel
Short-Term less than 1 year: 10
Non-US in own/other country: 273
Home staff: 25
Countries/Regions: Bolivia, Brazil, China (People's Republic of), Ghana, Indonesia, Japan, Kenya, South Korea, Malaysia, Mexico, Peru, Singapore, Turkey, Venezuela

NEW HOPE INTERNATIONAL

PO Box 25490
Colorado Springs, CO 80936 US
Phone: (719) 577-4450
Email: info@newhopeinternational.org
Website: newhopeinternational.org
A nondenominational support agency of Evangelical and Presbyterian tradition engaged in youth programs, childcare/orphanage programs, correspondence courses, leadership development, support of national workers and translation work. (DPE)
Purpose: . . . to establish a strong national NHI ministry in six former Communist countries: Czech Republic, Slovakia, Ukraine, Moldova, Hungary, and Romania.
Year Founded in US: 1974
Fully Supported US Personnel Working Cross-Culturally
More than 4 years: 3
1–4 years: 3
Other Personnel
Short-Term less than 1 year: 150
Tentmakers/BAM: 18
Non-US in own/other country: 34
Home staff: 8
Countries/Regions: Czech Republic, Eastern Europe, Hungary, Moldova, Romania, Slovakia, Ukraine

NEW HOPE UGANDA MINISTRIES

PO Box 154
Belle Fourche, SD 57717 US
Phone: (800) 611-6486
Email: office@nhum.org
Website: newhopeuganda.org
A nondenominational sending agency of Evangelical tradition engaged in Bible teaching, camping programs, childcare or orphanage, disabled ministry, theological education, and youth ministry.
Purpose: . . . to bring the Fatherhood of God to the fatherless.
Year Founded in US: 1992
Income for International Min:
$1,998,103
Fully Supported US Personnel Working Cross-Culturally
More than 4 years: 29
1–4 years: 4
Non-residential: 7
Other Personnel
Short-Term less than 1 year: 123
Non-US in own/other country: 154
Home staff: 5
Countries/Regions: Uganda

NEW LIFE ADVANCE INTERNATIONAL

PO Box 35857
Houston, TX 77235 US
Phone: (832) 242-7750
Email: kwheeler@nlai.com
Website: nlai.org
A nondenominational sending agency of Charismatic and Evangelical tradition engaged in childcare or orphanage, community development, church, school or general Christian education, theological education, addressing human trafficking, and leadership development.
Purpose: . . . to help children at risk be rescued, to equip leaders and see communities transformed to the Glory of God!

Year Founded in US: 1954
Income for International Min:
$1,325,037
Fully Supported US Personnel Working Cross-Culturally
More than 4 years: 14
X-C workers in US: 2
Other Personnel
Short-Term less than 1 year: 153
Home staff: 3
Countries/Regions: Guatemala, Kyrgyzstan

NEW LIFE INTERNATIONAL
6764 S. Bloomington Trail
Underwood, IN 47177 US
Phone: (812) 752-7474
Email: pam.sandlin@waterfortheworld.com
Website: waterfortheworld.com
A nondenominational specialized agency of Evangelical tradition engaged in community development and relief & aid.
Purpose: . . . to focus on local and international evangelism, experiencing Christ through discipleship and ministry through Christian service.
Year Founded in US: 1998
Income for International Min:
$330,786
Other Personnel
Short-Term less than 1 year: 7
Home staff: 4
Countries/Regions: Global Ministry

NEW MISSION SYSTEMS INTERNATIONAL
2701 Cleveland Ave, Ste. 200
Fort Myers, FL 33901 US
Phone: (239) 337-4336
Email: info@nmsi.org
Website: nmsi.org
Associations: Missio Nexus
A nondenominational sending agency of Christian (Restoration Movement) and

Evangelical tradition engaged in business as mission, church development, church planting (establishing), community development, discipleship, and youth ministry.
Purpose: . . . to proclaim Christ and make disciples globally, with a vision of joining with God to restore His dominion on earth, as evidenced by people of all nations worshiping God, experiencing continuous life transformation, fulfilling their God-given purpose
Year Founded in US: 1989
Income for International Min:
$4,668,650
Fully Supported US Personnel Working Cross-Culturally
More than 4 years: 115
1–4 years: 5
X-C workers in US: 4
Non-residential: 6
Other Personnel
Short-Term less than 1 year: 46
Tentmakers/BAM: 2
Non-US in own/other country: 36
Home staff: 2
Countries/Regions: Cambodia, Chile, Egypt, Ethiopia, Germany, Global Ministry, Haiti, Indonesia, Italy, Kenya, Macedonia, Malawi, Mexico, Middle East, Morocco, Myanmar (Burma), New Zealand, Russia, Rwanda, Thailand, Turkey, Uganda, Ukraine, Uzbekistan, Zambia, Zimbabwe

NEW TRIBES MISSION (US)
See Ethnos360

NEW TRIBES MISSION OF CANADA
313363 Hwy. 6 S.
Durham, ON N0G 1R0 CA
Phone: (519) 369-2622
Email: ntmc@ntmc.ca
Website: canada.ntm.org/
A nondenominational sending agency of Evangelical tradition engaged in church

planting (encompasses literacy, linguistics, teaching, etc.), discipleship, linguistics, missionary training, Bible translation and translation work. (DPE)

Purpose: . . . to assist the ministry of the local church through the mobilizing, equipping, and coordinating of believers to evangelize unreached people groups, translate Scripture, and see indigenous New Testament churches established.

Year Founded in CA: 1969
Income for International Min:
  $5,100,000
Fully Supported CA Personnel Working Cross-Culturally
  More than 4 years: 126
  1–4 years: 5
Other Personnel
  Short-Term less than 1 year: 4
  Home staff: 60
Countries/Regions: Africa, Asia, Latin America, Oceania, United Kingdom

NEW WINESKINS MISSIONARY NETWORK
P.O. Box 278
Ambridge, PA 15003-0278 US
Phone: (724) 266-2810
Email: jenny@newwineskins.org
Website: newwineskins.org
A denominational service agency of Anglican or Episcopal tradition engaged in association of missions, missionary & worker training, networking, partnership, or coordination, prayer-intercession, services for mission organizations, and equipping the church to go.

Purpose: . . . to help Anglicans to be more knowledgeable, active, and effective in fulfilling our Lord's Great Commission to make disciples of all nations.

Year Founded in US: 1974
Income for International Min:
  $24,000

Fully Supported US Personnel Working Cross-Culturally
  More than 4 years: 1
  X-C workers in US: 1
Other Personnel
  Short-Term less than 1 year: 1
  Home staff: 2
Countries/Regions: Global Ministry

NEXT WORLDWIDE
PO Box 271130
Flower Mound, TX 75028 US
Phone: (972) 255-4100
Email: wes.searcy@nextworldwide.org
Website: nextworldwide.org
Associations: Missio Nexus
A nondenominational service agency of Evangelical tradition engaged in church planting (establishing), discipleship, personal or small group evangelism, leadership development, recruiting or mobilizing for mission, and STM trip coordination.

Purpose: . . . to partner with church planters to establish new churches by using short-term trips that serve as a strategic catalyst for the local church and trip participants.

Year Founded in US: 2005
Income for International Min:
  $720,000
Other Personnel
  Short-Term less than 1 year: 405
  Home staff: 11

NIÑOS DE MEXICO
PO Box 309, 410 S Oak St
Union, MO 63084 US
Phone: (636) 583-2000
Email: ndm@ninosdemexico.org
Website: ninosdemexico.org
A nondenominational sending agency of Christian (Restoration Movement) tradition engaged in childcare or orphanage, church planting (establishing), church, school or

general Christian education, personal or small group evangelism, medical ministry, including dental or public health, and STM trip coordination.

Purpose: . . . to share the Gospel message of salvation through Jesus Christ with as many people as possible by raising at-risk children in Mexico to love God and grow to be mature educated Spirit-filled Christians with the ability and passion to evangelize their culture.

Year Founded in US: 1967
Income for International Min:
  $1,173,757

Other Personnel
  Short-Term less than 1 year: 184
  Home staff: 4
Countries/Regions: Mexico

NORTH AMERICAN BAPTIST CONFERENCE – WORLDWIDE OUTREACH

1219 Pleasant Grove Blvd
Roseville, CA 95678 US
Phone: (916) 797-6222
Email: nabmissions@nabconf.org
Website: nabconference.org

A denominational sending agency of Baptist tradition engaged in church planting, childcare/orphanage programs, children at risk, development, discipleship and theological education. (DPE)

Purpose: . . . to glorify God by making disciples of Jesus Christ at home and internationally.

Income for International Min:
  $2,626,575

Fully Supported US Personnel Working Cross-Culturally
  More than 4 years: 28
  1–4 years: 2
  Non-residential: 1

Other Personnel
  Short-Term less than 1 year: 227
  Non-US in own/other country: 15
  Home staff: 4
Countries/Regions: Brazil, Cameroon, Japan, Mexico, Nigeria

NORTHERN CANADA EVANGELICAL MISSION INC.

PO Box 3030
Prince Albert, SK S6V 7V4 CA
Phone: (306) 764-3388
Email: ncem@ncem.ca
Website: ncem.ca
Associations: Missio Nexus

An interdenominational sending agency of Evangelical tradition engaged in Bible teaching, radio or TV broadcasting, camping programs, church development, church planting (establishing), and tentmaking & related.

Purpose: . . . to fulfill the Great Commission of Jesus Christ among and in partnership with the Aboriginal Peoples of Canada and related people groups.

Year Founded in CA: 1946

Fully Supported CA Personnel Working Cross-Culturally
  More than 4 years: 20
  X-C workers in CA: 77

Other Personnel
  Non-CA in own/other country: 61
Countries/Regions: Canada, United States of America

NORTHWEST HAITI CHRISTIAN MISSION

7301 N Georgetown Rd, Ste. 190
Indianapolis, IN 46268 US
Phone: (317) 228-8770
Email: info@nwhcm.org
Website: nwhcm.org

A nondenominational service agency of Christian (Restoration Movement) tradition engaged in childcare or orphanage, church development, community development, disabled ministry, church, school or general Christian education, and medical ministry, including dental or public health.

Purpose: . . . to partner with local churches in Northwest Haiti to bring the people out of spiritual, physical and social poverty to demonstrate love for all

Year Founded in US: 1979

Fully Supported US Personnel Working Cross-Culturally
  More than 4 years: 7
  1–4 years: 4
  Non-residential: 1
Other Personnel
  Short-Term less than 1 year: 510
  Home staff: 3
Countries/Regions: Haiti

OM CANADA

Formerly: Operation Mobilization
84 West St.
Port Colborne, ON L3K 4C8 CA
Phone: (877) 487-7777
Email: info@om.org
Website: om.org

A sending agency of Evangelical tradition engaged in short-term programs, broadcasting, business as mission, mobilization for mission, missionary training and training. (DPE)

Purpose: . . . to motivate, develop, and equip people for world evangelization, and to strengthen and help plant churches, especially among the unreached in the Middle East, South and Central Asia, and Europe.

Year Founded in CA: 1957
Income for International Min:
  $2,200,000

Fully Supported CA Personnel Working Cross-Culturally
  More than 4 years: 31
  1–4 years: 47

Other Personnel
  Short-Term less than 1 year: 150
Countries/Regions: Afghanistan, Africa, Asia, Austria, Bosnia and Herzegovina, Central Asia, France, India, Middle East, Myanmar (Burma), Nepal, Pakistan, Sweden, Switzerland, Unspecified Country, Uruguay, Western Europe

OMF INTERNATIONAL

10 W. Dry Creek Circle
Littleton, CO 80120 US
Phone: (303) 730-4160
Email: debbie.coop@omfmail.com
Website: omf.org/us/
Associations: Missio Nexus

A nondenominational sending agency of Evangelical tradition engaged in Bible teaching, CPM, discipleship, theological education, personal or small group evangelism, and medical ministry, including dental or public health.

Purpose: . . . to see an indigenous biblical church movement in each people group of East Asia, evangelizing their own people and reaching out in mission to other peoples.

Year Founded in US: 1890
Income for International Min:
  $11,086,056

Fully Supported US Personnel Working Cross-Culturally
  More than 4 years: 240
  1–4 years: 13
  X-C workers in US: 16
Other Personnel
  Short-Term less than 1 year: 118
  Tentmakers/BAM: 9
  Home staff: 53
Countries/Regions: East Asia, Global Ministry, Japan, Philippines, Singapore, Southeast Asia, Taiwan (China), Thailand

OMF INTERNATIONAL – CANADA
21-5155 Spectrum Way
Mississauga, ON L4W 5A1 CA
Phone: (905) 568-9971
Email: omfcanada@omfmail.com
Website: omf.ca
Associations: Missio Nexus
An interdenominational sending agency
of Evangelical tradition engaged in Bible
teaching, community development,
discipleship, personal or small group
evangelism, leadership development, and
STM trip coordination.
Purpose: . . . to inspire and enable
Canadian Christians to participate in the
intentional evangelization of East Asia's
peoples.
Year Founded in CA: 1888
Income for International Min:
    $2,167,847
*Fully Supported CA Personnel Working
Cross-Culturally*
    More than 4 years: 81
    X-C workers in CA: 4
Other Personnel
    Short-Term less than 1 year: 42
    Non-CA in own/other country: 81
    Home staff: 32
Countries/Regions: Cambodia,
Indonesia, Japan, Philippines, Singapore,
Southeast Asia, Taiwan (China), Thailand,
United States of America

OMS INTERNATIONAL – CANADA
1295 North Service Rd
Burlington, ON L7R 4L9 CA
Phone: (800) 784-7077
Email: mail@omscanada.org
Website: omscanada.org
An interdenominational sending agency
of Methodist and Wesleyan tradition
engaged in church planting, broadcasting,
theological education, evangelism, support
of national workers and support of national
churches. (DPE)

Income for International Min:
    $1,000,000
*Fully Supported CA Personnel Working
Cross-Culturally*
    More than 4 years: 13
    1–4 years: 4
Other Personnel
    Short-Term less than 1 year: 16
    Tentmakers/BAM: 2
    Home staff: 6
Countries/Regions: Asia, Haiti,
Hungary

OMSC
Formerly: Overseas Ministries Study
Center
490 Prospect Street
New Haven, CT 06511 US
Phone: (203) 624-6672
Email: study@omsc.org
Website: omsc.org
A nondenominational service agency of
Ecumenical tradition engaged in leadership
development, literature production,
member care, missionary & worker
training, networking, partnership, or
coordination, and research.
Purpose: . . . to provide residential
programs for the renewal of missionaries
and international church leaders,
advancement of mission scholarship
through research and publication, and
continuing education in cross-cultural
Christian ministries.
Year Founded in US: 1922
Other Personnel
    Home staff: 19

ON THE GO MINISTRIES/
KEITH COOK TEAM
PO Box 963
Springfield, TN 37172 US
Phone: (615) 299-0222
Email: joancook@onthego.org
Website: onthego.org

A transdenominational support agency of Baptist and Evangelical tradition engaged in evangelism, theological education, leadership development, short-term programs and training. (DPE)

Purpose: . . . to be On the Go sharing Christ across the street and around the world.

Year Founded in US: 1974
Income for International Min:
   $350,000

Fully Supported US Personnel Working Cross-Culturally
   More than 4 years: 4
   1–4 years: 2
   Non-residential: 16

Other Personnel
   Short-Term less than 1 year: 1500
   Tentmakers/BAM: 3
   Non-US in own/other country: 2
   Home staff: 4

Countries/Regions: United Arab Emirates

ONE ANOTHER MINISTRIES INTERNATIONAL

P.O. Box 2430
Orange, CA 92859 US
Phone: (714) 602-3373
Email: info@OneAnother.com
Website: OneAnother.com
Associations: Missio Nexus

A nondenominational service agency of Evangelical tradition engaged in counseling, leadership development, member care, missionary & worker training, and services for mission organizations.

Purpose: . . . to proclaim the message of Jesus Christ and provide professional training, consulting, counseling, and resourcing for the development and care of mission organizations and their members, churches on the mission field, and their leaders.

Year Founded in US: 1997
Income for International Min:
   $265,000

Fully Supported US Personnel Working Cross-Culturally
   More than 4 years: 4

Other Personnel
   Tentmakers/BAM: 1

Countries/Regions: Global Ministry

ONE CHALLENGE

Formerly: OC International
PO Box 36900
Colorado Springs, CO 80936-6900 US
Phone: (719) 592-9292
Email: info@oci.org
Website: OneChallenge.org
Associations: Missio Nexus

An interdenominational sending agency of Evangelical tradition engaged in CPM, DMM, leadership development, networking, partnership, or coordination, research, and mission mobilization.

Purpose: . . . to serve, equip, and connect the body of Christ and its leaders to advance God's kingdom among all peoples.

Year Founded in US: 1950
Income for International Min:
   $10,434,498

Fully Supported US Personnel Working Cross-Culturally
   More than 4 years: 161
   1–4 years: 1
   X-C workers in US: 1
   Non-residential: 5

Other Personnel
   Short-Term less than 1 year: 30
   Non-US in own/other country: 23
   Home staff: 47

Countries/Regions: Brazil, Bulgaria, Central Asia, East Asia, Eastern Europe and Eurasia, Germany, Global Ministry, Guatemala, Mexico, Middle East, North Africa, Philippines, Romania, South Africa,

South America, South Asia, South Korea, Southeast Asia, Spain, Sub-Saharan Africa, Taiwan (China), Ukraine, Western Europe

ONE CHILD MATTERS
Formerly: Mission of Mercy
PO Box 62600
Colorado Springs, CO 80962 US
Phone: (800) 864-0200
Email: info@onechildmatters.org
Website: onechildmatters.org

A nondenominational support agency of Evangelical tradition engaged in childcare or orphanage, children's ministry, discipleship, church, school or general Christian education, and youth ministry.

Purpose: . . . to rescue forgotten children with Jesus' love.
Year Founded in US: 1954
Income for International Min:
  $14,962,511
Other Personnel
  Home staff: 18
Countries/Regions: Bangladesh, Cambodia, Dominican Republic, Ethiopia, Global Ministry, Haiti, Honduras, India, Jordan, Kenya, Lebanon, Nepal, Nicaragua, Philippines, Swaziland, Zimbabwe

ONE MISSION SOCIETY
Formerly: OMS International
941 Fry Road
Greenwood, IN 46142 US
Phone: (317) 888-3333
Email: tvanabeele@onemissionsociety.org
Website: onemissionsociety.org
Associations: Missio Nexus

A nondenominational sending agency of Evangelical tradition engaged in Bible teaching, CPM, DMM, personal or small group evangelism, partnership development, and recruiting or mobilizing for mission. (FPC-PE)

Purpose: . . . to inspire and equip Christians to make disciples of Jesus Christ, multiplying dynamic communities of believers around the world.
Year Founded in US: 1901
Countries/Regions: Australia, Brazil, China (People's Republic of), Colombia, Ecuador, Haiti, Hong Kong (China), Hungary, India, Indonesia, Ireland (Republic of), Japan, Kazakhstan, South Korea, Mexico, Mozambique, Philippines, Russia, South Africa, Spain, Taiwan (China), Ukraine, United Kingdom, Unspecified Country, Uruguay

ONE WORLD MISSIONS
16848 Leyte St NE
Andover, Mn 55304 US
Phone: (612) 636-8434
Email: staff@oneworldmissions.com
Website: oneworldmissions.com
Associations: Missio Nexus

An interdenominational service agency of Evangelical tradition engaged in leadership development, management consulting or training, networking, partnership, or coordination, recruiting or mobilizing for mission, and catalyzing mission movements.

Purpose: . . . to catalyze church planting, discipleship and mission movements among the nations. We are working to establish networks made up of church and mission leaders providing a broad platform for mission to be carried out by anyone and everyone to anywhere

ONEHOPE
600 SW 3rd St.
Pompano Beach, FL 33060 US
Phone: (954) 975-7777
Email: info@onehope.net
Website: onehope.net

A nondenominational sending agency engaged in evangelism, Bible distribution, mission-related research and video/film production/distribution. (DPE)

Purpose: . . . to affect destiny by providing God's eternal Word to all children and youth of the world.

Income for International Min: $20,038,303

Other Personnel
Short-Term less than 1 year: 574
Home staff: 127

Countries/Regions: Angola, Argentina, Armenia, Benin, Brazil, Bulgaria, Burkina Faso, Cambodia, Cameroon, Chile, China (People's Republic of), Colombia, Democratic Republic of Congo, Cuba, Dominican Republic, Ecuador, Ghana, Haiti, Honduras, India, Indonesia, Japan, Kenya, Lesotho, Madagascar, Malaysia, Mexico, Middle East, Mozambique, Nicaragua, Niger, Nigeria, Peru, Philippines, Romania, Russia, Sierra Leone, South Africa, Spain, Swaziland, Taiwan (China), Tanzania, Thailand, Togo, Uganda, Ukraine, United Kingdom, Venezuela

ONEWAY MINISTRIES
PO Box 2211
Napaville, IL 60567 US
Phone: (630) 626-4990
Email: Rich@owm.org
Website: OWM.org
Associations: Missio Nexus

A nondenominational service agency of Evangelical tradition engaged in audio recording or distribution, Bible teaching, radio or TV broadcasting, CPM, and prayer-intercession.

Purpose: . . . to activate God's people to exalt Jesus Christ and spread his gospel to the masses.

Year Founded in US: 2007
Income for International Min: $50,000

Other Personnel
Short-Term less than 1 year: 1
Home staff: 1

OPEN AIR CAMPAIGNERS – OVERSEAS MINISTRIES (OAC-OM)
PO Box 4454
St. Augustine, FL 32085 US
Phone: (904) 827-9715
Email: djwils39@bellsouth.net
Website: oacom.org

An interdenominational service agency of Baptist and Brethren tradition engaged in mass evangelism and STM trip coordination.

Purpose: . . . to preach the Gospel to the unreached through open air and other outreaches in partnership with the church.

Year Founded in US: 1990
Income for International Min: $412,272

Other Personnel
Short-Term less than 1 year: 14
Non-US in own/other country: 40
Home staff: 1

Countries/Regions: Bahamas, Bolivia, Brazil, Ecuador, India, Jamaica, Kenya, Mexico, Paraguay, Peru, Russia, Ukraine

OPEN DOOR BAPTIST MISSIONS
1115 Pelham Rd.
Greenville, SC 29615 US
Phone: (864) 297-7890
Email: info@odbm.org
Website: odbm.org

A nondenominational sending agency of Baptist and Independent tradition engaged in church planting, Christian education, theological education and evangelism. (DPE)

Purpose: . . . to promote the work of Christ in regions that have been closed to the Gospel or that presently have little or no fundamental gospel witness.

Income for International Min:
  $1,000,000
Fully Supported US Personnel Working Cross-Culturally
  More than 4 years: 43
Other Personnel
  Short-Term less than 1 year: 1
  Tentmakers/BAM: 1
  Non-US in own/other country: 5
  Home staff: 4
Countries/Regions: Asia, Cameroon, France, Ghana, Haiti, Japan, Lithuania, Middle East, Peru, Puerto Rico, South Africa, Spain, Taiwan (China), Uganda, United Kingdom

OPEN DOORS USA
PO Box 27001
Santa Ana, CA 92799 US
Phone: (949) 752-6600
Email: usa@opendoors.org
Website: opendoorsusa.org
A support agency of Evangelical tradition engaged in Bible distribution, justice, leadership development, literature distribution and support of national churches. (DPE)
Purpose: . . . to strengthen and equip the Body of Christ living under or facing restriction and persecution because of their faith in Jesus Christ, and to encourage their involvement in world evangelism.
Year Founded in US: 1973
Income for International Min:
  $6,813,818
Other Personnel
  Short-Term less than 1 year: 50
  Home staff: 41

OPEN DOORS WITH BROTHER ANDREW – CANADA
8-19 Brownridge Rd.
Halton Hills, ON L7G 0C6 CA
Phone: (905) 636-0944
Email: opendoorsca@od.org
Website: opendoorsca.org
A transdenominational support agency of Evangelical tradition engaged in Bible distribution, theological education, literature distribution, literature production, support of national churches and training. (DPE)
Purpose: . . . to serve persecuted Christians worldwide.

OPERATION BLESSING INTERNATIONAL RELIEF AND DEVELOPMENT CORPORATION
977 Centerville Turnpike
Virginia Beach, VA 23463 US
Phone: (757) 226-3401
Email: operation.blessing@ob.org
Website: ob.org
A nondenominational relief agency that has helped more than 184.9 million people in 96 countries, distributing more than $1.1 billion in goods. Engaged in hunger relief, medical aid, disaster relief, children's programs and community development that will make a significant, long-term impact. Operating methodology focuses on capacity building and collaboration between indigenously-staffed field offices and local indigenous partners (including other NGOs, government agencies, community-based social service agencies, and grassroots relief groups). (DPE)
Purpose: . . . to demonstrate God's love by alleviating human need and suffering in the United States and around the world.
Other Personnel
  Home staff: 85

OPERATION BOOTSTRAP AFRICA

625 Fourth Ave South, Suite 110
Minneapolis, MN 55415 US
Phone: (612) 871-4980
Email: info@operationbootstrapafrica.org
Website: bootstrapafrica.org/
A support agency of Lutheran and
Methodist tradition engaged in
community development and international
development & relief services. (DPE)
Purpose: . . . to partner with Africans in
educating their children.
Income for International Min:
   $726,409
Other Personnel
   Home staff: 2

OPERATION MOBILIZATION

285 Lynnwood Ave
Tyrone, GA 30290 US
Phone: (770) 631-0432
Email: info.us@om.org
Website: omusa.org/
Associations: Missio Nexus
A nondenominational sending agency of
Evangelical tradition engaged in church
planting (establishing), community
development, justice or peace issues,
leadership development, missionary &
worker training, and tentmaking & related.
Purpose: . . . to see multiplying
fellowships of Christ-followers established
among the unreached and forgotten.
Year Founded in US: 1957
Income for International Min:
   $21,329,054
*Fully Supported US Personnel Working
Cross-Culturally*
   More than 4 years: 190
   1–4 years: 191
Other Personnel
   Short-Term less than 1 year: 148
   Non-US in own/other country: 2757
   Home staff: 226

Countries/Regions: Albania, Angola,
Argentina, Australia, Austria, Belgium,
Bosnia and Herzegovina, Brazil, Canada,
Caribbean, Central America, Chad, Chile,
China (People's Republic of), Costa Rica,
Czech Republic, Denmark, Eastern Europe
and Eurasia, Ecuador, Faroe Islands,
Finland, France, Germany, Ghana, Global
Ministry, Greece, Hong Kong (China),
Hungary, Ireland (Republic of), Italy, Japan,
Madagascar, Malawi, Malaysia, Mexico,
Middle East, Moldova, Myanmar (Burma),
Namibia, Nepal, Netherlands, New
Zealand, Norway, Pakistan, Papua New
Guinea, Paraguay, Philippines, Poland,
Portugal, Romania, Russia, Singapore,
South Africa, South America, South
Asia, South Korea, Southeast Asia, Spain,
Sweden, Switzerland, Taiwan (China),
Tanzania, Thailand, Ukraine, United
Kingdom, Uruguay, Zambia, Zimbabwe

OPPORTUNITY INTERNATIONAL

550 West Van Buren St
Chicago, IL 60607 US
Phone: (800) 793-9455
Email: getinfo@opportunity.org
Website: opportunity.org
An interdenominational service agency
of Ecumenical tradition engaged in
microfinancing, leadership development,
funds transmission and training, working in
26 countries. (DPE)
Purpose: . . . to provide opportunities
for people in chronic poverty to transform
their lives.
Income for International Min:
   $112,064,000
Other Personnel
   Home staff: 65

OPPORTUNITY INTERNATIONAL CANADA

10 Four Seasons Place, Suite 610
Toronto, ON M9B 6H7 CA
Phone: (877) 867-2448
Email: info@opportunityinternational.ca
Website: opportunityinternational.ca

A service agency engaged in justice, business as mission, discipleship, HIV/AIDS and training. (DPE)

Purpose: . . . to provide opportunities for people in chronic poverty to improve their lives.

Year Founded in CA: 1998
Income for International Min:
$2,979,892

Other Personnel
Short-Term less than 1 year: 8
Home staff: 7

ORPHANETWORK

2624 Southern Blvd., Suite 101
Virginia Beach, VA 23452 US
Phone: (757) 333-7200
Email: dick.anderson@orphanetwork.org
Website: orphanetwork.org

A nondenominational specialized agency of Evangelical tradition engaged in childcare/orphanage programs, children at risk and short-term programs. (DPE)

Purpose: . . . to rescue abandoned children . . . to prevent at-risk children from being abandoned . . . to share Christ with everyone.

Income for International Min:
$1,500,000

Other Personnel
Short-Term less than 1 year: 800
Non-US in own/other country: 1
Home staff: 2
Countries/Regions: Nicaragua

ORPHANOS FOUNDATION

PO Box 1057
Cordova, TN 38088 US
Phone: (901) 458-9500
Email: info@orphanos.org
Website: orphanos.org
Associations: Missio Nexus

A nondenominational support agency of Reformed tradition engaged in childcare or orphanage and children's ministry.

Purpose: . . . to glorify Jesus Christ and serve His purpose on earth through a concentration, in the name of Jesus Christ, on meeting the needs of children in the world, with a particular emphasis on orphaned children.

Year Founded in US: 1997
Income for International Min:
$1,588,251

Fully Supported US Personnel Working Cross-Culturally
More than 4 years: 8
1–4 years: 4
Non-residential: 2

Other Personnel
Short-Term less than 1 year: 22
Non-US in own/other country: 12
Home staff: 5

Countries/Regions: Belize, Bolivia, Brazil, Cambodia, Colombia, Jamaica, South Korea, Kyrgyzstan, Mexico, North Africa, Peru, Russia

ORTHODOX PRESBYTERIAN CHURCH – COMMITTEE ON FOREIGN MISSIONS

607 N. Easton Rd., Bldg. E
Willow Grove, PA 19090 US
Phone: (215) 830-0900
Email: OPForeignMissions@opc.org
Website: opc.org

A denominational sending agency committed to the establishment of indigenous churches in the Presbyterian and Reformed tradition, primarily through the ministry of the Word. Actively engaged in church planting, theological education, evangelism and literature distribution, medicine, and national church support. Medical ministries of mercy supplement the gospel proclamation. (DPE)

Purpose: . . . to establish a healthy indigenous national church that is firmly and fully committed to the Reformed standards; that is self-supporting, self-governing and self-propagating; with whom the OPC may have fraternal relations; that is itself sending out foreign missionaries to other nations; which no longer needs the services of OP foreign missionaries.

Year Founded in US: 1940
Income for International Min:
   $1,700,000
Fully Supported US Personnel Working Cross-Culturally
   More than 4 years: 26
   1–4 years: 11
   Non-residential: 2
Other Personnel
   Short-Term less than 1 year: 45
   Tentmakers/BAM: 12
   Home staff: 5
Countries/Regions: China (People's Republic of), Eritrea, Ethiopia, Haiti, Japan, Kenya, South Korea, Suriname, Uganda

OUR DAILY BREAD
Formerly: RBC Ministries
3000 Kraft Ave SE
Grand Rapids, MI 49512 US
Phone: (616) 942-5741
Email: odb@odb.org
Website: rbc.org

A nondenominational service agency of Evangelical tradition engaged in radio or TV broadcasting, literature distribution, and literature production.

Purpose: . . . to make the life-changing wisdom of the Bible understandable and accessible to all.
Year Founded in US: 1938
Fully Supported US Personnel Working Cross-Culturally
   More than 4 years: 16
Other Personnel
   Home staff: 300
Countries/Regions: Fiji, Hong Kong (China), India, Indonesia, Jamaica, Japan, Malaysia, Mexico, New Zealand, Philippines, Russia, Singapore, Spain, Thailand, Ukraine, United Kingdom

OUTREACH CANADA
7201 72nd St Unit 2
Delta, BC V4G 1M5 CA
Phone: (604) 952-0050
Email: ckraft@outreach.ca
Website: outreach.ca
Associations: Missio Nexus

An interdenominational service agency of Evangelical tradition engaged in business as mission, discipleship, leadership development, member care, networking, partnership, or coordination, and recruiting or mobilizing for mission.

Purpose: . . . to accelerate the completion of the Great Commission, desiring to see the Godly transformation of individuals, families, churches, communities and nations through the presence of Christ.
Year Founded in CA: 1977
Fully Supported CA Personnel Working Cross-Culturally
   More than 4 years: 2
   1–4 years: 2
   X-C workers in CA: 30
   Non-residential: 3
Other Personnel
   Short-Term less than 1 year: 2
   Home staff: 3

Countries/Regions: Global Ministry, Russia

OUTREACH TO ASIA NATIONALS
PO Box 2440
Winchester, VA 22604 US
Phone: (540) 665-6418
Email: secretary@otaninfo.org
Website: otan.org
Associations: Missio Nexus
A denominational heritage support agency of Baptist tradition engaged in Bible distribution, Bible teaching, CPM, DMM, national worker support, and persecuted church.
Purpose: . . . to serve, train, equip, and empower national church workers in Asia as they plant evangelistic, disciple-making, and reproducing churches among unreached and least-reached people groups.
Year Founded in US: 1986
Fully Supported US Personnel Working Cross-Culturally
   More than 4 years: 10
   1–4 years: 13
   Non-residential: 18
Other Personnel
   Tentmakers/BAM: 23
   Non-US in own/other country: 85
Countries/Regions: Central America, Central Asia, East Asia, Global Ministry, Middle East, Southeast Asia

OVERSEAS COUNCIL INTERNATIONAL
3830 East Southport Rd. Ste. B
Indianapolis, IN 46237 US
Phone: (317) 788-7250
Email: info@overseas.org
Website: overseas.org
An interdenominational support agency of Evangelical tradition engaged in establishing partnerships between Western Christians and non-Western students and

evangelical theological schools. Affiliated organizations in Australia, Canada, Europe, New Zealand, and UK. (DPE)
Purpose: . . . to equip biblical leaders to be effective pastors, teachers, evangelists, missionaries and Christian leaders in their own countries.
Income for International Min:
   $3,370,383
Other Personnel
   Home staff: 28

PALM MISSIONARY MINISTRIES INC.
1702 Parks Lake Rd.
Lake Wales, FL 33898-8430 US
Phone: (863) 632-0230
Email: art@palmministries.org
Website: palmministries.com
An interdenominational sending agency of Evangelical tradition engaged in support of national workers, Christian education, evangelism, literacy work, support of national churches and short-term programs. (DPE)
Purpose: . . . to enable and facilitate the development of national missionaries and workers to go into all nations.
Year Founded in US: 1987
Income for International Min:
   $229,151
Fully Supported US Personnel Working Cross-Culturally
   More than 4 years: 2
Other Personnel
   Short-Term less than 1 year: 50
   Tentmakers/BAM: 2
   Non-US in own/other country: 39
   Home staff: 5
Countries/Regions: Argentina, Bolivia, Colombia, Ecuador, Mexico, Spain

PAN AMERICAN MISSIONS
PO Box 710097
Santee, CA 92072-0097 US
Phone: (619) 469-0970
Email: dllasher@cox.net
Website: panamericanmissions.com/
An interdenominational support agency
of Baptist and Wesleyan tradition engaged
in Bible distribution, childcare/orphanage
programs and church planting. (DPE)
Purpose: . . . ministers in Mexico and
other Spanish-speaking countries of Latin
America for the establishing and building
up of indigenous churches.
Income for International Min:
  $33,000
*Fully Supported US Personnel Working
Cross-Culturally*
  More than 4 years: 2
Other Personnel
  Home staff: 2
Countries/Regions: Mexico

PARACLETE MISSION GROUP INC.
PO Box 63450
Colorado Springs, CO 80962 US
Phone: (719) 302-2500
Email: info@paraclete.net
Website: paraclete.net
Associations: Missio Nexus
An interdenominational sending agency
of Evangelical tradition engaged in
counseling, leadership development,
management consulting or training,
member care, missionary & worker
training, and spiritual renewal.
Purpose: . . . to come alongside Christian
leaders around the world.
Year Founded in US: 1988
*Fully Supported US Personnel Working
Cross-Culturally*
  Non-residential: 83

Other Personnel
  Short-Term less than 1 year: 2
  Home staff: 3
Countries/Regions: Albania, Austria,
Azerbaijan, Belarus, Belgium, Bolivia,
Bulgaria, Central Asia, Chad, Colombia,
Costa Rica, Croatia, Czech Republic,
Dominican Republic, East Asia, Ethiopia,
France, Georgia, Germany, Ghana,
Greece, Guatemala, Haiti, Ireland
(Republic of), Italy, Japan, Kenya, Kosovo,
Latvia, Lesotho, Lithuania, Malta, Middle
East, Moldova, Montenegro, Netherlands,
Panama, Peru, Poland, Romania, Russia,
Senegal, Serbia, Slovakia, Slovenia,
South Africa, South Asia, Southeast
Asia, Sweden, Thailand, Ukraine, United
Kingdom

PARADIGM SHIFT
3472 Research Pky Ste. 104-401
Colorado Springs, CO 80920 US
Phone: (719) 321-2477
Email: jedd@shiftingparadigm.org
Website: shiftingparadigms.org
A nondenominational sending agency of
Evangelical tradition engaged in business
as mission, development, discipleship,
evangelism and leadership development.
(DPE)
Purpose: . . . to train local churches
and ministries in developing countries to
provide business training, microcredit,
mentoring and discipleship to the urban
poor.
*Fully Supported US Personnel Working
Cross-Culturally*
  1–4 years: 6
Other Personnel
  Short-Term less than 1 year: 6
  Home staff: 1
Countries/Regions: South Africa

PARTNERS IN ASIAN MISSIONS

PO Box 531011
Birmingham, AL 35253 US
Phone: (205) 854-8418
Email: js1@quickbox.com
Website: pam-ee.org

A nondenominational support agency of Reformed tradition engaged in support of national workers, childcare/orphanage programs, church construction, church planting, evangelism and leadership development. (DPE)

Purpose: . . . to mobilize and equip top leaders in every Asian country for developing and implementing an effective national church-planting project . . . to enlist groups that will take responsibility for evangelization of a particular geographic territory or ethnolinguistic group.

Year Founded in US: 1972
Income for International Min:
$150,000
Fully Supported US Personnel Working Cross-Culturally
Non-residential: 1
Other Personnel
Non-US in own/other country: 159
Home staff: 1
Countries/Regions: Asia

PARTNERS IN BIBLE TRANSLATION

PO Box 455
Richmond, OH 43944 US
Phone: (740) 314-7400
Email: kssawka@gmail.com
Website: PartnersInBibleTranslation.org

An interdenominational service agency of Evangelical and Independent tradition engaged in literacy and Bible translation.

Purpose: . . . to strengthen the body of Christ worldwide through the promotion of pioneer Bible translation, increased literacy, and foreign missionary work.

Year Founded in US: 2015

Income for International Min:
$80,000
Fully Supported US Personnel Working Cross-Culturally
More than 4 years: 2
Other Personnel
Non-US in own/other country: 3
Home staff: 2
Countries/Regions: Zambia

PARTNERS INTERNATIONAL

1117 E Westview Court
Spokane, WA 99218 US
Phone: (509) 343-4050
Email: lyndaj@partnersintl.org
Website: partnersintl.org

An interdenominational sending agency of Evangelical tradition engaged in Bible teaching, church planting (establishing), community development, discipleship, personal or small group evangelism, and missionary & worker training.

Purpose: . . . to connect the global Christian community to bring the Gospel of Jesus Christ to the least reached, least resourced nations on earth.

Year Founded in US: 1943
Income for International Min:
$14,061,896
Other Personnel
Home staff: 26

PARTNERS INTERNATIONAL CANADA

56 - 8500 Torbram Rd.
Brampton, ON L6T 5C6 CA
Phone: (905) 458-1202
Email: brentm@partnersinternational.ca
Website: partnersinternational.ca

A nondenominational support agency of Evangelical tradition engaged in support of national workers, childcare/orphanage programs, church planting, development, theological education and partnership development. (DPE)

Purpose: . . . to bring Canadians into partnership with indigenous Christian ministries to advance the Kingdom of God.

Year Founded in CA: 1963

Income for International Min:
$3,840,000

Fully Supported CA Personnel Working Cross-Culturally
1–4 years: 1
Non-residential: 3

Other Personnel
Short-Term less than 1 year: 80
Non-CA in own/other country: 1
Home staff: 17

Countries/Regions: Bangladesh, Bhutan, Bolivia, Brazil, China (People's Republic of), Cuba, India, Indonesia, Lebanon, Myanmar (Burma), Nepal, Nigeria, Pakistan, Peru, Senegal, South Africa, Thailand

PARTNERS RELIEF & DEVELOPMENT

1532 Galena St. #225
Aurora, CO 80010 US
Phone: (720) 289-1418
Email: maureen.beighey@partners.ngo
Website: partners.ngo

A nondenominational support agency of Evangelical tradition engaged in agricultural assistance, childcare or orphanage, church, school or general Christian education, addressing human trafficking, medical ministry, including dental or public health, and relief & aid.

Purpose: . . . to see free full lives for children affected by war and oppression.

Year Founded in US: 1995

Income for International Min:
$1,677,920

Fully Supported US Personnel Working Cross-Culturally
More than 4 years: 2
1–4 years: 11

Other Personnel
Short-Term less than 1 year: 30
Home staff: 2

Countries/Regions: Myanmar (Burma)

PARTNERS WORLDWIDE

6139 Tahoe Dr. SE
Grand Rapids, MI 49546 US
Phone: (616) 818-4900
Email: dougs@partnersworldwide.org
Website: partnersworldwide.org

A specialized agency of Reformed tradition engaged in business as mission, development, management consulting/ training and partnership development. (DPE)

Purpose: . . . to encourage, equip, and connect business and professional people in global partnerships that grow enterprises and create sustainable jobs, transforming the lives of all involved.

Year Founded in US: 1994

Income for International Min:
$2,460,861

Countries/Regions: Kenya, Uganda

PENTECOSTAL CHURCH OF GOD-WORLD MISSIONS DEPARTMENT

PO Box 211866
Bedford, TX 76095 US
Phone: (817) 554-5900
Email: wm@pcg.org
Website: pcg.org

A denominational sending agency of Pentecostal tradition engaged in Bible distribution, church construction or financing, church planting (establishing), mass evangelism, literature distribution, and national worker support. (FPC-PE)

Year Founded in US: 1919

PENTECOSTAL FREE WILL BAPTIST CHURCH INC. – WORLD WITNESS DEPT.

PO Box 1568
Dunn, NC 28335 US
Phone: (910) 892-4161
Email: preston@pfwb.org
Website: pfwb.org

A denominational sending agency of Holiness and Pentecostal tradition engaged in youth programs, missionary education, theological education, support of national churches, church planting and Christian education. (DPE)
Year Founded in US: 1959
Fully Supported US Personnel Working Cross-Culturally
   More than 4 years: 2
   Non-residential: 2
Other Personnel
   Short-Term less than 1 year: 40
   Tentmakers/BAM: 1
   Non-US in own/other country: 10
   Home staff: 11
Countries/Regions: Costa Rica, Dominican Republic, Guatemala, Honduras, Mexico, Nicaragua, Nigeria, Peru, Philippines, Puerto Rico, Venezuela

PEOPLE INTERNATIONAL USA

PO Box 3005
Vancouver, WA 98668-3005 US
Phone: (360) 859-4584
Email: peoplefinance@msn.com
Website: gopeople.org

An interdenominational sending agency of Evangelical tradition engaged in childcare or orphanage, church planting (establishing), discipleship, mass evangelism, leadership development, and Bible translation.
Purpose: . . . to unveil God's glory to Central Asian Muslims by establishing and enabling His Church.
Year Founded in US: 1987

Fully Supported US Personnel Working Cross-Culturally
   More than 4 years: 25
Other Personnel
   Home staff: 4
Countries/Regions: Afghanistan, Hong Kong (China), Kazakhstan, Kyrgyzstan, Tajikistan, Turkey

PERIMETER CHURCH – GLOBAL OUTREACH

9500 Medlock Bridge Rd.
Duluth, GA 30097 US
Phone: (678) 405-2270
Email: go@perimeter.org
Website: perimeter.org/

A denominational support agency of Presbyterian tradition engaged in support of national churches, development, discipleship, theological education, leadership development and partnership development. (DPE)
Purpose: . . . to partner with externally focused churches and church planters to make mature and equipped followers of Jesus Christ deployed for global city transformation.
Income for International Min:
   $1,100,000
Fully Supported US Personnel Working Cross-Culturally
   Non-residential: 3
Other Personnel
   Short-Term less than 1 year: 298
   Home staff: 13
Countries/Regions: China (People's Republic of), India, Russia, Tanzania, Thailand

PIC INTERNATIONAL (PARTNERS IN CHRIST INTERNATIONAL)

Formerly: Partners in Christ Intl.
PO Box 237
Tempe, AZ 85280 US
Phone: (480) 731-9170
Email: partnersinchrist@qwest.net
Website: picinternational.org

A nondenominational sending agency of Evangelical tradition engaged in leadership development.

Purpose: . . . to empower and equip national churches to create their own vision and strategy for ministry, mission, and community transformation.

Year Founded in US: 1986

Fully Supported US Personnel Working Cross-Culturally
  1–4 years: 8
Other Personnel
  Home staff: 3

Countries/Regions: Cuba, El Salvador, Guatemala, India, Mexico, Nicaragua, Slovenia

PILGRIM

2200 6th Ave. #804
Seattle, WA 98121 US
Phone: (206) 706-0350
Email: helen@pilgrimafrica.org
Website: pilgrimafrica.org

A nondenominational service agency of Evangelical tradition engaged in development, agricultural programs, Christian education, medical work, psychological counseling and relief and/or rehabilitation. (DPE)

Purpose: . . . to restore hope, dignity, and love to the needy, that God may be glorified.

Year Founded in US: 2004
Income for International Min:
  $11,488,520

Fully Supported US Personnel Working Cross-Culturally
  Non-residential: 14
Other Personnel
  Home staff: 5

PILLAR OF FIRE MISSIONS INTERNATIONAL

10 Chapel Drive
Zarephath, NJ 08890 US
Phone: (732) 356-0102
Email: info@pillar.org
Website: pillar.org

A sending agency of Holiness tradition engaged in Christian education, church construction, theological education and support of national workers. (DPE)

Income for International Min:
  $113,204
Other Personnel
  Home staff: 4

PIONEER BIBLE TRANSLATORS

7255 W. Camp Wisdom Rd
Dallas, TX 75236 US
Phone: (214) 699-4300
Email: pbt@pbti.org
Website: pioneerbible.org

A nondenominational sending agency of Christian (Restoration Movement) tradition engaged in mass evangelism, literacy, and Bible translation.

Purpose: . . . to disciple the nations by providing Scripture in the language of the people, developing mother-tongue literacy programs, establishing and strengthening congregations, and training leadership among nationals for partnership in reaching our goals.

Year Founded in US: 1976

Fully Supported US Personnel Working Cross-Culturally
  More than 4 years: 71

Other Personnel
Home staff: 27
Countries/Regions: Guinea, Papua New Guinea, Tanzania, Ukraine, Vanuatu

PIONEER CLUBS
PO Box 788
Wheaton, IL 60189-0788 US
Phone: (630) 293-1600
Email: info@pioneerclubs.org
Website: pioneerclubs.org

A nondenominational and interdenominational service agency of Evangelical tradition engaged in children's programs and camping programs. (DPE)

Purpose: . . . to serve God by providing the most effective and educationally sound programs to help children follow Christ in every aspect of life.

Other Personnel
Home staff: 25

PIONEERS CANADA
51 Byron Ave
Dorchester, ON N0L 1G2 CA
Phone: (519) 268-8778
Email: info@pioneers.ca
Website: pioneers.ca
Associations: Missio Nexus

A nondenominational sending agency of Evangelical tradition engaged in church planting (establishing), CPM, discipleship, and personal or small group evangelism.

Purpose: . . . to mobilize teams to glorify God among unreached peoples by initiating church-planting movements in partnership with local churches.

Year Founded in CA: 1993

Fully Supported CA Personnel Working Cross-Culturally
More than 4 years: 68
1–4 years: 3
X-C workers in CA: 28
Non-residential: 2

Other Personnel
Home staff: 27
Countries/Regions: Afghanistan, Algeria, Austria, Bolivia, Brazil, Bulgaria, Chad, China (People's Republic of), Egypt, France, Georgia, India, Indonesia, Japan, Jordan, Lebanon, Morocco, Peru, Tajikistan, Thailand, Turkey, United Arab Emirates, United Kingdom, United States of America

PIONEERS USA
10123 William Carey Drive
Orlando, FL 32832 US
Phone: (407) 382-6000
Email: info@pioneers.org
Website: pioneers.org
Associations: Missio Nexus

An interdenominational sending agency of Evangelical tradition engaged in business as mission, church planting (establishing), CPM, discipleship, personal or small group evangelism, and tentmaking & related.

Purpose: . . . to mobilize teams to glorify God among unreached peoples by initiating church-planting movements in partnership with local churches.

Year Founded in US: 1979
Income for International Min:
$46,840,000

Fully Supported US Personnel Working Cross-Culturally
More than 4 years: 921
X-C workers in US: 46
Non-residential: 52

Other Personnel
Short-Term less than 1 year: 116
Tentmakers/BAM: 30
Non-US in own/other country: 30
Home staff: 193

Countries/Regions: Central America, Central Asia, East Asia, Eastern Europe and Eurasia, Global Ministry, Middle East, North Africa, Oceania, South America, South Asia, Southeast Asia, Sub-Saharan Africa, Western Europe

POLISH CHRISTIAN MINISTRIES
1212 Schucks Rd
Bel Air, MD 21015 US
Phone: (410) 688-3294
Email: pcm@pcmusa.org
Website: pcmusa.org
A nondenominational support agency of
Christian (Restoration Movement) tradition
engaged in Bible teaching, church planting
(establishing), discipleship, personal or
small group evangelism, fund raising or
transmission, and STM trip coordination.
Purpose: . . . to assist Polish Christians
in becoming healthy, growing,
self-supporting, and reproducing
congregations.
Year Founded in US: 1954
Income for International Min:
   $509,046
*Fully Supported US Personnel Working
Cross-Culturally*
   More than 4 years: 1
   Non-residential: 3
Other Personnel
   Short-Term less than 1 year: 45
   Home staff: 4
Countries/Regions: Poland

POWER TO CHANGE MINISTRIES
20385 64th Avenue
Langley, BC V2Y 1N5 CA
Phone: (604) 514-2000
Email: give@p2c.com
Website: p2c.com
An interdenominational sending agency
of Evangelical tradition engaged in
Bible teaching, church development,
discipleship, personal or small group
evangelism, missionary & worker training,
and partnership development. (FPC-PE)
Purpose: . . . to help people know Jesus
and experience his power to change the
world across Canada and throughout the
world.

Year Founded in CA: 1967
*Fully Supported CA Personnel Working
Cross-Culturally*
   More than 4 years: 23
   1–4 years: 21
   X-C workers in CA: 150
Countries/Regions: Africa, Asia, India,
Japan, Panama, Philippines, Russia, South
Africa, United Kingdom

PRAKASH ASSOCIATION USA
2130 Stoney Point Farms Rd.
Cumming, GA 30041 US
Phone: (831) 234-9568
Email: prakash4india@bellsouth.net
Website: prakash4india.org
An interdenominational support
agency of Baptist tradition engaged in
vocational training, agricultural programs,
development, leadership development and
youth programs. (DPE)
Purpose: . . . to empower marginalized
young Indian nationals by teaching
marketable trades and life skills so they
can build self-supporting, spiritually
vibrant, transformed lives.
Year Founded in US: 1968
Income for International Min:
   $200,000
*Fully Supported US Personnel Working
Cross-Culturally*
   Non-residential: 1
Other Personnel
   Non-US in own/other country: 40
   Home staff: 3
Countries/Regions: India

PRAYER BAPTIST MISSIONS INTERNATIONAL INC.
PO Box 160849
Boiling Springs, SC 29349 US
Phone: (864) 599-5132
Email: pbmioffice@gmail.com
Website: prayerbaptistmissions.com

A denominational sending agency of Baptist and Fundamentalist tradition engaged in Bible distribution, church planting (establishing), discipleship, mass evangelism, and literature distribution.

Purpose: . . . to unite independent, fundamental Baptist churches with like-minded missionaries for the purpose of evangelizing the lost and establishing churches worldwide.

Year Founded in US: 1989

Fully Supported US Personnel Working Cross-Culturally
   More than 4 years: 14
Other Personnel
   Home staff: 4
Countries/Regions: Canada, Germany, Guyana, Honduras, Kenya, Mexico, South Sudan, Uganda

PRECEPT MINISTRIES INTERNATIONAL
PO Box 182218
Chattanooga, TN 37422 US
Phone: (423) 892-6814
Email: info@precept.org
Website: precept.org

A nondenominational sending agency of Baptist and Evangelical tradition engaged in inductive Bible study materials, broadcasting, discipleship, leadership development, training and translation work. (DPE)

Purpose: . . . to establish people in God's Word.

Fully Supported US Personnel Working Cross-Culturally
   More than 4 years: 2
   Non-residential: 7
Other Personnel
   Short-Term less than 1 year: 9
   Non-US in own/other country: 153
   Home staff: 109

Countries/Regions: Afghanistan, Angola, Argentina, Armenia, Australia, Bahamas, Bolivia, Brazil, Bulgaria, Chile, China (People's Republic of), Colombia, Costa Rica, Cuba, Czech Republic, Ecuador, Egypt, El Salvador, Estonia, Germany, Guatemala, Guinea-Bissau, Honduras, Hungary, India, Iran, Iraq, Ireland (Republic of), Israel, Italy, Kenya, South Korea, Macedonia, Mexico, Moldova, Mozambique, New Zealand, Nicaragua, Panama, Peru, Philippines, Poland, Portugal, Romania, Russia, Serbia, Singapore, Slovakia, South Africa, Syria, Taiwan (China), Tajikistan, Ukraine, United Kingdom, Uzbekistan, Venezuela

PRECIOUS SEED MINISTRIES INC.
1115 S Maryland St
Alton, TX 78573 US
Phone: (956) 585-9966
Email: wymanpylant@yahoo.com
Website: wymanpministries.com

A nondenominational support agency of Evangelical tradition engaged in childcare or orphanage, church construction or financing, church planting (establishing), church, school or general Christian education, personal or small group evangelism, and relief.

Purpose: . . . to reach out to the spiritually lost with God's love and salvation as well as aiding the homeless, orphaned and otherwise suffering people.

Year Founded in US: 1984

Fully Supported US Personnel Working Cross-Culturally
   More than 4 years: 1
Other Personnel
   Non-US in own/other country: 10
Countries/Regions: Mexico, Nicaragua

PRESBYTERIAN CHURCH (USA) WORLDWIDE MINISTRIES

100 Witherspoon St.
Louisville, KY 40202 US
Phone: (502) 569-5000
Email: hunter.farrell@pcusa.org
Website: pcusa.org/worldmission

A denominational sending agency of Presbyterian and Reformed tradition engaged in mobilization for mission, development, leadership development, medical work, partnership development and relief and/or rehabilitation. (DPE)

Purpose: . . . to share the transforming power of the Gospel of Jesus Christ and to carry out this mission by being committed to the whole church, the whole Gospel and the whole inhabited earth . . . assist the church in the quest for Christian unity and ecumenical commitment . . . nourish and strengthen the global perspective and mission effort of the General Assembly Council, the Divisions and the church-at-large.

Income for International Min:
  $40,000,000
Fully Supported US Personnel Working Cross-Culturally
  More than 4 years: 350
  1–4 years: 385
  Non-residential: 375
Countries/Regions: Africa, Asia, Australia, Europe, Latin America, Unspecified Country

PRESBYTERIAN MISSION INTERNATIONAL (PMI)

12330 Conway Rd
St. Louis, MO 63141 US
Phone: (314) 392-4120
Email: pmi@covenantseminary.edu
Website: pmiweb.org

An interdenominational sending agency of Presbyterian and Reformed tradition engaged in childcare or orphanage, church planting (establishing), mass evangelism, and national worker support.

Purpose: . . . to enhance worldwide Reformed and Presbyterian gospel ministry through relationships with nationals who labor in evangelism, church planting, leadership training, holistic ministries, and connecting churches internationally.
Year Founded in US: 1988
Fully Supported US Personnel Working Cross-Culturally
  More than 4 years: 12
Other Personnel
  Home staff: 2
Countries/Regions: Brazil, France, Hungary, India, Italy, Japan, Kenya, Netherlands, New Zealand, Philippines, Thailand, Ukraine

PRESBYTERIAN MISSIONARY UNION

PO Box 879
Bonners Ferry, ID 83805 US
Phone: (208) 267-9608
Email: office@presbyterianmissions.org
Website: presbyterianmissions.org

A denominational sending agency of Presbyterian and Reformed tradition engaged in church planting, evangelism, leadership development, support of national workers, short-term programs and translation work. (DPE)

Purpose: . . . to establish and strengthen indigenous Bible believing churches, related institutions, and works agreeable to the (Westminster) doctrinal standards and principles of (Presbyterian) church government.

Income for International Min:
  $101,200
Fully Supported US Personnel Working Cross-Culturally
  More than 4 years: 4
  Non-residential: 1

Other Personnel
Short-Term less than 1 year: 12
Tentmakers/BAM: 1
Non-US in own/other country: 4
Home staff: 2
Countries/Regions: Asia, Australia, Bolivia, Cambodia, Myanmar (Burma)

PRIMITIVE METHODIST CHURCH IN THE USA – INTERNATIONAL MISSION BOARD

4210 Ernest Drive
Wesley Chapel, FL 33543 US
Phone: (813) 404-2750
Email: paula1ssbg@gmail.com
Website: primitivemethodistchurch.org/imb.html

A denominational sending agency of Methodist tradition engaged in church planting, Bible translation, Christian education and evangelism. (DPE)

Fully Supported US Personnel Working Cross-Culturally
Non-residential: 1
Countries/Regions: Dominican Republic, Guatemala, Papua New Guinea, Spain

PROBE MINISTRIES INTERNATIONAL

2001 W. Plano Pkwy, Ste. 2000
Plano, TX 75075 US
Phone: (972) 941-4565
Email: info@probe.org
Website: probe.org

A nondenominational service agency of Evangelical tradition engaged in apologetics, church, school or general Christian education, theological education, and research.

Purpose: . . . to free culturally captive Christians, and build confident ambassadors for Christ.

Year Founded in US: 1973

PROCLAIM! INTERNATIONAL INC.

PO Box 56888
Jacksonville, FL 32241 US
Phone: (904) 739-0065
Email: info@proclaiminternational.com
Website: proclaiminternational.com

A sending agency of Evangelical tradition engaged in evangelism, broadcasting, support of national churches and mobilization for mission. (DPE)

Purpose: . . . to proclaim the Gospel with creativity, humility and boldness, in obedience to the authority of Jesus Christ and labor alongside believers of integrity, by bringing our gifts to serve so that the Church may express itself in its fullness by doing all things with excellence and above all to 'love one another' providing ourselves to be His disciples.

Year Founded in US: 2000
Income for International Min:
$1,233,000

Fully Supported US Personnel Working Cross-Culturally
More than 4 years: 13
1–4 years: 2
Non-residential: 8
Other Personnel
Short-Term less than 1 year: 17
Non-US in own/other country: 5
Home staff: 1
Countries/Regions: Africa, Croatia, Eastern Europe, Germany, Peru, Spain

PROGRESSIVE NATIONAL BAPTIST CONVENTION INC. (PNBC) – MISSIONS

601 50th St., NE
Washington, DC 20019 US
Phone: (202) 396-0558
Email: info@pnbc.org
Website: pnbc.org

A denominational support agency of Baptist tradition engaged in justice, Christian education, evangelism, literature production, training and youth programs. (DPE)

Purpose: . . . to develop, support, and empower Christian churches, communities, and PNBC partners to improve the quality of life of people domestically and internationally.

Year Founded in US: 1961

Other Personnel
  Home staff: 1
Countries/Regions: Haiti, Jamaica, Kenya, South Africa, Tanzania, United Kingdom

PROJECT AMAZON
PO Box 3253
Peoria, IL 61612 US
Phone: (309) 263-2299
Website: projectamazon.org

An interdenominational sending agency of Charismatic and Evangelical tradition engaged in evangelism, business as mission, church planting, discipleship, medical work and training. (DPE)

Purpose: . . . to glorify God, fulfilling the Great Commission by planting nationally led churches, emphasizing disciple making; the training, equipping, and sending of nationals; ministering to the whole person—spirit, soul, and body; and focusing on the Amazon basin.

Income for International Min:
  $1,678,102

Fully Supported US Personnel Working Cross-Culturally
  More than 4 years: 40
  1–4 years: 1
Other Personnel
  Short-Term less than 1 year: 82
  Non-US in own/other country: 5
  Home staff: 3
Countries/Regions: Brazil, Japan

PROJECT AMAZON CANADA SOCIETY
13401 108 Ave, Suite 360
Surrey, BC V3T 5T3 CA
Phone: (250) 919-4142
Website: projectamazon.org

The Canadian partner of Project AmaZon in the US. See Project AmaZon for statistical information. (DPE)

PROJECT WORLDREACH / TRAIN & MULTIPLY
271-1865 Dilworth Dr
Kelowna, BC VIY 9T1 CA
Phone: (604) 538-0307
Email: lloyd@trainandmutiply.com
Website: trainandmultiply.com/

A nondenominational support agency of Evangelical tradition engaged in church planting (establishing), CPM, and leadership development.

Purpose: . . . to focus all possible resources to reach the world for Christ.

Year Founded in CA: 1993
Countries/Regions: Afghanistan, Aruba, Australia, Austria, Bangladesh, Belgium, Benin, Bhutan, Bolivia, Bosnia and Herzegovina, Botswana, Brazil, Bulgaria, Cambodia, Cameroon, Central African Republic, Chile, China (People's Republic of), Colombia, Democratic Republic of Congo, Cuba, Dominican Republic, Ecuador, Egypt, Estonia, Fiji, France, Gambia, Germany, Greece, Haiti, Honduras, Hong Kong (China), Hungary, India, Indonesia, Israel, Jamaica, Japan, Kenya, South Korea, Laos, Liberia, Madagascar, Malawi, Malaysia, Mexico, Mongolia, Mozambique, Myanmar (Burma), Namibia, Nepal, New Zealand, Nicaragua, Nigeria, Oman, Pakistan, Palestine, Panama, Papua New Guinea, Paraguay, Peru, Philippines, Russia, Rwanda, Sierra Leone, Singapore, Solomon Islands, South Africa, South Sudan, Spain,

Sri Lanka, Switzerland, Taiwan (China), Tajikistan, Tanzania, Thailand, Togo, Tonga, Turkey, Uganda, Ukraine, United States of America, Vietnam, Zambia, Zimbabwe

PROVIDENCE MISSION HOMES INC.

PO Box 40727
Pasadena, CA 91114 US
Phone: (626) 398-2487
Email: providencehomes1@yahoo.com
Website: providencemissionhomes.com

A nondenominational specialized agency of Evangelical tradition engaged in furloughed missionary support. (DPE)

Other Personnel
Home staff: 1

PUBLICATIONS CHRÉTIENNES (CHRISTIAN PUBLISHING IN FRENCH)

230, rue lupien
Trois-rivières, PQ G8T 6W4 CA
Phone: (819) 378-4023
Email: info@pubchret.org
Website: publicationschretiennes.com

A nondenominational service agency of Evangelical and Reformed tradition engaged in literature distribution, literature production, and translation.

Purpose: . . . to publish and distribute the Bible and other Christian books in the French language that share the pertinence and necessity of faith in Jesus Christ while encouraging spiritual growth.

Year Founded in CA: 1958

Other Personnel
Short-Term less than 1 year: 2
Home staff: 5

RAISE INTERNATIONAL INC.

274 E. Eau Gallie Blvd, #337
Indian Harbour Beach, FL 32937 US
Phone: (888) 511-0118
Email: info@raise.international
Website: raise.international

A nondenominational support agency of Christian (Restoration Movement) and Methodist tradition engaged in agricultural assistance, community development, and STM trip coordination.

Purpose: . . . to develop communities to overcome poverty.

Year Founded in US: 2012
Income for International Min:
$254,675

Fully Supported US Personnel Working Cross-Culturally
X-C workers in US: 1
Non-residential: 1

Other Personnel
Short-Term less than 1 year: 43
Non-US in own/other country: 2
Home staff: 1

Countries/Regions: Jamaica

RAVI ZACHARIAS INTERNATIONAL MINISTRIES INC.

4725 Peachtree Corners Cir.
Norcross, GA 30092-2586 US
Phone: (770) 449-6766
Email: rzim@rzim.com
Website: rzim.org

An interdenominational specialized agency of Evangelical tradition engaged in evangelism, apologetics, discipleship, TEE, relief and/or rehabilitation and training. (DPE)

Purpose: . . . to support, expand, and enhance the preaching, teaching, and vision of Ravi Zacharias, distinctive in its strong evangelistic and apologetic foundation, intended to touch both the heart and the intellect of the thinkers and opinion-makers of society . . . to reach and challenge those who shape the ideas of a culture with the credibility of the Gospel of Jesus Christ.

Year Founded in US: 1986
Income for International Min:
$2,300,000
Fully Supported US Personnel Working Cross-Culturally
Non-residential: 2
Other Personnel
Non-US in own/other country: 22
Home staff: 41
Countries/Regions: Asia, Europe, Hong Kong (China), India, Middle East

REACH A VILLAGE
Formerly: Firstfruits International Ministries
P.O. Box 577
Park Forest, IL 60466 US
Phone: (708) 679-0237
Email: rcraft@reachavillage.org
Website: reachavillage.org
Associations: Missio Nexus

A nondenominational support agency of Evangelical tradition engaged in Bible distribution, children's ministry, church planting (establishing), discipleship, personal or small group evangelism, and literature distribution.

Purpose: . . . to provide training and Biblical resources to local Christians who spread the Gospel, disciple believers, and establish churches in unreached areas.

Year Founded in US: 2012
Income for International Min:
$605,490

Other Personnel
Non-US in own/other country: 67
Home staff: 4
Countries/Regions: Armenia, Belarus, Bulgaria, Cambodia, China (People's Republic of), Lithuania, Macedonia, Moldova, Myanmar (Burma), Philippines, Poland, Romania, Russia, Serbia, Thailand, Ukraine

REACH BEYOND
Formerly: HCJB Global
1065 Garden of the Gods Rd
Colorado Springs, CO 80907 US
Phone: (719) 590-9800
Email: info@reachbeyond.org
Website: reachbeyond.org
Associations: Missio Nexus

A nondenominational service agency of Evangelical tradition engaged in radio or TV broadcasting, community development, mass evangelism, leadership development, medical ministry, including dental or public health, and partnership development.

Purpose: . . . to serve with global partners as the voice and hands of Jesus

Year Founded in US: 1931
Income for International Min:
$15,113,866
Fully Supported US Personnel Working Cross-Culturally
More than 4 years: 95
1–4 years: 2
X-C workers in US: 9
Non-residential: 3
Other Personnel
Short-Term less than 1 year: 159
Non-US in own/other country: 39
Home staff: 61
Countries/Regions: Argentina, Australia, Central Asia, Croatia, Czech Republic, Eastern Europe and Eurasia, Ecuador, France, Ghana, Global Ministry, Guatemala, Japan, Kenya, North Africa,

THE
VOICE &
HANDS
OF JESUS.
TOGETHER.

REACHBEYOND.ORG

Papua New Guinea, Romania, South
Africa, South America, Southeast Asia,
United Kingdom

REACHACROSS
P.O. Box 2047
Lexington, SC 29071 US
Phone: (803) 358-2330
Email: info.us@ReachAcross.net
Website: ReachAcross.us
Associations: Missio Nexus

A nondenominational sending agency of
Evangelical tradition engaged in CPM,
DMM, discipleship, personal or small
group evangelism, relief & aid, and TESOL
or TEFL.

Purpose: . . . to share the Gospel with
Muslims, serving them in practical ways,
and discipling them to follow Jesus.
Year Founded in US: 1964
Income for International Min:
    $1,475,012
*Fully Supported US Personnel Working
Cross-Culturally*
    More than 4 years: 11
    1–4 years: 13
    X-C workers in US: 3
Other Personnel
    Short-Term less than 1 year: 18
    Tentmakers/BAM: 1
    Non-US in own/other country: 65
    Home staff: 5
Countries/Regions: Canada, Global
Ministry, Middle East, North Africa, South
Asia, Southeast Asia, Western Europe

REACHGLOBAL
901 E. 78th St.
Minneapolis, MN 55420 US
Phone: (952) 854-1300
Email: reachglobal@efca.org
Website: wwwgoreachglobal.com
Associations: Missio Nexus

A denominational sending agency of
Congregational tradition engaged in

business as mission, church planting
(establishing), TEE or other extension
education, and leadership development.
Purpose: . . . to glorify God by
multiplying healthy churches among all
people.
Year Founded in US: 1887
*Fully Supported US Personnel Working
Cross-Culturally*
    More than 4 years: 336
    1–4 years: 53
Other Personnel
    Home staff: 82
Countries/Regions: Austria, Belgium,
Bosnia and Herzegovina, Brazil, Bulgaria,
Cameroon, Canada, Central African
Republic, China (People's Republic of),
Democratic Republic of Congo, Costa
Rica, Cyprus, Czech Republic, France,
Germany, Global Ministry, Greece,
Guadeloupe, Haiti, Hungary, India,
Indonesia, Italy, Japan, Jordan, Lebanon,
Macau (China), Malaysia, Mexico,
Mongolia, Netherlands, Panama, Peru,
Philippines, Poland, Portugal, Romania,
Slovakia, Spain, Tajikistan, Tanzania,
Thailand, Turkey, Ukraine

REACHING INDIANS
MINISTRIES INTERNATIONAL
1949 Old Elm Road
Lindenhurst, IL 60046 US
Phone: (847) 265-0630
Email: ministry@rimi.org
Website: rimi.org

An interdenominational support agency of
Fundamental and Independent tradition
engaged in evangelism, childcare/
orphanage programs, missionary
education, theological education, support
of national churches and support of
national workers. (DPE)

Purpose: . . . to expand Christ's kingdom through evangelism and church planting, which is further advanced by leadership development and compassion services.

Income for International Min:
$149,472

Other Personnel
Short-Term less than 1 year: 20
Non-US in own/other country: 810
Home staff: 6
Countries/Regions: India

REACHING JAPAN TOGETHER (RJT)
1340-J Patton Avenue
Asheville, NC 28806 US
Email: RJTAJapan@hotmail.com
Website: rjta.upgjapanmissions.com

A nondenominational support agency of Evangelical tradition engaged in Church Planting (Establishing), Discipleship, Environmental Mission, Networking, Partnership or Coordination, Short-Term Mission Trip Coordination, Tentmaking and related.

Purpose: . . . to help missionaries thrive as they fulfill the Great Commission by responsibly reaching out with the gospel to the unreached and under-reached in Japan.

Year Founded in US: 2012
Income for International Min:
$90,000

Fully Supported US Personnel Working Cross-Culturally
More than 4 years: 2

Other Personnel
Short-Term less than 1 year: 41
Non-US in own/other country: 1
Home staff: 1
Countries/Regions: Japan

REAL IMPACT MISSIONS
PO Box 1532
Gainesville, GA 30503 US
Phone: (800) 774-6746
Email: GoInfo@realimpact.com
Website: realimpact.com

An interdenominational service agency of Evangelical and Independent tradition engaged in childcare or orphanage, community development, student evangelism, addressing human trafficking, medical ministry, including dental or public health, and STM trip coordination.

Purpose: . . . to mobilize individuals and groups for short-term mission trips around the world, which includes strategic evangelism, community development projects, mobile medical clinics, and disaster response teams.

Year Founded in US: 1997
Income for International Min:
$500,000

Fully Supported US Personnel Working Cross-Culturally
Non-residential: 4

Other Personnel
Short-Term less than 1 year: 318
Home staff: 6
Countries/Regions: Global Ministry

RECIPROCAL MINISTRIES INTERNATIONAL
5475 Lee St, Ste. 301
Lehigh Acres, Fl 33971 US
Phone: (239) 368-8390
Email: dan.shoemaker@rmibridge.org
Website: rmibridge.org

A nondenominational sending agency of Baptist and Evangelical tradition engaged in church planting (establishing), community development, discipleship, church, school or general Christian education, partnership development, and STM trip coordination.

Purpose: . . . to mobilize global partnerships to transform lives in Christ.

Year Founded in US: 1988

Income for International Min:
$1,591,000

Fully Supported US Personnel Working Cross-Culturally
More than 4 years: 4
1–4 years: 5

Other Personnel
Short-Term less than 1 year: 304
Non-US in own/other country: 38
Home staff: 7

Countries/Regions: Haiti

REFORMED BAPTIST MISSION SERVICES

P O Box 289
Carlisle, PA 17013 US
Phone: (717) 249-7473
Email: arbca@reformedbaptist.com
Website: arbca.com/rbms

A mission service coordinating member churches to assist one another to send missionaries and plant churches worldwide. (DPE)

Purpose: . . . to advance Christ's kingdom by providing an association in which churches of common confession may find mutual encouragement, assistance, edification and counsel, and to participate in cooperative efforts in church planting, foreign missions, ministerial training, publications and other endeavors deemed appropriate by the Association (ARBCA).

Year Founded in US: 1985

Income for International Min:
$674,213

Fully Supported US Personnel Working Cross-Culturally
More than 4 years: 3

Other Personnel
Non-US in own/other country: 22
Home staff: 3

Countries/Regions: Argentina, Asia, Chile, Colombia, France, Ireland (Republic of), Israel, Jamaica, Kenya, Switzerland, United Kingdom, Unspecified Country

REFORMED CHURCH IN AMERICA – GENERAL SYNOD COUNCIL – GLOBAL MISSION

4500 60th Street, SE
Grand Rapids, Mi 49512 US
Phone: (616) 541-0882
Email: kbogerd@rca.org
Website: rca.org

A denominational sending agency of Evangelical and Reformed tradition engaged in audio recording or distribution, community development, theological education, justice or peace issues, leadership development, and medical ministry, including dental or public health.

Purpose: . . . to equip congregations for ministry—a thousand churches in a million ways doing one thing—following Christ in mission, in a lost and broken world so loved by God.

Year Founded in US: 1857

Income for International Min:
$7,000,000

Fully Supported US Personnel Working Cross-Culturally
More than 4 years: 41
X-C workers in US: 3

Other Personnel
Short-Term less than 1 year: 476
Non-US in own/other country: 19
Home staff: 13

Countries/Regions: Bahrain, Bangladesh, Cambodia, Canada, Colombia, Dominican Republic, Ethiopia, Guatemala, Honduras, Hungary, India, Israel, Italy, Japan, Kenya, Lebanon, Malawi, Mexico, Myanmar (Burma), Nicaragua, Niger, Oman, Peru, Romania, South Sudan, Taiwan (China), Tanzania, Thailand, Turkey

REFORMED EPISCOPAL BOARD OF FOREIGN MISSIONS
4142 Dayflower Dr.
Katy, TX 77449 US
Phone: (800) 732-3433
Email: royalrec1@aol.com
Website: recus.org
A denominational sending agency of Anglican tradition engaged in church planting (establishing), medical ministry, including dental or public health, and Bible translation.
Purpose: . . . to set as the highest priority, biblical worship and declaring commitment to the work of evangelism, the bold and unadulterated proclamation of salvation by grace through faith in the Lord Jesus Christ.
Year Founded in US: 1892
Fully Supported US Personnel Working Cross-Culturally
   More than 4 years: 3
Countries/Regions: Croatia, Cuba, Germany

REHOBOTH MINISTRIES INC.
PO Box 11049
Goldsboro, NC 27532 US
Phone: (910) 703-3098
Email: pgiba3@aol.com
Website: rehobothhaiti.com/
A sending agency of Charismatic and Christian (Restoration Movement) tradition engaged in discipleship, broadcasting, Christian education and theological education. (DPE)
Income for International Min:
   $48,000
Fully Supported US Personnel Working Cross-Culturally
   More than 4 years: 2
Other Personnel
   Non-US in own/other country: 21
Countries/Regions: Haiti

RELIANT MISSION INC.
Formerly: Great Commission Ministries Inc.
11002 Lake Hart Dr, Ste. 100
Orlando, FL 32832-7106 US
Phone: (407) 671-9700
Email: info@reliant.org
Website: reliant.org
Associations: Missio Nexus
A nondenominational service agency of Christian (Plymouth Brethren) and Evangelical tradition engaged in personal or small group evangelism, student evangelism, international student ministry, leadership development, and recruiting or mobilizing for mission.
Purpose: . . . to partner with missional churches and Gospel-centered nonprofits to mobilize support-based missionaries for the Great Commission.
Year Founded in US: 1989
Income for International Min:
   $3,276,380
Fully Supported US Personnel Working Cross-Culturally
   More than 4 years: 18
   1–4 years: 17
   X-C workers in US: 15
Other Personnel
   Home staff: 3
Countries/Regions: Costa Rica, El Salvador, Germany, Honduras, India, Italy, Japan, Kenya, Mexico, Netherlands, Rwanda, Southeast Asia, Spain, Sweden, Thailand, Ukraine, United Kingdom

RESOURCE LEADERSHIP INTERNATIONAL
5335 Gainsberg Road
Bowser, BC V0R 1G0 CA
Phone: (778) 424-2231
Email: administrator@resourceleadership.com
Website: resourceleadership.com

A nondenominational support agency of Evangelical tradition engaged in theological education, leadership development, and literature production.

Purpose: . . . to assist resilient schools that sustain effective theological education and serve the Church in their region.

Year Founded in CA: 1979

Fully Supported CA Personnel Working Cross-Culturally
  Non-residential: 1
Other Personnel
  Non-CA in own/other country: 4
  Home staff: 4
Countries/Regions: Caribbean, Central America, Global Ministry, South America, Vietnam

RESOURCING CHRISTIAN EDUCATION INTERNATIONAL

PO Box 4528
Wheaton, IL 60189 US
Phone: (630) 580-5514
Email: info@rce-international.org
Website: rce-international.org

A nondenominational support agency of Evangelical and Independent tradition engaged in international Christian education (K-12 type schools) church/school, evangelism and TESOL. (DPE)

Purpose: . . . to serve international Christian education ministries in their mission of providing exceptional educational opportunities with a biblical foundation and Christian worldview.

Income for International Min:
  $3,238,754
Other Personnel
  Non-US in own/other country: 150
  Home staff: 2
Countries/Regions: Austria, Colombia, Czech Republic, Ecuador, Japan, Poland, Portugal, Russia, Spain, Ukraine

RIO GRANDE BIBLE INSTITUTE INC.

4300 S. US Hwy. 281
Edinburg, TX 78539-9650 US
Phone: (956) 360-8100
Email: rgbimail@riogrande.edu
Website: riogrande.edu

A nondenominational service agency of Independent tradition engaged in theological education, broadcasting, correspondence courses, missionary education, leadership development and video/film production/distribution. (DPE)

Purpose: . . . exists to glorify God by serving the Hispanic church through equipping leaders, edifying believers, and evangelizing the lost.

Year Founded in US: 1947

Other Personnel
  Short-Term less than 1 year: 84
  Home staff: 118

RIPE FOR HARVEST INC.

1375 E. Grand Ave, #333
Arroyo Grande, CA 93420 US
Phone: (480) 373-9387
Email: rfhphoenix@gmail.com
Website: ripeforharvest.org

A nondenominational sending agency of Evangelical tradition engaged in church planting (establishing), discipleship, mass evangelism, and tentmaking & related.

Purpose: . . . to conduct church services and related missions/ministries in obedience to the Great Commission as found in Matthew 28:18–20.

Year Founded in US: 1979

Fully Supported US Personnel Working Cross-Culturally
  More than 4 years: 33
Other Personnel
  Home staff: 7

Countries/Regions: Afghanistan, Bolivia, Cambodia, Canada, Chile, Czech Republic, Denmark, Ecuador, Ethiopia, France, Haiti, Honduras, Hong Kong (China), Hungary, India, Israel, Japan, Kazakhstan, Kenya, Mexico, Nicaragua, Paraguay, Philippines, Russia, Sierra Leone, South Korea, Spain, Sub-Saharan Africa, Thailand, Tunisia, Ukraine, Zambia, Zimbabwe

ROMANIAN MISSIONARY SOCIETY
PO Box 527
Wheaton, IL 60189-0527 US
Phone: (630) 665-6503
Email: rms@rmsonline.org
Website: rmsonline.org
An interdenominational sending agency of Baptist and Presbyterian tradition engaged in evangelism, broadcasting, children's programs, theological education, literature production and support of national workers. (DPE)
Purpose: . . . to support Christian projects and ministries in Romania.
Income for International Min:
  $425,000
Fully Supported US Personnel Working Cross-Culturally
  Non-residential: 2
Other Personnel
  Short-Term less than 1 year: 1
  Non-US in own/other country: 70
  Home staff: 3
Countries/Regions: Romania

ROSEDALE MENNONITE MISSIONS
2120 E 5th Ave
Columbus, OH 43219 US
Phone: (614) 258-4780
Email: info@rmmoffice.org
Website: rmmweb.org
Associations: Missio Nexus
A denominational sending agency of Mennonite or Anabaptist tradition engaged

in business as mission, church planting (establishing), discipleship, missionary & worker training, tentmaking & related, and youth ministry. (FPC-PE)
Purpose: . . . to establish locally rooted and led, rapidly reproducing churches, prioritizing people groups and locations that are least reached with the Good News.
Fully Supported US Personnel Working Cross-Culturally
  More than 4 years: 25
Other Personnel
  Short-Term less than 1 year: 70
  Tentmakers/BAM: 9
  Non-US in own/other country: 2
  Home staff: 21
Countries/Regions: Africa, Albania, Asia, Bangladesh, Middle East, Spain, Thailand

RP GLOBAL MISSIONS
Formerly: Foreign Mission Board of the Reformed Presbyterian Church of North America
3307 5th Ave.
Beaver Falls, PA 15010 US
Phone: (724) 384-8327
Email: serveChrist@rpglobalmissions.org
Website: rpglobalmissions.org
Associations: Missio Nexus
A denominational sending agency of Presbyterian and Reformed tradition engaged in church planting (establishing), CPM, discipleship, church, school or general Christian education, personal or small group evangelism, and STM trip coordination.
Purpose: . . . to carry on the work of missions in a fashion that is truly Biblical in its objectives, its motives and its methods.
Year Founded in US: 1871
Income for International Min:
  $420,000

Fully Supported US Personnel Working Cross-Culturally
  More than 4 years: 4
  1–4 years: 5
  X-C workers in US: 10
  Non-residential: 8
Other Personnel
  Short-Term less than 1 year: 65
  Tentmakers/BAM: 9
  Non-US in own/other country: 6
  Home staff: 1
Countries/Regions: Central Asia, Cyprus, East Asia, Japan, South Korea, Liberia, South Asia, South Sudan

RREACH

Formerly: Ramesh Richard Evangelism and Church Helps Intl
17110 Dallas Parkway, Ste. 230
Dallas, TX 75248 US
Phone: (972) 528-6100
Email: ramesh@rreach.org
Website: rreach.org
Associations: Missio Nexus

A nondenominational service agency of Reformed tradition engaged in mass evangelism, personal or small group evangelism, Internet evangelism, leadership development, networking, partnership, or coordination, and pastoral training.

Purpose: . . . to change the way people think and hear about the Lord Jesus Christ to the glory of the Father and by the power of the Holy Spirit.

Year Founded in US: 1987
Income for International Min:
  $2,301,717
Other Personnel
  Home staff: 9

RUSSIAN BIBLE SOCIETY INC.

PO Box 6068
Asheville, NC 28816 US
Phone: (828) 681-0370
Email: russianbibles@bellsouth.net

An interdenominational specialized agency of Baptist and Fundamentalist tradition engaged in Bible distribution, literature distribution, literature production, and Bible & other translation. (FPC-PE)

Purpose: . . . to continue providing the Synodal Translation of the Russian Bible, and its translation into many of the minority languages of Russia.

Year Founded in US: 1944
Income for International Min:
  $325,257
Other Personnel
  Home staff: 3

RUSSIAN CHRISTIAN RADIO INC. (OR RCR)

PO Box 1667
Estes Park, CO 80517 US
Phone: (770) 864-6464
Email: info@rcr-us.org
Website: rcrm.org

A nondenominational specialized agency of Evangelical tradition engaged in audio recording or distribution, radio or TV broadcasting, personal or small group evangelism, literature distribution, literature production, and drug & alcohol rehab centers.

Purpose: . . . to spread the Gospel of Jesus Christ, reaching hopeless and broken Russian-speaking people with the transforming love and power of Jesus Christ.

Income for International Min:
  $216,980
Other Personnel
  Short-Term less than 1 year: 20
  Non-US in own/other country: 15
  Home staff: 3
Countries/Regions: Russia

SALEM MINISTRIES INTERNATIONAL

4 Dogwood Crescent
Toronto, ON M1P 3N6 CA
Phone: (416) 993-3556
Email: philipselampal@gmail.com
Website: salemmercyhome.org

A nondenominational support agency of Evangelical and Pentecostal tradition engaged in Bible distribution, childcare or orphanage, church planting (establishing), theological education, mass evangelism, and literature production.

Purpose: . . . to reach the lost at any cost by providing the good news to everyone everywhere.

Year Founded in CA: 2011
Fully Supported CA Personnel Working Cross-Culturally
   More than 4 years: 3
   1–4 years: 10
   Non-residential: 7
Other Personnel
   Short-Term less than 1 year: 11
   Tentmakers/BAM: 4
   Non-CA in own/other country: 16
Countries/Regions: India, United States of America

SALVATION ARMY – CANADA AND BERMUDA TERRITORY, THE

2 Overlea Blvd.
Toronto, ON M4H 1P4 CA
Phone: (416) 425-2111
Email: donor_questions@can.salvationarmy.org
Website: salvationarmy.ca

A denominational sending agency of Evangelical and Wesleyan tradition engaged in relief and/or rehabilitation, camping programs, childcare/orphanage programs, children's programs, church planting, development, Christian education, evangelism, leadership development, and medical work. (DPE)

Year Founded in CA: 1909
Income for International Min:
   $10,000,000
Fully Supported CA Personnel Working Cross-Culturally
   More than 4 years: 22
   1–4 years: 16
   Non-residential: 2
Other Personnel
   Short-Term less than 1 year: 123
Countries/Regions: Africa, Argentina, Australia, Bangladesh, Caribbean, Chile, France, Germany, Pakistan, Papua New Guinea, Russia, Spain, United Kingdom

SAMARITAN'S PURSE

PO Box 3000
Boone, NC 28607 US
Phone: (828) 262-1980
Email: info@samaritan.org
Website: samaritanspurse.org

A nondenominational specialized agency of Evangelical tradition engaged in agricultural assistance, children's ministry, church, school or general Christian education, medical ministry, including dental or public health, persecuted church, and international disaster relief.

Purpose: . . . to provide spiritual and physical aid to hurting people around the world, of people who are victims of war, poverty, natural disasters, disease, and famine with the purpose of sharing God's love through His Son, Jesus Christ.

Year Founded in US: 1970
Fully Supported US Personnel Working Cross-Culturally
   More than 4 years: 5
   1–4 years: 101
Countries/Regions: Bolivia, Cambodia, Democratic Republic of Congo, Ecuador, Ethiopia, Honduras, Iraq, Kenya, Kosovo, Liberia, Mexico, Mongolia, Mozambique, Myanmar (Burma), Niger, Philippines, Sudan, Uganda, Vietnam

SAMARITAN'S PURSE – CANADA
20 Hopewell Way NE
Calgary, AB T3J 5H5 CA
Phone: (800) 663-6500
Email: canada@samaritan.org
Website: samaritanspurse.ca

A nondenominational service agency of Evangelical tradition engaged in relief, development, HIV/AIDS, medical work, partnership development and short-term programs. (DPE)

Purpose: . . . to provide spiritual and physical aid to hurting people around the world . . . to meet the needs of people who are victims of war, poverty, natural disasters, disease, and famine with the purpose of sharing the Good News of God's love through His Son, Jesus Christ . . . to serve the Church worldwide to promote the Gospel of the Lord Jesus Christ.

Income for International Min:
  $39,457,964

Fully Supported CA Personnel Working Cross-Culturally
  Non-residential: 10

Other Personnel
  Short-Term less than 1 year: 496
  Home staff: 73

Countries/Regions: Afghanistan, Cambodia, Hong Kong (China), Jordan, Kosovo, Liberia, Myanmar (Burma), Nepal, Niger, Sudan, Thailand, Vietnam

SAND INTERNATIONAL
PO Box 566
Crete, IL 60417 US
Phone: (708) 367-1605
Email: sand_ministries@yahoo.com

A nondenominational support agency of Evangelical and Pentecostal tradition engaged in agricultural assistance, Bible teaching, community development, church, school or general Christian education, leadership development, and missionary & worker training.

Purpose: . . . to improve the social, physical, and spiritual well-being of individuals, communities, and churches around the world by equipping, training, and demonstrating a "Two-Handed" Gospel of God's love.

Year Founded in US: 1982
Income for International Min:
  $4,000

Other Personnel
  Tentmakers/BAM: 3

Countries/Regions: India, Poland

SANMA (SOUTH ASIA NATIVE MISSIONARY ALLIANCE)
2100 N. Hwy. 360, Ste. 600B
Grand Prairie, TX 75050 US
Phone: (817) 561-6868
Email: contact@sanma.org
Website: sanma.org

A nondenominational service agency of Christian (Plymouth Brethren) tradition engaged in Bible distribution, Bible teaching, community development, church, school or general Christian education, addressing human trafficking, and Bible translation.

Purpose: . . . to design and implement programs that help build sustainable communities and ministries through occupational Christian missions.

Year Founded in US: 1998
Income for International Min:
  $280,355

Fully Supported US Personnel Working Cross-Culturally
  More than 4 years: 1
  1–4 years: 1
  X-C workers in US: 1

Other Personnel
  Short-Term less than 1 year: 1
  Tentmakers/BAM: 37
  Home staff: 2

Countries/Regions: India

SAT-7 NORTH AMERICA

PO Box 2770
Easton, MD 21601 US
Phone: (866) 744-7287
Email: usa@sat7.org
Website: sat7usa.org
Associations: Missio Nexus

An interdenominational specialized agency of Evangelical tradition engaged in Bible teaching, radio or TV broadcasting, children's ministry, theological education, persecuted church, and video-film production or distribution.

Purpose: . . . to provide the churches and Christians of the Middle East and North Africa an opportunity to witness to Jesus Christ through inspirational, informative, and educational television services.

Year Founded in US: 1998
Income for International Min:
$17,080,555

Fully Supported US Personnel Working Cross-Culturally
X-C workers in US: 2
Non-residential: 32

Other Personnel
Short-Term less than 1 year: 9
Non-US in own/other country: 4
Home staff: 14

Countries/Regions: Middle East, North Africa

SCORE INTERNATIONAL

Formerly: Youth on Mission merged with us in 2012
PO Box 9994
Chattanooga, TN 37412 US
Phone: (423) 894-7111
Email: info@scoreintl.org
Website: scoreintl.org

A nondenominational sending agency of Baptist and Evangelical tradition engaged in church planting (establishing), community development, discipleship, mass evangelism, STM trip coordination, and sports ministry.

Purpose: . . . to glorify God through missions in obedience to the Great Commission.

Year Founded in US: 1984

Fully Supported US Personnel Working Cross-Culturally
X-C workers in US: 4

Other Personnel
Short-Term less than 1 year: 6580
Home staff: 12

SCRIPTURE UNION USA

PO Box 215
Valley Forge, PA 19481 US
Phone: (800) 621-5267
Email: info@scriptureunion.org
Website: scriptureunion.org

A service agency of Evangelical tradition engaged in literature distribution, children's programs, discipleship, funds transmission, support of national workers and Bible engagement. (DPE)

Purpose: . . . to help children, young people, and their families know God's love, follow Jesus, and meet with Him daily in His Word.

Year Founded in US: 1959
Income for International Min:
$924,381

SCRIPTURES IN USE

101 S. La Canada, Ste. #49-D
Green Valley, AZ 85614 US
Phone: (520) 648-6400
Email: kentkiefer@siutraining.org
Website: scripturesinuse.org
Associations: Missio Nexus

An interdenominational support agency of Evangelical tradition engaged in church planting (establishing), CPM, DMM, discipleship, missionary & worker training, and orality or storying.

Purpose: . . . to equip and train indigenous, local and regional partner organizations worldwide to communicate the Scriptures using oral Bible strategies in order to evangelize, disciple and plant churches among unreached people groups.

Year Founded in US: 1986
Income for International Min:
$1,098,337
Fully Supported US Personnel Working Cross-Culturally
More than 4 years: 78
1–4 years: 21
X-C workers in US: 6
Non-residential: 99
Other Personnel
Short-Term less than 1 year: 16
Non-US in own/other country: 16700
Home staff: 10
Countries/Regions: Bhutan, Bolivia, Burkina Faso, Cameroon, Chad, Ethiopia, Ghana, Guinea-Bissau, India, Kenya, Kyrgyzstan, Malaysia, Myanmar (Burma), Nepal, Niger, Nigeria, Pakistan, Peru, Russia, Senegal, Tajikistan, Uganda, Uzbekistan, Vietnam

SEED COMPANY
220 Westway Pl, Ste. 100
Arlington, TX 76018 US
Phone: (817) 557-2121
Email: info@tsco.org
Website: theseedcompany.org/
Associations: Missio Nexus

A nondenominational service agency of Evangelical tradition engaged in Bible translation.
Purpose: . . . to accelerate Scripture translation and impact for people without God's Word through Great Commission partnerships.
Year Founded in US: 1993

SELF-HELP INTERNATIONAL
703 2nd Ave NW
Waverly, IA 50677 US
Phone: (319) 352-4040
Email: susan@selfhelpinternational.org
Website: selfhelpinternational.org

A denominational heritage service agency of Methodist tradition engaged in agricultural assistance, community development, leadership development, relief & aid, micro-finance, and clean water.
Purpose: . . . to alleviate hunger by helping people help themselves, by assisting small scale farmers and related enterprises in developing countries to become self-reliant.
Year Founded in US: 1955
Income for International Min:
$349,411
Other Personnel
Short-Term less than 1 year: 18
Non-US in own/other country: 9
Home staff: 2
Countries/Regions: Dominican Republic, East Asia, Guatemala, Haiti, Kenya, Lebanon, Papua New Guinea, Peru, Zambia

SEND INTERNATIONAL INC.
P.O. Box 513
Farmington, MI 48332 US
Phone: (248) 477-4210
Email: info@send.org
Website: send.org
Associations: Missio Nexus

An interdenominational sending agency of Evangelical tradition engaged in church planting (establishing), discipleship, theological education, personal or small group evangelism, leadership development, and tentmaking & related.
Purpose: . . . to mobilize God's people and engage the unreached in order to establish reproducing churches.

Year Founded in US: 1947
Income for International Min:
$12,696,029
Fully Supported US Personnel Working Cross-Culturally
More than 4 years: 275
1–4 years: 8
X-C workers in US: 4
Other Personnel
Short-Term less than 1 year: 102
Tentmakers/BAM: 10
Non-US in own/other country: 93
Home staff: 59
Countries/Regions: Albania, Bulgaria, Central Asia, China (People's Republic of), Croatia, Czech Republic, Germany, Global Ministry, Hong Kong (China), Hungary, Japan, Kosovo, Macedonia, Mexico, North Africa, Philippines, Poland, Romania, Russia, Slovenia, Spain, Taiwan (China), Thailand, Turkey, Uganda, Ukraine

SEND INTERNATIONAL OF CANADA
1-22423 Jefferies Road, RR 5
Komoka, ON N0L 1R0 CA
Phone: (519) 657-6775
Email: info@sendcanada.org
Website: send.org/canada
Associations: Missio Nexus
An interdenominational sending agency of Baptist and Evangelical tradition engaged in camping programs, church planting (establishing), community development, discipleship, recruiting or mobilizing for mission, and TESOL or TEFL.
Purpose: . . . to mobilize God's people to engage the unreached in order to establish reproducing churches.
Year Founded in CA: 1963
Income for International Min:
$3,394,530

Fully Supported CA Personnel Working Cross-Culturally
More than 4 years: 31
1–4 years: 6
X-C workers in CA: 5
Non-residential: 2
Other Personnel
Short-Term less than 1 year: 70
Home staff: 15
Countries/Regions: Japan, Macau (China), Macedonia, Philippines, Russia, Spain, Taiwan (China), Thailand, Uganda, Ukraine, United States of America

SENTINEL GROUP, THE
PO Box 2255
Lynnwood, WA 98036 US
Phone: (800) 668-5657
Email: info@sentinelgroup.org
Website: sentinelgroup.org
A nondenominational support agency of Charismatic and Evangelical tradition engaged in video/DVD production/distribution, missions information service, mission-related research and training. (DPE)
Purpose: . . . to help the Church pray knowledgeably for end-time global evangelization and to enable communities to discover the pathway to genuine revival and societal transformation.
Income for International Min:
$509,000
Other Personnel
Home staff: 16

SERGE
Formerly: World Harvest Mission
101 West Ave, Ste. 305
Jenkintown, PA 19046-2039 US
Phone: (215) 885-1811
Email: info@serge.org
Website: serge.org
Associations: Missio Nexus
A nondenominational sending agency of Evangelical and Reformed tradition

engaged in business as mission, church planting (establishing), personal or small group evangelism, literature production, medical ministry, including dental or public health, and spiritual renewal.

Purpose: . . . to lay down our lives to proclaim the kingdom of Jesus Christ through preaching, healing, and equipping.

Income for International Min: $11,482,466

Fully Supported US Personnel Working Cross-Culturally
  More than 4 years: 72
Other Personnel
  Short-Term less than 1 year: 86
  Home staff: 32

Countries/Regions: Chile, Czech Republic, Germany, Hungary, India, Ireland (Republic of), Italy, Kenya, Netherlands, Romania, Spain, Uganda, Ukraine, United Kingdom

SERVANT PARTNERS

Formerly: Urban Leadership Foundation
PO Box 3144
Pomona, CA 91769 US
Phone: (626) 398-1010
Email: info@servantpartners.org
Website: servantpartners.org

An interdenominational sending agency of Evangelical tradition engaged in church planting (establishing), community development, personal or small group evangelism, justice or peace issues, leadership development, and missionary & worker training.

Purpose: . . . to create churches that transform their urban poor communities.

Year Founded in US: 1993

Income for International Min: $1,400,000

Fully Supported US Personnel Working Cross-Culturally
  More than 4 years: 29
  X-C workers in US: 28
Other Personnel
  Non-US in own/other country: 12
  Home staff: 16

SERVANTS IN FAITH & TECHNOLOGY (SIFAT)

2944 County Rd. 113
Lineville, AL 36266 US
Phone: (256) 396-2015
Email: info@sifat.org
Website: sifat.org

An interdenominational service agency of Ecumenical and Evangelical tradition engaged in camping programs, community development, leadership development, missionary & worker training, technical training, and youth ministry.

Purpose: . . . to share God's love through service, education, and personal involvement with a needy world.

Year Founded in US: 1979

Other Personnel
  Non-US in own/other country: 7
  Home staff: 18

Countries/Regions: Bolivia, Ecuador, Uganda

SERVE GLOBALLY – THE EVANGELICAL COVENANT CHURCH

8303 West Higgins Rd.
Chicago, IL 60631 US
Phone: (773) 784-3000
Email: servegolbally@covchurch.org
Website: covchurch.org/serveglobally

A denominational sending agency of Evangelical tradition engaged in Bible teaching, community development, justice or peace issues, recruiting or mobilizing for mission, relief & aid, and STM trip coordination.

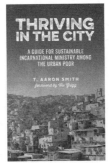

Purpose: . . . to make and deepen disciples, start and strengthen churches, develop leaders, love mercy and do justice, and serve globally—that is, join the rest of the global church in engaging in God's mission.

Year Founded in US: 1885

Fully Supported US Personnel Working Cross-Culturally
   More than 4 years: 67
   1–4 years: 29
   Non-residential: 9

Other Personnel
   Short-Term less than 1 year: 505
   Home staff: 22

Countries/Regions: Cameroon, Central African Republic, China (People's Republic of), Colombia, Democratic Republic of Congo, Czech Republic, Dominican Republic, Ecuador, France, Germany, Global Ministry, Japan, Kenya, Mexico, Mozambique, Nicaragua, Russia, South Sudan, Sweden, Taiwan (China), Thailand

SERVENOW

Formerly: MediaServe
5225 North Academy Blvd, Suite 206
Colorado Springs, CO 80918 US
Phone: (719) 900-1800
Email: office@weservenow.org
Website: weservenow.org

A nondenominational specialized agency of Evangelical tradition engaged in Bible distribution, children's ministry, discipleship, addressing human trafficking, literature distribution, and relief & aid.

Purpose: . . . to serve people in need by caring for orphans, widows, underprivileged children and youth as well as equipping the Church for greater fulfillment of its ministry, and providing humanitarian assistance where needed.

Year Founded in US: 2012

Income for International Min:
   $2,126,282

Other Personnel
   Home staff: 6

SERVLIFE INTERNATIONAL

PO Box 20596
Indianapolis, IN 46220-0596 US
Phone: (317) 544-0484
Email: info@servlife.org
Website: servlife.org

An interdenominational support agency of Evangelical tradition engaged in church planting (establishing), fund raising or transmission, and national worker support.

Purpose: . . . to propel reconciliation and justice by building global community to plant churches, care for children, and fight poverty.

Year Founded in US: 1996

Fully Supported US Personnel Working Cross-Culturally
   More than 4 years: 2

Countries/Regions: India, Nepal

SEVENTH DAY BAPTIST MISSIONARY SOCIETY

P.O. Box 156
Ashaway, RI 02804-0011 US
Phone: (401) 596-4326
Email: info@sdbmissions.org
Website: sdbmissions.org

A denominational sending agency of Baptist tradition engaged in church planting (establishing), fund raising or transmission, leadership development, medical ministry, including dental or public health, relief & aid, and STM trip coordination.

Purpose: . . . to coordinate and carry out . . . the message of salvation through faith in Christ to all who will hear, so they may accept Him as Savior.

Year Founded in US: 1818

Income for International Min:
   $120,488

Other Personnel
  Short-Term less than 1 year: 20
  Non-US in own/other country: 1
  Home staff: 2
Countries/Regions: Jamaica

SEVENTH-DAY ADVENTISTS – GENERAL CONFERENCE – GLOBAL MISSION

12501 Old Columbia Pike
Silver Spring, MD 20904-6601 US
Phone: (301) 680-6005
Email: kajiurar@gc.adventist.org
Website: adventistmission.com

A denominational sending agency of Adventist tradition engaged in evangelism, broadcasting, Christian education, literature production, medical work and mobilization for mission. (DPE)

Purpose: . . . to communicate to all peoples the everlasting Gospel of God's love as revealed in the life, death, resurrection, and high priestly ministry of Jesus Christ.

Year Founded in US: 1904
Income for International Min:
  $53,959,359
Fully Supported US Personnel Working Cross-Culturally
  More than 4 years: 331
  1–4 years: 127
Other Personnel
  Short-Term less than 1 year: 348
  Non-US in own/other country: 499
Countries/Regions: Afghanistan, Albania, Algeria, Angola, Antigua and Barbuda, Argentina, Armenia, Australia, Austria, Bangladesh, Bolivia, Botswana, Brazil, Burkina Faso, Cambodia, Cameroon, Chad, Chile, Colombia, Democratic Republic of Congo, Costa Rica, Côte d'Ivoire, Cyprus, Denmark, Djibouti, Dominican Republic, Ecuador, Egypt, Equatorial Guinea, Ethiopia, France, French Guiana, French Polynesia, Gambia, Georgia, Germany, Ghana, Greece, Guam, Guinea-Bissau, Guyana, Haiti, Honduras, Hong Kong (China), India, Indonesia, Israel, Jamaica, Japan, Kazakhstan, Kenya, North Korea, South Korea, Kuwait, Laos, Lebanon, Lesotho, Liberia, Madagascar, Malawi, Mali, Marshall Islands, Mauritania, Mexico, Federated States of Micronesia, Mongolia, Mozambique, Myanmar (Burma), Nepal, New Caledonia, Nicaragua, Niger, Nigeria, Oceania, Pakistan, Palau, Papua New Guinea, Paraguay, Peru, Philippines, Puerto Rico, Russia, Rwanda, Saint Vincent and the Grenadines, São Tomé and Príncipe, Senegal, Sierra Leone, Singapore, Sint Maarten, Solomon Islands, South Africa, Spain, Sudan, Switzerland, Taiwan (China), Tanzania, Thailand, Togo, Trinidad and Tobago, Tunisia, Turkey, Uganda, Ukraine, United Arab Emirates, United Kingdom, Venezuela, Vietnam, Yemen, Zambia, Zimbabwe

SGM CANADA

1885 Clements Rd, #226
Pickering, ON L1W 3V4 CA
Phone: (905) 683-6482
Email: canada@sgmlifewords.com
Website: sgmcanada.ca

A support agency engaged in Bible engagement & advocacy, Bible distribution, literature distribution, literature production, partnership development and mission-related research. (DPE)

Purpose: . . . to connect Canadians with the Bible and each other.

Year Founded in CA: 1951
Other Personnel
  Home staff: 7

SHELTER FOR LIFE INTL. INC.
10201 Wayzata Blvd. #230
Minnetonka, MN 55305 US
Phone: (763) 253-4085
Email: info@shelter.org
Website: shelter.orgt
Associations: Accord Network

A nondenominational specialized agency of Evangelical tradition engaged in agricultural assistance, TEE or other extension education, and partnership development.

Purpose: . . . to demonstrate God's love by enabling people affected by conflict and disaster to rebuild their communities and restore their lives.

Year Founded in US: 1989

Other Personnel
   Non-US in own/other country: 4
   Home staff: 6
Countries/Regions: Afghanistan, Liberia, Senegal, Tajikistan

SHEPHERD'S SUPPORT INC.
PO Box 701233
San Antonio, TX 78270 US
Phone: (210) 347-4432
Email: info@shepherdssupport.com
Website: shepherdssupport.com

An interdenominational support agency of Evangelical tradition engaged in Bible teaching, leadership development, member care, national worker support, and marriage & family support.

Purpose: . . . to encourage and equip spiritual leaders through educational, economic, and medical support.

Year Founded in US: 2006
Income for International Min:
   $120,000
Other Personnel
   Short-Term less than 1 year: 19
   Home staff: 3

Countries/Regions: Central Asia, East Asia, Eastern Europe and Eurasia, North Africa, South America, South Asia, Southeast Asia, Sub-Saharan Africa

SHIELD OF FAITH MISSION INTERNATIONAL
PO Box 144
Bend, OR 97709 US
Phone: (541) 382-7081
Email: sfmi@sfmiusa.org
Website: sfmiusa.org

A nondenominational sending agency of Evangelical tradition engaged in Bible teaching, discipleship, mass evangelism, literature distribution, missionary & worker training, and tentmaking & related.

Purpose: . . . to advance the kingdom of God through the ministry of reconciliation.

Year Founded in US: 1953
Income for International Min:
   $38,000
Fully Supported US Personnel Working Cross-Culturally
   More than 4 years: 14
   1–4 years: 1
   X-C workers in US: 4
   Non-residential: 20
Other Personnel
   Short-Term less than 1 year: 11
   Tentmakers/BAM: 5
   Non-US in own/other country: 7
   Home staff: 1
Countries/Regions: Bangladesh, Bolivia, Burkina Faso, Canada, Central Asia, Côte d'Ivoire, Ghana, Kenya, South Korea, Laos, Mexico, Myanmar (Burma), Nigeria, Peru, Togo

SIDNEY AND HELEN CORRELL MINISTRIES (DBA CORRELL MISSIONARY MINISTRIES)
Formerly: Christ's Mandate for Missions
PO 7705
Charlotte, NC 28241 US
Phone: (704) 517-2557
Email: missionsbase@gmail.com
Website: eaglemissions.org
A nondenominational support agency of Charismatic and Evangelical tradition engaged in church planting (establishing), personal or small group evangelism, leadership development, national worker support, persecuted church, and STM trip coordination.
Purpose: . . . to add many of the most effective high-impact missionary teams and base support to this growing and powerful missionary force and to network with other missions to see the Great Commission fulfilled and the gospel of the kingdom preached in every nati
Year Founded in US: 1978
Income for International Min:
$734,000
Fully Supported US Personnel Working Cross-Culturally
X-C workers in US: 512
Other Personnel
Short-Term less than 1 year: 173
Home staff: 7

SIM CANADA
10 Huntingdale Blvd
Scarborough, ON M1W 2S5 CA
Phone: (416) 497-2444
Email: info@sim.ca
Website: sim.ca
Associations: Missio Nexus
An interdenominational sending agency of Evangelical tradition engaged in church planting (establishing), TEE or other extension education, evangelism, HIV/AIDS ministry, leadership development, and national worker support.
Purpose: . . . to engage in church planting, development, theological education, HIV/AIDS, medical work and support of national churches.
Year Founded in CA: 1893
Fully Supported CA Personnel Working Cross-Culturally
More than 4 years: 98
Other Personnel
Home staff: 64
Countries/Regions: Angola, Benin, Bolivia, Botswana, Burkina Faso, Chile, Ethiopia, Ghana, Niger, Nigeria, Paraguay, Senegal, South Africa, Sudan, Zambia

SIM USA
PO Box 7900
Charlotte, NC 28241-7900 US
Phone: (704) 588-4300
Email: info@sim.org
Website: simusa.org
Associations: Missio Nexus
An interdenominational sending agency of Evangelical tradition engaged in business as mission, church planting (establishing), theological education, medical ministry, including dental or public health, sports ministry, and youth ministry.
Purpose: . . . to make disciples of the Lord Jesus Christ in communities where He is least known.
Year Founded in US: 1926
Income for International Min:
$11,900,918
Fully Supported US Personnel Working Cross-Culturally
More than 4 years: 489
1–4 years: 41
X-C workers in US: 18
Non-residential: 10

Other Personnel
  Short-Term less than 1 year: 100
  Home staff: 254
Countries/Regions: Angola, Bangladesh, Benin, Bolivia, Botswana, Burkina Faso, Cameroon, Chile, China (People's Republic of), Ecuador, Ethiopia, France, Ghana, Global Ministry, Guinea, India, Japan, Kenya, Liberia, Malawi, Mali, Mozambique, Namibia, Nepal, Niger, Nigeria, North Africa, Paraguay, Peru, Philippines, Senegal, South Africa, South Korea, South Sudan, Southeast Asia, Tanzania, Thailand, Togo, Uganda, Uruguay, Zambia, Zimbabwe

SLAVIC GOSPEL ASSOCIATION
6151 Commonwealth Dr.
Loves Park, IL 61111 US
Phone: (815) 282-8900
Email: info@sga.org
Website: sga.org
Associations: Missio Nexus

An interdenominational support agency of Evangelical tradition engaged in Bible distribution, children's ministry, church planting (establishing), theological education, literature distribution, and national worker support. (FPC-PE)

Purpose: . . . to help the evangelical churches make disciples of the people of the lands of Russia for our Lord and Savior, Jesus Christ, through prayer, strategic ministry, and financial assistance.

Year Founded in US: 1934
Other Personnel
  Home staff: 28

SLAVIC GOSPEL ASSOCIATION – CANADA
55 Fleming Dr., Ste. #26
Cambridge, ON N1T 2A9 CA
Phone: (519) 621-3553
Email: canada@sga.org
Website: sgacanada.ca
Associations: Missio Nexus

An interdenominational sending agency of Baptist and Evangelical tradition engaged in Bible distribution, childcare or orphanage, church planting (establishing), TEE or other extension education, literature production, and national worker support.

Purpose: . . . to serve the churches that Christ is building in Russia, Ukraine and CIS.

Year Founded in CA: 1947
Fully Supported CA Personnel Working Cross-Culturally
  More than 4 years: 3
Other Personnel
  Home staff: 3
Countries/Regions: Belarus, Russia, Ukraine

SLAVIC MISSIONARY SERVICE INC.
PO Box 469
Annandale, NJ 08801 US
Phone: (732) 873-8981
Email: sms@smsinternational.org
Website: smsinternational.org

An interdenominational support agency of Baptist and Evangelical tradition engaged in radio or TV broadcasting, church construction or financing, church planting (establishing), fund raising or transmission, and national worker support.

Purpose: . . . to expedite the missionary work among Slavic people worldwide
Year Founded in US: 1933

Fully Supported US Personnel Working Cross-Culturally
   More than 4 years: 4
Other Personnel
   Home staff: 4
Countries/Regions: Belarus, Moldova, Russia, Ukraine

SOCIETY OF ANGLICAN MISSIONARIES AND SENDERS (SAMS USA)

Formerly: South American Missionary Society
PO Box 399
Ambridge, PA 15003 US
Phone: (724) 266-0669
Email: info@sams-usa.org
Website: sams-usa.org
Associations: Missio Nexus

A denominational sending agency of Anglican or Episcopal tradition engaged in childcare or orphanage, church planting (establishing), community development, discipleship, church, school or general Christian education, and theological education.

Purpose: . . . to see a global Anglican family walking together in the ways of Jesus to spread Kingdom change throughout our communities.

Year Founded in US: 1976
Income for International Min:
   $2,100,000
Fully Supported US Personnel Working Cross-Culturally
   X-C workers in US: 2
Other Personnel
   Short-Term less than 1 year: 45
   Home staff: 9

SOURCE OF LIGHT MINISTRIES INTL. INC.

1011 Mission Rd
Madison, GA 30650 US
Phone: (706) 342-0397
Email: slm@sourcelight.org
Website: sourcelight.org
Associations: ANAM

An interdenominational sending agency of Baptist tradition engaged in church planting (establishing), correspondence courses, TEE or other extension education, and literature distribution.

Purpose: . . . to bring people of every nation, language and ethnicity into a mature relationship with Jesus Christ and into fellowship with a local church family through disseminating Gospel literature, portions of Scripture and Bible correspondence courses.

Year Founded in US: 1952
Other Personnel
   Non-US in own/other country: 28
   Home staff: 55
Countries/Regions: Argentina, Bolivia, Chile, Democratic Republic of Congo, Côte d'Ivoire, Ethiopia, Ghana, Haiti, India, Indonesia, Jamaica, Japan, Kenya, Liberia, Mexico, Myanmar (Burma), Nigeria, Peru, Philippines, Romania, Singapore, South Africa, Togo, Uganda

SOUTH AFRICAN CHRISTIAN MISSION INC.

PO Box 100
Stroh, IN 46789 US
Phone: (260) 351-4626
Email: sacm@sacmonline.org
Website: sacmonline.org

A nondenominational sending agency of Christian (Restoration Movement) tradition engaged in Bible distribution, Bible teaching, radio or TV broadcasting, children's ministry, church, school or general Christian education, and personal or small group evangelism.

Purpose: . . . to further the Kingdom of God and His only begotten Son, Jesus Christ, through the spreading of the Gospel, for the saving of the souls of mankind, and to establish churches after the New Testament pattern.

Year Founded in US: 1972
Income for International Min:
  $94,000

Fully Supported US Personnel Working Cross-Culturally
  More than 4 years: 1
Other Personnel
  Short-Term less than 1 year: 6
  Tentmakers/BAM: 7
Countries/Regions: South Africa

SOUTH AMERICA MISSION
1021 Maxwell Mill Rd, Ste. B
Fort Mill, SC 29708 US
Phone: (803) 802-8580
Email: samusa@southamericamission.org
Website: southamericamission.org
Associations: Missio Nexus

An interdenominational sending agency of Evangelical tradition engaged in aviation, CPM, discipleship, church, school or general Christian education, leadership development, and holistic ministry.

Purpose: . . . to see dynamic churches multiplied across South America that transform local communities and the world by embodying the Kingdom of God.

Year Founded in US: 1914
Income for International Min:
  $4,421,352
Fully Supported US Personnel Working Cross-Culturally
  More than 4 years: 72
  1–4 years: 15
  X-C workers in US: 2
  Non-residential: 2

Other Personnel
  Short-Term less than 1 year: 169
  Non-US in own/other country: 17
  Home staff: 13
Countries/Regions: Bolivia, Brazil, Colombia, Paraguay, Peru

SOUTH AMERICAN MISSIONARY SOCIETY IN CANADA
PO Box 21082
Barrie, ON L4M 6J1 CA
Phone: (905) 855-9018
Email: office@samscanada.ca
Website: samscanada.ca

A denominational sending agency of Anglican and Evangelical tradition engaged in mobilization for mission, evangelism, leadership development and support of national workers. (DPE)

Purpose: . . . to find and send those whom God is calling to the mission field, and to widen and deepen the missionary vision of Canadian Anglicans.

Year Founded in CA: 1980
Income for International Min:
  $9,980,000
Other Personnel
  Short-Term less than 1 year: 2
  Home staff: 3

SOWERS INTERNATIONAL, THE
5677 N. Red Hills Ave
Meridian, ID 83646 US
Phone: (208) 906-2936
Email: gwynn@sower.org
Website: sower.org

An interdenominational support agency of Evangelical tradition engaged in Bible distribution, mass evangelism, missionary & worker training, national worker support, and STM trip coordination.

Purpose: . . . to reach the lost and mobilize the found.

Year Founded in US: 1993

Fully Supported US Personnel Working Cross-Culturally
More than 4 years: 5
Other Personnel
Non-US in own/other country: 9
Home staff: 1
Countries/Regions: Brazil, Cambodia, China (People's Republic of), Colombia, Costa Rica, Global Ministry, Guatemala, Mexico, Myanmar (Burma), Philippines

SPANISH AMERICAN EVANGELISTIC MINISTRIES
650 Linwood Dr
El Paso, TX 79928 US
Phone: (915) 852-2525
Email: staff@saeministries.com
Website: saeministries.com
A denominational service agency of Christian (Restoration Movement) tradition engaged in Bible distribution, business as mission, mass evangelism, literature distribution, and literature production. (FPC-PE)
Purpose: . . . to help evangelistic outreach worldwide . . . to develop a program of benevolence . . . to give a full accounting to all supporting churches.
Year Founded in US: 1964
Other Personnel
Home staff: 3

SPANISH WORLD MINISTRIES
PO Box 542
Winona Lake, IN 46590 US
Phone: (547) 267-8821
Email: info@spanishworld.org
Website: spanishworld.org
A nondenominational support agency of Independent tradition engaged in audio recording or distribution, radio or TV broadcasting, church planting (establishing), correspondence courses, counseling, mass evangelism.

Purpose: . . . to assist local churches in the Spanish speaking world, to carry out the ministry of communicating the Gospel of Christ, and to edify those who believe.
Year Founded in US: 1958
Income for International Min:
$190,000
Other Personnel
Non-US in own/other country: 17
Countries/Regions: Bolivia, Chile, Colombia, Cuba, Dominican Republic, Ecuador, Guatemala, Honduras, Mexico, Paraguay, Peru, Uruguay, Venezuela

SPIRITUAL OVERSEERS SERVICE INTERNATIONAL
PO Box 5985
La Quinta, CA 92248 US
Phone: (760) 345-0906
Email: richfrazer@gmail.com
Website: sosinternational.us
An interdenominational support agency of Evangelical tradition engaged in leadership development, children's programs, support of national churches and training. (DPE)
Income for International Min:
$100,000
Fully Supported US Personnel Working Cross-Culturally
Non-residential: 7
Other Personnel
Short-Term less than 1 year: 3
Non-US in own/other country: 1
Home staff: 3
Countries/Regions: India

SPORTS & REC PLUS
2288 Gunbarrel Rd, Ste. 154-235
Chattanooga, TN 37421 US
Phone: (571) 278-5987
Email: sportsrecplus@cs.com
Website: sportsrecplus.org
A denominational specialized agency of Baptist and Evangelical tradition engaged in church planting (establishing),

discipleship, mass evangelism, medical ministry, including dental or public health, STM trip coordination, and sports ministry. (FPC-PE)

Purpose: . . . to help churches and mission organizations use sports and all forms of recreational activities for outreach, evangelism, church planting and church growth.

Year Founded in US: 1995
Other Personnel
    Home staff: 2

STANDARDS OF EXCELLENCE IN SHORT-TERM MISSION (SOE)
Formerly: DELTA Ministries Intl
1400 NE 136th Ave, Ste. 201
Vancouver, WA 98684 US
Phone: (360) 360-1865
Email: admin@soe.org
Website: soe.org
Associations: Missio Nexus

An interdenominational service agency with a denominational heritage of Baptist and Evangelical tradition engaged in children's ministry, mass evangelism, personal or small group evangelism, medical ministry, including dental or public health, and STM trip coordination.

Purpose: . . . to see lives transformed for the Gospel's sake in all the world through construction, medical and agricultural missions and to serve as a missions resource for the local church as it cultivates Christ-like character in individuals.

Year Founded in US: 1979
Income for International Min:
    $1,138,947
Other Personnel
    Short-Term less than 1 year: 571
    Home staff: 10

STEER INC.
PO Box 1236
Bismarck, ND 58502 US
Phone: (701) 258-4911
Email: steerinc@steerinc.com
Website: steerinc.com

A nondenominational support agency of Evangelical tradition engaged in supporting organizations. (FPC-PE)

Purpose: . . . to advance the work of the Lord Jesus Christ on earth by providing financial support for member mission societies to take the Gospel to all nations of the world before the coming of Jesus Christ.

STEM INTERNATIONAL
PO Box 386001
Minneapolis, MN 55438-6001 US
Phone: (952) 996-1385
Email: info@stemintl.org
Website: stemintl.org

An interdenominational support agency of Christian (Restoration Movement) tradition engaged in evangelism, children's programs, literature distribution, support of national workers, mobilization for mission and short-term programs. (DPE)

Purpose: . . . to extend God's glory through strategic partnerships in short-term mission outreaches, training, and publications

Income for International Min:
    $372,047
Fully Supported US Personnel Working Cross-Culturally
    More than 4 years: 4
    Non-residential: 2
Other Personnel
    Short-Term less than 1 year: 845
    Home staff: 26
Countries/Regions: Belize, Dominican Republic, Haiti, Honduras, Jamaica, Mexico, Paraguay, Trinidad and Tobago, Venezuela

STRAIGHTWAY INC.
45000 Teal Ct, Ste. 200
Highland, MI 48357 US
Phone: (800) 729 2636
Email: dgregg@straightway.com
Website: straightway.com

A nondenominational service agency of Baptist and Presbyterian tradition engaged in services for mission organizations, and relocation & transportation service. (FPC-PE)

Purpose: . . . to provide transportation with a mission.
Year Founded in US: 1968

SUPREME TASK INTERNATIONAL INC.
PO Box 490245
Lawrenceville, GA 30049 US
Phone: (678) 377-0179
Email: supremetask@aol.com
Website: supremetask.org

An interdenominational support agency of Charismatic tradition engaged in discipleship, development, leadership development, literacy work, medical work and relief and/or rehabilitation. (DPE)

Purpose: . . . to train and aid nationals to reach North India with the Gospel.
Year Founded in US: 1989
Income for International Min:
$170,000
Fully Supported US Personnel Working Cross-Culturally
More than 4 years: 2
Other Personnel
Short-Term less than 1 year: 10
Non-US in own/other country: 30
Home staff: 2
Countries/Regions: India

SURFING THE NATIONS
PO Box 860366
Wahiawa, HI 96786 US
Phone: (808) 622-6234
Email: info@surfingthenations.com
Website: surfingthenations.com

An interdenominational specialized agency of Charismatic tradition engaged in short-term programs, discipleship, evangelism, leadership development, relief and/or rehabilitation and youth programs. (DPE)

Purpose: . . . to use the sport of surfing as a tool to communicate the Gospel locally and internationally.
Year Founded in US: 2003
Income for International Min:
$246,380
Fully Supported US Personnel Working Cross-Culturally
Non-residential: 8
Other Personnel
Short-Term less than 1 year: 102
Non-US in own/other country: 2
Home staff: 11
Countries/Regions: Bangladesh, Indonesia, Sri Lanka

TAIWAN HARVEST 119
17595 Harvard Ave, Ste. C235
Irvine, CA 92614 US
Phone: (949) 954-0141
Email: taiwanharvest119@gmail.com
Website: taiwanharvest119.com
Associations: Missio Nexus

An interdenominational sending agency of Baptist and Reformed tradition engaged in children's ministry, CPM, discipleship, missionary & worker training, orality or storying, and recruiting or mobilizing for mission.

Purpose: . . . to take possession of the west coast of Taiwan for Jesus through planting transformational Christian Communities—like lighthouses—in every neighborhood.

TAIWAN HARVEST
豐收 119

Taking possession of the west coast of Taiwan for Jesus through—

- Training Lighthouse Teams how to win the hearts of the people along the west coast of Taiwan for Christ
- Saturating towns with God's Story
- Nurturing transformational Christian Communities, like lighthouses, in every neighborhood

INQUIRIES:taiwanharvest119@gmail.com
Follow us at taiwanharvest119.com!

Mark and Ruth Harbour,33 yrs. church planting in Taiwan, with Executive Committee—(L to R) Rita Chen, Rev. Caleb Yu, Ruth, Mark, Rev. Timothy Tang, Rev. Samuel Hsu, Rev. Caspar Liu, Rev. Steve Hsieh

*JOIN A LIGHTHOUSE TEAM (Minimum 3 to 5 year commitment)
*HOST A TAIWAN HARVEST 119 PRAYER MEETING
*COME FOR A SEMESTER TO DO COMMUNITY SERVICE PROJECTS
*HELP US REACH VIETNAMESE AND INDONESIAN BRIDES & WORKERS

"And Jesus went about all the cities and villages, teaching in their synagogues, and preaching the gospel of the kingdom, and healing every sickness and every disease among the people." (Matt. 9:35)

Year Founded in US: 2015
Income for International Min:
$3,375
Fully Supported US Personnel Working Cross-Culturally
More than 4 years: 2
Other Personnel
Short-Term less than 1 year: 1
Non-US in own/other country: 1
Home staff: 1
Countries/Regions: Taiwan (China)

TALKING BIBLES INTERNATIONAL
PO Box 906
Escondido, CA 92033 US
Phone: (760) 745-8105
Email: info@talkingbibles.org
Website: talkingbibles.org
A nondenominational specialized agency of Reformed tradition engaged in audio recording/distribution, Bible distribution and leadership development. (DPE)
Purpose: . . . A Talking Bible in every language and village . . . A Talking Bible on Sunday in every church.
Income for International Min:
$456,093
Fully Supported US Personnel Working Cross-Culturally
More than 4 years: 2
Other Personnel
Short-Term less than 1 year: 3
Non-US in own/other country: 5
Home staff: 3
Countries/Regions: Africa, India, Unspecified Country

TCM INTERNATIONAL INSTITUTE
PO Box 24560, 6337 Hollister Drive
Indianapolis, IN 46224 US
Phone: (317) 299-0333
Email: tcm@tcmi.org
Website: tcmi.org
Associations: Missio Nexus

A nondenominational support agency of Christian (Restoration Movement) tradition engaged in DMM, discipleship, theological education, and leadership development. (FPC-PE)
Purpose: . . . to develop Christian leaders for significant service through higher learning.
Year Founded in US: 1957
Income for International Min:
$3,056,404
Fully Supported US Personnel Working Cross-Culturally
More than 4 years: 4
1–4 years: 8
Other Personnel
Short-Term less than 1 year: 214
Non-US in own/other country: 10
Home staff: 10
Countries/Regions: Austria, Belarus, Bulgaria, Czech Republic, Estonia, Hungary, Moldova, Poland, Romania, Russia, Ukraine

TEACHBEYOND CANADA
2121 Henderson Hwy.
Winnipeg, MB R2G 1P8 CA
Phone: (204) 334-0055
Email: jtm@janzteam.org
Website: teachbeyond.org
A nondenominational sending agency of Evangelical tradition engaged in Christian education, business as mission, camping programs, evangelism, member care and mobilization for mission. (DPE)
Purpose: . . . to provide transformational education services to children and adults regardless of gender, ethnicity, or religion in order to promote holistic personal growth and enduring social benefit.
Income for International Min:
$1,646,862

Fully Supported CA Personnel Working Cross-Culturally
  More than 4 years: 36
  1–4 years: 14
Other Personnel
  Short-Term less than 1 year: 34
  Non-CA in own/other country: 3
  Home staff: 9
Countries/Regions: Belarus, Bolivia, Brazil, Germany, Malaysia, Mexico, Moldova, Paraguay, Switzerland

TEACHBEYOND USA
PO Box 6248
Bloomingdale, IL 60108 US
Phone: (800) 381-0076
Email: info@teachbeyond.org
Website: teachbeyond.org
Associations: Missio Nexus

A nondenominational sending agency of Evangelical tradition engaged in business as mission, church, school or general Christian education, management consulting or training, recruiting or mobilizing for mission, STM trip coordination, and TESOL or TEFL.

Purpose: . . . to offer teaching and learning services to all regardless of gender, ethnicity, or religion in order to promote holistic personal growth and enduring social benefit.

Year Founded in US: 1980
Income for International Min:
  $9,054,648
Fully Supported US Personnel Working Cross-Culturally
  More than 4 years: 475
  1–4 years: 161
Other Personnel
  Home staff: 22
Countries/Regions: Global Ministry

TEAM (THE EVANGELICAL ALLIANCE MISSION)
400 S. Main Place
Carol Stream, IL 60188 US
Phone: (630) 653-5300
Email: info@team.org
Website: team.org
Associations: Missio Nexus

An interdenominational sending agency of Evangelical tradition engaged in church planting (establishing), discipleship, theological education, personal or small group evangelism, leadership development, and medical ministry, including dental or public health.

Purpose: . . . to help churches send missionaries to establish reproducing churches among the nations to the glory of God. We seek to do this wherever the most people have the greatest need in collaboration with churches anywhere.

Year Founded in US: 1890
Income for International Min:
  $27,409,000
Fully Supported US Personnel Working Cross-Culturally
  More than 4 years: 575
  1–4 years: 106
  X-C workers in US: 12
  Non-residential: 2
Other Personnel
  Short-Term less than 1 year: 125
  Non-US in own/other country: 4
  Home staff: 138
Countries/Regions: Australia, Austria, Brazil, Central Asia, Chad, Costa Rica, Czech Republic, East Asia, France, Germany, Global Ministry, Greece, Guatemala, Honduras, Ireland (Republic of), Italy, Japan, Mexico, Middle East, Mozambique, North Africa, Papua, Peru, Philippines, Portugal, South Africa, Southeast Asia, Spain, Sub-Saharan Africa, Taiwan (China), Turkey, Ukraine, Zimbabwe

TEAM EXPANSION INC.

4112 Old Routt Rd.
Louisville, KY 40299 US
Phone: (502) 719-0007
Email: info@teamexpansion.org
Website: teamexpansion.org
Associations: Missio Nexus

A nondenominational sending agency of Christian (Restoration Movement) tradition engaged in CPM, DMM, personal or small group evangelism, leadership development, networking, partnership, or coordination, recruiting or mobilizing for mission.

Purpose: . . . to multiple disciples and churches among the unreached.

Year Founded in US: 1978

Fully Supported US Personnel Working Cross-Culturally
    More than 4 years: 142
    1–4 years: 4
    X-C workers in US: 18
    Non-residential: 4

Other Personnel
    Short-Term less than 1 year: 24
    Tentmakers/BAM: 2
    Non-US in own/other country: 20
    Home staff: 30

Countries/Regions: Central Asia, East Asia, Eastern Europe and Eurasia, Ecuador, Ghana, Ireland (Republic of), Italy, Japan, Mexico, Middle East, Mongolia, North Africa, Philippines, South Asia, Southeast Asia, Spain, Sub-Saharan Africa, Taiwan (China), Tanzania, Venezuela

TEAM OF CANADA

Formerly: The Evangelical Alliance Mission of Canada
#372-16 Midlake Blvd SE
Calgary, AB T2X 2X7 CA
Phone: (800) 295-4160
Email: info@teamcanada.org
Website: teamcanada.org
Associations: Missio Nexus

An interdenominational sending agency of Evangelical tradition engaged in church planting (establishing), discipleship, personal or small group evangelism, leadership development, and TESOL or TEFL.

Purpose: . . . to help churches send missionaries to establish reproducing churches among the nations to the glory of God. We seek to do this wherever the most people have the greatest need in collaboration with churches anywhere.

Year Founded in CA: 1945

Fully Supported CA Personnel Working Cross-Culturally
    More than 4 years: 41
    1–4 years: 6

Other Personnel
    Short-Term less than 1 year: 33
    Home staff: 3

Countries/Regions: Global Ministry

TEAMS FOR MEDICAL MISSIONS

PO Box 215
Macungie, PA 18062 US
Phone: (610) 398-0070
Email: teams@t4mm.org
Website: t4mm.org
Associations: Missio Nexus

A nondenominational sending agency of Evangelical and Independent tradition engaged in children's ministry, theological education, personal or small group evangelism, medical ministry, including dental or public health, relief & aid, and youth ministry.

Purpose: . . . to strengthen Jamaican churches which will have the commitment, ability, and resources to make obedient disciples of Jesus Christ.

Fully Supported US Personnel Working Cross-Culturally
    More than 4 years: 5

Other Personnel
Short-Term less than 1 year: 80
Home staff: 3
Countries/Regions: Jamaica

TECH SERVE INTERNATIONAL INC.
P. O. Box 598, 13 Thomas Drive
Greenbrier, AR 72058 US
Phone: (501) 679-2120
Email: info@techserve.org
Website: techserve.org
A nondenominational specialized agency
of Evangelical tradition engaged in services
for mission organizations, and technical
assistance. (FPC-PE)
Purpose: . . . to support the technological
needs of contemporary missionaries and
ministries.
Other Personnel
Short-Term less than 1 year: 50
Home staff: 5

TEEN MISSION USA INC.
DBA MISSION JOURNEYS
940 Holly Springs Drive
Lexington, KY 40504 US
Phone: (859) 278-3202
Email: tmusa@teenmission.org
Website: missionjourneys.org
A nondenominational service agency
of Christian (Restoration Movement)
tradition engaged in church construction
or financing, church development, mass
evangelism, literature distribution, STM trip
coordination, and youth ministry. (FPC-PE)
Purpose: . . . to connect people to
worthwhile mission projects and to
challenge and change lives in churches
and communities throughout the world for
Christ.
Year Founded in US: 1970
Income for International Min:
$350,000

TEEN MISSIONS
INTERNATIONAL INC.
885 E. Hall Rd.
Merritt Island, FL 32953 US
Phone: (321) 453-0350
Email: info@teenmissions.net
Website: teenmissions.org
An interdenominational sending agency
engaged in short-term programs, children's
programs, development, Christian
education, missionary education, literacy
work, services for other agencies,
missionary training, training, video/film
production/distribution, youth programs,
children at risk, HIV/AIDS and sports
program ministry. (DPE)
Purpose: . . . to challenge, train, and
disciple young people, exposing them to
worldwide missions.
Income for International Min:
$2,926,115
*Fully Supported US Personnel Working
Cross-Culturally*
More than 4 years: 13
1–4 years: 17
Non-residential: 14
Other Personnel
Short-Term less than 1 year: 800
Non-US in own/other country: 173
Home staff: 40
Countries/Regions: Australia, Belize,
Brazil, Cambodia, Cameroon, Ecuador,
Honduras, India, Indonesia, Madagascar,
Malawi, Mongolia, New Zealand,
Philippines, Russia, South Africa, Tanzania,
Uganda, Zambia, Zimbabwe

THE BRETHREN CHURCH INC.
524 College Ave.
Ashland, OH 44805 US
Phone: (419) 289-1708
Email: brethren@brethrenchurch.org
Website: brethrenchurch.org
A denominational sending agency of
Brethren tradition engaged in leadership

development, childcare/orphanage programs, church planting, missionary education, theological education and support of national churches. (DPE)

Purpose: . . . to embrace a new day of transformed leadership, resulting in transformed congregations, whose mission is the transformation of their communities in the power of the Holy Spirit.

Income for International Min: $730,000

Fully Supported US Personnel Working Cross-Culturally
   More than 4 years: 1
   Non-residential: 1
Other Personnel
   Short-Term less than 1 year: 100
   Non-US in own/other country: 168
   Home staff: 7
Countries/Regions: Argentina, Chile, Colombia, India, Malaysia, Mexico, Paraguay, Peru, Philippines, Spain

THE CENTERS FOR APOLOGETICS RESEARCH (CFAR)
P O Box 1196
San Juan Capistrano, CA 92693 US
Phone: (949) 496-2000
Email: centersforapologetics@gmail.com
Website: TheCenters.org
A nondenominational service agency of Evangelical tradition engaged in apologetics, radio or TV broadcasting, theological education, Internet discipleship or training, literature production, and research.

Purpose: . . . to equip Christians in the developing world for discernment, the defense of the faith, and cult evangelism.

Year Founded in US: 1998
Other Personnel
   Non-US in own/other country: 12
   Home staff: 2
Countries/Regions: Brazil, Ethiopia, Hungary, Russia, Uganda, Ukraine

THE CHRISTIAN AND MISSIONARY ALLIANCE
8595 Explorer Driver
Colorado Springs, CO 80920 US
Phone: (719) 599-5999
Email: im@cmalliance.org
Website: cmalliance.org
Associations: Missio Nexus

A denominational sending agency of Evangelical tradition engaged in church planting (establishing), discipleship, theological education, personal or small group evangelism, and leadership development. (FPC-PE)

Purpose: . . . to know Jesus Christ; exalt Him as Savior, sanctifier, healer, and coming king; and complete His Great Commission.

Year Founded in US: 1887
Income for International Min: $38,050,624

Fully Supported US Personnel Working Cross-Culturally
   More than 4 years: 888
Other Personnel
   Short-Term less than 1 year: 1729
   Tentmakers/BAM: 151
   Home staff: 22
Countries/Regions: Africa, Asia, Central Asia, Europe, Latin America, Unspecified Country

THE ESTHER SCHOOL – DYNAMIC YOUTH MINISTRIES
1333 Alger St SE
Grand Rapids, MI 49507 US
Phone: (616) 241-5616
Email: info@estherschool.org
Website: estherschool.org
A nondenominational support agency of Presbyterian and Reformed tradition engaged in church, school or general Christian education.

Purpose: . . . to provide a holistic, Christian education that develops the passion and skills students need to become servant leaders in the Kingdom of God.

Income for International Min:
$450,000

Other Personnel
Short-Term less than 1 year: 53
Home staff: 1

THE FREE METHODIST CHURCH IN CANADA
4315 Village Centre Court
Mississauga, ON L4Z 1S2 CA
Phone: (905) 848-2600
Email: info@fmcic.ca
Website: fmcic.ca
Associations: Missio Nexus

A denominational sending agency of Evangelical and Methodist tradition engaged in childcare or orphanage, church planting (establishing), leadership development, partnership development, and relief & aid.

Purpose: . . . to establish a healthy church within the reach of all people in Canada and beyond.

Year Founded in CA: 1876
Income for International Min:
$322,557

Fully Supported CA Personnel Working Cross-Culturally
More than 4 years: 6
Non-residential: 1
Other Personnel
Short-Term less than 1 year: 12
Tentmakers/BAM: 2
Non-CA in own/other country: 30
Home staff: 2
Countries/Regions: Cambodia, Ghana, Global Ministry, Kenya, Niger, Sri Lanka, Taiwan (China), Thailand

THE GOD'S STORY PROJECT
PO Box 187
Hemet, CA 92546 US
Phone: (951) 658-1619
Email: info@gods-story.org
Website: gods-story.org

A nondenominational sending agency of Evangelical tradition engaged in audio recording or distribution, Bible teaching, discipleship, orality or storying, Bible translation, and video-film production or distribution. (FPC-PE)

Purpose: . . . to promote the video's translation into foreign languages and to advance and oversee its distribution around the world, along with the use of Simply The Story and TGSP's other accompanying tools.

Year Founded in US: 1998
Income for International Min:
$400,000

Other Personnel
Short-Term less than 1 year: 60
Tentmakers/BAM: 4
Non-US in own/other country: 11
Countries/Regions: Ethiopia, India, Kenya, Myanmar (Burma), Nepal, Uganda, Zambia

THE INNER-CITY CHURCH PLANTING MISSION
P.O. Box 7 -
Grandville, MI 49504 US
Phone: (616) 970-4432
Email: danielschutte@sbcglobal.net
Website: citiesforchrist.org

An interdenominational sending agency of Baptist and Brethren tradition engaged in audio recording or distribution, church planting (establishing), discipleship, mass evangelism, personal or small group evangelism, and literature distribution.

Purpose: . . . to bring glory to the Lord Jesus Christ, edification to the saints, and salvation to the spiritually lost through the distribution of His gospel and His word.
Year Founded in US: 1980
Income for International Min:
  $5,000
Other Personnel
  Home staff: 4

THE KERUSSO INSTITUTE FOR GLOBAL LEADERS

P.O. Box 6871
McKinney, TX 75071 US
Phone: (469) 307-3087
Email: jay@kerussoinstitute.org
Website: kerussofoundation.org
An interdenominational service agency of Baptist and Evangelical tradition engaged in TEE or other extension education, and leadership development.
Purpose: . . . to build a movement of mature, authentic, servant-hearted, Global Leaders who bring the truth and transforming power of the gospel to their communities, countries, the region, and the world through multiplying and self-sustaining strategies.
Year Founded in US: 2008
Income for International Min:
  $176,000
Fully Supported US Personnel Working Cross-Culturally
  Non-residential: 8
Other Personnel
  Short-Term less than 1 year: 2
  Non-US in own/other country: 3
  Home staff: 3
Countries/Regions: Burundi, Cambodia, China (People's Republic of), Hong Kong (China), India, Vietnam

THE MASTER'S FOUNDATION

1290 Eglinton Ave. E, Ste. 5
Missisauga, ON L4W 1K8 CA
Phone: (905) 602-1350
Email: sgw@globalserve.net
Website: mastersfoundation.org
An interdenominational support agency of Evangelical and Pentecostal tradition engaged in childcare/orphanage programs, Bible distribution, broadcasting, church construction, relief and/or rehabilitation and short-term programs. (DPE)
Year Founded in CA: 1983
Income for International Min:
  $447,601
Other Personnel
  Short-Term less than 1 year: 11
  Non-CA in own/other country: 9
Countries/Regions: Ukraine

THE MASTERS MISSION

PO Box 547, 2902 Mission Road
Robbinsville, NC 28771 US
Phone: (828) 479-6873
Email: tmmteasdale@uuplus.com
Website: mastersmission.org
A nondenominational sending agency of Baptist and Evangelical tradition engaged in Bible teaching, childcare or orphanage, church planting (establishing), community development, discipleship, and missionary & worker training. (FPC-PE)
Purpose: . . . to enable and inspire others to bring the love of God through Christ to all people.
Year Founded in US: 1979
Income for International Min:
  $757,227
Fully Supported US Personnel Working Cross-Culturally
  X-C workers in US: 4
Other Personnel
  Home staff: 9

Countries/Regions: Democratic Republic of Congo, Ecuador, India, Israel, Kazakhstan, Kenya, Nigeria, Romania, Uganda

THE NAVIGATORS
P.O. Box 6000
Colorado Springs, CO 80934 US
Phone: (719) 594-2582
Email: navmissions@navigators.org
Website: navmissions.org
Associations: Accord Network, Missio Nexus

A nondenominational sending agency of Evangelical tradition engaged in DMM, discipleship, personal or small group evangelism, and leadership development.

Purpose: . . . to advance the Gospel of Jesus and His Kingdom into the nations through spiritual generations of laborers living and discipling among the lost.

Year Founded in US: 1933
Income for International Min:
  $3,037,000

Fully Supported US Personnel Working Cross-Culturally
  More than 4 years: 287
  X-C workers in US: 115

Other Personnel
  Short-Term less than 1 year: 280
  Non-US in own/other country: 266
  Home staff: 19

Countries/Regions: Argentina, Australia, Brazil, Bulgaria, Burundi, Cameroon, Canada, Colombia, Dominican Republic, France, Ghana, Global Ministry, Hungary, Italy, Jamaica, Japan, Kenya, Latvia, Mexico, Mongolia, Netherlands, New Zealand, Philippines, Slovakia, Spain, Thailand, Uganda, Uruguay

THE PENTECOSTAL ASSEMBLIES OF CANADA
2450 Milltower Court
Mississauga, ON L5N 5Z6 CA
Phone: (905) 542-7400
Email: info@paoc.org
Website: paoc.org
Associations: Missio Nexus

A denominational sending agency of Pentecostal tradition engaged in childcare or orphanage, church planting (establishing), discipleship, personal or small group evangelism, missionary & worker training, and recruiting or mobilizing for mission.

Purpose: . . . to glorify God by making disciples everywhere by proclaiming and practising the gospel of Jesus Christ in the power of the Holy Spirit.

Year Founded in CA: 1919
Income for International Min:
  $18,300,000

Fully Supported CA Personnel Working Cross-Culturally
  More than 4 years: 200
  1–4 years: 32
  X-C workers in CA: 12

Other Personnel
  Short-Term less than 1 year: 35
  Non-CA in own/other country: 16
  Home staff: 17

Countries/Regions: Angola, Bangladesh, Brazil, Cambodia, Caribbean, Central America, Cuba, Dominican Republic, Eastern Europe and Eurasia, El Salvador, Estonia, Ethiopia, France, Germany, Global Ministry, Guatemala, Guinea, Haiti, Honduras, India, Israel, Italy, Jamaica, Japan, Kenya, Lithuania, Malawi, Malaysia, Mozambique, Oceania, Peru, Philippines, Romania, Russia, Senegal, Slovakia, South Africa, South America, South Asia, Southeast Asia, Spain, Sri Lanka, Sub-Saharan Africa, Switzerland,

For two-thirds of a century, Navigators have served around the globe. We're **launching and developing new generations** to sacrificially advance Jesus' Kingdom among the nations.

THE NAVIGATORS®

Living and discipling in over 50 nations

Community and collegiate missions

Community-based discipleship with those in poverty

Professionals working with nationals to build nations

Missional business

Teaching English

Tanzania, Thailand, Turkey, Uganda, Ukraine, United Kingdom, Zambia, Zimbabwe

THE PRESBYTERIAN CHURCH IN CANADA

50 Wynford Drive
Toronto, ON M3C 1J7 CA
Phone: (416) 441-1111
Email: im@presbyterian.ca
Website: presbyterian.ca

A denominational sending agency of Presbyterian tradition engaged in community development, TEE or other extension education, theological education, leadership development, partnership development, and Bible translation.

Purpose: . . . as God sent Christ to us, to proclaim Christ in word and deed through evangelism, the offer of salvation to all people in the power of the Holy Spirit, to be received through faith in Christ.

Year Founded in CA: 1875
Income for International Min:
    $1,370,000

Fully Supported CA Personnel Working Cross-Culturally
    More than 4 years: 2
    1–4 years: 10
    Non-residential: 2
Other Personnel
    Short-Term less than 1 year: 23
    Non-CA in own/other country: 1
    Home staff: 2
Countries/Regions: Hungary, India, Japan, Kyrgyzstan, Malawi, Nepal, Nicaragua, Pakistan, Taiwan (China), Ukraine

THE SALVATION ARMY USA NATIONAL HEADQUARTERS

615 Slaters Lane
Alexandria, VA 22314 US
Phone: (703) 684-5500
Email: SAWSO.Communications@usn.salvationarmy.org
Website: salvationarmyusa.org/
Associations: Accord Network

A denominational sending agency of Evangelical tradition engaged in childcare or orphanage, church, school or general Christian education, addressing human trafficking, medical ministry, including dental or public health, relief & aid, and technical assistance.

Purpose: . . . to preach the gospel of Jesus Christ and to meet human needs in His name without discrimination.

Year Founded in US: 1880
Income for International Min:
    $38,700,651

Fully Supported US Personnel Working Cross-Culturally
    More than 4 years: 12
    1–4 years: 60
Other Personnel
    Short-Term less than 1 year: 23
    Home staff: 28
Countries/Regions: Argentina, Australia, Brazil, Canada, Costa Rica, Estonia, Haiti, Indonesia, Italy, Jamaica, Japan, Kenya, Moldova, New Zealand, Nigeria, Peru, Singapore, South Africa, South Korea, Spain, Switzerland, Tanzania, Thailand, Trinidad and Tobago, United Kingdom, Zambia

THE UPSTREAM COLLECTIVE

PO Box 23871
Knoxville, TN 37933 US
Phone: (865) 230-3949
Email: info@theupstreamcollective.org
Website: theupstreamcollective.org

A nondenominational service agency of Evangelical tradition engaged in business as mission, theological education, member care, missionary & worker training, and partnership development.

Purpose: . . . to equip churches to more effectively send out their members to reach the nations next door and all over the world by teaching them essential skills that will enable them to think and act like missionaries.

Year Founded in US: 2009

Other Personnel
  Short-Term less than 1 year: 14
  Home staff: 6

THE VOICE OF THE MARTYRS

PO Box 443
Bartlesville, Ok 74005-0443 US
Phone: (918) 337-8015
Email: thevoice@vom-usa.org
Website: persecution.com

A nondenominational specialized agency of Ecumenical and Evangelical tradition engaged in Bible distribution, church planting (establishing), personal or small group evangelism, national worker support, persecuted church, and relief & aid.

Purpose: . . . to serve persecuted Christians through spiritual and practical assistance and leading other members of the body of Christ into fellowship with them.

Year Founded in US: 1967
Income for International Min:
  $35,631,000

Fully Supported US Personnel Working Cross-Culturally
  More than 4 years: 39

Other Personnel
  Non-US in own/other country: 23
  Home staff: 9

Countries/Regions: Caribbean, East Asia, Eastern Europe and Eurasia, Global Ministry, Middle East, North Africa, South America, South Asia, Southeast Asia, Sub-Saharan Africa

THE WARAY-WARAY PROJECT

414 Highland Drive
Bartlesville, OK 74003 US
Phone: (918) 336-0750
Email: mail.waray@yahoo.com
Website: waray.org

A nondenominational service agency of Christian (Restoration Movement) tradition engaged in radio or TV broadcasting, church planting (establishing), personal or small group evangelism, and relief & aid.

Purpose: . . . to assist Filipino natives in evangelizing the Waray-Waray tribal group.

Income for International Min:
  $16,000

Other Personnel
  Non-US in own/other country: 9
Countries/Regions: Philippines

THE WORD FOR THE WORLD (TWFTW)

PO Box 26363
Colorado Springs, CO 80936 US
Phone: (719) 594-2052
Email: admin-us@twftw.org
Website: twftw.org

A nondenominational sending agency of Evangelical tradition engaged in Bible translation. (FPC-PE)

Purpose: . . . to enable persons, ministries and organizations from language communities that do not have the Bible in their own language yet to take responsibility for Bible translation and related activities and to ensure its availability and accessibility.

thrive
empowering global women

www.thriveministry.org
info@thriveministry.org
(303) 985-2148

Providing retreats and resources to
encourage **YOUR** missionary women.

"*I had lost sight of the God I serve and who I was in Him. All I knew for sure was that something needed to be different. Then I arrived at a THRIVE retreat. God began to break through the fog in my heart and I sensed it again... hope! I believe Thrive quite literally saved my life.*" - Global Woman Serving in Cape Town

Fully Supported US Personnel Working Cross-Culturally
  More than 4 years: 4
Other Personnel
  Non-US in own/other country: 103
Countries/Regions: Democratic Republic of Congo, Ethiopia, India, Malawi, Slovakia, South Africa, Tanzania, United Kingdom, Zambia, Zimbabwe

THINGS TO COME MISSION
P.O. Box 127
Beech Grove, IN 46107 US
Phone: (317) 783-0300
Email: tcm@tcmusa.org
Website: tcmusa.org
A denominational sending agency of Evangelical and Independent tradition engaged in Bible teaching, children's ministry, church development, church planting (establishing), theological education, and personal or small group evangelism.
Purpose: . . . to prepare people for Christ's return through the methods of the Apostle Paul.
Year Founded in US: 1955
Income for International Min:
  $1,012,730
Fully Supported US Personnel Working Cross-Culturally
  More than 4 years: 13
  1–4 years: 3
  X-C workers in US: 2
  Non-residential: 2
Other Personnel
  Short-Term less than 1 year: 17
  Non-US in own/other country: 49
  Home staff: 1
Countries/Regions: Brazil, Cambodia, Global Ministry, Indonesia, Kenya, Malaysia, Myanmar (Burma), Philippines, Singapore, South Africa, Southeast Asia, Thailand, Uganda, United Kingdom

THRIVE
Formerly: Women of the Harvest
P.O. Box 151297
Lakewood, CO 80215-9297 US
Phone: (303) 985-2148
Email: kris@thriveministry.org
Website: thriveministry.org
Associations: Missio Nexus
A nondenominational service agency of Christian (Restoration Movement) tradition engaged in Online Information, networking, partnership, or coordination, prayer-intercession, STM trip coordination, and spiritual renewal.
Purpose: . . . to encourage and empower global women to thrive and to be their advocate.
Year Founded in US: 1977
Income for International Min:
  $715,278
Other Personnel
  Short-Term less than 1 year: 120
  Home staff: 10

TIME MINISTRIES
Formerly: Teen Institute of Missionary Evangelism
PO Box 61408
Vancouver, WA 98666 US
Phone: (214) 828-1113
Email: timeministries@timeministries.org
Website: timeministries.org
Associations: Missio Nexus
A nondenominational sending agency of Evangelical tradition engaged in children's ministry, discipleship, personal or small group evangelism, STM trip coordination, sports ministry, and serve the local church.
Purpose: . . . to glorify God through changing lives by leading short-term groups to the mission field to serve local churches in need of additional resources and personnel.
Income for International Min:
  $641,082

Fully Supported US Personnel Working Cross-Culturally
    More than 4 years: 5
Other Personnel
    Short-Term less than 1 year: 360
    Non-US in own/other country: 7
    Home staff: 5
Countries/Regions: Dominican Republic, Mexico

TIMOTHY LEADERSHIP TRAINING INSTITUTE
3300 Burton Street SE, Ste. 105
Grand Rapids, MI 49546 US
Phone: (616) 647-5554
Email: tlti@tlti.org
Website: tlti.org
A denominational heritage service agency of Christian Reformed tradition engaged in leadership development.
Purpose: . . . to equip ministry partners to train pastors, evangelists and lay leaders worldwide to make a global difference in their congregations and communities.
Year Founded in US: 1997
Fully Supported US Personnel Working Cross-Culturally
    More than 4 years: 2
    Non-residential: 1
Other Personnel
    Non-US in own/other country: 3
Countries/Regions: Global Ministry

TIMOTHY TWO PROJECT INTERNATIONAL
PO Box 7889
Wilmington, NC 28406-7889 US
Phone: (631) 855-3064
Email: steve@timothytwo.org
Website: TimothyTwo.org
An interdenominational service agency of Presbyterian and Reformed tradition engaged in Bible teaching, children's ministry, discipleship, and theological education.

Purpose: . . . to train indigenous pastors in the essential doctrines of the faith and to equip them to train others.
Year Founded in US: 2011
Other Personnel
    Short-Term less than 1 year: 5

TITUS INTERNATIONAL
1515 McBrien Rd.
Chattanooga, TN 37412 US
Phone: (423) 867-7079
Email: office@titusinternational.org
Website: titusinternational.org
A denominational heritage service agency of Baptist tradition engaged in camping programs, church planting (establishing), discipleship, personal or small group evangelism, medical ministry, including dental or public health, and missionary & worker training.
Purpose: . . . to train nationals to reach their world.
Year Founded in US: 1984
Income for International Min:
    $950,000
Fully Supported US Personnel Working Cross-Culturally
    More than 4 years: 16
    X-C workers in US: 3
Other Personnel
    Short-Term less than 1 year: 110
    Non-US in own/other country: 80
    Home staff: 3
Countries/Regions: Austria, Azerbaijan, Czech Republic, France, Moldova, Philippines, Romania, Russia, Ukraine

TMS GLOBAL
Formerly: The Mission Society
6234 Crooked Creek Rd
Norcross, GA 30092 US
Phone: (800) 478-8963
Email: info@themissionsociety.org
Associations: Missio Nexus

A nondenominational with a denominational heritage sending agency of Evangelical tradition engaged in church development, community development, discipleship, leadership development, and networking, partnership, or coordination.

Purpose: . . . to mobilize and deploy the body of Christ globally to join Jesus in His mission, especially among the least-reached peoples.

Fully Supported US Personnel Working Cross-Culturally
    More than 4 years: 102
    1–4 years: 4
    X-C workers in US: 4
    Non-residential: 27
Other Personnel
    Tentmakers/BAM: 8
    Non-US in own/other country: 6

Countries/Regions: Brazil, Canada, China (People's Republic of), Costa Rica, Ecuador, Egypt, Estonia, France, Ghana, Global Ministry, Guatemala, India, Israel, Jordan, Kazakhstan, Kenya, Kosovo, Liberia, Malawi, Mexico, Namibia, Nicaragua, Paraguay, Peru, Philippines, Russia, South Africa, South Sudan, Spain, Tanzania, Thailand, Togo, Turkey

TO EVERY TRIBE

PO Box 1572
Los Fresnos, TX 78566 US
Phone: (956) 233-4353
Email: contact@toeverytribe.org
Website: toeverytribe.org
Associations: Missio Nexus

A nondenominational sending agency of Baptist and Reformed tradition engaged in church planting (establishing), discipleship, missionary & worker training & sending, recruiting or mobilizing for mission, and STM trip coordination.

Purpose: . . . to extend the worship of Christ among all peoples by mobilizing the church, training disciplemakers, and sending missionary teams to plant churches among the unreached.

Year Founded in US: 2004

Fully Supported US Personnel Working Cross-Culturally
    More than 4 years: 28
    Non-residential: 22
Other Personnel
    Home staff: 18

Countries/Regions: Canada, Ireland (Republic of), Mexico, Papua New Guinea, Southeast Asia

TOUCH THE WORLD

1 Maple Street
Allendale, NJ 07401 US
Phone: (201) 760-9925
Email: jessek@touchtheworld.org
Website: touchtheworld.org

A nondenominational sending agency of Evangelical tradition engaged in community development, discipleship, STM trip coordination, and youth ministry. (FPC-PE)

Purpose: . . . to equip youth to live out the mission of God, everyday, everywhere.

Year Founded in US: 1991
Income for International Min:
    $167,000

Fully Supported US Personnel Working Cross-Culturally
    X-C workers in US: 4
Other Personnel
    Short-Term less than 1 year: 258
    Home staff: 9

TRAINING EVANGELISTIC LEADERSHIP
PO Box E
Denton, TX 76202 US
Phone: (940) 765-1449
Email: development@tel-intl.org
Website: tel-intl.org
An interdenominational sending agency of Evangelical tradition engaged in evangelism, mass, Bible memorization, discipleship and support of national workers. (DPE)
Purpose: . . . to minister alongside existing national churches called to develop multi-national gospel teams which major in evangelism, follow-up, and discipleship.
Income for International Min: $655,905
Fully Supported US Personnel Working Cross-Culturally
    More than 4 years: 21
    1–4 years: 1
Other Personnel
    Short-Term less than 1 year: 1
    Tentmakers/BAM: 1
    Non-US in own/other country: 48
    Home staff: 2
Countries/Regions: China (People's Republic of), India, Indonesia, Philippines, Vietnam

TRIBES AND NATIONS OUTREACH
PO Box 2174
Pasadena, CA 91102 US
Phone: (626) 584-0383
Email: tnousa@aol.com
Website: tno-asia.org
A nondenominational support agency of Charismatic and Pentecostal tradition engaged in training, agricultural programs, Bible distribution, church planting, medical work and short-term programs. (DPE)
Purpose: . . . to help build the body of Christ in Asia through training and other forms of encouragement.

Countries/Regions: Cambodia, China (People's Republic of), Hong Kong (China), India, Indonesia, Laos, Macau (China), Myanmar (Burma), Nepal, Philippines, Thailand, Vietnam

TWENTY-SIX:TWELVE
6420 Southwest Blvd, Ste. 212
Fort Worth, TX 76109 US
Phone: (817) 732-2615
Email: missions@twentysixtwelve.org
Website: twentysixtwelve.org
Associations: Missio Nexus
A nondenominational specialized agency of Evangelical tradition engaged in Bible distribution, community development, medical ministry, including dental or public health, relief & aid, and STM trip coordination.
Purpose: . . . to help employers provide opportunities for their employees to serve others - across the street and around the globe.
Year Founded in US: 2007
Other Personnel
    Short-Term less than 1 year: 41
    Home staff: 3

TWR
Formerly: Trans World Radio
PO Box 8700
Cary, NC 27511 US
Phone: (919) 460-3778
Email: info@twr.org
Website: twr.org
Associations: Accord Network, Missio Nexus
A nondenominational specialized agency of Evangelical and Independent tradition engaged in Bible teaching, radio or TV broadcasting, discipleship, mass evangelism, and video-film production or distribution. (FPC-PE)

Purpose: . . . to assist the Church to fulfill the commands of Jesus Christ to make disciples of all peoples by using and making available mass media.

Year Founded in US: 1952
Income for International Min:
$36,585,956
Fully Supported US Personnel Working Cross-Culturally
More than 4 years: 62
1–4 years: 3
Other Personnel
Short-Term less than 1 year: 11
Home staff: 246
Countries/Regions: Austria, Benin, Cambodia, Germany, Guam, Netherlands, Singapore, Sint Maarten, Slovakia, South Africa, Swaziland

TWR CANADA
Formerly: Trans World Radio Canada
Box 25324
London, ON N6C 6B1 CA
Phone: (519) 672-6510
Email: info@twrcanada.org
Website: twrcanada.org
A nondenominational service agency of Evangelical tradition engaged in audio recording or distribution, radio or TV broadcasting, Internet discipleship or training, member care, partnership development, and global media outreach.
Purpose: . . . to assist the Church to fulfill the command of Jesus Christ to make disciples of all peoples, and to do so by using and making available mass media.
Year Founded in CA: 1973
Fully Supported CA Personnel Working Cross-Culturally
More than 4 years: 4
Other Personnel
Short-Term less than 1 year: 19
Tentmakers/BAM: 1

Countries/Regions: Bolivia, China (People's Republic of), Netherlands, Sint Maarten, Swaziland

UB GLOBAL
Formerly: United Brethren in Christ
302 Lake Street
Huntington, IN 46750 US
Phone: (260) 356-2312
Email: info@ubglobal.org
Website: ubglobal.org
Associations: Missio Nexus
A denominational sending agency of Evangelical tradition engaged in church planting (establishing), discipleship, personal or small group evangelism, HIV/AIDS ministry, medical ministry, including dental or public health, and TESOL or TEFL.
Purpose: . . . to to mobilize local United Brethren churches in the USA and Canada for missions to serve within United Brethren mission projects, or to serve in other countries in partnership with qualified mission agencies.
Year Founded in US: 1800
Income for International Min:
$757,243
Fully Supported US Personnel Working Cross-Culturally
More than 4 years: 10
1–4 years: 7
Non-residential: 2
Other Personnel
Short-Term less than 1 year: 235
Non-US in own/other country: 5
Home staff: 7
Countries/Regions: Canada, China (People's Republic of), Costa Rica, Egypt, El Salvador, Germany, Guatemala, Haiti, Honduras, Hong Kong (China), India, Jamaica, Liberia, Macau (China), Mexico, Nicaragua, Philippines, Sierra Leone, South Africa, Thailand

UKRAINIAN CHILDREN'S CHRISTIAN FUND

10340 Freshwater Dr
Richmond, BC V7E 4H7 CA
Phone: (918) 791-1001
Email: info@ukrainianchildrensfund.org
Website: ukrainianchildrensfund.org

A denominational heritage support agency of Evangelical tradition engaged in childcare or orphanage, children's ministry, medical supplies, and relief & aid.

Purpose: . . . to engage in childcare/orphanage programs, children's programs, providing medical supplies and relief and/or rehabilitation.

Fully Supported CA Personnel Working Cross-Culturally
   More than 4 years: 2
Other Personnel
   Short-Term less than 1 year: 20
   Non-CA in own/other country: 14
Countries/Regions: Ukraine

UKRAINIAN CHILDRENS FUND

1629 Pine Dr.
Grove, OK 74344 US
Phone: (918) 791-1001
Email: info@ukrainianchildrensfund.org
Website: ukrainianchildrensfund.org

A support agency of Evangelical tradition engaged in childcare/orphanage programs, children's programs, providing medical supplies and relief and/or rehabilitation. (DPE)

Income for International Min:
   $10,000
Other Personnel
   Short-Term less than 1 year: 20
   Non-US in own/other country: 2
Countries/Regions: Ukraine

UNITED CHURCH OF CHRIST – GLOBAL MINISTRIES

700 Prospect Ave. E.
Cleveland, OH 44115 US
Phone: (216) 736-3210
Email: wcm@ucc.org
Website: ucc.org

A denominational sending agency of Christian (Restoration Movement) and Congregational tradition engaged in support of national churches, development, Christian education, theological education, leadership development and partnership development working in partnership with the Christian Church (Disciples of Christ) Global Ministries. Joint statistics found with Christian Church (Disciples of Christ) Global Ministries. (DPE)

UNITED EVANGELICAL CHURCHES

PO Box 1000
San Juan Bautista, CA 95045 US
Phone: (800) 595-4832
Email: admin@uecol.org
Website: uecol.org

A denominational heritage service agency of Charismatic and Evangelical tradition engaged in church planting (establishing), personal or small group evangelism, member care, and missionary & worker training.

Purpose: . . . to serve God by serving those who serve.

Year Founded in US: 1958
Fully Supported US Personnel Working Cross-Culturally
   More than 4 years: 5
Other Personnel
   Short-Term less than 1 year: 6
   Home staff: 3
Countries/Regions: Bolivia, Kenya, Philippines, Trinidad and Tobago

UNITED WORLD MISSION INC.

205 Regency Executive Park Dr, Ste 430
Charlotte, NC 28217 US
Phone: (704) 357-3355
Email: info@uwm.org
Website: uwm.org
Associations: Missio Nexus

A nondenominational sending agency of
Evangelical tradition engaged in church
planting (establishing), community
development, discipleship, theological
education, leadership development, and
missionary & worker training.

Purpose: . . . to see God change lives
and transform communities everywhere
by partnering to equip leaders, establish
churches, and engage in holistic mission.

Year Founded in US: 1946
Income for International Min:
  $15,510,000
*Fully Supported US Personnel Working
Cross-Culturally*
  More than 4 years: 290
  1–4 years: 15
  X-C workers in US: 6
  Non-residential: 20
Other Personnel
  Short-Term less than 1 year: 12
  Tentmakers/BAM: 7
  Non-US in own/other country: 305
  Home staff: 37
Countries/Regions: Argentina,
Belgium, Brazil, Central America, Central
Asia, Chile, Colombia, Democratic
Republic of Congo, Costa Rica, Cuba,
Czech Republic, Dominican Republic,
East Asia, Eastern Europe and Eurasia,
Ecuador, France, Germany, Greece,
Honduras, Hungary, Ireland (Republic of),
Italy, Kenya, Mali, Mexico, Middle East,
Panama, Paraguay, Peru, Romania, Russia,
Senegal, Slovenia, South Africa, Southeast
Asia, Spain, Sweden, Tanzania, Uganda,
United Kingdom, Venezuela

UNIVERSITY BIBLE FELLOWSHIP

6558 N Artesian Ave
Chicago, IL 60645-5328 US
Phone: (773) 338-1155
Email: ubfhqoffice@gmail.com
Website: ubf.org
Associations: Missio Nexus

A nondenominational sending agency
of Reformed tradition engaged in Bible
teaching, children's ministry, personal
or small group evangelism, student
evangelism, missionary & worker training,
and video-film production or distribution.

Purpose: . . . to study the Bible, grow in
the grace and knowledge of our Lord and
Savior Jesus Christ, and live according to
his teachings. We especially pray to reach
college students and help them grow as his
lifelong disciples.

Year Founded in US: 1975
Income for International Min:
  $114,079
Other Personnel
  Short-Term less than 1 year: 16
  Tentmakers/BAM: 1160
  Home staff: 24
Countries/Regions: Argentina,
Australia, Austria, Bangladesh, Belarus,
Belgium, Belize, Bolivia, Botswana, Brazil,
Brunei, Bulgaria, Cambodia, Cameroon,
Canada, Chile, Colombia, Croatia, Czech
Republic, Denmark, Dominican Republic,
East Asia, Ecuador, Egypt, El Salvador,
Ethiopia, Finland, France, Germany,
Ghana, Greece, Guatemala, Honduras,
Hungary, India, Indonesia, Ireland
(Republic of), Italy, Japan, Kazakhstan,
Kenya, Kyrgyzstan, Laos, Latvia, Libya,
Macedonia, Malaysia, Mexico, Middle
East, Mongolia, Morocco, Namibia, Nepal,
Netherlands, New Zealand, Nicaragua,
Nigeria, Norway, Panama, Papua New
Guinea, Paraguay, Peru, Philippines,
Poland, Portugal, Romania, Russia,
Serbia, Singapore, Slovakia, South Africa,

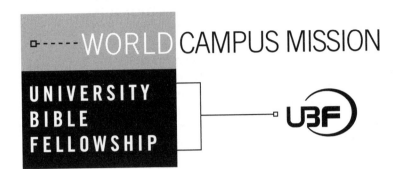

WORLD CAMPUS MISSION

UNIVERSITY
BIBLE
FELLOWSHIP

UBF

UBF is an international evangelical church (non-denominational) and network of house churches dedicated to Christ and his kingdom. Our main focus is to study the Bible, grow in the grace and knowledge of our Lord and Savior Jesus Christ, and live according to his teachings. We especially pray to reach college students and help them grow as his lifelong disciples. Our goal is to obey our Lord's commands to love one another and to go and make disciples of all nations (Jn 13:34; Mt 28:18-20). We pray that God may continue to call and raise lay missionaries through us and send them to the ends of the earth (Ac 1:8).

Website: ubf.org

One-to-One & Small Group Bible study
Weekly fellowship meetings
Morning Prayer meeting and Quiet Time
Sunday Worship Service
Bible School
Retreat
Christmas Worship Service
Leadership Development/Missionary Training
World Mission Report & International Conferences

South Sudan, Spain, Sri Lanka, Sweden, Switzerland, Taiwan (China), Tajikistan, Tanzania, Thailand, Uganda, Ukraine, United Kingdom, Uruguay, Uzbekistan, Venezuela, Vietnam, Zambia, Zimbabwe

VELLORE CHRISTIAN MEDICAL COLLEGE FOUNDATION INC.
475 Riverside Dr, Ste. 725
New York, NY 10115 US
Phone: (212) 870-2640
Email: foundation@vellorecmc.org
Website: vellorecmc.org
An interdenominational specialized agency of Ecumenical tradition engaged in fund raising or transmission. (FPC-PE)
Purpose: . . . to raise funds and provide support for programs, higher education, and medical research for the Christian Medical College in Vellore, India.

VENTURE INTERNATIONAL
P.O. Box 1582
Mesa, AZ 85211 US
Phone: (480) 730-2710
Email: info@ventureint.org
Website: ventureint.org
An interdenominational service agency of Evangelical tradition engaged in development, disability assistance programs, support of national churches, partnership development, relief and/or rehabilitation. (DPE)
Purpose: . . . serves as a bridge between those in need and those who want to help God's people in the Middle East; empowering and enhancing their work through strategic partnerships, emergency relief, small business creation and people development.
Other Personnel
    Non-US in own/other country: 51
    Home staff: 6
Countries/Regions: Egypt, Iraq, Israel, Jordan, Kyrgyzstan, Lebanon

VERNACULAR VIDEO MISSION INTERNATIONAL INC.
PO Box 22394
Minneapolis, MN 55422 US
Phone: (309) 338-1367
Email: info@vvmi.org
Website: vvmi.org
Associations: Missio Nexus
A nondenominational service agency of Evangelical tradition engaged in Bible distribution, networking, partnership, or coordination, prayer-intercession, STM trip coordination, technical assistance, and video-film production or distribution.
Purpose: . . . to partner with and equip ethnic Christians who proclaim the Gospel through video and other media in their common language.
Year Founded in US: 2000
Income for International Min:
    $68,552
Other Personnel
    Short-Term less than 1 year: 5
    Home staff: 2

VILLAGE MINISTRIES INTERNATIONAL
401 W Vandament Ave, Ste. 101
Yukon, OK 73099 US
Phone: (405) 634-4373
Email: vmi@villageministries.org
Website: villageministries.org
A nondenominational sending agency of Evangelical tradition engaged in Bible distribution, Bible teaching, literature distribution, persecuted church, STM trip coordination, and pastor training.
Purpose: . . . to take the Gospel and the teaching of God's Word to people in villages and remote cities that ordinarily would not be exposed to missionary activity or Bible teaching.
Year Founded in US: 1990
Income for International Min:
    $599,143

Fully Supported US Personnel Working Cross-Culturally
More than 4 years: 91
Other Personnel
Short-Term less than 1 year: 23
Tentmakers/BAM: 2
Non-US in own/other country: 91
Home staff: 4
Countries/Regions: Central America, Eastern Europe and Eurasia, South Asia, Southeast Asia, Sub-Saharan Africa

VILLAGE SCHOOLS INTERNATIONAL
Box 1929
Tomball, TX 77377 US
Phone: (281) 841-6555
Email: info@villageschools.org
Website: villageschools.org
Associations: Missio Nexus

An interdenominational support agency of Evangelical tradition engaged in community development, discipleship, church, school or general Christian education, student evangelism, HIV/AIDS ministry, and youth ministry.

Purpose: . . . to enable those in villages who would otherwise never get to go to school to have the opportunity to get an education and to send missionaries into villages where missionaries have never lived before to share the Gospel.

Year Founded in US: 2008
Income for International Min:
$2,223,856
Other Personnel
Short-Term less than 1 year: 18

VINEYARD CHURCH USA – MISSIONS
112 Harvard Ave., #265
Claremont, CA 91711 US
Phone: (909) 626-0773
Email: office@vineyardmissions.org
Website: vineyardmissions.org

A consortium of 8 different associations of Charismatic and Evangelical tradition engaged in church planting, evangelism, leadership development and support of national churches. There are approximately 380 Vineyard Churches outside the USA in 52 countries. The eight associations oversee the work being done in different areas of the world. (DPE)

Purpose: . . . to equip the saints for the advancement of the Kingdom of God through evangelizing and church planting.

VIRGINIA MENNONITE MISSIONS
601 Parkwood Drive
Harrisonburg, VA 22802 US
Phone: (540) 434-9727
Email: info@vmmissions.org
Website: vmmissions.org
Associations: Missio Nexus

A denominational sending agency of Mennonite or Anabaptist tradition engaged in church planting (establishing), discipleship, church, school or general Christian education, leadership development, missionary & worker training, and recruiting or mobilizing for mission.

Purpose: . . . to invite people to faithful living in Jesus Christ by forming and enabling congregations and individuals to continue God's reconciling work in the world.

Year Founded in US: 1919
Income for International Min:
$1,200,000
Fully Supported US Personnel Working Cross-Culturally
More than 4 years: 17
1–4 years: 6
X-C workers in US: 7
Other Personnel
Short-Term less than 1 year: 11
Non-US in own/other country: 23
Home staff: 13

Countries/Regions: Albania, Belize, Germany, Indonesia, Italy, Kosovo, Montenegro, Nicaragua, Thailand

VISION BEYOND BORDERS
100 Shepherd Trail Unit 12
Bozeman, MT 59715 US
Phone: (406) 587-2321
Email: info@visionbeyondborders.org
Website: visionbeyondborders.org
A nondenominational service agency of Evangelical tradition engaged in Bible distribution, childcare or orphanage, addressing human trafficking, literature distribution, medical supplies, and relief & aid.
Purpose: . . . to serve the worldwide church by providing the necessary tools and training for the local people to fulfill Christ's "Great Commission" in their own countries.
Fully Supported US Personnel Working Cross-Culturally
   Non-residential: 85
Other Personnel
   Short-Term less than 1 year: 98
   Non-US in own/other country: 15
Countries/Regions: Central America, China (People's Republic of), India, Laos, Myanmar (Burma), Romania, Vietnam

VISION MINISTRIES CANADA
145 Lincoln Road
Waterloo, ON N2J 2N8 CA
Phone: (519) 725-1212
Email: info@vision-ministries.org
Website: vision-ministries.org
A denominational heritage specialized agency of Christian (Plymouth Brethren) and Evangelical tradition engaged in church development, church planting (establishing), CPM, leadership development, and networking, partnership or coordination.

Purpose: . . . to move the mission of God forward by cultivating a collaborative network of churches who together with VMC are starting new churches, and helping existing churches fulfil their mandate more effectively.
Year Founded in CA: 1992
Income for International Min:
   $50,694
Other Personnel
   Short-Term less than 1 year: 5

VISIONLEDD O/A WORKING FOR ORPHANS AND WIDOWS
P.O Box 460
Burlington, ON L7R 3Y3 CA
Phone: (905) 319-8834
Email: info@wowmission.com
Website: wowmission.com
Associations: CCRDA
An interdenominational support agency of Evangelical tradition engaged in Bible teaching, childcare or orphanage, community development, church, school or general Christian education, HIV/AIDS ministry, and medical supplies. (FPC-PE)
Purpose: . . . to facilitate church planting and church planting equivalents, and equip African churches to care for orphans and widows.
Year Founded in CA: 1999
Income for International Min:
   $1,652,088
Other Personnel
   Short-Term less than 1 year: 15
   Home staff: 7
Countries/Regions: Malawi

VISIONSYNERGY
PO Box 232
Edmonds, WA 98020 US
Phone: (425) 673-5644
Email: dmansour@visionsynergy.net
Website: visionsynergy.net/
Associations: Missio Nexus

An interdenominational service agency of Evangelical tradition engaged in leadership development, networking, partnership, or coordination, and partnership development.

Purpose: . . . to accelerate the Great Commission by developing effective networks in high-priority sectors of world mission.

Year Founded in US: 2003
Income for International Min:
$1,593,480

Fully Supported US Personnel Working Cross-Culturally
More than 4 years: 2

Other Personnel
Short-Term less than 1 year: 2
Home staff: 7

Countries/Regions: Middle East, South Asia

VOICE OF THE MARTYRS INC., THE
P.O. Box 608
Streetsville, ON L5M 2C1 CA
Phone: (905) 670-9721
Email: thevoice@persecution.net
Website: vomcanada.com

A nondenominational support agency of Evangelical tradition engaged in persecution ministries, missions information service, justice, literature distribution, relief and/or rehabilitation and training. (DPE)

Purpose: . . . to glorify God by serving His persecuted Church.

Year Founded in CA: 1971
Income for International Min:
$1,645,818

Fully Supported CA Personnel Working Cross-Culturally
Non-residential: 2

Other Personnel
Home staff: 111

VOLUNTEERS IN MEDICAL MISSIONS
265 S. Cove Rd.
Seneca, SC 29672 US
Phone: (864) 885-9023
Email: missions@vimm.org
Website: vimm.org

A nondenominational sending agency of Evangelical and Christian tradition engaged in medical ministry, including dental or public health, and STM trip coordination. (FPC-PE)

Purpose: . . . to minister to the physical and spiritual needs of children and adults in developing countries throughout the world and provide opportunities for Christian medical professionals and other volunteers to experience missions firsthand.

Year Founded in US: 1986
Income for International Min:
$617,635

Fully Supported US Personnel Working Cross-Culturally
More than 4 years: 1

Other Personnel
Home staff: 3

Countries/Regions: Afghanistan

WALK THRU THE BIBLE MINISTRIES INC.
5550 Triangle Parkway, Suite 250
Peachtree Corners, GA 30092 US
Phone: (770) 458-9300
Email: info@walkthru.org
Website: walkthru.org

A nondenominational specialized agency of Evangelical tradition engaged in Bible teaching, radio or TV broadcasting, church construction or financing, literature production, missionary & worker training, and national worker support. (FPC-PE)

Purpose: . . . to help people everywhere live God's Word and love God's word.

Year Founded in US: 1976

Other Personnel

Non-US in own/other country: 275

Countries/Regions: Angola, Argentina, Armenia, Australia, Austria, Azerbaijan, Bahrain, Bangladesh, Belarus, Bhutan, Bolivia, Botswana, Brazil, Bulgaria, Cambodia, Cameroon, China (People's Republic of), Colombia, Democratic Republic of Congo, Costa Rica, Cuba, Dominican Republic, Ecuador, Egypt, El Salvador, Estonia, Ethiopia, Fiji, Georgia, Ghana, Guatemala, Haiti, Honduras, Hungary, India, Indonesia, Iraq, Ireland (Republic of), Israel, Japan, Jordan, Kazakhstan, Kenya, South Korea, Kuwait, Latvia, Lebanon, Lesotho, Liberia, Lithuania, Malawi, Malaysia, Mexico, Moldova, Mongolia, Morocco, Mozambique, Myanmar (Burma), Namibia, Nepal, Nigeria, Oman, Pakistan, Palestine, Peru, Philippines, Qatar, Romania, Russia, Saudi Arabia, Serbia, Sierra Leone, Singapore, South Africa, Sri Lanka, Sudan, Swaziland, Syria, Tanzania, Thailand, Togo, Tunisia, Uganda, Ukraine, United Arab Emirates, United Kingdom, Vietnam, Yemen, Zambia, Zimbabwe

WAYMAKERS

PO Box 203131

Austin, TX 78720 US

Phone: (512) 419-7729

Email: info@waymakers.org

Website: waymakers.org

An interdenominational specialized agency of Evangelical tradition engaged in leadership development, missionary & worker training, prayer-intercession, and recruiting or mobilizing for mission. (FPC-PE)

Purpose: . . . to impart vision and training for leaders of local movements of united prayer that will prepare communities for evangelization and spiritual awakening.

Year Founded in US: 1994

Income for International Min: $30,000

WAYMARKS RADIO MINISTRIES INTERNATIONAL

PO Box 2324

Macon, GA 31203 US

Phone: (478) 750-1422

Email: lorenwilson@juno.com

Website: waymarks.org

A specialized agency of Charismatic and Calvinist tradition engaged in broadcasting, radio and/or TV, audio recording/distribution, literature distribution, literature production and partnership development. (DPE)

Income for International Min: $500

Other Personnel

Short-Term less than 1 year: 1

Tentmakers/BAM: 1

Non-US in own/other country: 3

Home staff: 1

Countries/Regions: Malawi, Nigeria, Zimbabwe

WEC INTERNATIONAL

P.O. Box 1707, 709 Pennsylvania Ave.

Fort Washington, PA 19034 US

Phone: (215) 646-2322

Email: mailbox@wec-usa.org

Website: wec-usa.org

Associations: Missio Nexus

An interdenominational sending agency of Evangelical tradition engaged in arts in mission, children's ministry, CPM, missionary & worker training, STM trip coordination, and TESOL or TEFL.

Purpose: . . . to proclaim the gospel by word and deed, so that people come to a living faith in Jesus Christ as Saviour and Lord and become his disciples.

Year Founded in US: 1939

Income for International Min: $4,900,000

Fully Supported US Personnel Working Cross-Culturally
  More than 4 years: 118
  1–4 years: 12
  X-C workers in US: 17
  Non-residential: 2
Other Personnel
  Short-Term less than 1 year: 15
  Non-US in own/other country: 4
Countries/Regions: Brazil, Canada, Central Asia, Chad, Dominican Republic, East Asia, Equatorial Guinea, France, Gambia, Germany, Global Ministry, Japan, South Korea, Liberia, Mexico, Middle East, Philippines, Senegal, South America, South Asia, Southeast Asia, Spain, Taiwan (China), Thailand, Togo, United Kingdom, Vietnam

WEC INTERNATIONAL CANADA

37 Aberdeen Avenue
Hamilton, ON L8P 2M2 CA
Phone: (905) 529-0166
Email: info@wec-canada.org
Website: wec-canada.org
An interdenominational sending agency of Evangelical tradition engaged in personal or small group evangelism, member care, missionary & worker training, prayer-intercession, and recruiting or mobilizing for mission.
Purpose: . . . to see Christ known, loved and worshiped by the remaining unevangelized peoples of the world.
Year Founded in CA: 1936
Income for International Min:
  $1,890,000
Fully Supported CA Personnel Working Cross-Culturally
  More than 4 years: 61
  1–4 years: 6
  X-C workers in CA: 2
  Non-residential: 3

Other Personnel
  Short-Term less than 1 year: 1
  Non-CA in own/other country: 21
  Home staff: 13
Countries/Regions: Albania, Brazil, Cambodia, Central Asia, Democratic Republic of Congo, East Asia, Eastern Europe and Eurasia, Fiji, Gambia, Ghana, Global Ministry, Greece, Japan, Mali, Middle East, Netherlands, North Africa, Singapore, South Africa, South Asia, Spain, Thailand, United Kingdom, United States of America

WEINER MINISTRIES INTERNATIONAL

PO Box 1799
Gainesville, FL 32602 US
Phone: (352) 375-4455
Website: weinerministries.com
A nondenominational support agency of Charismatic tradition engaged in youth programs and training, discipleship, evangelism and mobilization for mission. (DPE)
Year Founded in US: 1991
Income for International Min:
  $433,938
Fully Supported US Personnel Working Cross-Culturally
  More than 4 years: 1
Other Personnel
  Home staff: 4

WHITE FIELDS

P.O. Box 1839
San Marcos, CA 92079 US
Phone: (760) 805-2084
Email: stevew@whitefields.org
Website: whitefields.org
A nondenominational service agency of Evangelical tradition engaged in church planting, support of national churches, partnership development and support of national workers. (DPE)

Purpose: . . . to provide collaborative start-up support to pastors planting local churches among their own people in other parts of the world.

Income for International Min:
$174,000

Other Personnel
Non-US in own/other country: 99
Home staff: 2

Countries/Regions: Argentina, Brazil, Ghana, Japan, Malawi, Myanmar (Burma), Paraguay, Philippines, Russia, South Africa, Zimbabwe

WHITE FIELDS MISSIONARY SOCIETY OF CANADA
PO Box 452
Coaldale, AB T1M 1M5 CA
Phone: (403) 345-4981
Website: whitefields.org

A service agency of Evangelical tradition engaged in church planting and evangelism. Countries of service and personnel information included in White Fields, Inc. (USA).

Purpose: . . . to provide collaborative start-up support to pastors and churches among their own people in other parts of the world.

Income for International Min:
$227,252

WISCONSIN EVANGELICAL LUTHERAN SYNOD – BOARD FOR WORLD MISSIONS
N16W2377 Stone Ridge Dr.
Waukesha, WI 53188 US
Phone: (414) 256-3233
Email: missionscontact@wels.net
Website: wels.net

A denominational sending agency of Lutheran tradition engaged in radio or TV broadcasting, church planting (establishing), correspondence courses,

TEE or other extension education, literature production, and partnership development.

Purpose: . . . to make disciples throughout the world . . . using the Gospel to win the lost for Christ and to nurture believers for lives of Christian service.

Year Founded in US: 1955

Fully Supported US Personnel Working Cross-Culturally
More than 4 years: 36

Other Personnel
Home staff: 10

Countries/Regions: Albania, Brazil, Bulgaria, Dominican Republic, Hong Kong (China), India, Indonesia, Japan, Malawi, Mexico, Russia, Taiwan (China), Thailand, Zambia

WITH OPEN EYES
4100 Coca Cola Plaza
Charlotte, NC 28211 US
Phone: (704) 442-7117
Email: savanna@withopeneyes.net
Website: withopeneyes.net

A nondenominational specialized agency of Independent tradition engaged in Bible teaching, church development, discipleship, mass evangelism, personal or small group evangelism, and recruiting or mobilizing for mission.

Purpose: . . . to accelerate the sharing and teaching of the good news of Jesus Christ to the unreached and underserved peoples of the world.

Year Founded in US: 2008

Fully Supported US Personnel Working Cross-Culturally
X-C workers in US: 1

Other Personnel
Short-Term less than 1 year: 60
Non-US in own/other country: 255
Home staff: 3

Countries/Regions: Democratic Republic of Congo, Ethiopia, Kenya, Rwanda, South Sudan, Sudan, Uganda

WOMEN IN THE WINDOW INTERNATIONAL

2101 Vista Parkway, Ste. 256
West Palm Beach, FL 33411 US
Phone: (561) 249-5377
Email: hannahc@womeninthewindow-intl.org
Website: womeninthewindow-intl.org/
Associations: Missio Nexus
A nondenominational specialized agency of Evangelical tradition engaged in Bible teaching, community development, discipleship, leadership development, spiritual renewal, and tentmaking & related.
Purpose: . . . to equip and empower women in the 10/40 Window and beyond to replace poverty and injustice with dignity and purpose in Christ.
Year Founded in US: 2013
Income for International Min:
$170,928
Other Personnel
    Short-Term less than 1 year: 32
    Home staff: 4

WOMEN OF HOPE INTERNATIONAL

187 Stateline Rd E, Ste. 17
Southaven, MS 38671-1702 US
Phone: (901) 775-9757
Email: admin@wohint.org
Website: WomenofHopeInternational.org
Associations: Missio Nexus
A nondenominational service agency of Presbyterian and Reformed tradition engaged in disabled ministry, discipleship, justice or peace issues, and management consulting or training.

Purpose: . . . to train and equip the Body of Christ to utilize a Biblical framework to promote the holistic transformation of women affected by disability with the Gospel throughout the developing world.
Year Founded in US: 2009
Income for International Min:
$470,743
Fully Supported US Personnel Working Cross-Culturally
    More than 4 years: 4
    Non-residential: 8
Other Personnel
    Short-Term less than 1 year: 6
    Non-US in own/other country: 12
    Home staff: 4
Countries/Regions: Sierra Leone, South Asia, Sub-Saharan Africa

WOMEN TO THE WORLD INC.

PMB 581, Ste. 103, 1860 Barnett Shoals Rd
Athens, GA 30605 US
Phone: (706) 548-0000
Email: survival@womentotheworld.org
Website: womentotheworld.org
A nondenominational specialized agency of Reformed tradition engaged in children's ministry, mass evangelism, addressing human trafficking, leadership development, national worker support, and partnership development.
Purpose: . . . to improve the lives of disenfranchised women throughout the developing world.
Year Founded in US: 1985
Other Personnel
    Non-US in own/other country: 4
    Home staff: 45
Countries/Regions: Afghanistan, Burkina Faso, Kenya, Turkey

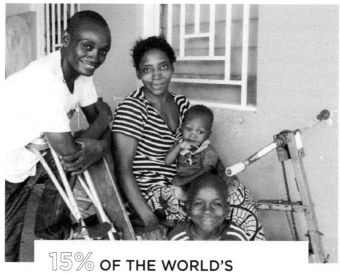

WORD & DEED
PO Box 157
Hudsonville, MI 49426 US
Phone: (866) 391-5728
Email: office@wordanddeed.org
Website: wordanddeed.org
Associations: CCRDA

A nondenominational support agency of Presbyterian and Reformed tradition engaged in Bible teaching, childcare or orphanage, church, school or general Christian education, medical ministry, including dental or public health, partnership development, and relief & development.

Purpose: . . . to help meet the physical and spiritual needs of those in the developing world in accordance with biblical principles.

Year Founded in US: 2000
Other Personnel
    Short-Term less than 1 year: 15
    Non-US in own/other country: 5
    Home staff: 1
Countries/Regions: Haiti, Malawi, Myanmar (Burma), South Africa

WORD & DEED
MINISTRIES CANADA
P.O. Box 20100
St. Thomas, ON N5P 4H4 CA
Phone: (519) 633-2333
Email: office@wordanddeed.org
Website: wordanddeed.org
Associations: CCRDA

A nondenominational service agency of Presbyterian and Reformed tradition engaged in Bible teaching, childcare or orphanage, church, school or general Christian education, medical ministry, including dental or public health, and partnership development.

Purpose: . . . to address the spiritual and physical needs of people in the developing world in accordance with biblical principles.

Year Founded in CA: 1994
Fully Supported CA Personnel Working Cross-Culturally
    More than 4 years: 2
Other Personnel
    Short-Term less than 1 year: 25
    Non-CA in own/other country: 3
    Home staff: 7
Countries/Regions: Malawi, South Africa

WORD OF LIFE FELLOWSHIP INC.
PO Box 600
Schroon Lake, NY 12870 US
Phone: (518) 494-6329
Email: imservices@wol.org
Website: wol.org

A nondenominational sending agency of Baptist tradition engaged in Bible teaching, camping programs, discipleship, personal or small group evangelism, STM trip coordination, and youth ministry.

Purpose: . . . to share the message of salvation with those who have never heard and help believers grow in their faith.

Year Founded in US: 1942
Income for International Min:
    $13,504,105
Fully Supported US Personnel Working Cross-Culturally
    More than 4 years: 153
    1–4 years: 33
    Non-residential: 1
Other Personnel
    Short-Term less than 1 year: 810
    Tentmakers/BAM: 36
    Non-US in own/other country: 886
    Home staff: 19

Countries/Regions: Anguilla, Argentina, Aruba, Australia, Austria, Bahamas, Belize, Bermuda, Bolivia, Brazil, Bulgaria, Canada, Caribbean, Cayman Islands, Central America, Central Asia, Chad, Chile, Costa Rica, Côte d'Ivoire, Curaçao, Czech Republic, Dominican Republic, Eastern Europe and Eurasia, Ecuador, El Salvador, Fiji, France, Germany, Ghana, Global Ministry, Greece, Guatemala, Honduras, Hungary, Italy, Jamaica, Japan, Kenya, Liberia, Lithuania, Mexico, Middle East, Mozambique, New Zealand, Nicaragua, Niger, Nigeria, Oceania, Panama, Papua New Guinea, Paraguay, Peru, Philippines, Poland, Portugal, Puerto Rico, Romania, Russia, Serbia, Sint Maarten, Slovakia, South Africa, South America, Spain, South Korea, Sub-Saharan Africa, Taiwan (China), Thailand, Togo, Trinidad and Tobago, Uganda, Ukraine, United Kingdom, Uruguay, Venezuela

WORD TO RUSSIA
PO Box 1521
West Sacramento, CA 95691 US
Phone: (916) 372-4610
Email: word2russia@gmail.com
Website: wordtorussia.org
A nondenominational support agency of Baptist and Evangelical tradition engaged in broadcasting, audio recording/distribution, camping programs, childcare/orphanage support, children's radio/music programs and literature distribution to Russian-speaking immigrants, with outreach in the former Soviet Union and Ukraine. Emphasis is on the children and youth. (DPE)
Year Founded in US: 1972
Income for International Min:
  $95,000

Fully Supported US Personnel Working Cross-Culturally
  More than 4 years: 5
  Non-residential: 1
Other Personnel
  Non-US in own/other country: 5
  Home staff: 2
Countries/Regions: Russia

WORLD CHRISTIAN MINISTRIES ASSOCIATION
10671 U.S. Hwy Route 301
Oxford, FL 34484 US
Phone: (434) 296-5263
Email: ron@worldchristianministries.org
Website: wcma-usa.org
A support agency of Pentecostal and Apostolic tradition engaged in literature distribution, Bible distribution, correspondence courses, theological education, literature production and seed grants. (DPE)
Year Founded in US: 2007
Income for International Min:
  $370,500

WORLD CHRISTIAN OUTREACH INC.
28720 Alessandro Blvd.
Moreno Valley, CA 92555 US
Phone: (951) 242-8795
Email: herpickstantonxp@roadrunner.com
Website: wcous.org
A nondenominational support agency of Evangelical tradition engaged in Christian education, childcare/orphanage programs, relief and/or rehabilitation and support of national workers. (DPE)
Year Founded in US: 1976
Income for International Min:
  $297,000
Fully Supported US Personnel Working Cross-Culturally
  1–4 years: 1

NO MATTER WHERE YOU'RE AT IN LIFE, THERE ARE ALWAYS OPPORTUNITIES TO SERVE. **WORD OF LIFE INTERNATIONAL MINISTRIES HAS SOMETHING FOR EVERYONE.**

Full-time missions
Families and individuals living and serving in over 70 countries.

Student Fusion
Short-term trips that allow high school students to make an impact and get plugged in to what God is doing around the world.

English 4 Life Schools
Teach English to students in South Korea, Taiwan, Japan, or Nicaragua.

Launch Program
College students, families, or retirees use everyday skills and abilities to serve. Trips range from 1 month to 2 years.

518.494.6329 · wol.org/missions · missions@wol.org

Other Personnel
Short-Term less than 1 year: 37
Tentmakers/BAM: 7
Non-US in own/other country: 15
Home staff: 1
Countries/Regions: Africa

WORLD COMPASSION SOCIETY
PO Box 1415
Medicine Hat, AB T1A 7N3 CA
Phone: (403) 526-8229
Website: worldcompassion.tv
A transdenominational specialized
agency of Charismatic and Independent
tradition engaged in church planting,
Bible distribution, discipleship, literature
distribution, relief and/or rehabilitation and
training. See World Compassion Terry Law
Ministries for statistical information.
Purpose: . . . to take the message of
Jesus Christ to nations that are hostile to
the Gospel, working with local bodies
of believers to support the spiritual and
physical transformation of lives.

WORLD COMPASSION
TERRY LAW MINISTRIES
PO Box 92
Tulsa, OK 74101-0092 US
Phone: (918) 492-2858
Email: joel@worldcompassion.tv
Website: worldcompassion.tv
A transdenominational specialized agency
of Charismatic tradition engaged in Bible
distribution, church planting (establishing),
discipleship, literature distribution, and
relief & aid.
Purpose: . . . to take the message of
Jesus Christ to nations that are hostile to
the Gospel, working with local bodies
of believers to support the spiritual and
physical transformation of lives.
Year Founded in US: 1969
Income for International Min:
$1,810,982

Other Personnel
Non-US in own/other country: 4
Home staff: 10
Countries/Regions: China (People's
Republic of), Cuba, Iraq, Myanmar (Burma)

WORLD CONCERN
19303 Fremont Ave. N.
Seattle, WA 98133 US
Phone: (800) 755-5022
Email: info@worldconcern.org
Website: worldconcern.org
A nondenominational sending agency of
Christian (Restoration Movement) tradition
engaged in relief and/or rehabilitation,
children at risk, development and HIV/
AIDS. (DPE)
Purpose: . . . to relieve human
suffering through disaster response and
development programs in the name of
Christ.
Income for International Min:
$48,818,000
*Fully Supported US Personnel Working
Cross-Culturally*
More than 4 years: 13
1–4 years: 19
Non-residential: 18
Other Personnel
Short-Term less than 1 year: 1
Non-US in own/other country: 858
Home staff: 26
Countries/Regions: Afghanistan, Africa,
Asia, Bangladesh, Bolivia, Burkina Faso,
Cambodia, Ethiopia, Haiti, Honduras,
Kenya, Laos, Myanmar (Burma), Peru,
Rwanda, Thailand, Uganda, Uzbekistan,
Vietnam

WORLD GOSPEL MISSION

3783 E State Rd 18
Marion, IN 46952 US
Phone: (765) 664-7331
Email: wgm@wgm.org
Website: wgm.org
Associations: Missio Nexus

An interdenominational sending agency of Holiness and Wesleyan tradition engaged in children's ministry, community development, church, school or general Christian education, TEE or other extension education, personal or small group evangelism, and medical ministry, including dental or public health.

Purpose: . . . to serve God in holiness and righteousness, connecting in ministry with churches worldwide to make disciples of Jesus Christ among all nations.

Year Founded in US: 1910
Income for International Min:
$16,744,455
Fully Supported US Personnel Working Cross-Culturally
More than 4 years: 118
1–4 years: 37
X-C workers in US: 40
Other Personnel
Non-US in own/other country: 1
Home staff: 42

WORLD HELP

PO Box 501
Forest, VA 24551 US
Phone: (434) 525-4657
Email: help@worldhelp.net
Website: worldhelp.net

A nondenominational support agency of Evangelical tradition engaged in child advocacy, Bible distribution, children's programs, church planting, leadership development and relief and/or rehabilitation. (DPE)

Purpose: . . . to fulfill the Great Commission and the Great Commandment through partnering, training, helping, and serving, especially in the unreached areas of the world.

Year Founded in US: 1992
Income for International Min:
$18,872,269
Other Personnel
Short-Term less than 1 year: 128
Home staff: 69

WORLD HOPE CANADA

PO Box 982
Kemptville, ON K0G 1J0 CA
Phone: (613) 482-1499
Email: contact@worldhope.ca
Website: worldhope.ca

A service agency of Wesleyan tradition engaged in trafficking/slavery issues, children at risk, development, partnership development and relief and/or rehabilitation. (DPE)

Purpose: . . . a faith based relief and development organization which seeks to bring hope and healing to a hurting world.

Year Founded in CA: 1999
Income for International Min:
$479,791
Fully Supported CA Personnel Working Cross-Culturally
More than 4 years: 2
Other Personnel
Short-Term less than 1 year: 75
Non-CA in own/other country: 12
Home staff: 2
Countries/Regions: Niger, Sierra Leone, Ukraine

WORLD HORIZONS

8 East Broad St.
Richmond, VA 23219 US
Phone: (804) 225-5517
Email: usinfo@worldhorizons.org
Website: worldhorizonsusa.org

A nondenominational support agency of Evangelical tradition engaged in arts in mission, business as mission, church planting (establishing), mass evangelism, and missionary & worker training.

Purpose: . . . to serve on behalf of souls as yet unsaved; churches as yet unplanted; missionaries as yet unsent . . . ministering through creative evangelism, church-planting, and the establishment of a trained missionary presence.

Year Founded in US: 1985

Fully Supported US Personnel Working Cross-Culturally
  More than 4 years: 45
Other Personnel
  Home staff: 7
Countries/Regions: Global Ministry

WORLD INDIGENOUS MISSIONS
PO Box 310627
New Braunfels, TX 78131-0627 US
Phone: (830) 629-0863
Email: wim@worldim.com
Website: worldim.com

An interdenominational sending agency of Charismatic and Evangelical tradition engaged in church planting, broadcasting, discipleship, evangelism, short-term programs and missionary training. (DPE)

Purpose: . . . to disciple the nations to reach the world.

Income for International Min:
  $1,741,262
Fully Supported US Personnel Working Cross-Culturally
  More than 4 years: 79
  1–4 years: 6
  Non-residential: 12

Other Personnel
  Short-Term less than 1 year: 53
  Tentmakers/BAM: 13
  Non-US in own/other country: 14
  Home staff: 4
Countries/Regions: Asia, Bolivia, Hungary, Indonesia, Mexico, Middle East, Philippines, Russia, Spain, Thailand, Venezuela

WORLD LINK MINISTRIES
PO Box 610607
Dallas, TX 75261 US
Phone: (972) 253-6800
Email: wlmsefovan@aol.com
Website: worldlinkministries.org

An interdenominational sending agency of Baptist and Evangelical tradition engaged in church planting, TEE, theological education, evangelism, leadership development and support of national workers. (DPE)

Year Founded in US: 1994

Fully Supported US Personnel Working Cross-Culturally
  More than 4 years: 10
Other Personnel
  Non-US in own/other country: 720
Countries/Regions: Africa, Cuba, Equatorial Guinea, Italy, Mexico, Romania, Spain, Ukraine, Vietnam

WORLD MISSION
4200 Alpine Avenue NW
Comstock Park, MI 49321 US
Phone: (616) 534-5689
Email: staff@worldmission.cc
Website: worldmission.cc

A nondenominational support agency of Evangelical and Reformed tradition engaged in audio recording/distribution, evangelism, leadership development, support of national churches and short-term programs. (DPE)

Year Founded in US: 1994
Income for International Min:
$265,900
Other Personnel
Short-Term less than 1 year: 2
Home staff: 4
Countries/Regions: Democratic
Republic of Congo, India, Mexico,
Myanmar (Burma), Nigeria

WORLD MISSION ASSOCIATES
2148 Embassy Drive
Lancaster, PA 17603 US
Phone: (717) 298-4198
Email: wmausa@wmausa.org
Website: wmausa.org/
Associations: Missio Nexus
A nondenominational service agency of
Evangelical tradition engaged in church
planting (establishing), CPM, DMM,
discipleship, orality or storying, and
promoting healthy, local self-reliance in
global missions.
Purpose: . . . to advance mission
practices through the lens of dignity,
sustainability, and multiplication.
Income for International Min:
$122,851
*Fully Supported US Personnel Working
Cross-Culturally*
Non-residential: 3
Other Personnel
Home staff: 2
Countries/Regions: Global Ministry

WORLD MISSION PRAYER LEAGUE
232 Clifton Avenue
Minneapolis, MN 55403 US
Phone: (612) 871-6843
Email: wmpl@wmpl.org
Website: wmpl.org
Associations: ALMA, Missio Nexus
A denominational sending agency of
Evangelical and Lutheran tradition
engaged in radio or TV broadcasting,

church planting (establishing), discipleship,
addressing human trafficking, medical
ministry, including dental or public health,
and Bible translation.
Purpose: . . . to know Christ, pray for
the advance of his kingdom, share the
gospel and ourselves with those who do
not know him, and encourage Christians
everywhere in this global task.
Year Founded in US: 1937
Income for International Min:
$2,705,000
*Fully Supported US Personnel Working
Cross-Culturally*
More than 4 years: 89
1–4 years: 10
X-C workers in US: 1
Other Personnel
Short-Term less than 1 year: 14
Tentmakers/BAM: 3
Non-US in own/other country: 9
Home staff: 26
Countries/Regions: Bangladesh,
Bolivia, Canada, Central Asia, Democratic
Republic of Congo, East Asia, Ecuador,
Eritrea, Ethiopia, Global Ministry, Hong
Kong (China), India, Japan, Kenya, Mexico,
Mongolia, Nepal, Nigeria, Pakistan, Peru,
Philippines, Russia, South Africa, South
Asia, South Sudan, Uganda

WORLD MISSIONARY ASSISTANCE PLAN
3025 N. Tarra Ave
Prescott, AZ 86301 US
Phone: (928) 515-2404
Email: frontdesk@world-map.com
Website: world-map.com
An interdenominational service agency
of Charismatic and Evangelical tradition
engaged in discipleship, TEE or other
extension education, leadership
development, literature production &
distribution, and translation. (FPC-PE)

Purpose: . . . to make disciples of all nations by equipping indigenous church leaders in Third-World nations through biblically-based, Spirit-filled teaching resources.
Year Founded in US: 1964
Other Personnel
  Home staff: 5

WORLD MISSIONARY PRESS INC.
PO Box 120, 19168 County Road 146
New Paris, IN 46553 US
Phone: (574) 831-2111
Email: mailroom@wmpress.org
Website: wmpress.org
An interdenominational service agency of Evangelical tradition engaged in literature distribution and production. (FPC-PE)
Purpose: . . . to provide Scripture and Bible study booklets, and New Testaments in a variety of languages.
Other Personnel
  Home staff: 50

WORLD MISSIONS & EVANGELISM
PO Box 790
Benton, KY 42025 US
Phone: (270) 527-8369
Email: life@christianfellowhip.org
Website: worldmissionsevangelism.com
A transdenominational sending agency of Evangelical tradition engaged in church planting, development, Christian education, funds transmission, leadership development and support of national workers. (DPE)(FPC16)
Income for International Min:
  $812,913
Fully Supported US Personnel Working Cross-Culturally
  More than 4 years: 23
  X-C workers in US: 4
  Non-residential: 9

Other Personnel
  Short-Term less than 1 year: 3
  Non-US in own/other country: 10
  Home staff: 4
Countries/Regions: Australia, Brunei, China (People's Republic of), Costa Rica, France, Germany, Guatemala, Honduras, Kenya, Mozambique, Philippines, Zimbabwe

WORLD ORPHANS
PO Box 1840
Castle Rock, CO 80104 US
Phone: (720) 362-4881
Email: info@worldorphans.org
Website: worldorphans.org
A specialized agency of Evangelical tradition engaged in childcare/orphanage, children at risk, HIV/AIDS and support of national churches. (DPE)
Purpose: . . . to rescue millions of orphaned and abandoned children, to strengthen thousands of indigenous churches, and to impact hundreds of communities with the Gospel of Jesus Christ . . . through the cost-effective empowerment of church-based orphan prevention, rescue, care, and transition programs in the least-reached areas of the world.
Fully Supported US Personnel Working Cross-Culturally
  More than 4 years: 7
Other Personnel
  Non-US in own/other country: 1
Countries/Regions: Guatemala, Iraq, Kenya

WORLD OUTREACH INTERNATIONAL – US
615 East Sego Lily Drive
Sandy, UT 84070 US
Phone: (801) 572-0211 x 11
Website: world-outreach.com

A nondenominational sending agency of Charismatic and Evangelical tradition engaged in church planting, childcare/orphanage programs, children's programs, discipleship, evangelism and leadership development. (DPE)

Purpose: . . . to impact least reached people groups with the Gospel of Jesus through raising leaders, evangelism, assisting emerging missions, children's ministry and humanitarian aid.

Fully Supported US Personnel Working Cross-Culturally
More than 4 years: 5
1–4 years: 2
Non-residential: 2
Other Personnel
Short-Term less than 1 year: 50
Tentmakers/BAM: 6
Home staff: 10
Countries/Regions: Burkina Faso, Indonesia, Tanzania, Vanuatu

WORLD PARTNERS USA
PO Box 9127
Fort Wayne, IN 46899 US
Phone: (260) 747-2027
Email: info@wpartners.org
Website: wpartners.org
Associations: Missio Nexus

A denominational sending agency of Evangelical tradition engaged in business as mission, church planting (establishing), discipleship, theological education, HIV/AIDS ministry, and leadership development.

Purpose: . . . to facilitate disciple-making movements thereby expanding the Church of Jesus Christ.

Year Founded in US: 1969
Fully Supported US Personnel Working Cross-Culturally
More than 4 years: 14

Other Personnel
Home staff: 5
Countries/Regions: Brunei, Cyprus, Ecuador, France, Guatemala, Indonesia, Ireland (Republic of), Russia, Sierra Leone, South Africa, Spain, Taiwan (China), Thailand, Uruguay

WORLD REACH INC.
PO Box 26155
Birmingham, AL 35260 US
Phone: (205) 979-2400
Email: info@world-reach.org
Website: world-reach.org
Associations: Missio Nexus

A nondenominational sending agency of Evangelical tradition engaged in church planting (establishing), discipleship, church, school or general Christian education, personal or small group evangelism, leadership development, and relief & aid.

Purpose: . . . to propagate the Christian faith around the world by introducing the lost to Jesus Christ and edifying and building up the body of believers.

Year Founded in US: 1982
Income for International Min:
$1,339,199
Fully Supported US Personnel Working Cross-Culturally
More than 4 years: 18
X-C workers in US: 2
Other Personnel
Short-Term less than 1 year: 91
Non-US in own/other country: 41
Home staff: 3
Countries/Regions: Albania, Argentina, Colombia, Eastern Europe and Eurasia, El Salvador, Germany, Global Ministry, Honduras, Kenya, Peru, Romania, Ukraine

WORLD RELIEF
7 E. Baltimore St.
Baltimore, MD 21202 US
Phone: (443) 451-1900
Email: worldrelief@wr.org
Website: worldrelief.org/us-offices

A transdenominational sending agency of
Christian (Restoration Movement) tradition
engaged in relief and/or rehabilitation,
development, agricultural programs,
business as mission, children at risk,
Christian education and HIV/AIDS. (DPE)

Purpose: . . . to work with, for, and from
the Church to alleviate human suffering,
poverty, and hunger worldwide in the
name of Jesus Christ.

Income for International Min:
  $28,300,000

*Fully Supported US Personnel Working
Cross-Culturally*
  More than 4 years: 10
  1–4 years: 23
Other Personnel
  Non-US in own/other country: 1196
  Home staff: 475

Countries/Regions: Burkina Faso,
Burundi, Cambodia, China (People's
Republic of), Republic of Congo, Grenada,
Haiti, India, Indonesia, Kenya, Kosovo,
Liberia, Malawi, Mongolia, Mozambique,
Nicaragua, Rwanda, Sierra Leone, Sudan,
Zimbabwe

WORLD RELIEF CANADA
#310 - 600 Alden Rd.
Markham, ON L3R 0E7 CA
Phone: (905) 415-8181
Email: worldrelief@worldrelief.ca
Website: worldrelief.ca

An interdenominational specialized agency
of Evangelical tradition engaged in relief
and/or rehabilitation, development and
partnership development. (DPE)

Purpose: . . . to respond to the relief and
developmental needs of the world's poor
in the name of Jesus Christ through our
global network of Christian organizations
in partnership with the Canadian and
overseas Church.

Income for International Min:
  $4,785,382

*Fully Supported CA Personnel Working
Cross-Culturally*
  More than 4 years: 2
Other Personnel
  Home staff: 13

Countries/Regions: Bangladesh,
Burundi, Cambodia, China (People's
Republic of), Democratic Republic of
Congo, Ethiopia, India, Kenya, Liberia,
Rwanda, Sudan, Tanzania, Vietnam

WORLD SERVANTS INC.
7130 Portland Avenue South
Richfield, MN 55423 US
Phone: (612) 866-0010
Email: info@worldservants.org
Website: worldservants.org

A nondenominational specialized
agency of Evangelical tradition engaged
in childcare or orphanage, community
development, personal or small group
evangelism, missionary & worker training,
recruiting or mobilizing for mission, and
STM trip coordination.

Purpose: . . . to mobilize a global
network of people to impact the world
through Jesus Christ by responding to
physical and spiritual needs and to develop
and facilitate life changing learning and
serving experiences that bring hope to the
world.

Year Founded in US: 1986
Income for International Min:
  $425,687

Fully Supported US Personnel Working Cross-Culturally
X-C workers in US: 3
Non-residential: 9
Other Personnel
Short-Term less than 1 year: 930
Home staff: 8
Countries/Regions: Canada, Caribbean, Dominican Republic, Ecuador, Global Ministry, Haiti, Jamaica, Kenya, Mexico, Peru, Puerto Rico, South America, Sub-Saharan Africa

WORLD TEAM CANADA
7575 Danbro Cres.
Mississauga, ON L5N 6P9 CA
Phone: (905) 821-6300
Email: wt-canada@worldteam.org
Website: worldteam.org
Associations: Missio Nexus
An interdenominational sending agency of Evangelical tradition engaged in church planting (establishing), mass evangelism, leadership development, partnership development, and Bible translation.
Purpose: . . . to glorify God by working together to establish reproducing churches focusing on unreached peoples of the world.
Fully Supported CA Personnel Working Cross-Culturally
More than 4 years: 22
Other Personnel
Home staff: 4
Countries/Regions: Cambodia, Cameroon, Cuba, Haiti, Italy, Papua, Peru, Spain

WORLD TEAM US
1431 Stuckert Rd
Warrington, PA 18976 US
Phone: (215) 491-4900
Email: wt-usa@worldteam.org
Website: worldteam.org
Associations: Missio Nexus

An interdenominational sending agency of Evangelical tradition engaged in aviation, church planting (establishing), discipleship, personal or small group evangelism, and Bible translation.
Purpose: . . . to glorify God by working together to establish reproducing churches focusing on unreached peoples of the world.
Year Founded in US: 1928
Income for International Min: $8,951,000
Fully Supported US Personnel Working Cross-Culturally
More than 4 years: 180
Other Personnel
Short-Term less than 1 year: 8
Home staff: 36
Countries/Regions: Brazil, Cambodia, Cameroon, Chile, Dominican Republic, France, Global Ministry, Greece, Haiti, Italy, Moldova, Mozambique, Papua, Peru, Philippines, Spain, Suriname, Taiwan (China), Trinidad and Tobago, United Kingdom

WORLD THRUST INTERNATIONAL
3545 Cruse Rd, Ste 309-A
Lawrenceville, GA 30044 US
Phone: (770) 923-5215
Email: info@worldthrust.com
Website: worldthrust.com
Associations: Missio Nexus
A nondenominational service agency of Evangelical tradition engaged in church development, theological education, leadership development, and church mobilization for world evangelization.
Purpose: . . . to see every local church in the world become a sending base for the Gospel of Christ so that a clear presentation and demonstration of it is available to all people.
Year Founded in US: 1984

Fully Supported US Personnel Working Cross-Culturally
More than 4 years: 2
Other Personnel
Home staff: 1
Countries/Regions: Global Ministry

WORLD VISION CANADA
1 World Dr.
Missisauga, ON L5T 2Y4 CA
Phone: (905) 565-6100
Email: info@worldvision.ca
Website: worldvision.ca
A transdenominational service agency of Evangelical tradition engaged in development, children's programs, relief and/or rehabilitation, training and youth programs. (DPE)
Purpose: . . . an international partnership of Christians . . . working with the poor and oppressed to promote human transformation, seek justice, and bear witness to the good news of the Kingdom of God . . . motivated by God's love for all people regardless of race, religion, gender or ethnicity.
Income for International Min:
$306,600,000
Fully Supported CA Personnel Working Cross-Culturally
Non-residential: 10
Other Personnel
Home staff: 552
Countries/Regions: Cambodia, Democratic Republic of Congo, Mali, Senegal, Uganda

WORLD VISION INC.
PO Box 9716
Federal Way, WA 98063-1000 US
Phone: (253) 815-1000
Email: info@worldvision.org
Website: worldvision.org
Associations: Accord Network

An interdenominational service agency of Evangelical tradition engaged in agricultural assistance, childcare or orphanage, justice or peace issues, leadership development, and relief & aid. (FPC-PE)
Purpose: . . . to follow our Lord and Savior Jesus Christ in working with the poor and oppressed to promote human transformation, seek justice, and bear witness to the Good News of the Kingdom of God.
Year Founded in US: 1950
Other Personnel
Home staff: 1150

WORLD WITNESS
918 S Pleasantburg Dr
Greenville, SC 29607 US
Phone: (864) 233-5226
Email: worldwitness@worldwitness.org
Website: worldwitness.org
Associations: Missio Nexus
A denominational sending agency of Presbyterian and Reformed tradition engaged in church planting (establishing), discipleship, church, school or general Christian education, and medical ministry, including dental or public health.
Purpose: . . . to plant healthy, reproducing God-glorifying churches, which are winsomely Reformed in doctrine and Presbyterian in structure, in defined communities across geographic and cultural boundaries.
Year Founded in US: 1907
Income for International Min:
$3,503,956
Fully Supported US Personnel Working Cross-Culturally
More than 4 years: 29
X-C workers in US: 8
Non-residential: 9

Other Personnel
Short-Term less than 1 year: 21
Home staff: 10
Countries/Regions: Eastern Europe
and Eurasia, Germany, Global Ministry,
Lithuania, Poland, South Asia, Spain,
United Kingdom

WORLD-WIDE MISSIONS
PO Box 8338
Redlands, CA 92375 US
Phone: (909) 793-2009
Email: info@world-widemissions.org
Website: world-widemissions.org
A support agency of Evangelical tradition
engaged in support of national workers,
childcare/orphanage programs, church
planting, Christian education, evangelism
and funds transmission. (DPE)
Purpose: . . . to touch the suffering
people of our world with the love of Jesus
Christ, changing forever the lives of men,
women, and children.
Income for International Min:
$11,396,421
*Fully Supported US Personnel Working
Cross-Culturally*
More than 4 years: 9
1–4 years: 5
Non-residential: 13
Other Personnel
Non-US in own/other country: 17
Home staff: 4
Countries/Regions: Bolivia, Brazil,
Republic of Congo, France, India, Jordan,
Kenya, Liberia, Macau (China), Mexico,
Nepal, Papua New Guinea, Peru,
Philippines, Turkey

WORLDVENTURE
1501 W. Mineral Ave.
Littleton, CO 80120 US
Phone: (720) 283-2000
Email: s.west@worldventure.com
Website: worldventure.com
Associations: Missio Nexus
A sending agency of Baptist and
Evangelical tradition engaged in church
planting (establishing), discipleship, church,
school or general Christian education,
theological education, leadership
development, and medical ministry,
including dental or public health.
Purpose: . . . to see people of all nations
transformed by Christ Jesus in partnership
with his church.
Year Founded in US: 1943
Income for International Min:
$31,377,290
*Fully Supported US Personnel Working
Cross-Culturally*
More than 4 years: 453
X-C workers in US: 41
Other Personnel
Short-Term less than 1 year: 11
Home staff: 82
Countries/Regions: Albania,
Argentina, Austria, Belgium, Bolivia,
Brazil, Cambodia, Canada, Central Asia,
Colombia, Costa Rica, Côte d'Ivoire,
Czech Republic, Ecuador, France,
Germany, Ghana, Guinea, Hong Kong
(China), Hungary, India, Indonesia,
Ireland (Republic of), Italy, Japan, Kenya,
Lithuania, Macedonia, Madagascar,
Malawi, Mali, Mexico, Middle East,
Mozambique, Nepal, Netherlands, New
Zealand, North Africa, Pakistan, Panama,
Philippines, Poland, Portugal, Romania,
Russia, Rwanda, Senegal, Singapore,
Slovenia, Spain, Taiwan (China), Tanzania,
Thailand, Uganda, Ukraine, United
Kingdom, Uruguay, Venezuela

WORLDVIEW

6012 SE Yamhill St
Portland, OR 97215 US
Phone: (503) 235-3818
Email: mark.hedinger@iiccworldview.org
Website: iiccworldview.org
Associations: Missio Nexus

A nondenominational service agency of
Evangelical tradition engaged in church,
school or general Christian education.
(FPC-PE)

Purpose: . . . to teach Jesus followers to
effectively share His message in cultures
and languages different than their own.

Year Founded in US: 1985

Other Personnel
   Short-Term less than 1 year: 3
   Home staff: 2

WORLDWIDE
DISCIPLESHIP ASSOC.

PO Box 142437
Fayetteville, GA 30214-6515 US
Phone: (770) 460-1337
Email: info@disciplebuilding.org
Website: disciplebuilding.org

An interdenominational support agency
of Evangelical tradition engaged in
discipleship and mass evangelism.

Purpose: . . . to serve the Church
worldwide by developing Christlike
character in people and equipping them
to disciple others according to the pattern
Jesus used to train his disciples.

Year Founded in US: 1974

*Fully Supported US Personnel Working
Cross-Culturally*
   More than 4 years: 4
Other Personnel
   Home staff: 13
Countries/Regions: Brazil, Kenya,
Tanzania, Uganda

WORLDWIDE LAB IMPROVEMENT

3607 Gembrit Cir
Kalamazoo, MI 49001 US
Phone: (269) 323-8407
Email: mail@wwlab.org
Website: wwlab.org

A nondenominational service agency of
Independent tradition engaged in medical
supplies and medical ministry, including
dental or public health. (FPC-PE)

Purpose: . . . to serve Jesus Christ by
providing mission hospitals, clinics, and
short-term teams in developing countries
with quality clinical laboratory equipment,
supplies, consulting, and on-site training at
reasonable cost.

Year Founded in US: 1995

Other Personnel
   Home staff: 2

WORLDWIDE MEDICAL-DENTAL
EVANGELICAL MISSION

1615 Farrier Trail
Clearwater, FL 33765 US
Phone: (727) 797-6830
Email: ssoliman98@yahoo.com
Website: mdemission.org

A specialized agency of Evangelical and
Fundamental tradition engaged in medical
work, Bible distribution, broadcasting,
church planting and evangelism. (DPE)

Purpose: . . . to use our professions
as dentists and physicians to spread the
Gospel and bring the lost to Christ . . .
to help the poor and needy . . . to plant
churches.

Other Personnel
   Short-Term less than 1 year: 8

WORLDWIDE TENTMAKERS INC.

2435 East North St., Ste. 1108
Greenville, SC 29615 US
Phone: (864) 370-0475
Email: office@worldwidetentmakers.com
Website: worldwidetentmakers.com
A service agency of Baptist tradition
engaged in business as mission,
management consulting/training,
tentmaking and TESOL. (DPE)
Purpose: . . . committed to assisting local
fundamentalist churches in the promotion,
preparation, and placement of self-
supporting witnesses worldwide.
Income for International Min:
  $250,000
*Fully Supported US Personnel Working
Cross-Culturally*
  More than 4 years: 4
  1–4 years: 5
  Non-residential: 9
Other Personnel
  Tentmakers/BAM: 2
  Non-US in own/other country: 9
  Home staff: 2
Countries/Regions: Asia, United
Kingdom

WYCLIFFE ASSOCIATES

P.O. Box 620143, 11450 Translation Way
Orlando, FL 32862 US
Phone: (800) 843-9673
Email: web@wycliffeassociates.org
Website: wycliffeassociates.org
A nondenominational service agency
of Evangelical tradition engaged in
community development, and Bible &
other translation.
Purpose: . . . to involve people in the
advancement of Bible translation and to
accelerate Bible translation through new
methodologies, technology, volunteers,
and the local church.
Year Founded in US: 1967

Income for International Min:
  $41,075,924
*Fully Supported US Personnel Working
Cross-Culturally*
  More than 4 years: 18
  1–4 years: 88
  X-C workers in US: 70
Other Personnel
  Non-US in own/other country: 80
  Home staff: 250
Countries/Regions: Caribbean, Central
America, Central Asia, East Asia, Eastern
Europe and Eurasia, Global Ministry,
Middle East, North Africa, Oceania, South
America, South Asia, Southeast Asia, Sub-
Saharan Africa, Western Europe

WYCLIFFE BIBLE TRANSLATORS OF CANADA INC.

4316 - 10 St. NE
Calgary, AB T2E 6K3 CA
Phone: (403) 250-5411
Email: info@wycliffe.ca
Website: wycliffe.ca/wycliffe
Associations: Missio Nexus
An interdenominational sending agency
of Evangelical tradition engaged in
Bible translation, Bible distribution,
development, linguistics, literacy work and
translation work. (DPE)
Purpose: . . . to empower indigenous
people worldwide for spiritual, personal
and social growth through Bible translation
and other language-related ministries.
Year Founded in CA: 1968
Income for International Min:
  $11,808,452
*Fully Supported CA Personnel Working
Cross-Culturally*
  More than 4 years: 239
Other Personnel
  Home staff: 12
Countries/Regions: Africa, Asia,
Austria, Brazil, Burkina Faso, Cameroon,
Central Asia, Chad, Democratic Republic

of Congo, Ethiopia, Ghana, Kenya, Latin America, Mali, Mexico, Mozambique, Netherlands, Nigeria, Papua New Guinea, Philippines, Senegal, South Pacific, Tanzania, Togo, United Kingdom, Unspecified Country

WYCLIFFE BIBLE TRANSLATORS USA
PO Box 628200
Orlando, FL 32862 US
Phone: (800) 992-5433
Email: info@wycliffe.org
Website: wycliffe.org
Associations: Missio Nexus

A nondenominational sending agency of Evangelical tradition engaged in community development, linguistics, literacy, prayer-intercession, recruiting or mobilizing for mission, and Bible translation. (FPC-PE)

Purpose: . . . to see a Bible translation program in progress in every language still needing one by 2025.

Year Founded in US: 1942
Fully Supported US Personnel Working Cross-Culturally
    More than 4 years: 1468
Countries/Regions: Australia, Bangladesh, Belgium, Belize, Benin, Brazil, Bulgaria, Burkina Faso, Cambodia, Cameroon, Central African Republic, Chad, Chile, Colombia, Democratic Republic of Congo, Costa Rica, Côte d'Ivoire, Ecuador, Ethiopia, Finland, France, Germany, Ghana, Guatemala, Guyana, Honduras, India, Indonesia, Kenya, Malawi, Malaysia, Mali, Mexico, Mozambique, New Zealand, Niger, Nigeria, Northern Mariana Islands, Papua New Guinea, Paraguay, Peru, Philippines, Romania, Senegal, Singapore, Solomon Islands, South Africa, Spain, Sweden, Switzerland, Tanzania, Thailand, Togo,

Trinidad and Tobago, Uganda, United Kingdom, Unspecified Country, Vanuatu, Vietnam

YOUNG LIFE
420 N Cascade Ave.
Colorado Springs, CO 80903 US
Phone: (719) 381-1890
Email: athomas@sc.younglife.org
Website: younglife.org

A nondenominational sending agency of Evangelical tradition engaged in camping programs, student evangelism, international student ministry, and youth ministry. (FPC-PE)

Purpose: . . . to introduce adolescents to Jesus Christ and help them grow in their faith by praying for young people and building personal relationships with them.

Year Founded in US: 1941
Fully Supported US Personnel Working Cross-Culturally
    More than 4 years: 39
    1–4 years: 47
Countries/Regions: Africa, Asia, Caribbean, Europe, Latin America, Russia, United Kingdom

YOUNG LIFE OF CANADA
#120 - 9440 202nd St.
Langley, BC V1M 4A6 CA
Phone: (604) 881-6023
Email: national@younglife.ca
Website: younglife.ca

A nondenominational support agency of Evangelical tradition engaged in youth programs, camping programs and discipleship. (DPE)

Purpose: . . . loving teenagers in their world encouraging them to know Jesus Christ.

Other Personnel
    Home staff: 8

Making the Bible accessible to *all people.*

Wycliffe Bible Translators believes every person deserves to experience God's Word in the language and form they understand best.

Learn more at **wycliffe.org.**

YOUTH FOR CHRIST CANADA
#308 - 8047 - 199 St.
Langley, BC V2Y 0E2 CA
Phone: (604) 637-3400
Email: tim.coles@yfccanada.org
Website: yfccanada.org
A nondenominational service agency of
Evangelical tradition engaged in DMM,
discipleship, personal or small group
evangelism, student evangelism, leadership
development, and youth ministry. (FPC-PE)
Purpose: . . . to participate in the body of
Christ in responsible evangelism of youth,
presenting them with the person, work and
teachings of Christ and discipling them into
the Church.
Year Founded in CA: 1972
*Fully Supported CA Personnel Working
Cross-Culturally*
    More than 4 years: 2
    1–4 years: 2
Countries/Regions: Argentina, United
Kingdom

YOUTH FOR CHRIST
INTERNATIONAL
PO Box 4555
Englewood, CO 80155-4555 US
Phone: (303) 843-9000
Email: info@yfci.org
Website: yfci.org
An interdenominational support agency
of Evangelical tradition engaged in youth
programs, discipleship, evangelism,
leadership development and training.
(DPE)

Purpose: . . . to see that every young
person in every people group in every
nation has the opportunity to make an
informed decision to be a follower of
Jesus Christ and become part of a local
church . . . to participate in the body of
Christ in responsible evangelism of youth,
presenting them with the person, work and
teachings of Christ and discipling them into
a local church.
Year Founded in US: 1992
Other Personnel
    Home staff: 13

YOUTH FOR CHRIST/USA
PO Box 4478
Englewood, CO 80155 US
Phone: (303) 843-9000
Email: worldinfo@yfc.net
Website: yfc.org
A nondenominational sending agency of
Evangelical tradition engaged in youth
evangelism and youth programs. (DPE)
Purpose: . . . facilitate USA citizens to
serve the YFC International movement in
reaching youth in nearly 100 countries in
the world.
Income for International Min:
    $4,500,000
*Fully Supported US Personnel Working
Cross-Culturally*
    More than 4 years: 92
    Non-residential: 6
Other Personnel
    Short-Term less than 1 year: 1400
    Home staff: 19
Countries/Regions: Africa, Australia,
Belgium, Bolivia, Brazil, Cayman Islands,
Europe, France, Germany, Guinea-Bissau,
Honduras, Ireland (Republic of), Italy,
Japan, Kenya, Middle East, New Zealand,
Philippines, Portugal, Rwanda, Slovakia,
South Africa, Spain, Switzerland, Thailand,
Uganda, United Kingdom

YOUTH MINISTRY INTERNATIONAL

1300 Envoy Circle, Ste. 1306
Louisville, KY 40299 US
Phone: (502) 493-9530
Email: info@ymitraining.com
Website: ymitraining.com
A nondenominational service agency
of Evangelical tradition engaged in
childcare or orphanage, theological
education, international student ministry,
leadership development, missionary &
worker training, and youth ministry.
Purpose: . . . to train national youth
workers for local churches within the
people groups of the world.
Year Founded in US: 1991
*Fully Supported US Personnel Working
Cross-Culturally*
More than 4 years: 10
Other Personnel
Non-US in own/other country: 8
Home staff: 5
Countries/Regions: Cuba, Global
Ministry, Indonesia, Kenya, Malaysia,
Nepal, Romania, Ukraine

YOUTH WITH A MISSION (YWAM)

Phone: (805) 642-5327
Email: info@ywam.org
Website: ywam.org
An interdenominational sending agency
of Charismatic and Evangelical tradition
engaged in youth programs, discipleship,
evangelism, missionary training and relief
and/or rehabilitation. (DPE)
*Fully Supported US Personnel Working
Cross-Culturally*
1–4 years: 1500
Other Personnel
Short-Term less than 1 year: 11325
Non-US in own/other country: 6162
Countries/Regions: Africa, Asia,
Australia, Europe, Latin America, Middle
East, New Zealand, Oceania

YOUTH WITH A MISSION CANADA INC.

PO Box 57100
Vancouver, BC V5K 5G6 CA
Phone: (604) 436-4433
Email: communications@ywamcanada.org
Website: ywamcanada.ca
An interdenominational sending agency
of Charismatic and Evangelical tradition
engaged in discipleship, evangelism,
mobilization for mission, short-term
programs and missionary training. (DPE)
Purpose: . . . to know God and to make
Him known.
Income for International Min:
$6,000,000
*Fully Supported CA Personnel Working
Cross-Culturally*
Non-residential: 13
Other Personnel
Home staff: 305

YUGO MINISTRIES (YOUTH UNLIMITED GOSPEL OUTREACH INC.)

PO Box 58
National City, CA 91951 US
Phone: (619) 336-9003 x3002
Email: outreach@yugo.org
Website: yugo.org
An interdenominational sending agency of
Evangelical tradition engaged in short-term
programs, childcare/orphanage programs,
evangelism, leadership development,
mobilization for mission and home
construction. (DPE)
Purpose: . . . to win the Mexican people
to Christ . . . to teach them to disciple
their neighbors . . . to challenge North
American Christians with world missions.
Year Founded in US: 1965
Income for International Min:
$2,060,000

Fully Supported US Personnel Working Cross-Culturally
   More than 4 years: 36
Other Personnel
   Tentmakers/BAM: 3
   Non-US in own/other country: 6
   Home staff: 8
Countries/Regions: Mexico

YUGO MINISTRIES CANADA
PO Box 68
Legal, AB T0G 1L0 CA
Phone: (780) 961-7625
Email: yugocanada@yugo.org
Website: yugo.org
An interdenominational sending agency of Baptist tradition engaged in short-term mission trips for youth & adults, childcare/orphanage programs, church planting, evangelism, support of national churches and support of national workers. (DPE)
Income for International Min:
   $243,563
Fully Supported CA Personnel Working Cross-Culturally
   More than 4 years: 6
   1–4 years: 4
Other Personnel
   Short-Term less than 1 year: 345
   Non-CA in own/other country: 1
   Home staff: 1
Countries/Regions: Mexico

ZION EVANGELICAL MINISTRIES OF AFRICA (ZEMA)
PO Box 727
Zion, IL 60999 US
Phone: (847) 872-7363
Email: zema@zema.org
Website: zema.org
Associations: Missio Nexus
A nondenominational sending agency of Evangelical tradition engaged in Bible distribution, camping programs, church, school or general Christian education, theological education, and STM trip coordination. (FPC-PE)
Purpose: . . . to know Christ and make Him known among the amaZioni of Southern Africa.
Year Founded in US: 1907
Income for International Min:
   $60,000
Fully Supported US Personnel Working Cross-Culturally
   More than 4 years: 12
   1–4 years: 3
Other Personnel
   Non-US in own/other country: 18
Countries/Regions: Mozambique, South Africa, Swaziland

Updates?
Questions?

Find information for updates and future editions of the Mission Handbook online.

MissioNexus.org/MissionHandbook

MISSIO NEXUS®

United we can do more!

Together we are building a Great Commission association that affirms our unique contributions and promotes generous collaboration for God's glory and the rejoicing of the nations.

Come with us.

CHAPTER 6
COUNTRIES OF ACTIVITY

This chapter lists the countries and continents where agencies reported field personnel engaged in ministry who are fully supported through either a US or Canadian sending agency. They are listed in alphabetical order according to the name most commonly recognized in North America. The organizations in each country or continent appear in alphabetical order.

Personnel numbers are separated into five categories. The first three categories are under the heading "Personnel from US or Canada" so represent those who are serving overseas and are fully supported with funds from their agency in the US or Canada. The "Other Countries" heading includes two categories: personnel who are not citizens of the US or Canada, but who are or are not citizens in the country of their ministry. These personnel are fully or partially supported by funds raised in the US or Canada by the associated agency.

| | | Personnel from US or Canada | | | Other Countries | |
	First Year	1–2 years	2–4 years	4+ years	Citizen	Not Citizen
Afghanistan						
EPC World Outreach				1		
Global Gates	2014			2		
Habitat for Humanity International			1			1
HOPE International	2004	1		1		
HOPE International Development Agency	2006				2	
Interserve USA	1962			22		
MEDA – Mennonite Economic Development Associates	2007				18	2
OM Canada		1		3		
People International USA				1		
Pioneers Canada			1			
Precept Ministries International						2
Ripe for Harvest Inc.				1		
Seventh-day Adventists – General Conference – Global Mission	1971					2
Shelter for Life Intl. Inc.					1	
Volunteers in Medical Missions				1		
Women to the World Inc.					1	
World Concern	1982	2		2	16	
Africa						
A.C.T. International	2006					2
ABWE Canada (Across Borders for World Evangelism)				2		
ACCI (Adventive Cross Cultural Initiatives) – US	2009		4			
African Enterprise Canada				3	3	
ARISE International Mission				4		
Bible League Canada	1980			5		
Canadian National Baptist Convention (CNBC)	2004					4
Christian and Missionary Alliance in Canada, The				11		
Christian Churches / Churches of Christ				4		
Cooperative Baptist Fellowship – Global Missions	1996			6		
endPoverty.org	1985				1	
Evangelical Christian Church in Canada, The	1988			1	1	
Fellowship of Companies for Christ International (FCCI)	2007				1	
Final Frontiers Foundation	1990				200	
Frontiers Canada	1984			6		
Gideons International, The					13	
Global Aid Network Inc. – Canada	2004		25	25		
globalLead					2	
Globe International	1993			2		
Good News Productions International	1995			2	8	
International Christian Ministries Canada (ICM)	1990		2	8	4	
InterServe Canada			4			
Mercy Ships		300	100	50	15	75

	First Year	Personnel from US or Canada			Other Countries	
		1–2 years	2–4 years	4+ years	Citizen	Not Citizen
Mission Aviation Fellowship	1961			2	2	
Navigators of Canada, The	1973			3		
New Tribes Mission of Canada				14		
OM Canada		2		5		
Power to Change Ministries	1998			2		
Presbyterian Church (USA) Worldwide Ministries			85	80		
Proclaim! International Inc.	2004			1		1
Rosedale Mennonite Missions	2007			5		
Salvation Army – Canada and Bermuda Territory, The			1	11		
Talking Bibles International	2002				1	
The Christian and Missionary Alliance	1996			182		
World Christian Outreach Inc.	1999		1	15		
World Concern	1980			30		
World Link Ministries	1993			2	6	
Wycliffe Bible Translators of Canada Inc.				5		
Young Life		2		4		
Youth for Christ/USA				2		
Youth With A Mission (YWAM)			127		733	
Albania						
Alongside Ministries International	1995			3	3	
Assemblies of God World Missions	1991	2		4		
BILD International				1	5	
Camino Global	2005			2	1	1
Campus Crusade for Christ (Cru in the US)		1		8		
Child Evangelism Fellowship Inc.				1		
Christian Aid Mission					21	
Church of God (Cleveland TN) World Missions	1993		2			2
Church of the Nazarene Inc.	1993			2		
Commission to Every Nation	2003			2		2
East European Missions Network				4		
Eastern Mennonite Missions	2013		2	2	2	
European Christian Mission Intl. – USA				12		
Evangelism Explosion III International Inc.	2015				1	
Fellowship of Evangelical Churches – International Ministries	1994			6		
Foursquare Missions International				2		
Global Missions (United Pentecostal Church Intl.)			1			
Global Partners (The Wesleyan Church World Headquarters)				10		
Globe International	1995			6		
Gospel Fellowship Association	1997			2		
Gospel Tide Broadcasting Association	2015				2	
Greater Grace World Outreach	1995	2				
International Pentecostal Holiness Church	2001		2		2	

	First Year	Personnel from US or Canada 1–2 years	2–4 years	4+ years	Other Countries Citizen	Not Citizen
International Teams U.S.A.		1		4		2
Operation Mobilization		2			3	14
Rosedale Mennonite Missions	2005			2		2
Seventh-day Adventists – General Conference – Global Mission	1992			2		
Virginia Mennonite Missions	1999	2	2	4	2	6
WEC International Canada	1993			1		
Wisconsin Evangelical Lutheran Synod – Board for World Missions				1		
World Reach Inc.	1999			2		
WorldVenture				4		
Algeria						
Christian Aid Mission	2005				6	
Pioneers Canada				2		
Seventh-day Adventists – General Conference – Global Mission	1905					2
American Samoa						
Global Missions (United Pentecostal Church Intl.)	1999		2			2
Andorra						
Elim Fellowship	2007			2		
Angola						
Assemblies of God World Missions	1983			2		
Canadian Baptist Ministries	1956			1	1	
Child Evangelism Fellowship Inc.				1		
Christian Church (Disciples of Christ) – Global Ministries			1			
Church of the Nazarene Inc.	1992			2		2
Evangelical Missionary Church of Canada	1996		2			
Mission Aviation Fellowship of Canada (MAFC)	1989	1		2		
Operation Mobilization					3	2
Precept Ministries International				1		
Seventh-day Adventists – General Conference – Global Mission	1924					2
SIM Canada				6		
SIM USA				7		
The Pentecostal Assemblies of Canada				2		
Anguilla						
Baptist International Missions Inc.				2		
Antigua and Barbuda						
Assemblies of God World Missions	1996	2		2		
Baptist International Missions Inc.				4		
BCM International	1995				1	
Biblical Ministries Worldwide				4		4
Global Outreach Mission Inc.				1		

	First Year	Personnel from US or Canada			Other Countries	
		1–2 years	2–4 years	4+ years	Citizen	Not Citizen
Seventh-day Adventists – General Conference – Global Mission	1944			2		2
Argentina						
ABWE International				5		
AMG International					2	
Assemblies of God World Missions	1910			28		
Avant Ministries	1911			4		
Awana Clubs International					3	
Baptist Bible Fellowship International – World Mission Service Center	1959			16		
Baptist General Conference of Canada	2007			1		
Baptist International Missions Inc.				6		
Baptist Mid-Missions	1987			8	2	
Baptist Missionary Association of America (BMAA)					2	
Biblical Ministries Worldwide				14		14
Canadian Baptist Ministries	2008			1		
Child Evangelism Fellowship Inc.				1		
Chosen People Ministries Inc.	1940			1	1	
Christian Aid Mission	1983				41	
Christian Churches / Churches of Christ				4	4	
Church of the Nazarene Inc.	1909			8	8	5
Converge				4		
Elim Fellowship	2000			2		
Encompass World Partners	1909				3	
Evangelism Explosion III International Inc.	2010				1	
Fellowship International Mission	2010			4	3	
Global Missions (United Pentecostal Church Intl.)	1967	2				4
Global Missions of Open Bible Churches	1961				1	
Global Outreach International	2001			5	3	
Globe International	2001			2		
Go Ye Fellowship	1968			1		1
Gospel Fellowship Association	2005			2		
Gospel Mission of South America Inc.	1970			8		
Gospel Mission of South America of Canada				1		1
Greater Grace World Outreach	1994			2		
IFCA World Missions					1	
Impact International Inc.	1959				2	
International Gospel Outreach	1973			5	4	1
International Teams U.S.A.						2
Life in Messiah International	2012			2		
LOGOI Ministries	1972				1	
Luis Palau Evangelistic Association					2	
Lutheran Church Missouri Synod – World Mission	1902			1		
Macedonia World Baptist Missions Inc.	2014			2		
Master's Resourcing Commission				1		

	First Year	Personnel from US or Canada				Other Countries	
		1–2 years	2–4 years	4+ years		Citizen	Not Citizen
Mennonite Mission Network	1917		2	6		10	
National Association of Congregational Christian Churches	1988					3	
On The Go Ministries/Keith Cook Team	1948			1			
Operation Mobilization		2				7	5
Palm Missionary Ministries Inc.	2006						2
Precept Ministries International							1
Reach Beyond							2
Reformed Baptist Mission Services							2
Salvation Army – Canada and Bermuda Territory, The				1			
Seventh-day Adventists – General Conference – Global Mission	1890						6
Source of Light Ministries Intl. Inc.						1	
Spanish World Ministries						1	
The Brethren Church Inc.	1941					3	
The Navigators				6			
The Salvation Army USA National Headquarters	1890		3				
United World Mission Inc.				2		2	
White Fields						12	
Word of Life Fellowship Inc.	1971			8		127	30
World Gospel Mission	1970	2		5			
World Reach Inc.	2008					2	
WorldVenture				6			
Youth for Christ Canada				2			
Armenia							
Assemblies of God World Missions	1999	4		4			
Baptist Missionary Association of America (BMAA)						2	
Child Evangelism Fellowship Inc.				2			
Church of the Nazarene Inc.	2002					1	1
Evangelism Explosion III International Inc.	2009					1	
Global Missions (United Pentecostal Church Intl.)			1				
Harvest Foundation							2
InterVarsity Christian Fellowship/USA			1				
Medical Ministry International	1990					1	
Precept Ministries International						1	
Reach A Village						4	
Seventh-day Adventists – General Conference – Global Mission	1990			1			1
Walk Thru the Bible Ministries Inc.	2000					1	
Aruba							
Assemblies of God World Missions	1992		2				
Church of God (Cleveland TN) World Missions	1968		2				
Global Missions (United Pentecostal Church Intl.)		2					3

	First Year	Personnel from US or Canada			Other Countries	
		1–2 years	2–4 years	4+ years	Citizen	Not Citizen
Asia						
ABWE Canada (Across Borders for World Evangelism)			2	1		
ACCI (Adventive Cross Cultural Initiatives) – US	2007			1		2
ARISE International Mission					5	
Asian Outreach International Canada					20	
BEE World (Biblical Education by Extension)	1994			7	2	
Café 1040 Inc.	2008	1	1			
Canadian National Baptist Convention (CNBC)	1991			2		8
CEIFA International	1995			13	13	
China Outreach Ministries Inc.	2005			2		2
Christian and Missionary Alliance in Canada, The				12		
Christian Churches / Churches of Christ				6	2	
Commission to Every Nation	2000		1	2	1	2
Compassion International Inc.		3	1	2		
Cooperative Baptist Fellowship – Global Missions	1993		3	12		
Fellowship of Companies for Christ International (FCCI)	2007				1	
Fellowship of Evangelical Churches – International Ministries	1994			2		
Final Frontiers Foundation	1986				550	
Frontiers Canada	1984			10	1	
Gideons International, The					7	
globalLead					3	
Go to Nations	1987			3	1	2
Gospel for Asia Inc.	1979				9523	
Hope for the Hungry	1981			2		
International Street Kids Outreach Ministries (ISKOM)	1998	1			164	
InterServe Canada	1975		15			
Lutheran Church Missouri Synod – World Mission				2		
Mission Aviation Fellowship	1992		2	20	2	
Mission ONE Inc.					100	
Missionary Athletes International	2008		1			
Navigators of Canada, The	1988		2	2		
New Tribes Mission of Canada		2		39		
OM Canada				3		
OMS International – Canada				4		
Open Door Baptist Missions	2002			7	2	
Partners in Asian Missions	1972				159	
Power to Change Ministries	1997	12	4	12		
Presbyterian Church (USA) Worldwide Ministries			70	65		
Presbyterian Missionary Union	2000			1		
Ravi Zacharias International Ministries Inc.	2004				1	3
Reformed Baptist Mission Services						2
Rosedale Mennonite Missions	2000			2		
The Christian and Missionary Alliance				287		

	First Year	Personnel from US or Canada			Other Countries	
		1–2 years	2–4 years	4+ years	Citizen	Not Citizen
World Concern					30	
World Indigenous Missions	1996			7		8
Worldwide Tentmakers Inc.	2004	3	2	2		7
Wycliffe Bible Translators of Canada Inc.				11		
Young Life		4	1	1		
Youth With A Mission (YWAM)			344		2694	
Australia						
ABWE International				16		
Advent Christian World Outreach	2012				1	
AMG International						2
Awana Clubs International					1	
Baptist Bible Fellowship International – World Mission Service Center	1968			22		
Baptist International Missions Inc.				14		
Baptist Mid-Missions	1968			4		
Biblical Ministries Worldwide				9		9
BILD International					1	
Campus Crusade for Christ (Cru in the US)		8		12		
Child Evangelism Fellowship Inc.				2		
Chosen People Ministries Inc.	1999				8	
Christian Aid Mission					38	
Christian Churches / Churches of Christ				20	4	
Church of God (Cleveland TN) World Missions	1976	2	2			4
Church of the Nazarene Inc.	1946			2		2
CMF International	2014		1			1
Compassio					2	
CRM					12	
Crossover Communications International	2014	2				
Development Associates Intl. (DAI)					1	
Elim Fellowship	1998			1		
Emmanuel Intl. Canada				1		
Fellowship International Mission	1994				2	
Foursquare Missions International	1929			2		
Global Frontier Missions	2015	4				
Global Missions (United Pentecostal Church Intl.)	1973		4			6
Global Outreach Mission Inc.	1994			2		
Global Partners (The Wesleyan Church World Headquarters)				2		
Global Recordings Network					30	6
Gospel Fellowship Association	1973			6		
Habitat for Humanity International	1988		1		1	
IFCA World Missions					1	
International Teams U.S.A.		2		3		17

	First Year	Personnel from US or Canada			Other Countries	
		1–2 years	2–4 years	4+ years	Citizen	Not Citizen
InterVarsity Christian Fellowship/USA			1			
Jews for Jesus				3		
Mennonite Mission Network	2000			1		
Mission Aviation Fellowship of Canada (MAFC)				3		
Mission to the World (PCA) Inc.	1984	1	1	20		
Missions Resource Network	1845			6		
One Mission Society						3
Operation Mobilization		1			35	14
Presbyterian Church (USA) Worldwide Ministries				2		
Presbyterian Missionary Union	2004			2		
Reach Beyond				2		
Salvation Army – Canada and Bermuda Territory, The	1996		3			
Seventh-day Adventists – General Conference – Global Mission	1885	3		3		7
TEAM (The Evangelical Alliance Mission)	1964			2		
Teen Missions International Inc.	1987		3	4		
The Navigators				8		
The Salvation Army USA National Headquarters	1881		2	1		
Word of Life Fellowship Inc.	1970			2		5
World Missions & Evangelism	2008			2		
Wycliffe Bible Translators USA				10		
Youth for Christ/USA				2		
Youth With A Mission (YWAM)			218			
Austria						
Action International Ministries	1987			1		1
Assemblies of God World Missions	1967	5		12		
Baptist International Missions Inc.				2		
Biblical Ministries Worldwide				2		2
Child Evangelism Fellowship Inc.				1		
Christian Churches / Churches of Christ			2	6	9	
Church of God (Cleveland TN) World Missions	1980			2		
Entrust	1979			4		
European Christian Mission Intl. – USA				10		
Foursquare Missions International	1993		2			
Global Missions (United Pentecostal Church Intl.)	1971		2			1
Global Outreach Mission Inc.				1		
Global Partners (The Wesleyan Church World Headquarters)				9		
Go Ye Fellowship	2002			2		2
Gospel Fellowship Association	1997	1		7		
Greater Europe Mission			2	7		
Greater Grace World Outreach	1984					
International Association For Refugees	2016			1		

	First Year	Personnel from US or Canada 1–2 years	2–4 years	4+ years	Other Countries Citizen	Not Citizen
International Teams Canada (Evangelical International Crusades Canada Inc.)				2		
International Teams U.S.A.	1978			28	4	4
MB Mission	1953			2		
MB Mission Canada	1953			2		
Mission to the World (PCA) Inc.	1991			2		
Missions Resource Network	1953			8		
OM Canada	1960	2				
Operation Mobilization		4			11	29
Pioneers Canada				2		
ReachGlobal				5		
Resourcing Christian Education International	2004				22	22
Seventh-day Adventists – General Conference – Global Mission	1902	1				
TCM International Institute	1957	6	2	4		
TEAM (The Evangelical Alliance Mission)	1963			6		
Titus International	2005			2		
TWR				12		
Word of Life Fellowship Inc.	1997			2	2	
WorldVenture				10		
Wycliffe Bible Translators of Canada Inc.				1		
Azerbaijan						
Global Missions (United Pentecostal Church Intl.)	2004		1			
Greater Grace World Outreach	1991				4	
Mission Eurasia					4	
Bahamas						
Baptist Bible Fellowship International – World Mission Service Center	1999			2		
Baptist International Missions Inc.				3		
Christ to the Nations				4		
Christian Churches / Churches of Christ				2		
Global Missions (United Pentecostal Church Intl.)						2
Helps Ministries	2016			2		
Macedonia World Baptist Missions Inc.	2006			2		
Missions Door					1	
Open Air Campaigners – Overseas Ministries (OAC-OM)	2012				1	
Precept Ministries International	2001				2	
Bahrain						
Church of God (Cleveland TN) World Missions	1984					2
Eastern Mennonite Missions	2015	1				
Interserve USA	1975			3		
Reformed Church in America – General Synod Council – Global Mission				3		
Bangladesh						
AMG International					16	
Awana Clubs International					6	

	First Year	Personnel from US or Canada			Other Countries	
		1–2 years	2–4 years	4+ years	Citizen	Not Citizen
Baptist Mid-Missions	1979				1	4
Beautiful Feet	2007				1	
BILD International					1	
Christian Aid Mission					90	
Christian Churches / Churches of Christ					2	
Christian Reformed World Missions	2004		2			
Church of the Nazarene Inc.	1992				1	
Compassion International Inc.	2004			1	33	
Cross-Cultural Ministries – Churches of God General Conference	1905				1	
Evangelical Friends Mission	2005				2	
Evangelism Explosion III International Inc.	2015				2	
Global Gates	2014			3		
Global Missions (United Pentecostal Church Intl.)	2004	2				
Global Recordings Network					4	
Habitat for Humanity International	1999	1				1
International Partnership Ministries Inc.	2004					6
Interserve USA	1852			4		
Liebenzell Mission of Canada	1974		2			
Mission to the World (PCA) Inc.				1		
Reformed Church in America – General Synod Council – Global Mission						2
Salvation Army – Canada and Bermuda Territory, The	1994		2	1		
Seventh-day Adventists – General Conference – Global Mission	1906					8
SIM USA				8		
Surfing the Nations	2004				1	
The Pentecostal Assemblies of Canada				2		
Walk Thru the Bible Ministries Inc.	2000				1	
World Concern	1978				251	
World Mission Prayer League	1972			6	1	1
Wycliffe Bible Translators USA				3		
Barbados						
Baptist International Missions Inc.				2		
Christian Churches / Churches of Christ				6		
Global Outreach International	2005			2		
IFCA World Missions					2	
National Baptist Convention USA Inc. – Foreign Mission Board	1975				1	
Belarus						
Campus Crusade for Christ (Cru in the US)				2		
Christian Aid Mission					48	
Christian Relief Fund, The	2005				1	
East European Missions Network					2	
Global Missions (United Pentecostal Church Intl.)	1990	2				
Greater Europe Mission				3		

	First Year	Personnel from US or Canada			Other Countries	
		1–2 years	2–4 years	4+ years	Citizen	Not Citizen
International Teams U.S.A.						2
Mission Eurasia					8	
Reach A Village					2	
Slavic Gospel Association – Canada				1		
Slavic Missionary Service Inc.				1		
TCM International Institute					1	
Walk Thru the Bible Ministries Inc.	2000				4	
Belgium						
Assemblies of God World Missions	1969	14		33		
Avant Ministries	1966			2		
Baptist Bible Fellowship International – World Mission Service Center	1962			4		
Child Evangelism Fellowship Inc.				2		
Christian Churches / Churches of Christ				1		
Church of God (Cleveland TN) World Missions	1973			5		
Cooperative Baptist Fellowship – Global Missions	1995			1		
Development Associates Intl. (DAI)					1	
European Christian Mission Intl. – USA				5		
FAIR				1		
Faith Christian Fellowship Intl.					1	
Global Missions (United Pentecostal Church Intl.)			2			
Global Outreach Mission Inc.				2		
Global Recordings Network					2	
Greater Europe Mission				3		
International Pentecostal Holiness Church	1999			6		
International Teams U.S.A.						2
InterVarsity Christian Fellowship/USA			1			
Link International Ministries	2008					1
Macedonia World Baptist Missions Inc.	2015			2		
Mission to the World (PCA) Inc.	2001		1	14		
Operation Mobilization		9			3	24
ReachGlobal				7		
United World Mission Inc.		1		4	2	3
WorldVenture				4		
Wycliffe Bible Translators USA				1		
Youth for Christ/USA				1		
Belize						
Assemblies of God World Missions	1950			6		
Avant Ministries	1955			2		
Baptist Bible Fellowship International – World Mission Service Center	1979			6		
Baptist International Missions Inc.				8		

	First Year	Personnel from US or Canada			Other Countries	
		1–2 years	2–4 years	4+ years	Citizen	Not Citizen
BCM International	1998				1	
Calvary Commission Inc.				6		
Child Evangelism Fellowship Inc.				2		
Christian Outreach International				1		
Church of God Ministries (Anderson) – Global Strategy	1989					2
Commission to Every Nation	2008			2		2
Congregational Methodist Missions				1		
Cooperative Baptist Fellowship – Global Missions	2008	2				
Eastern Mennonite Missions	2015		2			
Episcopal Church USA – Domestic & Foreign Missionary Society		17	9	42		
Equip Inc & Equip International	2014	2				
Evangelical Congregational Church – Global Ministries Commission				1		
Evangelical Mennonite Mission Conference	1965			1		
Friends United Meeting				2		
Global Missions (United Pentecostal Church Intl.)	1984		3			3
Global Outreach International	1991			11		
Global Outreach Mission Inc.				2		
International Pentecostal Holiness Church	2000			2		
Into All The World	1990			1		
Living Water Teaching						2
Macedonia World Baptist Missions Inc.	1998			2		
Mission to the World (PCA) Inc.	1996		8	5		
Missionary Ventures Intl.				2		
Missions Door					1	
Orphanos Foundation	2011			3		
Teen Missions International Inc.	2005		3			
Virginia Mennonite Missions	2005			1		1
Word of Life Fellowship Inc.	2009				3	3
Wycliffe Bible Translators USA				2		
Benin						
Assemblies of God World Missions	1937			4		
Child Evangelism Fellowship Inc.				1		
Christian Aid Mission	1996				550	
Evangel Bible Translators					2	
Evangelism Explosion III International Inc.	2011				4	
Faith Baptist Mission	2010			6		
Global Missions (United Pentecostal Church Intl.)	1988	2				4
Greater Grace World Outreach	2003					2
Literacy & Evangelism International				1	2	
Mennonite Mission Network	1985			2		
Mission ONE Inc.					1	
SIM Canada				7		

	First Year	Personnel from US or Canada			Other Countries	
		1–2 years	2–4 years	4+ years	Citizen	Not Citizen
SIM USA				3		
TWR				2		
Wycliffe Bible Translators USA				5		
Bermuda						
Word of Life Fellowship Inc.	1986			1	3	
Bhutan						
Christian Aid Mission					1	
Evangelical Friends Mission	2005				2	
FaithLife Ministries Inc.	2016					1
Global Missions (United Pentecostal Church Intl.)	2004		1			
Gospel Tide Broadcasting Association	2012				1	
India Gospel Outreach Inc.	1994				10	
International Partnership Ministries Inc.	2000					13
International Teams U.S.A.						2
Scriptures In Use	2013		2		200	
Walk Thru the Bible Ministries Inc.	2002				1	
Bolivia						
American Baptist International Ministries				2		
Apostolic Church of Pentecost of Canada (Global Harvest Missions)	2007			1		
Assemblies of God World Missions	1946	7		5		
Avant Ministries	1928			4		
Avant Ministries Canada	1928			8	1	
Awana Clubs International				2		
Baptist Bible Fellowship International – World Mission Service Center	1978			5		
Baptist International Missions Inc.				9		
Baptist International Outreach	2016			2		2
Baptist Missionary Association of America (BMAA)					2	
BCM International	2000				15	
Bright Hope	2007			1	1	
Canadian Baptist Ministries	1898			3	2	
Canadian South America Mission	1922			2	1	1
Catalyst Missions		2			2	
Child Evangelism Fellowship Inc.				1		
Christ for the City International	2005					2
Christian Aid Mission	1988				22	
Christian Discipleship International	2005					1
Christian Veterinary Mission	1983		1	4		
Church of God Ministries (Anderson) – Global Strategy	1976			2		
Church of the Nazarene Inc.	1945					2
Commission to Every Nation	2002		2			2
Commission To Every Nation-Canada	2013			2		
Compassion International Inc.	1975				55	
Cup of Cold Water Ministries	1978		3	6	4	5

	First Year	Personnel from US or Canada			Other Countries	
		1–2 years	2–4 years	4+ years	Citizen	Not Citizen
Ethnos360				25		
Evangelical Free Church of Canada Mission				13		
Evangelical Mennonite Conference	2012	1		2		
Evangelical Mennonite Mission Conference	1968			3	1	
Evangelism Explosion III International Inc.	2011			2		
Evangelistic Faith Mission Inc.	1977		2			
Fellowship International Mission	1998			2		
FH Canada	1998			2		
Food for the Hungry Inc.	1978		12	4		
Friends in Action Intl.				1		
Global Missions (United Pentecostal Church Intl.)	1974		4			4
Global Missions of Open Bible Churches	2013				1	
Global Outreach Mission Inc.		2		2		
Grace Ministries International	1951			2		
Harvest Foundation					3	
IFCA World Missions					1	
International Justice Mission	2006		1		9	
International Partnership Ministries Inc.	2000				5	
International Teams Canada (Evangelical International Crusades Canada Inc.)		1		1		
International Teams U.S.A.		4	2	3		3
Into All The World	2005			2		
LeaderTreks	2003	15				
Lifesong for Orphans	2013		1	4	28	
LOGOI Ministries	1972				1	
MAP International	1989				36	2
Medical Ministry International	2002				7	1
Medical Ministry International Canada Inc.	2006					2
Mennonite Mission Network	1974					1
Mission Generation Inc.	1995			2	55	
Mission to the World (PCA) Inc.				2		
Missionary Ventures Canada					1	
Missionary Ventures Intl.				2		
Missions Door					1	
Network of International Christian Schools	2002	30	10	10	40	
Open Air Campaigners – Overseas Ministries (OAC-OM)	2013				1	
Orphanos Foundation	2014			1	1	
Palm Missionary Ministries Inc.	2006			1		3
Pioneers Canada				2		
Precept Ministries International	1993				2	
Presbyterian Missionary Union	2004				2	
Ripe for Harvest Inc.					1	
Samaritan's Purse	2008	3				
Scriptures In Use	2001			4	800	

	First Year	Personnel from US or Canada			Other Countries	
		1–2 years	2–4 years	4+ years	Citizen	Not Citizen
Servants in Faith & Technology (SIFAT)					1	
Seventh-day Adventists – General Conference – Global Mission	1907	1				4
SIM Canada				7		
SIM USA		2		31		
Source of Light Ministries Intl. Inc.					1	
South America Mission	1926	1	5	24	3	4
Spanish World Ministries					1	
TWR Canada	2015			1		
United Evangelical Churches				1		
Word of Life Fellowship Inc.	1990				25	11
World Concern	1997	3	1	1	25	1
World Gospel Mission	1944	1		11	1	
World Indigenous Missions	1985			8		
World Mission Prayer League	1938			4		
World-Wide Missions	1962		1			
WorldVenture				2		
Youth for Christ/USA				3		
Bosnia and Herzegovina						
Campus Crusade for Christ (Cru in the US)		1		13		
Christian Churches / Churches of Christ			1	2		
Church of the Brethren – Global Mission Partnerships		2				
Elim Fellowship	1987			1		
European Christian Mission Intl. – USA				2		
Global Missions (United Pentecostal Church Intl.)			1			
Global Partners (The Wesleyan Church World Headquarters)				4		
International Teams U.S.A.				3		2
OM Canada		1				
Operation Mobilization		5				9
ReachGlobal				4		
Botswana						
Assemblies of God World Missions	1963	3		6		
Baptist Bible Fellowship International – World Mission Service Center	2001			4		
Baptist International Missions Inc.				2		
Baptist International Outreach	1992			4	4	
Campus Crusade for Christ (Cru in the US)		2		1		
Canadian National Baptist Convention (CNBC)	2004					2
Child Evangelism Fellowship Inc.				1		
Christian Church (Disciples of Christ) – Global Ministries			2			
Evangelism Explosion III International Inc.	2009				4	
Global Missions (United Pentecostal Church Intl.)	1980		2			2

	First Year	Personnel from US or Canada			Other Countries	
		1–2 years	2–4 years	4+ years	Citizen	Not Citizen
Habitat for Humanity International	1992		1			1
IFCA World Missions					1	
Independent Faith Mission Inc.				2		
Launch Out Ministries International	2007				3	
Mennonite Mission Network	1974		1			
Mission Aviation Fellowship of Canada (MAFC)		2		2		
Seventh-day Adventists – General Conference – Global Mission	1921			2		10
SIM Canada				1		
SIM USA				3		
Walk Thru the Bible Ministries Inc.	1999				2	
Brazil						
A.C.T. International	2001			3	2	1
ABWE Canada (Across Borders for World Evangelism)				4		
ABWE International				60		
ACCI (Adventive Cross Cultural Initiatives) – US	2009	2				
Action International Ministries	1991			14	9	6
Action International Ministries – Canada				2	2	
American Baptist International Ministries				2		
American Leprosy Missions				1		
AMG International					1	
Apostolic Church of Pentecost of Canada (Global Harvest Missions)	1995			1		
Assemblies of God World Missions	1910	1		11		
Association of Free Lutheran Congregations				7	2	
Avant Ministries	1911			12		
Avant Ministries Canada	1911			2		
Awana Clubs International					4	
Back to the Bible	2000				6	
Baptist Bible Fellowship International – World Mission Service Center	1952			21		
Baptist International Missions Inc.				38		
Baptist International Outreach	1995			3	2	1
Baptist Mid-Missions	1935			89	5	
Baptist Missionary Association of America (BMAA)					2	
BCM International	1987	2			7	
Be One Together	2011				3	
Bethany Gateways				7	1	
BILD International					1	
Brazil Gospel Fellowship Mission (BGFM)	1945		1	44		
Campus Crusade for Christ (Cru in the US)				1		
Canadian Baptist Ministries	1970			2		
Canadian South America Mission	1913		2			2
Child Evangelism Fellowship Inc.				1		
Christian Aid Mission	1977				100	

	First Year	Personnel from US or Canada			Other Countries	
		1–2 years	2–4 years	4+ years	Citizen	Not Citizen
Christian Broadcasting Network Inc., The	2004				4	
Christian Churches / Churches of Christ		1	4	28	6	
Christian Ministries International (CMI)				2		
Christians In Action Missions International	1960			2		
Church of God (Cleveland TN) World Missions	1951			4		
Church of the Brethren – Global Mission Partnerships		2	2			
Church of the Nazarene Inc.	1958				6	2
Churches of God – General Conference	1994			4		
CMF International	1957	2				2
Commission to Every Nation	2004			4		4
Compassion International Inc.	1974				49	
Converge				6		
Cross-Cultural Ministries – Churches of God General Conference	1994			1		
Crossworld	1931			22		
Crossworld Canada	1931			3		1
Emmanuel Intl. Canada				1		
Encompass World Partners	1949			2		
Equip Inc & Equip International	1996			3		
Ethnos360			5	80		
Evangelical Congregational Church – Global Ministries Commission				2		
Evangelical Missionary Church of Canada	1955			2		
Evangelism Explosion III International Inc.	2015				3	
FAIR				1		
FaithLife Ministries Inc.	2011				1	
Fellowship International Mission	1983			2	2	
FH Canada	1998		1			
Food for the Hungry Inc.	1997		2			
Free Methodist World Missions	1936			2		
Free Will Baptist International Missions	1957			2		
Global Missions (United Pentecostal Church Intl.)	1956		12			1
Global Missions of Open Bible Churches	1977				1	
Global Outreach International	2000			3		
Global Outreach Mission Inc.	1973			6		
Global Partners (The Wesleyan Church World Headquarters)				2		
Global Recordings Network					5	
Global Scholars	2003			3	1	2
Go Ye Fellowship	1962			4	2	2
Gospel Fellowship Association	1965			4		
Greater Grace World Outreach	2002				2	
Habitat for Humanity International	1987		1			1
Harvest Foundation					4	
IFCA World Missions					1	
International Street Kids Outreach Ministries (ISKOM)	1992			2	47	

		Personnel from US or Canada			Other Countries	
	First Year	1–2 years	2–4 years	4+ years	Citizen	Not Citizen
International Teams U.S.A.						1
Latin America Mission	2008			2		
Life Impact Inc.	2010			2	1	1
Living Water Teaching	2008			2		
Macedonia World Baptist Missions Inc.	1977			10	2	
Master's Resourcing Commission				1		
Mission Aviation Fellowship	1956		4			
Mission to the World (PCA) Inc.	1993			5		
Missions Door					1	
Network of International Christian Schools	1999	6	4	10	14	
North American Baptist Conference – Worldwide Outreach	1966					7
On The Go Ministries/Keith Cook Team	1958			2		
One Challenge	1963			4	1	
One Mission Society	1950			6		1
Open Air Campaigners – Overseas Ministries (OAC-OM)	1990			4		
Operation Mobilization					24	2
Orphanos Foundation	2007				2	
Pioneers Canada				2		
Precept Ministries International	2000				7	
Presbyterian Mission International (PMI)				1		
Project AmaZon	1977	1		38	5	
ReachGlobal				3		
Seventh-day Adventists – General Conference – Global Mission	1894					2
South America Mission	1914	1	2	10		
Sowers International, The					1	
TeachBeyond Canada			3		3	
TEAM (The Evangelical Alliance Mission)	1983			6		
Teen Missions International Inc.	1995		3	2	2	
The Centers for Apologetics Research (CFAR)					1	
The Navigators				5		
The Pentecostal Assemblies of Canada				4		
The Salvation Army USA National Headquarters	1922		2	2		
Things to Come Mission	1958			2	4	2
TMS Global	1998			4		
United World Mission Inc.				7	2	5
Walk Thru the Bible Ministries Inc.	2003				2	
WEC International				3		
WEC International Canada	1972			2	1	
White Fields					7	
Wisconsin Evangelical Lutheran Synod – Board for World Missions				3		
Word of Life Fellowship Inc.	1958	4		30	83	5

| | First Year | Personnel from US or Canada | | | Other Countries | |
		1–2 years	2–4 years	4+ years	Citizen	Not Citizen
World Team US				6		
World-Wide Missions	1965	1		6		
WorldVenture				13		
Worldwide Discipleship Assoc.				1		
Wycliffe Bible Translators of Canada Inc.				3		
Wycliffe Bible Translators USA				35		
Youth for Christ/USA	1950			2		
British Virgin Islands						
Foursquare Missions International				2		
Brunei						
Frontier Ventures			2			
World Missions & Evangelism	2013			2		
World Partners USA				1		
Bulgaria						
ABWE International				2		
American Baptist International Ministries				2		
AMG International					8	
Beautiful Feet	2015			2		
Christian Aid Mission					15	
Church of God (Cleveland TN) World Missions	1982			1		1
Church of the Nazarene Inc.	1994			3		
East European Missions Network					4	
Entrust	1979				2	
European Christian Mission Intl. – USA				4		
Evangelism Explosion III International Inc.	2015				1	
Far East Broadcasting Associates of Canada (FEB Canada)	2008		2			
Foursquare Missions International	1994			2		
Free Methodist World Missions	2007		2	4		
Free Will Baptist International Missions	2005			6	2	
Global Missions (United Pentecostal Church Intl.)	1991		1			
Global Scholars				1		1
Greater Europe Mission				2		
International Teams U.S.A.				3		5
InterVarsity Christian Fellowship/USA			2			
ISOH/IMPACT	1992			1		
Josiah Venture	2014			6	3	
Literacy & Evangelism International					1	
Ministry to Educate and Equip Intl. (MTEE)				2		
Mission to the World (PCA) Inc.	1994	1	3	18		
One Challenge	2003			1		
Pioneers Canada				1		
Precept Ministries International	1991				3	

	First Year	Personnel from US or Canada			Other Countries	
		1–2 years	2–4 years	4+ years	Citizen	Not Citizen
Reach A Village					3	
ReachGlobal				2		
SEND International Inc.	1993			4		2
TCM International Institute					1	
The Navigators				4		
Wisconsin Evangelical Lutheran Synod – Board for World Missions				1		
Word of Life Fellowship Inc.	2002				1	2
Wycliffe Bible Translators USA				4		
Burkina Faso						
Assemblies of God World Missions	1919			2		
Awana Clubs International					1	
Baptist Bible Fellowship International – World Mission Service Center	1994			6		
Baptist International Missions Inc.				2		
Child Evangelism Fellowship Inc.				1		
Christian Aid Mission	2008				20	
CMF International	2007			4		4
Commission to Every Nation	2009			2		2
Commission To Every Nation-Canada	2011			1	1	
Compassion International Inc.	2004				33	
ECHO	2012			4		
Evangelical Mennonite Conference	1976			2		
Evangelical Missionary Church of Canada	1996			1		
Evangelism Explosion III International Inc.	2011				4	
FaithLife Ministries Inc.	2015					1
FRIENDS in Action International – Canada	2000	1		1		
Friends in Action Intl.				1		
Global Missions (United Pentecostal Church Intl.)	1994		2			
Go to Nations	2003			3		3
Greater Grace World Outreach	2001				2	
International Gospel Outreach	1986			1		1
Living Word Missions				2		2
Macedonia World Baptist Missions Inc.	2006			2		
MB Mission	1990			2	3	
MB Mission Canada	1990				3	2
Mennonite Mission Network	1976	1			1	2
Scriptures In Use	2009			5	1100	
Seventh-day Adventists – General Conference – Global Mission	1972					4
Shield of Faith Mission International	1995			4		
SIM Canada				9		
SIM USA				12		
Women to the World Inc.					1	
World Concern	2003	4				

	First Year	Personnel from US or Canada			Other Countries	
		1–2 years	2–4 years	4+ years	Citizen	Not Citizen
World Outreach International – US	2002			1		
World Relief	1982	4			6	
Wycliffe Bible Translators of Canada Inc.				7		
Wycliffe Bible Translators USA				7		
Burundi						
Advent Christian World Outreach	2009				1	
Awana Clubs International					1	
Child Evangelism Fellowship Inc.				1		
Christian Aid Mission	1997				150	
Church of the Nazarene Inc.	1999					2
CRM					1	
Evangelism Explosion III International Inc.	2010				8	
Global Missions (United Pentecostal Church Intl.)		4				
Harvest Foundation						1
HOPE International	2008					1
International Gospel Outreach	2010	1				1
Literacy & Evangelism International					2	
MB Mission	2014					4
MB Mission Canada	2014			4		
The Navigators				2		
World Relief	1994			4	8	
Cambodia						
ABWE International				7		
Action International Ministries	2003			6		6
Assemblies of God World Missions	1990	9		20		
Baptist Bible Fellowship International – World Mission Service Center	1997			2		
Baptist International Missions Inc.				4		
Baptist International Outreach	2002			2	1	1
Baptist Mid-Missions	1998			8		
Baptist Missionary Association of America (BMAA)				2		
Beautiful Feet	2016			2		
BILD International				1	1	
Christian Aid Mission					68	
Christian and Missionary Alliance in Canada, The				6		
Christian Broadcasting Network Inc., The	2000				10	
Christian Reformed World Missions	2008			2		
Church of the Nazarene Inc.	1992			2		
Commission to Every Nation	2008		2			2
CRM				11	2	1
Crossworld	2004			8		
Crossworld Canada	2004			2	1	
Eastern Mennonite Missions	2008			4		
Encompass World Partners	2000			3	12	

	First Year	Personnel from US or Canada			Other Countries	
		1–2 years	2–4 years	4+ years	Citizen	Not Citizen
EPC World Outreach				1		
Ethnos360				2		
Evangelical Friends Church Southwest	1996		2		7	
Evangelism Explosion III International Inc.	2010				1	
Far East Broadcasting Associates of Canada (FEB Canada)	2009		2			
Far East Broadcasting Company					1	
FH Canada	2001		1			
Food for the Hungry Inc.	1991		2			
Foursquare Missions International				6		
Global Missions of Open Bible Churches	2007				1	
Global Outreach International	2006			2		
Global Partners (The Wesleyan Church World Headquarters)				4		
Gospel Fellowship Association	2000			4		
Helps Ministries	2014			5	2	
Holt International Children's Services Inc.					1	
HOPE International Development Agency	1992	1			5	
International Justice Mission	2000		3		13	1
International Teams U.S.A.				6		5
Interserve USA	2005			1		
InterVarsity Christian Fellowship/USA			1			
Lifesong for Orphans	2012	2			15	
Mission to the World (PCA) Inc.			3	7		
Missions Door					1	
New Mission Systems International	2009			1		
OMF International – Canada	1974			2		2
Orphanos Foundation	2015			1	1	
Presbyterian Missionary Union	2006			1		
Reach A Village					6	
Reformed Church in America – General Synod Council – Global Mission						2
Ripe for Harvest Inc.				1		
Samaritan's Purse	2003	2	4			
Seventh-day Adventists – General Conference – Global Mission	1991			8		2
Sowers International, The					1	
Teen Missions International Inc.	2003		2		2	2
The Free Methodist Church in Canada	1992			2		
The Pentecostal Assemblies of Canada		1		8		
Things to Come Mission	2007					4
TWR				4		
WEC International Canada	1992			3		1
World Concern	1991					2
World Relief	1989			2	318	3

	First Year	Personnel from US or Canada			Other Countries	
		1–2 years	2–4 years	4+ years	Citizen	Not Citizen
World Team Canada				2		
World Team US				27		
WorldVenture				1		
Wycliffe Bible Translators USA				4		
Cameroon						
Assemblies of God World Missions	1976	1		10		
Baptist International Missions Inc.				2		
Baptist Mid-Missions	2006			4		
Child Evangelism Fellowship Inc.				1		
Christian Aid Mission	2004				30	
Church of the Nazarene Inc.	1999			2		
Commission to Every Nation	1999			9	3	6
Converge				12		
Encompass World Partners	2003		2	7		
Evangelism Explosion III International Inc.	2010				6	
FaithLife Ministries Inc.	2013				1	
Global Missions (United Pentecostal Church Intl.)	1971		2			2
Global Outreach International	2002			2		
Global Recordings Network					2	
Gospel Fellowship Association	1987	2		16		
Health Teams International						
International Gospel Outreach	1986			1	0	1
International Pentecostal Holiness Church						
Lutheran Bible Translators of Canada	1980			3		1
Lutheran Brethren International Mission	1918					
Mailbox Club International Inc., The					1	
Medical Centers of West Africa (MCWA)	1989			2		
National Association of Congregational Christian Churches	2006				10	
North American Baptist Conference – Worldwide Outreach	1935			11		6
On The Go Ministries/Keith Cook Team	1923	4		6		
Open Door Baptist Missions	2007			1		
ReachGlobal				6		
Scriptures In Use	2010			3	400	
Serve Globally – The Evangelical Covenant Church			4	4		
Seventh-day Adventists – General Conference – Global Mission	1928	1		4		5
SIM USA				1		
Teen Missions International Inc.	2001			3	3	
The Navigators				2		
World Team Canada				4		
World Team US				15		
Wycliffe Bible Translators of Canada Inc.				21		

	First Year	Personnel from US or Canada			Other Countries	
		1–2 years	2–4 years	4+ years	Citizen	Not Citizen
Wycliffe Bible Translators USA				47		
Canada						
Allegheny Wesleyan Methodist Connection	1974				2	
Avant Ministries	1927			4		
Awana Clubs International					12	
Baptist Bible Fellowship International – World Mission Service Center	1971			14		
Baptist International Missions Inc.				35		
Baptist International Outreach	1994			6	1	5
Baptist Mid-Missions	1950			6	3	
Baptist Missionary Association of America (BMAA)					4	
BCM International	1942			1	23	
Biblical Ministries Worldwide				12		12
Chinese Christian Life Fellowship Inc.	2015				2	
Chosen People Ministries Inc.	1930			1	19	
Church of the Nazarene Inc.	1902				1	
Converge				4		
CRM				3		
Crossworld	1964			20		
Cup of Cold Water Ministries	2013			2		2
Engineering Ministries International (EMI)					6	
Equip Inc & Equip International	1997				7	
Ethnos360				2		
Faith Baptist Mission	2015			2		
Fellowship International Mission	2010			2		
Global Gates	2016			1		
Global Missions of Open Bible Churches	2006				1	
Global Recordings Network					1	
Greater Grace World Outreach	1980					2
InterAct Ministries	1967			27		
International Messengers		2	3	4	7	2
Jews for Jesus				2		1
Kidzana Ministries	2006			1		
Life in Messiah International	2006				3	
Literacy & Evangelism International				1		
Macedonia World Baptist Missions Inc.	1980			10		
Missions Door					1	
Northern Canada Evangelical Mission Inc.	1946			19	54	6
Operation Mobilization		4			36	28
Prayer Baptist Missions International Inc.				1		
ReachAcross					8	2
ReachGlobal				6		
Reformed Church in America – General Synod Council – Global Mission					1	

		Personnel from US or Canada			Other Countries	
	First Year	1–2 years	2–4 years	4+ years	Citizen	Not Citizen
Ripe for Harvest Inc.				1		
Servant Partners	2011			2	5	
Shield of Faith Mission International	2007				2	
The Navigators				7		
The Salvation Army USA National Headquarters	1882		2	4		
TMS Global	2008					2
To Every Tribe	2014			6		
Word of Life Fellowship Inc.	1984	1		6	47	
World Mission Prayer League	1969			6		
WorldVenture				2		
Cape Verde Islands						
Baptist International Missions Inc.				2		
Church of the Nazarene Inc.	1901				2	
Caribbean						
ABWE International				8		
Assemblies of God World Missions		0		2		
Awana Clubs International				1		
Baptist Bible Fellowship International – World Mission Service Center	1957			4		
Church of God (Cleveland TN) World Missions				2		
Communitas International	2010			2	1	
ECHO	1981			3		
Evangelical Congregational Church – Global Ministries Commission				2		
Final Frontiers Foundation	1989				3	
Foursquare Missions International				2		
Global Missions (United Pentecostal Church Intl.)	1974		8			
Grace Ministries International	2013				2	
Josue Yrion World Evangelism & Missions Inc.	2013				1	
Operation Mobilization		12			10	2
reSource Leadership International	2013					1
Salvation Army – Canada and Bermuda Territory, The		1				
The Pentecostal Assemblies of Canada		1				
The Voice of the Martyrs				3		
Word of Life Fellowship Inc.	2001				4	
Young Life			2	3		
Cayman Islands						
Baptist International Missions Inc.				2		
Christian Churches / Churches of Christ				2		
Church of God (Holiness) World Mission Dept. Inc.			2			
Global Missions of Open Bible Churches	1990				1	
InterVarsity Christian Fellowship/USA			1			
Youth for Christ/USA				1		

	First Year	Personnel from US or Canada			Other Countries	
		1–2 years	2–4 years	4+ years	Citizen	Not Citizen
Central African Republic						
Baptist Mid-Missions	1920			6		
Global Health Ministries	2008					1
Global Missions (United Pentecostal Church Intl.)	2000		2			
Global Recordings Network					2	
Living Word Missions				2		2
On The Go Ministries/Keith Cook Team	1974	1		1		1
ReachGlobal		1		4		
Serve Globally – The Evangelical Covenant Church				2		
Wycliffe Bible Translators USA				6		
Central America						
ABWE International				45		
Assemblies of God World Missions				2		
Awana Clubs International					1	
Christian Medical & Dental Associations				1		
Communitas International	2011			1	1	
Disciple Makers			4	10		
ECHO	1981			3		
Great Cities Missions				1		
Harvest Foundation					5	
Josue Yrion World Evangelism & Missions Inc.	2009				1	
Morelli Ministries Intl. Inc.				1		
Operation Mobilization					19	5
Outreach to Asia Nationals				2		
Pioneers USA				18		1
reSource Leadership International	2013					1
The Pentecostal Assemblies of Canada		4				
United World Mission Inc.				16		16
Village Ministries International	2006			4	1	3
Word of Life Fellowship Inc.						2
Wycliffe Associates	1967				1	
Central Asia						
Accelerating International Mission Strategies (AIMS)			1			
American Baptist International Ministries				2		
Anglican Frontier Missions				2	3	
Apostolic Church of Pentecost of Canada (Global Harvest Missions)	2014	3		3		
Asian Outreach International Canada				1	11	7
Assemblies of God World Missions		44		62		
Biblical Ministries Worldwide			12			12
CAMA Services	2016		2			
Canadian National Baptist Convention (CNBC)	1992					2

		Personnel from US or Canada			Other Countries	
	First Year	1–2 years	2–4 years	4+ years	Citizen	Not Citizen
China Ministries International				12		8
Christar	1991			5		
Christian Medical & Dental Associations				1		
Church Leadership Development International	2005				1	
Church of the Nazarene Inc.	2000			2		
CLC Ministries International	1997			2		
Converge				2		
CRM				2		
Crossworld		4		16		
East-West Ministries International	1995			7	1	
Evangelical Missionary Church of Canada	2004			1		
Final Frontiers Foundation	2004				15	
Foursquare Missions International				2		
Frontiers Canada	1984			9		
Go Ye Fellowship	1999			2		2
Harvest Foundation						2
InterServe Canada				32		
Lutheran Church Missouri Synod – World Mission				2		
Mission Aviation Fellowship of Canada (MAFC)				1		
Mission Catalyst Intl. Inc.		1				
OM Canada			4	2		
One Challenge						2
Outreach to Asia Nationals	1986				34	
Pioneers USA				73		2
Reach Beyond				4		
SEND International Inc.	2005			3		1
TEAM (The Evangelical Alliance Mission)				53		
Team Expansion Inc.	2012			2		
The Christian and Missionary Alliance				28		
United World Mission Inc.				8	2	6
WEC International				15		
WEC International Canada				3		1
Word of Life Fellowship Inc.	2007					2
World Mission Prayer League	1967			4		
WorldVenture				14		
Wycliffe Associates	2006				8	4
Wycliffe Bible Translators of Canada Inc.				45		
Chad						
Africa Inland Mission Canada Intl.			4			4
Assemblies of God World Missions	1995	2				
Baptist Mid-Missions	1925			2		
Child Evangelism Fellowship Inc.				1		

	First Year	Personnel from US or Canada			Other Countries	
		1–2 years	2–4 years	4+ years	Citizen	Not Citizen
Christian Aid Mission	2003				6	
Encompass World Partners	1966			6		
Global Recordings Network					2	
International Partnership Ministries Inc.	2000				9	
Living Word Missions				2	1	1
Lutheran Brethren International Mission	1918			10		
Mission Aviation Fellowship of Canada (MAFC)			1			
Operation Mobilization					2	2
Pioneers Canada				1		
Scriptures In Use	2014	3			300	
Seventh-day Adventists – General Conference – Global Mission	1870			1		1
TEAM (The Evangelical Alliance Mission)	1969			26		
WEC International		1		1		
Wycliffe Bible Translators of Canada Inc.				1		
Wycliffe Bible Translators USA				9		
Chile						
ABWE International		4		24		
American Baptist International Ministries				2		
Assemblies of God World Missions	1941	6		14		
Awana Clubs International					1	
Baptist Bible Fellowship International – World Mission Service Center	1954			8		
Baptist International Missions Inc.				4		
Baptist International Outreach	2013			2		2
Baptist Mid-Missions	1992			4		
BILD International				1		
Campus Crusade for Christ (Cru in the US)				2		
Child Evangelism Fellowship Inc.				1		
Christian Aid Mission	1998				16	
Christian Church (Disciples of Christ) – Global Ministries			1			
Christian Churches / Churches of Christ				32	4	
Church of God (Cleveland TN) World Missions	1954			3		
Church of the Nazarene Inc.	1962					2
CMF International	1988	1	6	3	2	8
Commission to Every Nation	2008			2	2	
Eastern Mennonite Missions	2005	1	2	4		
Encompass World Partners	1999					1
Evangelism Explosion III International Inc.	2010				4	
Far East Broadcasting Associates of Canada (FEB Canada)	2006			2		
Foursquare Missions International	1995			2		
Free Methodist World Missions	1986			1		

	First Year	Personnel from US or Canada			Other Countries	
		1–2 years	2–4 years	4+ years	Citizen	Not Citizen
Friendship International Ministries Inc.				1		
Global Missions (United Pentecostal Church Intl.)	1964		2			
Global Missions of Open Bible Churches	1982				1	
Global Outreach International	2001			1		
Global Outreach Mission Inc.				2		
Gospel Mission of South America Inc.	1923			10		
Gospel Mission of South America of Canada				2	2	2
Greater Grace World Outreach	1985				2	2
IBMGlobal	2015	2				
IFCA World Missions					1	
International Gospel Outreach	1975			2	2	
International Partnership Ministries Inc.	1999			16		
LOGOI Ministries	1972			2		
Macedonia World Baptist Missions Inc.	1995			7		3
Mission to the World (PCA) Inc.	1977			12		
Navigators of Canada, The	1983			2		
New Mission Systems International	2005			1	3	
Operation Mobilization		1			9	12
Precept Ministries International						1
Reformed Baptist Mission Services				2		
Ripe for Harvest Inc.				1		
Salvation Army – Canada and Bermuda Territory, The				1		
Serge				2		
Seventh-day Adventists – General Conference – Global Mission	1895			4		4
SIM Canada				2		
SIM USA				2		
Source of Light Ministries Intl. Inc.					1	
Spanish World Ministries					1	
The Brethren Church Inc.	2007				1	
United World Mission Inc.				2		2
Word of Life Fellowship Inc.	1977	1		2	17	
World Team US				2		
Wycliffe Bible Translators USA				2		
China, People's Republic of						
A.C.T. International	2006				1	2
All God's Children International	1995	2			25	
Baptist General Conference of Canada	2010			2		
Baptist International Outreach	2002			8	1	7
Baptist Missionary Association of America (BMAA)				5		2
Barnabas International				2		
BILD International				2		
China Partners	1996	4	5	5		1

	First Year	Personnel from US or Canada			Other Countries	
		1–2 years	2–4 years	4+ years	Citizen	Not Citizen
China Service Ventures	2007	1	1	3	2	
ChinaSource	1995			1		
Chinese Christian Life Fellowship Inc.	2009	1	1			
Christian Broadcasting Network Inc., The	1997	1	3	1	44	
Christian Church (Disciples of Christ) – Global Ministries				3		
Church of God (Cleveland TN) World Missions	1937			6		
Cooperative Baptist Fellowship – Global Missions	1996		3	4		
Crossover Communications International	2015				2	
Eastern Mennonite Missions	1998		1	4		
EPC World Outreach				6		
ERRC (Educational Resources & Referrals – China) US		1				46
ERRC Educational Society - Canada		1				46
Evangelical Christian Church in Canada, The	1975			1	1	
Evangelical Missionary Church of Canada	1991			5		
Food for the Hungry Inc.	1992		3	2		
Global Missions (United Pentecostal Church Intl.)						1
Global Outreach International	1992			13		
Globe International	2003			2		
Greater Grace World Outreach	1982					2
Habitat for Humanity International			2			2
Holt International Children's Services Inc.					18	
HOPE International	2000			1		1
Intercede International						2
International Friendships Inc.	1991		2		3	5
International Partnership Ministries Inc.	2005					5
International Students Inc (ISI)	2009	2				
Interserve USA	1870			16		
Lutheran Brethren International Mission	1901			2		
Macedonia World Baptist Missions Inc.	2002			1	1	
Mennonite Mission Network	1911			2		2
Network of International Christian Schools	1994	13	15	10	20	
On The Go Ministries/Keith Cook Team	1986	7		4		
One Mission Society	1999			3		2
Operation Mobilization		7			1	13
Orthodox Presbyterian Church – Committee on Foreign Missions	1994	4	2	4		
Partners International Canada	2009	1			1	
Pioneers Canada			1	19		
Precept Ministries International	1996					2
Reach A Village					10	
ReachGlobal		2		14		
SEND International Inc.	1991	2		16		6
Serve Globally – The Evangelical Covenant Church				5		
SIM USA				13		

		Personnel from US or Canada			Other Countries	
	First Year	1–2 years	2–4 years	4+ years	Citizen	Not Citizen
Sowers International, The					1	
TMS Global	1993			4		
Training Evangelistic Leadership	1985			10	7	
United Brethren in Christ	1932		4	2		
Walk Thru the Bible Ministries Inc.	2004				1	
World Compassion Terry Law Ministries					1	
World Gospel Mission	1910			2		
World Missions & Evangelism	1997			2		
World Relief					1	
Colombia						
ABWE International				11		
Action International Ministries	1992			2		5
Action International Ministries – Canada				4		1
Assemblies of God World Missions	1951	6		20		
Avant Ministries	1908			2		
Awana Clubs International					2	
Baptist Bible Fellowship International – World Mission Service Center	1971			6		
Baptist International Missions Inc.				4		
Brethren in Christ World Missions (BICWM)						2
Camino Global	2013	2			2	
Child Evangelism Fellowship Inc.				1		
Christ for the City International	1988		1	2	2	2
Christian Aid Mission	1985				50	
Christian Church (Disciples of Christ) – Global Ministries			1			
Christian Ministries International (CMI)				1		
Christians In Action Missions International	1969			2	4	
Church of God (Cleveland TN) World Missions	1954			3		
Church of the Nazarene Inc.	1975					2
Compassion International Inc.	1976				53	
CRM			1		1	
Equip Inc & Equip International	2012		1			
Ethnos360				32		
Evangelism Explosion III International Inc.	2010				5	
Far East Broadcasting Associates of Canada (FEB Canada)	1969			4	2	
Free Methodist World Missions	1994			2		
Global Missions (United Pentecostal Church Intl.)	1936		1			
Global Recordings Network					2	
Hope for the Hungry	1979			1		
IFCA World Missions	1965				1	
IN Network dba International Needs USA	1994				15	
International Teams U.S.A.				2		2
Latin America Mission	1961			2	4	

	First Year	Personnel from US or Canada			Other Countries	
		1–2 years	2–4 years	4+ years	Citizen	Not Citizen
Living Word Missions		1				1
LOGOI Ministries	1972				3	
Macedonia World Baptist Missions Inc.	2000		3	1		
Master's Resourcing Commission				1		
MB Mission	1945				1	
MB Mission Canada	1945				1	
Medical Ministry International	2004				1	
Mennonite Mission Network	1931		2	2	2	
Mission to the World (PCA) Inc.	2002	1	4			
One Mission Society	1943			6		2
Orphanos Foundation	2006				1	
Precept Ministries International	1995				4	
Reformed Baptist Mission Services						2
Reformed Church in America – General Synod Council – Global Mission				2		
Resourcing Christian Education International	2007				8	
Serve Globally – The Evangelical Covenant Church				5		
Seventh-day Adventists – General Conference – Global Mission	1921			1		3
South America Mission	1934		2	10	2	1
Sowers International, The					1	
Spanish World Ministries					1	
The Brethren Church Inc.	1975				2	
The Navigators				2		
United World Mission Inc.		2		17	5	14
World Reach Inc.	2005				4	
WorldVenture				1		
Wycliffe Bible Translators USA				12		
Comoros						
Advent Christian World Outreach	2006				1	
Africa Inland Mission Canada Intl.			2			2
African Enterprise	1975				15	
American Baptist International Ministries				14		
Assemblies of God World Missions	1921	0		11		
BCM International	2015				3	
BILD International				1		
Child Evangelism Fellowship Inc.				1		
Christian Aid Mission	2005				25	
Christian Mission for the Deaf	1990		2			
Church of the Nazarene Inc.	1990		2			2
Crossworld	1931		2			
Elim Fellowship	1984		1			
Empowering Lives International	2000				2	
Every Child Ministries Inc.	1985				21	
Global Missions (United Pentecostal Church Intl.)	1985		2			

	First Year	1–2 years	2–4 years	4+ years	Citizen	Not Citizen
		Personnel from US or Canada			Other Countries	
Global Recordings Network					1	
Greater Grace World Outreach	2005					6
Habitat for Humanity International	1974	1				1
Harvest Foundation					4	
HOPE International	2004		3	1		1
International Christian Ministries	2001				4	
Literacy & Evangelism International					2	
MB Mission	1913				6	
MB Mission Canada	1913				6	
Mission Aviation Fellowship	1961				22	
Congo, Democratic Republic of						
Advent Christian World Outreach	2006				1	
Africa Inland Mission Canada Intl.				2		2
African Enterprise	1975				15	
American Baptist International Ministries				14		
Assemblies of God World Missions	1921			11		
BCM International	2015				3	
BILD International				1		
Child Evangelism Fellowship Inc.				1		
Christian Aid Mission	2005				25	
Christian Mission for the Deaf	1990			2		
Church of the Nazarene Inc.	1990			2		2
Crossworld	1931			2		
Elim Fellowship	1984			1		
Empowering Lives International	2000				2	
Every Child Ministries Inc.	1985				21	
Global Missions (United Pentecostal Church Intl.)	1985		2			
Global Recordings Network					1	
Greater Grace World Outreach	2005					6
Habitat for Humanity International	1974	1				1
Harvest Foundation					4	
HOPE International	2004		3	1		1
International Christian Ministries	2001				4	
Literacy & Evangelism International					2	
MB Mission	1913				6	
MB Mission Canada	1913				6	
Mission Aviation Fellowship	1961				22	
National Association of Congregational Christian Churches	2004				8	
ReachGlobal				2		
Samaritan's Purse	1980	1	1			
Serve Globally – The Evangelical Covenant Church				7		
Seventh-day Adventists – General Conference – Global Mission	1965			2		12
Source of Light Ministries Intl. Inc.					2	
The Masters Mission	1986				2	
The Word for the World (TWFTW)	2004			14		

	First Year	Personnel from US or Canada			Other Countries	
		1–2 years	2–4 years	4+ years	Citizen	Not Citizen
United World Mission Inc.				5	5	
Walk Thru the Bible Ministries Inc.	2002				2	
With Open Eyes	2010				42	
World Mission Prayer League	2015			2		
Wycliffe Bible Translators of Canada Inc.				6		
Wycliffe Bible Translators USA				3		
Congo, Republic of						
Christian and Missionary Alliance in Canada, The				3		
FAIR				1		
Global Outreach Mission Inc.	1974	3		12		
HOPE International	2009					1
World Relief	1994		1		26	
World-Wide Missions	1961					2
Assemblies of God World Missions	1987			2		
Baptist Bible Fellowship International – World Mission Service Center	1957			2		
Evangelism Explosion III International Inc.	2014				1	
Costa Rica						
ABWE International				8		
American Baptist International Ministries				2		
Apostolic Church of Pentecost of Canada (Global Harvest Missions)					1	
Assemblies of God World Missions	1943	8		21		
Awana Clubs International					1	
Baptist Bible Fellowship International – World Mission Service Center	1970			12		
Baptist International Missions Inc.				2		
Baptist International Outreach	1992			2	2	
Baptist Missionary Association of America (BMAA)					1	
BILD International				1	1	1
Campus Crusade for Christ (Cru in the US)		2		6		
Casa Viva					500	
Children of Promise International			2	3		
Christ for the City International	1985	1	3	7	20	18
Christian Broadcasting Network Inc., The	1998				8	1
Christian Reformed World Missions	1981			3		
Church of the Nazarene Inc.	1964			6	4	5
Commission to Every Nation	1998		1	8	1	7
Commission To Every Nation-Canada	2013			1		
Converge				2		
Evangelism Explosion III International Inc.	2011				1	
Evangelistic Faith Mission Inc.	1982				2	
Food for the Hungry Inc.	1992		3			
Foursquare Missions International	1953			8		
Free Methodist World Missions	1990			4		

	First Year	Personnel from US or Canada			Other Countries	
		1–2 years	2–4 years	4+ years	Citizen	Not Citizen
Global Missions (United Pentecostal Church Intl.)	1975		2			2
Global Missions of Open Bible Churches	1999				1	
Global Outreach International	2002			2		
Global Outreach Mission Inc.		1		9		
Globe International	2006	1				
Go to Nations	1981			7	2	
Gospel Fellowship Association	1991			4		
Grace Ministries International	1986			2		2
Habitat for Humanity International	1987		45	6	37	14
Helps Ministries	2015			1	1	
Hope for the Hungry	1982			2		
International Pentecostal Holiness Church	1951			4		
International Teams Canada (Evangelical International Crusades Canada Inc.)				2		
International Teams U.S.A.	1993	5		15	7	11
Latin America Mission	1961			4	2	
LeaderTreks	2002	1	1			
Life Impact Inc.	2010			2		2
Mission Aviation Fellowship	1999		3		2	
Mission to the World (PCA) Inc.				1		
Missionary Ventures Intl.				1		
Missions Door					1	
Mutual Faith Ministries Intl.		1				
On The Go Ministries/Keith Cook Team	1998	1		1		1
Operation Mobilization		3			11	1
Pentecostal Free Will Baptist Church Inc. – World Witness Dept.					1	
Precept Ministries International	1994				3	
ReachGlobal		3		19		
Reliant Mission Inc.	2016	1				
Seventh-day Adventists – General Conference – Global Mission	1903			2		2
Sowers International, The					1	
TEAM (The Evangelical Alliance Mission)				4		
The Salvation Army USA National Headquarters	1907		2			
TMS Global	1987	1		2		
United World Mission Inc.				31	2	29
Word of Life Fellowship Inc.	1986				5	1
World Missions & Evangelism	2005			2		
WorldVenture				5		
Wycliffe Bible Translators USA				5		

Côte d'Ivoire

	First Year	Personnel from US or Canada			Other Countries	
Assemblies of God World Missions	1927			2		
Baptist Bible Fellowship International – World Mission Service Center	1988			2		

	First Year	Personnel from US or Canada			Other Countries	
		1–2 years	2–4 years	4+ years	Citizen	Not Citizen
Baptist International Missions Inc.				4		
Baptist Mid-Missions	1975			4		
Campus Crusade for Christ (Cru in the US)		5		3		
Child Evangelism Fellowship Inc.				1		
Christian Aid Mission	1990				4	
Christian Churches / Churches of Christ				6		
Church of God Ministries (Anderson) – Global Strategy	1997		2	2		
Church of the Nazarene Inc.	1987					
CityTeam Ministries – New Generations International					2	
CMF International	2002	3		2		5
Converge				2		
Development Associates Intl. (DAI)					1	
Evangelism Explosion III International Inc.	2014				2	
FaithLife Ministries Inc.	2013				1	
Global Missions (United Pentecostal Church Intl.)	1975		2			
Global Recordings Network					1	
Greater Grace World Outreach	2001				2	
International Gospel Outreach	1986		1		0	1
International Partnership Ministries Inc.	1999				13	
International Pentecostal Holiness Church	1993			2		
Link International Ministries	2004					1
Living Word Missions			2	2		
MAP International	1993				23	
Mutual Faith Ministries Intl.		1				
Seventh-day Adventists – General Conference – Global Mission	1946					6
Shield of Faith Mission International	1995			4		
Source of Light Ministries Intl. Inc.					1	
WorldVenture				14		
Wycliffe Bible Translators USA				2		
Croatia						
ABWE Canada (Across Borders for World Evangelism)	2001			2		
Advent Christian World Outreach	2006				1	
Assemblies of God World Missions	1992			6		
Baptist Bible Fellowship International – World Mission Service Center	1997			2		
Biblical Ministries Worldwide				4		4
Campus Crusade for Christ (Cru in the US)		7		8		
Canadian National Baptist Convention (CNBC)	1999					2
Child Evangelism Fellowship Inc.				2		
Church of God (Cleveland TN) World Missions	1968			2		
Church of the Nazarene Inc.	1999			2		
CRM					1	1
European Christian Mission Intl. – USA				9		

	First Year	Personnel from US or Canada			Other Countries	
		1–2 years	2–4 years	4+ years	Citizen	Not Citizen
Global Missions (United Pentecostal Church Intl.)			1			
Global Partners (The Wesleyan Church World Headquarters)			1	8		
Greater Europe Mission				3		
Greater Europe Mission Canada	1999			2		
Josiah Venture	2005			2	2	
Proclaim! International Inc.	1987		2		2	
Reach Beyond					2	
Reformed Episcopal Board of Foreign Missions				1		
SEND International Inc.	1995			4		1
Cuba						
AMG International					8	
Awana Clubs International					2	
Baptist Missionary Association of America (BMAA)						2
BCM International	1948			1		
BILD International				1	1	1
Calvary Commission Inc.				1		
Caring Partners International	1997				2	
Child Evangelism Fellowship Inc.				1		
Christian Aid Mission	1995				400	
Echocuba	1994			5	2	3
FaithLife Ministries Inc.	2013				1	
Global Missions (United Pentecostal Church Intl.)			2			
Global Missions of Open Bible Churches	1937			2	1	
Go to Nations	1992				1	
International Gospel Outreach	1999			6	4	2
International Partnership Ministries Inc.	1996				5	
International Teams U.S.A.						4
LOGOI Ministries	1972				4	
Missionary Ventures Canada					4	
PIC International (Partners in Christ International)		1				
Precept Ministries International					1	
Reformed Episcopal Board of Foreign Missions				1		
Spanish World Ministries					1	
The Pentecostal Assemblies of Canada				2		
United World Mission Inc.				1	1	
Walk Thru the Bible Ministries Inc.					1	
World Compassion Terry Law Ministries					1	
World Link Ministries	2000				430	
World Team Canada				2		
Youth Ministry International					3	
Cyprus						
AMG International	1984				3	3
Child Evangelism Fellowship Inc.				7		

	First Year	Personnel from US or Canada 1–2 years	2–4 years	4+ years	Other Countries Citizen	Not Citizen
Commission to Every Nation	2002		4			4
Crossover Communications International	2014	2				
Global Missions (United Pentecostal Church Intl.)	1989		2			
International Messengers			2			2
Interserve USA	2006			2		
Macedonia World Baptist Missions Inc.	1985			3		1
ReachGlobal		1		4		
RP Global Missions	1890					1
Seventh-day Adventists – General Conference – Global Mission	1932			3		8
World Partners USA				1		
Czech Republic						
ABWE International				3		
Alongside Ministries International			3			
Assemblies of God World Missions	1992	6		10		
Avant Ministries	2008			3		
Awana Clubs International					1	
Baptist Missionary Association of America (BMAA)				3		
Campus Crusade for Christ (Cru in the US)		4		2		
Christian Aid Mission					9	
Christian Churches / Churches of Christ				2		
Church of God (Cleveland TN) World Missions	2001	1		2		2
East European Missions Network					1	
Eastern Mennonite Missions	2011			1		
Encompass World Partners	1993					2
Entrust	1979			2		
Faith Christian Fellowship Intl.					1	
Foursquare Missions International				2		
Global Missions (United Pentecostal Church Intl.)	1995		2			
Global Partners (The Wesleyan Church World Headquarters)				15		
Global Scholars	1994		2	8		10
Greater Europe Mission				7		
Greater Grace World Outreach	1991				2	
IN Network dba International Needs USA	1995				6	
International Messengers				3	2	1
International Teams U.S.A.				3		
Josiah Venture	1993	11		25	75	1
Mission to the World (PCA) Inc.	1989			6		
Missions Resource Network	1990			7		
New Hope International	1971				2	
Operation Mobilization		3			3	2
Reach Beyond					2	
ReachGlobal				9		
Resourcing Christian Education International	2005				3	2

	First Year	Personnel from US or Canada			Other Countries	
		1–2 years	2–4 years	4+ years	Citizen	Not Citizen
Ripe for Harvest Inc.				1		
SEND International Inc.						1
Serge				2		
Serve Globally – The Evangelical Covenant Church			1	2		
TCM International Institute					1	
TEAM (The Evangelical Alliance Mission)	1990			16		
Titus International	2006			2		
United World Mission Inc.				6	6	
Word of Life Fellowship Inc.	1997			1	4	1
WorldVenture				2		
Denmark						
Biblical Ministries Worldwide				2		2
Child Evangelism Fellowship Inc.				2		
On The Go Ministries/Keith Cook Team	1995	1		2		
Operation Mobilization					5	
Ripe for Harvest Inc.				1		
Seventh-day Adventists – General Conference – Global Mission	1877	1				
Djibouti						
Harvest Foundation						1
Seventh-day Adventists – General Conference – Global Mission	1980					4
Dominica						
Awana Clubs International					1	
Christian Churches / Churches of Christ				5	15	
Church of the Nazarene Inc.	1974			2		
Gospel Fellowship Association	1994			2		
Dominican Republic						
Adventures in Missions	1990			2		
American Baptist International Ministries				5		
Assemblies of God World Missions	1933	5		13		
Awana Clubs International					1	
Baptist Bible Fellowship International – World Mission Service Center	1996			4		
Baptist International Missions Inc.				19		
Baptist Mid-Missions	1950			5		
Baptist Missionary Association of America (BMAA)				2	2	
BCM International	1994			1		
BILD International					1	1
Buckner International	2010			15		
Campus Crusade for Christ (Cru in the US)		6		4		
Christian Churches / Churches of Christ				12		
Christian Outreach International				1		

	First Year	Personnel from US or Canada			Other Countries	
		1–2 years	2–4 years	4+ years	Citizen	Not Citizen
Christian Reformed World Missions	1979			2		
Christian Relief Fund, The	1988				2	
Church of the Brethren – Global Mission Partnerships		2	1	2		
Church of the Nazarene Inc.	1974			2		1
Compassion International Inc.	1970				51	
Cross-Cultural Ministries – Churches of God General Conference	2011				1	
Crossworld	1949			5		
Evangelism Explosion III International Inc.	2010				7	
Evangelistic Faith Mission Inc.	1981	2				
Food for the Hungry Inc.	1979		3		1	
Foursquare Missions International				2		
Global Missions (United Pentecostal Church Intl.)	1965		4			2
Global Missions of Open Bible Churches	1986				1	
Global Outreach Mission Inc.				2		
Greater Grace World Outreach	2015				2	
Habitat for Humanity International	1987		1			1
Harvest Foundation					3	
International Partnership Ministries Inc.	1999				8	
International Pentecostal Holiness Church	1996			2		
Into All The World	2001			1		
Kids Alive International	1990	4	9	14	2	2
Literacy & Evangelism International						2
Medical Ministry International	1970			2	4	1
Medical Ministry International Canada Inc.	1980				2	2
Mission Possible USA	1992				23	
Missionary Ventures Intl.				5		
Missions Door					1	
Pentecostal Free Will Baptist Church Inc. – World Witness Dept.					1	
Reformed Church in America – General Synod Council – Global Mission				1		
Serve Globally – The Evangelical Covenant Church				1		
Seventh-day Adventists – General Conference – Global Mission	1908			2		4
Spanish World Ministries					1	
The Navigators				5		
The Pentecostal Assemblies of Canada		2		9		
TIME Ministries	1991			2	4	
United World Mission Inc.				2		2
WEC International		1			1	
Wisconsin Evangelical Lutheran Synod – Board for World Missions				1		
Word of Life Fellowship Inc.	1994	1		1	8	12
World Team US				4		

	First Year	Personnel from US or Canada			Other Countries	
		1–2 years	2–4 years	4+ years	Citizen	Not Citizen
East Asia						
ABWE International				34		
Assemblies of God World Missions		73		116		
Baptist International Missions Inc.				19		
Baptist Mid-Missions				14		
BCM International						2
Beautiful Feet	1999			16	1	1
Bethany Gateways		4		2	1	3
Campus Crusade for Christ (Cru in the US)		82		266		
Center for Mission Mobilization	2015		8	2	1	
Christar	1909	3	2	31		
Christar Canada				3		
Christian Medical & Dental Associations				1		
Church of the Nazarene Inc.				20		
CMF International	2002	4	1	2		7
CRM				4		
Crossworld				16		
Crossworld Canada				2		
East-West Ministries International		13	6	9		
Elim Fellowship	1998		1	24		
Evangelical Free Church of Canada Mission				2		
Evangelism Explosion III International Inc.	2010				160	
Free Methodist World Missions	1904		8	7		
Global Partners (The Wesleyan Church World Headquarters)				8		
Go Ye Fellowship	1934			6	1	5
iHope International	2010			2		
International Messengers				4	1	3
InterVarsity Christian Fellowship/USA			5			
Josue Yrion World Evangelism & Missions Inc.	2012				1	
Kids Alive International	1971			2		
Life Impact Inc.	2013			2		2
MB Mission				2	6	4
MB Mission Canada				4	6	2
Mission Catalyst Intl. Inc.		1				
Morelli Ministries Intl. Inc.				1		
OMF International			3	132		
One Challenge				24		
Outreach to Asia Nationals	1986	2	10	6	15	
Pioneers USA				182	3	
TEAM (The Evangelical Alliance Mission)				66		
Team Expansion Inc.	1989			10		

	First Year	Personnel from US or Canada			Other Countries	
		1–2 years	2–4 years	4+ years	Citizen	Not Citizen
The Voice of the Martyrs				7	4	
United World Mission Inc.	2005	2		11	1	12
WEC International				14		
WEC International Canada				7		
World Mission Prayer League	2007			11		1
Wycliffe Associates	2004		2	6	6	
Eastern Europe and Eurasia						
ABWE International				81		
Africa Inland Mission Canada Intl.	2016			2		
Agape Unlimited	1993			3	17	1
Assemblies of God World Missions		4		22		
Baptist International Missions Inc.				4		
Bethany Gateways		2				
Campus Crusade for Christ (Cru in the US)		6		8		
Christar	1991			12		
Christian Reformed World Missions	2005	2		3		
Communitas International	1992			2	10	1
CRM					23	
Crossworld		1		9		
Crossworld Canada				1		2
East European Missions Network		1		7	40	1
East-West Ministries International	1993		4	4	1	
Evangelical Free Church of Canada Mission			1	4		
Evangelism Explosion III International Inc.	1996			1		
Final Frontiers Foundation	1992				25	
Frontier Ventures				1		
GAIN (Global Aid Network)	1994				4	
International Christian Ministries Canada (ICM)	2000			2	4	
International Messengers			2	3		5
International Street Kids Outreach Ministries (ISKOM)	1998	1			21	
InterVarsity Christian Fellowship/USA			9			
Josue Yrion World Evangelism & Missions Inc.	2003				1	
MB Mission					1	
MB Mission Canada					1	
New Hope International	1971	3		3		
One Challenge				2		
Operation Mobilization				11	2	24
Pioneers USA				68	1	4
Proclaim! International Inc.	1987					1
Reach Beyond					1	2
Team Expansion Inc.	1999	1		14		
The Pentecostal Assemblies of Canada		1				

| | First Year | Personnel from US or Canada | | | Other Countries | |
		1–2 years	2–4 years	4+ years	Citizen	Not Citizen
The Voice of the Martyrs				2		
United World Mission Inc.				4		4
Village Ministries International	1992			2	2	
WEC International Canada				1		
Word of Life Fellowship Inc.				3	2	2
World Reach Inc.	2008					2
World Witness				4		
Wycliffe Associates	1980	1	3		5	
Ecuador						
ABWE International				8		
ACCI (Adventive Cross Cultural Initiatives) – US	2009		2			
Action International Ministries	1993			2	2	
Action International Ministries – Canada				2		
Apostolic Church of Pentecost of Canada (Global Harvest Missions)	2014			1		
Assemblies of God World Missions	1962	29		26		
Association of Free Lutheran Congregations				2		
Avant Ministries	1896			4		
Awana Clubs International					2	
Back to the Bible	1970				10	
Baptist Bible Fellowship International – World Mission Service Center	1975			10		
Baptist International Missions Inc.				4		
Baptist Mid-Missions	1988			1		
Baptist Missionary Association of America (BMAA)				2		
Biblical Ministries Worldwide				2		2
BILD International					1	1
Campus Crusade for Christ (Cru in the US)		1		2		
Caring Partners International	1998				2	
Child Evangelism Fellowship Inc.				2		
Christian Aid Mission	1997				31	
Christian and Missionary Alliance in Canada, The				5		
Christian Churches / Churches of Christ			4	4		
Christian Relief Fund, The	1990				1	
Christians In Action Missions International	1976			2		2
Church Ministries Intl.				1		
Church of God (Cleveland TN) World Missions	1971	4		8		2
Church of God Ministries (Anderson) – Global Strategy	1986			2		
Church of the Nazarene Inc.	1972			8		2
CMF International	2014		4		4	
Commission to Every Nation	2006		2	8	2	6
Commission To Every Nation-Canada	2008		1	1		
Compassion International Inc.	1974				53	
Crossworld	2000			6		

	First Year	Personnel from US or Canada			Other Countries	
		1–2 years	2–4 years	4+ years	Citizen	Not Citizen
Evangelical Friends Mission	2015	1				
Evangelism Explosion III International Inc.	2010				5	
Foursquare Missions International	1956			2		
Free Methodist World Missions	1981			2		
Global Missions (United Pentecostal Church Intl.)	1964		1			
Global Outreach International	1976			13		
Global Partners (The Wesleyan Church World Headquarters)				9		
Global Recordings Network						2
Globe International	2006			2		
Gospel Fellowship Association	2007			4		
Greater Grace World Outreach	1985				2	
Habitat for Humanity International	1998		1			1
IBMGlobal	2011			1		
IFCA World Missions					1	
International Pentecostal Holiness Church	2002			2	2	
International Teams Canada (Evangelical International Crusades Canada Inc.)		1				
International Teams U.S.A.	1994	5	1	18	6	9
InterVarsity Christian Fellowship/USA			1			
Jewish Awareness Ministries Inc.				2	1	1
Liebenzell Mission of Canada	1989					3
Liebenzell Mission of USA Inc.	1992			2		
MAP International	1988				17	
Medical Ministry International	1990				3	
Medical Ministry International Canada Inc.	2000				2	
Mennonite Mission Network	1969		2			2
Mission Aviation Fellowship	1948	3	8			
Mission to the World (PCA) Inc.	1975		2	8		
Missionary Ventures Intl.				4		
Missions Door					1	
One Mission Society	1952			7		8
Open Air Campaigners – Overseas Ministries (OAC-OM)	2001				2	
Operation Mobilization		3			11	3
Palm Missionary Ministries Inc.	1988			1	28	
Precept Ministries International					2	
Reach Beyond			2	49	1	12
Resourcing Christian Education International	2005				31	10
Ripe for Harvest Inc.				1		
Samaritan's Purse	2006		2			
Servants in Faith & Technology (SIFAT)					5	
Serve Globally – The Evangelical Covenant Church			6	5		
Seventh-day Adventists – General Conference – Global Mission	1916	1				

	First Year	Personnel from US or Canada			Other Countries	
		1–2 years	2–4 years	4+ years	Citizen	Not Citizen
SIM USA				15		
Spanish World Ministries					1	
Team Expansion Inc.	1989			4		
Teen Missions International Inc.	1997					2
The Masters Mission	2003			2		
TMS Global	2001			4		
United World Mission Inc.				10	3	7
Word of Life Fellowship Inc.	1970				9	5
World Mission Prayer League	1951			2		
World Partners USA				1		
WorldVenture				12		
Wycliffe Bible Translators USA				10		
Egypt						
Awana Clubs International					3	
Baptist International Outreach	2013			2		2
Baptist Missionary Association of America (BMAA)					1	
Christian Aid Mission	1990				40	
Christian Church (Disciples of Christ) – Global Ministries			2			
Christian Reformed World Missions	2012			2		
Development Associates Intl. (DAI)					1	
Elim Fellowship	1980			2		
Global Missions (United Pentecostal Church Intl.)	1950		2			
IN Network dba International Needs USA	1997				2	
International Christian Ministries	2003				4	
Interserve USA	1951			2		
Macedonia World Baptist Missions Inc.	2007			4		
Middle East Christian Outreach (MECO Canada)	1901			2		
New Mission Systems International	1997			2		
On The Go Ministries/Keith Cook Team	1967		2	2		
Pioneers Canada				2		
Seventh-day Adventists – General Conference – Global Mission	1879	2		4		4
United Brethren in Christ	2016	1				
Venture International	1994				2	
Walk Thru the Bible Ministries Inc.	2001				4	
El Salvador						
Apostolic Church of Pentecost of Canada (Global Harvest Missions)	2007			1		
Assemblies of God World Missions	1925	14		9		
Baptist International Missions Inc.				6		
Baptist Missionary Association of America (BMAA)					2	
Child Evangelism Fellowship Inc.				2		
Christian Relief Fund, The	1990				1	
Church of the Brethren – Global Mission Partnerships		1				

| | First Year | Personnel from US or Canada | | | Other Countries | |
		1–2 years	2–4 years	4+ years	Citizen	Not Citizen
Commission to Every Nation	2004			2	1	1
Compassion International Inc.	1977				51	
Evangelical Free Church of Canada Mission				3		
Evangelism Explosion III International Inc.	2010				2	
Foursquare Missions International	1973			5		
Full Gospel Evangelistic Association	2000		1	2		
Global Missions (United Pentecostal Church Intl.)	1975		1			9
Global Missions of Open Bible Churches	1973				1	
Global Partners (The Wesleyan Church World Headquarters)		1				
Harvesting In Spanish (HIS)				3		3
Impact International Inc.					2	
Living Water Teaching	1985			3		
Missions Door					1	
On The Go Ministries/Keith Cook Team	1985	1	1			
PIC International (Partners in Christ International)		1				
Precept Ministries International	1988				2	
Reliant Mission Inc.	2007	1		1		
The Pentecostal Assemblies of Canada		4		4		
Word of Life Fellowship Inc.	1993	2			6	4
World Reach Inc.	1996				1	
Equatorial Guinea						
Christian Aid Mission	2004				6	
Christian Churches / Churches of Christ				2		
Global Missions (United Pentecostal Church Intl.)			2			
Go to Nations	2004					2
Seventh-day Adventists – General Conference – Global Mission	1986			2		
WEC International				2		
World Link Ministries	2000				2	
Eritrea						
Christian Aid Mission	2009				20	
Orthodox Presbyterian Church – Committee on Foreign Missions	1944			4		
Estonia						
Alongside Ministries International				1	1	
Apostolic Church of Pentecost of Canada (Global Harvest Missions)	1990			1		
Assemblies of God World Missions	2001	4		6		
Baptist Bible Fellowship International – World Mission Service Center	2008			2		
Baptist International Missions Inc.				4		
Baptist Missionary Association of America (BMAA)				2		
Campus Crusade for Christ (Cru in the US)				2		
Child Evangelism Fellowship Inc.				2		

	First Year	Personnel from US or Canada			Other Countries	
		1–2 years	2–4 years	4+ years	Citizen	Not Citizen
Converge				3		
East European Missions Network					12	
Foursquare Missions International				6		
Greater Europe Mission				1		
Helps Ministries	2016			1		
International Pentecostal Holiness Church	2002			2		
Josiah Venture	2002			2	19	
Precept Ministries International	1994			1		
TCM International Institute					1	
The Pentecostal Assemblies of Canada				2		
The Salvation Army USA National Headquarters	1927		2			
TMS Global	2009			2		
Ethiopia						
African Enterprise	1975				12	
Assemblies of God World Missions	1975	12		13		
Awana Clubs International					1	
Baptist Bible Fellowship International – World Mission Service Center	1960			12		
Baptist International Outreach	1985			10	9	1
Baptist Mid-Missions	1993					2
BethanyKids	2012			2		
BILD International				1	3	
Blessing the Children International	2001				56	
Campus Crusade for Christ (Cru in the US)		5		2		
Center for Mission Mobilization	2012				2	
Children's HopeChest	2008				5	
Christian Churches / Churches of Christ				8	2	
Christian Veterinary Mission	1983			2		
Church of the Nazarene Inc.	1992			3	1	
CityTeam Ministries – New Generations International				1		2
CMF International	1963	5	4	13	1	21
Compassion International Inc.	1993				96	
Converge				1		
CrossWay International	2003				11	
Equip Inc & Equip International	1996		3	2		
Evangelical Free Church of Canada Mission				2		
FH Canada	2005		1			
Harvest Foundation					4	
Helimission Inc. – USA						3
Helps Ministries	2010			2	3	
Holt International Children's Services Inc.					60	
HOPE International Development Agency	1985				14	
IN Network dba International Needs USA	1996				6	
International Christian Ministries	2001				2	

	First Year	Personnel from US or Canada 1–2 years	2–4 years	4+ years	Other Countries Citizen	Not Citizen
International Crisis Aid					5	
International Gospel Outreach	2001			5	3	2
Into All The World	1999			2		
Lifesong for Orphans	2009		2	2	129	
MEDA – Mennonite Economic Development Associates	2008					1
Medical Ministry International	2004	1				
Mission ONE Inc.					37	
Mission to the World (PCA) Inc.	1990	2	6	4		
Missions Door					1	
New Mission Systems International	2010			1		1
On The Go Ministries/Keith Cook Team	1957			2		
Reformed Church in America – General Synod Council – Global Mission				2		
Ripe for Harvest Inc.				1		
Samaritan's Purse	2004	4		1		
Scriptures In Use	2014	2			200	
Seventh-day Adventists – General Conference – Global Mission	1907					15
SIM Canada				15		
SIM USA		7		49		
Source of Light Ministries Intl. Inc.					1	
The Centers for Apologetics Research (CFAR)					1	
The God's Story Project	2004					1
The Pentecostal Assemblies of Canada				4		
The Word for the World (TWFTW)	1995				37	
With Open Eyes	2010				23	
World Concern	1983			1	16	2
Wycliffe Bible Translators of Canada Inc.				3		
Wycliffe Bible Translators USA				11		
Europe						
ABWE Canada (Across Borders for World Evangelism)				3		
Canadian Baptist Ministries	1911			1		1
Canadian National Baptist Convention (CNBC)	2000			2		
Christian Aid Mission					9	
Church of God (Cleveland TN) World Missions				2		
Fellowship of Companies for Christ International (FCCI)	2005				1	
Final Frontiers Foundation	1992				25	
Frontiers Canada	1984			4	1	
Gideons International, The					21	
Global Missions (United Pentecostal Church Intl.)			6			23
Presbyterian Church (USA) Worldwide Ministries			40	37		
Ravi Zacharias International Ministries Inc.	1998				8	
The Christian and Missionary Alliance				186		
Young Life			17	8	14	

	First Year	Personnel from US or Canada				Other Countries	
		1–2 years	2–4 years	4+ years		Citizen	Not Citizen
Youth for Christ/USA				8			
Youth With A Mission (YWAM)			407			986	
Faroe Islands							
Operation Mobilization						2	
Fiji							
Assemblies of God World Missions	1918	4					
Awana Clubs International						1	
Baptist International Missions Inc.				8			
Biblical Ministries Worldwide				4			4
Child Evangelism Fellowship Inc.				3			
Church of God (Cleveland TN) World Missions	1990			2			
Church of the Nazarene Inc.	1995						
Evangelism Explosion III International Inc.	2009					25	
Global Missions (United Pentecostal Church Intl.)	1980		2				2
Habitat for Humanity International	1991		1				1
International Teams U.S.A.							2
Medical Ministry International	2003						1
Our Daily Bread				1			
WEC International Canada	1986			2			
Word of Life Fellowship Inc.	1986					2	
Finland							
Baptist Mid-Missions	1980			2			
Biblical Ministries Worldwide				8			8
Chosen People Ministries Inc.	2010					2	
Evangelism Explosion III International Inc.	2012					2	
Far East Broadcasting Company						1	
Global Missions (United Pentecostal Church Intl.)							4
Operation Mobilization		4				20	1
Wycliffe Bible Translators USA				6			
France							
A.C.T. International	2008			2			
ABWE International				5			
Alongside Ministries International		1	2	2			
Assemblies of God World Missions	1952	10		21			
Avant Ministries	1960			5			
Avant Ministries Canada	1960			7			
Baptist Bible Fellowship International – World Mission Service Center	1970			8			
Baptist International Missions Inc.				4			
Baptist Mid-Missions	1948			16	2		
Baptist Missionary Association of America (BMAA)				2			
BCM International	1988			4			2
Bethany Gateways		4	1	3		1	
Bibles and Literature in French	2005			2			

	First Year	Personnel from US or Canada			Other Countries	
		1–2 years	2–4 years	4+ years	Citizen	Not Citizen
BILD International					1	
Campus Crusade for Christ (Cru in the US)		10		23		
Child Evangelism Fellowship Inc.				2		
Chosen People Ministries Inc.	1960				1	
Christian and Missionary Alliance in Canada, The				3		
Christian Churches / Churches of Christ			1	5		
Church of God (Cleveland TN) World Missions	1960			3		
Church of the Brethren – Global Mission Partnerships		1				
Church of the Nazarene Inc.	1977			2		
Converge				2		
Crossworld	1962			19		2
Encompass World Partners	1951	3		15	5	
EPC World Outreach				3		
European Christian Mission Intl. – USA				14		
FAIR				6		
Far East Broadcasting Associates of Canada (FEB Canada)	1982			8	2	
Fellowship International Mission	2008			2		
Foursquare Missions International	1980			5	2	
Free Will Baptist International Missions	1966			12		
GAIN (Global Aid Network)	2008					2
Global Missions (United Pentecostal Church Intl.)	1930		8			
Global Outreach Mission Inc.	1946	1		38		
Go Ye Fellowship	2007			5	2	3
Greater Europe Mission			11	21		
Greater Grace World Outreach					2	
Helps Ministries	2006			2		
International Association For Refugees	2010		4	2		
International Pentecostal Holiness Church	1981			1		
International Teams U.S.A.				16		5
InterVarsity Christian Fellowship/USA			5			
Jews for Jesus	1992				2	1
Life in Messiah International	1998				4	
Master's Resourcing Commission				1		
MB Mission	2001			4		5
MB Mission Canada	2001			3		6
Mennonite Mission Network	1953			3		
Mission to the World (PCA) Inc.	1978	2	1	22		
Missions to Military Inc.				7		
OM Canada				1		
Open Door Baptist Missions	2008			1		
Operation Mobilization		8			2	13
Pioneers Canada				2		

	First Year	Personnel from US or Canada			Other Countries	
		1–2 years	2–4 years	4+ years	Citizen	Not Citizen
Presbyterian Mission International (PMI)				1		
ReachGlobal		1		17		
Reformed Baptist Mission Services						2
Ripe for Harvest Inc.				1		
Salvation Army – Canada and Bermuda Territory, The	1994		2			
Servant Partners	2010			2		
Serve Globally – The Evangelical Covenant Church			2	6		
Seventh-day Adventists – General Conference – Global Mission	1876					2
SIM USA				2		
TEAM (The Evangelical Alliance Mission)	1952			24		
The Navigators				4		
The Pentecostal Assemblies of Canada				2		
TMS Global	1995			2		
United World Mission Inc.		1		3		4
WEC International		1		1		
Word of Life Fellowship Inc.	1999	1		3	7	3
World Missions & Evangelism	1996			1		
World Partners USA				1		
World Team US				22		
World-Wide Missions			1			
WorldVenture				9		
Wycliffe Bible Translators USA				13		
Youth for Christ/USA	1949			2		
French Guiana						
Global Missions (United Pentecostal Church Intl.)	1991		2			
Seventh-day Adventists – General Conference – Global Mission	1946					2
French Polynesia						
Seventh-day Adventists – General Conference – Global Mission	1891					2
Gabon						
Assemblies of God World Missions	2000	2		2		
Christian Aid Mission	2009				2	
Global Missions (United Pentecostal Church Intl.)	2001		2			
Global Outreach Mission Inc.				1		
Greater Grace World Outreach	2008					2
Missionary Ventures Intl.				1		
Gambia						
Child Evangelism Fellowship Inc.				2		
Christian Aid Mission	1988				15	
Eastern Mennonite Missions	2015		2			
Global Missions (United Pentecostal Church Intl.)	2003		2			
Global Recordings Network					2	

	First Year	Personnel from US or Canada			Other Countries	
		1–2 years	2–4 years	4+ years	Citizen	Not Citizen
International Gospel Outreach	1986			1		1
Living Word Missions				1	1	
Seventh-day Adventists – General Conference – Global Mission	1973					2
WEC International		1		3		
WEC International Canada	1959			2		
Georgia						
Assemblies of God World Missions	1997	4		5		
Baptist International Missions Inc.				2		
Church Leadership Development International	1996				1	
Evangelism Explosion III International Inc.	2009				3	
Global Missions (United Pentecostal Church Intl.)						2
Greater Europe Mission				1		
International Gospel Outreach	1999			2	1	1
Mission Eurasia					4	
Pioneers Canada				2		
Seventh-day Adventists – General Conference – Global Mission	1886			2		
Germany						
A.C.T. International	2006					1
ABWE International				11		
Assemblies of God World Missions	1948	6		35		
Avant Ministries	1961			2		
Awana Clubs International				1	1	
Baptist Bible Fellowship International – World Mission Service Center	1970			16		
Baptist International Missions Inc.				20		
Baptist Mid-Missions	1949			20		
BCM International	1950				8	2
Be One Together	2011				2010	2
Bethany Gateways					2	
Biblical Ministries Worldwide				7		7
Cadence International	1973	3	9	25		
Campus Crusade for Christ (Cru in the US)		16		18		
Canadian National Baptist Convention (CNBC)						2
Child Evangelism Fellowship Inc.				4		
Chosen People Ministries Inc.	1995				19	
Christian Aid Mission					3	
Christian and Missionary Alliance in Canada, The				6		
Christian Churches / Churches of Christ			2	8		
Christians In Action Missions International	1975			1		
Church of God (Cleveland TN) World Missions	1936	2	2	10		4
Church of God Ministries (Anderson) – Global Strategy	1901	2		2		
Church of the Brethren – Global Mission Partnerships		1				

	First Year	Personnel from US or Canada			Other Countries	
		1–2 years	2–4 years	4+ years	Citizen	Not Citizen
Church of the Nazarene Inc.	1958				5	
CMF International	2008	3	4	3	1	9
Commission to Every Nation	2007		2			2
Converge				4		
CRM				4		
Crossover Communications International	2008					2
Crossworld	1976	1		7		
Eastern Mennonite Missions	2003	1		8	2	
Encompass World Partners	1969			4	2	
EPC World Outreach			1	2		
Ethnos360				1		
European Christian Mission Intl. – USA				17		
Evangelical Free Church of Canada Mission				2		
Faith Christian Fellowship Intl.					1	
Fellowship International Mission	2006			3		
Foursquare Missions International	1985			1		
Global Missions (United Pentecostal Church Intl.)	1960		4			
Global Outreach Mission Inc.	1946	1		6		
Globe International	1987			2		
Go Ye Fellowship	1980			4		4
Gospel Fellowship Association	1963	2		18		
Greater Europe Mission			10	24		
Greater Europe Mission Canada	1990			4		
International Pentecostal Holiness Church	1987		2	2		
InterVarsity Christian Fellowship/USA			1			
Jews for Jesus					3	2
Josiah Venture	2014			2		
Liebenzell Mission of Canada	1899		2			
Macedonia World Baptist Missions Inc.	2013			2		
MB Mission	1945			4	4	3
MB Mission Canada	1945			2	4	5
Mennonite Mission Network	2002		2	2		
Mission to the World (PCA) Inc.	1991		3	11		
New Mission Systems International	2002			6	4	
On The Go Ministries/Keith Cook Team	1972	3		6		
One Challenge	1981			4		
Operation Mobilization		2			80	22
Prayer Baptist Missions International Inc.				1		
Precept Ministries International	1992			1	1	1
Proclaim! International Inc.	1997			10		
ReachGlobal		11	2	16		
Reformed Episcopal Board of Foreign Missions				1		
Reliant Mission Inc.	1992			1		
Salvation Army – Canada and Bermuda Territory, The	1991			4		

	First Year	Personnel from US or Canada 1–2 years	2–4 years	4+ years	Other Countries Citizen	Not Citizen
Serge				3		
Serve Globally – The Evangelical Covenant Church		4				
Seventh-day Adventists – General Conference – Global Mission	1875	1				2
TeachBeyond Canada	1955	2	9	33		
TEAM (The Evangelical Alliance Mission)				13		
The Pentecostal Assemblies of Canada					2	
TWR				2		
United World Mission Inc.				5		5
Virginia Mennonite Missions	2012			2	1	1
WEC International						1
Word of Life Fellowship Inc.	1965	1		3	29	1
World Missions & Evangelism	2013			2		
World Reach Inc.	1988				2	
World Witness				3		
WorldVenture				7		
Wycliffe Bible Translators USA				57		
Youth for Christ/USA				9		
Ghana						
A.C.T. International	2007				4	
ABWE International		2				
Advent Christian World Outreach	1995				1	
African Enterprise	1972				22	
Agape Gospel Mission		2	4	4		
Allegheny Wesleyan Methodist Connection	1997			4		
American Baptist International Ministries				1		
American Leprosy Missions	2002					1
AMG International					2	
Apostolic Christian Church – Missionary Committee	1975					
Awana Clubs International					1	
Baptist International Missions Inc.				9		
Baptist Mid-Missions	1946			11	1	1
Baptist Missionary Association of America (BMAA)				2		
Bethany Gateways				2	1	1
Child Evangelism Fellowship Inc.				1		
Christian Aid Mission	1990				10	
Christian Broadcasting Network Inc., The	1999				2	
Christian Churches / Churches of Christ			1	13	2	
Christian Discipleship International	1985				4	
Christians In Action Missions International	1994				2	
Church of God (Cleveland TN) World Missions	1950	2		4		
Church of God (Holiness) World Mission Dept. Inc.			1		3	
Church of the Nazarene Inc.	1990			2		

	First Year	Personnel from US or Canada			Other Countries	
		1–2 years	2–4 years	4+ years	Citizen	Not Citizen
Compassion International Inc.	2005			1	40	
Development Associates Intl. (DAI)					1	
Evangel Bible Translators					2	
Evangelism Explosion III International Inc.	2010				9	
Every Child Ministries Inc.	1999			2	46	
FaithLife Ministries Inc.	2011				1	
Fellowship International Mission	2002				2	1
Global Missions (United Pentecostal Church Intl.)	1969	4				3
Global Missions of Open Bible Churches	1971				1	
Global Outreach Mission Inc.				1		
Go to Nations	2004					2
Greater Grace World Outreach					60	
Habitat for Humanity International	1987		1		1	
Harvest Foundation					2	
Hope for the Hungry	1984	1	2		6	
IN Network dba International Needs USA	1986				9	
International Gospel Outreach	1986			1		1
International Partnership Ministries Inc.	1995				22	
International Pentecostal Holiness Church	1992			2		
InterVarsity Christian Fellowship/USA			1			
Literacy & Evangelism International					2	
Macedonia World Baptist Missions Inc.	2010			2		
Medical Ministry International	1990				2	
Mission ONE Inc.					1	
Mutual Faith Ministries Intl.		1				
National Association of Congregational Christian Churches	1992				74	
National Baptist Convention of America – Foreign Mission Board	1984				45	
Network of International Christian Schools	2006	12	8	4	20	
Open Door Baptist Missions	2006			2		
Operation Mobilization					24	
Reach Beyond				6		2
Scriptures In Use	2008			6	1400	
Self-Help International	1989				5	
Seventh-day Adventists – General Conference – Global Mission	1894					6
Shield of Faith Mission International	2009			2		
SIM Canada					5	
SIM USA					4	
Source of Light Ministries Intl. Inc.					1	
Team Expansion Inc.	2008			4		
The Free Methodist Church in Canada	2006				10	
The Navigators				1		
TMS Global	1987			5		

	First Year	Personnel from US or Canada			Other Countries	
		1–2 years	2–4 years	4+ years	Citizen	Not Citizen
WEC International Canada	1940			2		
White Fields					3	
Word of Life Fellowship Inc.	2003				1	1
WorldVenture				4		
Wycliffe Bible Translators of Canada Inc.				3		
Wycliffe Bible Translators USA				1		
Global Ministry						
AEGA Ministries Int'l Inc. (Association of Evangelical Gospel Assemblies)	1989			10	45	
Africa Inland Mission				18		
Africa Inland Mission Canada Intl.	1953			31	29	2
American Baptist International Ministries				9		
Anglican Frontier Missions				5		
Assemblies of God World Missions		92		182		
Baptist Bible Fellowship International – World Mission Service Center				32		
Baptist General Conference of Canada	2013			2		
Baptist International Missions Inc.				2		
Baptist International Outreach	1985			7		
Baptist Mid-Missions				33		
Baptist Missionary Association of America (BMAA)				4		
Bethany Gateways				2		
Campus Crusade for Christ (Cru in the US)		2		13		
Caring for Others	2004			2		
Christar	2015			8		
Christian Ministries International (CMI)					28	
CMF International	2001			1		1
Commission To Every Nation-Canada	2009					2
Communitas International	1968			10		1
Crossworld				2		
Disciple Makers					1	
Entrust				45		
Ethnos360				28		
Every Home for Christ					1000	500
Fellowship International Mission				7		3
Foursquare Missions International				2		
Free Will Baptist International Missions				6		
Friends of Israel Gospel Ministry Inc.					32	
Frontiers				578		
Global Training Network	2004	22	31	30		1
Go Ye Fellowship				7		
GOGF Ministries					2	

	Personnel from US or Canada				Other Countries	
	First Year	1–2 years	2–4 years	4+ years	Citizen	Not Citizen
Gospel Revival Ministries	1980				1100	
Gospelink Inc.					1300	
Harvest Foundation					43	2
Hellenic Ministries USA				15	12	
iHope International	2010			2		
IMB of the Southern Baptist Convention	1845	557	778	2337		
Independent Faith Mission Inc.				47	14	
International Board of Jewish Missions Inc.		9		8	3	
International Project	1999	20	2	9		
InterVarsity Christian Fellowship/USA			1			
JAARS Inc.				500		5
Kidzana Ministries	1998			5		
Lutheran Bible Translators Inc.					94	
Mission Services Association Inc.	1946			4		
Missionary Ventures Canada					1	
Mobile Member Care Team	2000	1		2		
New Mission Systems International	1995	3		53		
New Wineskins Missionary Network	1974			1		
One Another Ministries International	1997			4		
One Challenge				42		
One Child Matters						
Operation Mobilization				53		469
Outreach Canada	2007		2			
Pioneers USA				63	1	
Reach Beyond				8		5
ReachAcross	1951			7		
ReachGlobal		10		89		
SEND International Inc.	1947			45		4
SIM USA				15		
Sowers International, The				5		
TeachBeyond USA		161		475		
TEAM (The Evangelical Alliance Mission)		100				
TEAM of Canada		6		41		
The Navigators				147	266	
The Pentecostal Assemblies of Canada				16		
The Voice of the Martyrs				11	3	
Things to Come Mission				7		
Timothy Leadership Training Institute	1997			2	3	
WEC International				7		
Word of Life Fellowship Inc.				12		
World Horizons				45		
World Mission Prayer League	1937			25		

	First Year	Personnel from US or Canada			Other Countries	
		1–2 years	2–4 years	4+ years	Citizen	Not Citizen
World Reach Inc.	1982			11		
World Team US				26		
World Thrust International				2		
Youth Ministry International				4		
Greece						
ABWE International				2		
AMG International	1945			6	401	
Assemblies of God World Missions	1935	4		6		
Baptist Bible Fellowship International – World Mission Service Center	1993			4		
Baptist International Missions Inc.				2		
Campus Crusade for Christ (Cru in the US)		4		6		
Child Evangelism Fellowship Inc.				2		
Church of God (Cleveland TN) World Missions	1972			2		
Cooperative Baptist Fellowship – Global Missions	2003			2		
Fellowship International Mission	2003				2	
Foursquare Missions International	1952			2		
Free Methodist World Missions	2000			2		
Global Missions (United Pentecostal Church Intl.)	1975		4			1
Greater Europe Mission				7		
Hellenic Ministries/USA	1980	2	6	6	10	15
International Teams Canada (Evangelical International Crusades Canada Inc.)		1				
International Teams U.S.A.	1984			9	4	11
Operation Mobilization					1	8
ReachGlobal				2		
Seventh-day Adventists – General Conference – Global Mission	1907					2
TEAM (The Evangelical Alliance Mission)	2014			2		
United World Mission Inc.				2		2
WEC International Canada						1
Word of Life Fellowship Inc.	2007					2
World Team US				2		
Grenada						
Baptist International Missions Inc.				2		
Christian Churches / Churches of Christ				2		
Church of the Nazarene Inc.	1977					
Foursquare Missions International	1987			1		
Global Missions (United Pentecostal Church Intl.)						2
Global Missions of Open Bible Churches	1971				1	
World Relief		2				
Guadeloupe						
Christian Church (Disciples of Christ) – Global Ministries			1			
ReachGlobal				1		

	First Year	Personnel from US or Canada 1–2 years	2–4 years	4+ years	Other Countries Citizen	Not Citizen
Guam						
Baptist Bible Fellowship International – World Mission Service Center	1975			2		
Baptist Mid-Missions	1981			1		
Biblical Ministries Worldwide				2		2
Elim Fellowship	2002			4		
Foursquare Missions International	2002			2		
Global Missions (United Pentecostal Church Intl.)						2
Liebenzell Mission of USA Inc.	1991			1		
Mission to the World (PCA) Inc.	1996			2		
On The Go Ministries/Keith Cook Team	1961			2		
Seventh-day Adventists – General Conference – Global Mission	1930	1		50		9
TWR		1		9		
Guatemala						
All God's Children International	2000	1			130	1
AMG International	1978	2	4	2	460	
Assemblies of God World Missions	1935	3		12		
Awana Clubs International					2	
Baptist Bible Fellowship International – World Mission Service Center	1975			5		
Baptist International Missions Inc.				2		
Baptist Missionary Association of America (BMAA)					2	
BILD International					1	1
Buckner International	2004	1			40	
Camino Global	1899			32	1	3
Camino Global Ministries Canada	1899			2		
Caring Partners International	1994				4	
CAUSE Canada	1984				17	
Child Evangelism Fellowship Inc.				1		
Children of Promise International			2	1		
Christian Aid Mission	1983				10	
Christian and Missionary Alliance in Canada, The			4	2		
Christian Church (Disciples of Christ) – Global Ministries			1			
Christian Churches / Churches of Christ				2	2	
Christian Reformed World Missions	2003			2		
Christian Relief Fund, The	1992				1	
Christians In Action Missions International	1970			2	1	
Church of God (Cleveland TN) World Missions	1934			2		
Church of the Brethren – Global Mission Partnerships	1980	2				
Church of the Nazarene Inc.	1904			6	4	5
Commission to Every Nation	1995		10	52	9	53
Commission To Every Nation-Canada	2009			13		
Compassion International Inc.	1976				53	
CRM				3	4	

	First Year	Personnel from US or Canada			Other Countries	
		1–2 years	2–4 years	4+ years	Citizen	Not Citizen
Cup of Cold Water Ministries	2014			1		1
Eastern Mennonite Missions	1995		2	2		
EPC World Outreach				1		
Evangel Bible Translators					2	
Evangelical Missionary Church of Canada	1993			2		
Evangelism Explosion III International Inc.	2011				2	
Evangelistic Faith Mission Inc.	1960		2			
FAIR				4		
Faith Christian Fellowship Intl.					1	
Food for the Hungry Inc.	1976		3	3	1	
Foursquare Missions International				2		
Global Action				2		
Global Missions (United Pentecostal Church Intl.)	1977		3			4
Global Missions of Open Bible Churches	1975				1	
Global Outreach International	1998			1		
Global Outreach Mission Inc.				11		
Globe International	1980			6		
Go to Nations	1987	2		11	6	
Holt International Children's Services Inc.					1	
Hope for the Hungry	1980			1		
Hope Haven International Ministries	2008			1	10	
Identify	2013				1	
Impact International Inc.	1970				2	
International Gospel Outreach	1984			2		2
International Justice Mission	2005				10	
International Partnership Ministries Inc.	2002				4	
International Pentecostal Holiness Church	1995			2		
Kids Alive International	1993	1	1	10		
Lifesong for Orphans	2012	1		3	47	
Literacy & Evangelism International					5	
Living Water Teaching	1979	1	1	5	4	
Living Word Missions				2		2
Lutheran Church Missouri Synod – World Mission	1947			1		
Medical Teams International	2009				1	
Mission Aviation Fellowship	1977		2			
Missionary Ventures Canada					2	
Missionary Ventures Intl.				8		
Missions Door					1	
Mutual Faith Ministries Intl.		2				
New Life Advance International	1976			12		
One Challenge	1991			6	2	
Paraclete Mission Group Inc.						
Pentecostal Free Will Baptist Church Inc. – World Witness Dept.					1	

	First Year	Personnel from US or Canada			Other Countries	
		1–2 years	2–4 years	4+ years	Citizen	Not Citizen
PIC International (Partners in Christ International)		1				
Precept Ministries International	1983				1	1
Reach Beyond				2		
Reformed Church in America – General Synod Council – Global Mission					1	
Sowers International, The					1	
Spanish World Ministries					1	
TEAM (The Evangelical Alliance Mission)				7		
The Pentecostal Assemblies of Canada		3			2	
World Missions & Evangelism	2011			3		
World Orphans	2008			2		
World Partners USA				1		
Wycliffe Bible Translators USA				9		
Guinea						
CAMA Services	1990			2	1	
Child Evangelism Fellowship Inc.				1		
Christian Aid Mission	2008				1	
Christian and Missionary Alliance in Canada, The				6		
Christian Churches / Churches of Christ			5	15		
Christian Reformed World Missions	1984			3		
FaithLife Ministries Inc.	2015					1
Global Missions of Open Bible Churches	1952			2	1	
Harvest Foundation					1	
International Gospel Outreach	1986			1		1
National Baptist Convention USA Inc. – Foreign Mission Board	1990			2	23	
Pioneer Bible Translators				27		
SIM USA				8		
The Pentecostal Assemblies of Canada				1		
WorldVenture				7		
Guinea-Bissau						
Christian Aid Mission	2003				25	
Christians In Action Missions International	2002					4
Church of the Nazarene Inc.	2004					2
Eastern Mennonite Missions	2013		2			
Hisportic Christian Mission						1
International Gospel Outreach	1986			1		1
Scriptures In Use	2009			6	1200	
Seventh-day Adventists – General Conference – Global Mission	1975			2		2
Youth for Christ/USA				6		
Guyana						
Baptist International Missions Inc.				2		
BCM International	1993			4		

	First Year	Personnel from US or Canada			Other Countries	
		1–2 years	2–4 years	4+ years	Citizen	Not Citizen
Christian Churches / Churches of Christ					2	
Church of the Nazarene Inc.	1946				2	
Crossworld	1949		2			
Global Missions (United Pentecostal Church Intl.)	1976	2				2
Global Missions of Open Bible Churches	1997				1	
Global Outreach International	1994		5			
Global Partners (The Wesleyan Church World Headquarters)				1		
IFCA World Missions	2002		2		4	
International Pentecostal Holiness Church	1996		2			
Lott Carey Baptist Foreign Mission Convention	1961				25	
Macedonia World Baptist Missions Inc.	1997		2			
On The Go Ministries/Keith Cook Team	1914		2			
Prayer Baptist Missions International Inc.				1		
Seventh-day Adventists – General Conference – Global Mission	1883		3			2
Wycliffe Bible Translators USA			2			
Haiti						
Advent Christian World Outreach	2014				1	
Allegheny Wesleyan Methodist Connection	1968		3			
American Baptist International Ministries			2			2
AMG International					25	
Assemblies of God World Missions	1957	5	3			
Awana Clubs International					1	
Baptist Bible Fellowship International – World Mission Service Center	1982		2			
Baptist Haiti Mission	1946		13			1
Baptist International Missions Inc.			4			
Baptist Mid-Missions	1934				4	
Baptist Missionary Association of America (BMAA)			2			
Beyond Borders	1993				15	
Bright Hope	1995	1				
Caribbean Baptist Mission Society	1993	6				
Child Evangelism Fellowship Inc.			2			
Childcare Worldwide	1983				13	
Children of Promise International			6			
Children's Lifeline	1989	2				
Christian Aid Ministries (CAM)	1988	3	4	11	38	
Christian Church (Disciples of Christ) – Global Ministries			2			
Christian Churches / Churches of Christ			4	4	30	
Christian Discipleship International	2006				1	
Christian Emergency Relief Teams (CERT) International	2015					
Christian Flights International	1977		1	1	100	
Christian Outreach International					1	
Christian Reformed World Missions	1985		2	2		

	First Year	Personnel from US or Canada 1–2 years	2–4 years	4+ years	Other Countries Citizen	Not Citizen
Christian Relief Fund, The	1998				2	
Christian Veterinary Mission	1980			2		
Church of God (Cleveland TN) World Missions	1933	1		2		
Church of God (Holiness) World Mission Dept. Inc.					32	
Church of God Ministries (Anderson) – Global Strategy	1968	2				
Church of the Nazarene Inc.	1950				1	5
Churches of God – General Conference	1967			4		
Colorado Haiti Project Inc.					23	
Compassion International Inc.	1968				71	
Congregational Methodist Missions				1		
Cooperative Baptist Fellowship – Global Missions	2005			2		
Cross-Cultural Ministries – Churches of God General Conference	1967			1	1	
Crossworld	1943			9		
Crossworld Canada	1943			1		
Elim Fellowship	1988			2		
Emmanuel Intl. Canada				1		
Eternal Hope in Haiti				4		
FOCAS (Foundation of Compassionate American Samaritans)	1986				8	
For Haiti with Love Inc.	1969			7	6	1
Foursquare Missions International	1984					
Free Methodist World Missions	1964			2		
Global Missions (United Pentecostal Church Intl.)	1966		2			
Global Outreach International	1988			8		
Global Outreach Mission Inc.				2		
Global Partners (The Wesleyan Church World Headquarters)				16		
Globe International	2002			2		
Good Shepherd Ministries Inc.	1975			2	48	
Grace Mission Inc.	1981			4	95	
Greater Grace World Outreach	1980				4	
Haiti Arise – Canada	2003			2		
Haiti Lutheran Mission Society					75	
Haitian Christian Outreach	1985				1	
Harvest Foundation					1	
Harvest International Inc.	1986		2		2	
Help for Haiti Inc.	1995				1	2
Hope for the Hungry	1982			5	2	
HOPE International	2006	2			1	
Intercede International					2	
International Child Care (Canada) Inc.	1967		4	2		
International Faith Missions	1984	6	6			1
International Partnership Ministries Inc.	1982				31	
Kids Alive International	2002		1	1		
KORE Foundation	2012			5	25	

	First Year	Personnel from US or Canada			Other Countries	
		1–2 years	2–4 years	4+ years	Citizen	Not Citizen
Lifesong for Orphans	2015			2	55	
Macedonia World Baptist Missions Inc.	1984			2		
Medical Ministry International	1990	1				
Medical Ministry International Canada Inc.	2004					2
Mission Aviation Fellowship	1986		12			
Mission Aviation Fellowship of Canada (MAFC)				1		
Mission Possible USA	1979				225	
Mission to the World (PCA) Inc.				2		
Missionary Ventures Intl.				1		
Missions Door					1	
National Association of Congregational Christian Churches	1997				3	2
National Baptist Convention of America – Foreign Mission Board	1975				25	
New Mission Systems International	2003				7	
Northwest Haiti Christian Mission	1979	2	2	7		
OMS International – Canada		4		8		
One Mission Society	1958		1	10		6
Open Door Baptist Missions	1994			6		
Orthodox Presbyterian Church – Committee on Foreign Missions	2004			2		
ReachGlobal		3		3		
Reciprocal Ministries International	1981	1	4	4	38	
Rehoboth Ministries Inc.	1983			2	20	1
Ripe for Harvest Inc.				1		
Seventh-day Adventists – General Conference – Global Mission	1905			2		
Source of Light Ministries Intl. Inc.					2	
STEM International	1985			4		
The Pentecostal Assemblies of Canada				2		
The Salvation Army USA National Headquarters	1950			2		
Word & Deed	2011					2
Word & Deed Ministries Canada	2011			2		
World Concern	1995				120	
World Relief	1987				18	1
World Team Canada				2		
World Team US				4		
Honduras						
Action International Ministries – Canada						1
Advent Christian World Outreach	1990			1		
American Baptist International Ministries					1	
Apostolic Church of Pentecost of Canada (Global Harvest Missions)	2004				1	
Assemblies of God World Missions	1940	4		11		1
Awana Clubs International					1	

	First Year	Personnel from US or Canada			Other Countries	
		1–2 years	2–4 years	4+ years	Citizen	Not Citizen
Baptist Bible Fellowship International – World Mission Service Center	1974			5		
Baptist General Conference of Canada	2014			2		
Baptist International Missions Inc.				17		
Baptist Medical & Dental Mission International Inc. (BMDMI)	1974	12	4	7	39	2
Baptist Mid-Missions	1954			6	1	
Baptist Missionary Association of America (BMAA)					2	
Bethany Gateways				2		
Biblical Ministries Worldwide				2		2
Brethren in Christ World Missions (BICWM)	1989			2		
Buckner International	2009				10	
Camino Global	1896	1		18	1	1
Camino Global Ministries Canada	1896			1		
CAUSE Canada	1995	1			6	1
Christian Aid Mission	1983				300	
Christian Churches / Churches of Christ		2		19	2	
Christian Outreach International				1		
Christian Reformed World Missions	1971			1		
Christian Relief Fund, The	1984				4	
Christians In Action Missions International	1978			1		2
Church of God (Cleveland TN) World Missions	1944	2		5		
Church of God Ministries (Anderson) – Global Strategy	1972			1		
Church of God of the Apostolic Faith Inc., The				1		
Church of the Brethren – Global Mission Partnerships	1981	1				
Commission to Every Nation	2004				1	1
Commission To Every Nation-Canada	2015		2			
Compassion International Inc.	1974				51	
CRM				2		
Eastern Mennonite Missions	2013			4		
Equip Inc & Equip International	2010			4		
Evangelical Free Church of Canada Mission				2		
Evangelism Explosion III International Inc.	2011				2	
Evangelistic Faith Mission Inc.	1968		2	1		
Far East Broadcasting Associates of Canada (FEB Canada)	2006		1			
Full Gospel Evangelistic Association	1970			2		
General Baptists International	1995			8		
Global Action				2		
Global Missions (United Pentecostal Church Intl.)	1997		4			
Global Outreach International	1990			11		
Global Outreach Mission Inc.				5		
Globe International	1986			2		
Go to Nations	1989			2	1	
Harvest Foundation					1	
Impact International Inc.	1970			4		

	First Year	Personnel from US or Canada			Other Countries	
		1–2 years	2–4 years	4+ years	Citizen	Not Citizen
International Gospel Outreach	1986			1		1
International Pentecostal Holiness Church	1993			2	2	
International Teams U.S.A.				2		
ISOH/IMPACT	2004			1		
Latin America Mission	2005	2		2		
Living Water Teaching	1983			3		
Macedonia World Baptist Missions Inc.	2011			3		
Medical Ministry International	1971				2	
Mission On The Move	2000	2	2		5	
Mission to the World (PCA) Inc.	2001		4			
Missionary Ventures Intl.				4		
Missions Door					1	
Moravian Church in North America – Board of World Mission	1994				2	
National Association of Congregational Christian Churches	1974				9	
On The Go Ministries/Keith Cook Team		1				
Pentecostal Free Will Baptist Church Inc. – World Witness Dept.					1	
Prayer Baptist Missions International Inc.				2		
Precept Ministries International						1
Reformed Church in America – General Synod Council – Global Mission					2	
Reliant Mission Inc.	2013		1			
Ripe for Harvest Inc.				1		
Samaritan's Purse	2000	1				
Servant Partners	2006			3		
Seventh-day Adventists – General Conference – Global Mission	1891			2		2
Spanish World Ministries					2	
TEAM (The Evangelical Alliance Mission)				3		
Teen Missions International Inc.	1987		2		2	
The Pentecostal Assemblies of Canada				6		
United World Mission Inc.				4		4
Walk Thru the Bible Ministries Inc.	2002				4	
Word of Life Fellowship Inc.	1998				7	2
World Concern	1998			1		1
World Gospel Mission	1944	2		17		
World Missions & Evangelism	1988				8	
World Reach Inc.	1982			1	8	
Wycliffe Bible Translators USA				2		
Youth for Christ/USA				3		
Hong Kong (China)						
American Baptist International Ministries				2		
Awana Clubs International					1	

	First Year	Personnel from US or Canada			Other Countries	
		1–2 years	2–4 years	4+ years	Citizen	Not Citizen
Baptist Bible Fellowship International – World Mission Service Center	1969			4		
Baptist International Missions Inc.				2		
Baptist International Outreach	2014			2		2
Baptist Mid-Missions	1952					
Baptist Missionary Association of America (BMAA)						2
Biblical Ministries Worldwide				7		7
BILD International					1	
Child Evangelism Fellowship Inc.				1		
Chinese Christian Life Fellowship Inc.	2014				1	
Chosen People Ministries Inc.	1930			4		
Christian Broadcasting Network Inc., The	2004		1	11		
Christian Church (Disciples of Christ) – Global Ministries			2			
Christian Churches / Churches of Christ				10	4	
Evangelize China Fellowship Inc.					1	
FAIR				1		
Foursquare Missions International	1936			2		
Global Missions (United Pentecostal Church Intl.)	1976		2			
Habitat for Humanity International			2			2
International Gospel Outreach	2001			2		2
International Students Inc (ISI)					2	
Life in Messiah International	2015				1	
Mission to the World (PCA) Inc.	1982			2		
On The Go Ministries/Keith Cook Team	1890	1		6	2	
One Mission Society	1954			5		1
Operation Mobilization					26	4
Our Daily Bread				1		
People International USA				1		
Ravi Zacharias International Ministries Inc.	2008					1
Ripe for Harvest Inc.				1		
SEND International Inc.	1988				4	
Seventh-day Adventists – General Conference – Global Mission	1888			14		4
Wisconsin Evangelical Lutheran Synod – Board for World Missions				2		
World Mission Prayer League	1977		2			
WorldVenture				4		
Hungary						
A.C.T. International	2003			1		
ABWE International		2		8		
American Baptist International Ministries				4		
Assemblies of God World Missions	1926			8		
Baptist Bible Fellowship International – World Mission Service Center	1990			2		

	First Year	Personnel from US or Canada			Other Countries	
		1–2 years	2–4 years	4+ years	Citizen	Not Citizen
Barnabas International		2				
BCM International	1993					2
Campus Crusade for Christ (Cru in the US)		1		62		
Child Evangelism Fellowship Inc.				1		
Christian Aid Mission					8	
Christian and Missionary Alliance in Canada, The				4		
Christian Church (Disciples of Christ) – Global Ministries			3			
Church of the Brethren – Global Mission Partnerships		1				
Church of the Nazarene Inc.	1996			2		
Cooperative Baptist Fellowship – Global Missions	1994		2	2		
CRM				1	6	
Entrust	1979			7	2	
European Christian Mission Intl. – USA				2		
Evangelical Free Church of Canada Mission				4		
Evangelical Missionary Church of Canada	2007			2		
Evangelism Explosion III International Inc.	2011				3	
Fellowship of Evangelical Churches – International Ministries	2000			2		
Foursquare Missions International				2		
Free Methodist World Missions	1995			2		
Friendship International Ministries Inc.				4		
Global Missions of Open Bible Churches	1979			2	1	
Greater Europe Mission				3		
Greater Europe Mission Canada	1994			3		
Greater Grace World Outreach	1990				5	
Habitat for Humanity International	1994	25		4	15	14
International Messengers				9	7	2
International Pentecostal Holiness Church	1989			4		
Jews for Jesus	2011			1	3	
Josiah Venture	2012		3	2	1	
Navigators of Canada, The	1981			2		
New Hope International	1971				2	
OMS International – Canada				1		
One Mission Society	1992			8		1
Operation Mobilization		4			9	4
Presbyterian Mission International (PMI)				1		
ReachGlobal		3		15		
Reformed Church in America – General Synod Council – Global Mission				2	1	
Ripe for Harvest Inc.				1		
SEND International Inc.	1994			8		
Serge				2		
TCM International Institute					1	

	First Year	Personnel from US or Canada 1–2 years	2–4 years	4+ years	Other Countries Citizen	Not Citizen
The Centers for Apologetics Research (CFAR)					1	
The Navigators				2		
The Presbyterian Church in Canada	2000					1
United World Mission Inc.			3	14	1	16
Word of Life Fellowship Inc.	1987	3		3	17	2
World Gospel Mission	1992	2		3		
World Indigenous Missions	1997			2		
WorldVenture				6		
Iceland						
Assemblies of God World Missions	1992	2		2		
Greater Europe Mission				2		
India						
ABWE International				8		
Action International Ministries	1994			1	8	2
Action International Ministries – Canada				2	5	
ACTS International Ministries Inc.	2004				1	
Advent Christian World Outreach	1880				3	
American Baptist International Ministries				2		
American Leprosy Missions	1906					
AMG International	1970				6400	
Apostolic Church of Pentecost of Canada (Global Harvest Missions)	1998				1	
Association of Free Lutheran Congregations				2	2	
Audio Scripture Ministries	2005			1	1	
Avant Ministries	2013				2	
Awana Clubs International					13	
Back to the Bible	1970				46	
Baptist General Conference of Canada	2015			2		
Baptist Mid-Missions	1935			6	9	
Baptist Missionary Association of America (BMAA)				2	4	
BCM International	1972				238	
Bibles For The World Inc.	1972				400	
BILD International				3	15	
Canadian Baptist Ministries	1874				4	
CEIFA International	2006			2	2	
Childcare Worldwide	1981				155	
Christ for India Inc.	1981			1		
Christ to the Nations				1		
Christian Broadcasting Network Inc., The	1997		1		151	
Christian Church (Disciples of Christ) – Global Ministries			2			
Christian Churches / Churches of Christ				17	35	
Christian Discipleship International	1992				7	
Christian Relief Fund, The	1974				12	
Christian Veterinary Mission	2015	1				

	First Year	Personnel from US or Canada			Other Countries	
		1–2 years	2–4 years	4+ years	Citizen	Not Citizen
Christians In Action Missions International	1977				8	
Church Leadership Development International	1996				3	
Church of the Nazarene Inc.	1898				2	
CMF International	2015	2			1	1
Commission to Every Nation	1999					1
Compassion International Inc.	1968				129	
Converge				1		
Cooperative Baptist Fellowship – Global Missions	2001	1	2	4		
Cross-Cultural Ministries – Churches of God General Conference	1898				1	
Cup of Cold Water Ministries	2012			4	2	2
Development Associates Intl. (DAI)					1	
Eastern Mennonite Missions	2009			3		
Engineering Ministries International (EMI)					15	
EPC World Outreach				5		
Equip Inc & Equip International	2016	2				
Evangel Bible Translators					20	
Evangelical Christian Church in Canada, The	1989			1	1	
Evangelical Friends Mission	1992	2			2	
Evangelism Explosion III International Inc.	2009				20	
Evangelism Resources Inc.	1990				2	
FAIR		1		17		
Faith Christian Fellowship Intl.					2	
FaithLife Ministries Inc.	2003				3	
Far East Broadcasting Associates of Canada (FEB Canada)	2008		3		2	
Fishhook International	2008				4	
Food for the Hungry Inc.	1998		1			
Free Will Baptist International Missions	1935			1		
Freedom Firm				2	30	
Friends in Action Intl.				1		
General Baptists International	1982				1	
Global Action				3		
Global Frontier Missions	2012		4			
Global Gates	2016			3		
Global Missions (United Pentecostal Church Intl.)	1909		1			3
Global Missions of Open Bible Churches	1928			2	2	
Global Outreach International	1977			4		
Global Outreach Mission Inc.		1		8		
Global Partners (The Wesleyan Church World Headquarters)				2		
Global Recordings Network					4	3
Globe International	1989			7		
Go to Nations	1987				10	
Good News for India	1987				350	
Good News Productions International	1989			2	10	

	First Year	Personnel from US or Canada			Other Countries	
		1–2 years	2–4 years	4+ years	Citizen	Not Citizen
Gospel Outreach Ministries Intl.	1988				250	
Gospel Tide Broadcasting Association	1978				7	
Greater Grace World Outreach	1984				24	
Habitat for Humanity International	1983		22		1	21
Harvest Foundation					4	
Harvest International Inc.	2002				2	
Harvest Mission to the Unreached					120	
HBI Global Partners	1984				595	
Helps Ministries	2010				2	1
Hope for the Hungry	1990				6	
HOPE International				1		
IFCA World Missions	1966			3		
IN Network dba International Needs USA	1979				7	
In Touch Mission International	2009	1			1	
India Evangelical Mission Inc.	1966	1		2	64	
India Gospel League	1948				347	
India Gospel Outreach Inc.	1984			1	2500	
India Partners	2001				1	
Intercede International					12	
International Gospel Outreach	1982			6	4	2
International Justice Mission	2000		6		82	1
International Partnership Ministries Inc.	1983				108	
International Pentecostal Holiness Church	1911			2		
Interserve USA	1852			8		
Kinship United						
Lifesong for Orphans	2009				56	
Literacy & Evangelism International					2	1
Lott Carey Baptist Foreign Mission Convention	1948				350	
Macedonia World Baptist Missions Inc.	2010			4		
Mailbox Club International Inc., The					1	
MB Mission	1889				14	11
MB Mission Canada	1889	2		7	16	
Mission India	1981				2	
Mission of Mercy Canada	1954	1	3			
Mission ONE Inc.					68	
Mission to the World (PCA) Inc.	1973			10		
National Association of Congregational Christian Churches	1967				3	
OM Canada				1		
On The Go Ministries/Keith Cook Team	1842			1		
One Mission Society	1941			1		1
Open Air Campaigners – Overseas Ministries (OAC-OM)	1987				18	
Our Daily Bread				1		
PIC International (Partners in Christ International)		1				

	First Year	Personnel from US or Canada			Other Countries	
		1–2 years	2–4 years	4+ years	Citizen	Not Citizen
Pioneers Canada				1		
Power to Change Ministries	1996	2		2		
Prakash Association USA	1968				40	
Precept Ministries International	2000				5	
Presbyterian Mission International (PMI)				1		
Ravi Zacharias International Ministries Inc.	1986				8	
ReachGlobal		2		2		
Reaching Indians Ministries International	1993				810	
Reformed Church in America – General Synod Council – Global Mission				4		
Reliant Mission Inc.	2012		2	2		
Ripe for Harvest Inc.				1		
Salem Ministries International	1970	5	5	2	5	3
Sanma (South Asia Native Missionary Alliance)	1998	0	1	1	0	0
Scriptures In Use	1996			10	2000	
Serge				2		
ServLife International				1		
Seventh-day Adventists – General Conference – Global Mission	1895		1	8		10
SIM USA		1		10		
Source of Light Ministries Intl. Inc.					1	
Spiritual Overseers Service International	1985				1	
Supreme Task International Inc.	1989			2	30	
Talking Bibles International	1997				4	
Teen Missions International Inc.	1982				12	
The Brethren Church Inc.	1969				150	
The God's Story Project	2000				1	
The Kerusso Institute for Global Leaders	2011				2	
The Masters Mission	1993				2	
The Pentecostal Assemblies of Canada				5	2	2
The Word for the World (TWFTW)	2008					2
TMS Global	1995		1	13		
Training Evangelistic Leadership	1975		1	2	16	
United Brethren in Christ	1974			1		
Walk Thru the Bible Ministries Inc.	1998				21	
Wisconsin Evangelical Lutheran Synod – Board for World Missions				2		
World Mission Prayer League	1904			4	1	
World Relief	2000	1			2	1
World-Wide Missions	1965				2	
WorldVenture				4		
Wycliffe Bible Translators USA				2		
Indonesia						
AMG International	1975				493	
Assemblies of God World Missions	1920	19		26		

	First Year	Personnel from US or Canada			Other Countries	
		1–2 years	2–4 years	4+ years	Citizen	Not Citizen
Awana Clubs International					7	
Back to the Bible	2003				9	
Baptist Bible Fellowship International – World Mission Service Center	1972			2		
Baptist International Missions Inc.				7		
Baptist Mid-Missions	1952			2		
Baptist Missionary Association of America (BMAA)				1		
BCM International	2002				9	
Biblical Ministries Worldwide				6		6
BILD International					1	1
CAMA Services	1989			4		
Canadian Baptist Ministries	1973			3		
Catalyst Missions			2		1	
Christian Aid Mission					148	
Christian and Missionary Alliance in Canada, The				10		
Christian Broadcasting Network Inc., The	1998			1	216	1
Christian Church (Disciples of Christ) – Global Ministries			1			
Christian Churches / Churches of Christ				15		
Church of God (Cleveland TN) World Missions	1967			2		
Church of the Nazarene Inc.	1973			8		
CityTeam Ministries – New Generations International						3
CMF International	1979	2		7	2	5
Compassion International Inc.	1968				126	
Crossover Communications International	2015	1				
Eastern Mennonite Missions	2015		2			
EPC World Outreach				3		
Evangelism Explosion III International Inc.	2012				29	
Far East Broadcasting Associates of Canada (FEB Canada)	2008			2		
Far East Broadcasting Company					1	
FH Canada	2005	2				1
Frontier Ventures				2		
Global Missions (United Pentecostal Church Intl.)	1938		2			
Global Recordings Network					4	
Globe International	1989			2		
Go Ye Fellowship	1938			3	1	2
Habitat for Humanity International			2			2
Helimission Inc. – USA		3	1	1		4
Indopartners Agency	2003		3			2
Intercede International					6	
International Teams U.S.A.				3		18
Interserve USA	2007			1		
Living Word Missions				1		2
Macedonia World Baptist Missions Inc.	1986			4		

	First Year	Personnel from US or Canada			Other Countries	
		1–2 years	2–4 years	4+ years	Citizen	Not Citizen
MAP International	2005				6	1
Medical Teams International	2005					1
Mission Aviation Fellowship	1952	5	3	70		
Mission Aviation Fellowship of Canada (MAFC)		2		7		
Missionary Ventures Intl.				2		
Mustard Seed International	1972			7		
Navigators of Canada, The	2008			2		
Network of International Christian Schools	1956	5	8	9	15	
New Mission Systems International	2010			2		
OMF International – Canada	1952			2		2
On The Go Ministries/Keith Cook Team	1970			1		
One Mission Society	1971			9		6
Our Daily Bread				1		
Pioneers Canada				4		
ReachGlobal				5		
Seventh-day Adventists – General Conference – Global Mission	1900			4		2
Source of Light Ministries Intl. Inc.					1	
TEAM (The Evangelical Alliance Mission)	1951			16		
Teen Missions International Inc.	2000				38	2
The Salvation Army USA National Headquarters	1894			2		
Things to Come Mission	1973				2	
Training Evangelistic Leadership	1976			3	8	
Virginia Mennonite Missions	2010			2	1	1
Walk Thru the Bible Ministries Inc.	2001			6		
Wisconsin Evangelical Lutheran Synod – Board for World Missions				1		
World Indigenous Missions	1995			4	2	
World Outreach International – US	2004	2				
World Partners USA				1		
World Relief	2004	2				
World Team Canada				4		
World Team US				15		
WorldVenture				19		
Wycliffe Bible Translators USA				95		
Youth Ministry International					1	
Iran						
Crossover Communications International	1999					1
Global Gates	2015			2		
Iraq						
Christian Aid Mission					25	
Entrust	2003				4	
Free Methodist World Missions	2003			2		
International Partnership Ministries Inc.	2001				2	
Samaritan's Purse	2003	1				
Venture International	2003				25	

	First Year	Personnel from US or Canada			Other Countries	
		1–2 years	2–4 years	4+ years	Citizen	Not Citizen
World Compassion Terry Law Ministries					1	
World Orphans	2007			5		
Ireland, Republic of						
ABWE International		2		7		
Assemblies of God World Missions	1978	13		11		
Baptist Bible Fellowship International – World Mission Service Center	1977			3		
Baptist International Missions Inc.				10		
Baptist Mid-Missions	1978					
BCM International	1965	7			6	
Campus Crusade for Christ (Cru in the US)				5		
Christian Churches / Churches of Christ		1		6		
Church of God (Cleveland TN) World Missions	1995	2		4		
Church of the Brethren – Global Mission Partnerships		5				
Church of the Nazarene Inc.	1987			1	1	1
Commission to Every Nation	2008					2
Crossworld	1980			7		
Crossworld Canada	1980			4		
Encompass World Partners	2002			2	1	
EPC World Outreach				1		
European Christian Mission Intl. – USA				13		
Evangelical Friends Mission	1998	3				
Evangelical Missionary Church of Canada	2005			1		
FAIR				4		
Faith Christian Fellowship Intl.					1	
Fellowship International Mission	2015			2		
Foursquare Missions International	2000			3		
Global Outreach Mission Inc.	1965			9		
Greater Europe Mission			3	8		
Greater Europe Mission Canada		1				
International Teams U.S.A.				4		
Mission to the World (PCA) Inc.	1995	1		4		
Missionary Ventures Intl.				1		
Operation Mobilization		24			4	34
Precept Ministries International	2002			4		
Reformed Baptist Mission Services					2	
Serge				16		
TEAM (The Evangelical Alliance Mission)	1994		2	1		
Team Expansion Inc.	1987			4		
To Every Tribe	2017			2		
United World Mission Inc.				2		2
World Partners USA				1		
WorldVenture				14		
Youth for Christ/USA				1		

	First Year	Personnel from US or Canada			Other Countries	
		1–2 years	2–4 years	4+ years	Citizen	Not Citizen
Israel						
A.C.T. International	2008					2
Baptist Bible Fellowship International – World Mission Service Center	2004			2		
Child Evangelism Fellowship Inc.				2		
Chosen People Ministries Inc.	1933			7	15	
Christian Aid Ministries (CAM)	2008	1		2		
Christian Churches / Churches of Christ				2	1	
Church of the Nazarene Inc.	1921			2		
Davar Partners International				1	5	
Global Missions (United Pentecostal Church Intl.)			2			4
Globe International	2001			6		
Great Commission Media Ministries	2001				2	2
High Adventure Ministries					3	
Hope for the Hungry	1982				2	
Independent Faith Mission Inc.				2		
International Teams U.S.A.				2		2
InterVarsity Christian Fellowship/USA			1			
Jewish Awareness Ministries Inc.				4	2	2
Jews for Jesus	1994				15	8
Life in Messiah International	1979			3	3	
Mennonite Mission Network	1953		1	1	1	
Messianic Jewish Movement International Inc. The (MJMI)					7	
Mission Eurasia					2	
Missionary Ventures Intl.				1		
Precept Ministries International	1995				4	
Reformed Baptist Mission Services					2	
Reformed Church in America – General Synod Council – Global Mission				2		
Ripe for Harvest Inc.				1		
Seventh-day Adventists – General Conference – Global Mission	1898					4
The Masters Mission	1990				2	
The Pentecostal Assemblies of Canada				2		
TMS Global	2006				1	
Venture International	1989				3	
Italy						
ABWE International				10		
ACCI (Adventive Cross Cultural Initiatives) – US	2004				2	
AMG International	2002			2		
Assemblies of God World Missions	1908	14		20		
Aurora Mission Inc.	1998	4	9	2		
Avant Ministries	1950			13	2	

	First Year	Personnel from US or Canada 1–2 years	2–4 years	4+ years	Other Countries Citizen	Not Citizen
Baptist Bible Fellowship International – World Mission Service Center	1978			4		
Baptist International Missions Inc.				6		
Baptist International Outreach	2016			2		2
Baptist Mid-Missions	1951			6		
BCM International	1963				1	1
BCM International (Canada) Inc.	1951					2
Biblical Ministries Worldwide				4		4
Cadence International	1980		2			
Campus Crusade for Christ (Cru in the US)		6		21		
Christian Churches / Churches of Christ				14	6	
Christian Veterinary Mission	2016	1				
Church of God (Cleveland TN) World Missions	1959			2		2
CRM			2			
Crossworld	1974			18		
Crossworld Canada	1974			1		
European Christian Mission Intl. – USA				5		
Evangelical Missionary Church of Canada	1998			1		
Far East Broadcasting Associates of Canada (FEB Canada)	1980			2		
Global Missions (United Pentecostal Church Intl.)	1959		1			
Globe International	2002			2		
Gospel Fellowship Association	1983			2		
Greater Europe Mission				2		
IBMGlobal	2012		2			
IFCA World Missions	1927			1		
International Gospel Outreach	1999			2		2
International Teams U.S.A.		2				
Italy for Christ Inc.	1983			2	3	
Life Impact Inc.	2005			1		1
Macedonia World Baptist Missions Inc.	2010			2		
Mission to the World (PCA) Inc.	1988			2		
New Mission Systems International	2014			2		
Operation Mobilization					6	9
Precept Ministries International	2007			2		
Presbyterian Mission International (PMI)				1		
ReachGlobal		1		3		
Reformed Church in America – General Synod Council – Global Mission				1	1	
Reliant Mission Inc.	1997	3		4		
Serge				2		
TEAM (The Evangelical Alliance Mission)	1981			30		
Team Expansion Inc.	2000	1		4	1	
The Navigators				2		
The Pentecostal Assemblies of Canada				2		

	First Year	Personnel from US or Canada			Other Countries	
		1–2 years	2–4 years	4+ years	Citizen	Not Citizen
The Salvation Army USA National Headquarters	1887		2			
United World Mission Inc.			2		1	1
Virginia Mennonite Missions	2014		2			2
Word of Life Fellowship Inc.	1985				1	3
World Link Ministries	2005		2		7	
World Team Canada			2			
World Team US			3			
WorldVenture			8			
Youth for Christ/USA			4			
Jamaica						
ABWE International			4			
Awana Clubs International					1	
Back to the Bible	1958		3			
Baptist Bible Fellowship International – World Mission Service Center	1972		2			
Baptist International Missions Inc.			3			
BCM International	1995		2			
Christian Churches / Churches of Christ			12		6	
Christian Relief Fund, The	1999		1			
CSI Ministries Inc.	1987	1				
Evangelism Explosion III International Inc.	2010				7	
Faith Christian Fellowship Intl.					2	
Foursquare Missions International	1964		2			
Global Missions of Open Bible Churches	1949				1	
Global Outreach Mission Inc.			2			
Go to Nations	1985				1	
Lott Carey Baptist Foreign Mission Convention	1995				10	
Lutheran Church Missouri Synod – World Mission	1993		2			
Medical Ministry International	1970				1	
National Baptist Convention of America – Foreign Mission Board	1945				38	
On The Go Ministries/Keith Cook Team	1990		2			
Open Air Campaigners – Overseas Ministries (OAC-OM)	1984				3	
Orphanos Foundation		2	1			
Our Daily Bread				1		
RAISE International Inc.	2010				2	
Reformed Baptist Mission Services					2	
Seventh Day Baptist Missionary Society	2014				1	
Seventh-day Adventists – General Conference – Global Mission	1893		12			
Source of Light Ministries Intl. Inc.					2	
TEAMS for Medical Missions	1992		5			
The Navigators			3			

	First Year	1–2 years	2–4 years	4+ years	Citizen	Not Citizen
		Personnel from US or Canada			Other Countries	
The Pentecostal Assemblies of Canada				2		
The Salvation Army USA National Headquarters	1887	2				
United Brethren in Christ	1945			4		
Japan						
A.C.T. International	2005				1	2
ABWE International				11		
Advent Christian World Outreach	1949				1	4
American Baptist International Ministries				2	1	
Asian Access	1967		4	23	2	
Assemblies of God World Missions	1913	14		30		
Awana Clubs International					3	
Back to the Bible	2004				1	
Baptist Bible Fellowship International – World Mission Service Center	1948			18		
Baptist International Missions Inc.				47		
Baptist Mid-Missions	1949			4	7	
Baptist Missionary Association of America (BMAA)					2	
Barnabas International						
Bethany Gateways		2		1	5	2
Biblical Ministries Worldwide				4		4
BILD International					1	
Cadence International	1960	3	2	9		
Campus Crusade for Christ (Cru in the US)		5		4		
Child Evangelism Fellowship Inc.				1		
Christian and Missionary Alliance in Canada, The				8		
Christian Church (Disciples of Christ) – Global Ministries			3			
Christian Churches / Churches of Christ			4	30		
Christian Reformed World Missions	1951			6		
Christians In Action Missions International	1957					6
Church of God Ministries (Anderson) – Global Strategy	1908			1		
Church of the Brethren – Global Mission Partnerships	1981	2				
Church of the Nazarene Inc.	1905			2		
Converge				8		
CRM		2				
Elim Fellowship	2015			2		
Encompass World Partners	1984			3		
Equip Inc & Equip International	1998			1		
Evangelical Free Church of Canada Mission				3		
Far East Broadcasting Associates of Canada (FEB Canada)	1963			6		
Fellowship International Mission	1985			6	4	
Foursquare Missions International	1950			8		
Free Methodist World Missions	1895			2		

	First Year	Personnel from US or Canada			Other Countries	
		1–2 years	2–4 years	4+ years	Citizen	Not Citizen
Free Will Baptist International Missions	1954			17		
Global Missions (United Pentecostal Church Intl.)	1900	8				4
Global Missions of Open Bible Churches	1950				1	
Global Partners (The Wesleyan Church World Headquarters)				2		
Global Scholars	2004			1		1
Gospel Fellowship Association	1958			1		
Helps Ministries	2012			2	1	
Hope for the Hungry	1981			1		
IBMGlobal	2014		2			
International Pentecostal Holiness Church	1989			4		
International Teams U.S.A.						8
InterVarsity Christian Fellowship/USA			2			
Japanese Evangelical Missionary Society (JEMS)		3		15		
Liberty Corner Mission	1951			1		6
Lutheran Brethren International Mission	1949			2		
Lutheran Church Missouri Synod – World Mission	1948	9		7		
Macedonia World Baptist Missions Inc.	2001			2		
MB Mission	1950					4
MB Mission Canada	1950			4		
Mennonite Mission Network	1949			3		
Mission to the World (PCA) Inc.	1985		5	36		
Network of International Christian Schools	1998	4	4	4	5	
North American Baptist Conference – Worldwide Outreach	1951			9		
OMF International				15		
OMF International – Canada	1951			8	1	7
On The Go Ministries/Keith Cook Team	1892	13		13	2	
One Mission Society	1922			12		3
Open Door Baptist Missions	2008			1		
Operation Mobilization					6	13
Orthodox Presbyterian Church – Committee on Foreign Missions	1938			6		
Our Daily Bread				1		
Pioneers Canada				3		
Power to Change Ministries	2002			2		
Presbyterian Mission International (PMI)				1		
Project AmaZon	1987			2		
ReachGlobal		1		14		
Reaching Japan Together (RJT)				2	1	
Reformed Church in America – General Synod Council – Global Mission				2		2
Reliant Mission Inc.	2012	2	1	2		
Resourcing Christian Education International					16	4
Ripe for Harvest Inc.				1		
RP Global Missions	1945	1	1	4		

	First Year	Personnel from US or Canada 1–2 years	2–4 years	4+ years	Other Countries Citizen	Not Citizen
SEND International Inc.	1947	1		52		7
SEND International of Canada				3		
Serve Globally – The Evangelical Covenant Church			2	6		
Seventh-day Adventists – General Conference – Global Mission	1896	2	1	3	1	
SIM USA		4		18		
Source of Light Ministries Intl. Inc.					1	
TEAM (The Evangelical Alliance Mission)	1891			57		
Team Expansion Inc.	2002			7		
The Navigators				32		
The Pentecostal Assemblies of Canada				4		
The Presbyterian Church in Canada	1927		1			
The Salvation Army USA National Headquarters	1895		2	1		
Walk Thru the Bible Ministries Inc.	2002				1	
WEC International				2		
WEC International Canada	1950			2		
White Fields					7	
Wisconsin Evangelical Lutheran Synod – Board for World Missions				3		
Word of Life Fellowship Inc.	1981	1		4	5	
World Gospel Mission	1952	1		3		
World Mission Prayer League	2012		1			
WorldVenture				20		
Youth for Christ/USA				1		
Jordan						
Baptist Missionary Association of America (BMAA)					2	
CAMA Services	2012		2	2		
Child Evangelism Fellowship Inc.				1		
Christian Aid Mission					77	
Church of the Nazarene Inc.	1950			2	3	1
Crossover Communications International	2007				2	
EPC World Outreach				1		
Evangelism Explosion III International Inc.	2009				2	
Global Missions (United Pentecostal Church Intl.)	1955		2			
Global Outreach Mission Inc.				3		
Habitat for Humanity International	2002		1			1
Intercede International					2	
Interserve USA	1951			4		
Medical Ministry International	2005					1
Medical Ministry International Canada Inc.	2000					2
Pioneers Canada				6		
ReachGlobal				4		
TMS Global	2011	2		5		
Venture International	1998				2	
World-Wide Missions	1987				1	

	First Year	Personnel from US or Canada 1–2 years	2–4 years	4+ years	Other Countries Citizen	Not Citizen
Kazakhstan						
All God's Children International					12	
Awana Clubs International					1	
Christian Aid Mission					31	
Christian Broadcasting Network Inc., The	1995				2	
Elim Fellowship	2010			2		
Evangelism Explosion III International Inc.	2011				1	
FAIR				2		
Far East Broadcasting Associates of Canada (FEB Canada)	2001			2		
Global Missions (United Pentecostal Church Intl.)			1			
Global Scholars				1		1
Greater Grace World Outreach	2001					1
Mission Eurasia					4	
One Mission Society	2003			1		1
People International USA				6		
Ripe for Harvest Inc.				1		
Seventh-day Adventists – General Conference – Global Mission	1886			2		2
The Masters Mission	1993			2		
TMS Global	1993			1		
Kenya						
A.C.T. International	2006			2		
ACM International	1996			5		
Advent Christian World Outreach	2001				1	
Adventures in Missions	1999	1		3		
Africa Inland Mission Canada Intl.		1		14		15
African Enterprise	1970				48	
Assemblies of God World Missions	1967	11		30		
Avant Ministries Canada	2015			2		
Awana Clubs International					5	
Baptist Bible Fellowship International – World Mission Service Center	1971			22		
Baptist International Missions Inc.				2		
Baptist Mid-Missions	2004				2	
Bethany Gateways		8	3	3	1	
BethanyKids	2001				28	2
Biblical Ministries Worldwide				2	2	
Bright Hope	1994			1	1	
Buckner International	2001				25	
Canadian Baptist Ministries	1970			5		
Care of Creation Inc.	2003			2	6	
Center for Mission Mobilization	2014			12	3	
Child Evangelism Fellowship Inc.				5		
Childcare Worldwide	1984				60	

	First Year	Personnel from US or Canada			Other Countries	
		1–2 years	2–4 years	4+ years	Citizen	Not Citizen
Christ to the Nations				1		
Christian Aid Mission	1985				2000	
Christian Church (Disciples of Christ) – Global Ministries			1			
Christian Churches / Churches of Christ		2	3	35	8	
Christian Discipleship International	1990				1	
Christian Reformed World Missions	2008			2		
Christian Relief Fund, The	1994				5	
Christian Veterinary Mission	1980			2		
Church of God (Cleveland TN) World Missions	1977			9		4
Church of God Ministries (Anderson) – Global Strategy	1922			2		
Church of the Nazarene Inc.	1984			9		2
CMF International	1977	15	2	18	2	33
Commission to Every Nation	2009					2
Compassion International Inc.	1980				79	
Cooperative Baptist Fellowship – Global Missions	1999			2		
CRM				2		
Cross-Cultural Ministries – Churches of God General Conference	2007				1	
CrossWay International	2002				1	
Crossworld	1996			2		
Daystar U.S.	1988			4		
Eastern Mennonite Missions	2008		2	2		
Elim Fellowship	1972			15		
Empowering Lives International	1996			2	50	
Entrust	2004					3
Equip Inc & Equip International	1998			2		
Evangelical Congregational Church – Global Ministries Commission				5		
Evangelism Explosion III International Inc.	2010				6	
Faith Christian Fellowship Intl.					2	
FaithLife Ministries Inc.	2005				3	
Far East Broadcasting Associates of Canada (FEB Canada)	1998			6		
Food for the Hungry Inc.	1976		4	1		
Foursquare Missions International	1982			2		
Free Methodist World Missions	1994		4	5		
Free Will Baptist International Missions	2016			2		
Freedom to Lead International	2014					
Friends United Meeting		1	1	1	1	
Full Gospel Evangelistic Association	2000			1	2	
Global Missions (United Pentecostal Church Intl.)	1972		4			1
Global Missions of Open Bible Churches	1969				1	
Global Outreach International	2002			7		
Global Recordings Network					4	
Global Recordings Network Canada					4	
Globe International	1987			2		

	First Year	Personnel from US or Canada			Other Countries	
		1–2 years	2–4 years	4+ years	Citizen	Not Citizen
Go Ye Fellowship	1996			5	1	4
Greater Grace World Outreach	2005				4	1
Habitat for Humanity International	1985		1			1
Harvest Foundation					3	
Harvest International Inc.	2005		2			
Heart of the Bride Ministries		2				
Hope for the Hungry	1985				1	
IN Network dba International Needs USA	2006				3	
Independent Faith Mission Inc.				6		
Intercede International					6	
International Christian Ministries	1986			2		
International Gospel Outreach	1983			7	5	2
International Justice Mission	2001				14	
International Pentecostal Holiness Church	1972			6	2	
International Teams U.S.A.				2		7
InterVarsity Christian Fellowship/USA			1			
Into All The World	2001			2		
Kids Alive International	2001					1
Leadership Vistas International Ministries						2
Link International Ministries	1989				13	
Literacy & Evangelism International					3	
Lott Carey Baptist Foreign Mission Convention	1985				50	
Lutheran Church Missouri Synod – World Mission	1999			2		
Macedonia World Baptist Missions Inc.	2004			2	2	
Mailbox Club International Inc., The					1	
MAP International	1987				21	1
Mission Aviation Fellowship of Canada (MAFC)				2		
Mission On The Move	2007				2	
Mission ONE Inc.					42	
Mission to the World (PCA) Inc.	1977			2		
Missions Door					1	
National Association of Congregational Christian Churches	1990				36	
Network of International Christian Schools	1996	12	12	8	20	
New Mission Systems International	1997			1	5	
On The Go Ministries/Keith Cook Team	1969			4		1
Open Air Campaigners – Overseas Ministries (OAC-OM)	2009				3	
Prayer Baptist Missions International Inc.				2		
Presbyterian Mission International (PMI)				1		
Reach Beyond					1	2
Reformed Baptist Mission Services						2
Reformed Church in America – General Synod Council – Global Mission				2		
Reliant Mission Inc.	2015	1				

	First Year	Personnel from US or Canada 1–2 years	2–4 years	4+ years	Other Countries Citizen	Not Citizen
Ripe for Harvest Inc.				1		
Samaritan's Purse	1995	5	1	2		
Scriptures In Use	2006			6	2000	
Serge				6		
Serve Globally – The Evangelical Covenant Church			2			
Seventh-day Adventists – General Conference – Global Mission	1906			21		31
SIM USA		2		41		
Source of Light Ministries Intl. Inc.					2	
The Free Methodist Church in Canada	1992			1		
The God's Story Project	2005				3	
The Masters Mission	1979			20	2	2
The Navigators				8		
The Pentecostal Assemblies of Canada				15		
The Salvation Army USA National Headquarters	1921		2			
Things to Come Mission	1984				4	2
TMS Global	2004			6	1	
United Evangelical Churches				1		
United World Mission Inc.		1		5		6
Walk Thru the Bible Ministries Inc.	1999				2	
With Open Eyes	2010				57	
Women to the World Inc.					1	
Word of Life Fellowship Inc.	1970	1			21	1
World Concern	1984	3	1	3	66	
World Gospel Mission	1927	19		34		
World Mission Prayer League	1968			3		
World Missions & Evangelism	1996			2		
World Orphans	2008				1	
World Reach Inc.	1983				11	
World Relief	1998				11	1
World Relief Canada				2		
World-Wide Missions	1963				2	
WorldVenture				15		
Worldwide Discipleship Assoc.				1		
Wycliffe Bible Translators of Canada Inc.				3		
Wycliffe Bible Translators USA				30		
Youth for Christ/USA				3		
Youth Ministry International					2	
Kiribati						
Baptist International Missions, Inc.				4		
Korea, North						
Go to Nations	2004				1	
Seventh-day Adventists – General Conference – Global Mission				2		

	First Year	Personnel from US or Canada			Other Countries	
		1–2 years	2–4 years	4+ years	Citizen	Not Citizen
Korea, South						
Assemblies of God World Missions	1928	1		2		
Awana Clubs International					4	
Baptist Bible Fellowship International – World Mission Service Center	1958			6		
Baptist International Missions Inc.				2		
Cadence International	1975			4		
Chosen People Ministries Inc.	2014				4	
Christian Churches / Churches of Christ				4	6	
Christians In Action Missions International	1957			2		
Church of the Nazarene Inc.	1948				1	1
CRM					5	
Faith Christian Fellowship Intl.					1	
Far East Broadcasting Company					1	
Global Missions (United Pentecostal Church Intl.)	1985		1			
Global Missions of Open Bible Churches	2006				1	
Global Recordings Network					1	
Go Ye Fellowship	1994		1			1
Gospel Fellowship Association	1967	1		4		
Independent Faith Mission Inc.				2		
Macedonia World Baptist Missions Inc.	1999			2		
Mennonite Mission Network	1983		1			
Mission to the World (PCA) Inc.				2		
Network of International Christian Schools	1983	40	20	80	95	
On The Go Ministries/Keith Cook Team	1961		2			
One Challenge	2009				2	
One Mission Society	1907			2		
Operation Mobilization		3			35	
Orphanos Foundation	2006				2	
Precept Ministries International	1987				13	
Ripe for Harvest Inc.				1		
Seventh-day Adventists – General Conference – Global Mission	1904	53	22	10		3
SIM USA				2		
The Salvation Army USA National Headquarters	1908		2			
Walk Thru the Bible Ministries Inc.	2000				4	
WEC International		1		2		
Word of Life Fellowship Inc.	1989	2		14	16	
Kosovo						
Alongside Ministries International			1		1	
BILD International				1	1	
CAMA Services	1999			4		
Christian Churches / Churches of Christ				2	1	
Church of the Nazarene Inc.	2005			2		

		Personnel from US or Canada			Other Countries	
	First Year	1–2 years	2–4 years	4+ years	Citizen	Not Citizen
Global Outreach Mission Inc.				1		
Gospel Tide Broadcasting Association	2015				2	
Greater Europe Mission				1		
International Teams U.S.A.				2		
Mercy Projects				1	1	
Samaritan's Purse	1999	1				
SEND International Inc.	2004			3		
TMS Global	2014			8		
Virginia Mennonite Missions	2013			2		2
World Relief	2000		1		14	
Seventh-day Adventists – General Conference – Global Mission	1978					2
Kyrgyzstan						
Christian Aid Mission					8	
Eastern Mennonite Missions	2010			2		
Encompass World Partners	1997			5		
EPC World Outreach				1		
Greater Grace World Outreach	1999				3	
Macedonia World Baptist Missions Inc.	2005			2		
Mission Eurasia					8	
New Life Advance International	2007			2		
Orphanos Foundation	2015	1				
People International USA				3		
Scriptures In Use	2012			2	100	
The Presbyterian Church in Canada	2006			2		
Venture International	1992				17	
Laos						
Christian Aid Mission					63	
Christian Church (Disciples of Christ) – Global Ministries			1			
Eastern Mennonite Missions	2006		2	4		
Globe International	2005			2		
Mission Aviation Fellowship of Canada (MAFC)				1		
Seventh-day Adventists – General Conference – Global Mission	1919					2
World Concern	1990				29	1
Fellowship of Companies for Christ International (FCCI)	2005				1	
Final Frontiers Foundation	1989				180	
Gideons International, The					17	
globalLead						1
International Christian Ministries Canada (ICM)	2008			2	2	
New Tribes Mission of Canada				31		
Presbyterian Church (USA) Worldwide Ministries			90	88		
The Christian and Missionary Alliance				144		
Wycliffe Bible Translators of Canada Inc.				19		

	First Year	Personnel from US or Canada			Other Countries	
		1–2 years	2–4 years	4+ years	Citizen	Not Citizen
Young Life		7	4	10		
Youth With A Mission (YWAM)			303		1668	
Latvia						
Assemblies of God World Missions	1926			3		
Awana Clubs International					1	
Bridge Builders International	1994			5		5
Campus Crusade for Christ (Cru in the US)				2		
Chosen People Ministries Inc.	1930				5	
East European Missions Network			1	4		
Global Missions (United Pentecostal Church Intl.)						4
Go to Nations	1989			1	1	
Greater Europe Mission				1		
Greater Europe Mission Canada	2003			4		
Josiah Venture	2004		3	4	15	1
Mission to the World (PCA) Inc.			4	2		
The Navigators				2		
Walk Thru the Bible Ministries Inc.	2000				1	
Lebanon						
A.C.T. International	2006					1
American Baptist International Ministries				3		
AMG International					4	
Baptist Missionary Association of America (BMAA)					6	
Canadian Baptist Ministries	2005			2		
Christian Aid Mission					20	
Church of the Nazarene Inc.	1950			1	1	
EPC World Outreach				5		
Global Missions (United Pentecostal Church Intl.)	1992	2				2
Heart for Lebanon Foundation	2006				54	
International Partnership Ministries Inc.	1998				4	
Kids Alive International	1950			3	1	
Mennonite Mission Network	1967	2				
Mutual Faith Ministries Intl.		1				
On The Go Ministries/Keith Cook Team	1969	1				
Pioneers Canada				3		
ReachGlobal				2		
Reformed Church in America – General Synod Council – Global Mission				1		
Seventh-day Adventists – General Conference – Global Mission	1970					4
Venture International	1987				2	
Lesotho						
Assemblies of God World Missions	1950			2		
Christian Church (Disciples of Christ) – Global Ministries			1			

	First Year	Personnel from US or Canada			Other Countries	
		1–2 years	2–4 years	4+ years	Citizen	Not Citizen
Evangelism Explosion III International Inc.	2015				2	
Global Missions (United Pentecostal Church Intl.)	1996	2				
Habitat for Humanity International	1986	1				1
Mission Aviation Fellowship	1980			13		
Mission Aviation Fellowship of Canada (MAFC)				1		
Seventh-day Adventists – General Conference – Global Mission	1899		1	2		2
Walk Thru the Bible Ministries Inc.	1999				1	
Liberia						
ABWE Canada (Across Borders for World Evangelism)	2002			1		
Advent Christian World Outreach	1988				1	
Assemblies of God World Missions	1908			2		
Awana Clubs International					1	
Baptist Mid-Missions	1931			2		
Baptist Missionary Association of America (BMAA)					1	
Beautiful Feet	2015			2		
Child Evangelism Fellowship Inc.				1		
Christian Aid Ministries (CAM)	1995	1	6	3	40	
Christian Aid Mission	1998				60	
Christian Churches / Churches of Christ				2		
Christian Discipleship International	1985				1	
Christian Relief Fund, The	1997				1	
Church of God (Cleveland TN) World Missions	1974					4
Commission to Every Nation	2007				2	
CrossWay International	2002				11	
Development Associates Intl. (DAI)					1	
Equip Canada	1997			2		
Evangel Bible Translators					1	
Evangelical Free Church of Canada Mission				2		
Evangelism Explosion III International Inc.	2011				4	
FaithLife Ministries Inc.	2012				1	
Global Missions (United Pentecostal Church Intl.)	1924	2				
Global Missions of Open Bible Churches	1935				1	
Global Recordings Network					2	
Greater Grace World Outreach	1987				10	
Intercede International					2	
International Gospel Outreach	1986			1		1
International Partnership Ministries Inc.	1997				21	
Lifesong for Orphans	2009				43	
Living Word Missions				2	1	1
Lott Carey Baptist Foreign Mission Convention	1908				100	
Medical Teams International	2003				1	3
Missions Door					1	
Mutual Faith Ministries Intl.		1				
On The Go Ministries/Keith Cook Team	1862	1		1		

	First Year	Personnel from US or Canada			Other Countries	
		1–2 years	2–4 years	4+ years	Citizen	Not Citizen
Samaritan's Purse	2003	11				
Seventh-day Adventists – General Conference – Global Mission	1927					2
Shelter for Life Intl. Inc.					1	
SIM USA				8		
Source of Light Ministries Intl. Inc.					1	
TMS Global	2015			4		
Walk Thru the Bible Ministries Inc.	2004				1	
WEC International		2				
World Relief	2000					1
World-Wide Missions	1961				4	
Libya						
Christian Aid Mission	2005				13	
Liechtenstein						
Assemblies of God World Missions	1992			5		
Baptist Bible Fellowship International – World Mission Service Center	1991			2		
Campus Crusade for Christ (Cru in the US)				3		
Christ to the Nations				1		
Christian Reformed World Missions	2015			2		
Global Missions (United Pentecostal Church Intl.)						7
Global Scholars	2003	2	1			3
Greater Grace World Outreach	1996					
MB Mission	1991				2	
MB Mission Canada	1991				2	
Mennonite Mission Network	1995			3		
Open Door Baptist Missions	1992			2		
Reach A Village					3	
The Pentecostal Assemblies of Canada				2		
World Witness				2		
WorldVenture				2		
Luxembourg						
Biblical Ministries Worldwide				4		4
Greater Europe Mission				1		
Greater Europe Mission Canada	1977			2		
Macau (China)						
Christians In Action Missions International	1973			1	1	
Lutheran Church Missouri Synod – World Mission	1988			3		
Mennonite Mission Network	1995					4
ReachGlobal				4		
SEND International of Canada				1		
United Brethren in Christ	1987			2		
World-Wide Missions				1		

	First Year	Personnel from US or Canada			Other Countries	
		1–2 years	2–4 years	4+ years	Citizen	Not Citizen
Macedonia						
Assemblies of God World Missions	1991			4		
BILD International				1	1	
Campus Crusade for Christ (Cru in the US)				6		
Cooperative Baptist Fellowship – Global Missions	1998			2		
Evangelism Explosion III International Inc.	2009				1	
Global Missions (United Pentecostal Church Intl.)		1				
Global Partners (The Wesleyan Church World Headquarters)				4		
Greater Europe Mission				4		
New Mission Systems International	2009			5		
Reach A Village					1	
SEND International Inc.	1993			15		
SEND International of Canada				1		
WorldVenture				6		
Madagascar						
Africa Inland Mission Canada Intl.			3	1		4
Assemblies of God World Missions	1989			10		
Baptist Bible Fellowship International – World Mission Service Center	2014			2		
Baptist International Missions Inc.				4		
BethanyKids	2011				1	
Child Evangelism Fellowship Inc.				1		
Commission To Every Nation-Canada	2015	2				
Evangelical Missionary Church of Canada	2015			2		
Global Health Ministries	2007				1	
Global Missions (United Pentecostal Church Intl.)	1970	2				1
Helimission Inc. – USA						5
IFCA World Missions					1	
Mission Aviation Fellowship of Canada (MAFC)			1	1		
On The Go Ministries/Keith Cook Team	1888		1	5		
Operation Mobilization					6	
Seventh-day Adventists – General Conference – Global Mission	1926			2		15
Teen Missions International Inc.	1997				15	
WorldVenture				7		
Malawi						
Action International Ministries	2006			3		
Advent Christian World Outreach	2002				1	
African Enterprise	1972				32	
Apostolic Church of Pentecost of Canada (Global Harvest Missions)					1	
Assemblies of God World Missions	1944			2		
Awana Clubs International					1	
Brethren in Christ World Missions (BICWM)	1983			6		

	First Year	Personnel from US or Canada			Other Countries	
		1–2 years	2–4 years	4+ years	Citizen	Not Citizen
Child Evangelism Fellowship Inc.				1		
Christian Aid Mission	1986				30	
Christian Relief Fund, The	1978				1	
Church of God Ministries (Anderson) – Global Strategy	1992		2			
Church of the Nazarene Inc.	1957			2		2
Emmanuel Intl. Canada				1		
EurAsian Baptist Mission	2004			2	4	
Evangelism Explosion III International Inc.	2010				14	
Faith Christian Fellowship Intl.					2	
Forgotten Voices Intl.					3	
Global Missions (United Pentecostal Church Intl.)			2			2
Grace Ministries International	2013			4		4
Greater Grace World Outreach	2012			2		1
Habitat for Humanity International	1986		1			1
IFCA World Missions					1	
International Association For Refugees	2009			2		
International Pentecostal Holiness Church	1950			4		
Liebenzell Mission of Canada	1993		1			
Literacy & Evangelism International					2	
Missionary Ventures Canada					1	
National Baptist Convention USA Inc. – Foreign Mission Board	1900				25	
New Mission Systems International	2000				2	
Operation Mobilization		0			4	4
Reformed Church in America – General Synod Council – Global Mission				1		
Seventh-day Adventists – General Conference – Global Mission	1902	1		1		12
SIM USA		1		8		
Teen Missions International Inc.	1988		2		25	2
The Pentecostal Assemblies of Canada				4		
The Presbyterian Church in Canada	1983		2			
The Word for the World (TWFTW)	1994				11	
TMS Global	2014			2		
Waymarks Radio Ministries International	2008				1	
White Fields					1	
Wisconsin Evangelical Lutheran Synod – Board for World Missions				7		
Word & Deed	2002				2	
Word & Deed Ministries Canada	2002				2	
World Relief	1988			1	86	
WorldVenture				2		
Wycliffe Bible Translators USA				2		
Malaysia						
Advent Christian World Outreach	1959				1	
Assemblies of God World Missions	1928			2		

	First Year	Personnel from US or Canada			Other Countries	
		1–2 years	2–4 years	4+ years	Citizen	Not Citizen
Center for Mission Mobilization	2015			4		
Christian and Missionary Alliance in Canada, The				9		
Church of God (Cleveland TN) World Missions	1991			4		
Elim Fellowship	1981			2		
EPC World Outreach				4		
Evangelism Explosion III International Inc.	2009				1	
Food for the Hungry Inc.	2000			2		
Global Missions (United Pentecostal Church Intl.)	1975		1			
Globe International	1983			2		
Missionary Ventures Intl.				1		
Network of International Christian Schools	2012	1	2			
Operation Mobilization					6	
Our Daily Bread				1		
Partners International	2009					
ReachGlobal				1		
Scriptures In Use	2014	2			100	
TeachBeyond Canada				1		
The Brethren Church Inc.	1972				1	
The Pentecostal Assemblies of Canada				2		
Things to Come Mission	2010	1		2		
Wycliffe Bible Translators USA				22		
Youth Ministry International				2		
Mali						
Apostolic Church of Pentecost of Canada (Global Harvest Missions)	2016					1
Assemblies of God World Missions	1987	5		8		
Avant Ministries	1919			3		
Avant Ministries Canada	1919			1		
CAMA Services	1984	1		2		
Child Evangelism Fellowship Inc.				1		
Christ for the City International	2004					1
Christian Aid Mission	2007				15	
Christian Churches / Churches of Christ				2		
Christian Reformed World Missions	1984		2	3		
Church of the Nazarene Inc.	2007					2
Evangelism Explosion III International Inc.	2010				4	
Faith Baptist Mission	2010			4		
FaithLife Ministries Inc.	2015					1
Global Gates	2012			2		
Greater Grace World Outreach	2011				2	
Harvest Foundation				1		
Seventh-day Adventists – General Conference – Global Mission	1982					2
SIM USA				3		
United World Mission Inc.				2		2

	First Year	Personnel from US or Canada			Other Countries	
		1–2 years	2–4 years	4+ years	Citizen	Not Citizen
WEC International Canada				2		
WorldVenture				4		
Wycliffe Bible Translators of Canada Inc.				2		
Wycliffe Bible Translators USA				4		
Malta						
Assemblies of God World Missions	1985	1		4		
Baptist Mid-Missions	2005			4		
Global Missions (United Pentecostal Church Intl.)	2002		2			
International Association For Refugees	2014					2
Marshall Islands						
Assemblies of God World Missions	1961			2		
Gospel Fellowship Association	1988			4		
Independent Faith Mission Inc.				2		
Missionary Ventures Intl.				2		
Seventh-day Adventists – General Conference – Global Mission	1969			3		
Mauritania						
Christian Aid Mission	2004				40	
Global Recordings Network						1
Seventh-day Adventists – General Conference – Global Mission	1992					2
Mauritius						
Global Missions (United Pentecostal Church Intl.)			2			
Mexico						
ABWE International				7		
Action International Ministries	1990			6	2	4
Advent Christian World Outreach	1987				3	
Adventures in Missions	1989			10		
American Baptist International Ministries				3		
AMG International	1978			3		
AMOR Ministries	1980	37			8	2
Apostolic Church of Pentecost of Canada (Global Harvest Missions)	1987			1	1	
Assemblies of God World Missions	1915	4		46		
Association of Free Lutheran Congregations				2	1	
Awana Clubs International				6		
Baptist Bible Fellowship International – World Mission Service Center	1946			56		
Baptist International Missions Inc.				36		
Baptist International Outreach	1999			4	2	2
Baptist Mid-Missions	1960			7		
Baptist Missionary Association of America (BMAA)				8		
BCM International	1975				4	1
Bethany Gateways				4		
Biblical Ministries Worldwide				7		7

	First Year	Personnel from US or Canada			Other Countries	
		1–2 years	2–4 years	4+ years	Citizen	Not Citizen
Brethren in Christ World Missions (BICWM)	1993			2		
Buckner International	2008				10	
Calvary Commission Inc.				10		
Camino Global	1955	1		37		
Camino Global Ministries Canada	1955	1		3		
Canadian National Baptist Convention (CNBC)	1985					4
Child Evangelism Fellowship Inc.				1		
Children of Promise International			3	5		
Children's Haven Intl.				22		
Christ for Children International	1992	1	1	5	3	
Christ for the City International	1988				5	6
Christian Aid Mission	1982			14		
Christian and Missionary Alliance in Canada, The			3	12		
Christian Broadcasting Network Inc., The	1998			4		
Christian Church (Disciples of Christ) – Global Ministries			2			
Christian Churches / Churches of Christ			4	50	20	
Christian Discipleship International	2002					1
Christian Fellowship Union Inc.	1944			2		
Christian Reformed World Missions	1962	2		12		
Christian Relief Fund, The	1999				1	
Christians In Action Missions International	1957			2		
Church of God (Cleveland TN) World Missions	1932	1				
Church of God of the Apostolic Faith Inc., The				1		
Church of the Brethren – Global Mission Partnerships			1			
Church of the Nazarene Inc.	1903			2	3	1
CMF International	1980	7	3	11	2	19
CMTS Ministries	1986				2	
ComCare International	1997			2	2	
Commission to Every Nation	1994	5	18	41	11	50
Commission To Every Nation-Canada	2011			6		
Compassion International Inc.	1980				42	
Congregational Methodist Missions				2		
Converge				10		
Cooperative Baptist Fellowship – Global Missions	2008	2				
Cross-Cultural Ministries – Churches of God General Conference	2012				1	
Crossworld	1971			4		
DeNike Ministries	1992			1		
Elim Fellowship	1976			9		
Encompass World Partners	1951				24	
Equip Inc & Equip International	1996			2		
Ethnos360			2	66		
Evangelical Free Church of Canada Mission				3		
Evangelical Friends Mission	1976			2		
Evangelical Mennonite Conference	1954	1		6		

	First Year	Personnel from US or Canada			Other Countries	
		1–2 years	2–4 years	4+ years	Citizen	Not Citizen
Evangelical Mennonite Mission Conference	1978			1		
Evangelical Methodist Church Inc. – Board of Missions	1946			5		
Evangelical Mission Ministries	1954			4	3	
Evangelical Missionary Church of Canada	2004			8		
Evangelism Explosion III International Inc.	2012				1	
Faith Christian Fellowship Intl.					2	
Far East Broadcasting Associates of Canada (FEB Canada)	2005			4		
Fellowship International Mission	1988	1		15	4	
Flying Doctors of America	1990					
Forward Edge International				1		
Foundation for His Ministry				20		
Foursquare Missions International	1943			17	1	
Full Gospel Evangelistic Association	1950			5		
General Baptists International	2003			4		
Global Missions (United Pentecostal Church Intl.)			9			15
Global Missions of Open Bible Churches	1965		4	2	1	
Global Outreach International	2000			9		
Global Outreach Mission Inc.				10		
Global Partners (The Wesleyan Church World Headquarters)				1		
Global Recordings Network					4	
Global Scholars	2004		1	1		2
Globe International	1985	1		11		
Go to Nations	1985			7	1	
Go Ye Fellowship	2004			8	1	7
Good News Productions International	1996		2	2	4	
Gospel Fellowship Association	1967	2		9		
Grace Mission Inc.	1988				6	
Impact International Inc.	1970				4	
Independent Faith Mission Inc.				2		
International Gospel Outreach	1982			4	1	3
International Partnership Ministries Inc.	1992					2
International Pentecostal Holiness Church	1930			6		
International Teams U.S.A.		3		13		6
InterVarsity Christian Fellowship/USA			1			
Latin America Mission	1961			1		
Latin American Lutheran Mission	1942			3	1	
Life in Messiah International	1977				5	
Lifesong for Orphans	2012				4	
LOGOI Ministries	1972				2	
Macedonia World Baptist Missions Inc.	1981			8		
Master's Resourcing Commission				1		
MB Mission	1950		2		3	7
MB Mission Canada	1950			7	3	2
Medical Ministry International	1970				1	1

		Personnel from US or Canada			Other Countries	
	First Year	1–2 years	2–4 years	4+ years	Citizen	Not Citizen
Medical Teams International	1985		1			
Mexican Medical Ministries	1963			13	8	3
Mexico Medical Missions	2001				10	35
Mission Aviation Fellowship	1945		2	2		
Mission On The Move	1986			2	10	
Mission to the World (PCA) Inc.	1977	3	9	49		
Missionary Gospel Fellowship	1959	2	4	11	2	15
Missionary Ventures Canada						2
Missionary Ventures Intl.				4		
Missions Door					1	
National Association of Congregational Christian Churches	1962			1	28	
Network of International Christian Schools	2015	2	2		10	
New Mission Systems International	2007			6	1	
Niños de Mexico	1967		3	6	25	
North American Baptist Conference – Worldwide Outreach	1992			8		
On The Go Ministries/Keith Cook Team	1956	1		2	1	
One Challenge	1967			2		
One Mission Society	1990			9		2
Open Air Campaigners – Overseas Ministries (OAC-OM)	2005			3		
Operation Mobilization		0			13	3
Orphanos Foundation				1	1	2
Our Daily Bread				1		
Palm Missionary Ministries Inc.	2006			4		
Pan American Missions	1960			2		
Pentecostal Free Will Baptist Church Inc. – World Witness Dept.				1		
PIC International (Partners in Christ International)		1				
Prayer Baptist Missions International Inc.				3		
Precept Ministries International	1980				1	3
Precious Seed Ministries Inc.	1966			1	8	
ReachGlobal				6		
Reformed Church in America – General Synod Council – Global Mission					1	
Reliant Mission Inc.	2015	1				
Ripe for Harvest Inc.				1		
Samaritan's Purse	2007	4				
SEND International Inc.	2016			2		
Servant Partners	2004			1		
Serve Globally – The Evangelical Covenant Church		1		9		
Seventh-day Adventists – General Conference – Global Mission	1893	1		12		22
Shield of Faith Mission International	1972			4	3	2
Source of Light Ministries Intl. Inc.				1		

	First Year	Personnel from US or Canada			Other Countries	
		1–2 years	2–4 years	4+ years	Citizen	Not Citizen
Sowers International, The					1	
Spanish World Ministries					2	
TEAM (The Evangelical Alliance Mission)	1982			26		
Team Expansion Inc.	2012			2	2	
The Brethren Church Inc.	1995			1	3	
The Navigators				8		
TIME Ministries	1968			3	3	
TMS Global	1986				2	
To Every Tribe	2004			12		
United World Mission Inc.		2	1	25	7	21
Walk Thru the Bible Ministries Inc.	2000			4		
WEC International		2		14		
Wisconsin Evangelical Lutheran Synod – Board for World Missions				2		
Word of Life Fellowship Inc.	1983	2			27	20
World Gospel Mission	1949			5		
World Indigenous Missions	1982			30		
World Link Ministries	2008			25		
World Mission Prayer League	1943		2	2		
World-Wide Missions					2	
WorldVenture				2		
Wycliffe Bible Translators of Canada Inc.				9		
Wycliffe Bible Translators USA				49		
YUGO Ministries (Youth Unlimited Gospel Outreach Inc.)	1964			36	5	1
YUGO Ministries Canada	2004	2	2	6	1	
Micronesia, Federated States of						
Assemblies of God World Missions	2010			5		
Baptist International Missions Inc.				2		
Baptist Mid-Missions	1997			2		
Child Evangelism Fellowship Inc.				2		
Conservative Congregational Christian Conference-Missions Committee				4		
Global Missions (United Pentecostal Church Intl.)			2			
Seventh-day Adventists – General Conference – Global Mission	1979	1	2	2		
Middle East						
ABWE Canada (Across Borders for World Evangelism)	1989			2		
ABWE International				18		
Anglican Frontier Missions		4	1	1	1	
Assemblies of God World Missions		23		56		
Baptist Mid-Missions					2	
Beautiful Feet	2016			2		
Café 1040 Inc.	2001	5				
Canadian Baptist Ministries	1978			2		

	First Year	Personnel from US or Canada			Other Countries	
		1–2 years	2–4 years	4+ years	Citizen	Not Citizen
Canadian National Baptist Convention (CNBC)	2004			2		
Christar	1975	9	8	44		1
Christar Canada				6		
Christian and Missionary Alliance in Canada, The			2	26		
Christian Discipleship International	1990				2	
Christian Medical & Dental Associations				1		
Christian Veterinary Mission	2016	2				
Church of God Ministries (Anderson) – Global Strategy				2		
Cooperative Baptist Fellowship – Global Missions	1994			7		
CRM		2			52	
Crossworld				2		
Crossworld Canada				2		
East-West Ministries International		28	12	3	2	
EPC World Outreach				1		
Far East Broadcasting Associates of Canada (FEB Canada)	1990		2			
Fellowship of Evangelical Churches – International Ministries	2007			2		
Final Frontiers Foundation	2004				10	
Foursquare Missions International				2		
Frontiers Canada	1984			8		
Global Missions (United Pentecostal Church Intl.)	1992		2			2
Global Partners (The Wesleyan Church World Headquarters)			1	26		
Go Ye Fellowship	2002			2		2
Greater Grace World Outreach	2013					2
International Friendships Inc.			2			
InterServe Canada				4		
Liebenzell Mission of USA Inc.	2002		1			
Life Impact Inc.	2015			2		2
Mennonite Mission Network	2007		2			
Middle East Christian Outreach (MECO Canada)		2		2		
Mission Catalyst Intl. Inc.		1				
Mission ONE Inc.					9	
New Mission Systems International	2016				2	
OM Canada		2		6		
One Challenge				4		
Open Door Baptist Missions	1997			5		
Operation Mobilization				78	52	190
Outreach to Asia Nationals	1996			2	5	
Pioneers USA				49		2
Ravi Zacharias International Ministries Inc.	2007				1	
ReachAcross	1951					3
Rosedale Mennonite Missions	1981			7		

	First Year	Personnel from US or Canada			Other Countries	
		1–2 years	2–4 years	4+ years	Citizen	Not Citizen
SAT-7 North America	1996				1	1
Servant Partners	2012			4		
TEAM (The Evangelical Alliance Mission)				38		
Team Expansion Inc.	2012			19		
The Voice of the Martyrs				6	4	
United World Mission Inc.	2015			4		4
visionSynergy	2003			1		
WEC International				10		
WEC International Canada		1		12		3
Word of Life Fellowship Inc.	2007					2
World Indigenous Missions	2001		6			
WorldVenture				17		
Wycliffe Associates	2009			2		
Youth for Christ/USA				6		
Youth With A Mission (YWAM)			48		11	
Moldova						
Assemblies of God World Missions	1991	4		6		
Awana Clubs International					1	
Baptist International Evangelistic Ministries					8	2
Baptist International Missions Inc.				2		
Child Evangelism Fellowship Inc.				1		
Christian Aid Ministries (CAM)			3			
CRM					4	
Crossover Communications International	1991	2				
EurAsian Baptist Mission	1993			2	6	
Evangelism Explosion III International Inc.	2012				2	
For God's Children Intl.					4	
Friends in Action Intl.				1		
Global Outreach International	2004			2	1	
Ministry to Educate and Equip Intl. (MTEE)				1		
Mission Eurasia					8	
New Hope International	1992				3	
Operation Mobilization		8			43	7
Precept Ministries International	1994				8	
Reach A Village					3	
Slavic Missionary Service Inc.				1		
TCM International Institute					1	
TeachBeyond Canada				2		
The Salvation Army USA National Headquarters	1994	2				
Titus International	1995			1	45	
Walk Thru the Bible Ministries Inc.	2000				1	
World Team US				6		

		Personnel from US or Canada			Other Countries	
	First Year	1–2 years	2–4 years	4+ years	Citizen	Not Citizen
Mongolia						
Assemblies of God World Missions	1993	2		4		
Baptist International Missions Inc.				8		
BILD International					1	
CAMA Services	2000			2		
Campus Crusade for Christ (Cru in the US)				2		
Christian Veterinary Mission	1994	2		4		2
Church of the Nazarene Inc.						4
Cup of Cold Water Ministries	1998		2	4		6
Evangelical Missionary Church of Canada	2004			2		
Evangelism Explosion III International Inc.	2015				1	
Far East Broadcasting Company					1	
Food for the Hungry Inc.	1997		2			
Habitat for Humanity International	2000		1			1
International Gospel Outreach	2013			2	0	2
Literacy & Evangelism International						2
Mennonite Mission Network	1993			4		2
Mission Aviation Fellowship of Canada (MAFC)				1		
Mission Eurasia					1	
ReachGlobal				2		
Samaritan's Purse	2005	3				
Seventh-day Adventists – General Conference – Global Mission	1931			2		4
Teen Missions International Inc.	1997				1	
The Navigators				2		
World Mission Prayer League	1993			4		
World Relief	2002		1			
Montenegro						
Campus Crusade for Christ (Cru in the US)		3		2		
Virginia Mennonite Missions	2012			2		2
Morocco						
Christian Aid Mission	2005				30	
Eastern Mennonite Missions	2015		1			
Global Missions (United Pentecostal Church Intl.)			1			2
Macedonia World Baptist Missions Inc.	2006					2
New Mission Systems International	2015			2		
Pioneers Canada				2		
Walk Thru the Bible Ministries Inc.	2002				1	
Mozambique						
Advent Christian World Outreach	2011				1	
AMG International					2	
Assemblies of God World Missions	1975	2		8		
Awana Clubs International					2	
Baptist International Missions Inc.				2		

	First Year	Personnel from US or Canada			Other Countries	
		1–2 years	2–4 years	4+ years	Citizen	Not Citizen
Baptist Mid-Missions	2005			3		1
BCM International	2013				1	
Child Evangelism Fellowship Inc.				1		
Christian Aid Mission	2003				100	
Christian Churches / Churches of Christ			2	6		
Church of the Nazarene Inc.	1922				4	2
Commission to Every Nation	2005	1		4		5
Entrust	2004				1	
Evangelism Explosion III International Inc.	2015				3	
Global Missions (United Pentecostal Church Intl.)			2			
Global Outreach International	2002			2		
Global Partners (The Wesleyan Church World Headquarters)				2		
Globe International	2000			2		
Grace Ministries International	2016					2
Greater Grace World Outreach	2003				2	
Habitat for Humanity International	2000		1			1
Medical Teams International	2009	1				
Mission Aviation Fellowship	1999			4		
One Mission Society	1994			8		3
Precept Ministries International					2	
Samaritan's Purse	2000	4				
Serve Globally – The Evangelical Covenant Church			2			
Seventh-day Adventists – General Conference – Global Mission	1935			1		1
SIM USA				8		
TEAM (The Evangelical Alliance Mission)				6		
The Pentecostal Assemblies of Canada				2		
Walk Thru the Bible Ministries Inc.	1999				3	
Word of Life Fellowship Inc.	2009				2	10
World Missions & Evangelism	2005			6		
World Relief	1987		1		383	5
World Team US				2		
WorldVenture				12		
Wycliffe Bible Translators of Canada Inc.				6		
Wycliffe Bible Translators USA				8		
Zion Evangelical Ministries of Africa (ZEMA)	2008					4
Myanmar (Burma)						
ACTS International Ministries Inc.	1991				2	
Advent Christian World Outreach	2005				1	
American Leprosy Missions	1906				1	
AMG International		1			4	
Awana Clubs International					1	
Baptist Mid-Missions	2015			2		
Baptist Missionary Association of America (BMAA)				4		

	First Year	Personnel from US or Canada 1–2 years	2–4 years	4+ years	Other Countries Citizen	Not Citizen
BCM International	1991				9	
BILD International					1	
CAMA Services	2012				1	
Christian Aid Mission					626	
Christian Churches / Churches of Christ					8	
Christian Discipleship International	2007				2	
Equip Inc & Equip International	2015	2				
Evangel Bible Translators					6	
Global Outreach International	2003			2	1	
Global Outreach Mission Inc.				5		
Global Recordings Network					3	
Good News Productions International	1999				2	
Harvest Foundation					1	
Intercede International					2	
International Gospel Outreach	2012			1		1
International Partnership Ministries Inc.	1993				29	
National Association of Congregational Christian Churches	1999				7	
New Mission Systems International	1999			7	3	
OM Canada		1				
Operation Mobilization		1			9	6
Partners Relief & Development	1995	7	4	2		
Presbyterian Missionary Union	2005				2	
Reach A Village					3	
Reformed Church in America – General Synod Council – Global Mission					1	
Samaritan's Purse	2008	3				
Scriptures In Use	2015	2			100	
Seventh-day Adventists – General Conference – Global Mission	1919					2
Source of Light Ministries Intl. Inc.					1	
Sowers International, The					1	
The God's Story Project	2003				2	
Things to Come Mission	2014				2	
Walk Thru the Bible Ministries Inc.	1999				2	
White Fields					9	
World Compassion Terry Law Ministries					1	
World Concern	1994				94	
Namibia						
Assemblies of God World Missions	1979			4		
Baptist International Missions Inc.				2		
Child Evangelism Fellowship Inc.				3		
Church of the Nazarene Inc.	1973			2		
Evangelism Explosion III International Inc.	2011				2	
Global Missions (United Pentecostal Church Intl.)	1986		2			

	First Year	Personnel from US or Canada 1–2 years	2–4 years	4+ years	Other Countries Citizen	Not Citizen
On The Go Ministries/Keith Cook Team	1983	6		1		
Operation Mobilization					6	3
SIM USA			1			
TMS Global	2010		2			
Walk Thru the Bible Ministries Inc.	1999				2	
Nepal						
ABWE International			2			
ACTS International Ministries Inc.	2005				3	
All God's Children International					3	
American Leprosy Missions	1982		1			
Awana Clubs International					9	
Back to the Bible	2001				2	
Baptist International Missions Inc.			6			
BCM International	1993				5	
BILD International					1	
CEIFA International	2006		2		2	
Child Evangelism Fellowship Inc.			1			
Christian Aid Mission					570	
Christian Discipleship International	2008				1	
Christian Reformed World Missions	2007		2			
Development Associates Intl. (DAI)					1	
Elim Fellowship	2016		2			
Evangelical Friends Mission	1994		2			4
Evangelism Explosion III International Inc.	2009				2	
FaithLife Ministries Inc.	2012				1	
Global Missions (United Pentecostal Church Intl.)	1992	1			1	
Global Partners (The Wesleyan Church World Headquarters)		2				
Global Recordings Network					7	
Globe International	2002		2			
Go to Nations	1996		1			1
Gospel Tide Broadcasting Association	2004				2	
Greater Grace World Outreach	1997	2			4	
Habitat for Humanity International	1997	1				1
Harvest Foundation					1	
HBI Global Partners					10	
Holt International Children's Services Inc.					1	
IN Network dba International Needs USA	1975				22	
India Gospel Outreach Inc.	1994				30	
Intercede International					4	2
International Gospel Outreach	2005		2			2
International Partnership Ministries Inc.	1999				18	4
International Teams U.S.A.			2			3
Mennonite Mission Network	1956		1			1

	First Year	Personnel from US or Canada			Other Countries	
		1–2 years	2–4 years	4+ years	Citizen	Not Citizen
Mission ONE Inc.					2	
OM Canada		1				
Operation Mobilization		8			36	31
Scriptures In Use	2010			6	800	
ServLife International				1		
Seventh-day Adventists – General Conference – Global Mission	1957			3		12
SIM USA				3		
The God's Story Project	2003				2	
The Presbyterian Church in Canada	1974		2			
Walk Thru the Bible Ministries Inc.	1999				2	
World Mission Prayer League	1954			6	1	
World-Wide Missions				1	1	
WorldVenture				2		
Youth Ministry International					1	
Netherlands						
Assemblies of God World Missions	1975	6		18		
Baptist Mid-Missions	1954			4		
BCM International	1950				18	
BCM International (Canada) Inc.	1950					1
Bethany Gateways				1	1	
Biblical Ministries Worldwide			2		2	
Chosen People Ministries Inc.	2010				2	
Christian and Missionary Alliance in Canada, The				1		
Church of God Ministries (Anderson) – Global Strategy	1914		2			
Church of the Brethren – Global Mission Partnerships		1				
Church of the Nazarene Inc.	1967				2	
Cooperative Baptist Fellowship – Global Missions	1996			2		
Eastern Mennonite Missions	2014			2		
European Christian Mission Intl. – USA				18		
Far East Broadcasting Associates of Canada (FEB Canada)	2003	2				
Global Missions (United Pentecostal Church Intl.)			2			7
Global Outreach Mission Inc.				1		
Go to Nations	1991	2				
Gospel Fellowship Association				2		
Greater Europe Mission				2		
International Pentecostal Holiness Church	2003			2		
International Teams U.S.A.						6
InterVarsity Christian Fellowship/USA			1			
Life in Messiah International	2005			2		
Operation Mobilization		1			54	11
Presbyterian Mission International (PMI)				1		
ReachGlobal				1		

	First Year	Personnel from US or Canada			Other Countries	
		1–2 years	2–4 years	4+ years	Citizen	Not Citizen
Reliant Mission Inc.	2002			2		
Serge				2		
The Navigators				4		
TWR				8		
TWR Canada	1993			1		
WEC International Canada	1948			2		
WorldVenture				2		
Wycliffe Bible Translators of Canada Inc.				2		
New Caledonia						
Global Missions (United Pentecostal Church Intl.)	2002		2			
Seventh-day Adventists – General Conference – Global Mission	1925					2
New Zealand						
ACCI (Adventive Cross Cultural Initiatives) – US	2009			4		
Action International Ministries – Canada				2		
Advent Christian World Outreach	1992		2	1		
Adventures in Missions	2004	1		2		
Baptist Bible Fellowship International – World Mission Service Center	1971			14		
Baptist International Missions Inc.				8		
Baptist Mid-Missions	1973			6		
Biblical Ministries Worldwide			11		11	
Campus Crusade for Christ (Cru in the US)		1		14		
Chosen People Ministries Inc.	2011			2	4	
Christian Churches / Churches of Christ				8		
Church of God Ministries (Anderson) – Global Strategy	1999	2				
Compassio					1	
Crossover Communications International	2011				1	
Elim Fellowship	2000			2		
Fellowship International Mission	1995			1	1	
Global Missions (United Pentecostal Church Intl.)	1969	3				12
Gospel Fellowship Association	1998			2		
International Teams U.S.A.				2	4	
Missions Resource Network	1844			6		
New Mission Systems International	2015			9		
Operation Mobilization		3			3	4
Our Daily Bread				1		
Precept Ministries International	1990				2	1
Presbyterian Mission International (PMI)				1		
Teen Missions International Inc.	1990				2	
The Navigators				12		
The Salvation Army USA National Headquarters	1883		2			
Word of Life Fellowship Inc.	1983	2		2	11	
WorldVenture				2		

	First Year	Personnel from US or Canada 1–2 years	2–4 years	4+ years	Other Countries Citizen	Not Citizen
Wycliffe Bible Translators USA				2		
Youth for Christ/USA				3		
Youth With A Mission (YWAM)			41			
Nicaragua						
ABWE International		1		24		
American Baptist International Ministries				4		
Assemblies of God World Missions	1912	9		18		
Baptist Bible Fellowship International – World Mission Service Center	1969			10		
Baptist International Missions Inc.				12		
Baptist Medical & Dental Mission International Inc. (BMDMI)	1989	3	2	2	43	
Baptist Missionary Association of America (BMAA)					2	
Camino Global	1900			1		
Christ for the City International	2002		4		1	2
Christian Aid Ministries (CAM)	1988		10		1	20
Christian Reformed World Missions	1973			2		
Christian Relief Fund, The	1997				4	
Christian Veterinary Mission	2007			2		
Church of God (Cleveland TN) World Missions	1950	2				
Commission to Every Nation	2000			2		2
Compassion International Inc.	2002				40	
CrossWay International	2004				4	
Equip Inc & Equip International	1997			2		
Evangelism Explosion III International Inc.	2010				3	
Food for the Hungry Inc.	1994		4			1
Forward Edge International				5		
Friends in Action Intl.				1		
Full Gospel Evangelistic Association	1960			2		
Global Health Outreach	2008				2	
Global Missions (United Pentecostal Church Intl.)	1971		2			1
Global Missions of Open Bible Churches	2003				2	
Global Outreach International	2001			2		
Globe International	1996	1		3		
Grace Ministries International	2013			4		2
Greater Grace World Outreach	2014				2	
Habitat for Humanity International	1984		1			1
International Gospel Outreach	1999			10	8	2
International Pentecostal Holiness Church	1994			1		
International Teams U.S.A.						1
Living Water Teaching	1986				2	
Macedonia World Baptist Missions Inc.	2014			2		
Mailbox Club International Inc., The					1	
Master's Resourcing Commission				1		
MEDA – Mennonite Economic Development Associates	1995				47	1
Medical Ministry International	2007	1				

	First Year	Personnel from US or Canada			Other Countries	
		1–2 years	2–4 years	4+ years	Citizen	Not Citizen
Mission to the World (PCA) Inc.	2002			2		
Missionary Ventures Canada						3
Missionary Ventures Intl.				6		
Missions Door					1	
National Baptist Convention USA Inc. – Foreign Mission Board	1958			2		
ORPHANetwork	2000				1	
Pentecostal Free Will Baptist Church Inc. – World Witness Dept.				1		
PIC International (Partners in Christ International)		2				
Precept Ministries International						1
Precious Seed Ministries Inc.	1972			2		
Reformed Church in America – General Synod Council – Global Mission				2		
Ripe for Harvest Inc.				1		
Self-Help International	1999			4		
Servant Partners	2011			5		2
Serve Globally – The Evangelical Covenant Church		1				
Seventh-day Adventists – General Conference – Global Mission	1928	1				2
The Presbyterian Church in Canada	1985	1				
TMS Global	2006			2		
Virginia Mennonite Missions	2014	2				2
Word of Life Fellowship Inc.	2007			1	3	3
World Relief	1991			1	23	
Niger						
Amazon Outreach	2008				3	
Assemblies of God World Missions	1991			2		
Baptist International Missions Inc.				2		
CAMA Services	2016		1			
Campus Crusade for Christ (Cru in the US)				1		
Canadian National Baptist Convention (CNBC)	2004					2
Child Evangelism Fellowship Inc.				1		
Christian Aid Mission	2005				35	
Christian and Missionary Alliance in Canada, The				10		
Elim Fellowship	1977			4		
Evangelism Explosion III International Inc.	2011				1	
Faith Baptist Mission	2010			7		
FaithLife Ministries Inc.	2015					1
Fellowship International Mission	1976			1		
Global Missions (United Pentecostal Church Intl.)	1999		2			
Global Partners (The Wesleyan Church World Headquarters)				4		
Go to Nations	2004	1				
Greater Grace World Outreach	2008				2	

	First Year	Personnel from US or Canada 1–2 years	2–4 years	4+ years	Other Countries Citizen	Not Citizen
Reformed Church in America – General Synod Council – Global Mission				3		
Samaritan's Purse	2005	1				
Scriptures In Use	2014		4		500	
Seventh-day Adventists – General Conference – Global Mission	1987					2
SIM Canada				13		
SIM USA		3		71		
The Free Methodist Church in Canada	2007			2		
Wycliffe Bible Translators USA				6		
Nigeria						
Advent Christian World Outreach	1966				1	
Awana Clubs International					1	
Baptist International Missions Inc.				2		
Baptist International Outreach	1985			4	4	
Beautiful Feet	2016			2		
BILD International					1	
Child Evangelism Fellowship Inc.				1		
Christian Aid Mission	1986				500	
Christian Broadcasting Network Inc., The	1997				20	
Christian Churches / Churches of Christ				2		
Christian Reformed World Missions	1940	2		10		
Church of God (Cleveland TN) World Missions	1951	2				
Church of the Brethren – Global Mission Partnerships		8	3			
Converge				3		
CRM					15	
Development Associates Intl. (DAI)					1	
Elim Fellowship	1977			2		
Equip Canada	2005			2		
Equip Inc & Equip International	1996				4	
Evangelical Missionary Church of Canada	1986			6		
Evangelism Explosion III International Inc.	2013				5	
Evangelism Resources Inc.	1991		2			
Faith Baptist Mission	2010			2		
FaithLife Ministries Inc.	2010				1	
Fellowship International Mission	1977			2	2	
Food for the Hungry Inc.	2000		2			
Free Methodist World Missions	1989			1		
Global Missions (United Pentecostal Church Intl.)	1970		4			5
Global Missions of Open Bible Churches	1989				1	
Global Recordings Network					5	
Global Scholars	1988		2	4	1	5
Go to Nations	1992				17	
Gospel Tide Broadcasting Association	2009				1	
Harvest Foundation					1	

	First Year	Personnel from US or Canada			Other Countries	
		1–2 years	2–4 years	4+ years	Citizen	Not Citizen
Intercede International					2	
International Christian Ministries	2002				4	
Liebenzell Mission of USA Inc.	2005		1	2		
Link International Ministries	1989				12	
Literacy & Evangelism International					2	
Lott Carey Baptist Foreign Mission Convention	1965				100	
Lutheran Church Missouri Synod – World Mission	1936			2		
Mission ONE Inc.					1	
Missionary Ventures Intl.				1		
Mutual Faith Ministries Intl.		1				
National Association of Congregational Christian Churches	1973				10	
North American Baptist Conference – Worldwide Outreach	1939	2				2
On The Go Ministries/Keith Cook Team	1913			1		
Pentecostal Free Will Baptist Church Inc. – World Witness Dept.					1	
Scriptures In Use	2014		4		500	
Seventh-day Adventists – General Conference – Global Mission	1914	1	1	4		2
SIM Canada				10		
SIM USA		4		24		
Source of Light Ministries Intl. Inc.					1	
The Masters Mission	1987				5	
The Salvation Army USA National Headquarters	1920		2			
Walk Thru the Bible Ministries Inc.	2000				4	
Waymarks Radio Ministries International	1999				1	
Word of Life Fellowship Inc.	2000			2	8	
World Gospel Mission	2013	2				
World Mission Prayer League	2015		1			
Wycliffe Bible Translators of Canada Inc.				4		
Wycliffe Bible Translators USA				8		
North Africa						
ABWE International		3		4		
ACM International	2014			4		
Africa Inland Mission				62		8
Africa Inland Mission Canada Intl.				3		3
Anglican Frontier Missions		1				
Assemblies of God World Missions		39		51		
BILD International				1	1	
Campus Crusade for Christ (Cru in the US)		43		149		
Christar	1984			6		
Christian Medical & Dental Associations				1		
Evangelical Free Church of Canada Mission				1		

	First Year	Personnel from US or Canada			Other Countries	
		1–2 years	2–4 years	4+ years	Citizen	Not Citizen
Global Missions of Open Bible Churches				2		
International Messengers			5		5	
Josue Yrion World Evangelism & Missions Inc.	2014				2	
MB Mission					18	
MB Mission Canada					18	
Mission Catalyst Intl. Inc.		1				
One Challenge				2		
Orphanos Foundation	2012			2		
Pioneers USA				71		1
Reach Beyond				1		3
ReachAcross	1951		7		5	19
SAT-7 North America	1996				1	1
Servant Partners	2001			1		3
SIM USA				4		
TEAM (The Evangelical Alliance Mission)				4		
Team Expansion Inc.	1999	1	1	22		2
The Voice of the Martyrs				4		
WEC International Canada			1	7		2
WorldVenture				6		
Northern Mariana Islands						
Church of God Ministries (Anderson) – Global Strategy	2007					2
Far East Broadcasting Company					1	
General Baptists International	1947			2		
Wycliffe Bible Translators USA				2		
Norway						
ABWE International		1		3		
American Leprosy Missions						1
Compassio					1	
Global Missions (United Pentecostal Church Intl.)			2			3
International Pentecostal Holiness Church	1992			2		
International Teams U.S.A.						2
Master's Resourcing Commission				1		
Operation Mobilization		2			2	
Oceania						
Africa Inland Mission Canada Intl.			2			2
Assemblies of God World Missions				4		
Crossworld				1		2
Ethnos360				136		
Evangelism Explosion III International Inc.	1996				1	
Final Frontiers Foundation	2001				2	
Foursquare Missions International				2		

	First Year	Personnel from US or Canada 1–2 years	2–4 years	4+ years	Other Countries Citizen	Not Citizen
Global Missions (United Pentecostal Church Intl.)	2004		2			
Josue Yrion World Evangelism & Missions Inc.	2003				2	
New Tribes Mission of Canada		3		41		
Pioneers USA				6		
Seventh-day Adventists – General Conference – Global Mission	1930	1		2		
The Pentecostal Assemblies of Canada				2		
Word of Life Fellowship Inc.				2		
Wycliffe Associates	1974	3	24	6	8	
Wycliffe Bible Translators of Canada Inc.				14		
Youth With A Mission (YWAM)			12		70	
Oman						
Interserve USA	1951			1		
Reformed Church in America – General Synod Council – Global Mission				3		
Pakistan						
Awana Clubs International					6	
BILD International					1	
Child Evangelism Fellowship Inc.				1		
Christ to the Nations				1		
Christian Aid Mission					450	
Christian Churches / Churches of Christ					2	
Church of God (Cleveland TN) World Missions	1972	1				
EPC World Outreach				2		
Evangelism Explosion III International Inc.	2009				1	
FaithLife Ministries Inc.	2014				1	
Far East Broadcasting Associates of Canada (FEB Canada)	1969	1		6		
Full Gospel Evangelistic Association	2003	3				
Gate Breaker Ministries	2009				15	
Global Gates	2016			1		
Global Missions (United Pentecostal Church Intl.)	1971		2			
Global Recordings Network					6	
Greater Grace World Outreach	2008				4	
Intercede International						2
International Gospel Outreach	2015			2	2	
Interserve USA	1852			11	1	
Key Communications	1977				1	
MEDA – Mennonite Economic Development Associates	2007				6	1
Mission ONE Inc.					54	
OM Canada				1		
Operation Mobilization					44	3
Salvation Army – Canada and Bermuda Territory, The	1997		1			
Scriptures In Use	2002			6	1200	

	First Year	Personnel from US or Canada			Other Countries	
		1–2 years	2–4 years	4+ years	Citizen	Not Citizen
Seventh-day Adventists – General Conference – Global Mission	1914	1				4
The Presbyterian Church in Canada	1984		2			
World Mission Prayer League	1947			4		1
WorldVenture				3		
Palau						
Assemblies of God World Missions	1983			2		
Baptist International Missions Inc.				2		
Biblical Ministries Worldwide				4		4
Liebenzell Mission of USA Inc.	1965		1			
Seventh-day Adventists – General Conference – Global Mission	1930	1				
Palestine						
Christian Aid Mission					26	
Christian Church (Disciples of Christ) – Global Ministries			3			
Friends United Meeting			1			
Global Gates	2015			2		
Global Missions (United Pentecostal Church Intl.)			2			
On The Go Ministries/Keith Cook Team	1967	2	2			
Panama						
American Baptist International Ministries				1		
Assemblies of God World Missions	1967	5		18		
Awana Clubs International					1	
Baptist Bible Fellowship International – World Mission Service Center	1976			8		
Baptist International Missions Inc.				4		
Baptist Missionary Association of America (BMAA)					2	
Bethany Gateways			2			
Camino Global	1944			2		
Christian and Missionary Alliance in Canada, The				2		
Christian Churches / Churches of Christ		2		2		
Church of God (Cleveland TN) World Missions	1935			2		
Church of the Nazarene Inc.	1953			6	2	3
Evangelical Free Church of Canada Mission						
FaithLife Ministries Inc.	2012					1
Global Missions (United Pentecostal Church Intl.)	1980		2			1
Global Partners (The Wesleyan Church World Headquarters)				2		
Gospel Fellowship Association	2002			2		
IBMGlobal	2013		2			
International Pentecostal Holiness Church	1988			2		
Living Water Teaching	2001					2
Lutheran Church Missouri Synod – World Mission	1941			6		
Macedonia World Baptist Missions Inc.	2015			1		

	First Year	Personnel from US or Canada			Other Countries	
		1–2 years	2–4 years	4+ years	Citizen	Not Citizen
MB Mission	1961			2	2	2
MB Mission Canada	1961			2	2	2
Mission to the World (PCA) Inc.				2		
Missions Door					1	
National Baptist Convention of America – Foreign Mission Board	1969			4		
Power to Change Ministries	2006	2				
Precept Ministries International						1
ReachGlobal				6		
United World Mission Inc.				2		2
Word of Life Fellowship Inc.	1988		0	2	12	5
WorldVenture				2		
Papua New Guinea						
ABWE International		2		18		
Advent Christian World Outreach	2008				1	
Assemblies of God World Missions	2000	2		2		
Awana Clubs International					2	
Baptist Bible Fellowship International – World Mission Service Center	1961			6		
Baptist International Missions Inc.				2		
Baptist Mid-Missions	2004			2	1	
Baptist Missionary Association of America (BMAA)				6		
Christian Aid Mission					64	
Christian Churches / Churches of Christ			6	30		
Church of God (Holiness) World Mission Dept. Inc.			2			
Church of the Nazarene Inc.	1955			19		2
Ethnos360		26	24	213		
Evangelical Congregational Church – Global Ministries Commission				5		
Evangelical Missionary Church of Canada	1994			2		
Evangelism Explosion III International Inc.	2010				8	
Foursquare Missions International	1956			6		
FRIENDS in Action International – Canada	1998			2		
Friends in Action Intl.				1		
Global Missions (United Pentecostal Church Intl.)	1973					3
Global Missions of Open Bible Churches	1971				1	
Gospel Fellowship Association	1997	5		13		
Into All The World	2008	1				
Kids Alive International	1992			1		
Lutheran Church Missouri Synod – World Mission	1948			1		
Mission Aviation Fellowship of Canada (MAFC)			1	7		
Mission to the World (PCA) Inc.	1987		1	2		
On The Go Ministries/Keith Cook Team	1886			2		1
Operation Mobilization					7	

| | First Year | Personnel from US or Canada | | | Other Countries | |
		1–2 years	2–4 years	4+ years	Citizen	Not Citizen
Pioneer Bible Translators				33		
Reach Beyond				2		
Salvation Army – Canada and Bermuda Territory, The	1998	1				
Seventh-day Adventists – General Conference – Global Mission	1908					22
To Every Tribe	2004			6		
Word of Life Fellowship Inc.	2000				3	1
World Gospel Mission	1996			10		
World-Wide Missions	1975				1	
Wycliffe Bible Translators of Canada Inc.				23		
Wycliffe Bible Translators USA				205		
Paraguay						
ABWE International				4		
Assemblies of God World Missions	1944			6		
Baptist Bible Fellowship International – World Mission Service Center	1980			2		
Baptist International Missions Inc.				2		
Baptist Missionary Association of America (BMAA)						2
Christian Aid Mission	1984				24	
Church of God (Cleveland TN) World Missions	1954			2		
Church of God Ministries (Anderson) – Global Strategy	1974				1	
Church of the Nazarene Inc.	1980			3		2
Ethnos360				41		
Evangelical Mennonite Conference	1959			9		
Evangelical Missionary Church of Canada	2009			2		
Evangelism Explosion III International Inc.	2011				1	
Global Missions (United Pentecostal Church Intl.)	1973	2				6
Global Missions of Open Bible Churches	1982				1	
Global Outreach Mission Inc.				4		
Grace Ministries International	2015			2		2
IBMGlobal	2014	2				
International Pentecostal Holiness Church					2	
Living Water Teaching	1990			2		
MB Mission	1930			2		
Mission Generation Inc.	2009				3	2
Missionary Ventures Intl.				2		
Open Air Campaigners – Overseas Ministries (OAC-OM)	1992				2	
Operation Mobilization					3	3
Ripe for Harvest Inc.				1		
Seventh-day Adventists – General Conference – Global Mission	1900					2
SIM Canada				2		
SIM USA		2		17		
Spanish World Ministries					1	

	First Year	Personnel from US or Canada			Other Countries	
		1–2 years	2–4 years	4+ years	Citizen	Not Citizen
The Brethren Church Inc.	1989				1	
TMS Global	1987			8		
United World Mission Inc.			1	4		5
White Fields					6	
Word of Life Fellowship Inc.	1979			1	4	4
World Gospel Mission	1986			7		
Wycliffe Bible Translators USA				2		
Peru						
ABWE International				22		
Allegheny Wesleyan Methodist Connection	1972			3		
Amazon Focus Inc.	1995			2	10	
AMG International					6	
Assemblies of God World Missions	1919	5		12		
Baptist Bible Fellowship International – World Mission Service Center	1958			19		
Baptist International Missions Inc.				11		
Baptist International Outreach	1994			2		2
Baptist Mid-Missions	1937			40	1	
Baptist Missionary Association of America (BMAA)				4		
BCM International	1994				29	
BILD International					2	1
Buckner International	2006				15	
Canadian South America Mission	1926			1		2
Center for Mission Mobilization	2015			2		
Child Evangelism Fellowship Inc.				1		
Christ for the City International	1989	1		1	1	1
Christian Aid Mission	1980				451	
Christian Emergency Relief Teams (CERT) International	1993				3	
Christians In Action Missions International	1979					2
Church of God (Cleveland TN) World Missions	1947			2		
Church of the Nazarene Inc.	1914				2	2
CMF International	2014		4		4	
Commission to Every Nation	2004		6	4		10
Compassion International Inc.	1977				62	
Cooperative Baptist Fellowship – Global Missions	2008	2				
Eastern Mennonite Missions	2003		1	5		
Elim Fellowship	1999			1		
Evangelism Explosion III International Inc.	2011				1	
Fellowship International Mission				1		
FH Canada	2002		3			
Food for the Hungry Inc.	1982	2	8		3	
Foursquare Missions International	1981			4		
Global Missions (United Pentecostal Church Intl.)	1962		4			
Global Missions of Open Bible Churches	1980				1	
Global Outreach International	2005			2		

	First Year	Personnel from US or Canada			Other Countries	
		1–2 years	2–4 years	4+ years	Citizen	Not Citizen
Global Outreach Mission Inc.				4		
Go to Nations	1986			1	1	
Greater Grace World Outreach	2003				2	2
Harvest Foundation				4		
IBMGlobal	2015	2				
Impact International Inc.					2	
International Messengers			3	2	2	3
International Partnership Ministries Inc.	1996				25	
International Pentecostal Holiness Church	1996			2	2	
Into All The World	2009		1			
Kids Alive International	1990	0	0	7	4	4
Latin American Missions Association	2009				1	3
Literacy & Evangelism International				3	1	
LOGOI Ministries	1972				2	
Macedonia World Baptist Missions Inc.	2003			9		
MB Mission	1983			2		1
MB Mission Canada	1983			1		2
MEDA – Mennonite Economic Development Associates	1996				19	10
Medical Ministry International	1999	1			7	
Medical Ministry International Canada Inc.	2005				2	
Mission Generation Inc.	2010					
Mission to the World (PCA) Inc.	1987	2	10	34		
Missionary Ventures Canada		1			3	3
Missionary Ventures Intl.				8		
Missions Door					1	
Network of International Christian Schools	2001	10	5	5	10	
Open Air Campaigners – Overseas Ministries (OAC-OM)	2015				1	
Open Door Baptist Missions	2007			2		
Orphanos Foundation	2012					2
Pentecostal Free Will Baptist Church Inc. – World Witness Dept.					1	
Pioneers Canada				2		
Precept Ministries International	1992				5	
Proclaim! International Inc.	2004				1	
ReachGlobal		1		2		
Reformed Church in America – General Synod Council – Global Mission				2		
Scriptures In Use	2002			4	800	
Seventh-day Adventists – General Conference – Global Mission	1898	5				
Shield of Faith Mission International	2016		1			
SIM USA		2		23		
Source of Light Ministries Intl. Inc.					1	
South America Mission	1926	0	4	28	5	2

	First Year	Personnel from US or Canada			Other Countries	
		1–2 years	2–4 years	4+ years	Citizen	Not Citizen
Spanish World Ministries					2	
TEAM (The Evangelical Alliance Mission)	1975			4		
The Brethren Church Inc.	1992				2	
The Pentecostal Assemblies of Canada				2		
The Salvation Army USA National Headquarters	1910		2			
TMS Global	1996			7		
United World Mission Inc.		1		11	3	9
Word of Life Fellowship Inc.	1986			1	20	4
World Concern	1987				6	
World Gospel Mission	2007	2		2		
World Mission Prayer League	1985			2		
World Reach Inc.	1998			4	6	1
World Team Canada				4		
World Team US				2		
World-Wide Missions					2	
Wycliffe Bible Translators USA				45		
Philippines						
ABWE International				9		
ACSI (Association of Christian Schools International)	1998			1		
Action International Ministries	1974	2		23	1	1
Action International Ministries – Canada	1980			5		
Advent Christian World Outreach	1954			4		
All About Orphans (David Livingstone KURE Foundation)						
American Baptist International Ministries				4		
AMG International	1979				312	
Assemblies of God World Missions	1926	13		37		
Awana Clubs International					5	
Back to the Bible	1957				20	
Baptist Bible Fellowship International – World Mission Service Center	1948			40		
Baptist General Conference of Canada	1983		1	2		
Baptist International Missions Inc.				28		
Baptist International Outreach	2001			7	6	1
Baptist Missionary Association of America (BMAA)				12		
Barnabas International						
BCM International	1982				233	
Bethany Gateways		3				
Biblical Ministries Worldwide				2		2
Campus Crusade for Christ (Cru in the US)		1		13		
Child Evangelism Fellowship Inc.				1		
Christ to the Nations				1		
Christian Aid Mission					1671	

	First Year	Personnel from US or Canada 1–2 years	2–4 years	4+ years	Other Countries Citizen	Not Citizen
Christian and Missionary Alliance in Canada, The				1		
Christian Aviation and Radio Mission	1997				5	
Christian Broadcasting Network Inc., The	1976				129	
Christian Churches / Churches of Christ				40	10	
Christian Cultural Development Foundation	1985			2	4	2
Christian Discipleship International	2002				3	
Christian Reformed World Missions	1961			2		
Christians In Action Missions International	1977					2
Church of God (Cleveland TN) World Missions	1947			16		8
Church of the Nazarene Inc.	1946			13	3	4
Commission to Every Nation	1997		2	8	1	9
Commission To Every Nation-Canada	2009			2		
Compassion International Inc.	1972				78	
Converge				14		
Crossworld	1985			5	1	
Cybermissions	2001			2		
Emmanuel Intl. Canada				1		
Encompass World Partners	1984			2	4	
Ethnos360		2	3	59		
Evangelical Free Church of Canada Mission				2		
Evangelical Friends Mission	1979				1	
Evangelical Missionary Church of Canada	2005			2		
Evangelism Explosion III International Inc.	2013				4	
Evangelize China Fellowship Inc.					1	
FaithLife Ministries Inc.	2002				1	
Far East Broadcasting Associates of Canada (FEB Canada)	2003		2			
Far East Broadcasting Company					1	
Food for the Hungry Inc.	1982		3	1		
Foursquare Missions International	1927			2		
Free Methodist World Missions	1949			4		
General Baptists International	1957			6		
Global Adopt A People Campaign				6		
Global Missions (United Pentecostal Church Intl.)	1957		8			5
Global Missions of Open Bible Churches	1978				1	
Global Outreach International	2000			2		
Global Partners (The Wesleyan Church World Headquarters)				4		
Global Recordings Network					4	
Globe International	1986			2		
Go to Nations	1987	2		14	7	
Go Ye Fellowship	2000			4	4	
Good News Productions International	1995			1	4	
Gospel Fellowship Association	1978	6		15		
Greater Grace World Outreach	1997		2		1	
Habitat for Humanity International	1986		4		3	1
IFCA World Missions					1	

	First Year	Personnel from US or Canada			Other Countries	
		1–2 years	2–4 years	4+ years	Citizen	Not Citizen
IN Network dba International Needs USA	1977				1	
Independent Faith Mission Inc.				2		
Intercede International					8	
International Gospel Outreach	1998			4	2	2
International Justice Mission	2000	4			55	
International Partnership Ministries Inc.	2001				13	
International Pentecostal Holiness Church	1975			6		
International Teams U.S.A.	1981	4	2		32	152
Kids for Christ International	2007				4	
Living Word Missions				2	2	
MB Mission	2006				5	
MB Mission Canada	2006				5	
Medical Ministry International	1990				1	
Mission to the World (PCA) Inc.	1991			8		
Missionary Ventures Intl.				2		
Mutual Faith Ministries Intl.		1				
National Association of Congregational Christian Churches	1948				4	
OMF International				10		
OMF International – Canada	1964			7		7
One Challenge	1952			18		
One Child Matters						
One Mission Society	1982			6		1
Operation Mobilization		0			32	7
Our Daily Bread				1		
Pentecostal Free Will Baptist Church Inc. – World Witness Dept.				2		
Power to Change Ministries	1979			2		
Precept Ministries International	1996				2	
Presbyterian Mission International (PMI)				1		
Reach A Village					5	
ReachGlobal				5		
Ripe for Harvest Inc.				1		
Samaritan's Purse	1999	1				
SEND International Inc.	1946	3		16	21	3
SEND International of Canada				4		
Servant Partners	2003			1	2	
Seventh-day Adventists – General Conference – Global Mission	1906			22		31
SIM USA		1				
Source of Light Ministries Intl. Inc.					1	
Sowers International, The					1	
TEAM (The Evangelical Alliance Mission)	1986			14		
Team Expansion Inc.	2005			2		
Teen Missions International Inc.	1983				8	

	First Year	Personnel from US or Canada			Other Countries	
		1–2 years	2–4 years	4+ years	Citizen	Not Citizen
The Brethren Church Inc.	2003				4	
The Navigators				2		
The Pentecostal Assemblies of Canada				4		
The Waray-Waray Project	1992				9	
Things to Come Mission	1958	2			7	
TMS Global	2012			2		
Training Evangelistic Leadership	1977			4	12	
United Evangelical Churches				2		
Walk Thru the Bible Ministries Inc.	2000				68	
WEC International				2		
White Fields					43	
Word of Life Fellowship Inc.	1973	2		9	22	
World Indigenous Missions	1989			8		
World Mission Prayer League	1983			1	1	
World Missions & Evangelism	2006			1	1	
World Team US				18		
World-Wide Missions	1971		2			
WorldVenture				24		
Wycliffe Bible Translators of Canada Inc.				21		
Wycliffe Bible Translators USA	1960			119		
Youth for Christ/USA				1		
Poland						
ABWE International		2				
Assemblies of God World Missions	1925			8		
Avant Ministries	2004			3	1	
BCM International	1998		1	1	1	
Campus Crusade for Christ (Cru in the US)				2		
Child Evangelism Fellowship Inc.				1		
Christian Aid Mission					2	
Christian and Missionary Alliance in Canada, The				4		
Christian Church (Disciples of Christ) – Global Ministries			2			
Christian Churches / Churches of Christ				2	60	
Church of the Nazarene Inc.	1999			4		
Commission to Every Nation	1999			2	1	1
CRM				1	1	
East European Missions Network					2	
Elim Fellowship	1997			2		
Encompass World Partners	2015			2		
European Christian Mission Intl. – USA				4		
Far East Broadcasting Associates of Canada (FEB Canada)	2005			3		
Fellowship International Mission	2012			1		
Global Missions (United Pentecostal Church Intl.)			2			3
Global Outreach International	1997			2		

	First Year	Personnel from US or Canada			Other Countries	
		1–2 years	2–4 years	4+ years	Citizen	Not Citizen
Greater Europe Mission				1		
Greater Grace World Outreach	1985				2	
In Touch Mission International	1984			5	9	
International Messengers		6	13	34	37	16
Josiah Venture	1993			7	18	
Lutheran Church Missouri Synod – World Mission	1943			3		
Mailbox Club International Inc., The					2	
Operation Mobilization					4	1
Polish Christian Ministries	1954			1		
Reach A Village					3	
ReachGlobal				2		
Resourcing Christian Education International	2005				1	
SEND International Inc.	1991			11		4
TCM International Institute					1	
Word of Life Fellowship Inc.	1987			8	1	
World Witness				2		
WorldVenture				11		
Portugal						
ABWE Canada (Across Borders for World Evangelism)		1		3		
ABWE International		1		22		
Assemblies of God World Missions	1972	0		4		
Avant Ministries	2015			6		
Awana Clubs International					1	
Baptist Bible Fellowship International – World Mission Service Center	1987			10		
Baptist General Conference of Canada	1998			1		
BCM International	1991					2
Be One Together	2011				2	
Campus Crusade for Christ (Cru in the US)		1		4		
Christian Churches / Churches of Christ				4		
Church of the Nazarene Inc.	1973			6	2	
Encompass World Partners	1990			2	3	
European Christian Mission Intl. – USA				21		
Global Missions (United Pentecostal Church Intl.)	1972		4			
Greater Europe Mission				1		
Greater Europe Mission Canada	1996		2	2		
International Pentecostal Holiness Church	2001			2		
MB Mission	1986			2	4	1
MB Mission Canada	1986			1	4	2
Mission to the World (PCA) Inc.				3		
Operation Mobilization		2			2	6
ReachGlobal		2		4		
Resourcing Christian Education International	2006				4	
TEAM (The Evangelical Alliance Mission)	1942			5		

	First Year	Personnel from US or Canada			Other Countries	
		1–2 years	2–4 years	4+ years	Citizen	Not Citizen
Word of Life Fellowship Inc.	1976				6	11
WorldVenture				4		
Youth for Christ/USA	1996			2		
Puerto Rico						
Awana Clubs International					1	
Baptist Bible Fellowship International – World Mission Service Center	1955			2		
Baptist International Missions Inc.				4		
Baptist Missionary Association of America (BMAA)					2	
Biblical Ministries Worldwide				5		5
Campus Crusade for Christ (Cru in the US)		2				
Christian Churches / Churches of Christ				5	5	
Evangelism Explosion III International Inc.	2012				1	
Global Missions (United Pentecostal Church Intl.)	1964		2			
Global Missions of Open Bible Churches	1954				1	
Gospel Fellowship Association	1963			2		
Grace Ministries International	1964	1	1	2	1	
Greater Grace World Outreach	2006			2		
International Partnership Ministries Inc.	1999				2	
InterVarsity Christian Fellowship/USA			1			
Lutheran Church Missouri Synod – World Mission	1993			8		
Macedonia World Baptist Mission International	1995			1		
Macedonia World Baptist Missions Inc.	1991		6			1
Mission to the World (PCA) Inc.				4		
Open Door Baptist Missions	1995			2		
Pentecostal Free Will Baptist Church Inc. – World Witness Dept.					1	
Seventh-day Adventists – General Conference – Global Mission	1901			8		
Word of Life Fellowship Inc.	2010			1	1	2
Réunion						
Global Missions (United Pentecostal Church Intl.)	1999		2			
Romania						
ABWE Canada (Across Borders for World Evangelism)	2000			2		
ABWE International				16		
AMG International	1992				48	
Assemblies of God World Missions	1951	11		13		
Awana Clubs International					2	
Baptist Bible Fellowship International – World Mission Service Center	1990			4		
Baptist International Evangelistic Ministries					16	
Baptist International Missions Inc.				7		
Baptist International Outreach	2011			1		1
Baptist Mid-Missions	1990			8		
Baptist Missionary Association of America (BMAA)				4		

	First Year	Personnel from US or Canada			Other Countries	
		1–2 years	2–4 years	4+ years	Citizen	Not Citizen
BCM International	2009				2	
Biblical Ministries Worldwide				2		2
Calvary Commission Inc.				2		
CEIFA International	1990			1		1
Christ to the Nations				1		
Christian Aid Ministries (CAM)	1981		13		20	134
Christian Emergency Relief Teams (CERT) International	1990				30	
Christian Reformed World Missions	1990			2		
Church of God (Cleveland TN) World Missions	1922	2		2		
Church of the Nazarene Inc.	1992			3		
Commission to Every Nation	2001		1	2	1	2
CRM					4	
Crossworld	1993			1	2	
EPC World Outreach				1		
European Christian Mission Intl. – USA				11		
Evangelical Missionary Church of Canada	2003			7		
Evangelism Explosion III International Inc.	2010				7	
FAIR				1		
FH Canada	2000		2			
Food for the Hungry Inc.	1991		6	4		
For God's Children Intl.				2	3	
Friendship International Ministries Inc.				2		
Global Missions (United Pentecostal Church Intl.)	1995		2			1
Global Missions of Open Bible Churches	1992				1	
Global Outreach International	1988			14	2	2
Global Outreach Mission Inc.				2		
Global Scholars	1991				1	1
Greater Europe Mission			2	8		
Greater Grace World Outreach	1991				6	2
Harvest International Inc.	2005	2	2			
Heart To Heart International Ministries	1992		1	6		
Hope Haven International Ministries					4	
IN Network dba International Needs USA	1992				13	
In Touch Mission International	1967				6	
International Messengers		5	2	20	10	17
International Pentecostal Holiness Church	1996			2		
International Teams U.S.A.		3		6		13
InterVarsity Christian Fellowship/USA			3			
Josiah Venture	2003		2		6	
Mission to the World (PCA) Inc.	2001	2	2	7		
New Hope International	1971				9	
One Challenge	1996	1		2	2	
Operation Mobilization					13	9
Precept Ministries International					12	

	First Year	Personnel from US or Canada			Other Countries	
		1–2 years	2–4 years	4+ years	Citizen	Not Citizen
Reach A Village					5	
Reach Beyond				2		
ReachGlobal		1		10		
Reformed Church in America – General Synod Council – Global Mission				2		
Romanian Missionary Society	1968				70	
SEND International Inc.	1993			3		
Serge				2		
Source of Light Ministries Intl. Inc.					1	
TCM International Institute					1	
The Masters Mission	1999			2	2	
The Pentecostal Assemblies of Canada				4		
Titus International	1999			5	20	
United World Mission Inc.				2		2
Walk Thru the Bible Ministries Inc.	2000				2	
Word of Life Fellowship Inc.	1993				5	1
World Link Ministries	2002				70	
World Reach Inc.	1998					2
WorldVenture				4		
Wycliffe Bible Translators USA				1		
Youth Ministry International				2		
Russia						
A.C.T. International	2004					1
Assemblies of God World Missions	1990	13		23		
Avant Ministries	1993			2		
Awana Clubs International					5	
Baptist Bible Fellowship International – World Mission Service Center	1993			8		
Baptist International Evangelistic Ministries				3	40	2
Baptist International Missions Inc.				11		
Baptist Mid-Missions	1992			3		
BCM International					1	
Biblical Ministries Worldwide				2	1	1
Campus Crusade for Christ (Cru in the US)		7		17		
Center for Mission Mobilization	2014		2			
Child Evangelism Fellowship Inc.				1		
Children's HopeChest	1994			1	145	
Chosen People Ministries Inc.					5	
Christian Aid Mission					192	
Christian and Missionary Alliance in Canada, The				2		
Christian Broadcasting Network Inc., The	1992				8	
Christian Churches / Churches of Christ		2	4	16	6	
Christian Reformed World Missions	2000			2		

	First Year	Personnel from US or Canada			Other Countries	
		1–2 years	2–4 years	4+ years	Citizen	Not Citizen
Church of God (Cleveland TN) World Missions	1992			6		2
Church of the Nazarene Inc.	1992			1	2	
CIS- Christian Involvement In Service	2004				12	
Development Associates Intl. (DAI)					1	
East European Missions Network					8	
Entrust	1979			3	1	
EPC World Outreach				2		
Evangelical Christian Church in Canada, The	1993			1	1	
Evangelism Explosion III International Inc.	2010				11	
Faith Christian Fellowship Intl.					1	
Far East Broadcasting Company					1	
Foursquare Missions International				2		
Full Gospel Evangelistic Association	2002		2			
Global Missions (United Pentecostal Church Intl.)	1990		7			5
Global Outreach Mission Inc.				5		
Global Partners (The Wesleyan Church World Headquarters)				1		
Globe International	1995			2		
Go to Nations	1990	2		2		
Great Commission Media Ministries	1978				10	30
Greater Grace World Outreach	1990				6	1
IBMGlobal	2013		1			
InterAct Ministries	1991			3		
International Christian Ministries Canada (ICM)	2003			2	4	
International Gospel Outreach	1995			7		7
International Teams U.S.A.				4		5
Jews for Jesus	1993			3		
Lutheran Church Missouri Synod – World Mission	1992			5		
Mailbox Club International Inc., The					2	
Mercy Projects					6	
Mission Eurasia					8	
Missionary Ventures Intl.				1		
New Mission Systems International	2003				2	
On The Go Ministries/Keith Cook Team	1994	1		1		
One Mission Society	1993		1	5		8
Open Air Campaigners – Overseas Ministries (OAC-OM)	2003				1	
Operation Mobilization		2			15	12
Our Daily Bread				1		
Outreach Canada	2004			2		
Power to Change Ministries	1994			1		
Precept Ministries International	1994				3	
Reach A Village					7	
Resourcing Christian Education International	2005				11	

	First Year	Personnel from US or Canada			Other Countries	
		1–2 years	2–4 years	4+ years	Citizen	Not Citizen
Ripe for Harvest Inc.				1		
Russian Christian Radio Inc. (or RCR)					15	
Salvation Army – Canada and Bermuda Territory, The	1990		1			
Scriptures In Use	2012			2	300	
SEND International Inc.	1992	1		24		4
SEND International of Canada				6		
Serve Globally – The Evangelical Covenant Church			2			
Seventh-day Adventists – General Conference – Global Mission	1886			6		14
Slavic Gospel Association – Canada				1		
Slavic Missionary Service Inc.				1		
TCM International Institute					1	
The Centers for Apologetics Research (CFAR)					4	
The Pentecostal Assemblies of Canada				2	2	
TMS Global	1993			1		
United World Mission Inc.				4		4
Walk Thru the Bible Ministries Inc.	2000				21	
White Fields					2	
Wisconsin Evangelical Lutheran Synod – Board for World Missions				2		
Word To Russia				5	5	
World Indigenous Missions	1990			6		
World Mission Prayer League	2005			1		
World Partners USA				1		
WorldVenture				2		
Young Life				1		
Rwanda						
African Enterprise	1972				40	
Assemblies of God World Missions	1995			6		
Awana Clubs International					1	
Baptist General Conference of Canada	2012			2		
Baptist International Missions Inc.				2		
Canadian Baptist Ministries	1992			2	2	
Christian Discipleship International	2014				1	
Commission to Every Nation	2009		1			1
Commission To Every Nation-Canada	2015			2		
Compassion International Inc.	1980			2	66	
Elim Fellowship	2011			2		
Evangelical Free Church of Canada Mission			2			
Evangelical Friends Mission	1986			4		
Evangelism Explosion III International Inc.	2013				1	
Free Methodist World Missions	1942			1		
Global Missions (United Pentecostal Church Intl.)	1999		2			
Global Outreach International	1994			2		

	First Year	Personnel from US or Canada			Other Countries	
		1–2 years	2–4 years	4+ years	Citizen	Not Citizen
Greater Grace World Outreach	2004				2	
Harvest Foundation					4	
HOPE International	2005	1				1
International Gospel Outreach	2010			3	2	1
International Justice Mission	2007				14	2
International Teams Canada (Evangelical International Crusades Canada Inc.)				2		
International Teams U.S.A.						2
Leadership Vistas International Ministries						2
Missions Resource Network	2005		6			
New Mission Systems International	2015			2		
Reliant Mission Inc.	2014		1			
Seventh-day Adventists – General Conference – Global Mission	1920			6		9
With Open Eyes	2010				42	
World Concern	1995				2	
World Relief	1994	3	2	1	165	1
WorldVenture				12		
Youth for Christ/USA				4		
Saint Kitts and Nevis						
Macedonia World Baptist Missions Inc.	2002		2			
Saint Lucia						
ABWE International				2		
Baptist International Missions Inc.				2		
Saint Vincent and the Grenadines						
Baptist Mid-Missions	1946			1		
BCM International	1992				1	
Global Missions of Open Bible Churches	1981				1	
Macedonia World Baptist Missions Inc.	2011			2		
Seventh-day Adventists – General Conference – Global Mission	1889			2		
Samoa						
Baptist International Missions Inc.				3		
Global Missions (United Pentecostal Church Intl.)	1999		2			
São Tomé and Príncipe						
Baptist International Missions Inc.				2		
Seventh-day Adventists – General Conference – Global Mission	1938					2
Saudi Arabia						
Global Gates	2015			2		
International Gospel Outreach	2009			1		1
Senegal						
Assemblies of God World Missions	1956	6		12		
Avant Ministries	2011			4		
Baptist International Missions Inc.				4		

		Personnel from US or Canada			Other Countries	
	First Year	1–2 years	2–4 years	4+ years	Citizen	Not Citizen
Biblical Ministries Worldwide				2		2
CAMA Services	2007			2		
Campus Crusade for Christ (Cru in the US)		8		4		
Christian Aid Mission	1996				100	
Christian and Missionary Alliance in Canada, The				1		
Christian Broadcasting Network Inc., The	2004			2	1	
Church of the Nazarene Inc.	1988			4	1	
Converge				6		
Crossworld	2002			5		
Crossworld Canada	2002			3		
Fellowship International Mission	2000			2		
Habitat for Humanity International	2003		1			1
Intercede International						2
Mennonite Mission Network	1998			2	1	1
On The Go Ministries/Keith Cook Team	1976			7		3
Scriptures In Use	2006			6	1200	
Seventh-day Adventists – General Conference – Global Mission	1952					2
Shelter for Life Intl. Inc.					1	
SIM Canada				2		
SIM USA		2		10		
The Pentecostal Assemblies of Canada		1		6		
United World Mission Inc.				13		13
WEC International				2		
WorldVenture				26		
Wycliffe Bible Translators of Canada Inc.				3		
Wycliffe Bible Translators USA				9		
Serbia						
Assemblies of God World Missions	1993			2		
Child Evangelism Fellowship Inc.				2		
Christian and Missionary Alliance in Canada, The				2		
CRM		2		2		
European Christian Mission Intl. – USA				4		
Global Missions (United Pentecostal Church Intl.)			1			
Greater Grace World Outreach	2016					2
Josiah Venture	2003		1	1	3	
Precept Ministries International	1994			2		
Reach A Village				2		
Word of Life Fellowship Inc.	2006		1	2		
Seychelles						
Global Missions (United Pentecostal Church Intl.)	1988	2				
Sierra Leone						
Amazon Outreach	2000				1	
Assemblies of God World Missions	1920			4		

	First Year	Personnel from US or Canada			Other Countries	
		1–2 years	2–4 years	4+ years	Citizen	Not Citizen
Awana Clubs International					1	
BethanyKids	2013				2	
CAUSE Canada	1987	2	2		55	1
Christian Aid Mission	1988				15	
Christian Discipleship International	2012				2	
Christians In Action Missions International	1976				2	
CityTeam Ministries – New Generations International					2	
Evangelism Explosion III International Inc.	2012				5	
FaithLife Ministries Inc.	2012				1	
Global Missions (United Pentecostal Church Intl.)	1975		2			
Global Missions of Open Bible Churches	2002				1	
Global Outreach Mission Inc.				4		
Global Partners (The Wesleyan Church World Headquarters)				2		
Global Recordings Network					5	
International Christian Ministries	2001				2	1
International Gospel Outreach	1986			1		1
International Pentecostal Holiness Church						
Literacy & Evangelism International					2	
Living Word Missions				2	2	
Missions Door					1	
National Baptist Convention USA Inc. – Foreign Mission Board	1950				51	
Ripe for Harvest Inc.				1		
Seventh-day Adventists – General Conference – Global Mission	1905					2
Women of Hope International	2010			4	12	
World Partners USA				1		
World Relief	1994	1	1		27	1
Sint Maarten						
Christ to the Nations				2		
Global Outreach Mission Inc.				1		
Seventh-day Adventists – General Conference – Global Mission	1926			1		1
TWR				2		
TWR Canada	2013			1		
Singapore						
Advancing Native Missions	2008	1				
Assemblies of God World Missions	1926	0		6		
Awana Clubs International					1	
Baptist Bible Fellowship International – World Mission Service Center	1970			6		
Campus Crusade for Christ (Cru in the US)		1				
Child Evangelism Fellowship Inc.				1		
Christian Broadcasting Network Inc., The	1996				3	

		Personnel from US or Canada			Other Countries	
	First Year	1–2 years	2–4 years	4+ years	Citizen	Not Citizen
Christian Churches / Churches of Christ				4		
Church of God (Cleveland TN) World Missions	1989			2		2
Church of the Nazarene Inc.				5		2
Converge				2		
CRM					2	6
EPC World Outreach				1		
Ethnos360			2			
Evangelical Missionary Church of Canada	2011			2		
Faith Christian Fellowship Intl.					1	
Global Fellowship Inc.				1		
Global Missions (United Pentecostal Church Intl.)	1981		2			
Global Partners (The Wesleyan Church World Headquarters)				1		
Good News Productions International				2	2	
Habitat for Humanity International			15	3	9	9
International Pentecostal Holiness Church	1987			6		
InterVarsity Christian Fellowship/USA			1			
Mission to the World (PCA) Inc.				2		
Missionary Ventures Intl.				1		
Network of International Christian Schools	1993	15	15	20	10	
OMF International				8		
OMF International – Canada	1951			4		4
On The Go Ministries/Keith Cook Team	1966			1		
Operation Mobilization					15	
Our Daily Bread				1		
Precept Ministries International	1988				4	
Seventh-day Adventists – General Conference – Global Mission	1904			2		5
Source of Light Ministries Intl. Inc.					1	
The Salvation Army USA National Headquarters	1935		2			
Things to Come Mission	2016					2
TWR				4		
Walk Thru the Bible Ministries Inc.	1998				7	
WEC International Canada	1980			2		2
WorldVenture				3		
Wycliffe Bible Translators USA				10		
Slovakia						
ABWE International				4		
Assemblies of God World Missions	1960	1		4		
Awana Clubs International					1	
Baptist Bible Fellowship International – World Mission Service Center	1998			2		
Baptist Mid-Missions	1949			2		

	First Year	Personnel from US or Canada			Other Countries	
		1–2 years	2–4 years	4+ years	Citizen	Not Citizen
Campus Crusade for Christ (Cru in the US)				3		
Child Evangelism Fellowship Inc.				1		
Cooperative Baptist Fellowship – Global Missions	1996			2		
Crossworld	1993			2		
East European Missions Network		1			3	1
Entrust	1979			2	1	
Global Missions (United Pentecostal Church Intl.)	1930		2			2
Global Outreach International	2000			1		
Go Ye Fellowship	2002			2		2
IN Network dba International Needs USA	1993				5	
Josiah Venture	1997		1	9	14	
Life Impact Inc.	2010			1		1
Mission to the World (PCA) Inc.		3	2	11		
Navigators of Canada, The	1975			2		
New Hope International	1971				3	
On The Go Ministries/Keith Cook Team	1991		5	2		
Precept Ministries International	1991				1	
ReachGlobal				2		
The Navigators				2		
The Pentecostal Assemblies of Canada				2		
The Word for the World (TWFTW)	2003			2		
TWR				2		
Youth for Christ/USA				1		
Slovenia						
Assemblies of God World Missions	1933			2		
Avant Ministries	2009			4		
Avant Ministries Canada	2009			1		
Campus Crusade for Christ (Cru in the US)		8		9		
Child Evangelism Fellowship Inc.				1		
European Christian Mission Intl. – USA				7		
International Messengers				7		7
Josiah Venture	2001		3	16	8	
Macedonia World Baptist Missions Inc.	2013			2		
PIC International (Partners in Christ International)		1				
SEND International Inc.	1996			7		6
United World Mission Inc.				4	1	3
WorldVenture				2		
Solomon Islands						
Evangelism Explosion III International Inc.	2009				25	
Global Missions (United Pentecostal Church Intl.)	1991		2			
Seventh-day Adventists – General Conference – Global Mission	1914					4
Wycliffe Bible Translators USA				4		

	Personnel from US or Canada				Other Countries	
	First Year	1–2 years	2–4 years	4+ years	Citizen	Not Citizen
Somalia						
Emmanuel Intl. Canada				1		
Global Gates	2015			2		
South Africa						
Advent Christian World Outreach	1998				1	
African Enterprise	1962				48	
American Baptist International Ministries				2		
Assemblies of God World Missions	1917	17		30		
Awana Clubs International					1	
Baptist Bible Fellowship International – World Mission Service Center	1980			10		
Baptist International Missions Inc.				14		
Baptist International Outreach	1988			6	2	4
Baptist Mid-Missions	2010			2		2
BCM International	2002				7	
BethanyKids	2013				2	
Biblical Ministries Worldwide				24	4	20
Child Evangelism Fellowship Inc.				3		
Chosen People Ministries Inc.	2011				1	
Christian Aid Mission	1954				15	
Christian Broadcasting Network Inc., The	1997				3	
Christian Church (Disciples of Christ) – Global Ministries			4			
Christian Churches / Churches of Christ			3	32	4	
Christian Reformed World Missions	2013			2		
Christian Veterinary Mission	2008	1				
Church of God (Cleveland TN) World Missions	1951			1		1
Church of the Nazarene Inc.	1919			14	3	8
CityTeam Ministries – New Generations International				2		
Commission to Every Nation	2002	1		1		2
Cooperative Baptist Fellowship – Global Missions	1999			4		
CRM				4	6	1
Crossworld	1979			2	1	
Davar Partners International					17	
Development Associates Intl. (DAI)					1	
Eastern Mennonite Missions	2011	2				
Entrust	2004				2	1
Evangelical Missionary Church of Canada	2009			3		
Evangelism Explosion III International Inc.	2009				10	
Faith Christian Fellowship Intl.					1	
Global Missions (United Pentecostal Church Intl.)	1948	8				2
Global Partners (The Wesleyan Church World Headquarters)				2		
Global Recordings Network					1	2
Globe International	2000	1		2		

	First Year	Personnel from US or Canada			Other Countries	
		1–2 years	2–4 years	4+ years	Citizen	Not Citizen
Go to Nations	1995			2		
Gospel Fellowship Association	1988			2		
Greater Grace World Outreach	2001				4	
Habitat for Humanity International	1987	20		4	14	10
Helps Ministries	2014			5		
Hope for the Hungry	1980				2	
HOPE International Development Agency	1983				2	
IBMGlobal	2012		2			
IFCA World Missions	1989			2		
In Touch Mission International	1977			2	6	
Independent Faith Mission Inc.				12		
International Christian Ministries	2002				4	
International Messengers			1		1	
International Pentecostal Holiness Church	1911			19		
Into All The World	2003			4		
Jews for Jesus	1989				3	
Launch Out Ministries International	2005				3	1
LeaderTreks	2000		1			
Life Impact Inc.	2011			2	1	1
Lott Carey Baptist Foreign Mission Convention	1995				75	
Macedonia World Baptist Missions Inc.	2003			6		
Mailbox Club International Inc., The					3	
MB Mission	2004					2
MB Mission Canada	2004					2
Mennonite Mission Network	1982			4		
Mission to the World (PCA) Inc.	1997		2	24		
Missionary Ventures Intl.				1		
National Baptist Convention USA Inc. – Foreign Mission Board	1894	1			1	
On The Go Ministries/Keith Cook Team	1844	1		1	1	
One Challenge	1987			8		
One Mission Society						1
Open Door Baptist Missions	2003			6		
Operation Mobilization		24			121	65
Paraclete Mission Group Inc.						
Paradigm Shift	2009	6				
Power to Change Ministries	1988			2		
Precept Ministries International	1990				17	
Reach Beyond						2
Servant Partners	2008			3		
Seventh-day Adventists – General Conference – Global Mission	1887			2		15
SIM Canada				7		
SIM USA		6		11		
Source of Light Ministries Intl. Inc.					1	
South African Christian Mission Inc.	1959			1		

	First Year	Personnel from US or Canada			Other Countries	
		1–2 years	2–4 years	4+ years	Citizen	Not Citizen
TEAM (The Evangelical Alliance Mission)	1892			19		
Teen Missions International Inc.	1985	2			2	1
The Pentecostal Assemblies of Canada				9	2	
The Salvation Army USA National Headquarters	1883	4				
The Word for the World (TWFTW)	1981				6	
Things to Come Mission	1989				4	2
TMS Global	2011			2		
TWR		2		15		
United Brethren in Christ	2014			1		
United World Mission Inc.				16		16
Walk Thru the Bible Ministries Inc.	1999				44	
WEC International Canada	1955			1		4
White Fields					6	
Word & Deed	2006				1	
Word & Deed Ministries Canada	2006				1	
Word of Life Fellowship Inc.	1998	3		11	2	
World Mission Prayer League	2015				2	
World Partners USA				1		
Wycliffe Bible Translators USA				4		
Youth for Christ/USA	1977			5		
Zion Evangelical Ministries of Africa (ZEMA)	1907		3	8	10	2
South America						
ABWE International				136		
Assemblies of God World Missions		15		94		
Campus Crusade for Christ (Cru in the US)				6		
Christian Medical & Dental Associations				1		
Church of God (Cleveland TN) World Missions				2		
Church of God Ministries (Anderson) – Global Strategy				2		
Communitas International	2005			3	3	1
Evangelical Christian Church in Canada, The	1978			1	1	
Evangelism Explosion III International Inc.	1996				1	
Foursquare Missions International				2		
Global Missions of Open Bible Churches				2		
Global Training Network					2	
Great Cities Missions				1		
Harvest Foundation					12	
Impact International Inc.				4		
Josue Yrion World Evangelism & Missions Inc.	2003				6	
Luis Palau Evangelistic Association					13	
Morelli Ministries Intl. Inc.				1		
One Challenge				2		
Operation Mobilization					7	2

	First Year	Personnel from US or Canada			Other Countries	
		1–2 years	2–4 years	4+ years	Citizen	Not Citizen
Pioneers USA				37	1	
Reach Beyond				4		
reSource Leadership International	2013					1
The Pentecostal Assemblies of Canada		1				
The Voice of the Martyrs				1		
WEC International					2	
Word of Life Fellowship Inc.				1	5	
Wycliffe Associates	1967			3		
South Asia						
ABWE International				40		
Accelerating International Mission Strategies (AIMS)			5	10		
Apostolic Church of Pentecost of Canada (Global Harvest Missions)	2014	3		3		
Assemblies of God World Missions		51		85		
Awana Clubs International					1	
Baptist Bible Fellowship International – World Mission Service Center				50		
Beautiful Feet	2005				1	
Campus Crusade for Christ (Cru in the US)		12		4		
Christar	1930	1	7	12		
Christar Canada				6		
Christian Medical & Dental Associations				1		
CRM				1		
East-West Ministries International	1990	2				
Evangelistic Faith Mission Inc.	2013		2			
Foursquare Missions International				2		
Global Fellowship Inc.				7		
Global Training Network				2		
Harvest Bridge	2014	1	1			
iHope International	2011				2	
InterVarsity Christian Fellowship/USA			2			
Josue Yrion World Evangelism & Missions Inc.	1991				30	
Mission Catalyst Intl. Inc.		1				
One Challenge					3	
Operation Mobilization				48	40	200
Pioneers USA				101	4	1
ReachAcross	1957		2	4	6	4
Servant Partners	2004			2		
Team Expansion Inc.	2010			5	2	
The Pentecostal Assemblies of Canada		2			2	
The Voice of the Martyrs				2	2	
Village Ministries International	1997			27	27	

	First Year	Personnel from US or Canada			Other Countries	
		1–2 years	2–4 years	4+ years	Citizen	Not Citizen
visionSynergy	2003			1		
WEC International		2		7		
WEC International Canada			1	4	1	
World Mission Prayer League	1990			2		
World Witness				2		
Wycliffe Associates	1985	2	2		27	
South Sudan						
Africa Inland Mission Canada Intl.				2		2
Baptist Bible Fellowship International – World Mission Service Center	2012			2		
Baptist International Missions Inc.				2		
Campus Crusade for Christ (Cru in the US)				11		
East African Ministries	2009			1	61	22
Empowering Lives International	2005			1		
Four Corners Ministries	2016			1		
IBMGlobal	2014		2			
International Gospel Outreach	2003			3		3
Prayer Baptist Missions International Inc.				1		
Reformed Church in America – General Synod Council – Global Mission						2
RP Global Missions	2006		3	4		1
Serve Globally – The Evangelical Covenant Church				1		
SIM USA				23		
TMS Global	2012			3		
With Open Eyes	2010				31	
World Gospel Mission	2006			2		
World Mission Prayer League	2009		2			
Southeast Asia						
Accelerating International Mission Strategies (AIMS)			2			
American Baptist International Ministries				4		
Apostolic Church of Pentecost of Canada (Global Harvest Missions)	1998			1		
Assemblies of God World Missions		29		60		
Awana Clubs International				1	1	
Baptist International Missions Inc.				12		
Beautiful Feet	2001			8		
Bethany Gateways				8	2	
CAMA Services	1990		1	4		
Campus Crusade for Christ (Cru in the US)				3		
Christar	1975			25		
Christar Canada				2		
Christian Medical & Dental Associations				1		
Christian Veterinary Mission	2015	2				
Church of the Nazarene Inc.				2		

	First Year	Personnel from US or Canada			Other Countries	
		1–2 years	2–4 years	4+ years	Citizen	Not Citizen
CMF International	1979	2		9	2	9
Crossworld				4		
Disciple Makers				2	300	
Earth Mission Inc.				2		
Evangelism Explosion III International Inc.	1996			1		
Firefall International Inc.	2006	3	2	2		
Foursquare Missions International				2		
Harvest Foundation					7	
iHope International	2010			2		
Josue Yrion World Evangelism & Missions Inc.	2007				3	
MB Mission					5	
MB Mission Canada					5	
Mission Catalyst Intl. Inc.		1				
OMF International			7	31		
OMF International – Canada	1866			36	2	34
One Challenge				32		
Operation Mobilization		4			9	52
Outreach to Asia Nationals	1986		1		28	3
Pioneers USA				168	5	
Reach Beyond				10		1
ReachAcross	2014	1			1	
Reliant Mission Inc.	2013		2			
SIM USA				2		
TEAM (The Evangelical Alliance Mission)				27		
Team Expansion Inc.	1996			16		
The Pentecostal Assemblies of Canada		5		6		
The Voice of the Martyrs				1	2	
Things to Come Mission	2011					6
To Every Tribe	2014			2		
United World Mission Inc.	2005			20	2	18
Village Ministries International	2009			4	3	1
WEC International				2		
Wycliffe Associates	1997	9	8	4	21	
Spain						
ABWE International				25		
Action International Ministries	2003			3		3
AMG International	1989			1	2	4
Assemblies of God World Missions	1932	37		50		
Avant Ministries	1966			29		
Avant Ministries Canada	1966			8		
Baptist Bible Fellowship International – World Mission Service Center	1970			14		
Baptist International Missions Inc.				8		
Baptist Mid-Missions	1979			13	2	

	Personnel from US or Canada				Other Countries	
	First Year	1–2 years	2–4 years	4+ years	Citizen	Not Citizen
BCM International	1947				4	
BCM International (Canada) Inc.	1949					1
Biblical Ministries Worldwide				6		6
Brethren in Christ World Missions (BICWM)	1988			3		
Cadence International	1974		2			
CAMA Services	2016			2		
Camino Global	1971			17	5	4
Campus Crusade for Christ (Cru in the US)				12		
Christ for the City International	1994			2		
Christian and Missionary Alliance in Canada, The				1		
Christian Churches / Churches of Christ				1		
Christian Fellowship Union Inc.	1999			2		
Church of God (Cleveland TN) World Missions	1937			4		9
Church of the Nazarene Inc.	1981			2		2
CMF International	2004	5		5	2	8
Commission to Every Nation	2006			2	2	
Converge				4		
Cooperative Baptist Fellowship – Global Missions	2006		2			
CRM				15		1
Crossover Communications International	2011					2
Crossworld	1985			6		
Entrust	2016			1		
EPC World Outreach				1		
Equip Inc & Equip International	2004			2		
European Christian Mission Intl. – USA				53		
Evangelical Congregational Church – Global Ministries Commission				4		
Evangelical Methodist Church Inc. – Board of Missions	2004					1
Evangelical Missionary Church of Canada	2009			1		
Evangelism Explosion III International Inc.	2010				2	
Far East Broadcasting Associates of Canada (FEB Canada)	1980			2		
Fellowship of Evangelical Churches – International Ministries	2008			2		
Foursquare Missions International	1975			3		
Free Methodist World Missions	2005			5		
Free Will Baptist International Missions	1971			11	2	
Global Missions (United Pentecostal Church Intl.)			6			8
Global Missions of Open Bible Churches	1969				1	
Global Outreach Mission Inc.		1				
Global Recordings Network						4
Gospel Fellowship Association	1978			4		
Greater Europe Mission			3	5		
Helps Ministries	2015			2		
International Partnership Ministries Inc.	2000				2	
International Pentecostal Holiness Church	1988			4		

	First Year	Personnel from US or Canada			Other Countries	
		1–2 years	2–4 years	4+ years	Citizen	Not Citizen
International Teams U.S.A.		2	1	6		1
Macedonia World Baptist Missions Inc.	2006			3		1
Master's Resourcing Commission				1		
Mennonite Mission Network	1972			3	1	
Mission to the World (PCA) Inc.	1983		5	8		
One Challenge	1995				1	2
One Mission Society	1972			11		3
Open Door Baptist Missions	1999			4	2	
Operation Mobilization		1			2	4
Our Daily Bread				1		
Palm Missionary Ministries Inc.	2001					2
Proclaim! International Inc.	2004			2		
ReachGlobal				2		
Reliant Mission Inc.	2008			1		
Resourcing Christian Education International	2007				3	4
Ripe for Harvest Inc.				1		
Rosedale Mennonite Missions	2008			4		
Salvation Army – Canada and Bermuda Territory, The	1998			2		
SEND International Inc.	1987			15		13
SEND International of Canada			1	2		
Serge				6		
Seventh-day Adventists – General Conference – Global Mission	1903	1				
TEAM (The Evangelical Alliance Mission)	1952		4	32		
Team Expansion Inc.	2007			8		3
The Brethren Church Inc.	2005				1	
The Navigators				6		
The Pentecostal Assemblies of Canada				3		
The Salvation Army USA National Headquarters	1971		4			
TMS Global	2013			2		
United World Mission Inc.				6	1	5
WEC International				12		
WEC International Canada	1968			3		3
Word of Life Fellowship Inc.	1977			2	2	9
World Indigenous Missions	1993			6		
World Link Ministries	1985			6	30	
World Partners USA				1		
World Team Canada				2		
World Team US				11		
World Witness				10		
WorldVenture				21		
Wycliffe Bible Translators USA				10		
Youth for Christ/USA	1982			4		

| | First Year | Personnel from US or Canada | | | Other Countries | |
		1–2 years	2–4 years	4+ years	Citizen	Not Citizen
Sri Lanka						
Awana Clubs International					1	
Back to the Bible	1955				34	
BCM International	1994				10	
Bethany Gateways		1				
BILD International					1	
Christian Aid Mission					40	
Church of God Ministries (Anderson) – Global Strategy	1990	2				
CMF International	2014		2		1	1
Faith Christian Fellowship Intl.					1	
Global Missions (United Pentecostal Church Intl.)	1949		2			3
Globe International	1984			2		
Habitat for Humanity International	1994		1			1
Hope for the Hungry	1982				3	
Medical Teams International	2005	2	2			
Surfing the Nations	1999				1	
The Free Methodist Church in Canada	2004				20	
The Pentecostal Assemblies of Canada				2		
Walk Thru the Bible Ministries Inc.	1999				2	
Sub-Saharan Africa						
Accelerating International Mission Strategies (AIMS)				2		
Africa Inland Mission				408		189
African Leadership Development	1997				5	
Anglican Frontier Missions					2	
Assemblies of God World Missions		22		56		
Baptist Bible Fellowship International – World Mission Service Center	1980			10		
Baptist International Missions Inc.				3		
BASIC Ministries Inc.	1992				50	
Beautiful Feet	2003			5	1	
CAMA Services	2003			2		
Campus Crusade for Christ (Cru in the US)				8		
Christian Medical & Dental Associations				1		
East-West Ministries International		2				
Ethnos360			90			
Evangelism Explosion III International Inc.	1996			1		
Every Child Ministries Inc.	1985			7		
Foursquare Missions International				2		
Global Training Network				2		
Harvest Foundation					19	
iHope International	2010			2		
Josue Yrion World Evangelism & Missions Inc.	2001			4		
MB Mission					1	

	First Year	Personnel from US or Canada			Other Countries	
		1–2 years	2–4 years	4+ years	Citizen	Not Citizen
MB Mission Canada					1	
Mobile Member Care Team	2000		4	1		1
One Challenge				4		2
Pioneers USA				41	3	
Ripe for Harvest Inc.				1		
TEAM (The Evangelical Alliance Mission)				23		4
Team Expansion Inc.	2005			3		2
The Pentecostal Assemblies of Canada		3		7		
The Voice of the Martyrs				2	8	
Village Ministries International	1990			54	54	
Word of Life Fellowship Inc.				3	2	1
Wycliffe Associates	1967		30			
Sudan						
Catalyst Missions		2			1	
Christian Aid Mission	2003				15	
Evangelical Missionary Church of Canada	2007			2		
Global Missions (United Pentecostal Church Intl.)	2004		2			
Global Outreach International	2004			1		
In Touch Mission International	1998				2	
Intercede International					2	
Mission ONE Inc.					42	
Samaritan's Purse	1997	25	14	2		
Seventh-day Adventists – General Conference – Global Mission	1978			6		2
SIM Canada				1		
Walk Thru the Bible Ministries Inc.	2001				1	
With Open Eyes	2010				12	
World Relief	1999	3			90	3
Suriname						
BCM International	1975			2	1	
Beautiful Feet	2011			2		
Child Evangelism Fellowship Inc.				1		
Commission to Every Nation	2006	1		2	2	1
Evangelism Explosion III International Inc.	2010				1	
Global Missions (United Pentecostal Church Intl.)	2003		2			2
Global Missions of Open Bible Churches	2005				1	
Independent Faith Mission Inc.				7		
Orthodox Presbyterian Church – Committee on Foreign Missions	1987			2		
World Team US				3		
Swaziland						
Adventures in Missions	2004	1		6		
Assemblies of God World Missions	1984	2		4		
BCM International	1972				2	

	First Year	Personnel from US or Canada			Other Countries	
		1–2 years	2–4 years	4+ years	Citizen	Not Citizen
Children's HopeChest	2006				6	2
Evangelism Explosion III International Inc.	2011				4	
Global Missions (United Pentecostal Church Intl.)	1982		2			
Global Partners (The Wesleyan Church World Headquarters)				3		
Launch Out Ministries International	2005				1	2
Missionary Ventures Canada					2	
National Baptist Convention USA Inc. – Foreign Mission Board	1971	1			27	
TWR				2		
TWR Canada	1997			1		
Walk Thru the Bible Ministries Inc.	2000				2	
Zion Evangelical Ministries of Africa (ZEMA)	2006			4		2
Sweden						
Assemblies of God World Missions	1988			2		
Biblical Ministries Worldwide				2		2
Campus Crusade for Christ (Cru in the US)		5		10		
Commission to Every Nation	2007		2			1
Converge				4		
Cross-Cultural Ministries – Churches of God General Conference	2005			1		
Crossworld	1984			2		
European Christian Mission Intl. – USA				4		
Fellowship International Mission	1977			2		
Global Missions (United Pentecostal Church Intl.)						2
Greater Europe Mission			1	4		
Mission to the World (PCA) Inc.	1999			2		
OM Canada			1			
Operation Mobilization		4			25	14
Reliant Mission Inc.	2012			1		
Serve Globally – The Evangelical Covenant Church			2	2		
United World Mission Inc.				2		2
Wycliffe Bible Translators USA				2		
Switzerland						
Assemblies of God World Missions	1967	2		2		
Child Evangelism Fellowship Inc.				6		
Church of the Nazarene Inc.	1978			5		3
Global Missions (United Pentecostal Church Intl.)			2			2
Global Outreach Mission Inc.				1		
Greater Europe Mission				1		
InterVarsity Christian Fellowship/USA		1				
Jews for Jesus	2010				2	
Living Word Missions				2	1	1

	First Year	Personnel from US or Canada			Other Countries	
		1–2 years	2–4 years	4+ years	Citizen	Not Citizen
OM Canada		2				
Operation Mobilization					33	3
Reformed Baptist Mission Services					2	
Seventh-day Adventists – General Conference – Global Mission	1870					2
The Pentecostal Assemblies of Canada				2		
The Salvation Army USA National Headquarters	1882		2			
Wycliffe Bible Translators USA				8		
Youth for Christ/USA				7		
Syria						
Christian Aid Mission					14	
Taiwan (China)						
ABWE International				2		
Apostolic Church of Pentecost of Canada (Global Harvest Missions)	1963			1		
Assemblies of God World Missions	1948	1		8		
Awana Clubs International					1	
Baptist Bible Fellowship International – World Mission Service Center	1946			10		
Baptist International Missions Inc.				2		
Baptist Mid-Missions	1972			4		
Beautiful Feet	1997			1		
Christian and Missionary Alliance in Canada, The				6		
Christian Churches / Churches of Christ			2	21		
EPC World Outreach				1		
Foursquare Missions International	1988			2		
Free Methodist World Missions	1952			5		
Global Missions (United Pentecostal Church Intl.)			4			
Globe International	2000			2		
Hope for the Hungry	2003			2		
International Partnership Ministries Inc.	2002			1	1	
International Teams U.S.A.						7
Liberty Corner Mission	1952			2		3
Lutheran Brethren International Mission	1951			4		
Lutheran Church Missouri Synod – World Mission	1951			9		
Macedonia World Baptist Missions Inc.	1982			4		
Mission to the World (PCA) Inc.	1977	1		12		
OMF International			1	14		
OMF International – Canada	1951			3		3
One Challenge	1951			2	1	
One Mission Society	1950			5		2
Open Door Baptist Missions	2005			1		1
Operation Mobilization					7	2
Precept Ministries International	1990			1	2	

	First Year	Personnel from US or Canada			Other Countries	
		1–2 years	2–4 years	4+ years	Citizen	Not Citizen
Reformed Church in America – General Synod Council – Global Mission				2		
SEND International Inc.	1965			7		8
SEND International of Canada				1		
Serve Globally – The Evangelical Covenant Church				2		
Seventh-day Adventists – General Conference – Global Mission	1902	2	1	8		1
Taiwan Harvest 119	2016			2	1	
TEAM (The Evangelical Alliance Mission)	1951			9		
Team Expansion Inc.	1997			11	1	
The Presbyterian Church in Canada	1872	1				
WEC International				1		
Wisconsin Evangelical Lutheran Synod – Board for World Missions				1		
Word of Life Fellowship Inc.	2006	3		1		3
World Partners USA				1		
World Team US				4		
WorldVenture				15		
Tajikistan						
Avant Ministries	2007			2		
Biblical Ministries Worldwide				2		2
Eastern Mennonite Missions	2013					
Evangelism Explosion III International Inc.	2012				1	
Greater Grace World Outreach	2005				1	
Interserve USA	1993			3		
ISOH/IMPACT	1996			2		
MEDA – Mennonite Economic Development Associates	2004				7	1
Mission Eurasia					4	
People International USA				2		
Pioneers Canada				2		
Precept Ministries International					1	
ReachGlobal				3		
Scriptures In Use	2012			2	100	
Shelter for Life Intl. Inc.					1	
Tanzania						
A.C.T. International	2006					2
ACM International	2003			2		
Advent Christian World Outreach	2010				1	
Africa Inland Mission Canada Intl.				12		12
African Enterprise	1970				16	
Assemblies of God World Missions	1940	13		17		
Avant Ministries	2012			4		
Awana Clubs International					3	
Baptist Bible Fellowship International – World Mission Service Center	1988			8		

	First Year	Personnel from US or Canada			Other Countries	
		1–2 years	2–4 years	4+ years	Citizen	Not Citizen
Baptist International Missions Inc.				7		
Baptist International Outreach	2010			1	1	
Campus Crusade for Christ (Cru in the US)		1				
Care of Creation Inc.						2
Christian Aid Mission	1990				80	
Christian Churches / Churches of Christ				21		
Christian Discipleship International	2006				1	
Christian Veterinary Mission	2014	1				
Church of God Ministries (Anderson) – Global Strategy	1959	2				
CMF International	1984	2	4	6		12
Commission to Every Nation	2009		2			2
Commission To Every Nation-Canada	2010	1	1	2		
Compassion International Inc.	1999				65	
Eastern Mennonite Missions	2012			4		
ECHO	2011	2		1	8	
Elim Fellowship	1983			8		
Emmanuel Intl. Canada				1		
Empowering Lives International	1988		1		3	
Evangelism Explosion III International Inc.	2011				8	
FaithLife Ministries Inc.	2012				1	
Global Missions (United Pentecostal Church Intl.)	1980		4			1
Go to Nations	2005			6		
Go Ye Fellowship	2004			2	1	1
Grace Ministries International	1962			14		
Greater Grace World Outreach	1999				2	
Habitat for Humanity International	1986		3			3
Indopartners Agency	2005			5		
International Christian Ministries	1994	2			2	4
International Gospel Outreach	1999	4		1		5
International Pentecostal Holiness Church	1996			4		
Into All The World	2005			2		
Launch Out Ministries International	2006				5	
Lifesong for Orphans	1997				36	
MEDA – Mennonite Economic Development Associates	1991				68	2
Mission ONE Inc.					2	
Moravian Church in North America – Board of World Mission	2003					2
On The Go Ministries/Keith Cook Team	1924	1	2	19		
Operation Mobilization		0			7	5
Pioneer Bible Translators				6		
ReachGlobal		5		21		
Reformed Church in America – General Synod Council – Global Mission				2		
Seventh-day Adventists – General Conference – Global Mission	1903			4		7

	First Year	Personnel from US or Canada			Other Countries	
		1–2 years	2–4 years	4+ years	Citizen	Not Citizen
SIM USA				2		
Team Expansion Inc.	1998			2		4
Teen Missions International Inc.	2000			1	2	
The Pentecostal Assemblies of Canada				3		2
The Salvation Army USA National Headquarters	1933		2			
The Word for the World (TWFTW)	2004				26	2
TMS Global	1999			1		
United World Mission Inc.				2		2
Walk Thru the Bible Ministries Inc.	2000				2	
World Outreach International – US	1986			2		
WorldVenture				2		
Worldwide Discipleship Assoc.				1		
Wycliffe Bible Translators of Canada Inc.				5		
Wycliffe Bible Translators USA				20		
Thailand						
ABWE International		1		32		
Advent Christian World Outreach	2009				1	
American Baptist International Ministries				14		1
AMG International	1976				76	13
Assemblies of God World Missions	1968	10		43		
Avant Ministries	2015			1		3
Avant Ministries Canada	2015			4		
Baptist Bible Fellowship International – World Mission Service Center	1983			6		
Baptist International Missions Inc.				14		
Baptist Mid-Missions	1998			3	1	
Baptist Missionary Association of America (BMAA)				5	1	
Barnabas International				2		
Bethany Gateways		13	2	6		1
Cadence International	1967			4		
Campus Crusade for Christ (Cru in the US)		1		11		
Christian Aid Mission					123	
Christian and Missionary Alliance in Canada, The				4		
Christian Broadcasting Network Inc., The	1999	1		1	47	3
Christian Church (Disciples of Christ) – Global Ministries			1			
Christian Churches / Churches of Christ		2		41	12	
Christian Ministries International (CMI)				1		
Christian Veterinary Mission	1999			3		
Church of God Ministries (Anderson) – Global Strategy	1975			2		
Church of the Nazarene Inc.	1989			7		4
CLC Ministries International	1958			2		
CMF International	1994		4	4	2	6
Commission to Every Nation	2001			4		4

	First Year	Personnel from US or Canada			Other Countries	
		1–2 years	2–4 years	4+ years	Citizen	Not Citizen
Compassio					34	
Compassion International Inc.	1970	1			58	
Converge				5		
Crossworld	2013	2		2		
Eastern Mennonite Missions	2010			3		
ECHO	2009	1		3	8	
Elim Fellowship	2004			2		
Encompass World Partners	2005			6		
Entrust	2015			2		
EPC World Outreach				3		
Ethnos360				25		
Evangelical Congregational Church – Global Ministries Commission				3		
Evangelical Free Church of Canada Mission				2		
Evangelical Missionary Church of Canada	2013			4		
Evangelism Explosion III International Inc.	2015				2	
FH Canada	1998		2	2		
Food for the Hungry Inc.	2004		2	2		
Foursquare Missions International	1987			13		
Free Methodist World Missions	2000	2		6		
Global Gates	2016			2		
Global Missions (United Pentecostal Church Intl.)	1968		6			
Global Missions of Open Bible Churches	2017		2			
Global Outreach Mission Inc.				2		
Global Partners (The Wesleyan Church World Headquarters)				2		
Global Recordings Network				5	5	2
Globe International	1992			6		
Go to Nations	1988			3		2
Go Ye Fellowship	2013			4	1	3
Good News Productions International	1998			4		2
Greater Grace World Outreach	1989				5	
Habitat for Humanity International	1998		21	5	14	12
Helps Ministries	2006			7	4	
IBMGlobal	2011			2		2
Intercede International						2
International Justice Mission	2000				9	
International Pentecostal Holiness Church	1988			4		
International Teams U.S.A.						9
Kids for Christ International	2002				1	
Launch Out Ministries International	2008	2				
Living Word Missions				5	1	4
Macedonia World Baptist Missions Inc.	2006			2		
MB Mission	1992			10	67	15
MB Mission Canada	1992			11	67	14
Mennonite Mission Network	1967					2

		Personnel from US or Canada			Other Countries	
	First Year	1–2 years	2–4 years	4+ years	Citizen	Not Citizen
Mission ONE Inc.					47	
Mission to the World (PCA) Inc.	2000		2	8		
Missionary Ventures Intl.				2		
Navigators of Canada, The	2007			2		
New Mission Systems International	2008	2		6	2	
OMF International			2	30		
OMF International – Canada	1951			18	1	17
On The Go Ministries/Keith Cook Team	1975					2
Operation Mobilization		2			1	1
Our Daily Bread				1		
Pioneers Canada				2		
Presbyterian Mission International (PMI)				1		
Reach A Village					2	
ReachGlobal				3		
Reformed Church in America – General Synod Council – Global Mission						1
Reliant Mission Inc.	2007	1		1		
Ripe for Harvest Inc.				1		
Rosedale Mennonite Missions	2004			5		
SEND International Inc.	2010			4		6
SEND International of Canada				4		
Servant Partners	2003			3		
Serve Globally – The Evangelical Covenant Church				10		
Seventh-day Adventists – General Conference – Global Mission	1919	9	4	20	1	19
SIM USA		4		9		
The Free Methodist Church in Canada	1999			1		
The Navigators				4		
The Pentecostal Assemblies of Canada		2		18		
The Salvation Army USA National Headquarters			2			
Things to Come Mission	2008			2		2
TMS Global	2010			6		
United Brethren in Christ	1993	2				5
Virginia Mennonite Missions	2014			2		2
WEC International				5		
WEC International Canada	1947	1			1	
Wisconsin Evangelical Lutheran Synod – Board for World Missions				2		
Word of Life Fellowship Inc.	2008			2		
World Concern	1980		2	4	15	
World Indigenous Missions	1999			4		4
World Partners USA				1		
WorldVenture				7		
Wycliffe Bible Translators USA				93		

	First Year	Personnel from US or Canada			Other Countries	
		1–2 years	2–4 years	4+ years	Citizen	Not Citizen
Youth for Christ/USA				2		
Timor Leste						
Christian Church (Disciples of Christ) – Global Ministries			3			
Togo						
ABWE Canada (Across Borders for World Evangelism)				4		
Assemblies of God World Missions	1937	3		11		
Baptist International Missions Inc.				3		
Christian Aid Mission	1995				230	
Church of the Nazarene Inc.	1998					2
Compassion International Inc.	2008				11	
Crossworld Canada	2015				2	
Development Associates Intl. (DAI)					1	
Evangelism Explosion III International Inc.	2010				3	
FaithLife Ministries Inc.	2014				1	
Fellowship International Mission	2011	1		1		
Global Missions (United Pentecostal Church Intl.)	1972		2			
Global Recordings Network					2	
Greater Grace World Outreach	1990				2	
Harvest Foundation					1	
International Partnership Ministries Inc.	1994				16	
Lutheran Church Missouri Synod – World Mission	1980			2		
Mission ONE Inc.					1	
Seventh-day Adventists – General Conference – Global Mission	1964			4		2
SIM USA				2		
Source of Light Ministries Intl. Inc.					1	
TMS Global	2005			2		
WEC International				2		
Wycliffe Bible Translators of Canada Inc.				1		
Wycliffe Bible Translators USA				7		
Tonga						
Assemblies of God World Missions	1975	2		2		
Evangelism Explosion III International Inc.	2010				5	
Global Missions (United Pentecostal Church Intl.)			2			1
Trinidad and Tobago						
ABWE Canada (Across Borders for World Evangelism)	2002			2		
ABWE International				6		
Apostolic Church of Pentecost of Canada (Global Harvest Missions)	1977			1		
Back to the Bible	1996				1	
Baptist International Missions Inc.				9		
Church of the Nazarene Inc.	1926				1	1
Commission to Every Nation	2008			4		4

	First Year	Personnel from US or Canada			Other Countries	
		1–2 years	2–4 years	4+ years	Citizen	Not Citizen
Global Missions (United Pentecostal Church Intl.)			2			
Global Missions of Open Bible Churches	1954			2	1	
Mission to the World (PCA) Inc.				2		
Seventh-day Adventists – General Conference – Global Mission	1893			4		3
The Salvation Army USA National Headquarters	1901	2				
United Evangelical Churches				1		
World Team US				4		
Wycliffe Bible Translators USA				1		
Tunisia						
Macedonia World Baptist Missions Inc.	2013			2		
Ripe for Harvest Inc.				1		
Seventh-day Adventists – General Conference – Global Mission	1928					2
Turkey						
AMG International	1977				2	
Avant Ministries	2013			16		
Barnabas International			2			
Christian Church (Disciples of Christ) – Global Ministries			3			
Crossover Communications International	1971		2	6	3	8
East European Missions Network				2		
Eastern Mennonite Missions	2015		2			
Encompass World Partners	2002			2	1	1
Entrust	2005					2
Faith Christian Fellowship Intl.					1	
Frontier Ventures				2		
Global Gates	2015			2		
Global Missions (United Pentecostal Church Intl.)			4			5
IBMGlobal	2011			2		2
IN Network dba International Needs USA	2001				5	
Intercede International					2	
International Pentecostal Holiness Church	2001				6	
International Teams U.S.A.				3		1
Interserve USA	1985			15	1	
MB Mission	2010			2	1	7
MB Mission Canada	2010			6	1	3
Navigators of Canada, The	1991			2		
Network of International Christian Schools	2004	9	8	15	8	
New Mission Systems International	2008			2		
People International USA				12		
Pioneers Canada				3		
ReachGlobal		2		2		
Reformed Church in America – General Synod Council – Global Mission				4		

	First Year	Personnel from US or Canada			Other Countries	
		1–2 years	2–4 years	4+ years	Citizen	Not Citizen
SEND International Inc.	2001			3		
Seventh-day Adventists – General Conference – Global Mission	1889			2		2
The Pentecostal Assemblies of Canada				2		
TMS Global	2014			2		
Women to the World Inc.					1	
World-Wide Missions	1970			1		
Turkmenistan						
Greater Grace World Outreach	1995				6	
Mission Eurasia					2	
Turks and Caicos Islands						
Baptist International Missions Inc.				2		
Uganda						
Action International Ministries	2002			2		1
Africa Inland Mission Canada Intl.				7		7
African Children's Mission	1989			2		
African Enterprise	1972				32	
AMG International					18	
Association of Free Lutheran Congregations				4		
Awana Clubs International					1	
Baptist Bible Fellowship International – World Mission Service Center	1986			2		
Baptist International Missions Inc.				31		
Beautiful Feet	2005			2		
BethanyKids	2013				1	
BILD International				1		
Bold Ventures	2006			2	23	
Bright Hope	1996				2	
Campus Crusade for Christ (Cru in the US)				2		
Childcare Worldwide	1985				47	
Children's HopeChest	2008				4	
Christian Aid Mission	1986				60	
Christian Relief Fund, The	1995				2	
Christian Veterinary Mission	1994	2	3			
Church of God Ministries (Anderson) – Global Strategy	1983			2		
Church of the Nazarene Inc.	1988			2		
Commission to Every Nation	2004	1				1
Compassion International Inc.	1980				86	
Cooperative Baptist Fellowship – Global Missions	2007	2				
Development Associates Intl. (DAI)					1	
Emmanuel Intl. Canada				1		
Engineering Ministries International (EMI)					30	
Equip Canada	2000			2		
Equip Inc & Equip International	2000			5		
Evangelism Explosion III International Inc.	2010				12	

	First Year	Personnel from US or Canada			Other Countries	
		1–2 years	2–4 years	4+ years	Citizen	Not Citizen
Every Child Ministries Inc.	2006	0	2	1	27	0
FaithLife Ministries Inc.	2008				7	1
Fellowship International Mission	1989			1	1	1
FH Canada	2002			1		
Forefront Experience	2015	2				
Four Corners Ministries	2009			4		
Global Missions (United Pentecostal Church Intl.)	1970		2			
Global Missions of Open Bible Churches	1983			2	1	
Global Outreach International	1984			22		
Global Partners (The Wesleyan Church World Headquarters)				2		
Global Scholars			2			2
Gospel Outbound	2008			1		
Greater Grace World Outreach	1996				32	
Habitat for Humanity International	1984	1				1
Harvest International Inc.	1996		2		2	
Heart of the Bride Ministries		2				
Helps Ministries	2015				4	
Hope for the Hungry	2002			2		
In Touch Mission International				1		2
International Christian Ministries	1988				6	
International Gospel Outreach	2014	2		2	2	2
International Justice Mission	2002		1		13	
International Messengers		2		10	10	2
International Pentecostal Holiness Church	2002			2		
International Teams U.S.A.						5
Into All The World	2002			1		
Leadership Vistas International Ministries						2
Lifesong for Orphans	2007				31	
Mailbox Club International Inc., The					2	
MAP International	2006				4	
Medical Teams International	2005				2	
Mission Aviation Fellowship	1961			6		
Mission Aviation Fellowship of Canada (MAFC)				2		
Mission ONE Inc.					2	
Mission to the World (PCA) Inc.	1983		2	10		
Missionary Ventures Intl.				1		
New Hope Uganda Ministries	1989		4	29	117	37
New Mission Systems International	2009			1		
Open Door Baptist Missions	2005			2		
Orthodox Presbyterian Church – Committee on Foreign Missions	1995	2	3	8		
Prayer Baptist Missions International Inc.				3		
Samaritan's Purse	1999	4	1			
Scriptures In Use	2014	2			200	·
SEND International Inc.	2003			1		

	First Year	Personnel from US or Canada 1–2 years	2–4 years	4+ years	Other Countries Citizen	Not Citizen
SEND International of Canada			1			
Serge				11		
Servant Partners	2014			2		
Servants in Faith & Technology (SIFAT)					1	
Seventh-day Adventists – General Conference – Global Mission	1926			2		8
SIM USA				1		
Source of Light Ministries Intl. Inc.					1	
Teen Missions International Inc.	1992			1	20	
The Centers for Apologetics Research (CFAR)				4		
The God's Story Project	2008				1	
The Masters Mission	1998				2	
The Navigators				1		
The Pentecostal Assemblies of Canada				4		
Things to Come Mission	2004			4		
United World Mission Inc.				3		3
Walk Thru the Bible Ministries Inc.	1999				3	
With Open Eyes	2010				48	
Word of Life Fellowship Inc.	2002			4	54	
World Concern	1985					1
World Gospel Mission	1992	6		14		
World Mission Prayer League	2014		2			
WorldVenture				25		
Worldwide Discipleship Assoc.				1		
Wycliffe Bible Translators USA				5		
Youth for Christ/USA				1		
Ukraine						
ABWE Canada (Across Borders for World Evangelism)	1993			2		
ACSI (Association of Christian Schools International)	1992			2		
Action International Ministries – Canada	2004			1		
Amazon Outreach	2001			2	8	
Assemblies of God World Missions	1993	8		20		
Avant Ministries	2015			2		
Awana Clubs International					9	
Baptist Bible Fellowship International – World Mission Service Center	1993			2		
Baptist International Evangelistic Ministries					25	
Baptist Missionary Association of America (BMAA)				2		
BCM International	1993				19	
Beautiful Feet	2014			2		
Campus Crusade for Christ (Cru in the US)				5		
Child Evangelism Fellowship Inc.				1		
Chosen People Ministries Inc.	1990				1	
Christian Aid Ministries (CAM)	2001		6	2	10	

	First Year	Personnel from US or Canada			Other Countries	
		1–2 years	2–4 years	4+ years	Citizen	Not Citizen
Christian Aid Mission					505	
Christian Broadcasting Network Inc., The	1991		2	1	180	
Christian Churches / Churches of Christ				30	8	
Christian Outreach International				1		
Christian Reformed World Missions	1990			2		
Christian Relief Fund, The	1997				2	
Church Leadership Development International	1994				2	
Church of God (Cleveland TN) World Missions	1992			3		2
Church of the Nazarene Inc.	1992			2		
CIS- Christian Involvement In Service	2004				9	
CMF International	1994	1		5		6
Commission to Every Nation	2005			2	1	1
Converge				1		
Cooperative Baptist Fellowship – Global Missions	2002			2		
Crossworld	2000			4		
Crossworld Canada	2000			2		
East European Missions Network					4	
European Christian Mission Intl. – USA				20		
Evangelical Congregational Church – Global Ministries Commission				1		
Evangelical Free Church of Canada Mission				2	4	
Evangelical Missionary Church of Canada	1983			2		
Global Action				2		
Global Missions (United Pentecostal Church Intl.)		1				
Global Missions of Open Bible Churches	1998			1	1	
Global Outreach International	2000			5		
Global Outreach Mission Inc.				2		
Globe International	2000			2		
Go to Nations	1992			2		
Good News Productions International	1997			2	2	
Great Commission Media Ministries	1986				4	
Greater Grace World Outreach	1991				8	2
Harvest International Inc.	1996		1		4	
Holt International Children's Services Inc.					8	
HOPE International	1998				1	
IBMGlobal	2015	2				
IFCA World Missions					1	
Intercede International						2
International Messengers		1	6	12	13	6
International Pentecostal Holiness Church	1990				9	
International Teams U.S.A.				9		3
InterVarsity Christian Fellowship/USA			3			
Jews for Jesus	1991				15	
Josiah Venture	2005		4	2	7	2

	First Year	Personnel from US or Canada			Other Countries	
		1–2 years	2–4 years	4+ years	Citizen	Not Citizen
Lifesong for Orphans	2001	0	0	0	46	0
MB Mission	2003				21	
MB Mission Canada	2003				21	
Mennonite Mission Network	1996			1		
Mercy Projects					28	
Ministry to Educate and Equip Intl. (MTEE)					50	
Mission Eurasia				2	34	
Mission to the World (PCA) Inc.	1993	2	9	21		
Missionary Athletes International	2005			1		
Missionary Ventures Canada					2	
Missions Door					1	
Missions Resource Network	1952			6		
Missions to Military Inc.				5		
New Hope International	1971				15	
New Mission Systems International	2009			1		
One Challenge	2013			1	1	
One Mission Society	2003			4		4
Open Air Campaigners – Overseas Ministries (OAC-OM)	2001				1	
Operation Mobilization		3			12	7
Our Daily Bread				1		
Pioneer Bible Translators				4		
Precept Ministries International	1994				5	
Presbyterian Mission International (PMI)				1		
Reach A Village					8	
ReachGlobal		1		2		
Reliant Mission Inc.	1994			2		
Resourcing Christian Education International	2005				9	
Ripe for Harvest Inc.				1		
SEND International Inc.	1992	1		32		2
SEND International of Canada				4		
Serge				2		
Seventh-day Adventists – General Conference – Global Mission	1886	2				
Slavic Gospel Association – Canada				1		
Slavic Missionary Service Inc.				1		
TCM International Institute					1	
TEAM (The Evangelical Alliance Mission)				4		
The Centers for Apologetics Research (CFAR)					1	
The Master's Foundation	1983				9	
The Pentecostal Assemblies of Canada				7		
The Presbyterian Church in Canada	2000	1				
Titus International	1993			6	15	

	First Year	Personnel from US or Canada			Other Countries	
		1–2 years	2–4 years	4+ years	Citizen	Not Citizen
Ukrainian Children's Christian Fund				2	14	
Ukrainian Childrens Fund	1995				2	
Walk Thru the Bible Ministries Inc.	1998				26	
Word of Life Fellowship Inc.	1992				29	1
World Gospel Mission	1997			3		
World Link Ministries	2002				50	
World Reach Inc.	1991				2	
WorldVenture				10		
Youth Ministry International				2	1	
United Arab Emirates						
Awana Clubs International				1		
Interserve USA	1951			2		
On The Go Ministries/Keith Cook Team	1974		2	4	2	
Pioneers Canada				3		
Seventh-day Adventists – General Conference – Global Mission	1987			2		
United Kingdom						
A.C.T. International	2005					2
ABWE Canada (Across Borders for World Evangelism)				2		
ABWE International				13		
Adventures in Missions	2005	1	1	2		
American Baptist International Ministries						2
American Leprosy Missions						1
Assemblies of God World Missions	2010	9		16		
Avant Ministries	1963			2		
Baptist Bible Fellowship International – World Mission Service Center	1982			45		
Baptist International Missions Inc.				22		
Baptist Mid-Missions	1972			8	2	
BCM International	1947	2		2	9	
Bethany Gateways				1	1	
Biblical Ministries Worldwide				18	4	14
Cadence International	1990			2		
Campus Crusade for Christ (Cru in the US)				9		
Chosen People Ministries Inc.	1940				4	
Christian Broadcasting Network Inc., The	1997				4	1
Christian Churches / Churches of Christ			6	20		
Christians In Action Missions International	1965			2		
Church of God (Cleveland TN) World Missions	1955					2
Church of God Ministries (Anderson) – Global Strategy	1898		2			
CMF International	1989	11	11	8	2	28
Compassio					2	
CRM				15	14	
Development Associates Intl. (DAI)				1		

	First Year	Personnel from US or Canada			Other Countries	
		1–2 years	2–4 years	4+ years	Citizen	Not Citizen
Eastern Mennonite Missions	1999			2		
Emmanuel Intl. Canada				1		
Encompass World Partners	1982			8		
Engineering Ministries International (EMI)					6	
Ethnos360				10		
European Christian Mission Intl. – USA				3		
Evangelism Explosion III International Inc.	2011				1	
FAIR				2		
Far East Broadcasting Company					1	
Fellowship of Evangelical Churches – International Ministries	2000			3		
Foursquare Missions International	1981			2		
Friendship International Ministries Inc.				1		
Global Missions (United Pentecostal Church Intl.)			6			14
Global Missions of Open Bible Churches	2004				1	
Global Outreach International	2000			5		
Global Outreach Mission Inc.				9		
Global Recordings Network					2	
Globe International	1994			10		
Go Ye Fellowship	2006			2	1	1
Gospel Fellowship Association	1972	1		17		
Greater Europe Mission			8	9	3	
Habitat for Humanity International	1994	1			1	
International Messengers				2		2
International Pentecostal Holiness Church	1978			8		
International Teams U.S.A.			1	13		15
InterServe Canada			2			
InterVarsity Christian Fellowship/USA			1			
Jews for Jesus	1992				3	
Luis Palau Evangelistic Association					3	
Macedonia World Baptist Missions Inc.	2001			3	1	
Mennonite Mission Network	1952					2
Mission to the World (PCA) Inc.	1990		7	28		
Missionary Ventures Intl.				2		
New Tribes Mission of Canada				1		
One Mission Society						7
OneHope						
Open Door Baptist Missions	2006			1		
Operation Mobilization		19			110	49
Our Daily Bread				1		
Pioneers Canada		1				
Power to Change Ministries	2008	1				
Precept Ministries International	1998				11	

	First Year	Personnel from US or Canada			Other Countries	
		1–2 years	2–4 years	4+ years	Citizen	Not Citizen
Reach Beyond				4	2	
Reformed Baptist Mission Services						2
Reliant Mission Inc.	2008			1		
Salvation Army – Canada and Bermuda Territory, The	1985		4	2		
Serge				14		
Seventh-day Adventists – General Conference – Global Mission	1902			6	1	13
The Pentecostal Assemblies of Canada				3		
The Salvation Army USA National Headquarters	1865	5	5			
The Word for the World (TWFTW)	2005				1	
Things to Come Mission	1970			2		
United World Mission Inc.				6	2	4
Walk Thru the Bible Ministries Inc.	2003			4		
WEC International		1		9		
WEC International Canada	1913			3	1	
Word of Life Fellowship Inc.	1980			2	1	2
World Team US				4		
World Witness				6		
WorldVenture				3		
Worldwide Tentmakers Inc.	1989			2		2
Wycliffe Bible Translators of Canada Inc.				5		
Wycliffe Bible Translators USA				12		
Young Life		2		6		
Youth for Christ Canada		2				
Youth for Christ/USA	1983			8		
United States of America						
Africa Inland Mission Canada Intl.				2		2
Camino Global Ministries Canada	1982			1		
Commission To Every Nation-Canada	2000			5	2	
Emmanuel Intl. Canada				1		
Evangelical Missionary Church of Canada	2014			8		
InterAct Ministries of Canada	1951			1		
Northern Canada Evangelical Mission Inc.	1946			1	1	
OMF International – Canada	1888			1	1	
Pioneers Canada				2		
Salem Ministries International	2001			1	5	3
SEND International of Canada			4	5		
WEC International Canada	1939			2		
Communitas International	2006			3		
Unspecified Country						
Bible League International					500	
Brethren in Christ World Missions (BICWM)				18		1
Christian and Missionary Alliance in Canada, The				13		

	First Year	Personnel from US or Canada			Other Countries	
		1–2 years	2–4 years	4+ years	Citizen	Not Citizen
Christian Churches / Churches of Christ		20	10	160	120	
Church of God (Cleveland TN) World Missions				18		
General Baptists International		7				
Global Scholars				8	1	7
globalLead	1997			1		
Gospel Fellowship Association	2005	14		4		
International Pentecostal Holiness Church		1		5	8	
International Teams Canada (Evangelical International Crusades Canada Inc.)				3		
International Teams U.S.A.		2		23		71
Lutheran Hour Ministries				1	290	
Middle East Media – USA				2	80	9
Mission to the World (PCA) Inc.		2	30	70		
OM Canada	1970	20	5	3		
One Mission Society						5
Presbyterian Church (USA) Worldwide Ministries			100	78		
Reformed Baptist Mission Services				3		
Talking Bibles International	1989			2		
The Christian and Missionary Alliance				61		
Weiner Ministries International	1991			1		
Wycliffe Bible Translators of Canada Inc.				16		
Wycliffe Bible Translators USA				405		
Uruguay						
Assemblies of God World Missions	1946	0		8		
Avant Ministries	2010			5		
Avant Ministries Canada	2010			4		
Baptist Bible Fellowship International – World Mission Service Center	1958			4		
Baptist International Missions Inc.				4		
Camino Global	2009			2		
Campus Crusade for Christ (Cru in the US)		3				
Christian Aid Mission	1983				7	
CMF International	2015	6			3	3
Converge				1		
Free Methodist World Missions	2016			2		
Free Will Baptist International Missions	1962			4		
Global Missions (United Pentecostal Church Intl.)	1932		2			
Global Missions of Open Bible Churches	1982				1	
Gospel Mission of South America Inc.	1970			6		
IFCA World Missions					1	
International Partnership Ministries Inc.	1999				3	3
LOGOI Ministries	1972				1	
Mailbox Club International Inc., The					1	
OM Canada				2		

	First Year	Personnel from US or Canada			Other Countries	
		1–2 years	2–4 years	4+ years	Citizen	Not Citizen
One Mission Society	2002			6		1
Operation Mobilization		0			2	4
SIM USA				2		
Spanish World Ministries					1	
The Navigators				4		
Word of Life Fellowship Inc.	1977				3	1
World Partners USA				1		
WorldVenture				2		
Uzbekistan						
Christian Aid Mission					28	
EPC World Outreach				1		
Evangelism Explosion III International Inc.	2010				4	
Food for the Hungry Inc.	2004		1			
Greater Grace World Outreach	1999				2	
Interserve USA	2007			2		
Mission Eurasia					4	
New Mission Systems International	2005			2		2
Precept Ministries International	1994				1	
Scriptures In Use	2006			6	800	
World Concern	1993	2		1	136	
Vanuatu						
Assemblies of God World Missions	1967	2		8		
Baptist Bible Fellowship International – World Mission Service Center	1999			2		
Biblical Ministries Worldwide				2		2
Church of the Nazarene Inc.	2001			2		2
Evangelism Explosion III International Inc.	2009				15	
Friends in Action Intl.				1		
Global Missions (United Pentecostal Church Intl.)	1970	5				
Global Recordings Network				2		
Pioneer Bible Translators				1		
World Outreach International – US	1995			2		
Wycliffe Bible Translators USA				6		
Venezuela						
Assemblies of God World Missions	1919	11		8		
Avant Ministries				1		
Awana Clubs International					3	
Baptist International Missions Inc.				4		
Baptist International Outreach	2015			2		2
Baptist Mid-Missions	1924			1	2	
Baptist Missionary Association of America (BMAA)					1	1
Children of Promise International			1	1		
Christian and Missionary Alliance in Canada, The				5		

	First Year	Personnel from US or Canada			Other Countries	
		1–2 years	2–4 years	4+ years	Citizen	Not Citizen
Christian Church (Disciples of Christ) – Global Ministries			1			
Christian Churches / Churches of Christ				15		
Church of God (Cleveland TN) World Missions	1966			3		2
CRM				5	4	1
Cross-Cultural Ministries – Churches of God General Conference	2008				1	
Far East Broadcasting Associates of Canada (FEB Canada)	1990			3		
Fellowship International Mission	1994			2		
Fellowship of Evangelical Churches – International Ministries	1980			3		
Foursquare Missions International	1953			2		
Global Missions (United Pentecostal Church Intl.)	1956	4				
Global Missions of Open Bible Churches	1993				1	
Harvest Foundation					1	
IFCA World Missions					1	
Impact International Inc.					2	
LOGOI Ministries	1972				3	
Lutheran Church Missouri Synod – World Mission	1951			3		
Macedonia World Baptist Missions Inc.	2000				2	2
Network of International Christian Schools	1990	3	3	7	6	
Pentecostal Free Will Baptist Church Inc. – World Witness Dept.					1	
Seventh-day Adventists – General Conference – Global Mission	1910			2		
Spanish World Ministries					1	
Team Expansion Inc.	1985			3	3	
United World Mission Inc.					1	1
Word of Life Fellowship Inc.	1979			1	5	3
World Indigenous Missions	1999			4		
WorldVenture					4	
Vietnam						
All God's Children International					10	
BILD International				1		
CAMA Services	1995			2		
Christian Aid Mission					289	
Church of God (Cleveland TN) World Missions	1995	1				
Church of God Ministries (Anderson) – Global Strategy	1999	2				
Church of the Brethren – Global Mission Partnerships				1		
Elim Fellowship	1997			4		
Encompass World Partners	2011			7		2
Evangelism Explosion III International Inc.	2010				45	
Global Outreach International	2003			2		
Globe International	2002			2		
Habitat for Humanity International		1				1

		Personnel from US or Canada			Other Countries	
	First Year	1–2 years	2–4 years	4+ years	Citizen	Not Citizen
Holt International Children's Services Inc.					13	
Hope Haven International Ministries					2	
IN Network dba International Needs USA	1991				18	
Intercede International						2
International Gospel Outreach	2003			1		1
reSource Leadership International	2011					1
Samaritan's Purse	2000		4			
Scriptures In Use	2010			4	400	
Seventh-day Adventists – General Conference – Global Mission	1937			1		1
The Kerusso Institute for Global Leaders	2016				1	
Training Evangelistic Leadership	1991			2	4	1
Vision Beyond Borders	1997					15
World Concern	1989	1			14	
World Link Ministries	2008				100	
Wycliffe Bible Translators USA				2		
Virgin Islands of the USA						
Baptist International Missions Inc.				2		
National Baptist Convention of America – Foreign Mission Board	1978				6	
Western Europe						
ABWE International				96		
Accelerating International Mission Strategies (AIMS)			2			
American Baptist International Ministries						2
Assemblies of God World Missions			0	44		
Awana Clubs International				1		
Baptist International Missions Inc.				2		
Campus Crusade for Christ (Cru in the US)				12		
Christar	1975		2	14		
Christar Canada				4		
Church of God Ministries (Anderson) – Global Strategy				2		
CLC Ministries International	1942			2		
Communitas International	1980	1		39	6	10
East-West Ministries International	1998	3		1	5	
Elim Fellowship	1982			1		
Foursquare Missions International				2		
InterVarsity Christian Fellowship/USA			1			
Josue Yrion World Evangelism & Missions Inc.	1995				4	
MB Mission					2	
MB Mission Canada					2	
OM Canada			5	4		
One Challenge				3	2	
Pioneers USA				44		1

	First Year	Personnel from US or Canada			Other Countries	
		1–2 years	2–4 years	4+ years	Citizen	Not Citizen
ReachAcross	1951		3		17	
Wycliffe Associates	1970		1			
Western Sahara						
Christian Aid Mission	2005				20	
Yemen						
Global Gates	2016			2		
Interserve USA				5		
Seventh-day Adventists – General Conference – Global Mission	1994			2		
Zambia						
Action International Ministries	2002		1	7		
Action International Ministries – Canada	2000	2		1		
Agathos International	2004	5		1	6	
Assemblies of God World Missions	1996	2		9		
Awana Clubs International					3	
Baptist Bible Fellowship International – World Mission Service Center	1989			13		
Baptist International Missions Inc.				6		
Baptist International Outreach	1985			10		10
Baptist Mid-Missions	1990			4	2	
BCM International	2007				1	
BIC Canada-Global	2015		5			
Brethren in Christ World Missions (BICWM)	1906			2		
Bright Hope	1998					1
Child Evangelism Fellowship Inc.				1		
Christian Aid Mission	1999				5	
Christian Relief Fund, The	2004				1	
Christian Veterinary Mission	2016	2				
Church of God (Cleveland TN) World Missions	1965			3		
Church of the Nazarene Inc.	1961			2	2	
Commission to Every Nation	2008			2		2
Evangelism Explosion III International Inc.	2015				3	
Forgotten Voices Intl.					11	
Global Missions (United Pentecostal Church Intl.)	1980		2			
Global Partners (The Wesleyan Church World Headquarters)			1	3		
Gospel Fellowship Association	2005	1		11		
Greater Grace World Outreach	2004				12	
Heart of the Bride Ministries		3				
IBMGlobal	2011	2	8	2		
IN Network dba International Needs USA	1985				3	
In Touch Mission International	1995			2	4	
Independent Faith Mission Inc.				7		
International Justice Mission	2004				11	
International Partnership Ministries Inc.	2002			2		
International Pentecostal Holiness Church	1950		2			
International Teams U.S.A.						2

	First Year	Personnel from US or Canada			Other Countries	
		1–2 years	2–4 years	4+ years	Citizen	Not Citizen
Kids Alive International	2001	1	2			
Launch Out Ministries International	2005				5	
Liebenzell Mission of USA Inc.	2011	1		2		
Lifesong for Orphans	2006	2	2	1	102	1
MEDA – Mennonite Economic Development Associates	2008				3	
Mission Aviation Fellowship of Canada (MAFC)			1	1		
Mission to the World (PCA) Inc.	2002			2		
Missionary Ventures Canada			1			
Missionary Ventures Intl.				2		
New Mission Systems International	2010			2	1	
Operation Mobilization		6			69	43
Partners in Bible Translation	2015			2	3	
Ripe for Harvest Inc.				1		
Seventh-day Adventists – General Conference – Global Mission	1905			2		8
SIM Canada				11		
SIM USA				12		
Teen Missions International Inc.	1993			2	30	
The God's Story Project	2002				1	
The Pentecostal Assemblies of Canada		2		4		
The Salvation Army USA National Headquarters	1922		1			
The Word for the World (TWFTW)	2004			2	2	
Walk Thru the Bible Ministries Inc.	1999				8	
Wisconsin Evangelical Lutheran Synod – Board for World Missions				8		
Zimbabwe						
African Enterprise	1972				14	
Apostolic Church of Pentecost of Canada (Global Harvest Missions)					1	
Assemblies of God World Missions	1968	2		2		
Awana Clubs International					3	
Baptist International Missions Inc.				2		
BCM International	1971				9	
Brethren in Christ World Missions (BICWM)	1898			2		
Child Evangelism Fellowship Inc.				1		
Christian Aid Mission	1954				15	
Christian Church (Disciples of Christ) – Global Ministries			2			
Christian Churches / Churches of Christ				34	14	
Evangelical Free Church of Canada Mission				4		
Evangelism Explosion III International Inc.	2010				5	
Faith Christian Fellowship Intl.					1	
Fellowship of Evangelical Churches – International Ministries	2009			1		
Forgotten Voices Intl.					7	

	First Year	Personnel from US or Canada			Other Countries	
		1–2 years	2–4 years	4+ years	Citizen	Not Citizen
Global Missions (United Pentecostal Church Intl.)	1968	2				1
Gospel Tide Broadcasting Association	1983				1	
Greater Grace World Outreach	2013	1				2
Harvest International Inc.	2008					2
Hope for the Hungry	1983				2	
Independent Faith Mission Inc.				3		
Lott Carey Baptist Foreign Mission Convention	1998				20	
New Mission Systems International	2007			1	1	
Operation Mobilization		0			14	0
Ripe for Harvest Inc.				1		
Seventh-day Adventists – General Conference – Global Mission	1894			3		12
SIM USA				1		
TEAM (The Evangelical Alliance Mission)				32		
The Pentecostal Assemblies of Canada				4		
The Word for the World (TWFTW)	1984				2	
Walk Thru the Bible Ministries Inc.	1999				6	
Waymarks Radio Ministries International					1	
White Fields					3	
World Missions & Evangelism	1998				1	
World Relief	2003				2	

MOODY
Theological
Seminary™

Ready to Put the Word into Action?

Transform your community as you earn a Master of Arts [Intercultural and Urban Studies] degree from Moody Theological Seminary. As you deepen your knowledge of the Word, you'll join a local and international network of scholars and churches. Choose this, or one of eight other accredited degrees including an online Master of Divinity.

Get started today!

(800) 588-8344 | moody.edu/mtsmission

CHAPTER 7

AGENCIES BY MINISTRY ACTIVITY OR CHURCH TRADITION

Another value of the *Mission Handbook* is the ability to locate a North American agency by a ministry activity category or church tradition/affiliation. This chapter provides the user with those indices. Agency responses on the survey helped define the listed categories. The organizations in each category appear in alphabetical order.

By Ministry Activity

Almost all agencies are involved in many types of ministry activities, so they may be listed under several categories. We asked those with more than six to indicate the six activities toward which they had committed the largest amount of resources. They are listed as such.

By Church Tradition

If an agency needs more than one generic or denominational category to describe its traditional doctrinal and/or ecclesiastical stance, the agency may appear under more than one category. The list is arranged alphabetically by church tradition and within each category by agency name.

MINISTRY ACTIVITY

ADOPTION
All God's Children International
Buckner International
Holt International Children's Services, Inc.
Lifesong for Orphans

ADVOCACY
Bread for the World
World Help

AGRICULTURAL ASSISTANCE
ADRA (Adventist Development
 and Relief Agency)
Agathos International
Bright Hope
CAMA Services
Care of Creation, Inc.
Christian Flights International
Christian Veterinary Mission
Church World Service
Cooperative Baptist Fellowship
 - Global Missions
Crossroads Christian
 Communications Inc. (ERDF)
CWE Missions
ECHO
Empowering Lives International
Equip Inc & Equip International
Equip, Canada
ERDO - Emergency Relief
 and Development
FARMS International, Inc.
Food for the Hungry, Inc.
FRIENDS in Action International - Canada
General Baptists International
Haiti Arise - Canada
Heifer Project International
Helps Ministries
HOPE International Development Agency

KORE Foundation
Lutheran World Relief
MEDA - Mennonite Economic
 Development Associates
Mennonite Economic Development
 Associates (MEDA)
Mercy Ships
Mission Without Borders Canada
Mustard Seed International
Partners Relief & Development
Pilgrim
Prakash Association, USA
RAISE International, Inc.
Samaritan's Purse
SAND International
Self-Help International
Shelter for Life Intl. Inc.
Tribes and Nations Outreach
World Relief
World Vision, Inc.

ARTS IN MISSION
A.C.T. International
Bridge Builders International
GoCorps
Greater Europe Mission
Jews for Jesus
Missionary TECH Team
WEC International
World Horizons

ASSOCIATION OF MISSIONS
Canadian Assemblies of God,
 General Conference
COMMA
Evangelical Friends Church Southwest
Great Commission Media Ministries
Japanese Evangelical Missionary
 Society (JEMS)
Middle East Christian Outreach
 (MECO Canada)

Mission to Children
New Wineskins Missionary Network

AUDIO RECORDING OR DISTRIBUTION

Alberto Mottesi Evangelistic
  Association, Inc.
Audio Scripture Ministries
Back to the Bible Canada
Celebrant Singers
Chinese Christian Life Fellowship, Inc
Christian Aviation and Radio Mission
Davar Partners International
Far East Broadcasting Company
Friends of Israel Gospel Ministry Inc.
Galcom International Canada
Galcom International USA, Inc
Global Recordings Network
Global Recordings Network Canada
Good News Productions International
Gospel Tide Broadcasting Association
Hermano Pablo Ministries
Lutheran Bible Translators of Canada
Master's Resourcing Commission
Oneway Ministries
Reformed Church in America, General
  Synod Council, Global Mission
Russian Christian Radio, Inc. (or RCR)
Spanish World Ministries
Talking Bibles International
The God's Story Project
The Inner-city Church Planting Mission
TWR Canada
Waymarks Radio Ministries International
Word To Russia
World Mission

AVIATION

Africa Inland Mission
Air Mobile Ministries
Canadian South America Mission

Christian Aviation and Radio Mission
Ethnos360
Evangelical Congregational Church -
  Global Ministries Commission
Helimission, Inc. - USA
JAARS, Inc.
Mexico Medical Missions
Mission Aviation Fellowship
Mission Aviation Fellowship
  of Canada (MAFC)
Mission Safety International
Missionaire International
Missionary Flights Intl.
MMS Aviation (Missionary
  Maintenance Services)
South America Mission
World Team US

BIBLE & OTHER TRANSLATION

Gospel Literature International (GLINT)
Russian Bible Society, Inc.
Wycliffe Associates

BIBLE DISTRIBUTION

ACCI (Adventive Cross Cultural Initiatives)
Ambassadors for Christ, Inc.
Asian Outreach International Canada
Baptist International Evangelistic Ministries
Baptist International Missions, Inc.
Baptist International Outreach
BASIC Ministries, Inc
Bible League Canada
Bible League International
Bibles and Literature in French
Bibles For The World, Inc.
BLF Canada
Canadian Bible Society / La Societe
  Biblique Canadienne
CEIFA International
Central Yearly Meeting of Friends Missions
China Ministries International

Christian Aid Ministries (CAM)

Christian Emergency Relief Teams (CERT) International

Christian Resources Intl.

Church of God of the Apostolic Faith, Inc., The

CIS- Christian Involvement In Service

CLC Ministries International

CSM Canada Intl. (Christian Salvage Mission)

Davar Partners International

Door of Hope International

Equip Inc & Equip International

Equipping The Saints

Eternal Hope in Haiti

Evangel Bible Translators

Every Home for Christ

Final Frontiers Foundation

Firefall International Inc.

Fundamental Baptist Missions International

Gideons International, The

Global Gates

Global Media Outreach

Gospel for Asia Canada

Gospel Revival Ministries

Gospel Tide Broadcasting Association

Greater Europe Mission Canada

Harvesting In Spanish (HIS)

Intercede International

International Project

Italy for Christ, Inc.

Josue Yrion World Evangelism & Missions, Inc.

Kids for Christ International

Leadership Ministries Worldwide

Leadership Vistas International Ministries

Life in Messiah International

Living Hope Ministries International, Inc.

Living Water International

Lutheran Bible Translators of Canada

Lutheran Bible Translators, Inc.

Macedonian Missionary Service

Mission Eurasia

Missionary Flights Intl.

Multiplication Network Ministries

OneHope

Open Doors with Brother Andrew – Canada

Open Doors, USA

Outreach to Asia Nationals

Pan American Missions

Pentecostal Church of God-World Missions Department

Prayer Baptist Missions International, Inc.

Reach A Village

Russian Bible Society, Inc.

Salem Ministries International

Sanma (South Asia Native Missionary Alliance)

ServeNow

SGM Canada

Slavic Gospel Association

Slavic Gospel Association - Canada

South African Christian Mission, Inc.

Sowers International, The

Spanish American Evangelistic Ministries

Talking Bibles International

The Master's Foundation

The Voice of the Martyrs

Tribes and Nations Outreach

Twenty-six:Twelve

Vernacular Video Mission International, Inc.

Village Ministries International

Vision Beyond Borders

World Christian Ministries Association

World Compassion Society

World Compassion Terry Law Ministries

World Help

Worldwide Medical-Dental Evangelical Mission

Wycliffe Bible Translators of Canada, Inc.

Zion Evangelical Ministries of Africa (ZEMA)

BIBLE MEMORIZATION
Disciples International
Kids for Christ International
Navigators of Canada, The
Training Evangelistic Leadership

BIBLE TEACHING
10/40 Connections
Advent Christian World Outreach
Africa Inland Mission Canada Intl.
African Children's Mission
Agape Gospel Mission
Air Mobile Ministries
Association of Free Lutheran Congregations
Back to the Bible
Baptist Bible Fellowship International
  - World Mission Service Center
Baptist Haiti Mission
Baptist International Outreach
Baptist Missionary Association
  of America (BMAA)
BCM International
Be One Together
Bible Training Centre for Pastors
Bridge Builders International
Camino Global Ministries Canada
Caribbean Lifetime Mission
Catalyst Missions
Chaplaincy Endorsement Commission
  for the Christian Church and
  Churches of Christ
Children's Lifeline
Chinese Christian Life Fellowship, Inc
Chosen People Ministries (Canada)
Christian Discipleship International
Church Planting International
CIS- Christian Involvement In Service
Cross-Cultural Ministries, Churches
  of God General Conference
CrossWay International
CyberMissions

Davar Partners International
Discipleship International
East African Ministries
Elim Fellowship
ERRC (Educational Resources &
  Referrals - China) - US
Ethnos360
EurAsian Baptist Mission
Every Home for Christ
Far Corners Missions
Firefall International Inc.
Free Will Baptist International Missions
Freedom in Christ Ministries - USA
Global Missions of Open Bible Churches
Global Partners (The Wesleyan
  Church World Headquarters)
Gospel Outbound
Greater Europe Mission, Global Mission
Greater Grace World Outreach
Haitian Christian Outreach
Harvest Mission to the Unreached
Heart for Lebanon Foundation
Heart To Heart International Ministries
iHope International
International Faith Missions
International Project
InterVarsity Christian Fellowship/USA
Jews for Jesus
Josiah Venture
Josue Yrion World Evangelism
  & Missions, Inc.
Latin America Mission
Latin American Missions Association
Leadership Resources International
Leadership Vistas International Ministries
Life in Messiah International
LIFE International
Living Word Missions
Luke Society
Lutheran Bible Translators of Canada

Macedonia World Baptist
    Mission International
Mission Possible
Mission to Children
Mission Without Borders Canada
Missionary Gospel Fellowship
National Association of Congregational
    Christian Churches
New Hope Uganda Ministries
Northern Canada Evangelical Mission Inc
OMF International
OMF International - Canada
One Mission Society
Oneway Ministries
Outreach to Asia Nationals
Partners International
Polish Christian Ministries
Power to Change Ministries
Precept Ministries International
SAND International
Sanma (South Asia Native
    Missionary Alliance)
SAT-7 North America
Scripture Union, USA
Serve Globally
SGM Canada
Shepherd's Support, Inc.
Shield of Faith Mission International
South African Christian Mission, Inc.
The Evangelical Covenant Church
The God's Story Project
The Masters Mission
Things to Come Mission
Timothy Two Project International
TWR
University Bible Fellowship
Village Ministries International
Visionledd o/a Working for
    Orphans and Widows
Walk Thru the Bible Ministries, Inc.
With Open Eyes

Women in the Window International
Word & Deed
Word & Deed Ministries Canada
Word of Life Fellowship Inc

BIBLE TRANSLATION

Ambassadors for Christ, Inc.
Baptist Mid-Missions
Canadian Bible Society / La Societe
    Biblique Canadienne
Church of God (Holiness) World
    Mission Dept., Inc.
Deaf Missions International, Inc.
Door of Hope International
Ethnos360
Evangel Bible Translators
Evangelical Congregational Church -
    Global Ministries Commission
Faith Baptist Mission
Fundamental Baptist Missions International
Global Teams International, Inc
Helimission, Inc. - USA
In Touch Mission International
Independent Faith Mission Inc.
JAARS, Inc.
Liebenzell Mission of USA, Inc.
Lutheran Bible Translators of Canada
Lutheran Bible Translators, Inc.
Lutheran Brethren International Mission
New Tribes Mission of Canada
Partners in Bible Translation
People International USA
Pioneer Bible Translators
Primitive Methodist Church in the
    USA - International Mission Board
Reformed Episcopal Board
    of Foreign Missions
Sanma (South Asia Native
    Missionary Alliance)
Seed Company
The God's Story Project

The Presbyterian Church in Canada
The Word for the World (TWFTW)
World Mission Prayer League
World Team Canada
World Team US
Wycliffe Bible Translators of Canada, Inc.
Wycliffe Bible Translators USA

BROADCASTING

Alberto Mottesi Evangelistic
    Association, Inc.
Back to the Bible Canada
Crossroads Christian
    Communications Inc. (ERDF)
Evangelize China Fellowship, Inc.
Global Outreach Mission Inc. Canada
Global Outreach Mission, Inc.
Gospel for Asia Canada
Gospel for Asia, Inc.
Great Commission Media Ministries
Hermano Pablo Ministries
International Cooperating Ministries (ICM)
Jewish Awareness Ministries, Inc.
Lutheran Hour Ministries
Middle East Media - USA
OM Canada
OMS International - Canada
Precept Ministries International
Proclaim! International, Inc.
Rehoboth Ministries, Inc
Rio Grande Bible Institute, Inc.
Romanian Missionary Society
Seventh-day Adventists, General
    Conference - Global Mission
The Master's Foundation
Word To Russia
World Indigenous Missions
Worldwide Medical-Dental
    Evangelical Mission

BUSINESS AS MISSION

ACM International
Action International Ministries
Africa Inland Mission
Agathos International
Anglican Frontier Missions
Apostolic Church of Pentecost of
    Canada (Global Harvest Missions)
Avant Ministries
Baptist Bible Fellowship International
    - World Mission Service Center
Brethren in Christ World
    Missions (BICWM)
Café 1040, Inc.
Camino Global
Caribbean Baptist Mission Society
Christar
Christian and Missionary
    Alliance in Canada, The
CLC Ministries International
CRM
Crossworld
Crossworld Canada
Empowering Lives International
Encompass World Partners
EPC World Outreach
Evangelical Free Church of Canada Mission
Fellowship of Companies for
    Christ International (FCCI)
Fishhook International
Forefront Experience
Frontiers
Global Teams International, Inc
GoCorps
Gospel Outbound
Greater Europe Mission
HOPE International
IBMGlobal
InterServe Canada
Interserve USA
KORE Foundation

Latin America Mission
Latin American Missions Association
Lifesong for Orphans
MEDA - Mennonite Economic
    Development Associates
Mission ONE, Inc.
New Mission Systems International
OM Canada
Opportunity International Canada
Outreach Canada
Paradigm Shift
Partners Worldwide
Pioneers USA
Project AmaZon
Project AmaZon Canada Society
ReachGlobal
Rosedale Mennonite Missions
Serge
SIM USA
Spanish American Evangelistic Ministries
TeachBeyond Canada
TeachBeyond USA
The Upstream Collective
World Horizons
World Partners USA
World Relief
Worldwide Tentmakers, Inc.

CAMPING PROGRAMS
ABWE International
Action International Ministries - Canada
Alongside Ministries International
Avant Ministries
Avant Ministries Canada
BCM International
BCM International (Canada), Inc.
Brazil Gospel Fellowship Mission (BGFM)
Christian Mission for the Deaf
Deaf Missions International, Inc.
Echocuba
Engineering Ministries International (EMI)
For God's Children Intl.

Friendship International Ministries, Inc.
Gospel Fellowship Association
Greater Europe Mission Canada
Heart To Heart International Ministries
Hope Haven International Ministries
IBMGlobal
Inter-Varsity Christian
    Fellowship of Canada
InterAct Ministries of Canada
Japanese Evangelical Missionary
    Society (JEMS)
Jews for Jesus
Mercy Projects
Mission Without Borders Canada
New Hope Uganda Ministries
Northern Canada Evangelical Mission Inc
Pioneer Clubs
Salvation Army - Canada and
    Bermuda Territory, The
SEND International of Canada
Servants in Faith & Technology (SIFAT)
TeachBeyond Canada
Titus International
Word of Life Fellowship Inc
Word To Russia
Young Life
Young Life of Canada
Zion Evangelical Ministries
    of Africa (ZEMA)

CAMPUS MINISTRY
Inter-Varsity Christian
    Fellowship of Canada

CHILD ADVOCACY
World Help

CHILD SPONSORSHIP
Childcare Worldwide
Lifeline Christian Mission
Make Way Partners
Mercy Projects

CHILDCARE OR ORPHANAGE

Action International Ministries - Canada
African Leadership Development
Agape Gospel Mission
Agathos International
All About Orphans (David
  Livingstone KURE Foundation)
Baptist International Missions, Inc.
Barnabas Aid
BASIC Ministries, Inc
Bibles For The World, Inc.
BIC Canada-Global
Blessing the Children International
Bridge Builders International
Calvary Commission, Inc.
Caribbean Lifetime Mission
Childcare Worldwide
Children of Promise International
Children's Haven Intl.
Children's HopeChest
Children's Lifeline
Christ for India, Inc.
Christ for the City International
Christ to the Nations
Christian Aid Ministries (CAM)
Christian Relief Fund, The
Church of God (Cleveland, TN)
  World Missions
Commission to Every Nation
Commission To Every Nation-Canada
Cup of Cold Water Ministries
Door of Hope International
EBM International
Elim Fellowship
Empowering Lives International
Equip, Canada
ERDO - Emergency Relief
  and Development
Eternal Hope in Haiti, Global Mission
Evangelical Bible Mission
Evangelical Free Church of Canada Mission

Evangelize China Fellowship, Inc.
Every Child Ministries, Inc.
Far Corners Missions
Final Frontiers Foundation
Fishhook International
Forgotten Voices Intl.
Foundation for His Ministry
Friends United Meeting
General Baptists International
Global Aid Network, Inc. - Canada
Global Hope India
Global Missions of Open Bible Churches
Global Outreach International
Global Witness and Ministry-AME Church
Gospel Outreach Ministries Intl.
Gospelink, Inc.
Grace Mission Inc.
Harvest Bridge
Harvest International, Inc.
Harvesting In Spanish (HIS)
Heart of the Bride Ministries
Heart To Heart International Ministries
Holt International Children's Services, Inc.
Hope for the Hungry
IBMGlobal
iHope International
Impact Nations International Ministries
In Touch Mission International
Independent Gospel Missions:
  A Baptist Mission Agency
India Evangelical Mission Inc.
India Partners
Intercede International
International Child Care (Canada), Inc.
International Crisis Aid
International Faith Missions
International Partnership Ministries, Inc.
International Pentecostal Holiness Church
International Street Kids Outreach
  Ministries (ISKOM)
Kerus Global Education

Kids Alive International
Kinship United
Launch Out Ministries International
Lifesong for Orphans
Link International Ministries
Living Hope Ministries International, Inc.
Macedonia World Baptist Missions, Inc.
Make Way Partners
Mission Nannys
Mission On The Move
Mission Possible
Mission to Children
Mission Without Borders Canada
Mustard Seed International
National Association of Congregational
    Christian Churches
New Hope International
New Hope Uganda Ministries
New Life Advance International
Niños de Mexico
North American Baptist Conference
    - Worldwide Outreach
Northwest Haiti Christian Mission
One Child Matters
ORPHANetwork
Orphanos Foundation
Pan American Missions
Partners in Asian Missions
Partners International Canada
Partners Relief & Development
People International USA
Precious Seed Ministries Inc.
Presbyterian Mission International (PMI)
Reaching Indians Ministries International
Real Impact Missions
Salem Ministries International
Salvation Army - Canada and
    Bermuda Territory, The
Slavic Gospel Association - Canada
Society of Anglican Missionaries
    and Senders (SAMS USA)

The Brethren Church, Inc.
The Free Methodist Church in Canada
The Master's Foundation
The Masters Mission
The Pentecostal Assemblies of Canada
The Salvation Army USA
    National Headquarters
Ukrainian Children's Christian Fund
Ukrainian Childrens Fund
Vision Beyond Borders
Visionledd o/a Working for
    Orphans and Widows
Word & Deed
Word & Deed Ministries Canada
World Christian Outreach, Inc.
World Orphans
World Outreach International - US
World Servants, Inc.
World Vision, Inc.
World-Wide Missions
Youth Ministry International
YUGO Ministries (Youth Unlimited
    Gospel Outreach, Inc.)
YUGO Ministries Canada

CHILDREN AT RISK

ADRA (Adventist Development
    and Relief Agency)
CEIFA International
Childcare Worldwide
Children's HopeChest
Christ for Children International
Christ for the City International
COMHINA
Equip, Canada
ERDO - Emergency Relief
    and Development
Food for the Hungry, Inc.
GAIN (Global Aid Network)
Heart of the Bride Ministries
Holt International Children's Services, Inc.

International Street Kids Outreach
Ministries (ISKOM)
International Teams, U.S.A.
Kerus Global Education
Kids for Christ International
Living Hope Ministries International, Inc.
Mission Generation, Inc.
National Baptist Convention USA,
Inc. - Foreign Mission Board
Nazarene Compassion Ministries Canada
North American Baptist Conference
- Worldwide Outreach
ORPHANetwork
Teen Missions International, Inc.
World Concern
World Hope Canada
World Orphans
World Relief

CHILDREN'S MINISTRY
African Children's Mission
BCM International (Canada), Inc.
Bible League Canada
Cadence International
Children's Ministry International, Inc. (CMI)
China Service Ventures
Christ for Children International
Compassion International, Inc.
Evangelical Methodist Church,
Inc. - Board of Missions
FOCAS (Foundation of Compassionate
American Samaritans)
Food for the Hungry, Inc.
Go to Nations
Gospel for Asia, Inc.
Heart of the Bride Ministries
Holt International Children's Services, Inc.
International Child Care (Canada), Inc.
International Crisis Aid
International Teams, Canada (Evangelical
International Crusades Canada, Inc.)
ISOH/IMPACT

Kids for Christ International
Living Water Teaching
Mailbox Club International Inc., The
MAP International
Mexican Medical Ministries
Mission Generation, Inc.
Mission of Mercy Canada
Operation Blessing International Relief
and Development Corporation
Pioneer Clubs
Romanian Missionary Society
Salvation Army - Canada and
Bermuda Territory, The
Scripture Union, USA
Spiritual Overseers Service International
STEM International
Teen Missions International, Inc.
Ukrainian Childrens Fund
Word To Russia
World Help
World Outreach International - US
World Vision Canada

CHRISTIAN EDUCATION
ACSI (Association of Christian
Schools International)
Agape Gospel Mission
All About Orphans (David
Livingstone KURE Foundation)
Allegheny Wesleyan Methodist Connection
Association of Free Lutheran Congregations
Avant Ministries
Avant Ministries Canada
Baptist Haiti Mission
Baptist Missionary Association
of America (BMAA)
Barnabas Aid
BethanyKids Canada
Bibles For The World, Inc.
BIC Canada-Global
Blessing the Children International
Board of World Mission

Brazil Gospel Fellowship Mission (BGFM)
Care of Creation, Inc.
Childcare Worldwide
Children's Lifeline
Children's Ministry International, Inc. (CMI)
Chosen People Ministries (Canada)
Christian Church (Disciples of
    Christ) - Global Ministries
Christian Flights International
Christian Medical & Dental Associations
Christian Mission for the Deaf
Christian Reformed World Missions
Church of God (Holiness) World
    Mission Dept., Inc.
Church of the Brethren - Global
    Mission Partnerships
Churches of God, General Conference
Colorado Haiti Project Inc.
Commission to Every Nation
Commission To Every Nation-Canada
Compassion International, Inc.
Cross-Cultural Ministries, Churches
    of God General Conference
Cup of Cold Water Ministries
Daystar U.S., Global Mission
Discipleship International
East European Missions Network
EBM International
Echocuba
Effect Hope
Engineering Ministries International (EMI)
Enrich Missions, Inc
Episcopal Church USA - Domestic
    & Foreign Missionary Society
Evangelical Bible Mission
Evangelical Mennonite Mission Conference
Evangelical Mission Ministries
Evangelism Resources, Inc.
Evangelize China Fellowship, Inc.
Faith Baptist Mission
Faith Christian Fellowship Intl.

FH Canada
FOCAS (Foundation of Compassionate
    American Samaritans)
Four Corners Ministries
Fundamental Baptist Missions International
Gate Breaker Ministries
Global Missions of Open Bible Churches
Global Witness and Ministry-AME Church
Good News for India
Good Shepherd Ministries Intl.
Grace Mission Inc.
Great Commission Media Ministries
Greater Grace World Outreach
Haiti Lutheran Mission Society
Haitian Christian Outreach
Harvest Bridge
Harvest Foundation
Harvesting In Spanish (HIS)
Heart for Lebanon Foundation
Heart To Heart International Ministries
Identify
IN Network dba International Needs USA
India Partners
Indopartners Agency
Interaction International
Intercede International
International Child Care, USA
International Faith Missions
International Justice Mission
Jews for Jesus Canada
Joni and Friends
Joshua Expeditions
Kerus Global Education
Kids Alive International
Kids Around the World
Kids for Christ International
LeadaChild
Leadership Ministries Worldwide
Liebenzell Mission of USA, Inc.
Lifeline Christian Mission
Lifesong for Orphans

Luke Society

Lutheran Church-Missouri Synod, World Mission

Macedonia World Baptist Mission International

Macedonia World Baptist Missions, Inc.

Make Way Partners

Middle East Christian Outreach (MECO Canada)

Ministry to Educate and Equip Intl. (MTEE)

Mission Eurasia

Mission On The Move

Mission Possible

Mission Possible Canada

Mission Possible USA

Mission to Children

Missions Resource Network

Moravian Church in North America

Mustard Seed International

Mustard Seed Mission Canada, Inc.

National Association of Congregational Christian Churches

National Baptist Convention of America - Foreign Mission Board

National Baptist Convention USA, Inc. - Foreign Mission Board

National Religious Broadcasters

Network of International Christian Schools

New Life Advance International

Niños de Mexico

Northwest Haiti Christian Mission

One Child Matters

Open Door Baptist Missions

Palm Missionary Ministries, Inc.

Partners Relief & Development

Pentecostal Free Will Baptist Church, Inc. - World Witness Dept.

Pilgrim

Pillar of Fire Missions International

Precious Seed Ministries Inc.

Primitive Methodist Church in the USA - International Mission Board

Probe Ministries International

Progressive National Baptist Convention, Inc. (PNBC) - Missions

Reciprocal Ministries International

Rehoboth Ministries, Inc

Resourcing Christian Education International

RP Global Missions

Salvation Army - Canada and Bermuda Territory, The

Samaritan's Purse

SAND International

Sanma (South Asia Native Missionary Alliance)

Seventh-day Adventists, General Conference - Global Mission

Society of Anglican Missionaries and Senders (SAMS USA)

South African Christian Mission, Inc.

South America Mission

TeachBeyond Canada

TeachBeyond USA

Teen Missions International, Inc.

The Esther School - Dynamic Youth Ministries

The Salvation Army USA National Headquarters

United Church of Christ - Global Ministries

Village Schools International

Virginia Mennonite Missions

Visionledd o/a Working for Orphans and Widows

Word & Deed

Word & Deed Ministries Canada

World Christian Outreach, Inc.

World Gospel Mission

World Missions & Evangelism

World Reach, Inc

World Relief

World Witness

World-Wide Missions

WorldVenture

WorldView

Zion Evangelical Ministries
of Africa (ZEMA)

CHRISTIAN EDUCATIONAL TRAVEL

Joshua Expeditions

CHURCH CONSTRUCTION
OR FINANCING

Apostolic Christian Church -
Missionary Committee

Baptist International Evangelistic Ministries

Caribbean Baptist Mission Society

Christ for India, Inc.

Christ for the Nations, Inc.

Church Ministries Intl., Global Mission

Church of God (Cleveland, TN)
World Missions

Church of God of the Apostolic
Faith, Inc., The

CWE Missions

Evangelical Mission Ministries

Evangelize China Fellowship, Inc.

Global Missions of Open Bible Churches

Global Outreach International

Gospel Revival Ministries

Harvest International, Inc.

IBMGlobal

Macedonian Missionary Service

Missionary TECH Team

Nehemiah Teams International

Partners in Asian Missions

Pentecostal Church of God-World
Missions Department

Pillar of Fire Missions International

Precious Seed Ministries Inc.

Slavic Missionary Service, Inc.

Teen Mission, USA, Inc. dba
Mission Journeys

The Master's Foundation

Walk Thru the Bible Ministries, Inc.

CHURCH DEVELOPMENT

AEGA Ministries Int'l Inc (Association
of Evangelical Gospel Assemblies)

Allegheny Wesleyan Methodist Connection

AMG International

Association of Free Lutheran Congregations

Baptist General Conference of Canada

Baptist Haiti Mission

Baptist Mid-Missions

BCM International

BILD International

Camino Global

Caribbean Lifetime Mission

Caring Partners International

Catalyst Missions

Christian Reformed World Missions

Church of the Nazarene, Inc.

Commission to Every Nation

Converge

Eastern Mennonite Missions

EBM International

Echocuba

Encompass World Partners

Evangelical Bible Mission

Evangelical Mennonite Mission Conference

FARMS International, Inc.

Fellowship International Mission

Free Methodist World Missions

Global Frontier Missions

Global Training Network

Gospelink, Inc.

Haitian Christian Outreach

Harvest Foundation

HOPE International

International Faith Missions

Into All The World

Missionary Gospel Fellowship

New Mission Systems International

Northern Canada Evangelical Mission Inc

Northwest Haiti Christian Mission
Power to Change Ministries
Teen Mission, USA, Inc. dba
   Mission Journeys
Things to Come Mission
TMS Global
Vision Ministries Canada
With Open Eyes
World Thrust International

CHURCH MISSION DEVELOPMENT & MOBILIZATION
Global Focus

CHURCH PLANTING
A.C.T. International
ABWE Canada (Across Borders
   for World Evangelism)
ABWE International
ACCI (Adventive Cross Cultural Initiatives)
ACTS International Ministries, Inc.
Asian Outreach International Canada
Aurora Mission, Inc.
Baptist Medical & Dental Mission
   International, Inc. (BMDMI)
BCM International (Canada), Inc.
Bible League Canada
Brazil Gospel Fellowship Mission (BGFM)
Brethren in Christ World
   Missions (BICWM)
Canadian Baptist Ministries
Canadian National Baptist
   Convention (CNBC)
Canadian South America Mission
Caribbean Baptist Mission Society
CEIFA International
Central Yearly Meeting of Friends Missions
Christ for India, Inc.
Christian and Missionary
   Alliance in Canada, The
Christian Fellowship Union, Inc.
Christians In Action Missions International

Church Leadership Development
   International
Church of God (Cleveland, TN)
   World Missions
Churches of God, General Conference
CityTeam Ministries - New
   Generations International
Cumberland Presbyterian Church
   Board of Missions
DeNike Ministries
Evangelical Christian Church in Canada
Evangelical Congregational Church -
   Global Ministries Commission
Evangelical Covenant Church of Canada
Evangelical Friends Church Southwest
Evangelical Methodist Church,
   Inc. - Board of Missions
Evangelism Resources, Inc.
Far East Broadcasting Associates
   of Canada (FEB Canada)
Fellowship of Evangelical Churches
   - International Ministries
FRIENDS in Action International - Canada
Fundamental Baptist Mission
   of Trinidad & Tobago
Fundamental Baptist Missions International
General Baptists International
Global Aid Network, Inc. - Canada
Global Missions (United
   Pentecostal Church Intl.)
Global Outreach Mission Inc., Canada
Global Outreach Mission, Inc.
Global Teams International, Inc
Globe International
Go to Nations
Gospel Fellowship Association
Gospel for Asia Canada
Gospel for Asia, Inc.
Gospel Mission of South
   America of Canada
Gospel Mission of South America, Inc.
Gospel Outreach Ministries Intl.

Haiti Arise - Canada
Haiti Lutheran Mission Society
HBI Global Partners
Helimission, Inc. - USA
Hisportic Christian Mission
IFCA World Missions
India Gospel Outreach, Inc.
International Cooperating Ministries (ICM)
International Partnership Ministries, Inc.
International Teams, Canada (Evangelical
    International Crusades Canada, Inc.)
Kids for Christ International
Liberty Corner Mission
Liebenzell Mission of USA, Inc.
Link International Ministries
Lutheran Church-Missouri
    Synod, World Mission
Men for Missions International
Mennonite Mission Network
Messianic Jewish Movement
    International, Inc. The (MJMI)
Mission to the World (PCA), Inc.
Missions Door
Mustard Seed International
National Baptist Convention USA,
    Inc. - Foreign Mission Board
New Tribes Mission of Canada
North American Baptist Conference
    - Worldwide Outreach
OMS International - Canada
Open Door Baptist Missions
Orthodox Presbyterian Church -
    Committee on Foreign Missions
Pan American Missions
Partners in Asian Missions
Partners International Canada
Pentecostal Free Will Baptist Church,
    Inc. - World Witness Dept.
Presbyterian Missionary Union
Primitive Methodist Church in the
    USA - International Mission Board

Project AmaZon
Project AmaZon Canada Society
Reformed Baptist Mission Services
Salvation Army - Canada and
    Bermuda Territory, The
The Brethren Church, Inc.
Tribes and Nations Outreach
Vineyard Church USA - Missions
White Fields
White Fields Missionary Society
    of Canada, Global Mission
World Compassion Society
World Help
World Indigenous Missions
World Link Ministries
World Missions & Evangelism
World Outreach International - US
World-Wide Missions
Worldwide Medical-Dental
    Evangelical Mission
YUGO Ministries Canada

CHURCH PLANTING (ESTABLISHING)

20schemes
Advancing Native Missions
Advent Christian World Outreach
Agape Gospel Mission
Agape Unlimited
Alongside Ministries International
Anglican Frontier Missions
Apostolic Church of Pentecost of
    Canada (Global Harvest Missions)
Assemblies of God World Missions
Avant Ministries
Avant Ministries Canada
Awana Clubs International
Baptist Bible Fellowship International
    - World Mission Service Center
Baptist General Conference of Canada
Baptist International Evangelistic Ministries

Baptist International Missions, Inc.

Baptist International Outreach

Baptist Mid-Missions

Baptist Missionary Association
  of America (BMAA)

BASIC Ministries, Inc

BCM International

Be One Together

Bethany Gateways

Bible League International

Biblical Ministries Worldwide

BIC Canada-Global

BILD International

Bold Ventures

Boundless Ministries, Inc.

Bright Hope

Camino Global Ministries Canada

Caribbean Lifetime Mission

Catalyst Missions

Chosen People Ministries (Canada)

Chosen People Ministries, Inc.

Christ to the Nations

Christar

Christar Canada

Christian Aid Mission

Christian Discipleship International

Christian Veterinary Mission

Church Ministries Intl., Global Mission

Church of God (Holiness) World
  Mission Dept., Inc.

Church of God of the Apostolic
  Faith, Inc., The

Church of the Nazarene, Inc.

Church Planting International

CIS- Christian Involvement In Service

Commission To Every Nation-Canada

Communitas International

Congregational Methodist Missions

Converge

CRM

Cross-Cultural Ministries, Churches
  of God General Conference

Crossover Communications International

Crossworld

Crossworld Canada

Cup of Cold Water Ministries

Disciple Makers

e3 Partners Ministry

Eastern Mennonite Missions

Elim Fellowship

Encompass World Partners

EPC World Outreach

Ethnos360

EurAsian Baptist Mission

European Christian Mission Intl. - USA

Evangel Bible Translators

Evangelical Free Church of Canada Mission

Evangelical Friends Mission

Evangelical Mennonite Conference

Evangelical Mennonite Mission Conference

Evangelical Mission Ministries

Evangelistic Faith Mission, Inc.

Every Home for Christ

Faith Baptist Mission

Faith Christian Fellowship Intl.

Far Corners Missions

Fellowship International Mission

Final Frontiers Foundation

Fishhook International

Foundation for His Ministry

Four Corners Ministries

Free Methodist World Missions

Free Will Baptist International Missions

Frontiers Canada

Global Action, Inc.

Global Fellowship Inc.

Global Hope India

Global Missions of Open Bible Churches

Global Partners (The Wesleyan
  Church World Headquarters)

Go Ye Fellowship

GOGF Ministries
Good News for India
GoSendMe Global
Gospel Tide Broadcasting Association
Gospelink, Inc.
Grace Ministries International
Grace Mission Inc.
Great Cities Missions
Greater Grace World Outreach
Haitian Christian Outreach
Harvest Bridge
Harvest Mission to the Unreached
Hellenic Ministries USA
IBMGlobal
IMB of the Southern Baptist Convention
Impact International, Inc.
IN Network dba International Needs USA
Independent Faith Mission Inc.
Independent Gospel Missions:
   A Baptist Mission Agency
India Evangelical Mission Inc.
India Gospel League
InterAct Ministries
InterAct Ministries of Canada
Intercede International
International Pentecostal Holiness Church
Italy for Christ, Inc.
Josiah Venture
Key Communications
Latin America Mission
Liebenzell Mission of Canada
Lifeline Christian Mission
Living Word Missions
Luke Society
Lutheran Brethren International Mission
Macedonia World Baptist Missions, Inc.
Macedonian Missionary Service
Master's Resourcing Commission
Medical Ambassadors International
   (Lifewind International)
Mission Catalyst Intl. Inc.

Mission India
Mission ONE, Inc.
Morelli Ministries Intl. Inc.
Multiplication Network Ministries
National Association of Congregational
   Christian Churches
New Mission Systems International
NEXT Worldwide
Niños de Mexico
Northern Canada Evangelical Mission Inc
Operation Mobilization
Partners International
Pentecostal Church of God-World
   Missions Department
People International USA
Pioneers Canada
Pioneers USA
Polish Christian Ministries
Prayer Baptist Missions International, Inc.
Precious Seed Ministries Inc.
Presbyterian Mission International (PMI)
Project WorldReach / Train & Multiply
Reach A Village
ReachGlobal
Reaching Japan Together (RJT)
Reciprocal Ministries International
Reformed Episcopal Board
   of Foreign Missions
Ripe for Harvest, Inc.
Rosedale Mennonite Missions
RP Global Missions
Salem Ministries International
SCORE International
Scriptures In Use
SEND International of Canada
SEND International, Inc.
Serge
Servant Partners
ServLife International
Seventh Day Baptist Missionary Society

Sidney and Helen Correll Ministries
(dba Correll Missionary Ministries)
SIM Canada
SIM USA
Slavic Gospel Association
Slavic Gospel Association - Canada
Slavic Missionary Service, Inc.
Society of Anglican Missionaries
and Senders (SAMS USA)
Source of Light Ministries Intl. Inc.
Spanish World Ministries
Sports & Rec Plus
TEAM (The Evangelical Alliance Mission)
TEAM of Canada
The Christian and Missionary Alliance
The Free Methodist Church in Canada
The Inner-city Church Planting Mission
The Masters Mission
The Pentecostal Assemblies of Canada
The Voice of the Martyrs
The Waray-Waray Project
Things to Come Mission
Titus International
To Every Tribe
United Brethren in Christ
United Evangelical Churches
United World Mission, Inc.
Virginia Mennonite Missions
Vision Ministries Canada
Wisconsin Evangelical Lutheran
Synod, Board for World Missions
World Compassion Terry Law Ministries
World Horizons
World Mission Associates
World Mission Prayer League
World Partners USA
World Reach, Inc
World Team Canada
World Team US
World Witness
WorldVenture

CHURCH/SCHOOL/GENERAL CHRISTIAN EDUCATION

Agape Gospel Mission
Allegheny Wesleyan Methodist Connection
Association of Free Lutheran Congregations
Avant Ministries
Avant Ministries Canada
Baptist Haiti Mission
Baptist Missionary Association
of America (BMAA)
Barnabas Aid
BethanyKids Canada
Bibles For The World, Inc.
BIC Canada-Global
Blessing the Children International
Care of Creation, Inc.
Childcare Worldwide
Children's Lifeline
Chosen People Ministries (Canada)
Christian Medical & Dental Associations
Christian Reformed World Missions
Church of God (Holiness) World
Mission Dept., Inc.
Colorado Haiti Project Inc.
Commission to Every Nation
Commission To Every Nation-Canada
Cross-Cultural Ministries, Churches
of God General Conference
Cup of Cold Water Ministries
Daystar U.S., Global Mission
Discipleship International
East European Missions Network
EBM International
Echocuba
Effect Hope
Engineering Ministries International (EMI)
Enrich Missions, Inc
Evangelical Bible Mission
Evangelical Mennonite Mission Conference
Evangelical Mission Ministries
Faith Baptist Mission

Faith Christian Fellowship Intl.
Four Corners Ministries
Gate Breaker Ministries
Global Witness and Ministry-AME Church
Global Missions of Open Bible Churches
Good News for India
Good Shepherd Ministries Intl.
Grace Mission Inc.
Greater Grace World Outreach
Haitian Christian Outreach
Harvest Bridge
Harvest Foundation
Heart for Lebanon Foundation
Heart To Heart International Ministries
Identify
IN Network dba International Needs USA
Indopartners Agency
Intercede International
International Faith Missions
Jews for Jesus Canada
Joni and Friends
Kids Alive International
Kids Around the World
LeadaChild
Lifeline Christian Mission
Lifesong for Orphans
Luke Society
Macedonia World Baptist
    Mission International
Macedonia World Baptist Missions, Inc.
Make Way Partners
Middle East Christian Outreach
    (MECO Canada)
Ministry to Educate and Equip Intl. (MTEE)
Mission Eurasia
Mission On The Move
Mission Possible
Mission Possible Canada
Mission Possible USA
Mission to Children
Missions Resource Network

National Association of Congregational
    Christian Churches
National Religious Broadcasters
Network of International Christian Schools
New Life Advance International
Niños de Mexico
Northwest Haiti Christian Mission
One Child Matters
Partners Relief & Development
Precious Seed Ministries Inc.
Probe Ministries International
Reciprocal Ministries International
Resourcing Christian Education
    International
RP Global Missions
Samaritan's Purse
SAND International
Sanma (South Asia Native
    Missionary Alliance)
Society of Anglican Missionaries
    and Senders (SAMS USA)
South African Christian Mission, Inc.
South America Mission
TeachBeyond USA
The Esther School - Dynamic
    Youth Ministries
The Salvation Army USA
    National Headquarters
Village Schools International
Virginia Mennonite Missions
Visionledd o/a Working for
    Orphans and Widows
Word & Deed
Word & Deed Ministries Canada
World Gospel Mission
World Reach, Inc
World Witness
WorldVenture
WorldView
Zion Evangelical Ministries
    of Africa (ZEMA)

COMMUNITY DEVELOPMENT

ACM International
American Leprosy Missions
Assemblies of God World Missions
Baptist Haiti Mission
Beautiful Feet
Beyond Borders
Blessing the Children International
Bright Hope
Buckner International
CAMA Services
Camino Global
CAUSE Canada
Christian Veterinary Mission
CMF International
Commission to Every Nation
Commission To Every Nation-Canada
Cross-Cultural Ministries, Churches
    of God General Conference
Earth Mission, Inc.
East African Ministries
ECHO
Empowering Lives International
endPoverty.org
Enrich Missions, Inc
Equip Inc & Equip International
Equip, Canada
Evangelical Free Church of Canada Mission
Evangelical Mennonite Mission Conference
Evangelical Missionary Church of Canada
Every Child Ministries, Inc.
FAME
FARMS International, Inc.
Four Corners Ministries
Free Methodist World Missions
GoCorps
Good News for India
Haitian Christian Outreach
Heart for Lebanon Foundation
Helps Ministries
IN Network dba International Needs USA

India Gospel League
Interserve USA
Into All The World
Kinship United
KORE Foundation
Latin America Mission
Latin American Missions Association
Luke Society
Lutheran Brethren International Mission
MB Mission
MB Mission Canada
MEDA - Mennonite Economic
    Development Associates
Medical Ambassadors International
    (Lifewind International)
Mennonite Economic Development
    Associates (MEDA)
Mission ONE, Inc.
Missionary TECH Team
mPower Approach
New Life Advance International
New Life International
New Mission Systems International
Northwest Haiti Christian Mission
OMF International - Canada
Operation Blessing International Relief
    and Development Corporation
Operation Bootstrap Africa
Operation Mobilization
Partners International
RAISE International, Inc.
Reach Beyond
Real Impact Missions
Reciprocal Ministries International
Reformed Church in America, General
    Synod Council, Global Mission
SAND International
Sanma (South Asia Native
    Missionary Alliance)
SCORE International
Self-Help International

SEND International of Canada
Servant Partners
Servants in Faith & Technology (SIFAT)
Serve Globally
Society of Anglican Missionaries
    and Senders (SAMS USA)
The Evangelical Covenant Church
The Masters Mission
The Presbyterian Church in Canada
TMS Global
Touch the World
Twenty-six:Twelve
United World Mission, Inc.
Village Schools International
Visionledd o/a Working for
    Orphans and Widows
Women in the Window International
World Gospel Mission
World Servants, Inc.
Wycliffe Associates
Wycliffe Bible Translators USA

CONSTRUCTING CHURCHES & CHILDREN'S HOMES
Mission of Mercy Canada

CORRESPONDENCE COURSES
American Evangelical Christian Churches
BCM International (Canada), Inc.
Disciples International
Evangelical Christian Church
    in Canada, The
Evangelical Mission Ministries
Every Home for Christ
Good Shepherd Ministries Intl.
Gospel Fellowship Association
Gospel Tide Broadcasting Association
Impact Canada Ministries, Inc.
InterAct Ministries of Canada
Macedonian Missionary Service
Mailbox Club International Inc., The

Master's Resourcing Commission
Mission Without Borders Canada
New Hope International
Rio Grande Bible Institute, Inc.
Source of Light Ministries Intl. Inc.
Spanish World Ministries
Wisconsin Evangelical Lutheran
    Synod, Board for World Missions
World Christian Ministries Association

COUNSELING
African Enterprise
Alongside, Inc
Avant Ministries Canada
Barnabas International
Caring for Others
Chaplaincy Endorsement Commission
    for the Christian Church and
    Churches of Christ
Compassio
Forgotten Voices Intl.
Freedom in Christ Ministries - USA
Global Aid Network, Inc. - Canada
Life Impact Inc
Link Care Foundation
Mercy Ships
Mobile Member Care Team
Narramore Christian Foundation
One Another Ministries International
Paraclete Mission Group, Inc.
Pilgrim
Spanish World Ministries

CPM
10/40 Connections
Accelerating International
    Mission Strategies (AIMS)
Africa Inland Mission Canada Intl.
Ambassadors for Christ International
Anglican Frontier Missions

Apostolic Church of Pentecost of
  Canada (Global Harvest Missions)
Asian Access
Baptist International Outreach
Beautiful Feet
Beyond
BILD International
Campus Crusade for Christ (Cru in the US)
Caribbean Lifetime Mission
Christar Canada
CMF International
Communitas International
CRM
Crossover Communications International
Disciple Makers
East-West Ministries International
Eastern Mennonite Missions
EPC World Outreach
Evangelical Mennonite Conference
FARMS International, Inc.
Foursquare Missions International
Frontiers
Frontiers Canada
Global Gates
Greater Europe Mission
Greater Europe Mission Canada
IMB of the Southern Baptist Convention
Indopartners Agency
International Gospel Outreach
International Project
MB Mission
MB Mission Canada
Medical Centers of West Africa (MCWA)
Multiplication Network Ministries
OMF International
One Challenge
One Mission Society
Oneway Ministries
Outreach to Asia Nationals
Pioneers Canada
Pioneers USA

Project WorldReach / Train & Multiply
ReachAcross
RP Global Missions
Scriptures In Use
South America Mission
Taiwan Harvest 119
Team Expansion, Inc.
Vision Ministries Canada
WEC International
World Mission Associates

CRISIS MANAGEMENT & SECURITY
Crisis Consulting International
Mobile Member Care Team

DEAF-BLIND MINISTRIES
Biblical Ministries Worldwide

DEVELOPMENT
ADRA (Adventist Development
  and Relief Agency)
All About Orphans (David
  Livingstone KURE Foundation)
Canadian South America Mission
China Service Ventures
Christian Flights International
Christian Relief Fund, The
Church World Service
Crossroads Christian
  Communications Inc. (ERDF)
EMAS Canada
ERDO - Emergency Relief
  and Development
Evangelical Friends Mission
Food for the Hungry, Inc.
FRIENDS in Action International - Canada
Global Aid Network, Inc. - Canada
Habitat for Humanity Canada
Habitat for Humanity International
Heifer Project International
International Aid
International Association For Refugees

International Child Care (Canada), Inc.
International Crisis Aid
International Teams, U.S.A.
InterServe Canada
Kerus Global Education
Living Hope Ministries International, Inc.
Medical Teams International
Mexico Medical Missions
Mission of Mercy Canada
North American Baptist Conference
  - Worldwide Outreach
Pilgrim
Teen Missions International, Inc.
World Concern
World Relief
World Vision Canada
Wycliffe Bible Translators of Canada, Inc.
Youth for Christ, Canada
Youth Ministry International

DISABLED MINISTRY

American Leprosy Missions
BethanyKids
BethanyKids Canada
Bridge Builders International
CAUSE Canada
Christian Blind Mission
  International - Canada
Deaf Missions International, Inc.
Foundation for His Ministry
Go Ye Fellowship
Help for Haiti Inc.
Holt International Children's Services, Inc.
Hope Haven International Ministries
International Child Care (Canada), Inc.
Joni and Friends
Macedonia World Baptist
  Mission International
Macedonia World Baptist Missions, Inc.
New Hope Uganda Ministries
Northwest Haiti Christian Mission

Venture International
Women of Hope International

DISCIPLESHIP

A.C.T. International
ABWE Canada (Across Borders
  for World Evangelism)
ABWE International
ACCI (Adventive Cross Cultural Initiatives)
Action International Ministries - Canada
Advancing Native Missions
Advent Christian World Outreach
Adventures in Missions
Africa Inland Mission
Africa Inland Mission Canada Intl.
African Children's Mission
African Enterprise
Allegheny Wesleyan Methodist Connection
Alongside Ministries International
Amazon Focus, Inc.
American Baptist International Ministries
Apostolic Church in Canada, The
Apostolic Church of Pentecost of
  Canada (Global Harvest Missions)
Assemblies of God World Missions
Avant Ministries Canada
Awana Clubs International
Back to the Bible
Baptist Bible Fellowship International
  - World Mission Service Center
Baptist General Conference of Canada
Baptist Medical & Dental Mission
  International, Inc. (BMDMI)
Baptist Mid-Missions
Baptist Missionary Association
  of America (BMAA)
Be One Together
BEE World (Biblical Education
  by Extension)
BethanyKids
Bible League Canada

Biblical Ministries Worldwide

BLF Canada

Boundless Ministries, Inc.

Brethren in Christ World
    Missions (BICWM)

Cadence International

Café 1040, Inc.

Camino Global

Campus Crusade for Christ (Cru in the US)

Canadian Baptist Ministries

Canadian National Baptist
    Convention (CNBC)

Catalyst Missions

CBMC, Inc.

Chaplaincy Endorsement Commission
    for the Christian Church and
    Churches of Christ

Children's HopeChest

China Partners

Chosen People Ministries (Canada)

Christ for Children International

Christian Aid Mission

Christian Aviation and Radio Mission

Christian Discipleship International

Christian Fellowship Union, Inc.

Christian Medical & Dental Associations

Christian Ministries International (CMI)

Christian Reformed World Missions

Church of the Nazarene, Inc.

CityTeam Ministries - New
    Generations International

CMTS Ministries

Commission to Every Nation

Compassion Canada

Converge

CRM

Crossworld

Crossworld Canada

CULTURELink

CyberMissions

Davar Partners International

Development Associates Intl. (DAI)

Disciple Makers

Disciples International

Discipleship International

East European Missions Network

Eastern Mennonite Missions

Emmanuel Intl. Canada

Encompass World Partners

Entrust

EQUIP International Ministries

ERRC Educational Society - Canada

Eternal Hope in Haiti

Ethnos360

EurAsian Baptist Mission

European Christian Mission Intl. - USA

Evangelical Friends Mission

Evangelical Mennonite Mission Conference

Evangelical Methodist Church,
    Inc. - Board of Missions

Evangelical Missionary Church of Canada

Evangelism Explosion III International, Inc.

Faith Christian Fellowship Intl.

FaithLife Ministries, Inc.

Far East Broadcasting Associates
    of Canada (FEB Canada)

FARMS International, Inc.

Fellowship International Mission

Fellowship of Companies for
    Christ International (FCCI)

Fellowship of Evangelical Churches
    - International Ministries

Foundation for His Ministry

Four Corners Ministries

Foursquare Missions International

Freedom in Christ Ministries - USA

Friendship International Ministries, Inc.

Global Health Outreach

Global Media Outreach

Global Missions (United
    Pentecostal Church Intl.)

Global Missions of Open Bible Churches

Global Partners (The Wesleyan
   Church World Headquarters)
Global Recordings Network
Global Training Network
Globe International
Go Ye Fellowship
Good News for India
Good Shepherd Ministries Intl.
GoSendMe Global
Gospel Mission of South
   America of Canada
Gospel Tide Broadcasting Association
Greater Europe Mission Canada
Greater Europe Mission, Global Mission
Greater Grace World Outreach
Haitian Christian Outreach
Harvest Foundation
HBI Global Partners
Heart for Lebanon Foundation
Heart of the Bride Ministries
Heart To Heart International Ministries
Hellenic Ministries USA
HOPE International
iHope International
IMB of the Southern Baptist Convention
In Motion Ministries
India Gospel League
Indopartners Agency
InterAct Ministries
InterAct Ministries of Canada
International Friendships, Inc.
International Gospel Outreach
International Messengers
International Street Kids Outreach
   Ministries (ISKOM)
International Students, Inc (ISI)
International Teams, U.S.A.
Into All The World
Italy for Christ, Inc.
Jewish Awareness Ministries, Inc.
Jews for Jesus Canada

Kids for Christ International
Kidzana Ministries
LeadaChild
Liberty Corner Mission
Liebenzell Mission of Canada
Liebenzell Mission of USA, Inc.
Life in Messiah International
LIFE International
Lifesong for Orphans
Living Word Missions
LOGOI Ministries
Mailbox Club International Inc., The
Master's Resourcing Commission
MB Mission
MB Mission Canada
Medical Ministry International Canada, Inc
Messianic Jewish Movement
   International, Inc. The (MJMI)
Mission Catalyst Intl. Inc.
Mission On The Move
Mission ONE, Inc.
Mission Possible Canada
Missionary Athletes International
Missions Door
Missions to Military, Inc.
Morelli Ministries Intl. Inc.
National Association of Congregational
   Christian Churches
Navigators of Canada, The
Nehemiah Teams International
Network of International Christian Schools
New Mission Systems International
New Tribes Mission of Canada
NEXT Worldwide
North American Baptist Conference
   - Worldwide Outreach
OMF International
OMF International - Canada
One Child Matters
Opportunity International Canada
Outreach Canada

Paradigm Shift
Partners International
People International USA
Perimeter Church - Global Outreach
Pioneers Canada
Pioneers USA
Polish Christian Ministries
Power to Change Ministries
Prayer Baptist Missions International, Inc.
Precept Ministries International
Project AmaZon
Project AmaZon Canada Society
Ravi Zacharias International Ministries, Inc.
Reach A Village
ReachAcross
Reaching Japan Together (RJT)
Reciprocal Ministries International
Rehoboth Ministries, Inc
Ripe for Harvest, Inc.
Rosedale Mennonite Missions
RP Global Missions
SCORE International
Scripture Union, USA
Scriptures In Use
SEND International of Canada
SEND International, Inc.
ServeNow
Shield of Faith Mission International
Slavic Gospel Association
Society of Anglican Missionaries
    and Senders (SAMS USA)
South America Mission
Sports & Rec Plus
Supreme Task International, Inc.
Surfing the Nations
Taiwan Harvest 119
TCM International Institute
TEAM (The Evangelical Alliance Mission)
TEAM of Canada
The Centers for Apologetics
    Research (CFAR)

The Christian and Missionary Alliance
The God's Story Project
The Inner-city Church Planting Mission
The Masters Mission
The Navigators
The Pentecostal Assemblies of Canada
TIME Ministries
Timothy Two Project International
Titus International
TMS Global
To Every Tribe
Touch the World
Training Evangelistic Leadership
TWR
TWR Canada
United Brethren in Christ
United World Mission, Inc.
Village Schools International
Virginia Mennonite Missions
Weiner Ministries International
With Open Eyes
Women in the Window International
Women of Hope International
Word of Life Fellowship Inc
World Compassion Society
World Compassion Terry Law Ministries
World Indigenous Missions
World Mission Associates
World Mission Prayer League
World Missionary Assistance Plan
World Outreach International - US
World Partners USA
World Reach, Inc
World Team US
World Witness
WorldVenture
Worldwide Discipleship Assoc.
Young Life of Canada
Youth for Christ International
Youth for Christ, Canada

Youth With A Mission (YWAM)
Youth with a Mission Canada Inc.

DMM

ACM International
Ambassadors for Christ International
Apostolic Church of Pentecost of
  Canada (Global Harvest Missions)
Asian Access
Beautiful Feet
Christar Canada
CMF International
CRM
Disciple Makers
East-West Ministries International
EPC World Outreach
Evangelical Mennonite Conference
Evangelical Missionary Church of Canada
Forefront Experience
Frontiers
Frontiers Canada
Global Frontier Missions
International Project
Josiah Venture
Medical Centers of West Africa (MCWA)
Mission to Children
Missions Resource Network
One Challenge
One Mission Society
Outreach to Asia Nationals
ReachAcross
Scriptures In Use
TCM International Institute
Team Expansion, Inc.
The Navigators
World Mission Associates
Youth for Christ, Canada

DOMESTIC HELP & HOMESCHOOLING FOR MISSIONARY FAMILIES

Mission Nannys

ECONOMIC DEVELOPMENT

Latin America Mission
Mennonite Economic Development
  Associates (MEDA)

ENVIRONMENTAL MISSIONS

Care of Creation, Inc.
Christar
Reaching Japan Together (RJT)

EVANGELISM

A.C.T. International
ABWE Canada (Across Borders
  for World Evangelism)
ACCI (Adventive Cross Cultural
  Initiatives) - US
Advancing Native Missions
Alberto Mottesi Evangelistic
  Association, Inc.
Alongside Ministries International
Amazon Outreach
American Evangelical Christian Churches
Apostolic Christian Church -
  Missionary Committee
Awana Clubs International
Baptist Medical & Dental Mission
  International, Inc. (BMDMI)
BCM International (Canada), Inc.
BLF Canada
Brazil Gospel Fellowship Mission (BGFM)
Cadence International
Canadian National Baptist
  Convention (CNBC)
Caribbean Baptist Mission Society
CEIFA International
Central Yearly Meeting of Friends Missions
Children of Promise International

Children's Ministry International, Inc. (CMI)

China Outreach Ministries, Inc.

Christ for Children International

Christ for the City International

Christ for the Nations, Inc.

Christian and Missionary
Alliance in Canada, The

Christian Cultural Development
Foundation

Christians In Action Missions International

Church of God (Cleveland, TN)
World Missions

Commission To Every Nation-Canada

Compassion International, Inc.

CTI Music Ministries (Carpenter's
Tools International)

Disciples International

Episcopal Church USA - Domestic
& Foreign Missionary Society

ERRC Educational Society - Canada

Evangelical Covenant Church of Canada

Evangelical Lutheran Church in
America, Div. for Global Mission

Evangelical Methodist Church,
Inc. - Board of Missions

Evangelism Resources, Inc.

Evangelize China Fellowship, Inc.

Far East Broadcasting Associates
of Canada (FEB Canada)

Fellowship of Companies for
Christ International (FCCI)

Fellowship of Evangelical Churches
- International Ministries

FOCAS (Foundation of Compassionate
American Samaritans)

For His Glory Evangelistic Ministries

Friends in Action Intl.

Fundamental Baptist Mission
of Trinidad & Tobago

Fundamental Baptist Missions International

GAIN (Global Aid Network)

Gideons International, The

Global Missions (United
Pentecostal Church Intl.)

Global Outreach International

Global Outreach Mission Inc., Canada

Global Outreach Mission, Inc.

Global Scholars

globalLead

Globe International

Go to Nations

Good Shepherd Ministries, Inc.

Gospel Fellowship Association

Gospel for Asia Canada

Gospel Mission of South
America of Canada

Gospel Outreach Ministries Intl.

Great Commission Media Ministries

Harvest International, Inc.

Heart for Honduras

Heart of the Bride Ministries

Hermano Pablo Ministries

Impact Canada Ministries, Inc.

India Gospel Outreach, Inc.

Inter-Varsity Christian
Fellowship of Canada

International Partnership Ministries, Inc.

International Students, Inc (ISI)

International Teams, Canada (Evangelical
International Crusades Canada, Inc.)

Iranian Christians International

ISOH/IMPACT

Kids for Christ International

Liberty Corner Mission

Living Hope Ministries International, Inc.

Living Water International

Living Water Teaching

Lutheran Hour Ministries

Mailbox Club International Inc., The

Messianic Jewish Movement
International, Inc. The (MJMI)

Mexican Medical Ministries

Middle East Media - USA

Mission Generation, Inc.

Muslim Hope

Mustard Seed Mission Canada, Inc.

National Baptist Convention of
America - Foreign Mission Board

National Baptist Convention USA,
Inc. - Foreign Mission Board

Navigators of Canada, The

OMS International - Canada

On The Go Ministries/Keith Cook Team

OneHope

Open Door Baptist Missions

Orthodox Presbyterian Church -
Committee on Foreign Missions

Palm Missionary Ministries, Inc.

Paradigm Shift

Partners in Asian Missions

Presbyterian Missionary Union

Primitive Methodist Church in the
USA - International Mission Board

Proclaim! International, Inc.

Progressive National Baptist Convention,
Inc. (PNBC) - Missions

Project AmaZon

Project AmaZon Canada Society

Ravi Zacharias International Ministries, Inc.

Reaching Indians Ministries International

Resourcing Christian Education
International

Romanian Missionary Society

Salvation Army - Canada and
Bermuda Territory, The

Seventh-day Adventists, General
Conference - Global Mission

SIM Canada

South American Missionary
Society in Canada

STEM International

Surfing the Nations

TeachBeyond Canada

Vineyard Church USA - Missions

Weiner Ministries International

White Fields Missionary Society of Canada

World Indigenous Missions

World Link Ministries

World Mission

World Outreach International - US

World-Wide Missions

Worldwide Medical-Dental
Evangelical Mission

Youth for Christ International

Youth With A Mission (YWAM)

Youth with a Mission Canada Inc.

YUGO Ministries (Youth Unlimited
Gospel Outreach, Inc.)

YUGO Ministries Canada

EXTENSION EDUCATION

ACSI (Association of Christian
Schools International)

Alberto Mottesi Evangelistic
Association, Inc.

American Evangelical Christian Churches

BEE World (Biblical Education
by Extension)

Bibles For The World, Inc.

Bold Ventures

Brazil Gospel Fellowship Mission (BGFM)

Brethren in Christ World
Missions (BICWM)

CEIFA International

Christ to the Nations

Christian Outreach International

Church of God (Cleveland, TN)
World Missions

Church of God Ministries
(Anderson) - Global Strategy

Church of the Brethren - Global
Mission Partnerships

CrossWay International

CyberMissions

Daystar U.S.

EMAS Canada

Emmanuel Intl. Canada

Entrust

Eternal Hope in Haiti

Evangelical Christian Church in Canada

Evangelical Friends Church Southwest

Evangelical Mennonite Conference

Evangelistic Faith Mission, Inc.

Fellowship of Evangelical Churches
- International Ministries

Global Scholars

Good Shepherd Ministries, Inc.

International Christian Ministries

International Christian Ministries
Canada (ICM)

Liebenzell Mission of USA, Inc.

Lifewater International, Inc.

Lutheran Church-Missouri
Synod, World Mission

Ministry to Educate and Equip Intl. (MTEE)

Mission of Mercy Canada

Missions Door

Mustard Seed International

Ravi Zacharias International Ministries, Inc.

ReachGlobal

Shelter for Life Intl. Inc.

SIM Canada

Slavic Gospel Association - Canada

Source of Light Ministries Intl. Inc.

The Kerusso Institute for Global Leaders

The Presbyterian Church in Canada

Wisconsin Evangelical Lutheran
Synod, Board for World Missions

World Gospel Mission

World Link Ministries

World Missionary Assistance Plan

FINANCIAL AND OTHER SUPPORT

International Foundation for
EWHA Woman's University

FUND RAISING OR TRANSMISSION

A.C.T. International

ABWE Canada (Across Borders
for World Evangelism)

Apostolic Christian Church -
Missionary Committee

Barnabas Aid

Children of Promise International

Christian Mission for the Deaf

Crossroads Christian
Communications Inc. (ERDF)

East West Interknit

Evangelical Covenant Church of Canada

Fundamental Baptist Missions International

Globe International

IFCA World Missions

International Child Care, USA

International Pentecostal Holiness Church

MedSend

Opportunity International

Polish Christian Ministries

Scripture Union, USA

ServLife International

Seventh Day Baptist Missionary Society

Slavic Missionary Service, Inc.

Vellore Christian Medical
College Foundation, Inc.

World Missions & Evangelism

World-Wide Missions

FURLOUGHED MISSIONARY SUPPORT

CMTS Ministries

Episcopal Church USA - Domestic
& Foreign Missionary Society

Gospel Mission of South
America of Canada

Interaction International

National Baptist Convention USA,
Inc. - Foreign Mission Board

Providence Mission Homes, Inc.

GRANTS FOR CHRISTIAN HEALTHCARE PROFESSIONALS
MedSend

HEALTH & TECHNOLOGY EDUCATION
Earth Mission, Inc.

HIV/AIDS MINISTRY
ADRA (Adventist Development
    and Relief Agency)
Children's HopeChest
Christian Relief Fund, The
Church World Service
endPoverty.org
ERDO - Emergency Relief
    and Development
Food for the Hungry, Inc.
Global Scholars
Heart of the Bride Ministries
International Child Care, USA
Kerus Global Education
Launch Out Ministries International
Lott Carey Baptist Foreign
    Mission Convention
Medical Teams International
National Baptist Convention USA,
    Inc. - Foreign Mission Board
Nazarene Compassion Ministries Canada
Opportunity International Canada
Samaritan's Purse - Canada
Teen Missions International, Inc.
World Concern
World Orphans
World Relief

HOLISTIC MINISTRY
South America Mission

HOME BUILDING
Lifeline Christian Mission

HOUSING
Habitat for Humanity Canada
Habitat for Humanity International

HOUSING FOR MISSIONARIES
Cedar Lane Missionary Homes
D&D Missionary Homes Inc.
Missionary Retreat Fellowship
Providence Mission Homes, Inc.

HUMAN TRAFFICKING
10/40 Connections
American Baptist International Ministries
Beyond Borders
Compassio
Easy English Outreach
Every Child Ministries, Inc.
Freedom Firm
Gate Breaker Ministries
Global Health Outreach
Go Ye Fellowship
GoCorps
Impact Nations International Ministries
India Partners
International Crisis Aid
International Justice Mission
International Street Kids Outreach
    Ministries (ISKOM)
International Teams, U.S.A.
Interserve USA
Launch Out Ministries International
Lott Carey Baptist Foreign
    Mission Convention
Make Way Partners
New Life Advance International
Partners Relief & Development
Real Impact Missions
Sanma (South Asia Native
    Missionary Alliance)
ServeNow

The Salvation Army USA
  National Headquarters
Vision Beyond Borders
Women to the World, Inc.
World Hope Canada
World Mission Prayer League

IMPOVERISHED FAMILIES
Action International Ministries - Canada
Christ for Children International

INFORMATION OR JOURNALISM
Cumberland Presbyterian Church
  Board of Missions
Door of Hope International
Envoy International
Frontier Ventures
Global Focus
Global Impact Services
GMI
God Reports
International Child Care, USA
Media Associates International
Middle East Christian Outreach
  (MECO Canada)
Mission Services Association, Inc.
Sentinel Group, The
Voice of the Martyrs, Inc., The

INTERNATIONAL DISASTER RELIEF
Samaritan's Purse

INTERNATIONAL
STUDENT MINISTRY
ACM International
Allegheny Wesleyan Methodist Connection
Christian Veterinary Mission
CMF International
Forefront Experience
Go Ye Fellowship
International Friendships, Inc.
International Gospel Outreach

InterVarsity Christian Fellowship/USA
Missionary Gospel Fellowship
Network of International Christian Schools
Reliant Mission, Inc.
Young Life
Youth Ministry International

INTERNET DISCIPLESHIP
OR TRAINING
Camino Global
Christian Aviation and Radio Mission
CyberMissions
Discipleship International
Freedom in Christ Ministries - USA
Global Media Outreach
iHope International
Indopartners Agency
Jews for Jesus Canada
LIFE International
The Centers for Apologetics
  Research (CFAR)
TWR Canada

INTERNET EVANGELISM
Campus Crusade for Christ (Cru in the US)
Chinese Christian Life Fellowship, Inc
Christian Aviation and Radio Mission
CyberMissions
Global Media Outreach
Global Recordings Network
God Reports
Good News Productions International
Indopartners Agency
Jews for Jesus
Jews for Jesus Canada
Key Communications
Life in Messiah International
RREACH

JUSTICE OR PEACE ISSUES
2nd Mile Ministries
American Baptist International Ministries

Beyond Borders
Bread for the World
Café 1040, Inc.
Casa Viva
Christ In Youth
Christian Cultural Development
Foundation
Church of the Brethren - Global
Mission Partnerships
Church World Service
Compassio
Cooperative Baptist Fellowship
- Global Missions
Equip, Canada
ERDO - Emergency Relief
and Development
Food for the Hungry, Inc.
Heifer Project International
International Justice Mission
International Street Kids Outreach
Ministries (ISKOM)
Iranian Christians International
Micah Challenge USA
Open Doors, USA
Operation Mobilization
Opportunity International Canada
Progressive National Baptist Convention,
Inc. (PNBC) - Missions
Reformed Church in America, General
Synod Council, Global Mission
Servant Partners
Serve Globally
The Evangelical Covenant Church
Voice of the Martyrs, Inc., The
Women of Hope International
World Vision, Inc.

LEADERSHIP DEVELOPMENT

10/40 Connections
ACCI (Adventive Cross Cultural Initiatives)
ACSI (Association of Christian
Schools International)

Action International Ministries - Canada
ACTS International Ministries, Inc.
Advent Christian World Outreach
African Enterprise
African Enterprise Canada
African Leadership Development
Agape Gospel Mission
Alongside Ministries International
Amazon Focus, Inc.
Ambassadors for Christ International
American Baptist International Ministries
ARISE International Mission
Asian Access
Asian Outreach International Canada
Assemblies of God World Missions
Aurora Mission, Inc.
BCM International
Be One Together
BEE World (Biblical Education
by Extension)
Beyond Borders
Biblical Ministries Worldwide
BIC Canada-Global
BILD International
Board of World Mission
Bold Ventures
Boundless Ministries, Inc.
Brazil Gospel Fellowship Mission (BGFM)
Bridge Builders International
Bright Hope
Café 1040, Inc.
Canadian Assemblies of God,
General Conference
Canadian Baptist Ministries
Canadian South America Mission
CBMC, Inc.
Chaplaincy Endorsement Commission
for the Christian Church and
Churches of Christ
China Partners
ChinaSource

Christ for the City International

Christian and Missionary
Alliance in Canada, The

Christian Church (Disciples of
Christ) - Global Ministries

Christian Cultural Development
Foundation

Christian Fellowship Union, Inc.

Christian Medical & Dental Associations

Christian Ministries International (CMI)

Christian Reformed World Missions

Church Leadership Development
International

Church of God Ministries
(Anderson) - Global Strategy

Church of the Nazarene, Inc.

Church Planting International

Churches of God, General Conference

CIS- Christian Involvement In Service

CMF International

Colorado Haiti Project Inc.

COMHINA

Compassion Canada

Compassion International, Inc.

Congregational Methodist Missions

Cooperative Baptist Fellowship
- Global Missions

Crisis Consulting International

CRM

Crossworld

Crossworld Canada

CULTURELink

Cumberland Presbyterian Church
Board of Missions

Daystar U.S.

Development Associates Intl. (DAI)

Disciple Makers

Disciples International

e3 Partners Ministry

East African Ministries

East European Missions Network

Eastern Mennonite Missions

Emmanuel Intl. Canada

Emmaus Road International

Encompass World Partners

Entrust

Envoy International

EQUIP International Ministries

ERRC Educational Society - Canada

Evangelical Friends Church Southwest

Evangelical Lutheran Church in
America, Div. for Global Mission

Evangelical Mennonite Conference

Evangelical Missionary Church of Canada

Evangelism Resources, Inc.

Faith Christian Fellowship Intl.

FaithLife Ministries, Inc.

Far East Broadcasting Associates
of Canada (FEB Canada)

Fellowship International Mission

Fellowship of Companies for
Christ International (FCCI)

Fellowship of Evangelical Churches
- International Ministries

FH Canada

Firefall International Inc.

For His Glory Evangelistic Ministries

Forgotten Voices Intl.

Free Methodist World Missions

Freedom in Christ Ministries - USA

Freedom to Lead International

Friends United Meeting

Gate Breaker Ministries

Global Hope India

Global Missions (United
Pentecostal Church Intl.)

Global Outreach International

Global Partners (The Wesleyan
Church World Headquarters)

Global Spheres

Global Teams International, Inc

Global Training Network

globalLead
Globe International
GMI
Go to Nations
Gospel for Asia, Inc.
Gospel Mission of South America, Inc.
Gospel Outreach Ministries Intl.
Grace Ministries International
Great Commission Media Ministries
Harvest Foundation
HBI Global Partners
HOPE International Development Agency
In Motion Ministries
Independent Gospel Missions:
    A Baptist Mission Agency
India Evangelical Mission Inc.
India Gospel League
India Gospel Outreach, Inc.
InterAct Ministries
International Association For Refugees
International Christian Ministries
International Christian Ministries
    Canada (ICM)
International Faith Missions
International Pentecostal Holiness Church
Iranian Christians International
Italy for Christ, Inc.
JARON Ministries International
Kidzana Ministries
Latin America Mission
Latin American Lutheran Mission
Leadership Ministries Worldwide
Leadership Resources International
Leadership Training International
Leadership Vistas International Ministries
LeaderTreks
Liebenzell Mission of USA, Inc.
LIFE International
Link International Ministries
LOGOI Ministries
Lutheran Brethren International Mission

Lutheran Church-Missouri
    Synod, World Mission
Lutheran World Relief
Master's Resourcing Commission
Media Associates International
Medical Ambassadors International
    (Lifewind International)
Mennonite Mission Network
Mercy Ships
Mercy Ships Canada
Messianic Jewish Movement
    International, Inc. The (MJMI)
Ministry to Educate and Equip Intl. (MTEE)
Mission Catalyst Intl. Inc.
Mission Eurasia
Mission Generation, Inc.
Mission Possible
Mission Possible Canada
Mission Possible USA
Mission to the World (PCA), Inc.
Missionaire International
Missionary Gospel Fellowship
Missionary TECH Team
Missions Door
Moravian Church in North America
Multiplication Network Ministries
Mustard Seed Mission Canada, Inc.
Navigators of Canada, The
Nazarene Compassion Ministries Canada
Nehemiah Teams International
New Hope International
New Life Advance International
NEXT Worldwide
OMF International - Canada
OMSC
On The Go Ministries/Keith Cook Team
One Another Ministries International
One Challenge
One World Missions
Open Doors, USA
Operation Mobilization

Opportunity International
Outreach Canada
Paraclete Mission Group, Inc.
Paradigm Shift
Partners in Asian Missions
People International USA
Perimeter Church - Global Outreach
PIC International (Partners in
    Christ International)
Prakash Association, USA
Precept Ministries International
Presbyterian Church (USA),
    Worldwide Ministries
Presbyterian Missionary Union
Project WorldReach / Train & Multiply
Reach Beyond
ReachGlobal
Reformed Church in America, General
    Synod Council, Global Mission
Reliant Mission, Inc.
reSource Leadership International
Rio Grande Bible Institute, Inc.
RREACH
Salvation Army - Canada and
    Bermuda Territory, The
SAND International
Self-Help International
SEND International, Inc.
Servant Partners
Servants in Faith & Technology (SIFAT)
Seventh Day Baptist Missionary Society
Shepherd's Support, Inc.
Sidney and Helen Correll Ministries
    (dba Correll Missionary Ministries)
SIM Canada
South America Mission
South American Missionary
    Society in Canada
Spiritual Overseers Service International
Supreme Task International, Inc.
Surfing the Nations

Talking Bibles International
TCM International Institute
TEAM (The Evangelical Alliance Mission)
Team Expansion, Inc.
TEAM of Canada
The Brethren Church, Inc.
The Christian and Missionary Alliance
The Free Methodist Church in Canada
The Kerusso Institute for Global Leaders
The Navigators
The Presbyterian Church in Canada
Timothy Leadership Training Institute
TMS Global
United Church of Christ - Global Ministries
United World Mission, Inc.
Vineyard Church USA - Missions
Virginia Mennonite Missions
Vision Ministries Canada
visionSynergy
WayMakers
Women in the Window International
Women to the World, Inc.
World Help
World Link Ministries
World Mission
World Missionary Assistance Plan
World Missions & Evangelism
World Outreach International - US
World Partners USA
World Reach, Inc
World Team Canada
World Thrust International
World Vision, Inc.
WorldVenture
Youth for Christ International,
    Global Mission
Youth for Christ, Canada
Youth Ministry International
YUGO Ministries (Youth Unlimited
    Gospel Outreach, Inc.)

LINGUISTICS

Baptist Bible Translators Institute
Canadian Bible Society / La Societe
   Biblique Canadienne
Easy English Outreach
Mission Training International
New Tribes Mission of Canada
Wycliffe Bible Translators of Canada, Inc.
Wycliffe Bible Translators USA

LITERACY

Asian Outreach International Canada
Back to the Bible Canada
Beyond Borders
Bible League Canada
Bible League International
CAUSE Canada
Christian Literacy Associates
Church World Service
CLC Ministries International
Enrich Missions, Inc
Evangel Bible Translators
General Baptists International
Gospel Outreach Ministries Intl.
Literacy & Evangelism International
Lutheran Bible Translators of Canada
Lutheran Bible Translators, Inc.
Mission India
Palm Missionary Ministries, Inc.
Partners in Bible Translation
Pioneer Bible Translators
Supreme Task International, Inc.
Teen Missions International, Inc.
Wycliffe Bible Translators of Canada, Inc.
Wycliffe Bible Translators USA

LITERATURE DISTRIBUTION

Action International Ministries - Canada
Alberto Mottesi Evangelistic
   Association, Inc.
ARISE International Mission

Bible League Canada
Bibles and Literature in French
BLF Canada
Canadian Bible Society / La Societe
   Biblique Canadienne
CEIFA International
Child Evangelism Fellowship, Inc.
Christ for the Nations, Inc.
Christian Aid Ministries (CAM)
Christian Resources Intl.
Church Leadership Development
   International
Church of God of the Apostolic
   Faith, Inc., The
CLC Ministries International
Crescent Project
Disciples International
East West Interknit
Equip Inc & Equip International
Equipping The Saints
Evangelism Resources, Inc.
Every Home for Christ
Friends of Israel Gospel Ministry Inc.
Global Adopt A People Campaign
Good Shepherd Ministries, Inc.
Grace & Truth Inc.
Harvesting In Spanish (HIS)
Impact Canada Ministries, Inc.
International Board of Jewish Missions Inc
Iranian Christians International
Jewish Awareness Ministries, Inc.
Life in Messiah International
Living Word Missions
Lutheran Bible Translators of Canada
Lutheran Bible Translators, Inc.
Mailbox Club International Inc., The
Media Associates International
Missions to Military, Inc.
Open Doors with Brother
   Andrew – Canada
Open Doors, USA

Orthodox Presbyterian Church - Committee on Foreign Missions

Our Daily Bread

Pentecostal Church of God-World Missions Department

Prayer Baptist Missions International, Inc.

Publications Chrétiennes (Christian Publishing in French)

Reach A Village

Russian Bible Society, Inc.

Russian Christian Radio, Inc. (or RCR)

Scripture Union, USA

ServeNow

SGM Canada

Shield of Faith Mission International

Slavic Gospel Association

Source of Light Ministries Intl. Inc.

Spanish American Evangelistic Ministries

STEM International

Teen Mission, USA, Inc. dba Mission Journeys

The Inner-city Church Planting Mission

Village Ministries International

Vision Beyond Borders

Voice of the Martyrs, Inc., The

Waymarks Radio Ministries International

Word To Russia

World Christian Ministries Association

World Compassion Society

World Compassion Terry Law Ministries

World Missionary Assistance Plan

World Missionary Press, Inc.

LITERATURE PRODUCTION

Alberto Mottesi Evangelistic Association, Inc.

Ambassadors for Christ, Inc.

Aurora Mission, Inc.

Bethany Gateways

Bibles and Literature in French

BLF Canada

Canadian Bible Society / La Societe Biblique Canadienne

CEIFA International

Child Evangelism Fellowship, Inc.

Christ for the Nations, Inc.

CLC Ministries International

Crescent Project

Easy English Outreach

Friends of Israel Gospel Ministry Inc.

Friends United Meeting

Frontier Ventures

Global Adopt A People Campaign

Gospel for Asia Canada

Great Commission Center International

International Christian Ministries Canada (ICM)

Iranian Christians International

JARON Ministries International

Jewish Awareness Ministries, Inc.

Josue Yrion World Evangelism & Missions, Inc.

Key Communications

Kidzana Ministries

Leadership Ministries Worldwide

Living Word Missions

Lutheran Brethren International Mission

Media Associates International

Middle East Media - USA

OMSC

Open Doors with Brother Andrew – Canada

Our Daily Bread

Progressive National Baptist Convention, Inc. (PNBC) - Missions

Publications Chrétiennes (Christian Publishing in French)

reSource Leadership International

Romanian Missionary Society

Russian Bible Society, Inc.

Russian Christian Radio, Inc. (or RCR)

Salem Ministries International

Serge
Seventh-day Adventists, General
    Conference - Global Mission
SGM Canada
Slavic Gospel Association - Canada
Spanish American Evangelistic Ministries
The Centers for Apologetics
    Research (CFAR)
Walk Thru the Bible Ministries, Inc.
Waymarks Radio Ministries International
Wisconsin Evangelical Lutheran
    Synod, Board for World Missions
World Christian Ministries Association
World Missionary Assistance Plan
World Missionary Press, Inc.

MANAGEMENT CONSULTING OR TRAINING

ACSI (Association of Christian
    Schools International)
Christian Ministries International (CMI)
Crisis Consulting International
CULTURELink
FaithLife Ministries, Inc.
Fellowship of Companies for
    Christ International (FCCI)
Global Health Ministries
Health Partners International of Canada
LIFE International
Link Care Foundation
MEDA - Mennonite Economic
    Development Associates
Media Associates International
Mennonite Economic Development
    Associates (MEDA)
Mobile Member Care Team
One World Missions
Paraclete Mission Group, Inc.
Partners Worldwide
TeachBeyond USA
Women of Hope International
Worldwide Tentmakers, Inc.

MASS EVANGELISM

African Enterprise
African Enterprise Canada
Air Mobile Ministries
Allegheny Wesleyan Methodist Connection
Ambassadors for Christ International
AMG International
Assemblies of God World Missions
Baptist Bible Fellowship International
    - World Mission Service Center
BASIC Ministries, Inc
Boundless Ministries, Inc.
Calvary Commission, Inc.
Child Evangelism Fellowship, Inc.
China Ministries International
Chinese Christian Life Fellowship, Inc
Chosen People Ministries, Inc.
Christ to the Nations
Christian Aid Mission
Christian Laymen's Missionary
    Evangelism Association
Christian Medical & Dental Associations
Christian Outreach International
Church of God of the Apostolic
    Faith, Inc., The
Church of the Nazarene, Inc.
Congregational Methodist Missions
Crescent Project
CrossWay International
Deaf Missions International, Inc.
e3 Partners Ministry
East African Ministries
East-West Ministries International
EurAsian Baptist Mission
European Christian Mission Intl. - USA
Far Corners Missions
Far East Broadcasting Company
For God's Children Intl.
Foundation for His Ministry
Foursquare Missions International
Friendship International Ministries, Inc.

Global Action, Inc.
Global Fellowship Inc.
Global Media Outreach
Global Recordings Network
Good News Productions International
Gospel Revival Ministries
India Evangelical Mission Inc.
Intercede International
Intercomm, Inc.
Italy for Christ, Inc.
Jews for Jesus
Jews for Jesus Canada
Joni and Friends
Josiah Venture
Josue Yrion World Evangelism
    & Missions, Inc.
KORE Foundation
Luis Palau Evangelistic Association
Mission Eurasia
Mission India
Mission Possible
Missions to Military, Inc.
Morelli Ministries Intl. Inc.
Mutual Faith Ministries Intl.
Open Air Campaigners - Overseas
    Ministries (OAC-OM)
Pentecostal Church of God-World
    Missions Department
People International USA
Pioneer Bible Translators
Prayer Baptist Missions International, Inc.
Presbyterian Mission International (PMI)
Reach Beyond
Ripe for Harvest, Inc.
RREACH
Salem Ministries International
SCORE International
Shield of Faith Mission International
Sowers International, The
Spanish American Evangelistic Ministries
Spanish World Ministries

Sports & Rec Plus
Standards of Excellence in Short-
    Term Mission (SOE)
Teen Mission, USA, Inc. dba
    Mission Journeys
The Inner-city Church Planting Mission
Training Evangelistic Leadership
TWR
With Open Eyes
Women to the World, Inc.
World Horizons
World Team Canada
Worldwide Discipleship Assoc.

MEDIA OUTREACH
Intercomm, Inc.
TWR Canada

**MEDICAL MINISTRY: INCLUDING
DENTAL OR PUBLIC HEALTH**
Action International Ministries
Agape Unlimited
American Baptist International Ministries
American Leprosy Missions
AMG International
Azusa Pacific University -
    Mexico Outreach
Baptist Haiti Mission
Baptist Missionary Association
    of America (BMAA)
BethanyKids
BethanyKids Canada
Blessings International
Buckner International
Caring Partners International
CAUSE Canada
Children's Lifeline
Childspring International
Christ In Youth
Christar
Christian Dental Society

Christian Emergency Relief Teams
(CERT) International
Christian Medical & Dental Associations
Church of God (Holiness) World
Mission Dept., Inc.
Colorado Haiti Project Inc.
Commission To Every Nation-Canada
Converge
Cross-Cultural Ministries, Churches
of God General Conference
Cup of Cold Water Ministries
CWE Missions
Earth Mission, Inc.
EBM International
Effect Hope
Engineering Ministries International (EMI)
EPC World Outreach
Equip Inc & Equip International
Eternal Hope in Haiti
EurAsian Baptist Mission
Evangelical Bible Mission
Evangelical Free Church of Canada Mission
Evangelical Friends Mission
Evangelistic Faith Mission, Inc.
Faith Baptist Mission
FAME
Far Corners Missions
Flying Doctors of America
For Haiti with Love, Inc.
Global Health Outreach
Global Hope India
Global Partners (The Wesleyan
Church World Headquarters)
GoCorps
Health Partners International of Canada
Health Teams International
Identify
Impact Nations International Ministries
India Gospel League
International
International Faith Missions

Interserve USA
Lifeline Malawi
Luke Society
Macedonian Missionary Service
Medical Centers of West Africa (MCWA)
Medical Ministry International Canada, Inc
MedSend
Mennonite International
Health Association
Mercy Ships Canada
Mexican Medical Ministries
Mission Possible Canada
Mission Possible USA
mPower Approach
National Association of Congregational
Christian Churches
Niños de Mexico
Northwest Haiti Christian Mission
OMF International
Partners Relief & Development
Reach Beyond
Real Impact Missions
Reformed Church in America, General
Synod Council, Global Mission
Reformed Episcopal Board
of Foreign Missions
Samaritan's Purse
Serge
Seventh Day Baptist Missionary Society
SIM USA
Sports & Rec Plus
Standards of Excellence in Short-
Term Mission (SOE)
TEAM (The Evangelical Alliance Mission)
TEAMS for Medical Missions
The Salvation Army USA
National Headquarters
Titus International
Twenty-six:Twelve
United Brethren in Christ
Volunteers in Medical Missions

Word & Deed
Word & Deed Ministries Canada
World Gospel Mission
World Mission Prayer League
World Witness
WorldVenture
Worldwide Lab Improvement

MEDICAL SUPPLIES

Advancing Native Missions
Air Mobile Ministries
American Leprosy Missions
Awana Clubs International
Blessings International
Caribbean Baptist Mission Society
Caring Partners International
CEIFA International
Chosen Mission Project
Christ for India, Inc.
ComCare International
Effect Hope
Equipping The Saints
FAME
FH Canada
Flying Doctors of America
For Haiti with Love, Inc.
GAIN (Global Aid Network)
Global Health Ministries
Good Shepherd Ministries, Inc.
Haiti Arise - Canada
Harvest International, Inc.
Health Teams International
IMA World Health
International Aid
ISOH/IMPACT
Link International Ministries
MAP International
Medical Ministry International Canada, Inc
Medical Teams International
Men for Missions International

Mennonite International
   Health Association
Mercy Ships Canada
Mexican Medical Ministries
National Baptist Convention of
   America - Foreign Mission Board
Nazarene Compassion Ministries Canada
Orthodox Presbyterian Church -
   Committee on Foreign Missions
Ukrainian Children's Christian Fund
Ukrainian Childrens Fund
Vision Beyond Borders
Visionledd o/a Working for
   Orphans and Widows
Worldwide Lab Improvement

MEDICAL WORK

ABWE International
ADRA (Adventist Development
   and Relief Agency)
Agathos International
Amazon Outreach
Baptist Medical & Dental Mission
   International, Inc. (BMDMI)
Childcare Worldwide
China Service Ventures
Christian Aid Ministries (CAM)
Christian Flights International
Churches of God, General Conference
Compassion International, Inc.
EMAS Canada
Equip, Canada
Far East Broadcasting Associates
   of Canada (FEB Canada)
FOCAS (Foundation of Compassionate
   American Samaritans)
Friends United Meeting
Global Health Ministries
Global Outreach International
Global Outreach Mission Inc., Canada
Global Outreach Mission, Inc.
Good Shepherd Ministries, Inc.

Gospel Fellowship Association
Haiti Lutheran Mission Society
Harvesting In Spanish (HIS)
Heart for Honduras
India Partners
International Child Care (Canada), Inc.
International Crisis Aid
InterServe Canada
Lifewater International, Inc.
Living Water Teaching
Lott Carey Baptist Foreign
   Mission Convention
Medical Ministry International
Medical Teams International
Mercy Ships
Mexico Medical Missions
Mission to the World (PCA), Inc.
Mustard Seed International
National Baptist Convention of
   America - Foreign Mission Board
Nazarene Compassion Ministries Canada
Operation Blessing International Relief
   and Development Corporation
Pilgrim
Presbyterian Church (USA),
   Worldwide Ministries
Project AmaZon
Project AmaZon Canada Society
Salvation Army - Canada and
   Bermuda Territory, The
Samaritan's Purse - Canada
Seventh-day Adventists, General
   Conference - Global Mission
Supreme Task International, Inc.
Tribes and Nations Outreach
Worldwide Medical-Dental
   Evangelical Mission

MEMBER CARE

Anglican Frontier Missions
Apostolic Church in Canada, The
Avant Ministries

Avant Ministries Canada
Barnabas International
Caring for Others
Christian Medical & Dental Associations
Church of God Ministries
   (Anderson) - Global Strategy
Emmaus Road International
Evangelical Friends Church Southwest
Foursquare Missions International
Free Will Baptist International Missions
Frontiers
Full Gospel Evangelistic Association
Global Opportunities – Global Intent
Global Teams International, Inc
Great Cities Missions
Hope for the Hungry
Interaction International
Into All The World
Life Impact Inc
Link Care Foundation
Mission Training International
Missions Resource Network
Mobile Member Care Team
OMSC
One Another Ministries International
Outreach Canada
Paraclete Mission Group, Inc.
Shepherd's Support, Inc.
TeachBeyond Canada
The Upstream Collective
TWR Canada
United Evangelical Churches
WEC International Canada

MICRO-FINANCE
Bright Hope
Opportunity International
Self-Help International

**MINISTRY TO THE
MILITARY COMMUNITY**
Cadence International

MISSIONARY & WORKER TRAINING

2nd Mile Ministries
A.C.T. International
Accelerating International Mission Strategies (AIMS)
ACCI (Adventive Cross Cultural Initiatives) - US
Africa Inland Mission Canada Intl.
African Enterprise Canada
Asian Outreach International Canada
Baptist Bible Fellowship International - World Mission Service Center
Baptist Bible Translators Institute
Baptist International Missions, Inc.
Bethany Gateways
BethanyKids Canada
Board of World Mission
Bold Ventures
Café 1040, Inc.
Canadian Churches Forum for Global Ministries
Caring for Others
Catalyst Missions
CEIFA International
Center for Mission Mobilization
China Ministries International
ChinaSource
Chosen People Ministries, Inc.
Christ In Youth
Christ to the Nations
Christian Aid Mission
Christian Fellowship Union, Inc.
Christian Ministries International (CMI)
Christians In Action Missions International
Church of God Ministries (Anderson) - Global Strategy
Church of the Brethren - Global Mission Partnerships
COMMA
Crescent Project
Crisis Consulting International

CULTURELink
CyberMissions
DeNike Ministries
ECHO
Emmaus Road International
Entrust
Equip Inc & Equip International
ERRC Educational Society - Canada
Ethnos360
Far Corners Missions
Fishhook International
Forefront Experience
Foursquare Missions International
Frontiers
Gateway Training for Cross-cultural Service
Global Fellowship Inc.
Global Frontier Missions
Global Outreach International
Globe International
GMI
Go to Nations
GoSendMe Global
Gospel for Asia, Inc.
Gospel Outbound
Great Cities Missions
Great Commission Center International
Harvest Bridge
Harvest Foundation
Harvest Mission to the Unreached
Hope for the Hungry
IFCA World Missions
In Motion Ministries
Interaction International
International Board of Jewish Missions Inc
International Gospel Outreach
International Messengers
International Pentecostal Holiness Church
International Project
InterVarsity Christian Fellowship/USA
JAARS, Inc.
Jewish Awareness Ministries, Inc.

Jews for Jesus
Joni and Friends
Kids for Christ International
Kidzana Ministries
Liebenzell Mission of Canada
Lifesong for Orphans
Link Care Foundation
Literacy & Evangelism International
Living Water Teaching
MB Mission
MB Mission Canada
MedSend
Messianic Jewish Movement
    International, Inc. The (MJMI)
Middle East Media - USA
Mission Catalyst Intl. Inc.
Mission India
Mission Nannys
Mission Training International
MissionPREP Inc.
Missions Resource Network
MMS Aviation (Missionary
    Maintenance Services)
Mobile Member Care Team
Moravian Church in North America
Muslim Hope
New Tribes Mission of Canada
New Wineskins Missionary Network
OM Canada
OMSC
One Another Ministries International
Operation Mobilization
Paraclete Mission Group, Inc.
Partners International
Power to Change Ministries
Rosedale Mennonite Missions
SAND International
Scriptures In Use
Servant Partners
Servants in Faith & Technology (SIFAT)
Shield of Faith Mission International

Sowers International, The
Taiwan Harvest 119
Teen Missions International, Inc.
The Masters Mission
The Pentecostal Assemblies of Canada
The Upstream Collective
Titus International
To Every Tribe
United Evangelical Churches
United World Mission, Inc.
University Bible Fellowship
Virginia Mennonite Missions
Walk Thru the Bible Ministries, Inc.
WayMakers
WEC International
WEC International Canada
World Horizons
World Indigenous Missions
World Servants, Inc.
Youth Ministry International
Youth With A Mission (YWAM)
Youth with a Mission Canada, Inc.

MISSIONARY EDUCATION

Christ for the Nations, Inc.
COMHINA
Missionaire International
Mustard Seed Mission Canada, Inc.
Pentecostal Free Will Baptist Church,
    Inc. - World Witness Dept.
Reaching Indians Ministries International
Rio Grande Bible Institute, Inc.
Teen Missions International, Inc.
The Brethren Church, Inc.

MISSIONARY KIDS EDUCATION

Evangelical Congregational Church -
    Global Ministries Commission

MOBILIZATION FOR MISSION

A.C.T. International

ACCI (Adventive Cross Cultural
   Initiatives) - US
ARISE International Mission
Canadian National Baptist
   Convention (CNBC)
Children's HopeChest
Christians In Action Missions International
COMHINA
Evangelical Covenant Church of Canada
Global Health Ministries
Global Outreach Mission Inc., Canada
Global Teams International, Inc
IFCA World Missions
India Gospel Outreach, Inc.
International Students, Inc (ISI)
InterServe Canada
Kids for Christ International
Launch Out Ministries International
OM Canada
One Challenge
Presbyterian Church (USA),
   Worldwide Ministries
Proclaim! International, Inc.
Seventh-day Adventists, General
   Conference - Global Mission
South American Missionary
   Society in Canada
STEM International
TeachBeyond Canada
Weiner Ministries International
Youth with a Mission Canada, Inc.
YUGO Ministries (Youth Unlimited
   Gospel Outreach, Inc.)

MUSIC MINISTRY EVANGELISM & ETHNO-MUSICOLOGY

Celebrant Singers

NATIONAL CHURCH SUPPORT

ACCI (Adventive Cross Cultural Initiatives)
ACCI (Adventive Cross Cultural
   Initiatives) - US

ACTS International Ministries, Inc.
Amazon Outreach
American Evangelical Christian Churches
Apostolic Christian Church -
   Missionary Committee
Apostolic Church in Canada, The
Aurora Mission, Inc.
Baptist Medical & Dental Mission
   International, Inc. (BMDMI)
Canadian Assemblies of God,
   General Conference
Canadian National Baptist
   Convention (CNBC)
Children's Ministry International, Inc. (CMI)
Christ for the City International
Christian Fellowship Union, Inc.
Christians In Action Missions International
Church of God Ministries
   (Anderson) - Global Strategy
Church of the Brethren - Global
   Mission Partnerships
Churches of God, General Conference
Cooperative Baptist Fellowship
   - Global Missions
Episcopal Church USA - Domestic
   & Foreign Missionary Society
Evangelical Congregational Church -
   Global Ministries Commission
Friends United Meeting
Full Gospel Evangelistic Association
globalLead
IFCA World Missions
In Touch Mission International
International Child Care, USA
International Christian Ministries
   Canada (ICM)
International Cooperating Ministries (ICM)
International Teams, U.S.A.
Latin American Lutheran Mission
LOGOI Ministries
Lott Carey Baptist Foreign
   Mission Convention

Lutheran Church-Missouri Synod
Mennonite Mission Network
Mexico Medical Missions
Middle East Media - USA
Mission to the World (PCA), Inc.
Missionary Ventures Intl.
Missions Door
OMS International - Canada
Open Doors with Brother
    Andrew – Canada
Open Doors, USA
Orthodox Presbyterian Church -
    Committee on Foreign Missions
Pentecostal Free Will Baptist Church,
    Inc. - World Witness Dept.
Perimeter Church - Global Outreach
Proclaim! International, Inc.
Reaching Indians Ministries International
Spiritual Overseers Service International
The Brethren Church, Inc.
United Church of Christ - Global Ministries
Venture International
Vineyard Church USA - Missions
World Mission
World Orphans
YUGO Ministries Canada

NATIONAL WORKER SUPPORT

ACTS International Ministries, Inc.
All About Orphans (David
    Livingstone KURE Foundation)
AMG International
AMOR Ministries
Audio Scripture Ministries
Bibles For The World, Inc.
BIC Canada-Global
Calvary Commission, Inc.
Catalyst Missions
CEIFA International
Center for Mission Mobilization
Children of Promise International

China Ministries International
Christ for India, Inc.
Christ to the Nations
Christian Aid Mission
Christian Church (Disciples of
    Christ) - Global Ministries
Christian Cultural Development
    Foundation
Christian Laymen's Missionary
    Evangelism Association
Church of the United Brethren in Christ
Churches of God, General Conference
CIS- Christian Involvement In Service
Conservative Congregational Christian
    Conference-Missions Committee
CrossWay International
East West Interknit
European Christian Mission Intl. - USA
Evangelical Christian Church in Canada
Far East Broadcasting Company
Firefall International Inc.
FRIENDS in Action International - Canada
Friends in Action Intl.
Fundamental Baptist Mission
    of Trinidad & Tobago
Global Fellowship Inc.
Global Outreach Mission Inc., Canada
Global Outreach Mission, Inc.
globalLead
GOGF Ministries
Good News for India
Gospel for Asia Canada
Gospel for Asia, Inc.
Gospel Mission of South
    America of Canada
Gospel Outreach Ministries Intl.
Gospel Revival Ministries
Great Cities Missions
Harvest Mission to the Unreached
HBI Global Partners
Helps Ministries

IFCA World Missions
In Touch Mission International
Independent Gospel Missions:
   A Baptist Mission Agency
India Evangelical Mission Inc.
India Gospel Outreach, Inc.
International Association For Refugees
International Child Care, USA
Latin American Lutheran Mission
Link International Ministries
Medical Centers of West Africa (MCWA)
Mercy Projects
Mission Catalyst Intl. Inc.
Morelli Ministries Intl. Inc.
Mustard Seed Mission Canada, Inc.
New Hope International
OMS International - Canada
Outreach to Asia Nationals
Palm Missionary Ministries, Inc.
Palm Missionary Ministries, Inc.
Partners in Asian Missions
Partners International Canada
Pentecostal Church of God-World
   Missions Department
Pillar of Fire Missions International
Presbyterian Mission International (PMI)
Presbyterian Missionary Union
Reaching Indians Ministries International
Romanian Missionary Society
Scripture Union, USA
ServLife International
Shepherd's Support, Inc.
Sidney and Helen Correll Ministries
   (dba Correll Missionary Ministries)
SIM Canada
Slavic Gospel Association
Slavic Gospel Association - Canada
Slavic Missionary Service, Inc.
South American Missionary
   Society in Canada
Sowers International, The

STEM International
The Voice of the Martyrs
Training Evangelistic Leadership
Walk Thru the Bible Ministries, Inc.
Women to the World, Inc.
World Christian Outreach, Inc.
World Link Ministries
World Missions & Evangelism
World-Wide Missions
YUGO Ministries Canada

NETWORKING/PARTNERSHIP/ COORDINATION
10/40 Connections
Accelerating International
   Mission Strategies (AIMS)
Adventures in Missions
AEGA Ministries Int'l Inc (Association
   of Evangelical Gospel Assemblies)
Amazon Focus, Inc.
Asian Access
Baptist General Conference of Canada
Bethany Gateways
Beyond Borders
Bold Ventures
Bridge Builders International
Catalyst Services
Center for Mission Mobilization
COMMA
East European Missions Network
ECHO
Equipping The Saints
Frontier Ventures
Gate Breaker Ministries
Global Gates
Global Hope India
GMI
God Reports
Harvest Foundation
Issachar Initiative
Kids Around the World

LeadaChild
Link Care Foundation
Mission Aviation Fellowship
Mission Data International
Missions Resource Network
Mobile Member Care Team
National Religious Broadcasters
New Wineskins Missionary Network
OMSC
One Challenge
One World Missions
Outreach Canada
Overseas Council International
Reaching Japan Together (RJT)
RREACH
Team Expansion, Inc.
Thrive
TMS Global
Vernacular Video Mission
    International, Inc.
Vision Ministries Canada
visionSynergy

NEWS SERVICE
ASSIST (Aid to Special Saints
    in Strategic Times)

NUTRITION MINISTRIES
Lifeline Christian Mission

ORALITY OR STORYING
Davar Partners International
Freedom to Lead International
Global Recordings Network
IMB of the Southern Baptist Convention
Kids Around the World
Medical Ambassadors International
    (Lifewind International)
Scriptures In Use
Taiwan Harvest 119
The God's Story Project
World Mission Associates

ORPHAN CARE
All God's Children International
CIS- Christian Involvement In Service
Heart To Heart International Ministries

ORPHAN EDUCATION
Gospel Outbound

ORPHAN SPONSORSHIP PROGRAMS
Children's HopeChest
Word To Russia

PARTNERSHIP DEVELOPMENT
ABWE Canada (Across Borders
    for World Evangelism)
ACCI (Adventive Cross Cultural Initiatives)
Adventures in Missions
African Enterprise Canada
Agathos International
Alongside Ministries International
Amazon Focus, Inc.
Ambassadors for Christ, Inc.
AMOR Ministries
ARISE International Mission
Boundless Ministries, Inc.
Canadian National Baptist
    Convention (CNBC)
Catalyst Services
Center for Mission Mobilization
Child Evangelism Fellowship, Inc.
Childspring International
China Partners
ChinaSource
Christian Church (Disciples of
    Christ) - Global Ministries
Church Ministries Intl.
CityTeam Ministries - New
    Generations International
Colorado Haiti Project Inc.
COMHINA
Compassion Canada

Congregational Methodist Missions
Cumberland Presbyterian Church
   Board of Missions
Davar Partners International
DeNike Ministries
Development Associates Intl. (DAI)
East European Missions Network
Emmanuel Intl. Canada
Emmaus Road International
endPoverty.org
Envoy International
Episcopal Church USA - Domestic
   & Foreign Missionary Society
Eternal Hope in Haiti
Evangelical Lutheran Church in
   America, Div. for Global Mission
Faith Christian Fellowship Intl.
FH Canada
Free Will Baptist International Missions
Friends in Action Intl.
Global Health Ministries
Global Witness and Ministry-AME Church
Heart for Honduras
Helps Ministries
In Touch Mission International
India Partners
International Christian Ministries
International Partnership Associates
International Partnership Ministries, Inc.
Into All The World
ISOH/IMPACT
Issachar Initiative
KORE Foundation
LeadaChild
LIFE International
Lifewater International, Inc.
Living Water International
Luke Society
Lutheran Brethren International Mission
MAP International

Mennonite Economic Development
   Associates (MEDA)
Mennonite Mission Network
Mission of Mercy Canada
One Mission Society
Partners International Canada
Partners Worldwide
Perimeter Church - Global Outreach
Power to Change Ministries
Presbyterian Church (USA),
   Worldwide Ministries
Reach Beyond
Reciprocal Ministries International
Samaritan's Purse - Canada
SGM Canada
Shelter for Life Intl. Inc.
The Free Methodist Church in Canada
The Presbyterian Church in Canada
The Upstream Collective
TWR Canada
United Church of Christ - Global Ministries
Venture International
Vision Ministries Canada
visionSynergy
Waymarks Radio Ministries International
White Fields
Wisconsin Evangelical Lutheran
   Synod, Board for World Missions
Women to the World, Inc.
Word & Deed
Word & Deed Ministries Canada
World Hope Canada
World Relief Canada
World Team Canada

PERSECUTED CHURCH
Advancing Native Missions
Ambassadors for Christ International
Asian Access
Awana Clubs International
Barnabas Aid

Christian Aid Mission
FARMS International, Inc.
Final Frontiers Foundation
Firefall International Inc.
God Reports
Harvest Bridge
Intercede International
Iranian Christians International
Make Way Partners
Samaritan's Purse
SAT-7 North America
Sidney and Helen Correll Ministries
   (dba Correll Missionary Ministries)
The Voice of the Martyrs
Village Ministries International
Voice of the Martyrs, Inc., The

PERSONAL OR SMALL GROUP EVANGELISM

ABWE International
Africa Inland Mission
Agape Gospel Mission
Agape Unlimited
Air Mobile Ministries
Ambassadors for Christ International
Anglican Frontier Missions
Association of Free Lutheran Congregations
Azusa Pacific University -
   Mexico Outreach
Baptist General Conference of Canada
Baptist International Evangelistic Ministries
Baptist International Outreach
Baptist Mid-Missions
Bible League International
Biblical Ministries Worldwide
Bold Ventures
Bright Hope
Caring Partners International
CBMC, Inc.
China Partners
Chosen People Ministries (Canada)

Christar
Christian Emergency Relief Teams
   (CERT) International
Christian Literacy Associates
Christian Reformed World Missions
Church of God (Holiness) World
   Mission Dept., Inc.
Church Planting International
COMMA
Commission to Every Nation
Communitas International
Cross-Cultural Ministries, Churches
   of God General Conference
CrossWay International
East-West Ministries International
Elim Fellowship
Evangelical Free Church of Canada Mission
Evangelical Friends Mission
Evangelical Mennonite Conference
Evangelism Explosion III International, Inc.
Every Home for Christ
Fellowship International Mission
Fishhook International
Four Corners Ministries
Friends of Israel Gospel Ministry Inc.
Global Gates
Global Partners (The Wesleyan
   Church World Headquarters)
Global Recordings Network International
Go Ye Fellowship
Gospelink, Inc.
Grace Ministries International
Greater Europe Mission
Greater Grace World Outreach
Health Teams International
Helimission, Inc. - USA
Hellenic Ministries USA
High Adventure Ministries
IBMGlobal
Identify
Impact International, Inc.

In Motion Ministries
Independent Faith Mission Inc.
InterAct Ministries
InterAct Ministries of Canada
International Board of Jewish Missions Inc
International Messengers
International Project
Japanese Evangelical Missionary
    Society (JEMS)
Jewish Awareness Ministries, Inc.
Jews for Jesus Canada
Latin American Missions Association
Liebenzell Mission of Canada
Life in Messiah International
Literacy & Evangelism International
Medical Ambassadors International
    (Lifewind International)
Mission On The Move
Missionary Athletes International
Missionary Gospel Fellowship
NEXT Worldwide
Niños de Mexico
OMF International
OMF International - Canada
One Mission Society
Partners International
Pioneers Canada
Pioneers USA
Polish Christian Ministries
Power to Change Ministries
Precious Seed Ministries Inc.
Reach A Village
ReachAcross
Reliant Mission, Inc.
RP Global Missions
RREACH
Russian Christian Radio, Inc. (or RCR)
SEND International, Inc.
Serge
Servant Partners

Sidney and Helen Correll Ministries
    (dba Correll Missionary Ministries)
South African Christian Mission, Inc.
Standards of Excellence in Short-
    Term Mission (SOE)
TEAM (The Evangelical Alliance Mission)
Team Expansion, Inc.
TEAM of Canada
TEAMS for Medical Missions
The Christian and Missionary Alliance
The Inner-city Church Planting Mission
The Navigators
The Pentecostal Assemblies of Canada
The Voice of the Martyrs
The Waray-Waray Project
Things to Come Mission
TIME Ministries
Titus International
United Brethren in Christ
United Evangelical Churches
University Bible Fellowship
WEC International Canada
With Open Eyes
Word of Life Fellowship Inc
World Gospel Mission
World Reach, Inc
World Servants, Inc.
World Team US
Youth for Christ, Canada
Youth for Christ/USA

POVERTY EDUCATION
Bread for the World

PRAYER-INTERCESSION
Barnabas Aid
Earth Mission, Inc.
Fishhook International
Global Adopt A People Campaign
Global Frontier Missions
Global Gates

Global Media Outreach
Impact Nations International Ministries
InterVarsity Christian Fellowship/USA
Into All The World
Latin American Missions Association
LIFE International
Middle East Christian Outreach
(MECO Canada)
New Wineskins Missionary Network
Oneway Ministries
Thrive
Vernacular Video Mission
International, Inc.
WayMakers
WEC International Canada
Wycliffe Bible Translators USA

PRODUCTION OF HEARING AIDS
ComCare International

PROSTITUTION MINISTRY
Christian Cultural Development
Foundation

PUBLISHER & WRITER TRAINING
Media Associates International

RADIO OR TV BROADCASTING
ASSIST (Aid to Special Saints
in Strategic Times)
Back to the Bible
Celebrant Singers
Christian Aviation and Radio Mission
Christian Broadcasting Network Inc., The
Christian Laymen's Missionary
Evangelism Association
Deaf Missions International, Inc.
EBM International
Evangelical Bible Mission
Faith Baptist Mission
Far East Broadcasting Company

Foundation for His Ministry
Friends of Israel Gospel Ministry Inc.
Galcom International Canada
GOGF Ministries
Good News Productions International
Gospel Outbound
Gospel Tide Broadcasting Association
Grace Mission Inc.
Greater Grace World Outreach
High Adventure Ministries
Impact International, Inc.
International Board of Jewish Missions Inc
Joni and Friends
Key Communications
Link Care Foundation
Luis Palau Evangelistic Association
Macedonian Missionary Service
Master's Resourcing Commission
National Religious Broadcasters
Northern Canada Evangelical Mission Inc
Oneway Ministries
Our Daily Bread
Reach Beyond
Russian Christian Radio, Inc. (or RCR)
SAT-7 North America
Slavic Missionary Service, Inc.
South African Christian Mission, Inc.
Spanish World Ministries
The Centers for Apologetics
Research (CFAR)
The Waray-Waray Project
TWR
TWR Canada
Walk Thru the Bible Ministries, Inc.
Waymarks Radio Ministries International
Wisconsin Evangelical Lutheran
Synod, Board for World Missions
World Mission Prayer League

RECORDING BIBLE STORIES IN MINORITY LANGUAGES

Global Recording Network Canada

RECRUITING OR MOBILIZING FOR MISSION

Accelerating International Mission Strategies (AIMS)
Adventures in Missions
Assemblies of God World Missions
Azusa Pacific University - Mexico Outreach
Be One Together
Bethany Gateways
Boundless Ministries, Inc.
Catalyst Services
Center for Mission Mobilization
Chaplaincy Endorsement Commission for the Christian Church and Churches of Christ
Christ In Youth
Christian Churches / Churches of Christ
Christian Emergency Relief Teams (CERT) International
DualReach
East-West Ministries International
Eastern Mennonite Missions
Envoy International
Evangelical Mennonite Mission Conference
Forefront Experience
Frontier Ventures
Frontiers
Frontiers Canada
Global Adopt A People Campaign
Global Gates
GoCorps
God Reports
GoSendMe Global
International Messengers
InterVarsity Christian Fellowship/USA
JAARS, Inc.

Latin America Mission
MB Mission
MB Mission Canada
Middle East Christian Outreach (MECO Canada)
Missionary Ventures Canada
MissionNext
Missions Resource Network
NEXT Worldwide
One Mission Society
One World Missions
Outreach Canada
Reformed Baptist Mission Services
Reliant Mission, Inc.
SEND International of Canada
Serve Globally
Taiwan Harvest 119
TeachBeyond USA
Team Expansion, Inc.
The Evangelical Covenant Church
The Pentecostal Assemblies of Canada
To Every Tribe
Virginia Mennonite Missions
WayMakers
WEC International Canada
With Open Eyes
World Servants, Inc.
World Thrust International
Wycliffe Bible Translators USA

REENTRY TRAINING & LITERATURE FOR MISSIONARY CHILDREN

Narramore Christian Foundation

REFUGEE MINISTRY

International Association For Refugees
Iranian Christians International

RELIEF & AID

ACCI (Adventive Cross Cultural Initiatives) - US

ADRA (Adventist Development
  and Relief Agency)
African Enterprise
Agathos International
Air Mobile Ministries
AMOR Ministries
Apostolic Christian Church -
  Missionary Committee
Apostolic Church of Pentecost of
  Canada (Global Harvest Missions)
Barnabas Aid
BASIC Ministries, Inc
BethanyKids Canada
BIC Canada-Global
CAMA Services
CAUSE Canada
Childcare Worldwide
Children's Lifeline
Christian Aid Ministries (CAM)
Christian Outreach International
Christian Relief Fund, The
Church Planting International
Church World Service
CityTeam Ministries - New
  Generations International
Compassio
Crossroads Christian
  Communications Inc. (ERDF)
CrossWay International
Cumberland Presbyterian Church
  Board of Missions
Cup of Cold Water Ministries
Door of Hope International
Earth Mission, Inc.
East African Ministries
Effect Hope
Emmanuel Intl. Canada
Encompass World Partners
Engineering Ministries International (EMI)
Enrich Missions, Inc

ERDO - Emergency Relief
  and Development
Evangelical Lutheran Church in
  America, Div. for Global Mission
Evangelical Missionary Church of Canada
Evangelize China Fellowship, Inc.
FAIR
Far East Broadcasting Associates
  of Canada (FEB Canada)
FH Canada
For God's Children Intl.
Forward Edge International
GAIN (Global Aid Network)
Global Aid Network, Inc. - Canada
Global Outreach Mission, Inc.
Global Witness and Ministry-AME Church
GoSendMe Global
Gospel Outreach Ministries Intl.
Gospel Revival Ministries
Habitat for Humanity Canada
Habitat for Humanity International
Haiti Lutheran Mission Society
Harvest Bridge
Harvest Mission to the Unreached
HBI Global Partners
Health Partners International of Canada
Heart for Lebanon Foundation
Helimission, Inc. - USA
Help for Haiti Inc.
High Adventure Ministries
HOPE International Development Agency
Impact Nations International Ministries
IN Network dba International Needs USA
In Touch Mission International
International Aid
International Crisis Aid
International Justice Mission
International Teams, U.S.A.
ISOH/IMPACT
Kids Alive International
Kinship United

Launch Out Ministries International
Living Water International
Lutheran World Relief
Make Way Partners
MAP International
Medical Teams International
Middle East Christian Outreach
 (MECO Canada)
Mission Aviation Fellowship
Mission Eurasia
Mission of Mercy Canada
Mission Possible
Mission Without Borders Canada
Missionary Flights Intl.
Nazarene Compassion Ministries Canada
New Life International
Operation Blessing International Relief
 and Development Corporation
Operation Bootstrap Africa
Partners Relief & Development
Pilgrim
Precious Seed Ministries Inc.
Presbyterian Church (USA),
 Worldwide Ministries
Ravi Zacharias International Ministries, Inc.
ReachAcross
Salvation Army - Canada and
 Bermuda Territory, The
Samaritan's Purse - Canada
Self-Help International
Serve Globally
ServeNow
Seventh Day Baptist Missionary Society
Supreme Task International, Inc.
Surfing the Nations
TEAMS for Medical Missions
The Evangelical Covenant Church
The Free Methodist Church in Canada
The Master's Foundation
The Salvation Army USA
 National Headquarters

The Voice of the Martyrs
The Waray-Waray Project
Twenty-six:Twelve
Ukrainian Children's Christian Fund
Ukrainian Childrens Fund
Venture International
Vision Beyond Borders
Voice of the Martyrs, Inc., The
Word & Deed
World Christian Outreach, Inc.
World Compassion Society
World Compassion Terry Law Ministries
World Concern
World Help
World Hope Canada
World Reach, Inc
World Relief
World Relief Canada
World Vision Canada
World Vision, Inc.
Youth With A Mission (YWAM)

RELOCATION & TRANSPORTATION SERVICE
Straightway, Inc.

RESEARCH
American Leprosy Missions
ChinaSource
ECHO
Finishing the Task
Frontier Ventures
Global Impact Services
GMI
Gospel Outreach Ministries Intl.
Great Commission Center International
IMB of the Southern Baptist Convention
International Association For Refugees
Issachar Initiative
Mission Catalyst Intl. Inc.
OMSC

One Challenge
OneHope
Probe Ministries International
Sentinel Group, The
SGM Canada
The Centers for Apologetics
  Research (CFAR)

SERVICES FOR MISSION ORGANIZATIONS

AEGA Ministries Int'l Inc (Association
  of Evangelical Gospel Assemblies)
Catalyst Services
Center for Mission Mobilization
Children's Ministry International, Inc. (CMI)
ChinaSource
Christian Flights International
Christian Literacy Associates
Christian Missions In Many Lands, Inc.
Church Ministries Intl.
CLC Ministries International
CMTS Ministries
Crisis Consulting International
Crossroads Christian
  Communications Inc. (ERDF)
CULTURELink
D&D Missionary Homes Inc.
DeNike Ministries
DualReach
Echocuba
Envoy International
Equipping The Saints
Forefront Experience
Friends in Action Intl.
Frontier Ventures
Full Gospel Evangelistic Association
Global Adopt A People Campaign
Good Shepherd Ministries, Inc.
Harvest International, Inc.
Helimission, Inc. - USA
Help for Haiti Inc.

Hope for the Hungry
In Motion Ministries
Interaction International
International Aid
InterServe Canada
Issachar Initiative
JAARS, Inc.
Kerus Global Education
Literacy & Evangelism International
MATS International
MedSend
Mission Data International
Mission Safety International
Mission Services Association, Inc.
Mission Training International
Missionaire International
Missionary Expediters, Inc.
Missionary TECH Team
Muslim Hope
National Religious Broadcasters
Nehemiah Teams International
New Wineskins Missionary Network
One Another Ministries International
Straightway, Inc.
Tech Serve International, Inc.
Teen Missions International, Inc.

SHORT-TERM MEDICAL TEAMS
Medical Teams International

SPIRITUAL RENEWAL
African Enterprise
Buckner International
Chaplaincy Endorsement Commission
  for the Christian Church and
  Churches of Christ
Elim Fellowship
Emmaus Road International
Identify
Paraclete Mission Group, Inc.
Serge

Thrive
Women in the Window International

SPORTS MINISTRY
CAMA Services
Campus Crusade for Christ (Cru in the US)
Christian Outreach International
Firefall International Inc.
International Cooperating Ministries (ICM)
Missionary Athletes International
SCORE International
SIM USA
Sports & Rec Plus
Teen Missions International, Inc.
TIME Ministries

STM TRIP COORDINATION
ACCI (Adventive Cross Cultural
   Initiatives) - US
ACSI (Association of Christian
   Schools International)
Advent Christian World Outreach
Adventures in Missions
Agape Unlimited
Amazon Outreach
AMG International
AMOR Ministries
Association of Free Lutheran Congregations
Azusa Pacific University -
   Mexico Outreach
Blessing the Children International
BLF Canada
Board of World Mission
Buckner International
Calvary Commission, Inc.
Camino Global Ministries Canada
Caring Partners International
CEIFA International
Children's Haven Intl.
Children's Lifeline
Children's Ministry International, Inc. (CMI)

Chosen People Ministries, Inc.
Christ for the City International
Christ In Youth
Christian Emergency Relief Teams
   (CERT) International
Christian Flights International
Christian Outreach International
Christian Veterinary Mission
Christians In Action Missions International
Church Planting International
Congregational Methodist Missions
Conservative Congregational Christian
   Conference-Missions Committee
CSI Ministries, Inc.
CTI Music Ministries (Carpenter's
   Tools International)
CULTURELink
Cumberland Presbyterian Church
   Board of Missions
Cup of Cold Water Ministries
CWE Missions
DeNike Ministries
e3 Partners Ministry
East-West Ministries International
Easy English Outreach
EBM International
Echocuba
EMAS Canada
Empowering Lives International
Envoy International
ERRC (Educational Resources
   & Referrals - China) US
ERRC Educational Society - Canada
Evangelical Bible Mission
FAME
Final Frontiers Foundation
FOCAS (Foundation of Compassionate
   American Samaritans)
Forward Edge International
Four Corners Ministries
Foursquare Missions International

Free Methodist World Missions
Free Will Baptist International Missions
Friendship International Ministries, Inc.
GAIN (Global Aid Network)
Gate Breaker Ministries
General Baptists International
Global Action, Inc.
Global Frontier Missions
Global Health Outreach
Global Hope India
Global Outreach Mission Inc., Canada
Global Outreach Mission, Inc.
Global Witness and Ministry-AME Church
GoSendMe Global
Gospel Outreach Ministries Intl.
Grace Mission Inc.
Greater Europe Mission Canada
Habitat for Humanity Canada
Harvest International, Inc.
Harvesting In Spanish (HIS)
HBI Global Partners
Health Teams International
Heart for Honduras
Hope for the Hungry
Identify
Impact Nations International Ministries
In Motion Ministries
Independent Faith Mission Inc.
Independent Gospel Missions:
    A Baptist Mission Agency
India Partners
Indopartners Agency
International Child Care (Canada), Inc.
International Gospel Outreach
International Messengers
International Pentecostal Holiness Church
Japanese Evangelical Missionary
    Society (JEMS)
JARON Ministries International
Joni and Friends
Joshua Expeditions

Kids Alive International
Kids Around the World
KORE Foundation
Latin American Lutheran Mission
Launch Out Ministries International
Lifeline Christian Mission
Living Water International
Living Water Teaching
MB Mission
MB Mission Canada
Medical Ministry International Canada, Inc
Men for Missions International
Mennonite Mission Network
Mercy Projects
Mexican Medical Ministries
Mission Data International
Mission Possible Canada
Mission Possible USA
Missionary Ventures Canada
Missionary Ventures Intl.
Moravian Church in North America
MOST Ministries
Mutual Faith Ministries Intl.
Nehemiah Teams International
NEXT Worldwide
Niños de Mexico
OM Canada
OMF International - Canada
On The Go Ministries/Keith Cook Team
Open Air Campaigners - Overseas
    Ministries (OAC-OM)
ORPHANetwork
Palm Missionary Ministries, Inc.
Polish Christian Ministries
Presbyterian Missionary Union
RAISE International, Inc.
Reaching Japan Together (RJT)
Real Impact Missions
Reciprocal Ministries International
RP Global Missions
Samaritan's Purse - Canada

SCORE International
Serve Globally
Seventh Day Baptist Missionary Society
Sidney and Helen Correll Ministries
  (dba Correll Missionary Ministries)
Sowers International, The
Sports & Rec Plus
Standards of Excellence in Short-
  Term Mission (SOE)
STEM International
Surfing the Nations
TeachBeyond USA
Teen Mission, USA, Inc. dba
  Mission Journeys
Teen Missions International, Inc.
The Evangelical Covenant Church
The Master's Foundation
Thrive
TIME Ministries
To Every Tribe
Touch the World
Tribes and Nations Outreach
Twenty-six:Twelve
Vernacular Video Mission
  International, Inc.
Village Ministries International
Volunteers in Medical Missions
WEC International
Word of Life Fellowship Inc
World Indigenous Missions
World Mission
World Servants, Inc.
Youth with a Mission Canada, Inc.
YUGO Ministries (Youth Unlimited
  Gospel Outreach, Inc.)
YUGO Ministries Canada
Zion Evangelical Ministries
  of Africa (ZEMA)

STUDENT EVANGELISM

African Enterprise Canada
Campus Crusade for Christ (Cru in the US)

China Partners
East European Missions Network
Elim Fellowship
Enrich Missions, Inc
ERRC (Educational Resources
  & Referrals - China) US
Every Child Ministries, Inc.
International Friendships, Inc.
International Project
InterVarsity Christian Fellowship/USA
Italy for Christ, Inc.
Josiah Venture
Kidzana Ministries
Mission Possible USA
Network of International Christian Schools
Real Impact Missions
Reliant Mission, Inc.
University Bible Fellowship
Village Schools International
Young Life
Youth for Christ, Canada

SUPPORTING ORGANIZATIONS
Steer, Inc.

SURGICAL TRAINING PROGRAM
BethanyKids Canada

TECHNICAL ASSISTANCE
ARISE International Mission
Audio Scripture Ministries
Chosen Mission Project
CMTS Ministries
CyberMissions
Earth Mission, Inc.
ECHO
endPoverty.org
Engineering Ministries International (EMI)
Galcom International USA, Inc
GMI
Interserve USA
Lifewater International, Inc.

MEDA - Mennonite Economic
Development Associates
Mennonite Economic Development
Associates (MEDA)
Mission Aviation Fellowship
Missionary TECH Team
Servants in Faith & Technology (SIFAT)
Tech Serve International, Inc.
The Salvation Army USA
National Headquarters
Vernacular Video Mission
International, Inc.

TEE OR OTHER EXTENSION EDUCATION

Alberto Mottesi Evangelistic
Association, Inc.
BEE World (Biblical Education
by Extension)
Bibles For The World, Inc.
Board for World Missions
Bold Ventures
Brazil Gospel Fellowship Mission (BGFM)
Brethren in Christ World
Missions (BICWM)
CEIFA International
Christ to the Nations
Christian Outreach International
Church of God (Cleveland, TN)
World Missions
Church of God Ministries
(Anderson) - Global Strategy
Church of the Brethren - Global
Mission Partnerships
CrossWay International
CyberMissions
Daystar U.S.
Emmanuel Intl. Canada
Entrust
Eternal Hope in Haiti
Evangelical Christian Church
in Canada, The
Evangelical Friends Church Southwest

Evangelical Mennonite Conference
Evangelistic Faith Mission, Inc.
International Christian Ministries
Lutheran Church-Missouri Synod
Ministry to Educate and Equip Intl. (MTEE)
Missions Door
Mustard Seed International
Ravi Zacharias International Ministries, Inc.
ReachGlobal
Shelter for Life Intl. Inc.
SIM Canada
Slavic Gospel Association - Canada
Source of Light Ministries Intl. Inc.
The Kerusso Institute for Global Leaders
The Presbyterian Church in Canada
Wisconsin Evangelical Lutheran Synod
World Gospel Mission
World Link Ministries
World Mission
World Missionary Assistance Plan

TENTMAKING & RELATED

Anglican Frontier Missions
Christar
Christar Canada
Christian and Missionary
Alliance in Canada, The
Cooperative Baptist Fellowship
- Global Missions
InterServe Canada
mPower Approach
Northern Canada Evangelical Mission Inc
Operation Mobilization
Pioneers USA
Reaching Japan Together (RJT)
Ripe for Harvest, Inc.
Rosedale Mennonite Missions
SEND International, Inc.
Shield of Faith Mission International
Women in the Window International
Worldwide Tentmakers, Inc.

TESOL OR TEFL

Baptist Bible Translators Institute
Baptist International Outreach
CAMA Services
China Partners
Christar Canada
Christian Literacy Associates
Easy English Outreach
ERRC (Educational Resources
   & Referrals - China) US
Global Frontier Missions
Global Scholars
Haiti Arise - Canada
InterAct Ministries
International Messengers
Interserve USA
Kids for Christ International
Literacy & Evangelism International
ReachAcross
Resourcing Christian Education
   International
SEND International of Canada
TeachBeyond USA
TEAM of Canada
United Brethren in Christ
WEC International
Worldwide Tentmakers Inc.

THEOLOGICAL EDUCATION

ABWE Canada (Across Borders
   for World Evangelism)
ABWE International
Action International Ministries
ACTS International Ministries, Inc.
Africa Inland Mission
Africa Inland Mission Canada Intl.
American Baptist International Ministries
Aurora Mission, Inc.
Baptist Haiti Mission
Baptist International Evangelistic Ministries
Baptist Mid-Missions

Baptist Missionary Association
   of America (BMAA)
BEE World (Biblical Education
   by Extension)
Biblical Ministries Worldwide
BILD International
Brethren in Christ World
   Missions (BICWM)
Camino Global
Camino Global Ministries Canada
China Ministries International
Chinese Christian Life Fellowship, Inc
Chosen People Ministries, Inc.
Christ for India, Inc.
Christ for the Nations, Inc.
Christar Canada
Christian and Missionary
   Alliance in Canada, The
Christian Discipleship International
Christian Fellowship Union, Inc.
Church of God (Cleveland, TN)
   World Missions
Church of God Ministries
   (Anderson) - Global Strategy
Church of God of the Apostolic
   Faith, Inc., The
Church of the Nazarene, Inc.
Converge
Crossworld
Crossworld Canada
Daystar U.S.
DeNike Ministries
Development Associates Intl. (DAI)
Entrust
EPC World Outreach
Equip Inc & Equip International
ERRC (Educational Resources
   & Referrals - China) US
ERRC Educational Society - Canada
EurAsian Baptist Mission
European Christian Mission Intl. - USA

Evangelical Friends Mission
Evangelical Methodist Church,
    Inc. - Board of Missions
Evangelical Mission Ministries
Evangelical Missionary Church of Canada
Evangelism Explosion III International, Inc.
Faith Baptist Mission
Faith Christian Fellowship Intl.
Free Will Baptist International Missions
Friends United Meeting
General Synod Council
Global Missions International
Global Missions (United
    Pentecostal Church Intl.)
Global Scholars
Good News for India
Good Shepherd Ministries, Inc.
Gospel Fellowship Association
Gospel Mission of South America, Inc.
Gospelink, Inc.
Grace Ministries International
Haiti Arise - Canada
Haiti Lutheran Mission Society
iHope International
IMB of the Southern Baptist Convention
India Evangelical Mission Inc.
International Christian Ministries
International Christian Ministries
    Canada (ICM)
International Gospel Outreach
International Partnership Ministries, Inc.
JARON Ministries International
Josue Yrion World Evangelism
    & Missions, Inc.
LeadaChild
Leadership Vistas International Ministries
Liebenzell Mission of Canada
Liebenzell Mission of USA, Inc.
Living Water Teaching
LOGOI Ministries

Lott Carey Baptist Foreign
    Mission Convention
Lutheran Church-Missouri
    Synod, World Mission
Macedonia World Baptist
    Mission International
Macedonia World Baptist Missions, Inc.
MAP International
Mennonite Mission Network
Ministry to Educate and Equip Intl. (MTEE)
Mission Possible USA
Mission to the World (PCA), Inc.
Muslim Hope
New Hope Uganda Ministries
New Life Advance International
North American Baptist Conference
    - Worldwide Outreach
OMF International
OMS International - Canada
On The Go Ministries/Keith Cook Team
Open Door Baptist Missions
Open Doors with Brother
    Andrew – Canada
Orthodox Presbyterian Church -
    Committee on Foreign Missions
Partners International Canada
Pentecostal Free Will Baptist Church,
    Inc. - World Witness Dept.
Perimeter Church - Global Outreach
Pillar of Fire Missions International
Probe Ministries International
Reaching Indians Ministries International
Reformed Church in America
Rehoboth Ministries, Inc
reSource Leadership International
Rio Grande Bible Institute, Inc.
Romanian Missionary Society
Salem Ministries International
SAT-7 North America
SEND International, Inc.
SIM USA

Slavic Gospel Association
Society of Anglican Missionaries
and Senders (SAMS USA)
TCM International Institute
TEAM (The Evangelical Alliance Mission)
TEAMS for Medical Missions
The Brethren Church, Inc.
The Centers for Apologetics
Research (CFAR)
The Christian and Missionary Alliance
The Presbyterian Church in Canada
The Upstream Collective
Things to Come Mission
Timothy Two Project International
United Church of Christ - Global Ministries
United World Mission, Inc.
World Christian Ministries Association
World Link Ministries
World Mission
World Partners USA
World Thrust International
WorldVenture
Youth Ministry International
Zion Evangelical Ministries
of Africa (ZEMA)

TRAINING
Action International Ministries - Canada
ACTS International Ministries, Inc.
AEGA Ministries Int'l Inc (Association
of Evangelical Gospel Assemblies)
Audio Scripture Ministries
BCM International (Canada), Inc.
Christian Blind Mission
International - Canada
Christian Church (Disciples of
Christ) - Global Ministries
CityTeam Ministries - New
Generations International
endPoverty.org
Evangelical Christian Church in Canada

General Baptists International
Global Impact Services
Global Opportunities
Global Spheres
globalLead
Haiti Arise - Canada
Heifer Project International
HOPE International Development Agency
International Aid
International Students, Inc (ISI)
Kerus Global Education
Latin American Lutheran Mission
Leadership Ministries Worldwide
Lifewater International, Inc.
Living Water International
Mercy Ships
Missionaire International
On The Go Ministries/Keith Cook Team
Open Doors with Brother
Andrew – Canada
Opportunity International
Opportunity International Canada
Prakash Association, USA
Precept Ministries International
Progressive National Baptist Convention,
Inc. (PNBC) - Missions
Project AmaZon
Project AmaZon Canada Society
Ravi Zacharias International Ministries, Inc.
Sentinel Group, The
Spiritual Overseers Service International
Tribes and Nations Outreach
Voice of the Martyrs, Inc., The
Weiner Ministries International
World Compassion Society
World Vision Canada
Youth for Christ International

TRAINING INDIGENOUS LEADERS
20schemes
India Gospel Outreach, Inc.

TRAINING PASTORS & CHURCH LEADERS
Bible Training Centre for Pastors
Church Leadership Development
    International
Global Training Network
RREACH
Village Ministries International

TRANSLATION
BILD International
Good News Productions International
Leadership Ministries Worldwide
Living Word Missions
Middle East Media - USA
Multiplication Network Ministries
New Hope International
Precept Ministries International
Presbyterian Missionary Union
Publications Chrétiennes (Christian
    Publishing in French)
World Missionary Assistance Plan

UNREACHED TRIBES
Gospel Revival Ministries

URBAN POOR
CMF International

VETERINARY
Christian Veterinary Mission

WATER PROJECT
East African Ministries
Living Water International

YOUTH MINISTRY
2nd Mile Ministries
ACM International
AEGA Ministries Int'l Inc (Association
    of Evangelical Gospel Assemblies)
African Children's Mission

Alongside Ministries International
Association of Free Lutheran Congregations
Awana Clubs International
Board of World Mission
Cadence International
Canadian Assemblies of God,
    General Conference
CEIFA International
China Service Ventures
Christ In Youth
Commission To Every Nation-Canada
CTI Music Ministries (Carpenter's
    Tools International)
Door of Hope International
Episcopal Church USA - Domestic
    & Foreign Missionary Society
ERRC (Educational Resources
    & Referrals - China) US
For God's Children Intl.
Freedom in Christ Ministries - USA
Friendship International Ministries, Inc.
Global Action, Inc.
globalLead
GoCorps
Good Shepherd Ministries Intl.
Hellenic Ministries USA
Inter-Varsity Christian
    Fellowship of Canada
InterAct Ministries
InterAct Ministries of Canada
International Teams, Canada (Evangelical
    International Crusades Canada, Inc.)
Josiah Venture
Kerus Global Education
Kids Alive International
Latin American Missions Association
Living Water Teaching
Lott Carey Baptist Foreign
    Mission Convention
Mercy Projects
Mission On The Move

Mission to the World (PCA), Inc.
Missionaire International
Missionary Athletes International
Moravian Church in North America
Network of International Christian Schools
New Hope International
New Hope Uganda Ministries
New Mission Systems International
One Child Matters
Pentecostal Free Will Baptist Church,
    Inc. - World Witness Dept.
Prakash Association, USA
Progressive National Baptist Convention,
    Inc. (PNBC) - Missions
Rosedale Mennonite Missions
Servants in Faith & Technology (SIFAT)
SIM USA

Surfing the Nations
TEAMS for Medical Missions
Teen Mission, USA, Inc. dba
    Mission Journeys
Teen Missions International, Inc.
Touch the World
Village Schools International
Weiner Ministries International
Word of Life Fellowship Inc
World Vision Canada
Young Life
Young Life of Canada
Youth for Christ International
Youth for Christ, Canada
Youth for Christ/USA
Youth Ministry International
Youth With A Mission (YWAM)

CHURCH TRADITION

ADVENTIST
ADRA (Adventist Development
and Relief Agency)
Advent Christian World Outreach
Seventh-day Adventists, General
Conference - Global Mission

ANGLICAN
Anglican Frontier Missions
Christ for Children International
Episcopal Church USA - Domestic
& Foreign Missionary Society
New Wineskins Missionary Network
Reformed Episcopal Board
of Foreign Missions
Society of Anglican Missionaries
and Senders (SAMS USA)
South American Missionary
Society in Canada

BAPTIST
20schemes
ABWE Canada (Across Borders
for World Evangelism)
ABWE International
African Children's Mission
Amazon Outreach
American Baptist International Ministries
Aurora Mission, Inc.
Avant Ministries
Avant Ministries Canada
Awana Clubs International
Back to the Bible
Baptist Bible Fellowship International
- World Mission Service Center
Baptist Bible Translators Institute
Baptist General Conference of Canada
Baptist Haiti Mission
Baptist International Evangelistic Ministries
Baptist International Missions, Inc.

Baptist International Outreach
Baptist Medical & Dental Mission
International, Inc. (BMDMI)
Baptist Mid-Missions
Baptist Missionary Association
of America (BMAA)
Brazil Gospel Fellowship Mission (BGFM)
Bridge Builders International
Buckner International
Camino Global Ministries Canada
Canadian Baptist Ministries
Canadian National Baptist
Convention (CNBC)
Caribbean Baptist Mission Society
Catalyst Missions
Christ to the Nations
Christar Canada
Christian Discipleship International
Christian Emergency Relief
Teams (CERT), International
CIS- Christian Involvement In Service
Converge
Cooperative Baptist Fellowship
- Global Missions
Crossworld
Crossworld Canada
Envoy International
Eternal Hope in Haiti
EurAsian Baptist Mission
Evangelize China Fellowship, Inc.
FAIR
Faith Baptist Mission
Far East Broadcasting Associates
of Canada (FEB Canada)
Fellowship International Mission
Final Frontiers Foundation
Four Corners Ministries
Free Will Baptist International Missions
FRIENDS in Action International - Canada
Fundamental Baptist Mission
of Trinidad & Tobago

Fundamental Baptist Missions International
General Baptists International
Global Focus
Global Hope India
Global Recordings Network Canada
Good Shepherd Ministries, Inc.
GoSendMe Global
Gospel Mission of South
    America of Canada
Gospel Mission of South America, Inc.
HBI Global Partners
Heart of the Bride Ministries
IBMGlobal
Identify
IMB of the Southern Baptist Convention
Impact International, Inc.
Independent Faith Mission Inc.
Independent Gospel Missions:
    A Baptist Mission Agency
International Board of Jewish Missions Inc
International Partnership Ministries, Inc.
JARON Ministries International
Jewish Awareness Ministries, Inc.
Living Hope Ministries International, Inc.
Living Water International
Lott Carey Baptist Foreign
    Mission Convention
Macedonia World Baptist
    Mission International
Macedonia World Baptist Missions, Inc.
Missions Door
Missions to Military, Inc.
Muslim Hope
National Baptist Convention of
    America - Foreign Mission Board
National Baptist Convention USA,
    Inc. - Foreign Mission Board
North American Baptist Conference
    - Worldwide Outreach
On The Go Ministries/Keith Cook Team

Open Air Campaigners - Overseas
    Ministries (OAC-OM)
Open Door Baptist Missions
Outreach to Asia Nationals
Pan American Missions
Prakash Association, USA
Prayer Baptist Missions International, Inc.
Precept Ministries International
Progressive National Baptist Convention,
    Inc. (PNBC) - Missions
Reciprocal Ministries International
Reformed Baptist Mission Services
Romanian Missionary Society
Russian Bible Society, Inc.
SCORE International
SEND International of Canada
Seventh Day Baptist Missionary Society
Slavic Gospel Association - Canada
Slavic Missionary Service, Inc.
Source of Light Ministries Intl. Inc.
Sports & Rec Plus
Standards of Excellence in Short-
    Term Mission (SOE)
Straightway, Inc.
Taiwan Harvest 119
The Inner-city Church Planting Mission
The Kerusso Institute for Global Leaders
The Masters Mission
Titus International
To Every Tribe
Word of Life Fellowship Inc
Word To Russia
World Link Ministries
WorldVenture
Worldwide Tentmakers, Inc.
YUGO Ministries Canada

BRETHREN
BIC Canada-Global
Brethren in Christ World
    Missions (BICWM)

Christian Mission for the Deaf
Church of the Brethren - Global
  Mission Partnerships
Encompass World Partners
Forgotten Voices Intl.
GOGF Ministries
Grace & Truth Inc.
International Teams, Canada (Evangelical
  International Crusades Canada, Inc.)
Open Air Campaigners - Overseas
  Ministries (OAC-OM)
The Brethren Church, Inc.
The Inner-city Church Planting Mission

CHARISMATIC

Accelerating International
  Mission Strategies (AIMS)
Adventures in Missions
AEGA Ministries Int'l Inc (Association
  of Evangelical Gospel Assemblies)
Agape Gospel Mission
Apostolic Church in Canada, The
Bold Ventures
Calvary Commission, Inc.
Celebrant Singers
China Partners
Christ for India, Inc.
Christian Laymen's Missionary
  Evangelism Association
Christian Ministries International (CMI)
CyberMissions
DeNike Ministries
Easy English Outreach
Faith Christian Fellowship Intl.
Firefall International Inc.
FOCAS (Foundation of Compassionate
  American Samaritans)
Foundation for His Ministry
Foursquare Missions International
Full Gospel Evangelistic Association
Gate Breaker Ministries

Globe International
Go to Nations
Good News for India
Good Shepherd Ministries Intl.
Gospel Outbound
Haiti Arise - Canada
Helimission, Inc. - USA
Impact Nations International Ministries
India Gospel Outreach, Inc.
Leadership Training International
Living Word Missions
Master's Resourcing Commission
Messianic Jewish Movement
  International, Inc. The (MJMI)
Mission Catalyst Intl. Inc.
New Life Advance International
Project AmaZon
Project AmaZon Canada Society
Rehoboth Ministries, Inc
Sentinel Group, The
Sidney and Helen Correll Ministries
  (dba Correll Missionary Ministries)
Supreme Task International, Inc.
Surfing the Nations
Tribes and Nations Outreach
United Evangelical Churches
Vineyard Church USA - Missions
Waymarks Radio Ministries International
Weiner Ministries International
World Compassion Society
World Compassion Terry Law Ministries
World Indigenous Missions
World Missionary Assistance Plan
World Outreach International - US
Youth With A Mission (YWAM)
Youth with a Mission Canada, Inc.

CHRISTIAN

Christian Dental Society
MedSend
Volunteers in Medical Missions

CHRISTIAN (PLYMOUTH BRETHREN)

Christian Missions In Many Lands, Inc.
GOGF Ministries
Reliant Mission, Inc.
Sanma (South Asia Native
   Missionary Alliance)
Vision Ministries Canada

CHRISTIAN (RESTORATION MOVEMENT)

ACM International
Chaplaincy Endorsement Commission
   for the Christian Church and
   Churches of Christ
Childspring International
Christ In Youth
Christian Aviation and Radio Mission
Christian Church (Disciples of
   Christ) - Global Ministries
Christian Churches / Churches of Christ
Christian Relief Fund, The
CMF International
COMHINA
Disciple Makers
Evangelical Christian Church
   in Canada,The
FAME
For God's Children Intl.
Good News Productions International
Great Cities Missions
Hisportic Christian Mission
Identify
IMA World Health
Key Communications
Kids for Christ International
KORE Foundation
Lifeline Christian Mission
Mission Services Association, Inc.
Missions Resource Network
New Mission Systems International

Niños de Mexico
Northwest Haiti Christian Mission
Pioneer Bible Translators
Polish Christian Ministries
RAISE International, Inc.
South African Christian Mission, Inc.
Spanish American Evangelistic Ministries
STEM International
TCM International Institute
Team Expansion, Inc.
Teen Mission, USA, Inc. dba
   Mission Journeys
The Waray-Waray Project
Thrive
United Church of Christ - Global Ministries
World Concern
World Relief

CONGREGATIONAL

Conservative Congregational Christian
   Conference-Missions Committee
Effect Hope
Missions Resource Network
National Association of Congregational
   Christian Churches
ReachGlobal

ECUMENICAL

American Leprosy Missions
Beyond Borders
Bread for the World
Canadian Bible Society / La Societe
   Biblique Canadienne
Canadian Churches Forum
   for Global Ministries
Christian Cultural Development
   Foundation
Christian Dental Society
Christian Flights International
Church World Service
Engineering Ministries International (EMI)
Flying Doctors of America

Freedom Firm
Habitat for Humanity Canada
Habitat for Humanity International
Health Teams International
HOPE International
International Foundation for
    EWHA Woman's University
International Students, Inc (ISI)
Medical Teams International
Mercy Ships Canada
Moravian Church in North America,
    Board of World Mission
OMSC
Opportunity International
Servants in Faith & Technology (SIFAT)
The Voice of the Martyrs
Vellore Christian Medical
    College Foundation, Inc.

EPISCOPAL OR ANGLICAN
Colorado Haiti Project Inc.

EVANGELICAL
10/40 Connections
2nd Mile Ministries
A.C.T. International
ACCI (Adventive Cross Cultural Initiatives)
ACCI (Adventive Cross Cultural
    Initiatives) - US
ACSI (Association of Christian
    Schools International)
Action International Ministries
Action International Ministries - Canada
ACTS International Ministries, Inc.
Advancing Native Missions
Adventures in Missions
AEGA Ministries Int'l Inc (Association
    of Evangelical Gospel Assemblies)
Africa Inland Mission
Africa Inland Mission Canada Intl.
African Enterprise
African Enterprise Canada

African Leadership Development
Agape Unlimited
Agathos International
Air Mobile Ministries
Alberto Mottesi Evangelistic
    Association, Inc.
Alongside Ministries International
Alongside, Inc
Amazon Focus, Inc.
Ambassadors for Christ International
Ambassadors for Christ, Inc.
American Evangelical Christian Churches
AMOR Ministries
Anglican Frontier Missions
Asian Access
ASSIST (Aid to Special Saints
    in Strategic Times)
Audio Scripture Ministries
Avant Ministries Canada
Awana Clubs International
Azusa Pacific University -
    Mexico Outreach
Back to the Bible
Back to the Bible Canada
Barnabas International
BASIC Ministries, Inc
BCM International
BCM International (Canada), Inc.
Be One Together
Beautiful Feet
BEE World (Biblical Education
    by Extension)
Bethany Gateways
BethanyKids
BethanyKids Canada
Beyond
Bible League Canada
Bible League International
Bible Training Centre for Pastors
Bibles and Literature in French
Bibles For The World, Inc.

BILD International
Blessing the Children International
BLF Canada
Boundless Ministries, Inc.
Bright Hope
Cadence International
Café 1040, Inc.
Calvary Commission, Inc.
CAMA Services
Camino Global
Camino Global Ministries Canada
Campus Crusade for Christ (Cru in the US)
Canadian South America Mission
Care of Creation, Inc.
Caribbean Lifetime Mission
Caring for Others
Caring Partners International
Casa Viva
Catalyst Services
CBMC, Inc.
CEIFA International
Celebrant Singers
Center for Mission Mobilization
Childcare Worldwide
Children of Promise International
Children's Haven Intl.
Children's HopeChest
Children's Lifeline
China Ministries International
China Outreach Ministries, Inc.
ChinaSource
Chinese Christian Life Fellowship, Inc
Chosen Mission Project
Chosen People Ministries (Canada)
Chosen People Ministries, Inc.
Christ for the City International
Christ In Youth
Christar
Christar Canada
Christian Aid Mission

Christian and Missionary
  Alliance in Canada, The
Christian Blind Mission
  International - Canada
Christian Broadcasting Network Inc., The
Christian Discipleship International
Christian Fellowship Union, Inc.
Christian Literacy Associates
Christian Medical & Dental Associations
Christian Outreach International
Christian Resources Intl.
Christian Veterinary Mission
Christians In Action Missions International
Church Leadership Development
  International
Church Ministries Intl.
Church Planting International
Churches of God, General Conference
CIS- Christian Involvement In Service
CLC Ministries International
CMTS Ministries
ComCare International
COMMA
Commission to Every Nation
Commission To Every Nation-Canada
Communitas International
Compassio
Compassion Canada
Conservative Congregational Christian
  Conference-Missions Committee
Crescent Project
CRM
Crossover Communications International
Crossroads Christian
  Communications Inc. (ERDF)
CrossWay International
CSI Ministries, Inc.
CSM Canada Intl. (Christian
  Salvage Mission)
CTI Music Ministries (Carpenter's
  Tools International)

Cup of Cold Water Ministries
CWE Missions
D&D Missionary Homes Inc.
Davar Partners International
Daystar U.S.
Deaf Missions International, Inc.
Development Associates Intl. (DAI)
Disciples International
Discipleship International
DualReach
e3 Partners Ministry
Earth Mission, Inc.
East African Ministries
East West Interknit
East-West Ministries International
Easy English Outreach
ECHO
Echocuba
Effect Hope
Elim Fellowship
EMAS Canada
Emmanuel Intl. Canada
Emmaus Road International
Empowering Lives International
Encompass World Partners
endPoverty.org
Enrich Missions, Inc
Entrust
Envoy International
EPC World Outreach
Equip Inc & Equip International
Equip, Canada
Equipping The Saints
ERRC (Educational Resources
    & Referrals - China) US
ERRC Educational Society - Canada
Eternal Hope in Haiti
Ethnos360
European Christian Mission Intl. - USA
Evangelical Bible Mission,
    EBM International

Evangelical Covenant Church of Canada
Evangelical Free Church of Canada Mission
Evangelical Friends Mission
Evangelical Mennonite Conference
Evangelical Mennonite Mission Conference
Evangelical Mission Ministries
Evangelical Missionary Church of Canada
Evangelism Explosion III International, Inc.
Evangelism Resources, Inc.
Every Child Ministries, Inc.
Every Home for Christ
Far Corners Missions
Far East Broadcasting Company
FARMS International, Inc.
Fellowship International Mission
Fellowship of Companies for
    Christ International (FCCI)
Fellowship of Evangelical Churches
    - International Ministries
Finishing the Task
Firefall International Inc.
Fishhook International
Food for the Hungry, Inc.
For Haiti with Love, inc.
For His Glory Evangelistic Ministries
Forefront Experience
Forgotten Voices Intl.
Forward Edge International
Foundation for His Ministry
Freedom in Christ Ministries - USA
Freedom to Lead International
Friends in Action Intl.
Friends of Israel Gospel Ministry Inc.
Friendship International Ministries, Inc.
Frontier Ventures
Frontiers
Frontiers Canada
GAIN (Global Aid Network)
Galcom International Canada
Galcom International USA, Inc
Gateway Training for Cross-cultural Service

Gideons International, The
Global Action, Inc.
Global Adopt A People Campaign
Global Aid Network, Inc. - Canada
Global Fellowship Inc.
Global Frontier Missions
Global Gates
Global Health Outreach
Global Impact Services
Global Media Outreach
Global Outreach International
Global Outreach Mission Inc., Canada
Global Outreach Mission, Inc.
Global Recordings Network
Global Recordings Network Canada
Global Scholars
Global Spheres
Global Teams International, Inc
Global Training Network
globalLead
GMI
Go Ye Fellowship
GoCorps
God Reports
Gospel for Asia Canada
Gospel for Asia, Inc.
Gospel Literature International (GLINT)
Gospel Outreach Ministries Intl.
Gospel Tide Broadcasting Association
Gospelink, Inc.
Grace Ministries International
Grace Mission Inc.
Great Commission Center International
Great Commission Media Ministries
Greater Europe Mission
Greater Europe Mission Canada
Greater Grace World Outreach
Haitian Christian Outreach
Harvest Bridge
Harvest Foundation

Harvest International, Inc.
Harvesting In Spanish (HIS)
Health Partners International of Canada
Heart for Lebanon Foundation
Heart To Heart International Ministries
Hellenic Ministries USA
Help for Haiti Inc.
Helps Ministries
Hermano Pablo Ministries
High Adventure Ministries
Holt International Children's Services, Inc.
Hope for the Hungry
HOPE International Development Agency
iHope International
Impact Canada Ministries, Inc.
IN Network dba International Needs USA
In Touch Mission International
India Evangelical Mission Inc.
India Gospel League
Indopartners Agency
Inter-Varsity Christian
    Fellowship of Canada
InterAct Ministries
InterAct Ministries of Canada
Interaction International
Intercede International
Intercomm, Inc.
International Aid
International Association For Refugees
International Board of Jewish Missions Inc
International Child Care (Canada), Inc.
International Christian Ministries
International Christian Ministries
    Canada (ICM)
International Cooperating Ministries (ICM)
International Crisis Aid
International Faith Missions
International Friendships, Inc.
International Gospel Outreach
International Messengers
International Partnership Associates

International Project
International Street Kids Outreach
  Ministries (ISKOM)
International Teams, U.S.A.
InterServe Canada
Interserve USA
InterVarsity Christian Fellowship/USA
Into All The World
Iranian Christians International
Issachar Initiative
Italy for Christ, Inc.
JAARS, Inc.
Japanese Evangelical Missionary
  Society (JEMS)
Jews for Jesus
Jews for Jesus Canada
Joni and Friends
Joshua Expeditions
Josiah Venture
Josue Yrion World Evangelism
  & Missions, Inc.
Kids Alive International
Kids Around the World
Kidzana Ministries
Kinship United
Latin America Mission
Launch Out Ministries International
Leadership Ministries Worldwide
Leadership Resources International
Leadership Vistas International Ministries
Liberty Corner Mission
Liebenzell Mission of Canada
Liebenzell Mission of USA, Inc.
Life Impact Inc
Life in Messiah International
LIFE International
Lifeline Malawi
Lifesong for Orphans
Link Care Foundation
Link International Ministries
Literacy & Evangelism International

Living Water Teaching
Luis Palau Evangelistic Association
Lutheran Brethren International Mission
Macedonian Missionary Service
Mailbox Club International Inc., The
Make Way Partners
MATS International
Media Associates International
Medical Ambassadors International
  (Lifewind International)
Medical Centers of West Africa (MCWA)
Medical Ministry International Canada, Inc
MedSend
Mercy Projects
Mercy Ships
Mexican Medical Ministries
Mexico Medical Missions
Micah Challenge USA
Middle East Christian Outreach
  (MECO Canada)
Mission Aviation Fellowship
Mission Aviation Fellowship
  of Canada (MAFC)
Mission Data International
Mission Eurasia
Mission Generation, Inc.
Mission India
Mission Nannys
Mission On The Move
Mission ONE, Inc.
Mission Possible
Mission Possible Canada
Mission Possible USA
Mission Safety International
Mission to Children
Mission Training International
Mission Without Borders Canada
Missionaire International
Missionary Athletes International
Missionary Flights Intl.
Missionary Gospel Fellowship

Missionary Retreat Fellowship
Missionary Ventures Canada
Missionary Ventures Intl.
MissionNext
MissionPREP Inc.
MMS Aviation (Missionary
  Maintenance Services)
Mobile Member Care Team
mPower Approach
Multiplication Network Ministries
Mustard Seed International
Narramore Christian Foundation
National Religious Broadcasters
Navigators of Canada, The
Network of International Christian Schools
New Hope International
New Hope Uganda Ministries
New Life Advance International
New Life International
New Mission Systems International
New Tribes Mission of Canada
NEXT Worldwide
Northern Canada Evangelical Mission Inc
OM Canada
OMF International
OMF International - Canada
One Another Ministries International
One Challenge
One Child Matters
One Mission Society
One World Missions
Oneway Ministries
Open Doors with Brother
  Andrew – Canada
Open Doors, USA
Operation Blessing International Relief
  and Development Corporation
Operation Mobilization
ORPHANetwork
Our Daily Bread
Outreach Canada

Overseas Council International
Palm Missionary Ministries, Inc.
Paraclete Mission Group, Inc.
Paradigm Shift
Partners in Bible Translation
Partners International
Partners International Canada
Partners Relief & Development
People International USA
PIC International (Partners in
  Christ International)
Pilgrim
Pioneer Clubs
Pioneers Canada
Pioneers USA
Power to Change Ministries
Precious Seed Ministries Inc.
Probe Ministries International
Proclaim! International, Inc.
Project WorldReach / Train & Multiply
Providence Mission Homes, Inc.
Publications Chrétiennes (Christian
  Publishing in French)
Ravi Zacharias International Ministries, Inc.
Reach A Village
Reach Beyond
ReachAcross
Reaching Japan Together (RJT)
Real Impact Missions
Reciprocal Ministries International
Reformed Church in America, General
  Synod Council, Global Mission
Reliant Mission, Inc.
reSource Leadership International
Resourcing Christian Education
  International
Ripe for Harvest, Inc.
Russian Christian Radio, Inc. (or RCR)
Salem Ministries International
Salvation Army - Canada and
  Bermuda Territory, The

Samaritan's Purse
Samaritan's Purse - Canada
SAND International
SAT-7 North America
SCORE International
Scripture Union, USA
Scriptures In Use
Seed Company
SEND International of Canada
SEND International, Inc.
Serge
Servant Partners
Servants in Faith & Technology (SIFAT)
Serve Globally, The Evangelical
  Covenant Church
ServeNow
ServLife International
Shelter for Life Intl. Inc.
Shepherd's Support, Inc.
Shield of Faith Mission International
Sidney and Helen Correll Ministries
  (dba Correll Missionary Ministries)
SIM Canada
SIM USA
Slavic Gospel Association
Slavic Gospel Association - Canada
Slavic Missionary Service, Inc.
South America Mission
Sowers International, The
Spiritual Overseers Service International
Sports & Rec Plus
Standards of Excellence in Short-
  Term Mission (SOE)
Steer, Inc.
TeachBeyond Canada
TeachBeyond USA
TEAM (The Evangelical Alliance Mission)
TEAM of Canada
TEAMS for Medical Missions
Tech Serve International, Inc.
The Centers for Apologetics
  Research (CFAR)

The Christian and Missionary Alliance
The Free Methodist Church in Canada
The God's Story Project
The Kerusso Institute for Global Leaders
The Master's Foundation
The Masters Mission
The Navigators
The Salvation Army USA
  National Headquarters
The Upstream Collective
The Voice of the Martyrs
The Word for the World (TWFTW)
Things to Come Mission
TIME Ministries
TMS Global
Touch the World
Training Evangelistic Leadership
Twenty-six:Twelve
TWR
TWR Canada
Ukrainian Children's Christian Fund
Ukrainian Childrens Fund
United Brethren in Christ
United Evangelical Churches
United World Mission, Inc.
Venture International
Vernacular Video Mission
  International, Inc.
Village Ministries International
Village Schools International
Vision Beyond Borders
Vision Ministries Canada
Visionledd o/a Working for
  Orphans and Widows
visionSynergy
Voice of the Martyrs, Inc., The
Volunteers in Medical Missions
Walk Thru the Bible Ministries, Inc.
WayMakers
WEC International
WEC International Canada

White Fields
White Fields Missionary Society of Canada
Women in the Window International
World Christian Outreach, Inc.
World Help
World Horizons
World Mission
World Mission Associates
World Mission Prayer League
World Missionary Assistance Plan
World Missionary Press, Inc.
World Missions & Evangelism
World Orphans
World Partners USA
World Reach, Inc
World Relief Canada
World Servants, Inc.
World Team Canada
World Team US
World Thrust International
World Vision Canada
World Vision, Inc.
World-Wide Missions
WorldVenture
WorldView
Worldwide Discipleship Assoc.
Worldwide Medical-Dental
    Evangelical Mission
Wycliffe Associates
Wycliffe Bible Translators of Canada, Inc.
Wycliffe Bible Translators USA
Young Life
Young Life of Canada
Youth for Christ International
Youth for Christ, Canada
Youth for Christ/USA
Youth Ministry International
YUGO Ministries (Youth Unlimited
    Gospel Outreach, Inc.)
Zion Evangelical Ministries
    of Africa (ZEMA)

FRIENDS

BethanyKids
BethanyKids Canada
Central Yearly Meeting of Friends Missions
Evangelical Friends Church Southwest
Evangelical Friends Mission
Friends United Meeting

FUNDAMENTALIST

African Children's Mission
Christian Resources Intl.
CSM Canada Intl. (Christian
    Salvage Mission)
Gospel Fellowship Association
Missionary TECH Team
Nehemiah Teams International
Network of International Christian Schools
Prayer Baptist Missions International, Inc.
Reaching Indians Ministries International
Russian Bible Society, Inc.

HOLINESS

Church of God (Holiness) World
    Mission Dept., Inc.
Church of God Ministries
    (Anderson) - Global Strategy
Church of the Nazarene, Inc.
Evangelistic Faith Mission, Inc.
Fishhook International
International Pentecostal Holiness Church
ISOH/IMPACT
Nazarene Compassion Ministries Canada
Pentecostal Free Will Baptist Church,
    Inc. - World Witness Dept.
Pillar of Fire Missions International
World Gospel Mission

INDEPENDENT

All About Orphans (David
    Livingstone KURE Foundation)
All God's Children International
AMG International

Barnabas Aid
Bible League International
Biblical Ministries Worldwide
Blessings International
Bold Ventures
CAUSE Canada
Cedar Lane Missionary Homes
Child Evangelism Fellowship, Inc.
ChinaSource
Christ to the Nations
Commission To Every Nation-Canada
Communitas International
Crisis Consulting International
Crossworld
Crossworld Canada
CULTURELink
Gospel Revival Ministries
Haitian Christian Outreach
Harvest Mission to the Unreached
Health Partners International of Canada
Heifer Project International
iHope International
In Motion Ministries
Independent Gospel Missions:
    A Baptist Mission Agency
InterAct Ministries
InterAct Ministries of Canada
Josiah Venture
Mutual Faith Ministries Intl.
Partners in Bible Translation
Real Impact Missions
Rio Grande Bible Institute, Inc.
Spanish World Ministries
TEAMS for Medical Missions
Things to Come Mission
TWR
With Open Eyes
Worldwide Lab Improvement

LUTHERAN

Association of Free Lutheran Congregations
China Service Ventures
East European Missions Network
Evangelical Lutheran Church in
    America, Div. for Global Mission
FaithLife Ministries, Inc.
Global Health Ministries
Haiti Lutheran Mission Society
Heart for Honduras
Latin American Lutheran Mission
LeadaChild
Lutheran Bible Translators of Canada
Lutheran Bible Translators, Inc.
Lutheran Brethren International Mission
Lutheran Church-Missouri
    Synod, World Mission
Lutheran Hour Ministries
Lutheran World Relief
MOST Ministries
Operation Bootstrap Africa
Wisconsin Evangelical Lutheran
    Synod, Board for World Missions
World Mission Prayer League

MENNONITE OR ANABAPTIST

BIC Canada-Global
Christian Aid Ministries (CAM)
Eastern Mennonite Missions
Evangelical Mennonite Conference
Evangelical Mennonite Mission Conference
MB Mission
MB Mission Canada
MEDA - Mennonite Economic
    Development Associates
Mennonite Economic Development
    Associates (MEDA)
Mennonite International
    Health Association
Mennonite Mission Network
Rosedale Mennonite Missions
Virginia Mennonite Missions

METHODIST

Allegheny Wesleyan Methodist Connection
Congregational Methodist Missions
Empowering Lives International
Free Methodist World Missions
Global Witness and Ministry-AME Church
International Child Care, USA
OMS International - Canada
Primitive Methodist Church in the
    USA - International Mission Board
RAISE International, Inc.
Self-Help International
The Free Methodist Church in Canada

OTHER TRADITION

Apostolic Christian Church -
    Missionary Committee
Lifewater International, Inc.
Middle East Media - USA

PENTECOSTAL

Apostolic Church of Pentecost of
    Canada (Global Harvest Missions)
Assemblies of God World Missions
Blessing the Children International
Canadian Assemblies of God,
    General Conference
Caribbean Lifetime Mission
Christ for the Nations, Inc.
Church of God (Cleveland, TN)
    World Missions
Church of God of the Apostolic
    Faith, Inc., The
CyberMissions
Elim Fellowship
ERDO - Emergency Relief
    and Development
Evangel Bible Translators
Foursquare Missions International
Gate Breaker Ministries
Global Missions (United
    Pentecostal Church Intl.)

Global Missions of Open Bible Churches
Good News for India
Good Shepherd Ministries Intl.
Gospel Outbound
IFCA World Missions
International Pentecostal Holiness Church
Into All The World
Josue Yrion World Evangelism
    & Missions, Inc.
Latin American Missions Association
Master's Resourcing Commission
Ministry to Educate and Equip Intl. (MTEE)
Mission Aviation Fellowship
Mission of Mercy Canada
Morelli Ministries Intl. Inc.
Pentecostal Church of God-World
    Missions Department
Salem Ministries International
SAND International
The Pentecostal Assemblies of Canada
World Christian Ministries Association

PRESBYTERIAN

Alongside Ministries International
BASIC Ministries, Inc
Children's Ministry International, Inc. (CMI)
Cumberland Presbyterian Church
    Board of Missions
EPC World Outreach
Latin America Mission
Literacy & Evangelism International
Mission to the World (PCA), Inc.
Orthodox Presbyterian Church -
    Committee on Foreign Missions
Perimeter Church - Global Outreach
Presbyterian Church (USA),
    Worldwide Ministries
Presbyterian Mission International (PMI)
Presbyterian Missionary Union
RP Global Missions
Straightway, Inc.

The Esther School - Dynamic
  Youth Ministries
The Presbyterian Church in Canada
Timothy Two Project International
Women of Hope International
Word & Deed
Word & Deed Ministries Canada
World Witness

REFORMED
20schemes
Christian Reformed World Missions
Church Planting International
ERRC (Educational Resources
  & Referrals - China) US
Four Corners Ministries
Hope Haven International Ministries
Leadership Resources International
LOGOI Ministries
Luke Society
Orphanos Foundation
Partners in Asian Missions
Partners Worldwide
Presbyterian Mission International (PMI)
Publications Chrétiennes (Christian
  Publishing in French)
Reformed Church in America, General
  Synod Council, Global Mission
RP Global Missions
RREACH
Serge
Talking Bibles International
Taiwan Harvest 119
The Esther School - Dynamic
  Youth Ministries

Timothy Leadership Training Institute
Timothy Two Project International
To Every Tribe
University Bible Fellowship
Women of Hope International
Women to the World, Inc.
Word & Deed
Word & Deed Ministries Canada
World Witness

WESLEYAN
Allegheny Wesleyan Methodist Connection
Azusa Pacific University -
  Mexico Outreach
Church of God (Holiness) World
  Mission Dept., Inc.
Church of the Nazarene, Inc.
Congregational Methodist Missions
Cross-Cultural Ministries, Churches
  of God General Conference
Evangelical Bible Mission,
  EBM International
Evangelical Congregational Church -
  Global Ministries Commission
Evangelistic Faith Mission, Inc.
Evangelical Methodist Church,
  Inc. - Board of Missions
Free Methodist World Missions
Global Partners (The Wesleyan
  Church World Headquarters)
International Gospel Outreach
Men for Missions International
World Gospel Mission
World Hope Canada

APPENDIX A
Networks and Associations

North American

The past decade has seen an increased collaboration and networking by US and Canadian mission organizations between themselves within North America. Although Missio Nexus may be the largest association/network of members among ministries working worldwide, it is by no means the only one or even the most significant. Issue-specific networks especially continue to be birthed.

The following are some of the most significantly recognized North American-based networks that mission agencies most frequently mentioned with whom they are associated. This list does not include common accreditation bodies like the Evangelical Council for Financial Accountability (ECFA) and Canadian Council of Christian Charities (CCCC).

- Accord Network
  http://www.accordnetwork.org/
- ACT Alliance
  http://actalliance.org/
- Association of Lutheran Mission Agencies (ALMA)
  http://www.alma-online.org/
- Association of North American Missions (ANAM)
  http://www.anamissions.org/
- Canadian Christian Relief and Development Association (CCRDA)
  https://ccrda.ca/
- Coalition on the Support of Indigenous Ministries (COSIM)
  http://cosim.info/
- Fellowship of Missions (FOM)
  http://fellowshipofmissions.org/
- Missio Nexus
  https://missionexus.org/

Global and Regional

We live in an unprecedented period of mission history. The new paradigm of "from anywhere to everywhere" is by nature complex, resulting in an increasing need for North American ministries to partner with others around the globe for effective ministry. Networks are becoming a strategic tool for ministry leaders navigating the complexities of the globalized world of missions.

There are two basic categories of networks. The first is those that are geographically defined, and the second is those defined by a specific issue. There are far too many to list here. Therefore, explore the excellent website, www.LinkingGlobalVoices.com, for a comprehensive and extensive listing of global, regional, country, and issue-specific neteworks.

The following are listings also found on that site:
- Global and Regional Networks
- Country Level Networks
- Issue Specific Networks
- People Group Networks
- Calendar of Network Events

APPENDIX B
Questionnaire for the United States

The *North American Mission Handbook* reports on Protestant organizations in the U.S. and Canada that send missionaries, workers, funds, or other resources to other countries in the service of Jesus Christ. A local church qualifies if it functions as its own mission agency; directly sending and supporting long-term missionaries or workers to other countries without working through a separate organization.

If you also have a Canadian office, a separate questionnaire must be completed. Please check to confirm they also received the questionnaire. If not, give them the link to the Data Gathering page.

The anticipated release date is Fall 2017. Mission (or church) specific *results will not be posted online.*

Your information as you would like it to be listed in the *North American Mission Handbook*:
- Organization name and contact information are required.
- Other fields are recommended but optional.

Organization Name* _____

Mailing Address* _____

PO Box or Street Address _____

Street Address Line 2 _____

City _____ State / Province _____

Postal / Zip Code (5 digits only) _____ United States

Phone Number* _____

E-mail* _____

Web Site _____

Facebook Page _____

Twitter Handle _____

Year Founded _____ Year Founded in the U.S. _____

Are you registered as a 501(c)(3) with the IRS?*

❏ Yes
❏ No

Previous name or names of your organization, including mission organizations that have merged in:

_____

Denominational Orientation*

❏ Denominational
❏ Nondenominational
❏ Interdenominational
❏ Denominational heritage (a denominational connection is part of your history, but less significant now)
❏ Other _____

The doctrinal or ecclesiastical stance of your organization (or of your supporters). Please select one or two:

❏ Adventist
❏ Anglican
❏ Baptist
❏ Brethren
❏ Christian (Restoration Movement)
❏ Christian (Plymouth Brethren)
❏ Charismatic
❏ Conciliar
❏ Congregational
❏ Ecumenical
❏ Episcopal or Anglican
❏ Evangelical
❏ Friends
❏ Fundamentalist
❏ Holiness
❏ Independent
❏ Lutheran
❏ Mennonite or Anabaptist
❏ Methodist
❏ Moravian
❏ Pentecostal
❏ Presbyterian
❏ Reformed
❏ Wesleyan

Any associations of which you are a member:

❏ Accord Network (formerly AERDO)
❏ ACT Alliance
❏ Association of Lutheran Mission Agencies (ALMA)

❑ Association of North American Missions (ANAM)
❑ Canadian Christian Relief and Development Association (CCRDA)
❑ Consortium of Christian Relief and Development Associations (CCRDA)
❑ Fellowship of Missions (FOM)
❑ Missio Nexus (formerly EFMA/The Mission Exchange, IFMA/CrossGlobal Link)
❑ None
❑ Other _____

ACTIVITIES

Select at least one but not more than six of the following which describe the primary activities of your organization. If actively involved in more than six, check those to which the most resources are currently committed.*

❑ Adoption
❑ Agricultural Assistance
❑ Apologetics
❑ Arts in Mission
❑ Association of Missions
❑ Audio Recording or Distribution
❑ Aviation
❑ Bible Distribution
❑ Bible Teaching
❑ Broadcasting: Radio or TV
❑ Business as Mission
❑ Camping Programs
❑ Childcare or Orphanage
❑ Children's Ministry
❑ Church Construction or Financing

❑ Church Development
❑ Church Planting (Establishing)
❑ Church Planting Movements (CPM)
❑ Community Development
❑ Correspondence Courses
❑ Counseling
❑ Disabled Ministry
❑ Disciple-Making Movements (DMMs)
❑ Discipleship
❑ Education: Church, School or General Christian
❑ Education: TEE or Other Extension

- Education: Theological
- Environmental Missions
- Ethno-Musicology
- Evangelism: Mass
- Evangelism: Personal or Small Group
- Evangelism: Student
- Fund Raising or Transmission
- HIV/AIDS Ministry
- Human Trafficking
- Information or Journalism
- International Student Ministry
- Internet Discipleship or Training
- Internet Evangelism
- Justice or Peace Issues
- Leadership Development
- Linguistics
- Literacy
- Literature Distribution
- Literature Production
- Management Consulting or Training
- Medical Supplies
- Medical Ministry, including Dental or Public Health
- Member Care
- Missionary/Worker Training
- National Worker Support
- Networking, Partnership, or Coordination
- Orality or Storying
- Partnership Development
- Persecuted Church
- Prayer/Intercession
- Purchasing or Supply Services
- Recruiting or Mobilizing for Mission
- Relief and Aid
- Research
- Services for Mission Organizations
- Short-Term Mission Trip Coordination
- Spiritual Renewal
- Sports Ministry
- Technical Assistance
- Tentmaking and Related
- TESOL or TEFL
- Translation, Bible
- Translation, Other
- Video/Film Production or Distribution
- Youth Ministry
- Other _____

Which ONE (1) from those selected above is most commonly associated with your organization?*

_____

FINANCIAL DATA

Total income of your organization for all ministries (U.S. and international) in the last fiscal year, including gifts-in-kind: _____

From the total for all ministries reported in the prior question, the amount of income for international ministries: _____

From the total for international ministries reported in the prior question, the value received in the form of gifts-in-kind, merchandise, commodities and/or services: _____

PERSONNEL

The information about countries of service and field personnel from the U.S. and other countries are reported on Part 1 of data collecting. The questions below are for categories other than those on that report.

Referencing your *completed* Countries of Service report, all those international workers (missionaries + nonresidential missionary personnel + tentmakers or Christian professionals) who were:

    Married Men _____   Single Men _____

    Married Women _____   Single Women _____

Mission Trip *Participants*: those who went on international service projects or mission trips through your organization. They may have been partially or fully supported through your organization, or raised their own support.

In your most recent fiscal year, those who served:

    2 weeks or less _____

    More than two weeks but less than one year _____

Number of home staff or employees in the U.S. who support your international workers:

Full-time paid staff _____

Part-time paid staff or associates _____

The focus of the *Mission Handbook* is to compile statistics of U.S. organizations that send missionaries to countries outside of the U.S. However, recognizing the diaspora of the nations, what is the number of U.S. missionaries serving cross-culturally in the U.S.?   _____

CLOSING INFORMATION

Your organization's board approved mission statement:*
In 40 words or less describe your organization; what is distinctive about you? If you have a statement or slogan you often use, include that also.

Would your organization like to purchase an advertisement in the *North American Mission Handbook*?*

❑ Yes   ❑ Maybe   ❑ No

Please suggest mission organizations that may have been missed by the *Mission Handbook* in the past, or that might be missed because they are new, small, or not well known. This includes ministries based in the U.S. or Canada that primarily work overseas.

Organization name and point of contact #1 (If available, please include an email, phone and/or website.)

Organization name and point of contact #2 (If available, please include an email, phone and/or website.)

Organization name and point of contact #3 (If available, please include an email, phone and/or website.)

Additional comments about your organization or this survey:

Submitted by:*

_____   _____
First Name   Last Name

Position/Title:*_____

E-mail:*_____

Phone Number:*_____

Date:*_____
        Month   Day   Year

APPENDIX C
Questionnaire for Canada

The *North American Mission Handbook* reports on Protestant organisations in the Canada and U.S. that send missionaries, workers, funds, or other resources to other countries in the service of Jesus Christ. A local church qualifies if it functions as its own mission agency; directly sending and supporting long-term missionaries or workers to other countries without working through a separate organisation.

If you also have a U.S. office, a separate questionnaire must be completed. Please check to confirm they also received the questionnaire. If not, give them the link to the Data Gathering page.

The anticipated release date is Fall 2017. Mission (or church) specific *results will not be posted online.*

Your information as you would like it to be listed in the *North American Mission Handbook*:

- Organisation name and contact information are required.
- Other fields are recommended but optional.

Organisation Name* _____

Mailing Address* _____

PO Box or Street Address _____

Street Address Line 2 _____

City _____ State / Province _____

Postal / Zip Code (5 digits only) _____ Canada

Phone Number* _____

E-mail* _____

Web Site _____

Facebook Page _____

Twitter Handle _____

Year Founded _____ Year Founded in Canada _____

Are you a Registered Charity with the Canada Revenue Agency?*
- ❏ Yes
- ❏ No

Previous name or names of your organisation, including mission organisations that have merged in:

_____

Denominational Orientation*
- ❏ Denominational
- ❏ Nondenominational
- ❏ Interdenominational
- ❏ Denominational heritage (a denominational connection is part of your history, but less significant now)
- ❏ Other _____

The doctrinal or ecclesiastical stance of your organisation (or of your supporters). Please select one or two:

- ❏ Adventist
- ❏ Anglican
- ❏ Baptist
- ❏ Brethren
- ❏ Christian (Restoration Movement)
- ❏ Christian (Plymouth Brethren)
- ❏ Charismatic
- ❏ Conciliar
- ❏ Congregational
- ❏ Ecumenical
- ❏ Episcopal or Anglican
- ❏ Evangelical
- ❏ Friends
- ❏ Fundamentalist
- ❏ Holiness
- ❏ Independent
- ❏ Lutheran
- ❏ Mennonite or Anabaptist
- ❏ Methodist
- ❏ Moravian
- ❏ Pentecostal
- ❏ Presbyterian
- ❏ Reformed
- ❏ Wesleyan

Any associations of which you are a member:
- ❏ Accord Network (formerly AERDO)
- ❏ ACT Alliance
- ❏ Association of Lutheran Mission Agencies (ALMA)

- ❑ Association of North American Missions (ANAM)
- ❑ Canadian Christian Relief and Development Association (CCRDA)
- ❑ Consortium of Christian Relief and Development Associations (CCRDA)
- ❑ Fellowship of Missions (FOM)
- ❑ Missio Nexus (formerly EFMA/The Mission Exchange, IFMA/CrossGlobal Link)
- ❑ None
- ❑ Other _____

ACTIVITIES

Select at least one but not more than six of the following which describe the primary activities of your organisation. If actively involved in more than six, check those to which the most resources are currently committed.*

- ❑ Adoption
- ❑ Agricultural Assistance
- ❑ Apologetics
- ❑ Arts in Mission
- ❑ Association of Missions
- ❑ Audio Recording or Distribution
- ❑ Aviation
- ❑ Bible Distribution
- ❑ Bible Teaching
- ❑ Broadcasting: Radio or TV
- ❑ Business as Mission
- ❑ Camping Programs
- ❑ Childcare or Orphanage
- ❑ Children's Ministry
- ❑ Church Construction or Financing
- ❑ Church Development
- ❑ Church Planting (Establishing)
- ❑ Church Planting Movements (CPM)
- ❑ Community Development
- ❑ Correspondence Courses
- ❑ Counseling
- ❑ Disabled Ministry
- ❑ Disciple-Making Movements (DMMs)
- ❑ Discipleship
- ❑ Education: Church, School or General Christian
- ❑ Education: TEE or Other Extension
- ❑ Education: Theological

❑ Environmental
  Missions
❑ Ethno-Musicology
❑ Evangelism: Mass
❑ Evangelism: Personal
  or Small Group
❑ Evangelism: Student
❑ Fund Raising or
  Transmission
❑ HIV/AIDS Ministry
❑ Human Trafficking
❑ Information or
  Journalism
❑ International Student
  Ministry
❑ Internet Discipleship
  or Training
❑ Internet Evangelism
❑ Justice or Peace
  Issues
❑ Leadership
  Development
❑ Linguistics
❑ Literacy
❑ Literature
  Distribution
❑ Literature
  Production
❑ Management
  Consulting or
  Training
❑ Medical Supplies
❑ Medical Ministry,
  including Dental or
  Public Health
❑ Member Care

❑ Missionary/Worker
  Training
❑ National Worker
  Support
❑ Networking,
  Partnership, or
  Coordination
❑ Orality or Storying
❑ Partnership
  Development
❑ Persecuted Church
❑ Prayer/Intercession
❑ Purchasing or Supply
  Services
❑ Recruiting or Mobi-
  lizing for Mission
❑ Relief and Aid
❑ Research
❑ Services for Mission
  Organisations
❑ Short-Term Mission
  Trip Coordination
❑ Spiritual Renewal
❑ Sports Ministry
❑ Technical Assistance
❑ Tentmaking and
  Related
❑ TESOL or TEFL
❑ Translation, Bible
❑ Translation, Other
❑ Video/Film Produc-
  tion or Distribution
❑ Youth Ministry
❑ Other _____

Which ONE (1) from those selected above is most commonly associated with your organisation?*

_____

FINANCIAL DATA

Total income of your organisation for all ministries (Canadian and international) in the last fiscal year, including gifts-in-kind: _____

From the total for all ministries reported in the prior question, the amount of income for international ministries: _____

From the total for international ministries reported in the prior question, the value received in the form of gifts-in-kind, merchandise, commodities and/or services: _____

PERSONNEL

The information about countries of service and field personnel from the Canada and other countries are reported on Part 1 of data collecting. The questions below are for categories other than those on that report.

Referencing your *completed* Countries of Service report, all those international workers (missionaries + nonresidential missionary personnel + tentmakers or Christian professionals) who were:

Married Men _____   Single Men _____
Married Women _____   Single Women _____

Mission Trip *Participants*: those who went on international service projects or mission trips through your organisation. They may have been partially or fully supported through your organisation, or raised their own support.

In your most recent fiscal year, those who served:
2 weeks or less _____
More than two weeks but less than one year _____

Number of home staff or employees in Canada who support your international workers:

Full-time paid staff _____

Part-time paid staff or associates _____

The focus of the *Mission Handbook* is to compile statistics of Canadian organisations that send missionaries to countries outside of the Canada. However, recognizing the diaspora of the nations, what is the number of Canadian missionaries serving cross-culturally in the Canada? _____

CLOSING INFORMATION

Your organisation's board approved mission statement:*
In 40 words or less describe your organisation; what is distinctive about you? If you have a statement or slogan you often use, include that also.

Would your organisation like to purchase an advertisement in the *North American Mission Handbook*?*

❑ Yes   ❑ Maybe   ❑ No

Please suggest mission organisations that may have been missed by the *Mission Handbook* in the past, or that might be missed because they are new, small, or not well known. This includes ministries based in Canada or the U.S. that primarily work overseas.

Organisation name and point of contact #1 (If available, please include an email, phone and/or website.)

Organisation name and point of contact #2 (If available, please include an email, phone and/or website.)

Organisation name and point of contact #3 (If available, please include an email, phone and/or website.)

Additional comments about your organization or this survey:

Submitted by:*

_____   _____
First Name   Last Name

Position/Title:*_____

E-mail:*_____

Phone Number:*_____

Date:*_____
          Month   Day   Year